Bridges Not Walls

A Book About Interpersonal Communication

ELEVENTH EDITION

John Stewart
University of Dubuque

Mc
Graw
Hill

Connect
Learn
Succeed™

BRIDGES NOT WALLS, A BOOK ABOUT INTERPERSONAL COMMUNICATION,
ELEVENTH EDITION

Published by McGraw-Hill, a business unit of The McGraw-Hill Companies, Inc., 1221 Avenue of
the Americas, New York, NY 10020. Copyright © 2012 by The McGraw-Hill Companies, Inc. All
rights reserved. Previous editions © 2009, 2006, and 2002. No part of this publication may be
reproduced or distributed in any form or by any means, or stored in a database or retrieval system,
without the prior written consent of The McGraw-Hill Companies, Inc., including, but not limited
to, in any network or other electronic storage or transmission, or broadcast for distance learning.

Some ancillaries, including electronic and print components, may not be available to customers
outside the United States.

This book is printed on acid-free paper.

1 2 3 4 5 6 7 8 9 0 DOC/DOC 1 0 9 8 7 6 5 4 3 2 1

ISBN 978-0-07-353431-2
MHID 0-07-353431-5

Vice President & Editor-in-Chief: *Michael Ryan*
Vice President & Director of Specialized Publishing: *Janice M. Roerig-Blong*
Publisher: *David Patterson*
Senior Sponsoring Editor: *Debra B. Hash*
Director of Marketing & Sales: *Jennifer J. Lewis*
Project Manager: *Melissa M. Leick*
Design Coordinator: *Brenda A. Rolwes*
Media Project Manager: *Sridevi Palani*
Cover Designer: *Studio Montage, St. Louis, Missouri*
Cover Image: © *PhotoLink/Getty Images RF*
Buyer: *Laura Fuller*
Compositor: *Aptara®, Inc.*
Typeface: *10/12 Palatino*
Printer: *R. R. Donnelley*

All credits appearing on page or at the end of the book are considered to be an extension of the
copyright page.

Library of Congress Cataloging-in-Publication Data

Bridges not walls: a book about interpersonal communication / [edited by] John Stewart.—11th ed.
 p. cm.
ISBN 978-0-07-353431-2 (pbk.)
1. Interpersonal communication. I. Stewart, John Robert.
BF637.C45B74 2011
158.2—dc22

                                        2011013891

Books and People

Imagine yourself in a situation where you are alone, wholly alone on earth, and you are offered one of the two, books or [people]. I often hear [speakers] prizing their solitude, but that is only because there are still [people] somewhere on earth, even though in the far distance. I knew nothing of books when I came forth from the womb of my mother, and I shall die without books, with another human hand in my own. I do, indeed, close my door at times and surrender myself to a book, but only because I can open the door again and see a human being looking at me.

—Martin Buber

About the Editor

JOHN STEWART taught interpersonal communication at the University of Washington from 1969 to 2001. He attended Centralia Community College and Pacific Lutheran University, then earned his M.A. at Northwestern University and completed his Ph.D. at the University of Southern California in 1970. In 2001 John moved to the University of Dubuque in northeast Iowa, where he served as Vice President for Academic Affairs and Dean of the Graduate School. Now retired, he continues to teach interpersonal communication at UD. He has four children and six grandchildren and lives with his wife Becky in Dubuque and Skagit County, Washington.

Contents

PREFACE *xi*

Part One
FOUNDATIONS OF INTERPERSONAL COMMUNICATION

Chapter 1 Introduction to the Editor and to This Book   3

Chapter 2 Communication and Interpersonal Communication   13

John Stewart: *Communicating and Interpersonal Communicating* 14
Malcolm Parks: *Personal Relationships and Health* 42
Susan Scott: *Fierce Conversations* 52
Abdul K. Sinno, Rafic Sinno, and John Stewart: *Social Media: Where Interpersonal Communication Meets Mass Communication* 61

Chapter 3 Communication Building Identities   72

John Stewart, Karen E. Zediker, and Saskia Witteborn: *Constructing Identities* 73
Steve Duck and David T. McMahan: *Self and Identity: Transacting a Self in Interactions with Others* 85
Douglas Stone, Bruce Patton, and Sheila Heen: *Identity and Difficult Conversations* 91

Chapter 4   Verbal and Nonverbal Contact   100

    John Stewart and Carole Logan: *Verbal and Nonverbal*
        Dimensions of Talk   101
    Steve Duck and David T. McMahan: *Talk and Interpersonal*
        Relationships   127
    John Stewart: *Two of the Most Important Words*   139
    Ben Finzel: *Say What? Eight Words and Phrases to Avoid in LGBT*
        Communication   146
    Steve Duck and David T. McMahan: *What Are the Functions of Nonverbal*
        Communication?   150

Part Two
MAKING MEANING TOGETHER

Chapter 5   Inhaling: Perceiving and Listening   161

    John Stewart, Karen E. Zediker, and Saskia Witteborn: *Inhaling:*
        Perception   162
    Julia T. Wood: *It's Only Skin Deep: Stereotyping and Totalizing*
        Others   178
    Rebecca Z. Shafir: *Mindful Listening*   185
    John Stewart, Karen E. Zediker, and Saskia Witteborn: *Empathic and*
        Dialogic Listening   192

Chapter 6   Exhaling: Expressing and Disclosing   208

    David W. Johnson: *Being Open with and to Other People*   209
    Douglas Stone, Bruce Patton and Sheila Heen: *Expression: Speak for*
        Yourself with Clarity and Power   218

Part Three
RELATIONSHIPS

Chapter 7   Communicating with Family and Friends   233

    Julia T. Wood: *What's a Family, Anyway?*   234
    Deborah Tannen: *Separating Messages from Metamessages*
        in Family Talk   243
    Steve Duck: *Our Friends, Ourselves*   254
    William Paul Young: *Relationships and Power*   266

Chapter 8   Communicating with Intimate Partners   274

Laura K. Guerrero, Peter A. Andersen, and Walid A. Afifi, *Communicating*
          Closeness: Intimacy, Affection, and Social Support   275
Malcolm R. Parks: *Gender and Ethnic Similarities and Differences*
          in Relational Development   289
Lawrence A. Kurdek: *What Do We Know about Gay and Lesbian*
          Couples?   306
Erik Qualman: *Word of Mouth Goes World of Mouth*   314

Part Four
BRIDGES NOT WALLS

Chapter 9   Coping with Communication Walls   327

John Stewart, Karen E. Zediker, and Saskia Witteborn: *Deception,*
          Betrayal, and Aggression   328
Anita L. Vangelisti: *Messages That Hurt*   340
Jack R. Gibb: *Defensive Communication*   352
William W. Wilmot and Joyce L. Hocker: *Power: The Structure*
          of Conflict   359
Charles J. Wigley III: *Verbal Aggression Interventions:*
          What Should Be Done?   374

Chapter 10   Conflict: Turning Walls into Bridges   385

Joseph P. Folger, Marshall Scott Poole, and Randall K. Stutman:
          Conflict and Interaction   386
William W. Wilmot: *Communication Spirals, Paradoxes, and*
          Conundrums   399
Steve Duck: *Handling the Break-Up of Relationships*   415
Susan M. Campbell: *I Hear You, and I Have a Different Perspective*   423
Hugh and Gayle Prather: *How to Resolve Issues Unmemorably*   428

Chapter 11   Bridging Cultural Differences   438

Geert Hofstede and Gert Jan Hofstede: *The Individual and the Collective*
          in Society   439
David W. Johnson: *Building Relationships with Diverse Others*   453
David A. Anderson: *From Racism to Gracism*   465
Dawn O. Braithwaite and Charles A. Braithwaite: *"Which Is My Good*
          Leg?" Cultural Communication of Persons with Disabilities   470

Chapter 12   Promoting Dialogue   484

Karen E. Zediker and John Stewart: *Dialogue's Basic Tension*   485
Maggie Herzig and Laura Chasin: *Fostering Dialogue across Divides*   495
Jonathan Sacks: *Turning Enemies into Friends*   506
Martin Buber: *Elements of the Interhuman*   513

PHOTO CREDITS   *530*

INDEX   *531*

Preface

This eleventh edition of *Bridges Not Walls* maintains the approach and the basic format of the previous ten editions. The book's major divisions parallel those of most interpersonal communication courses and textbooks—foundations are first, followed by treatments of taking in cues and giving out cues (inhaling and exhaling), relationships, and building bridges not walls (difficult communication, conflict, cultural differences, dialogue). The underlying communication theory is relational, with an emphasis on identity-construction and interconnections among verbal and nonverbal cues. This edition keeps the chapter sequence and the articles that reviewers and other users appreciated. I have updated several chapters to reflect current communication concerns and directions of current research and teaching, and, as another aid to students, I have added bulleted "Main Ideas" at the end of the introduction to each reading.

Reviewers of past editions have appreciated the book's variety of voices, and this edition includes materials from 44 communication teacher-scholars, clinical and research psychologists, business communication experts, public communication practitioners, advocates/activists, and authors with a spiritual or religious focus. All these writings are consistent with the social construction approach to communication developed in Chapters 1 and 2, and all offer their ideas in readily accessible language.

Nineteen articles from the previous edition have been replaced by fifteen new essays. A new discussion of social media now concludes Chapter 2, and social media and interpersonal relationships are also discussed in Chapter 8, "Communicating with Intimate Partners."

This edition includes three selections from Steve Duck and David T. McMahan's *The Basics of Communication: A Relational Perspective*, all chosen because of the consistency between Duck and McMahan's approach to interpersonal communication and the one developed in *Bridges Not Walls*. Now, thanks in part to Duck and McMahan's writings, all the readings in Chapter 4, "Verbal and Nonverbal Contact," reflect the principle that verbal and nonverbal elements always occur together. This same chapter has also been updated by adding an essay that simplifies and applies the book's approach to communication by discussing specific uses of the words "and" and "next," and an essay that responds to reviewers' demands that lesbian, gay, bisexual and transgender (LGBT) communication be treated more extensively.

Two selections have been excerpted from Douglas Stone, Bruce Patton, and Sheila Heen's book that grew out of the Harvard Negotiation Project, *Difficult Conversations: How to Discuss What Matters Most*, again, because of the close fit between these authors' approach to communication and the one developed in *Bridges Not Walls*. Stone, Patton, and Heen make important new contributions to Chapter 3, "Communication Building Identities," and Chapter 6, "Exhaling: Expressing and Disclosing." There is also a new discussion of relationships and power from the best-selling "guy-meets-God novel," *The Shack*.

Laura Guerrero, Peter A. Andersen, and Walid A. Afifi's excellent discussion of intimacy now anchors Chapter 8, and the chapter is filled out with Malcolm R. Parks's *Gender and Ethnic Similarities and Differences in Relational Development*, the Qualman essay on social media, and a brief and readable review of what is known about gay and lesbian couples' communication that was originally published in *Current Directions in Psychological Science*.

Communication scholar-teacher Charles J. Wigley III's *Verbal Aggression Interventions: What Should Be Done?* extends Chapter 9, "Coping with Communication Walls," and Chapter 11, "Bridging Cultural Differences," now begins with Hofstede and Hofstede's classic distinction between individualist and collectivist cultures. The chapter is rounded out with a simple yet profound discussion by Christian pastor David A. Anderson of the difference between racism and "gracism."

Bridges Not Walls is still designed primarily for college students enrolled in interpersonal communication classes. But the materials discuss topics also included in social work, humanities, counseling, and sociology courses. A majority of the readings are authored by communication scholars and teachers, and there are also materials from authors in a range of disciplines.

Since the first edition of *Bridges Not Walls* was published in 1973, the approach to communication that has guided this collection of readings has treated "communication" as the term humans use for our collaborative processes of meaning-making. To say that humans are "social animals" is to say that we make sense of things *with others*, and "communication" is the general label for these processes. When I call these processes "collaborative," I obviously do not mean that humans always agree as we make meanings together, but only that we "co-labor," or work out meanings in response to one another. All this implies that communication is not simply an activity that one person performs or does "to" another but is a process that happens *between* people. For those with theoretical interests, these basic ideas can be found in primary works by Mikhail Bakhtin, Martin Buber, Martin Heidegger, Alfred Schutz, Hans-Georg Gadamer, and in writings by social construction theorists and practitioners.

Interpersonal communication is a subset of communication, a type or kind of contact that happens when the people involved talk and listen in ways that maximize the presence of the personal. This approach to interpersonal communication highlights the ways communication affects social and personal identities, it emphasizes the prominence of culture, and it foregrounds the close connection between quality of communication and quality of life. In other words, although communication can clearly be expressive and instrumental, this approach emphasizes that it is also person-building, which is to say that *who humans are* gets worked out in our verbal/nonverbal contact. Virtually all of the authors represented here acknowledge these features of communication, and many comment directly on them.

This is a book for people who want practical suggestions and skills that will help them communicate more effectively with their friends, partners, spouses, family, and co-workers. But unlike much of the self-help literature, *Bridges* resists the tendency to gloss over conceptual issues and to reduce interpersonal effectiveness to techniques or formulas. The authors of these readings recognize that there is much more to effective communication than simply "being open and honest." For example, there are thought-provoking discussions of the nature of interpersonal contact, the inseparability of verbal and nonverbal cues, identity management, listening, deception and betrayal, family intimacy, cultural diversity, and dialogue. *Bridges* also includes systematic treatments of self-awareness, functions of nonverbal behavior, social perception, disclosure, gender patterns, hurtful messages, and defensiveness. But no reading claims to offer the definitive "six steps" or "twelve easy techniques" for guaranteed success. The authors emphasize that the unique situation, the constancy of change, and especially the element of human choice all make it impossible to design and execute a purely technical approach to *human* relationships.

This point is rooted in the book's definition of its subject matter, which I've already sketched. *Bridges* does not define interpersonal communication as something that only happens in face-to-face settings, during discussions of weighty topics, or in long-term intimate relationships. Instead, the term "interpersonal" designates a kind or quality of contact that emerges between people whenever they are willing and able to highlight in their speaking and listening aspects of what makes them human. The editor's introduction in Chapter 1 and the first essay in Chapter 2 explain this definition, and subsequent readings extend and develop it. Throughout the book, the point is also made that different kinds or qualities of contact are appropriate in different situations. "More" interpersonal communicating is *not* always better. There is much more to it than that, as the readings in Chapters 10, 11, and 12 especially demonstrate. At the same time, materials in several chapters clarify how most people's personal, educational, and work lives could profit from increased interpersonal contact.

These theoretical and conceptual commitments are complemented by my desire to make the book as readable as possible. This is the main reason why few research articles from scholarly journals are included. As in all earlier editions, I have tried to select substantive materials that speak directly to the student reader. I continue to search for authors who "write with their ears," or talk with their readers. Selections from past editions by Susan Scott, Julia Wood, Susan Campbell, and Hugh and Gayle Prather, are included in this edition partly because they do this so well. I have also found this accessibility in some new authors, especially Duck and McMahan; Stone, Patton, and Heen; Finzel; and David Anderson.

New Features

No communication textbook published after 2009 can ignore social media, and this edition of *Bridges* includes two essays about this phenomenon. These readings acknowledge the pervasiveness of both horizontal (e.g., Twitter) and vertical (e.g., Facebook) social media, and describe how this phenomenon has shifted the classic model

$$\text{Sender-} \rightarrow \text{Message-} \rightarrow \text{Channel-} \rightarrow \text{Receiver-} \rightarrow \text{Effect}$$

to a model that looks like this:

$$\text{Channel-} \rightarrow \text{Sender-} \rightarrow \text{Message-} \rightarrow \text{Receiver-} \rightarrow \text{Effect.}$$

As Abdul and Rafic Sinno and I argue in Chapter 2, social media have also shifted the understanding of Marshall McLuhan's classic slogan, "The Medium is the Message/Massage" to "The Medium is the Mass Age." The readings on social media alert student readers to some of the dangers of heavy media multitasking, and they describe some ways social media are changing the dating scene.

Several reviewers of the tenth edition complained about the book's limited and dated treatment of LGBT communication, and this edition responds in several ways. Ben Finzel's simple and direct "Eight Words and Phrases to Avoid in LGBT Communication" should prompt lively classroom discussion of verbal cues, and Lawrence A. Kurdek's review of the scholarly literature on gay and lesbian couples enriches Chapter 8, "Communicating with Intimate Partners." LGBT communication is also treated by several other authors as an increasingly normal part of the contemporary communication terrain. Religiously-focused readers who are uncomfortable with these readings can, of course, ignore or omit them—this is a benefit of an anthology. But I hope that, instead, they will notice that this edition of *Bridges* also includes two readings from Christian-focused books, a fact that hopefully makes the point, albeit indirectly, that it is clearly possible both to affirm a Christian commitment and to actively support LGBT people. More importantly, I hope readers will use all these readings to encourage students to reflect on these important and increasingly inescapable social issues.

I have already mentioned that all the readings in Chapter 4, "Verbal and Nonverbal Contact," are now consistent with the initial point that Carole Logan and I make at the start of this chapter: That the verbal/nonverbal dichotomy does not accurately reflect what actually happens when people communicate, because the two kinds of cues always occur together. Duck and McMahan do a good job of making this point.

The chapter on "Expressing and Disclosing" has also been updated, and Chapter 8, "Communicating with Intimate Partners" has been more theoretically grounded and broadened beyond just considerations of gender.

Reviewers expressed appreciation for the coverage of conflict and other communication "walls" in Chapters 9 and 10, and this edition includes most of the readings they praised. I have added Charles J. Wigley III's helpful "Verbal Aggression Interventions: What Should Be Done?" They also praised essays by Malcolm Parks, Julia T. Wood, Deborah Tannen, Anita L. Vangelisti, Jack R. Gibb, William W. Wilmot, Dawn and Charles Braithwaite, and David W. Johnson, all of which have been kept.

Other Features

As in earlier editions, my introduction shows how *Bridges Not Walls* is different from the traditional, faceless, "objective" college textbook. I want readers to consider the potential for, and the limits of, interpersonal communicating between writer and reader. I also want them to remember that a book or essay is always somebody's point of view. I'd like readers to respond to what's here not as "true because it's printed in black and white" but as the thoughtful speech of a person addressing them. In the Introduction, I tell readers a little about myself, give a rationale for the way the book is put together, and argue for the link between quality of communication and quality of life.

I have shortened the introductions to most readings, and concluded each with a bulleted list of "Main Ideas," in order to further guide student reading. Two sets of questions still follow each reading. The first, "Review Questions," are designed to prompt the reader's recall of key ideas. If the student can respond to these, there is some clear indication that he or she understands what's in the reading. Then "Probes" ask the reader to take some additional steps by extending, criticizing, or applying the author's ideas. Some "Probes" also explore links between readings in various chapters.

Many of the readings include extensive bibliographies or references. There are lengthy lists of additional sources, for example, accompanying the readings that discuss the book's approach, personal relationships and health, verbal and nonverbal dimensions of talk, perception, listening, gender and ethnic similarities and differences, hurtful messages, verbal aggression, identity management, and communication with people with disabilities. A detailed index also locates and provides cross-references to authors and key ideas.

As before, I want to remind readers that this book *about* interpersonal communicating cannot substitute for direct contact between persons in the concrete, everyday world. This is why I've once again begun the book with Buber's comment about "Books and People" and ended with Hugh Prather's reflections on the world of ideas and the world of "messy mortals."

Acknowledgments

This book would not be possible without the cooperation of the authors and publishers of material reprinted here. Thanks to all of them for their permissions.

I am also grateful to reviewers of the earlier edition. The following people offered insightful comments that guided the revision process this time:

Laurie Bershire, Erie Community College
Rodney Carveth, Fitchburg State College
Maria C. Bridenbaugh, Regis University
Jethro S. De Lisle, Tacoma Community College
Derek Devries, Grand Rapids Community College
Nancy Grass Hemmert, Santa Monica College
Lowell Habel, Chapman University
Steven King, Ivy Tech Community College of Southern Indiana
Charles Korn, Northern Virginia Community College
Becky M. Mulvaney, Florida Atlantic University
Mary Nagy, Rutgers University of New Brunswick
Michele Poff, University of Washington–Seattle
John Radwan, Seton Hall University
Sarah E. Riley, University of Kentucky–Lexington
Kathleen Roberts, Duquesne University
Beth Rose, Mid America Nazarene University
Kenneth Troyer, Sterling College
Matthew S. Vorell, St. Cloud State University

Many people I am fortunate enough to contact regularly have also contributed in direct and indirect ways to what's here. I appreciate many current and past interpersonal communication teachers in the program at the University of Washington, including Milt Thomas, Lyall Crawford, Kathy Hendrix, Jeff Kerssen-Griep, Lisa Coutu, Roberta Gray, Laura Manning, Tasha Souza, Amanda Graham, Laura Black, Jodi Koenig Kellas, Andi Hamilton Zamora, and Aimee Carillo Rowe. I also deeply appreciate past contacts with colleagues who have supported and challenged my ideas, including Gerry Philipsen, Mac Parks, Barbara Warnick, Valerie Manusov, Jody Nyquist, Ken Cissna, Ron Arnett, Kim and Barnett Pearce, John Shotter, and, since 2001, new colleagues at the University of Dubuque, including Jeff Bullock, Bob Reid, Jenn Supple, Peter Smith, Brad Longfield, Henry Pitman, and Gail Hodge. I continue to notice how both the greatest tests and the most solid confirmations of what's in this book emerge in my most important living relationships with Becky, Lincoln, Marcia, Lisa, Brad, Barbara, Dorothy, Jamie, Josh, and other family members.

Two things that still have not changed through all these editions of *Bridges Not Walls* are my awareness of the difficulty and the necessity of interpersonal communicating and my excitement about the challenge of working toward achieving it. I hope that some of this excitement will rub off on you.

John Stewart
Dubuque, IA 2011

PART ONE

Foundations of Interpersonal Communication

CHAPTER 1

Introduction to the Editor and to This Book

Writing about interpersonal communication, especially in a book that's used mainly as a text, is difficult because it's almost impossible to practice what you preach. Like many other text authors and editors, I could think of you as just "reader" or "student" and of myself as just "editor" or "teacher" and proceed to tell you what I want you to know. But if I did, we'd have something a lot closer to *impersonal* rather than *interpersonal* communication.

Why? Because, if I write simply as "teacher," and address you simply as "student" or "reader," and if you respond the same way, we will be relating to each other only in terms of our social roles, not in terms of who we are *as persons*. If I use the vocabulary introduced in the next chapter, this kind of contact would connect us as interchangeable parts.

But there's more to it than that. Both you and I are *non*interchangeable, multidimensional persons with distinctive histories, ideas, convictions, wants, and needs. For my part, my name is John Stewart, I've taught college for over 40 years, and I am now semiretired and teaching part-time. Like many of you, my family is nontraditional, by "nuclear family" standards. My two daughters were born shortly after I finished high school and are in their late 40s, one son is 36, and another is 18. Two of my grandchildren are in their 20s, two are early teens, and Luke and Isaac are not yet in school. So one son, Lincoln, is an uncle to a niece and nephew older than he, and one son and four grandkids are "blended" into our family via second and third marriages. Julia T. Wood talks about this feature of 21st century families at the start of Chapter 7.

I'm a native of the northwestern United States who moved in 2001 to northeast Iowa. I love the smell of saltwater and the fizz it makes behind a quiet boat; the exhilaration of biking and downhill skiing; the dazzling brightness of a winter sun on Midwest snow; and the babble of a crowded family gathering. I dislike phony smiles, grandiose flattery or apologies, pretentious academicians, rules that are vaguely stated but rigidly enforced, oysters, and machinery that runs roughly. I also get impatient with people who have trouble saying what they mean and meaning what they say. I was raised in a small town in Washington State and now live most of the year on the Mississippi, right at the point where Iowa, Illinois, and Wisconsin meet. I like the challenges of helping people in my classes learn new and old ideas and I feel very fortunate to be retired and to have my family and health.

The longer I study and teach interpersonal communication, the more I'm struck by how much the person I am today has been molded by the relationships I've experienced. Some of the most important people in my life are no longer alive: for example, my dad and mom; my first real "boss," Marc Burdick; college teachers Peter Ristuben and "Prof." Karl; and Allen Clark, the friend who introduced me to Martin Buber's writings. Some others I've almost completely lost contact with, like high school and college teachers, co-workers in the pea cannery, and graduate school classmates. But many other relationships continue to teach and mold me, including those I have with Lincoln, my wife Becky, my sister Barbara, cousins Jim and Carol, and close friends Karen Zediker, Tim Milander, John Campbell, David Kendell, Father Ralph Carskadden, and Jeff Bullock. I've also been affected by relationships with many authors who have made themselves available in their writing, especially Martin Buber, Hans-Georg Gadamer, Mikhail Bakhtin, John Shotter, Eric Voegelin, Martin Heidegger, Parker Palmer, and Carl Rogers. Contacts with all these persons have helped shape me. At the same time, I sense the presence of a continuous "me" who's never static but who's firmly anchored in values, understandings, weaknesses, and strengths that make me who I am.

If I stuck to being just "writer" or "teacher," I could also skip the fact that I am as grateful and excited about doing this eleventh edition of *Bridges Not Walls* as I was about the first edition, and that I continue to be a little amazed that this book speaks to so many different people. Each mention of the book by a student who has read it or a teacher who has used it is a delight, and I especially like hearing from the communication graduate students and teachers who tell me that this was their introduction to the field. It's a gift to be able to share some ideas and feelings about interpersonal communication in this way, and I'm pleased that readers continue to allow me to talk relatively personally rather than just in the safe, sterile, and distant style of some "educational materials."

The impersonal approach I mentioned would also get in the way of the contact between you and me, because *you* are not simply "reader" or "student." Where were you born and raised, and how has that affected you? Are you reading this book because you want to or because somebody required it? If you're reading it as part of a college course, how do you expect the course to turn out? Challenging? Boring? Threatening? Useful? Inhibiting? Exciting? How do you generally feel about required texts? About going to school? What groups have you been in or are you a part of? A sports team? A neighborhood gang? A band? Campfire or Scouts? Natural Helpers? A church group? A sorority or fraternity? Alateen? What important choices have you made recently? To end a relationship? Move? Change majors? Quit work? Make a new commitment?

I'm not saying that you have to pry into the intimate details of somebody's life before you can communicate with him or her, but I am saying that interpersonal communication happens between *persons,* not between roles, masks, or stereotypes. Interpersonal communication can happen between you and me only to the degree that each of us makes available some of what makes us a person *and* at the same time is aware of some of what makes the other a person, too.

One way to conceptualize what I'm saying is to think about what could be called your Contact Quotient, or CQ. Your CQ is a measure of how you connect with another person. It's the quotient that expresses the ratio between the quality of contact you experience and the quality of contact that's possible. In other words,

$$\frac{\text{Richness or quality of contact achieved}}{\text{Richness or quality of contact possible}}$$

A husband and wife who have been married for 40 years have a huge CQ denominator (the figure below the line)—let's say 10,000. When one is giving the other the silent treatment, their numerator (the figure above the line) is painfully small—maybe 15. So their CQ in this instance would be 15/10,000—pretty low. But when they spend an afternoon and evening together in conversation, mutually enjoyed activities, and lovemaking, their numerator is very high—perhaps 9,500—and their CQ approaches 10,000/10,000. You and I, on the other hand, have a pretty small denominator. This means that the absolute quality of contact we can achieve by way of this book is relatively low. But we can still work toward a CQ of unity—maybe 100/100—and this is one of my goals in this introduction and the other materials I've written for this book.

It's going to be difficult, though, to maximize the CQ between you and me. I can continue to tell you some of who I am, but I don't know whether what I write is what you need in order to know me as me. In addition, I know almost nothing about what makes you a person—nothing about your choices, feelings, hopes, fears, insights, or blind spots—your individuality. This is why *writing* about interpersonal communication can sometimes be frustrating. Interpersonal communication can be discussed in print, but not much of it can happen here.

More can happen, though, than usually does with a textbook. Our relationship can be at least a little closer to interpersonal than it often is. I will work toward this end by continuing to share some of what I'm thinking and feeling in my introductions to the readings, in the Review Questions and Probes at the end of each selection, and in the essays I've authored or co-authored. I hope you'll be willing to make yourself available by becoming involved enough in this book to recognize clearly which ideas and skills are worthwhile for you and which are not. I also hope you'll be willing and able to make yourself available to other persons reading this book, so they can benefit from your insights and you can benefit from theirs.

WHY APPROACH INTERPERSONAL COMMUNICATION THIS WAY?

Before we begin breaking human communication down into manageable parts, I want to talk about a couple of beliefs that guide my selection and organization of the materials in this book. I believe that when you know something about this book's rationale, it'll be easier for you to understand what's being said about each topic, and you'll be in a better position to accept what works for you, while leaving aside the rest.

Quality of Communication and Quality of Life

One of my basic assumptions is that *there's a direct link between the quality of your communication and the quality of your life.* I can best explain this idea with a little bit more of my history.

After high school, I attended a community college for two years and then transferred to a four-year college to finish my degree. I took a basic speech communication course at both schools and noticed that in each, something was missing. The teachers emphasized how to inform others and persuade them to do what you want. They showed our classes how to research and outline ideas, how to move and gesture effectively, and how to use vocal variety to keep our listeners' attention. Students were required to write papers and give speeches to demonstrate that they'd mastered these skills. But the courses seemed to overlook something important. Neither the textbooks nor the instructors said anything about the connection between the quality of your communication and the quality of your life.

Other texts and teachers did. In my literature and anthropology classes, I read that "no human is an island" and that "the human is a social animal." Psychology books reported studies of infants who suffered profoundly when they were deprived of touch, talk, or other kinds of contact. A philosophy text made the same point in these words: "communication means life or death to persons.... Both the individual and society derive their basic meaning from the relations that exist between [persons]. It is through dialogue that [humans] accomplish the miracle of personhood and community."[1]

The communication texts and teachers promised that they could help students learn to make ideas clear, be entertaining, and persuade others to agree with them. But they seemed to miss the impact of the point being made in literature, anthropology, psychology, and philosophy. If humans really are social beings, then *communication is where humanness happens.* In other words, although communication is definitely a way to express ideas, get things done, and entertain, convince, and persuade others, it's also more than that. It's the process that defines who we are. As a result, *if we experience mainly distant, objective, impersonal communicating, we're liable to grow up pretty one-sided, but if we experience our share of close, supportive, interpersonal communicating, we're likely to develop more of our human potential.* This is how the quality of your communication affects the quality of your life.

One reason I started teaching interpersonal communication is that I figured out the truth of this idea, and this same point has motivated me to edit this book. I've also been impressed with some research that supports this reason for studying interpersonal communication. Malcolm Parks reviews this research in the next chapter.

As Parks notes, medical doctors have done some of the most impressive studies. James J. Lynch was co-director of the Psychophysiological Clinic and Laboratories at the University of Maryland School of Medicine when he introduced one of his books with these words:

> As we shall see, study after study reveals that human dialogue not only affects our hearts significantly but can even alter the biochemistry of individual tissues at the farthest extremities of the body. Since blood flows through every human tissue, the entire body is influenced by dialogue.[2]

In other words, Lynch is saying that the quality of your communication affects the *physical* quality of your life. One of his important discoveries was that blood pressure changes much more rapidly and frequently than people used to believe, and that some of the most significant blood pressure changes occur when people speak and are spoken to. Computerized instruments permitted Lynch and other researchers to monitor blood pressure constantly and to map the effects of a person's entering the room, engaging in nonverbal contact, reading aloud, and conversing. Speech appears to directly affect blood pressure; in one study, the mean arterial pressure of healthy nurses went from 92 when they were quiet to 100 when they "talked calmly."[3] Listening has the opposite effect. Rather than just returning to baseline when a person stops speaking, blood pressure actually drops below baseline when one concentrates on the other person.[4] And this happens only when we talk with people; "conversation" with pets does not produce the same result.[5]

What conclusions can be drawn from evidence like this? Lynch put it this way:

> Human companionship does affect our heart, and ... there is reflected in our hearts a biological basis for our need for loving human relationships, which we fail to fulfill at our peril.... The ultimate decision is simple: we must either learn to live together or increase our chances of prematurely dying alone.[6]

In other words, if you view quality of life physically, it becomes apparent that there's more to it than ample food, warm clothing, shelter, education, and modern conveniences. The quality of your existence is linked directly to the quality of your communication.

If you go beyond physical quality of life, the same point can be made even more strongly. In fact, nonmedical people have been talking about the link between the quality of your communication and the quality of your life for many years. For example, to paraphrase the philosopher Martin Buber:

> The unique thing about the human world is that something is continually happening between one person and another, something that never happens in the animal or plant world.... *Humans are made human by that happening....* This special event begins by one human turning to another, seeing him or her as this particular other being, and offering to communicate with the other in a mutual way, building from the individual world each person experiences to a world they share together.[7]

Jesuit psychologist John Powell put the same idea in simpler terms: "What I am, at any given moment in the process of my becoming a person, will be determined by my relationships with those who love me or refuse to love me, with those I love or refuse to love."[8]

"Okay," you might be saying, "I don't disagree with the lofty ideals expressed by all these people, and I can see how quality of life and quality of communication are related, but let's be a little practical. It's not always *possible* to treat everybody as a personal friend, and more importantly, it's not always *wise*. So you can't realistically expect your communication always to be friendly and supportive. Impersonal communication happens all the time, and often it's exactly the right kind of communication to have."

I agree. And this is an important point. Many factors make interpersonal communication difficult or even impossible. Role definitions, status relationships, cultural differences, physical surroundings, and even the amount of time available can all be obstacles to interpersonal contact. Lack of awareness and lack of skills can also affect your CQ. One person may want to connect interpersonally with someone else but may simply not know how to do it.

In other situations, it may be possible but, as you point out, it may not be wise. The power relationships or amount of hostility may make it too risky. Everyday communication also includes a great deal of deception. One study concluded that 62 percent of statements made in conversations could be classified as deceptive, and in two other large surveys, more than one-third of the respondents admitted to lying to close friends about important topics.[9] The bottom line is that all of our contacts certainly cannot be interpersonal, but in most cases, more of them could be. And if they were, the quality of our lives would be enhanced.

Human Being Results from Human Contact

The second, closely related basic assumption behind the materials in this book is that *there is a basic movement in the human world, and it is toward relation, not division.* This might sound a little vague, but I think it'll get clearer if you bear with me for a couple of paragraphs. First, I believe that human life is a process and that the general kind of process we humans are engaged in is growing into fully developed persons. So far, no big deal, right?

Second, humans are relational, not solitary, beings. We fundamentally need contact with other persons. If you could combine a human egg and sperm in a completely impersonal environment, what you'd end up with would not be a person. This is different from cloning. I'm thinking about an artificial womb, machine-assisted birth, mechanical feeding and changing, and so on. Why wouldn't the being that was created this way be a person? Because in order to become a person, the human needs to experience relationships with other persons. This point can't be proved experimentally, of course, because it would be unethical to treat any human organism that way. But some empirical evidence supports this claim; I'm thinking of studies of "feral," or "wild," children—children discovered after they'd been raised for a time by wolves or other animals. One book tells about the Wild Boy of Aveyron, a "remarkable creature" who came out of the woods near a small village in southern France on January 9, 1800, and was captured while digging for vegetables in a village garden. According to the people who knew him, the creature

> was human in bodily form and walked erect. Everything else about him suggested an animal. He was naked except for the tatters of a shirt and showed no modesty, no awareness of himself as a human person related in any way to the people who had captured him. He could not speak and made only weird, meaningless cries. Though very short, he appeared to be a boy of about eleven or twelve.[10]

The creature was taken to a distinguished physician named Dr. Pinel, one of the founders of psychiatry. The doctor was unable to help, partly because "the boy had no human sense of being in the world. He had no sense of himself as a person related to other persons."[11] The "savage of Aveyron" made progress toward becoming human only after he was taken on as a project by another medical doctor named Jean-Marc Gaspard Itard. Itard's first move was to place the boy in a foster family, in the care of a mature, loving mother, Mme. Guerin. In this household, the boy was able to learn to "use his own chamber pot," dress himself, come when he was called, and even associate some letters of the alphabet with some pictures.

Itard's first report about his year of efforts to socialize the wild boy emphasized the importance of human contact in becoming a person. Itard described in detail events that demonstrate the significance of "the feeling of friendship" between him and the boy and especially between the boy and Mme. Guerin: "Perhaps I shall be understood if people remember the major influence on a child of those endless cooings and caresses, those kindly nothings which come naturally from a mother's heart and which bring forth the first smiles and joys in a human life."[12] Without this contact, the young human organism was a creature, a savage. With contact, he began to develop into a person.

Accounts like this one help make the point that *human being results from human contact.* Our genes give us the potential to develop into humans, but without contact, this potential cannot be realized. People definitely are affected by solitude, meditation, and quiet reflection, but mostly because those individualized activities happen in the context of ongoing relationships. As many writers have pointed out, we are molded by our contacts with nature, our contacts with other humans, and our contacts with whatever supreme being, higher power, or god we believe in. This book focuses on the second kind—our contacts with people.

This is *why* there is a direct connection between the quality of your communication and the quality of your life. This is also why I encourage you to think about your communicating in terms of its Contact Quotient. You certainly cannot have the same quality of contact with everybody you meet, in every situation. But you can recognize the quality of contact that's possible between you and the other person(s) and work toward a CQ of 1/1.

Again, I'm not saying that if everybody just holds hands, smiles, and stares at the sunset, all conflict will disappear and the world will be a happy place. But the kind of communicating discussed in this book is not just a trendy, pop-psychology, Western, white, middle-class exercise in narcissism or New Age good feeling. It's grounded in some basic beliefs about who human beings are and what communication means in human life—regardless of ethnicity, gender, class, or age. In the first reading of Chapter 2, I say more about this point. When you read those pages, you might want to refer to the two assumptions I just described.

PREVIEW OF THE BOOK

So far I've tried to say that for me, interpersonal communication differs from impersonal communication in that it consists of *contact between (inter) persons.* This means that for interpersonal communication to happen, each participant has to be willing and able to talk and listen in ways that maximize the presence of the personal. This willingness and ability will happen only when the people involved (1) are familiar with the foundations of interpersonal communication, (2) are willing and able to accurately perceive and listen to themselves and others, and to make themselves and their ideas available to others, (3) recognize how the basic communication processes work in various relationships, and (4) have some resources to deal with communication difficulties.

This is why I've organized *Bridges Not Walls* into four sections, or parts; the readings in each part are designed to do what I've just outlined. So the next three chapters, which complete Part One, explore the rest of the foundations—your overall view of the communication process (Chapter 2), the communicative or social nature of who we are (Chapter 3), and the verbal and nonverbal parts of the process (Chapter 4). Part Two is organized around the metaphor "inhaling-exhaling." I explain the reasons for this metaphor in the introduction to Chapter 5. Basically, I use the term *inhaling* to highlight the perception and listening parts of the communication process and *exhaling* to focus attention on the messages that are expressed. The allusion to breathing emphasizes the impossibility, in actual practice, of separating these two processes.

Chapter 5 treats various parts of inhaling, including person perception and listening. Chapter 6 is made up of articles discussing self-expression and self-disclosure. Together, Parts One and Two lay out the general communication process and specific information about each of its main subparts.

The last two sections of this book focus on application. The two chapters of Part Three discuss applications to relationships. There are four readings about family and friend relationships in Chapter 7, and four treatments of communication between intimate partners in Chapter 8. Next are the four chapters that make up Part Four, "Bridges Not Walls," where 25 different authors grapple with some of the most difficult situations where communication knowledge and skills are applied. Chapter 9 focuses on some of the kinds of communication that generate walls: hurtful messages, deception, betrayal, aggression, defensiveness, and power. Then in Chapter 10, eight authors offer suggestions about how to manage conflict by turning walls like these into bridges. This is followed by a chapter that focuses on the special difficulties that often emerge in contacts between members of different cultures—ethnic groups, genders, ages, and so on. Finally, Chapter 12 describes dialogue, a kind of communicating that, at the beginning of the 21st century, many people are offering as the best way to build bridges not walls.

Before each reading, some introductory comments guide your reading and I bullet each selection's main ideas. At the end of each reading, I've also included two kinds of questions. Review Questions prompt your recall of key ideas. Probes are questions intended to provoke your thinking and discussion, especially about how the ideas in the reading relate (1) to your own life experience and (2) to ideas in other readings.

One final note: A few of the essays that I have reprinted here were written before people learned about the destructive potential of the historical male bias in the English language. As a result, when these authors mean "humanity," "humans," or "humankind," they write *man* or *mankind.* And when they are using a pronoun to refer to a person in the abstract, it's always *he* rather than *she* or *he and she.* Wherever possible, I've tried to delete offensive uses or to substitute terms in brackets.

I also hope that you can have some fun with at least parts of what's ahead. Sometimes the topics are serious, and occasionally the concepts are complex. But this book is about familiar activities that all of us engage in just about all the time. By the time you're finished with it, you should be an even more effective communicator than you already are. This kind of learning can be exciting!

NOTES

1. Reuel Howe, *The Miracle of Dialogue* (New York: Seabury, 1963), cited in *The Human Dialogue,* ed. F. W. Matson and A. Montagu (New York: Free Press, 1968), pp. 148–49.
2. James J. Lynch, *The Language of the Heart: The Body's Response to Human Dialogue* (New York: Basic Books, 1985), p. 3.
3. Lynch, pp. 123–24.
4. Lynch, pp. 160ff.
5. Lynch, pp. 150–55.
6. James J. Lynch, *The Broken Heart: The Medical Consequences of Loneliness* (New York: Basic Books, 1977), p. 14.
7. Paraphrased from Martin Buber, *Between Man and Man* (New York: Macmillan, 1965), p. 203.
8. John Powell, *Why Am I Afraid to Tell You Who I Am?* (Chicago: Argus Communications, 1969), p. 43.
9. H. Dan O'Hair and Michael J. Cody, "Deception," in *The Dark Side of Interpersonal Communication,* ed. W. R. Cupach and B. H. Spitzberg (Hillsdale, NJ: Lawrence Erlbaum, 1994), pp. 183–84.
10. Roger Shattuck, *The Forbidden Experiment: The Story of the Wild Boy of Aveyron* (New York: Farrar, Straus and Giroux, 1980), p. 5.
11. Shattuck, p. 37.
12. Shattuck, p. 119.

CHAPTER 2

Communication and Interpersonal Communication

Communicating and Interpersonal Communicating

John Stewart

One of the best courses I took during my first year of college was Introduction to Philosophy. Part of the appeal was the teacher. He knew his topic, and he loved to teach it. But as I discovered a few years later, I also enjoyed the course because I liked the kind of thinking that was going on in the materials we read and the discussions we had. As I continued through college, I supplemented my communication courses with other work in philosophy. The topics I talk about in this essay reflect this dual interest.

One definition of philosophy is "the systematic critique of presuppositions." This means that philosophers are interested in first principles, basic understandings, and underlying assumptions. If you've read much philosophy, you may have the impression that it can be stuffy or even nitpicky. But it can also be exciting and important, because the philosopher says something like, "Hold it! Before you go off to spin a complicated web of explanations about something important—like how people should treat each other, principles of economics and business, or how people communicate—try to get clear about some *basic* things. When you're talking about human communication, for example, what are you assuming about what actually gets passed between people as they communicate? Ideas? Meanings? Or just light and sound waves?" The philosopher might say, "Since meanings are internal, and all that gets exchanged are light and sound, one person can communicate only with *his or her perceptions of* another person. This means I can *never* communicate directly with you. All I can do, when it comes right down to it, is communicate with myself!"

Basic issues like these intrigue me, mainly because they have so many practical effects. Our assumptions about things "leak" out in everything we do. For example, do you know somebody who fundamentally believes that it's a dog-eat-dog world? Watch him or her walk. Listen to the way that person answers the phone. Look at his or her typical facial expression. People's everyday choices about both big and small beliefs and actions grow out of their assumptions—about what's right, what's important, what's honorable, what will provide the best income, or whatever.

So it's important to think about these assumptions and to change them when they aren't working well. I know that many potentially exciting conversations have been squelched by someone's insistence that all participants "define their terms." But I also know that a great deal of fuzziness can be cleared up and many unhealthy choices can be revised when a conversation starts with some shared understandings about the assumptions behind what's being discussed.

In the following essay, I describe my definition of the topic of this book—interpersonal communication. I begin with a six-part description of communication in general that includes a practical implication of each of the six parts. Then I discuss interpersonal communication as a subset of the more general term.

As you'll notice, the views of communication and interpersonal communication that I develop here extend the point I made in Chapter 1 about quality of communication and quality of life. One of the most important things I want to emphasize throughout this book

is that communication functions partly to negotiate identities, or sel
who we are emerges in our listening and talking. This is why the rea
extended explanation of how human worlds or realities are collabo
(built, modified, torn down, rebuilt) in communication. And the defin
communication grows out of this point. In brief, as I put it, interperse
happens when the people involved talk and listen in ways that maximize the presence of
the personal.

16   th

The reading is a little long, and I apologize for that. But I'm using it to frame everything
that follows in this book.

MAIN IDEAS

- It's important to pay attention to your basic view of communication, because it "leaks
out" in your communication behavior.
- Linear, causal, content-based views of communication are misleading and
inaccurate.
- Communication is best viewed as the continuous, complex, collaborative process of
verbal and nonverbal meaning-making.
- One implication of this view is that no one person controls a communication event or
causes a communication outcome.
- Principles of causality—and attendant fault and blame—cannot accurately be applied
to human communication events.
- A second implication is that choices communicators make reveal their ethical stan-
dards and commitments.
- A third implication is that culture always affects communication.
- A fourth is that human identities are always in play.
- A fifth is that the most influential communication events are often the most
common.
- A sixth is that the single most important communication skill is nexting.
- Interpersonal communication can be understood as one end of a continuum that has
impersonal communication at the other end.
- Interpersonal communication is the kind or quality of contact that happens when
the people involved talk and listen in ways that maximize the presence of the
personal.
- "The personal" consists of five qualities: uniqueness, unmeasurability, responsiveness,
reflectiveness, and addressability.
- To the degree that communicators are able to "give out" and "take in" appropriate
features of "the personal," the contact between them will be interpersonal.

Communication is an intriguing topic to study because, on the one hand,
you and I have been doing it since at least the day we were born, so we
have some claim to being "experts," and on the other hand, many of the
difficulties that people experience are communication difficulties, which suggests that we all have a lot to learn. If your communication life is trouble-free,

⌐ book and the course it is probably a part of might not be for you. But if your experience is anything like mine, you might be interested in some help. After over 45 years of communication study and teaching, I still experience plenty of misunderstandings, but I've found that some basic insights about what communication is and how it works can smooth many of the rough spots. That's why this introduction describes the general subject matter of communication and this book's specific focus, interpersonal communication. I think you'll discover that there are some common ways of thinking about these topics that can actually make things harder rather than easier. And there are some important features of communication and interpersonal communication that significantly affect how they work.

COMMUNICATING[1]

In the most general sense, the terms "communication" and "communicating" label *the continuous, complex, collaborative process of verbal and nonverbal meaning-making*. When somebody says, "She's a good communicator" or "We communicate well," it basically means that contacts with these persons tend to go smoothly and that there aren't many confusions or misunderstandings, which is to say that the meanings the people build together generally work okay. By the same token, people talk about "poor communication" when they experience confusing, ambiguous, frustrating, disrespectful, or incomplete meanings.

The word "continuous" in the definition reminds us that communication was going on when we were born and it will continue after we're dead. "Complex" means that there are many elements or dimensions of every communicative event, including facial expression, tone of voice, choice of words, past history, and social roles, among dozens of other factors. The words "verbal and nonverbal" highlight the two basic codes that humans work with. And the term "collaborative" just means that we co-labor, or work together on the meanings we make. Even when two parties are in the midst of a violent disagreement, they are still co-constructing their meanings of anger, hostility, fairness, and respect. So whether you're talking about written or spoken communication, face-to-face or digital, conflict or cooperation, the process basically involves humans making meaning together.

Meaning is what makes the human world different from the spaces inhabited by other living beings—worms, dogs and cats, and even, so far as we now know, chimpanzees, whales, and dolphins. Since humans live in worlds of meaning—rather than worlds made up of only objects or things—communication is a major part of human living.

To clarify this idea that humans live in worlds of meaning, consider the part of your world that's your "home." If someone asked you to describe your home, you probably wouldn't just talk about how many square feet it has, how tall it is, how far it is from your home to some prominent landmark, or what color the bedroom walls are (objective features). Instead, you'd talk about what it *means* to live in a place this small or this big, what you think and feel about the wall color, and what it *means* to live where your home is located. And the meanings of all these parts of our worlds get built up (constructed) and changed in communication—the written and oral, verbal and nonverbal contact people have with each other.

When each of us was born, this process of meaning-making was going on all around us, and we entered it kind of like a chunk of potato when it's plopped into a pot of simmering soup. The soup was there before we were born, it will be simmering all the time we're alive, and these communication processes will continue after we die. As individuals and groups, we certainly affect our worlds more than a chunk of potato affects a pot of soup. But each of us is also a participant in an ongoing process that we do not completely control, a process as old and as vast as the history of humanity. All the time, everywhere, in all the contacts that make us social animals, humans are constructing meaning together, and "communication" is the name of this ongoing process.

Interpersonal communication is a subset of this general process, a particular kind or type of communication. I'll describe what it is later. But first I want to explain six important features of all kinds of communication, the first of which I've already introduced, and an important implication or practical application of each of the six:

Six Features of Communication

1. **Meaning:** Humans live in worlds of meaning, and communication is the process of collaboratively making these meanings.
   Implication 1: No one person can completely control a communication event, and no single person or action causes—or can be blamed for—a communication outcome.
2. **Choice:** All communication involves choices, some of which we actively consider, and others that seem almost automatic.
   Implication 2: The choices communicators make reveal their ethical standards and commitments.
3. **Culture:** Culture and communication are intertwined. Ethnicity, gender, age, social class, sexual orientation, and other cultural features always affect communication and are affected by it.
   Implication 3: Your cultures, and mine, affect what I say about communication in this book and how you respond to it.
4. **Identities:** Some of the most important meanings people collaboratively construct are identities; all communicating involves negotiating identities, or selves.
   Implication 4: Identity messages are always in play.
5. **Conversation:** The most influential communication events are conversations.
   Implication 5: The most ordinary communication events are often the most significant.

6. **Nexting:** The most important single communication skill is "nexting." *Implication 6:* Whenever you face a communication challenge or problem, the most useful question you can ask yourself is, "What can I help to happen next?"

1. Meaning: Humans Live in Worlds of Meaning, and Communication Is the Process of Collaboratively Making These Meanings

When I introduced this idea, you might have thought it was kind of strange. Most people don't give much thought to their definition of *communication,* and if pressed, a person who's new to this subject matter might just say that communication basically means "getting your ideas across," or "sending and receiving messages." In fact, there's a widespread belief in many cultures that communication

- Begins when a sender gets an idea he or she wants to communicate.
- Works by having the sender translate the idea into words or some other kind of message.
- Requires the receiver to perceive the message and retranslate it into an idea.
- Can be evaluated in terms of the match, fit, or, fidelity between message sent and message received.
- Can be analyzed by figuring out who *caused* its successes or failures (who's responsible, who gets the credit, who's at fault or to blame).

According to this definition, the general process of communication can be diagrammed this way:

$$\text{Idea}_1 \rightarrow \text{Message Sent} \rightarrow \text{Message Received} \rightarrow \text{Idea}_2$$

When idea$_2$ is the same as idea$_1$, then communication is successful. When the two ideas don't match, there's a misunderstanding that's somebody's "fault."

This might sound like a fairly reasonable, even accurate, understanding of communication. **But all these common beliefs about communication are misleading, and if you act on them, you're likely to have problems.**

Let's consider each briefly.

Communication Consists Mainly of "Getting Your Ideas Across"   This belief focuses attention on the topic or content of the communication—the ideas people talk about. And it's reasonable to believe that idea transmission or information sharing is the most important function of communication. But to test this belief, look for a minute at an excerpt from an actual conversation:

JOHN: So what do you THINK about the bicycles on campus?
JUDY: I think they're terrible.

JOHN: Sure is about a MILLION of 'em.

JUDY: Eh, heh.

JOHN: (Overlapping Judy) Duzit SEEM to you ... there's a lot more people this year?

JUDY: The re-yeah, for sure.

JOHN: (Overlapping) Go-GOD, there seems to be a mILLion people.

JUDY: Yeah. (brief pause) YEah, there's way too many. I can't ... at TIMES the bicycles get so bad I just get off mine and ... hhh ... give up.

JOHN: (Overlapping) Oh, really ...

JOHN: I dunno, when I DODGE one then I have to DODGE another one, 'n it's an endless cycle.

JUDY: Yeah (brief pause), oh they're TERrible.

JOHN: 'S so many people.

JUDY: Um hmm.[2]

The content of this conversation—bicycles on campus—is only a small part of what's going on here. John and Judy are college students who have just met, and they are using the topic of bicycles in part to figure out who they are to and for each other. In fact, the most important parts of this conversation are probably not John's and Judy's ideas about bicycles, but the commonality that their similar opinions creates, combined with the subtle power relationship that's constructed when John defines the topic and overlaps Judy's talk, and Judy is willing to go along with this slightly one-up/one-down relationship. In other words, especially if you remember that John and Judy don't know each other well, you'd probably agree that the most important features of this conversation are what communication researchers call the *identity messages* or *relationship messages* (implication 4). These are the verbal and nonverbal indicators of how John defines himself, how he views Judy, and what he thinks Judy thinks of him, along with Judy's verbal and nonverbal ways of defining herself, what she thinks of John, and what she thinks John thinks of her. These messages about the identities, or selves, of the persons involved and their relationships with each other are at least as important as the idea content, and often more so. So the first part of the common definition of communication is misleading because human communication always involves more than simply getting ideas across.

Communication Works by Having the Sender Translate the Idea into Words or Some Other Kind of Message   This belief assumes that speech happens when a speaker changes a mental idea into spoken words. But this conversation didn't just "start" when John got a nonverbal idea about bicycles in his head. He's encountering Judy in a particular context—in this case, they're both volunteer subjects in a communication experiment. Their social, political, and religious cultures help define how similar-age men and women strangers relate to one another, and they're probably each looking for ways to make the encounter as comfortable as possible. So the topic of bicycles emerges out of a context much broader than John's mind. In addition, before John spoke, there was probably no clearly identifiable, singular piece of mental content (an idea) located somewhere in his brain. The phenomena called "ideas" are complex and always changing; they're made up not simply of synapse patterns or cognitions but of words, intonations, stresses, pauses, and facial expressions; and they change as they are being uttered. This means that *there is no unitary, identifiable thing inside a person's head (an idea) that gets translated or encoded into spoken words.*

Communication Requires the Receiver to Perceive the Message and Retranslate It into an Idea   This belief suggests that listeners are doing the same things that speakers are, only in reverse. But again, human communication is not this simple. First, notice that neither John nor Judy is simply "sender" or "receiver" at any point in this exchange; in fact, they're both sending and receiving at every moment. *As she speaks,* Judy is noticing John's response (she is receiving) and is modifying what she says and how she says it. John is doing the same thing. *As he listens,* he's "saying" things to Judy with his face and body. And this goes on all the time. Human communicators are always sending and receiving simultaneously. As a result, each communicator has the opportunity to change how things are going at any time in the process. When this excerpt of the conversation ends, John and Judy are at a point of potential change, and the next utterance may move them closer together or further apart. John could pick up on Judy's disclosure that she is a cyclist, for example, or Judy could introduce a new topic that's more important to her than this one. The point is, much more is going on here than back-and-forth translation and retranslation of individual ideas.

Communication Can Be Evaluated in Terms of the Match, Fit, or Fidelity Between Message Sent and Message Received   This belief suggests that it is possible to isolate and define John's and Judy's mental contents (ideas) to figure out how well they match or fit. But since ideas are so fluid and dynamic, and since communication happens as much in talk as in people's heads, the fidelity model doesn't fit living conversation very well. In order to apply this notion of matching or fitting, you'd have to slow down and distort the exchange to the point where it wouldn't be anything like what actually happened. Communication success has more to do with the people's ability to continue relating smoothly with each other than with matching mental contents.

Communication Problems Can Be Analyzed by Identifying Fault and Blame To say that a problem is somebody's "fault" is to say that she or he *caused* it, just as a temperature below 0°C causes water to freeze, or pushing down on one end of a lever causes the other end to rise. In other words, this belief assumes that human communication is governed by laws of cause and effect. But is it? If Judy noticed the one-up/one-down power relationship with John, she might believe that it's John's fault because he asserted power by taking on the roles of topic definer and overlapping speaker.[3] John, on the other hand, might think that any power imbalance between them is due to Judy's initial silence or to her willingness to go along with his topic choice. Who's right? Whose fault is it, really? Who's really to blame?

One problem with questions like these is that they require somebody to identify where the exchange *started*, so they can determine what's "cause" and what's "effect." But as I've already noted, some of what's going on in a conversation is as old as the participants themselves, or older. And this is literally always true. Every single thing the participants say and do may be understood as a *response to* what preceded it in their lives. No living human is the original Adam or Eve, the first one to disturb the cosmic silence of the universe. An enormous amount of communication precedes everything all of us communicate.[4] Even the first "hi" in a relationship can be understood as a response to a smile, the situation, or a lesson your parents taught you about being polite. In John and Judy's conversation, some of what's said can be traced back to the gender definitions that each of them developed when they were growing up. And these influences could be traced back to John's and Judy's parents' definitions of themselves, which came in part from *their* parents, and so on. This is the kind of complex mess a search for original causes can suck you into. And for the sake of argument, let's assume that John and Judy finally agree on just where the exchange started and whose fault some part of it was. What then? Will the resulting guilt feelings or an apology from the accused party fix the problem? Not usually. Even when people agree on fault and blame, that agreement doesn't usually improve things much. The reason is that human communication is much too complex to be profitably analyzed into simple cause–effect, fault–blame sequences.

In short, two things can be learned from this brief example:

- Some of the most common understandings or definitions of human communication are plausible but misleading.
- Since the way you think about or define something determines what you experience, and what you experience determines the responses you make (in other words, assumptions, as I said before, "leak" out in all our beliefs and behaviors), it's important to have a workable definition of human communication so you can respond in ways that help you communicate effectively.

The main reason that this common definition of communication is misleading is that it's oversimplified.

Communication Is the Continuous, Complex, Collaborative Process of Verbal and Nonverbal Meaning-Making   As I mentioned before, it's *continuous* because humans are always making meaning—figuring out, making sense of, or interpreting what's happening. It's *complex* because it involves not just words and ideas but also intonation, facial expression, eye contact, touch, and several other nonverbal elements, and it always includes identity and relationship messages, culture and gender cues, more or less hidden agendas, unspoken expectations, and literally dozens of other features that usually become apparent only when they create problems. It's *collaborative*, because we do it with other people; we don't communicate alone.[5] "Co-labor-ating" just means working together, and collaboration can be as anonymous as obeying traffic laws and speaking the local language, or as intimate as attending to your partner's lovemaking preferences.

Implication 1: No One Person Can Completely Control a Communication Event, and No Single Person or Action Causes—or Can Be Blamed for—a Communication Outcome   Many people come to communication classes or workshops wanting to learn how to "do it right." They want to know how to *solve* the communication problems they experience—get their parents off their backs; eliminate misunderstandings with roommates, co-workers, or dating partners; deal with a critical and complaining boss; end a painful relationship; become a masterful salesperson. These people are disappointed, and some are even angry, when they learn that it isn't that simple. They are even more uncomfortable when they learn that it's an illusion to believe that surefire techniques of human communication even exist! As philosopher William Barrett put it over 30 years ago in his book *The Illusion of Technique*, "Technical thinking cannot deal with our human problems."[6]

I don't mean that technical thinking is hopeless or that there's nothing to be gained from scientific and social scientific experiments. But one direct implication of the recognition that communication is a *collaborative* process is that no one person can completely control any communication event and no technique or set of communication moves can definitely determine its outcome.

Regardless of how clearly I write or speak, you may still interpret me in a variety of ways. Regardless of how carefully I plan a meeting, one or more people are likely to have agendas very different from mine. Even a successful dictator whose orders are consistently followed can't control how people feel about his or her demands.

I believe that your skill as a communicator will be enhanced if you try to manage your expectations about control and perfection. The more you understand how communication works and the more communication skills you develop, the more effective and competent you will be. It is possible to learn how to give and get criticism gracefully, to manage conflict effectively, and to develop relationships smoothly. But not 100 percent of the time.

Cause–effect, fault–blame thinking is one of the oversimplifications people often fall into. I won't repeat what I said in the discussion of John and Judy's communication, but I do want to reemphasize it in this context. Problems obviously happen in communication, and the choices of the people involved help create, maintain, worsen, and solve these problems. But when you understand that communication is *continuous, complex,* and *collaborative*, you cannot coherently blame one person or one set of actions for whatever you might see as problematic. For one thing, fault and blame ignore the continuousness of communication. In order to say someone is at fault, you need to assume that whatever happened *began with the guilty person's action.* But all the people involved have been engaged in communication literally since they were born and have developed and reinforced each other's ways of speaking, listening, and interpreting since at least the time they met. So the person whom you say is at fault because he didn't call you back to confirm the meeting may be remembering your complaints about "getting all those annoying calls" and your insistence that it's only necessary to call if meeting plans change.

Fault and blame also ignore the fact that communication is collaborative. When directions are unclear, for example, it's due to both the direction-giver and the direction-receiver. Did the receiver ask about what confused her? Did the giver check the receiver's understanding? It may have seemed perfectly legitimate to one person to assume that everybody understood that the meeting was at 8:00 P.M. and not 8:00 A.M., for example, or that the family would gather for the holiday dinner just like they had in the past. But others might have radically different assumptions that lead to significantly different interpretations.

Does this mean that when there are problems, nobody's responsible? Does this idea eliminate any possibility of accountability? No, not at all. Individual responses still make a difference, and some are definitely more ethical, appropriate, or humane than others. But I'm trying to replace the oversimplified and distorted notions of fault and blame with a broader focus on both or all "sides" of the communication process. I do not mean to replace "It's his fault" with "It's her fault," "It's both of their faults," or "It's nobody's fault." Instead, I encourage you to give up the notion of fault altogether, at least when you're thinking or talking about human communication.

Another way to put this point is to say that this view of communication redefines what responsibility means. Traditionally, being responsible means that you *caused* something to happen, that it was your fault. But from the perspective I'm developing here, responsibility means *ability to respond,* not fault, blame, or credit. It means *"response-able."* You are response-able when you have the willingness and the ability to contribute in some way to how things are unfolding, rather than ignoring what's going on or dropping out of the event. "Irresponsible" people are not responsive; they act without taking into account what else is going on or how their actions may influence others. Responsible (response-able) actions consider the larger wholes that they help make up. This idea is related to the basic skill of "nexting" that's discussed in feature 6.

2. Choice: All Communication Involves Choices, Some of Which People Actively Consider, and Others That Seem Almost Automatic

Human meanings are inherently ethical because they involve choices. Individually and collectively, humans create and abide by guidelines for evaluating actions as right or wrong, good or bad, and appropriate or inappropriate.

These ethical standards influence people's actions but do not always determine them. Interpersonal communication, as I'll explain, involves reflective and responsive choices.

Some of the choices people make don't feel much like choices. For example, shaking hands and bowing are two culturally influenced actions that one may choose to engage in when meeting another person for a business lunch. Although decisions about how long and how firmly to shake a hand or how deep to bow may be something you actively consider, the initial behavior of shaking or bowing may not be. You may not actively choose the tone of voice you use with your sibling in the same way you may consider how to talk with your best friend, because the norms for interaction in your family culture may be taken for granted, but not in your friendship.

Implication 2: The Choices Communicators Make Reveal Their Ethical Standards and Commitments Consider the issue of shoplifting food from a grocery store, for example. Many people admit to stealing a candy bar as a kid, a choice made for the thrill, as a response to peer pressure, or just because they wanted one and didn't have the money at the time. They might have had an ethical standard that stealing was wrong and another, competing standard that the adrenaline rush, fitting in with friends, or immediate gratification was good. They had to choose between competing standards, and in this case, the stealing-is-wrong ethic carried less weight. Other people cannot understand how anyone could ever decide to steal. For these people, the stealing-is-wrong ethical standard is more heavily weighted, perhaps in response to explicit lessons from family, teachers, or a religious community. But whether you would or would not steal something from a grocery store, how would you evaluate an individual who had been involuntarily unemployed for months, exhausted the resources of the local food bank, and had decided that the only way members of her family would eat today would be if she took a loaf of bread and a jar of peanut butter without paying for them? In this case, is the stealing right or wrong? A good or bad choice? An appropriate or inappropriate action?

The point is that there are always competing forces in human lives and that part of what it means to be human is to make meaningful choices among them. All of our choices are made within the context of our personal experience and are evaluated in relation to cultural norms and expectations. Standards for evaluation can differ from person to person, family to family, and culture to culture over time.

3. Culture: Culture and Communication Are Intertwined. Ethnicity, Gender, Age, Social Class, Sexual Orientation, and Other Cultural Features Always Affect Communication and Are Affected by It

When many people think about culture, they envision a group's customs, cooking, and clothing, but there's much more to it than that. In a very general sense, culture provides you with ways to make meaning. One way to talk about culture is to say that *culture means shared norms, values, and beliefs related to how people live and how people communicate.* These shared values, norms, and beliefs influence every part of people's lives.

Dating, for example, is one context in which the interaction of culture and communication can be observed. In some cultures, dating is a means to an end—a way to select a life partner, and whom you date is your business. In other cultures, it would be inappropriate to bring someone home to meet the folks, because "the folks" (parents, community members, or tribal leaders) will already have made arrangements for marriage.

When you think about culture this way, you'll realize that it involves much more than just national identity. People who share ways of living and speaking—who belong to "the same culture"—can be members of different ethnic groups. Even two members of the same family (for example, a heterosexual brother and his lesbian sister) inhabit different cultures.

Especially today, with the increasing globalization of sports, music, media, business, education, and religion; with the explosion of international communication via the Internet and the Web; and with the growing recognition in education and business that diversity in organizations is a strength rather than a threat, culture is on almost everybody's minds. This is partly why I say that culture figures prominently in communication.

But there is a more basic reason: Culture becomes concrete in communication. What it *means* to belong to a culture is to communicate in certain ways—to use certain expressions that members of other cultures don't use, to prefer certain kinds of meetings, to honor certain styles of speaking, to maintain certain distances, to touch in certain ways, and so on. This means that your culture is present in your communicating and other people's cultures are present in their communicating, too.

Implication 3: Your Cultures—and Mine—Affect What I Say About Communication in This Book and How You Respond to It   Importantly for each author in this book—and for you as reader—*our* cultures are present in our communicating, too. I consider myself to be culturally Western, Anglo, middle class, late middle-aged, heterosexual, gendered, a parent, and a teacher-scholar. This means that my communication content and style in this book will embody these cultural features (and others I am not aware of). You'll get cultural information about some of the other authors in this book, and none about other authors. If you do *not* identify yourself culturally with an author, you may legitimately ask, "How are this person's ideas relevant to me? If culture and communication are so intertwined, what can I—an African-American, perhaps, or Latino, 20-year-old, gay or lesbian, engineering or chemistry student—learn from writings by this person?"

Enough, I hope, to keep you reading. This book offers some knowledge and skills about communication that are supported by evidence from a variety of cultures, and its authors speak from positions in cultures with fairly large memberships and fairly wide ranges of influence. If you are not a member of one or more of the cultures an author belongs to, this material can still be useful to you in at least two ways: (1) You can test generalizations against your experience in your own cultures to determine which apply and which don't, and (2) when an author's ideas don't apply in one or more of your cultures, you can use them to enhance your ability to communicate with people in the cultures the author inhabits.

For example, my first three claims about human communication are that humans live in worlds of meaning that are constructed in communicating, that choices embody ethical standards, and that culture figures prominently in all communication. I believe that there is ample evidence to demonstrate that these points are true about all people in all cultures, *not* just Western, Anglo, middle-class, late middle-aged, heterosexual, gendered, parent, and teacher–scholar cultures. Do you? I encourage you to test these generalizations against your own experience and to discuss the results with your instructor and classmates. On the other hand, as just one example, this book's readings about nonverbal communication may contain some generalizations about space or eye contact that don't ring true for one or more of your cultures. If so, you can combine your understanding of your own culture with what the author says about hers or his and then use this knowledge about space or eye contact in the author's culture to enhance your ability to communicate outside your own culture, with people in the culture the author inhabits.

4. Identities: Some of the Most Important Meanings People Collaboratively Create Are Identities; All Communicating Involves Negotiating Identities, or Selves

Communication theorist and teacher John Shotter emphasizes this point when he says that our "ways of being, our 'selves,' are produced in our ... ways of interrelating ourselves to each other—these are the terms in which we are socially accountable in our society—and these 'traditional' or 'basic' (dominant) ways of talking are productive of our 'traditional' or 'basic' psychological and social [identities]."[7] In other words, who we are—our identities—is built in our communicating. People come to each encounter with an identifiable "self," built through past interactions, and *as we talk,* we adapt ourselves to fit the topic we're discussing and the people we're talking with, and we are changed by what happens to us as we communicate.

The way communication and identity are closely related became especially apparent in a conversation I had with a friend who was going through a painful divorce. "Mary Kay is not the person she used to be," Dale said. "Sometimes I hardly know her. I wish we could communicate and enjoy each other like we did when we were first married."

The times Dale was remembering were before Mary Kay was a mother, before she completed medical school, before she suffered through her residency in an urban hospital 2,000 miles from home, before she joined a prestigious medical clinic, and before she became a full-fledged practicing physician. They were also before Dale was a dad, before he started his import–export business, before he became active in his state professional association, and before he began attending church regularly. Dale was forgetting that Mary Kay could not possibly still be "the person she used to be." Neither could he. Both of them had experienced many relationships that changed them decisively. Mary Kay had been treated like a medical student—required to cram scientific information into her head and spout it on command—and like a first-year resident—forced to go without sleep, stand up to authoritarian doctors, and cope with hospital administrators. Now nurses obey her, many patients highly respect her for her skills, and prestigious doctors treat her like an equal. And she's treated as a mom by her son. Dale has also experienced many different relationships, and he's changed, too. He's treated as a boss by his employees and as "a respected American businessman" by his Japanese customers. Because of the contacts both have experienced, each is a different person. And the process continues as both Mary Kay and Dale continue to be changed by their communication.

Obviously, these identity changes are limited. Most people don't change their gender, ethnicity, or family of origin. But some changes are inevitable over time, and others can happen in the short term. For example, a woman can communicate in ways that say she is more feminine—or more masculine—than her conversation partner and as a person with greater or less authority or power than her conversation partner has. The other person's responses will contribute to the identity as it's negotiated verbally and nonverbally.

Consider the difference, for example, between "Shut the door, stupid!" and "Please close the door." The command projects the identity of a superior speaking to a subordinate. On the other hand, the request identifies the speaker as an equal to the person being addressed. The person who's told to "Shut the door, stupid!" may silently comply, in which case he or she is reinforcing part of the identities of superior and subordinate. Or the person may respond, "Shut it yourself!" which is a negotiation move that says, in effect, "You're not my superior; we're equals."

Implication 4: Identity Messages Are Always in Play   The point is that *identity negotiation, or the collaborative construction of selves, is going on whenever people communicate.* It definitely is not the *only* thing that's happening, but it's one of the very important processes, and it often gets overlooked. When it does, troubles usually result. By contrast, people who are aware of identity negotiation processes can communicate more effectively and successfully in many different situations. So whenever you communicate—on the telephone, via e-mail, face-to-face, in meetings, even in front of the television—part of what is happening is identity negotiation.

Communication content is important, too, and sometimes problems can be solved only when the parties involved have more or better information. Policies may be out of date, data may be incomplete, and people may have misread or misheard key instructions. In these cases, the people involved may need to complete, refine, or recalibrate the information they're working with.

But as I noted, effective communicators understand and manage what they're verbally and nonverbally "saying" about *who they are* to the people they're communicating with. Identities are communicated in many different ways. Topic choice and vocabulary are important. Grooming and dress also contribute to this process, as people offer definitions of themselves using nose rings and other body piercing, tatoos, starched white shirts or blouses, and conservative business suits. Tone of voice is similarly identity-defining. Some people foster misunderstanding by unknowingly sounding like they're skeptical, hostile, or bored, and other tones of voice can help their listeners feel genuinely appreciated and supported. Facial expressions also help define a person as attentive, careful, positive, or their opposites.

Especially when you're troubleshooting—or just trying to live through—a disagreement or conflict, it usually works best to start by understanding the identities that are in play. Who might be getting defined as inattentive, insensitive, or incompetent? What communication moves make one person appear more important, trustworthy, moral, or thorough than the other? Does everybody involved feel able to influence the ways they're viewed by the others? Or are identities being treated as unchangable? By the time you've worked through this book, you should have a wealth of ideas and practical skills for constructively managing how you define yourself and how others define you.

5. Conversation: The Most Influential Communication Events Are Conversations

If you had to identify one event that humans all over the world engage in characteristically—because they're humans—routinely, naturally, and almost constantly, what would it be? We all breathe, but so do other animals. We eat and drink, but not constantly, and again, other animals do too. The one activity that marks us as human and that occupies a large part of our personal and occupational lives is conversation, verbal and nonverbal exchange in real time, either face-to-face or mediated by some electronic medium (e.g., a computer or handheld device).

For a long time, people who studied communication and language tended to overlook this point. Language scholars focused on rules of grammar and syntax, dictionary definitions, and other features of writing, and speech research and teaching paid primary attention to public speaking and deliberation in law courts and legislatures. But in the last third of the 20th century, an increasing number of scholars and teachers have shown how written and formal kinds of communicating are derived from the most basic human activity, informal conversation. For example, two well-known psychologists from Stanford University began a report of their National Science Foundation–supported research with these words:

> Conversation is the fundamental site of language use. For many people, even for whole societies, it is the only site, and it is the primary one for children acquiring language. From this perspective other arenas of language use—novels, newspapers, lectures, street signs, rituals—are derivative or secondary.[8]

Another respected scholar puts it more simply. "Conversation," he writes, "is sociological bedrock,"[9] the absolute foundation or base for everything humans do as social beings. This explains the sense of the title of one of communication theorist John Shotter's books, *Conversational Realities: Constructing Life Through Language*.[10] Shotter's book explains in detail how human realities get constructed in communication—my feature 1—and emphasizes that the most characteristic form of this communication is *conversation*.

Implication 5: The Most Ordinary Communication Events Are Often the Most Significant   The reason I highlight this idea as one of the six main points about human communication is that it justifies paying close attention to something common and ordinary. The fact that humans engage in conversation so constantly, and so often almost without thinking, is part of what makes the process so important. As organizational theorist and trainer Peter Senge puts it, effective conversation is "the single greatest learning tool in your organization—more important than computers or sophisticated research."[11] Whether in a living group, a family-run shop, a small work team, or a multinational corporation, the real organizational structure and rules—as contrasted with what's on the organizational chart—get defined in the subtleties of verbal and nonverbal conversation. (Susan Scott makes this point later in this chapter.) Superior and subordinate status get negotiated in face-to-face contacts. Key decisions are heavily influenced by brief informal contacts in the bathrooms and halls as much as they are by formal presentations in meetings. Similarly, conversation is the primary way families have of making decisions and negotiating differences. And children become effective participants in play groups, classrooms, sports teams, and their own families by learning how to converse well.

This means that one very important way to improve your communication competence is to pay close attention to the most common and everyday kind of communicating—conversation. When you do, you'll discover that you already have a great deal of experience with many of the concepts and skills this book discusses. This means that you have a solid foundation to build on. Even if you don't believe you're very good at conversation, you've done it often and well enough, and it's going on around you so much, that you can build on the experiences you have. One way is with the sixth feature of communication.

6. Nexting: The Most Important Single Communication Skill Is "Nexting"

Nexting is a strange term, I admit. But it's the best one I've come up with for this skill. If, as you read this section, you come up with a better one, please let me know. You can e-mail me at jstewart@dbq.edu.

By "nexting" I *mean doing something helpful next, responding fruitfully to what's just happened, taking an additional step in the communication process.* If you've grasped how I've described communication so far, this is the most important single skill you can build on this understanding. Here's why:

Since you realize that communication is complex, continuous, and collaborative, you'll always recognize that, no matter what's happened before and no matter how bad things currently look, you always have the option to try a *next step*. No matter how many times the same insult has been repeated, the next response can be creative rather than retaliatory. No matter how long the parties have not been speaking to each other, the next time they meet, one of them could speak. No matter how ingrained and toxic the pattern is that two groups are caught in, the next move one side makes could be positive. No matter how much you feel "thrown" by what the other person just said and did, if you give yourself a little time to regroup, you can make a next move that could help get the relationship back on track. No matter how little power the system gives you, your next communication choice can maximize the power you have. Even when it is very difficult not to strike back, your next comment could conceivably be helpful rather than abusive.

When you understand that communication is continuous and collaborative, you'll recognize the potential value of what you do next. Why? Because since no one person determines all the outcomes of a communication event, you can help determine some outcomes, even if you feel almost powerless. Since no one person is 100 percent to blame or at fault, and all parties share response-ability, your next contribution can affect what's happening. Since all communication is collaborative—remember, even prizefighters are co-labor-ating—your next communication move can make a change in the situation, or at least keep the conversation going.

Implication 6: Whenever You Face a Communication Challenge or Problem, the Most Useful Question You Can Ask Yourself Is, "What Can I Help to Happen Next?" You can apply the skill of nexting by remembering that no human system is ever completely determined or cast in stone. Regardless of how well or badly things are going between you and someone else, remember that what you do next will help maintain or destroy this quality. In some cases you may not *want* to try to improve a bad situation or to maintain a good one. You may have tried to make positive contributions and have been continually rebuffed, and you may be out of patience, resources, or caring. You may in this particular case decide not to make a positive, supportive, or conciliatory move. You may also decide to let silence remain, to keep your distance, or to let the hostility fester. But if you understand the world-constructing nature of human communication, you can understand these options for what they are—*responses*, choices, decisions about what you are going to do *next*. They have their benefits and their consequences, just as other responses would.

To put it simply, people who understand communication to be the kind of process I've outlined so far are not generally thrown off balance by communication difficulties. They understand that the most important thing to consider is what they are going to do *next*.

INTERPERSONAL COMMUNICATING

As I said at the start of this chapter, interpersonal communication is a subset of communication in general. This means that collaboration, choices, culture, identities, conversation, and nexting are all parts of interpersonal communicating, too. The kind of communication I'm calling "interpersonal" doesn't happen all the time, but it can take place in families, between friends, during an argument, in business situations, and in the classroom. It can also happen on the telephone, online, among jurors, at a party, across a bargaining table, and even during public speeches or presentations. The main characteristic of interpersonal communication is that the people involved are contacting each other *as persons.* This might sound pretty simple, but again, there's a little more to it than you might think.

For one thing, as you and I move through our daily lives, we tend to relate with others in two different ways. Sometimes we treat others and are treated by them *impersonally* as role-fillers (bank teller, receptionist, employer, bus driver, etc.). And sometimes we connect with others *personally,* as a unique individual (not just role-filler or cultural representative). I don't mean that there are sharp divisions; sometimes we move back and forth between impersonal and interpersonal contact. But these two terms can anchor a sliding scale or continuum that models the qualities or kinds of communication that people experience.

QUALITIES OF COMMUNICATION

Impersonal ———————————————————— Interpersonal

The left side of the continuum, the impersonal side, is characterized by communication that is based on exchanges that minimize the presence of the communicators' personal identities. Impersonal communication is the label I use to describe your typical experiences at the bank, convenience store, and fast-food restaurant, and in front of the most screens. In these situations, people usually connect in ways that emphasize their social roles—teller/customer, buyer/seller, server/diner, and so on. Even though human beings are obviously involved, they all function pretty much like interchangeable parts of an automobile or computer. So long as the teller, buyer, or server knows his or her job (social role), and so long as the customer, seller, or diner remains in his or her role, it doesn't matter much who they are as individuals.

Often, of course, this is exactly the best kind of communicating to have. For one thing, it's efficient. Nobody wants to wait in line while the Burger King cashier has a personal chat with each customer. It's also often the most appropriate kind of communicating. We don't ordinarily approach bank tellers, ticket sellers, or driver's license clerks expecting or wanting to have a deep conversation.

Some impersonal communicating also takes place with people we know well. It is not unusual to engage in efficient, issue-centered communication with people we care about. We also engage in generic greeting rituals with our best friends and family members as well as strangers. It's not uncommon to hear parents involve role-based communication patterns with their children (e.g., "Because I'm the mom, that's why!"). The important point is that impersonal communicating is a common, normal, useful, and often appropriate way of relating.

But some of almost every day's communicating also fits near the right-hand end of the scale. During a committee meeting or team activity, you may contact another person as a unique individual, and you may get treated that way by him or her. The same kind of communicating can happen in your conversations with a dating partner, a parent, a sibling, your roommate, co-workers, or close friends.

No one's communication life can be packaged into neat boxes; that's why the model is a sliding scale. At one moment you may be contacting someone impersonally, and at the next moment your communication may become interpersonal. But what I've said so far clarifies what I mean when I define interpersonal communication, the main topic of this book, as *the type or kind of communication that happens when the people involved talk and listen in ways that maximize the presence of the personal.*

Notice that this definition is not based on the number of people involved or whether they are in the same place. I believe that it is possible to communicate interpersonally in groups and via texting, e-mail, and social media. When communication emphasizes the persons involved rather than just their roles or stereotypical characteristics, interpersonal communication is happening.

Features of the Personal

So what do I mean by "the personal"? Many philosophers, anthropologists, and communication scholars have defined what it means to be a person and how persons differ from other kinds of animals. One widely recognized description was created by a philosopher of communication named Martin Buber. (Buber was born in 1878; lived in Austria, Germany, and Israel; visited the United States a couple of times; and died in 1965.) He suggested that there are five qualities, or characteristics, that distinguish persons across many—though perhaps not all—cultures: uniqueness, measurability, responsiveness, reflectiveness, and addressability.[12] These five define what I mean by "the personal," and I will use the five and their opposites to distinguish *impersonal* from *interpersonal* communicating.

Unique   Uniqueness means noninterchangeability. We, as persons, can be treated as if we were interchangeable parts, but each of us is unique in a couple of ways, genetically and experientially. The main that reason that cloning experiments are controversial is that they threaten this quality. Unless they are cloned or are identical twins, the probability that two persons would have the same genetic materials is 1 in 10 to the ten-thousandth power. That's less than one chance in a billion trillion!

But cloning wouldn't really threaten uniqueness, because even when persons have the same biological raw material, each experiences the world differently. For example, recall identical twins you've known. Both twins might see the same film in the same theater on the same night at the same time, sitting next to each other. Both might leave the theater at the same time and say exactly the same words about it: "I liked that film." At a superficial level, someone might suggest that the experiences of the two are, in this situation, interchangeable. But additional talk will show that they aren't. Did both twins like the film for the same reasons? Did they recall the same experiences as they interpreted the film? Will the film have the same effect on both of them? Will both remember the same things about it? If you asked the twins these questions, you'd get different answers, and you'd discover what you probably knew before you began the process: Each human is unique.

When people are communicating with each other impersonally, they're overlooking most of this uniqueness and focusing on the similarities among all those who play a given social role. All of us naturally and constantly fill many different roles—student, daughter or son, sibling, employee, and so on. And role relationships are an inescapable part of communicating. But the sliding scale emphasizes that people can move from impersonal communication to interpersonal contact.

So the first feature that distinguishes *persons* is experiential and, in most cases, genetic uniqueness. Some cultures downplay this feature, but most Western cultures emphasize it. The more present this feature is in your communicating, the farther your communication is toward the right-hand side of the impersonal-interpersonal continuum.

Unmeasurable   Objects are measurable; they fit within boundaries. An event is of a certain duration; it lasts a measurable amount of time. Even extremely complex objects, such as sophisticated supercomputers, and 100-story buildings, can be completely described in space-and-time terms. This is what blueprints do. They record all the measurements necessary to re-create the object—length, height, width, mass, specific gravity, amperage, voltage, velocity, circumference, hardness, ductility, malleability, conductivity, and so on. Although it's difficult to measure some things directly—the temperature of a kiss, the velocity of a photon, the duration of an explosion—no object or event has any parts that are unmeasurable, in theory at least.

It's different with persons. Even if a medical team accurately identifies your height, weight, temperature, blood pressure, serum cholesterol level, hemoglobin count, and all your other data right down to the electric potential in your seventh cranial nerve, the team will not have exhaustively accounted for the person you are, because there are parts of you that can't be measured. Many scientists, social scientists, philosophers, and theologians have made this point. Some cognitive scientists, for example, include in their model of the person components they call "schematas," or "cognitive patterns" that don't have any space-and-time (measurable) existence, but that can be inferred from observations of behavior. Others call the unmeasurable elements of a person the "human spirit," "psyche," or "soul." But whatever you call it, it's there.

Emotions or feelings are the clearest observable evidence of this unmeasurable part. Although instruments can measure things related to feelings—brain waves, sweaty palms, heart rate, paper-and-pencil responses—what the measurements record is a long way from the feelings themselves. "Pulse 110, respiration 72, Likert rating 5.39, palmar conductivity 0.036 ohms" may be accurate, but it doesn't quite capture what's going on inside when you encounter somebody you can't stand or greet somebody you love.

One other thing: These emotions or feelings are *always* a part of what we are experiencing. Psychologists and educators agree that it's unrealistic to try to separate the intellectual or objective aspect of a person or a subject matter from the affective or emotional parts. This is because humans are always thinking *and* feeling. As one writer puts it, "It should be apparent that there is no intellectual learning without some sort of feeling and there are no feelings without the mind's somehow being involved."[13]

Even though feelings are always present, some communication acknowledges them and some communication doesn't. The cashier who's dedicated to her social role will greet people with a smile and wish them a "nice day" even if she feels lousy. Servers in a restaurant are taught not to bring their feelings to work. Two persons who are in a minority may share similar feelings of isolation or exclusion, but they may or may not talk about them. On the other hand, when people are communicating interpersonally, some of their feelings are in play. This does not mean that you have to wear your heart on your sleeve to communicate interpersonally. It just means that when people are making interpersonal contact, some feelings are appropriately acknowledged and shared.

Responsive   Humans are thoroughly and uniquely responsive beings. Objects can only react; they cannot respond. They cannot choose what to do next. Automatic pilots, photoelectric switches, personal and industrial robots, thermostats, and computers can sometimes seem to operate on their own or turn themselves off and on, but they too are dependent on actions initiated outside them. The computers and robots have to be programmed, the thermostat reacts to temperature, which reacts to the sun's rays, which are affected by the earth's rotation, and so on. Similarly, a ball can go only where it's kicked, and if you were good enough at physics calculations, you could figure out how far and where it would go, on the basis of weight, velocity, aerodynamics, the shape of your shoe, atmospheric conditions, and so on.

But what if you were to kick a person? You cannot accurately predict what will happen, because, when persons are involved, the outcome depends on *response, not simply reaction.* If you tap my knee, you may cause a reflex jerk, but the feelings that occur are not completely predictable, and the behavior or actions that accompany my reflex may be anything from giggles to a slap in the face.

The range of responses is limited, of course. We can't instantly change sex, become three years younger, or memorize the contents of Wikipedia. But we can decide whether to use a conventional word or an obscene one; we can choose how to prioritize our time commitments; and, as will be discussed, choice is even a part of the feelings we experience.

In fact, the more you realize your freedom and power to respond rather than simply react, the more of a person you can be. Sometimes it's easy to get out of touch with this freedom and power. You feel like saying, "I *had* to shout back; he was making me look silly!" or "I just *couldn't* say anything!" These statements make it sound like you don't have any choice, like what you do is completely *caused* by what another person does. But as the discussions of fault and blame and nexting noted, even when circumstances are exerting pressure, persons still have some freedom and power to choose how to respond. It may mean resisting a culturally rooted preference or breaking some well-established habit patterns, and it may take lots of practice, but it's possible to become aware of your responses and, when you want to, to change them. The reason it's important to learn this skill is that when you believe you're just reacting, you've lost touch with part of what it means to be a person. So, all communication involves choices because persons are responsive, and the more you remember and act on this feature, the more interpersonal your communicating can become.

Reflective   A fourth distinguishing characteristic is that persons are reflective. Being reflective means not only that we are aware of what's around us but also that we can be aware of our awareness. As one author puts it, "No matter how much of yourself you are able to objectify and examine, the quintessential, living part of yourself will always elude you, i.e., the part of you that is conducting the examination,"[14] the reflective part. Wrenches, rocks, and rowboats aren't aware at all. Dogs, cats, armadillos, and giraffes are all aware of their environments, but we don't have any evidence that they are aware of their awareness. So far as we know, only humans compose and save histories of their lives, elaborately bury their dead, explore their extrasensory powers, question the meaning of life, and speculate about the past and future. And only humans are aware that we do all these things.

Reflection is not a process that affects only philosophers and people who know that they don't have long to live. Healthy, "ordinary" people reflect, too. I wonder from time to time whether I'm spending my work time wisely and whether I'm making the right parenting decisions. Sometimes you probably wonder what you'll be doing five years from now. Before you make an important decision, you ask questions of yourself and others about priorities and probable consequences. On clear days, you may notice the beauty of the landscape around you and reflect on how fortunate you are to live where you do. Like all persons, you ask questions and reflect.

When people ignore the fact that persons are reflective, their communication usually shows it. For example, you may stick with superficial topics—the weather, recent news items, gossip. On the other hand, when you're aware of your own and others' reflectiveness, you can respond to more of what's going on as you communicate. Questions can be a clear indicator that a person is reflecting. Often people who express their opinions with absolute certainty have forgotten to reflect, to ask what they might be unsure of and what they might not have thought about. But the reflective person will often explicitly express appropriate reservations and qualifications—"I think this is the right thing to do, but I'm not absolutely sure," or "I know I don't want to lie to him, but I'm not sure how or when to tell him."

Addressable   Beings who are addressable are fundamentally *linguistic,* which, as Carole Logan and I explain in Chapter 4, means that we inhabit at least one language. Humans live in a world made up of people more- or less-effectively talking and listening with each other. We don't just "have" or "use" language like a tool, but we inhabit it like a fish inhabits water. Addressable beings can recognize when they are addressed, that is, when they are called or spoken to in language, and can also respond in language. Addressability is what makes the difference between talking *to* and talking *with.* Neither baseball bats nor dogs and cats are addressable, because you can talk to them, but not with them. You can call them, curse them, scold them, and praise them, but you cannot carry on a mutual conversation, even with an "almost human" pet.

Communication theorist John Shotter talks about this feature of human communication under the heading of "addressivity," which he defines as "the quality of being directed toward someone."[15] "Addressed" speech is directed or "aimed" speech, and one characteristic of persons is that they can recognize address and respond in kind. So, for example, as you sit in an audience of several hundred, the speaker can single you out for immediate contact: "Holly Tartar? Are you here? Your question is about job programs, and I want to try to answer it now." Or even more commonly and more directly, you may sit across from a friend and know from the friend's eyes, the touch of his hand, and his voice that he means *you;* he's *present* with you; you are being addressed.

Definition of Interpersonal Communication

Remember that communicators are always both talking and listening, sending and receiving, giving off cues and taking them in—Part Two of this book calls it "exhaling" and "inhaling." These five features—unique, unmeasurable, responsive, reflective, and addressable—can be used to describe how communicators engage in these exhaling and inhaling processes. That is, these five can describe what people are giving out (exhaling) and what they are taking in (inhaling). And, as I noted a few paragraphs earlier, **the term *interpersonal* labels the kind of communication that happens when the people involved talk and listen in ways that maximize the presence of the personal.** When communicators give and receive or talk and listen in ways that emphasize their uniqueness, unmeasureability, responsiveness, reflectiveness, and addressability, then the communication between them is interpersonal. When they listen and talk in ways that highlight the opposites of these five features—interchangeability, measurable aspects, reactivity, unreflectiveness—and imperviousness—their communicating fits on the impersonal end of the sliding scale.

Interpersonal communication is easiest when there are only two of you and you already know and trust each other. But it can also occur early in a relationship—even at first meeting—and, as I've already mentioned, it can occur over the telephone, during an argument, on the job, on social media, and even in public speaking or presentation situations. The important thing is not how many people there are or where they're located, but the peoples' willingness and ability to choose personal over impersonal communication attitudes and behaviors.

Importantly, the terms *impersonal* and *interpersonal* are *descriptive*, not *prescriptive*. Interpersonal communication can be appropriate, effective, or "good" in some situations, and "bad" in others, and the same goes for impersonal contact. The point of this simple model is to give you some control over where your communication is on the impersonal–interpersonal scale.

So the basic definition of interpersonal communication is pretty simple. It's the counterpart of impersonal communication. But as you'll see, I base this book's entire approach on this simple definition. As I've already explained in Chapter 1, each major division of the book, each chapter, and each reading extend a part of the approach to communication, and to interpersonal communication, that I've outlined here. So although this book contains writings by 44 different people, we all view interpersonal communication in similar ways. As a result, by the time you're finished with the book, you ought to have developed not only a deeper understanding of interpersonal communication but also a more powerful and effective sense of how to help make it happen when you want to.

BETWEEN

The backstory: Two lovers, forced by prior commitments to be 2,000 miles apart for six weeks, talk by phone every day. Although they understand that "absence makes the heart grow fonder" and "pain builds character," they dislike the separation. Three weeks into the separation, he writes a poem for her and when he reads it to her over the phone, she cries. After their conversation about that poem, he writes this one.

"You make me cry."
"You make me write."
Lovers touching over miles,
Each reports a personal truth,
And each distorts what's real.

Her tears aren't caused by him,
Like hammer drives a nail
Or the moon moves tides.
His writing's not caused by her,

Like heat boils water,
Or a lever lifts a weight.
Neither makes the other cry or write.

Crying happens when her love meets his words.
Writing blooms from his love of words and her.
Both emerge between.

Her crying shows her love:
Others wouldn't weep,
Some wouldn't even read.
His writing shows his love:
Others might tweet or sing.
Some wouldn't even blink

So it is between these two,
And everywhere that humans walk.
Count all that's individual,
Track each psychic piece,
Trace every singularity,
And what remains counts most:
The syn- in synergy
The function in math,
The green when yellow meets blue—
The between.

Don't shape your world to fit the lie
That "person" equals "island,"
That Adam's only one,
Separate, individual,
Disconnected from partner Eve.

Asian thinkers have it right:
The smallest human unit's two.
We're products of connections.
What's real for each is co- and syn-
Jill's world is built with Jack
And his with her.

So what?
Don't shift from blame to guilt—
"It's all my fault" or "I screwed up."
That's just another lie,
Obscuring what's between.
Instead, refigure fault and blame,
Re-own your role in joys and pains,
Embrace your partnered life.

REVIEW QUESTIONS

1. According to this reading, what is the main distinction between the world inhabited by a dog, cat, chimpanzee, or dolphin and the world inhabited by a human?
2. Why is it misleading to think about human communication in terms of senders and receivers?
3. Complete the sentence: Communication is the c_____, c_____, c_____ process of verbal and _____ meaning-making.
4. According to this reading, what's the difference between responsibility and response-ability?
5. List three qualities in addition to ethnicity that make up a person's culture.
6. True or false: Identity negotiation is the only process that's occurring when humans communicate. Explain.
7. Define *nexting*, and give an example of it from your own communication experience.
8. What is the clearest example of the unmeasurable part of persons?
9. What's the difference between a reaction and a response?
10. The presence of questions in one's communicating is a clear example of which of the following: uniqueness, unmeasurability, responsiveness, reflectiveness, or addressability?
11. Complete the following: This reading defines *interpersonal communication* as the kind of _____ that happens when the people involved _____ and _____ in ways that _____ the presence of the _____.
12. Describe which main points of this reading are made by the poem, "Between."

PROBES

1. At the start of this reading, I outline five common but misleading ideas about communication: that it happens between sender and receiver, that it starts when an idea is translated into a message, that it continues when a message is retranslated into another idea, that it can be evaluated in terms of fidelity, and that it can be understood in terms of cause and effect. Which of these five are part(s) of your understanding of communication? Which are you least willing to give up or change?
2. How often does your communication focus on issues of fault and blame? How productive are these discussions? What alternative do you hear me proposing here?
3. Paraphrase the point I make when I say that collaboration doesn't necessarily mean agreement.
4. Implication 1 says, "No one person can completely control a communication event, and no single person or action causes—or can be blamed for—a communication outcome." How do you respond to this claim?

5. How would you describe the greatest cultural distance between you and the author of this reading? Where are you and this author culturally closest?
6. Describe the identity that you understand me (the author of this reading and the editor of this book) to be trying to develop so far in this book.
7. Without reading ahead to Chapter 3, which do you believe are more important in the identity negotiation process, verbal or nonverbal cues?
8. Which of the five features of the personal—uniqueness, unmeasurability, responsiveness, reflectiveness, or addressability—do you believe is most important in interpersonal communicating?

NOTES

1. "Communica*tion*" or "communica*ting*?" I started with the "-ion" form because it's a little more familiar. But many "-ion" words, like *education, expression, persuasion,* and *sensation,* call to mind the finished product rather than the ongoing process. Education, for example, is something I get at school and expression is something that comes from my voice or body. "Educa*ting,*" on the other hand, calls to mind events, occurrences, and processes, just like such terms as *singing, laughing, arguing,* and *making love.* It's helpful to remember that the topics of this reading are processes. This is why the reading title and main headings use the "-ing" forms.
2. Adapted from an example in Douglas W. Maynard, "Perspective-Display Sequences in Conversation," *Western Journal of Speech Communication* 53 (1989), p. 107.
3. Interruptions, or overlapping speech, can manifest a variety of power relationships between conversation partners. Sometimes overlaps can be supportive, and at other times they are denigrating. See, for example, Deborah Tannen, *Talking from 9 to 5* (New York: Morrow, 1994), pp. 232–34.
4. Russian communication theorist Mikhail Bakhtin put it this way: "Any concrete utterance is a link in the chain of speech communication of a particular sphere.... Each utterance is filled with echoes and reverberation of other utterances to which it is related by the communality of the sphere of speech communication.... The speaker is not Adam, and therefore the subject of his speech itself inevitably becomes the arena where his opinions meet those of his partners." *Speech Genres and Other Essays,* trans. Vern W. McGee, ed. Caryl Emerson and Michael Holquist (Austin: Univ. of Texas Press, 1986), pp. 91, 94.
5. Some people call talking to yourself or thinking out loud "intrapersonal communication," or communication "within" one person. I prefer

to reserve the term *communication* for what happens between two or more people. The main reason is that *common* or *commune* is the root of *communication,* and you can't make something common that's not divided or separated. While any one person obviously has various "parts" or "sides," I think it's most useful to understand the human as a whole, a unity captured by such terms as *I, me,* or *the person.* Talking to yourself and thinking out loud are important processes, but they are fundamentally different from connecting with an *other,* someone who is not you. In addition, I want to emphasize that humans are, first and foremost, "social animals," relational beings. Humans become who we are in our contacts with others, not mainly as a result of thinking and talking to ourselves.

6. William Barrett, *The Illusion of Technique: A Search for Meaning in a Technological Civilization* (Garden City, NY: Anchor Doubleday, 1978), p. xx.

7. John Shotter, "Epilogue," *Conversational Realities: Constructing Life Through Language* (London: Sage, 1993), p. 180.

8. Herbert H. Clark and Deanna Wilkes-Gibbs, "Referring as a Collaborative Process," *Cognition* 22 (1986), p. 1.

9. Emanuel A. Schegloff, "Discourse as an Interactional Achievement III: The Omnirelevance of Action," *Research on Language and Social Interaction* 28 (1995), pp. 186–87.

10. Shotter, 1993.

11. Peter M. Senge, Art Kleiner, Charlotte Roberts, Richard B. Ross, and Bryan J. Smith, *The Fifth Discipline Fieldbook: Strategies and Tools for Building a Learning Organization* (New York: Doubleday, 1994), p. 14.

12. Buber was an international citizen whose major book has been translated into over 20 languages. So he believed that his definition of the person applied across cultures. Some people in cultures that emphasize group identity (e.g., Japan) believe that Buber's emphasis on the individual was misleading. But most people in Western cultures think that his description fits their experience pretty well. What do you think? See Martin Buber, *I and Thou,* trans. Walter Kaufmann (New York: Scribners, 1970).

13. For a discussion of this point, see George Isaac Brown, *Human Teaching for Human Learning: An Introduction to Confluent Education* (New York: Viking Press, 1971).

14. Fredrick Buechner, *Wishful Thinking: A Theological ABC* (New York: Harper Collins, 1973), p. 64.

15. John Shotter, *Cultural Politics of Everyday Life: Social Constructionism, Rhetoric and Knowing of the Third Kind* (Toronto: Univ. of Toronto Press, 1993), p. 176.

Personal Relationships and Health
Malcolm Parks

Mac Parks is a communication professional whose research and teaching have substantially increased our understanding of how personal networks affect interpersonal relationships. In this excerpt from his 2007 book, he greatly expands my point that there is an important relationship between the quality of your communication and the quality of your life.

Parks reviews extensive research that connects interpersonal communication with five aspects of mental and physical health: social skill deficits, violence and suicide, cardiovascular difficulties, immune system malfunctions, and risky health practices.

In each case, he summarizes findings from social scientific research, which means that the list of references at the end of this reading could support a detailed research paper. But the connections he draws are even more impressive than the references.

Parents' communication, for example, can cripple the chances of their children to succeed. Sexual abuse may be a precursor to eating disorders. Violent spouses tend to raise children who create violent marriages. Divorce can be a precursor of violence and abuse in young adults' romantic relationships. Suicide is often linked to the absence of lasting interpersonal relationships. Disruptions in significant relationships can lead to disruptions in the body's immune system. And poor interpersonal relationships can promote, or at least fail to discourage, risky and destructive behavior such as smoking, careless driving, and unsafe sex.

The point of this reading is not to scare you but to underscore the close connection between the quality of your communication and the quality of your life. This article focuses on physiological and psychological aspects of your life. As Parks concludes, "personal relationships, then, are much more than private arrangements. They are linked to the physical and mental health of their participants ..."

The articles at the end of this book, in Chapters 11 and 12, extend this point to apply to our lives as cultural members and our lives as world citizens. Remember Parks' essay when you read about the life-destroying relationships between Christians and Muslims, Shiites and Sunnis, Hamas and Fatah, and Jews and Palestinians. At all levels, for all persons, the relationships between quality of communication and quality of life are profound.

MAIN IDEAS

- Inadequate or distorted interpersonal relationships can have dramatic negative effects on physical and mental health.
- Poor relationships cripple peoples' abilities to empathize, regulate emotional expression, manage conflict, and effectively presuade others.
- Violence and suicide are often linked to interpersonal deficits.
- Inadequate interpersonal relationships contribute to cardiovascular disease.

- Interpersonal stress reduces the effectiveness of human immune systems and often leads to infection or stimulates autoimmune disease.
- Poor interpersonal relationships promote risky health practices like smoking, overeating, and substance abuse.

Inadequate or disordered interpersonal relationships can kill, sometimes slowly, sometimes swiftly. Although the idea that physical and mental well-being are linked to the quality of social life dates from antiquity, the connection has been demonstrated in convincing fashion by research in the life and social sciences over the last 40 years. Classic works, such as Alexander's (1950) *Psychosomatic Medicine,* perpetuated the idea that specific psychological conflicts were associated with specific diseases. Although this view is still influential in the popular press, researchers have now moved beyond this rather mechanical model. In fact the entire concept of a *psychosomatic disease* may be misleading because it implies that some diseases have psychological components while others do not (Plaut & Friedman, 1981). It is more accurate to think of interpersonal and psychological factors as altering the person's susceptibility to illness or injury in general rather than as causing specific types of disease.

By the late 1980s, research evidence on the dangers of inadequate or disordered personal relationships was as strong as the evidence against cigarette smoking was when the U.S. government issued its first warnings in 1964 (House, Landis, & Umberson, 1988). But even this comparison is probably conservative. More linkages come into view when we fully liberate ourselves from the biomedical and psychosomatic models.

I believe that there are at least five interrelated pathways linking the quality of our personal relationships with our physical and mental health. Disrupted or inadequate personal relationships are associated with: (a) social skill deficits, (b) violence and suicide, (c) stress-induced illnesses of the cardiovascular system, (d) malfunctions in the immune system, and (e) risky health practices.

SOCIAL SKILL DEFICITS

As social animals, we are born with a strong foundation for the acquisition of social skills. Yet additional learning and practice are required for nearly all of the social skills needed to manage complex interactions—perspective-taking, turn-taking, regulating emotional expression, constructing persuasive strategies, managing conflict, and so on. Interactions with family and peers in childhood and adolescence are among the most important arenas in which we develop these skills. When these early relationships are disordered, then important learning opportunities are lost or distorted and a variety of illnesses may result. This means that many illnesses, particularly mental illnesses may result. This means that many illnesses, particularly mental illnesses, can properly be thought of as interpersonal illnesses (Segrin, 2001).

The damaging effects of interactions with those with poor social skills can be found all across the literature on mental illness. Children who are rejected by their parents, for example, are more likely to have difficulty regulating their own emotional expression and engaging in interaction (Cohn, Campbell, Matias, & Hopkins, 1990). Similarly, parents who are simultaneously highly controlling and yet unable to express affection toward their children may be setting their children up for lifelong deficits in social skills that manifest themselves in a wide range of mental health and relational problems (Hudson & Rapee, 2000). Adolescents with a history of negative interactions with parents, for example, are more likely to behave coercively and abusively with dating partners years later (Kim, Conger, Lorenz, & Elder, 2001).

This is not to suggest that people are necessarily victims of their early relationships. Early relationships matter, but critics have rightly faulted approaches to mental illnesses that place too much importance on childhood relationships (e.g., Coyne, 1999). Regardless of when they occur, interpersonal relationships serve as arenas for developing or damaging social skills. They are "rolling laboratories" in which the level of skills found in relationships at one point in life help determine the level of skills in relationships at the next point. Social skill deficits can thus be self-perpetuating.

In some cases, it is not merely the lack of positive models that leads to mental and physical illness, but the presence of negative models. Sexual abuse, for instance, is thought to be a precursor to eating disorders partly because it reduces its victims' sense of social competency (Mallinckrodt, McCreary, & Robertson, 1995). It is no wonder, then, that physical and sexual abuse in childhood are strongly linked to mental and physical illnesses across the adult life cycle (Dinwiddie et al., 2000).

VIOLENCE AND SUICIDE

Violence and abuse in personal relationships pose profound problems for society (for a survey, see Harvey & Weber, 2002). Those with inadequate or dysfunctional personal relationships are particularly susceptible to violence, either by their own hand or the hands of others. Some simply carry violent patterns from previous relationships. Violence in dating relationships, for example, is linked both to a history of family violence and to having friends who treat their dating partners abusively (Arriaga & Foshee, 2004). Similarly, spouses in violent marriages frequently grew up in families with a history of violence and abuse (Bergman & Brismar, 1993). Even nonviolent families may fail to provide positive models of conflict management. Parental neglect and divorce are also precursors of violence and abuse in young adults' romantic relationships (Billingham & Notebaert, 1993; Straus & Savage, 2005). People in dysfunctional relationships are themselves more likely to be victims of violence. They may have more people mad at them, but they may also just be more vulnerable and isolated. For example, school children who do not have a reciprocated friendship are more likely to be bullied by their classmates (Boulton, Trueman, Chau, Whitehand, & Amatya,

1999). More generally, data both from the United States and other countries indicates that people who are divorced or separated are far more likely to be homicide victims than people who are married (Lynch, 1977; Wilson & Daly, 1993).

Over a century ago Durkheim (1897/1951) hypothesized that people committed suicide because they were no longer integrated into the larger social institutions that give their lives meaning. Although we now consider suicide from a number of different perspectives, it is clear that being or feeling disconnected from friends and family contributes to suicide. Some of the most disturbing evidence comes from counselors who report that suicidal behavior among elementary school children is frequently a response to the divorce, illness, or death of parents or other significant relatives (D. E. Matter & R. M. Matter, 1984). In her study of people whom the police had rescued from suicide in Vienna, Margarethe von Andics (1947) painted the attempted suicide as a person who was either unable to form lasting relationships or unable to recover from their loss. More broadly based studies also support the link between suicide and inadequate or disordered personal relationships (Beautrais, Joyce, & Mulder, 1996; Trout, 1980). Demographic data reveals that divorced people have consistently had higher suicide rates over the last 25 years than people who are married, despite the fact that divorce has become more socially acceptable during that time (Stack, 1990).

CARDIOVASCULAR DISEASE

Poor personal relationships break people's hearts—literally. A large and varied body of evidence testifies to the effects of dysfunctional, inadequate personal relationships on cardiovascular disease. The conflict-laden, aggressive, unsupportive, and unsupportable "Type A" personality was formally recognized as a risk factor in coronary disease by the National Blood, Heart, and Lung Institute in the early 1980s. Global personality types, however, are crude measures because they are so far removed from social interaction itself. And indeed, the evidence linking Type A behavior to cardiovascular disease is far from consistent (Suls & Wan, 1993).

More powerful predictors of cardiovascular disease emerge when we look at the give and take of the social support process. Cardiovascular activity appears to be quite sensitive to changes in the nature of interpersonal communication (Lynch, 1985). Blood pressure changes less in reaction to stress, for example, in children whose family communication patterns are open and emotionally expressive, than in families where interpersonal communication is closed (Wright et al., 1993). Adult men reported less angina pectoris (severe pain radiating from the heart area to the left shoulder and arm) when they perceived their wives as supportive than when they perceived their wives as unsupportive (Medalie & Goldbourt, 1976).

All this implies that death from cardiovascular disease should be more common among those with disrupted or inadequate personal relationships. And indeed it is. Studies in a number of countries consistently reveal that cardiovascular disease is both more common and more likely to be fatal among people who experience high levels of family conflict, are divorced, separated, have few friends, and/or who have little involvement in informal and formal groups (Ebrahim, Wannamethee, McCallum, Walker, & Shaper, 1995; Orth-Gomer et al., 2000; Rosengren et al., 2004). These are not small risk factors. High psychosocial stress poses risks as great as high blood pressure and obesity....

IMMUNE SYSTEM MALFUNCTIONS

The immune system is our body's private physician, curing and protecting us from a host of diseases (Desowitz, 1987). Although the complex interplay of the immune system's components is far from understood, research over the last 40 years demonstrates convincingly that disruptions in significant relationships cause significant disruptions in the immune system. This effect takes at least two forms: immunosuppression and autoimmune disease.

In everyday language, we would say that a person experiencing immunosuppression has a low resistance to disease. The ability to form an immune response to foreign cells or toxins entering the body is reduced. This occurs in large part because of disruptions in the various neuropeptides, neurotransmitters, and neuroendocrines that regulate immune responses (Fleshner & Laudenslager, 2004). People are simply more likely to get sick during periods of interpersonal stress because their immune systems are not as effective at warding off and recovering from disease. This was illustrated quite clearly in an early study by Meyer and Haggerty (1962), who tracked respiratory infections in 16 families over the course of a year. They found that respiratory illnesses were four times more common during periods of stressful family interaction than during less stressful periods.

Studies conducted over the past 30 years have consistently shown that chronic stress reduces immunity (Segerstrom & Miller, 2004). Immunosuppression has been associated with a variety of interpersonal and psychological conditions including depression, loneliness, family conflict, role conflict, separation from family and peers, divorce, and bereavement (Kaplan, 1991). Moreover, the consequences of this immunosuppression can be fatal. Divorced people for example, are far more likely to die of pneumonia than married people (Lynch, 1977).

The second major effect of interpersonal factors on the immune system is to stimulate autoimmune disease. In these diseases the body attacks itself. The immune system fails to distinguish properly between what is self and what is foreign. Consequently, the immune system produces antibodies that mistakenly injure the body's own tissue. The onset and severity of autoimmune diseases appears to vary with interpersonal events. Rheumatoid arthritis, for instance, progresses more rapidly and is more disabling among people who experience high levels of anger, depression, or stress (Latman & Walls, 1996; Solomon, 1985). These emotional disturbances may be caused by a variety of factors, of course, but the most common stressor identified in the literature is disrupted relationships with spouses or parents. Conversely, the presence of supportive relationships, especially ones in which the interaction helps the sufferer feel in greater control of his or her disease, is associated with better coping and less severe episodes (e.g., Evers, Kraaimaat, Geene, Jacobs, & Bijlsma, 2003; Holtzman, Newth, & Delongis, 2004).

Just as a lack of support worsens autoimmune disease, the disease itself limits social participation. Thus people with rheumatoid arthritis report significant reductions across the entire range of their social activities (P. P. Katz, 1995). For some, the net result is a vicious cycle of increasing social isolation and worsening disease.

RISKY HEALTH PRACTICES

Poor interpersonal relationships promote, or at least fail to discourage, risky and plainly destructive behavior. Failure to seek needed health care or to follow treatment regimens are common forms. People whose friends and family are unsupportive, for example, are less successful when it comes to smoking cessation, taking high blood pressure medication, maintaining control over diabetes, and losing weight (Gorin et al., 2005; Hanson, De Guire, Schinkel, & Kolterman, 1995; Umberson, 1987).

People may also be more prone to engage in risky activities or to engage in activities in unsafe ways if they lack commitments to positive personal relationships. For example, recently separated or divorced people are nearly three times more likely than married people to be involved in a traffic accident (Lagarde et al., 2004). Divorced parents or parents who are distracted by relational problems may provide less supervision and instruction to their children, making their children more susceptible to accidents, injury, or unsafe sexual practices. Teenagers who come from families with poor supervision and cohesiveness, for example, are more likely to drink and drive than teenagers whose parents provide better supervision (Augustyn & Simons-Morton, 1995). Another study found that a greater proportion of 12- to 14-year-olds from recently divorced families had engaged in sexual intercourse than from intact or stepparent families (Flewelling & Bauman, 1990). Even in intact families, poor mother–daughter communication is among the most powerful predictors of teenage pregnancy (Adolph, Ramos, Linton, & Grimes, 1995; Silva & Ross, 2002).

Death from drug and alcohol abuse is far more common among people with disordered personal relationships (Risser, Bonsch, & Schneider, 1996). Disordered relationships are both the product and cause of drug and alcohol abuse. Certainly some people do cope with their relational inadequacies and losses by turning to drugs and alcohol. Compared to children from intact families, children from divorced families are more likely to try drugs and alcohol, to have drug and alcohol problems, and perhaps worst of all, to perpetuate the entire cycle by having greater difficulty forming stable relationships of their own (Flewelling & Bauman, 1990; Jeynes, 2001; Needle, Su, & Doherty, 1990).

The cycle continues when these people become parents themselves. The children of parents who abuse alcohol or drugs are at far greater risk for accidents and injuries. A study of house fires in Scotland between 1980 and 1990, for instance, indicated that parental alcohol abuse was a significant contributor to the death of children (Squires & Busuttil, 1995). Another study in the United States reported that children whose mothers were problem drinkers were over twice as likely to have serious accidents and injuries as children whose mothers are not problem drinkers. The risks were even higher when both parents were problem drinkers or when the problem drinker was also a single mother (Bijur, Kurzon, Overpeck, & Scheidt, 1992).

These findings remind us that negative social and health outcomes typically appear together—drinking, school problems, violence, suicide, psychological disorders, and so on. Yet to the extent that these problems are the consequence of low interpersonal skills and poor social relationships, all can be addressed by interventions that build communicative skills and provide a social support network. Indeed, programs that focus on exactly these factors have proven successful in enhancing self-esteem, improving school performance, decreasing drug use, and reducing suicide potential among adolescents (e.g., Eggert, Thompson, Herting, Nicholas, & Dicker, 1994; E. A. Thompson, Eggert, Randell, & Pike, 2001).

Personal relationships, then, are much more than private arrangements. They are linked to the physical and mental health of their participants and, by virtue of the social and economic roles they play, to the vitality of society as a whole. This recognition has grown slowly as the study of personal relationships has evolved over the past 100 years.

REVIEW QUESTIONS

1. The lack of positive models of interpersonal communication can promote illness, as well as the presence of what?
2. What relationship does Parks suggest between bullying and childhood friendships?
3. What is the relationship between disrupted or inadequate personal relationships and cardiovascular disease?
4. How can family stress affect family members' respiratory illnesses?
5. What are some other illnesses that are worsened by stress?

PROBES

1. If you were to base a "Family Communication" workshop on the content of this reading, what topics would you address in your workshop?
2. In the "Social Skill Deficits" section, Parks notes that "people are [not] necessarily victims of their early relationships." What point is he making here about causality (fault and blame) in interpersonal relationships?
3. Summarize the evidence in this essay about the possible effects of divorce.
4. What are the implications of this essay for the importance of premarital counseling and education?
5. What connections do you see between the quality of your communication and the quality of your life?

REFERENCES

Adolph, C., Ramos, D. E., Linton, K. L., & Grimes, D. A. (1995). Pregnancy among Hispanic teenagers: Is good parental communication a deterrent? *Contraception, 51*(5), 303–306.

Alexander, F. (1950). *Psychosomatic medicine.* New York: Norton.

Arriaga, X. B., & Foshee, V. A. (2004). Adolescent dating violence: Do adolescents follow in their friends', or their parents', footsteps? *Journal of Interpersonal Violence, 19,* 162–184.

Augustyn, M., & Simons-Morton, B. G. (1995). Adolescent drinking and driving: Etiology and interpretation. *Journal of Drug Education, 25,* 41–59.

Beautrais, A. L., Joyce, P. R., & Mulder, R. T. (1996). Risk factors for serious suicide attempts among youths aged 13 through 24 years. *Journal of the American Academy of Child and Adolescent Psychiatry, 35,* 1174–1182.

Bergman, B., & Brismar, B. (1993). Assailants and victims: A comparative study of male wife-beaters and battered males. *Journal of Addictive Diseases, 12*(4), 1–10.

Bijur, P. E., Kurzon, M., Overpeck, M. D., & Scheidt, P. C. (1992). Parental alcohol use, problem drinking, and children's injuries. *Journal of the American Medical Association, 267,* 3166–3171.

Billingham, R. E., & Notebaert, N. L. (1993). Divorce and dating violence revisited: Multivariate analyses using Straus's conflict tactics subscores. *Psychological Reports, 73,* 679–684.

Boulton, M. J., Trueman, M., Chau, C., Whitehand, C., & Amatya, K. (1999). Concurrent and longitudinal links between friendship and peer victimization: Implications for befriending interventions. *Journal of Adolescence, 22,* 461–466.

Cohn, J. F., Campbell, S. B., Matias, R., & Hopkins, J. (1990). Face-to-face interactions of postpartum depressed and nondepressed mother-infant pairs at 2 months. *Developmental Psychology, 26,* 15–23.

Coyne, J. C. (1999). Thinking interactionally about depression: A radical restatement. In T. Joiner & J. C. Coyne (Eds.), *The interactional nature of depression* (pp. 365–392). Washington, DC: American Psychological Association.

Desowitz, R. S. (1987). *The thorn in the starfish: How the human immune system works.* New York: Norton.

Dinwiddie, S. H., Heath, A. C., Dunne, M. P., Bucholz, K. K., Madden, P. A. F., Slutske, W. S., et al. (2000). Early sexual abuse and lifetime psychopathology: A co-twin-control study. *Psychological Medicine, 30,* 41–52.

Durkheim, E. (1951). *Suicide.* New York: Free Press. (Original work published 1897).

Ebrahim, S., Wannamethee, G., McCallum, A., Walker, M., & Shaper, A. G. (1995). Marital status, change in marital status, and mortality in middle-aged British men. *American Journal of Epidemiology, 142,* 834–842.

Eggert, L. L., Thompson, E. A., Herting, J. R., Nicolas, L. J., & Dicker, B. G. (1994). Preventing adolescent drug abuse and high school dropout through an intensive school-based social network development program. *American Journal of Health Promotion, 8,* 202–215.

Evers, A., Kraaimaat, F. W., Greene, R., Jacobs, J., & Bijlsma, J. (2003). Pain coping and social support as predictors of long-term functional disability and pain in early rheumatoid arthritis. *Behaviour Research & Therapy, 41,* 1295–1310.

Fleshner, M., & Laudenslager, M. L. (2004). Psychoneuroimmunology: Then and now. *Behavioral & Cognitive Neuroscience Reviews, 3*(2), 114–130.

Flewelling, R. L., & Bauman, K. E. (1990). Family structure as a predictor of initial substance use and sexual intercourse in early adolescence. *Journal of Marriage and the Family, 52,* 171–181.

Gorin, A., Phelan, S., Tate, D., Sherwood, N., Jeffery, R., & Wing, R. (2005). Involving support partners in obesity treatment. *Journal of Consulting and Clinical Psychology, 73,* 341–343.

Hanson, C. L., De Guire, M. J., Schinkel, A. M., & Kolterman, O. G. (1995). Empirical validation for a family-centered model of care. *Diabetes Care, 18*(10), 1347–1356.

Harvey, J. H., & Weber, A. L. (2002). *Odyssey of the heart: Close relationships in the 21st century* (2nd ed.). Mahwah, NJ: Lawrence Erlbaum Associates.

Holtzman, S., Newth, S., & Delongis, A. (2004). The role of social support in coping with daily pain among patients with rheumatoid arthritis. *Journal of Health Psychology, 9,* 677–695.

House, J., Landis, K., & Umberson, D. (1988). Social relationships and health. *Science, 241*(4865), 540–545.

Hudson, J. L., & Rapee, R. M. (2000). The origins of social phobia. *Behavior Modification, 24*(1), 102–129.

Jeynes, W. H. (2001). The effects of recent parental divorce on their children's consumption of marijuana and cocaine. *Journal of Divorce and Remarriage, 35*(3–4), 43–65.

Kaplan, H. B. (1991). Social psychology of the immune system: A conceptual framework and review of the literature. *Social Science and Medicine, 33,* 909–923.

Katz, P. P. (1995). The impact of rheumatoid arthritis on life activities. *Arthritis Care and Research, 8,* 272–278.

Kim, K. J., Conger, R., Lorenz, F. O., & Elder, G. H. (2001). Parent-adolescent reciprocity in negative affect and its relation to early adult social development. *Developmental Psychology, 37,* 775–790.

Lagarde, E., Chastang, J. F., Gueguen, A., Coeuret-Pellicer, M., Chiron, M., & Lafont, S. (2004). Emotional stress and traffic accidents: The impact of separation and divorce. *Epidemiology, 15,* 762–766.

Latman, N. S., & Walls, R. (1996). Personality and stress: An exploratory comparison of rheumatoid arthritis and osteoarthritis. *Archives of Physical and Medical Rehabilitation, 77,* 796–800.

Lynch, J. J. (1977). *The broken heart: The medical consequences of loneliness.* New York: Basic Books.

Lynch, J. J. (1985). *The language of the heart.* New York: Basic Books.

Mallinckrodt, B., McCreary, B. A., & Robertson, A. K. (1995). Co-occurrence of eating disorders and incest: The role of attachment, family environment, and social competencies. *Journal of Counseling Psychology, 42,* 178–186.

Matter, D. E., & Matter, R. M. (1984). Suicide among elementary school children: A serious concern for counselors. *Elementary School Guidance and Counseling, 18,* 260–267.

Medalie, J. H., & Goldbourt, U. (1976). Angina pectoris among 10,000 men. II. Psychosocial and other risk factors as evidenced by a multivariate analysis of a five-year incidence study. *American Journal of Medicine, 60,* 910–921.

Meyer, R. J., & Haggerty, R. J. (1962). Streptococcal infections in families. Factors altering individual susceptibility. *Pediatrics, 29,* 536–549.

Needle, R. H., Su, S. S., & Doherty, W. J. (1990). Divorce, remarriage, and adolescent substance use: A prospective longitudinal study. *Journal of Marriage and the Family, 52,* 157–169.

Orth-Gomer, K., Wamala, S. P., Horsten, M., Schenck-Gustafsson, K., Schneiderman, N., & Mittleman, M. A. (2000). Marital stress worsens prognosis in women with coronary heart disease: The Stockholm Female Coronary Risk Study. *Journal of the American Medical Association, 284,* 3008–3014.

Plaut, S. M., & Friedman, S. B. (1981). Psychosocial factors in infectious disease. In R. Ader (Ed.), *Psychoneuroimmunolgy* (pp. 3–30). New York: Academic Press.

Risser, D., Bonsch, A., & Schneider, B. (1996). Family background of drug-related deaths: A descriptive study based on interviews with relatives of deceased drug users. *Journal of Forensic Science, 41,* 960–962.

Rosengren, A., Hawken, S., Ôunpuu, S., Silwa, K., Zubain, M., Almahmeed, W. A., et al. (2004). Association of psychosocial risk factors with risk of acute myocardial infarction in 11,119 cases and 13,648 controls from 52 countries (the Interheart Study): Case-control study. *Lancet, 364,* 953–962.

Segerstrom, S. C., & Miller, G. E. (2004). Psychological stress and the human immune system: A meta-analytic study of 30 years of inquiry. *Psychological Bulletin, 130,* 601–630.

Segrin, C. (2001). *Interpersonal processes in psychological problems.* New York: Guilford Press.

Silva, M., & Ross, I. (2002). Association of perceived parental attitudes towards premarital sex with initiation of sexual intercourse in adolescence. *Psychological Reports, 91*(3, Pt. 1), 781–784.

Solomon, G. F. (1985). The emerging field of psychoneuroimmunology: With a special note on AIDS. *Advances, 2,* 6–19.

Squires, T., & Busuttil, A. (1995). Child fatalities in Scottish house fires 1980–1990: A case of child neglect? *Child Abuse and Neglect, 19,* 865–873.

Stack, S. (1990). New micro-level data on the impact of divorce on suicide, 1959–1980: A test of two theories. *Journal of Marriage and the Family, 52,* 119–127.

Straus, M. A., & Savage, S. A. (2005). Neglectful behavior by parents in the life history of university students in 17 countries and its relation to violence against dating partners. *Child Maltreatment: Journal of the American Professional Society on the Abuse of Children, 10*(2), 124–135.

Suls, J., & Wan, C. K. (1993). The relationship between trait hostility and cardiovascular reactivity: A quantitative review and analysis. *Psychophysiology, 30,* 615–626.

Thompson, E. A., Eggert, L. L., Randell, B. P., & Pike, K. C. (2001). Evaluation of indicated suicide risk prevention approaches for potential high school dropouts. *American Journal of Public Health, 91,* 742–752.

Trout, D. L. (1980). The role of social isolation in suicide. *Suicide and Life-Threatening Behavior, 10,* 10–23.

Umberson, D. (1987). Family status and health behaviors: Social control as a dimension of social integration. *Journal of Health & Social Behavior, 28,* 306–319.

Von Andics, M. (1947). *Suicide and the meaning of life.* London: W. Hodge.

Wilson, M., & Daly, M. (1993). Spousal homicide risk and estrangement. *Violence and Victims, 8,* 3–16.

Wright, L. B., Treiber, F. A., Davis, H., Strong, W. B., Levy, M., Van Huss, E., et al. (1993). Relationship between family environment and children's hemodynamic responses to stress: A longitudinal evaluation. *Behavioral Medicine, 19,* 115–121.

Fierce Conversations

Susan Scott

Susan Scott is an executive educator who has helped clients around the world transform the cultures of their organizations. In this excerpt from her best-selling book, she explains how, as I noted earlier in the chapter, conversations are the most important communication events people experience. As she puts it, "our work, our relationships, and, in fact, our very lives succeed or fail gradually, then suddenly, one conversation at a time."

Although Scott's primary audience is businesspeople rather than college students, her main points apply to everyone. Regardless of your station in life, when you face an important challenge, your first step should be to resist what she calls the "accountability shuffle" of blaming others, and your second should be to "identify the conversations out there with your name on them and resolve to have them with all the courage, grace, and vulnerability they require." If life is good, you can also realize that you got here "gradually, then suddenly, one *successful* conversation at a time." And her advice applies as much to experiences at home as it does to experiences at work.

Scott reinforces what other authors in this chapter have also said: Relationships exist in the conversations that make them up. Whether you're thinking about a dating relationship, a marriage relationship, a work relationship, or a family relationship, "the conversation is the relationship." Relationship problems begin in specific conversations, negative spirals can be tracked through conversations, and improvement can occur when conversations change.

By "fierce conversation," Scott explains that she means intense, strong, powerful, passionate, eager, and robust conversation. "Fierce" does not mean angry or hostile; it emphasizes the importance of being genuinely present and authentic in as many as possible of the conversations you experience. Scott urges her readers to embrace the possibility that fierce conversations are opportunities to be known, seen, and changed.

Near the end of this reading, Scott tells her story of discovering the importance of conversation while working with business leaders on issues that undercut their effectiveness. As she explains, her brief and superficial explanation of what she did for a living was "I ran think tanks for corporate leaders and worked with them one-to-one." But "what I really did was extend an intimate invitation to my clients, that of conversation." And most clients experienced significant improvement in their effectiveness and their job satisfaction.

This reading ends with a challenge for you to begin working to make more of your conversations genuinely authentic or "fierce." The rest of Scott's 290-page book effectively details how to do this. But as a contribution to the second chapter of this book, I hope her words emphasize how crucially important it is for you to pay attention to the communication events that most define your reality and determine your success and happiness: conversations.

MAIN IDEAS

- Our work, our relationships, and our very lives succeed or fail *one conversation at a time.*
- While no single conversation is guaranteed to change the trajectory of a business, career, marriage, or life, any single conversation *can.*
- Inventory your important relationships by asking, "How did we get here?" and identify key conversations.
- Consider which conversations will change the trajectory of a troubled relationship or keep a wonderful one where it is.
- Recognize that each relationship is *made up of* conversations.
- *Fierce* conversation is not menacing or threatening; it is robust, strong, passionate, "one in which we ... make it real."
- You can mold your relationship future positively by engaging in more "fierce" conversations.
- The author discovered the effectiveness of this approach in her own work life.

O ver ten thousand hours of one-to-one conversations with industry leaders, as well as workshops with men and women from all walks of life confronting issues of relationship and life direction, have convinced me that our work, our relationships, and, in fact, our very lives succeed or fail gradually, then suddenly, *one conversation at a time.*

Equally provocative has been my realization that while no single conversation is guaranteed to change the trajectory of a business, a career, a marriage, or a life, any single conversation *can.* . . .

Whether you intend to maintain positive results in your life or turn things around, considering all of the conversations you need to have could feel a bit discouraging, so let's take the curse off the somewhat daunting field of "communications." I'd like you to simply take it *one conversation at a time,* beginning with the person who next stands in front of you. Perhaps there are very few conversations in between you and what you desire.

. . . Once you get the hang of it, once you master the courage and the skills and, more important, enjoy the benefits of fierce conversations, there will be no going back. It could change the world. It will certainly change *your* world.

When *Here* Is Troubling

Be patient with yourself. You got here—wherever "here" is—one conversation at a time. Allow the changes needed at home or at work to reveal themselves one conversation at a time.

Sometimes *here* just happens. Following the high-tech carnage, crashing economies, corporate layoffs, and terrorist attacks of 2001, which altered our individual and collective realities in a heartbeat, it would be easy to conclude that life has grown too unpredictable, that there's nothing to do but hang on and muddle through as best you can.

Perhaps you received a major wake-up call. You lost your biggest customer—the one that counted for 40 percent of your net profit. Or you lost your most valued employee. Or you lost your job, and it wasn't due to a layoff. You lost the loyalty of your team. You lost your eighteen-year marriage, or the cohesiveness of your family.

Perhaps your company is experiencing turnover, turf wars, rumors, departments not cooperating with one another, long overdue reports and projects, strategic plans that still aren't off the ground, and lots of very good reasons and excuses why things can't be any different or better.

To experience what happens for many individuals and organizations facing challenges, put your right arm out and point your finger, then visualize pointing it at someone who is the bane of your professional or personal life right now. That's called the *accountability shuffle.* He did it, she did it, they did it to me.

Blame isn't the answer, nor is cocooning in the perceived safety of your home. Once you reflect on the path that led you to a disappointing or difficult point and place in time, you may remember, often in vivid detail, the conversation that set things in motion, ensuring that you would end up exactly where you find yourself today. It is very likely that you arrived at this destination one *failed* conversation at a time.

Ask yourself, "How did I get *here?* How is it that I find myself in a company, a role, a relationship, or a life from which I've absented my spirit? How did I lose my way?"

So many times I've heard people say, "We never addressed the real issue, never came to terms with reality." Or, "We never stated our needs. We never told each other what we were really thinking and feeling. In the end, there were so many things we needed to talk about, the wheels came off the cart."

In February 2002, Robert Kaiser and David Ottaway wrote an article for the *Washington Post* about the fragility of U.S.–Saudi ties. Brent Scowcroft, national security adviser to the first President Bush, is quoted as saying, "Have we [the United States and Saudi Arabia] understood each other particularly well? ... Probably not. And I think, in a sense, we probably avoid talking about the things that are the real problems between us because it's a very polite relationship. We don't get all that much below the surface."

Take your finger and touch your nose. This is where the resolution begins. This is the accountable position. If you want to make progress toward a better "here" in your professional or personal life, identify the conversations out there with your name on them and resolve to have them with all the courage, grace, and vulnerability they require.

When *Here* Is Wonderful

And on the positive side, you finally landed that huge customer, the one your competition would kill for. Or you successfully recruited a valuable new employee. Or you discovered that your team is committed to you at the deepest level. Or you just received a promotion. Or you enjoy a deeply fulfilling relationship. You are clear and passionate about your life.

You got to this good place in your life, this satisfying career path, this terrific relationship, gradually, then suddenly, one *successful* conversation at a time. Perhaps one marvelously *fierce* conversation at a time. And now you are determined to ensure the quality of your ongoing conversations with the people central to your success and happiness.

If you want better results at home or at work, you've come to the right place. After reading this, gathering your courage, and working with the tools we'll explore together, you will return to your colleagues at work, to your partner at home, and, most important, to your *self*, prepared to engage in ongoing, groundbreaking conversations that will profoundly transform your life.

While it was tempting to give in to suggestions that I write two books—*Fierce Conversations in the Workplace* and *Fierce Conversations at Home*—breaking this material into two books would have been a mistake. Perhaps you've bought into the premise that we respond differently depending on whom we are with, that our work and home personas are really quite different. Perhaps you pay fierce attention to conversations at work but slip into a conversational coma at home, convinced there's nothing new, interesting, or energizing to discuss, preferring the company of the remote control. Perhaps you leave your warmth, playfulness, and authenticity at home and prop up an automaton at your desk at work, afraid to let your authentic self show up lest you be judged as poor fodder for the corporate feast. Perhaps you've told yourself that conversations at work are unavoidably and substantially different from conversations at home. That that's just the way it has to be. This is not true.

Each of us must discard the notion that we respond differently depending on whom we're with and that our work and home conversations are really quite different.

When you squeeze an orange, what comes out of it? Orange juice. Why? Because that's what's inside it. The orange doesn't care whether it's on a boardroom table or beside the kitchen sink. It doesn't leak orange juice at home and tomato juice at work.

When we get squeezed—*when things aren't going well for us*—what comes out of us? Whatever's inside us. To pretend that what's going on in our personal lives can be boxed, taped shut, and left in the garage while we are at work is hogwash. It seeps in everywhere. Who we are is who we are, all over the place. So if your conversations at work are yielding disappointing results, I'd be willing to bet you're getting similar results at home. The principles and skills needed to engage in conversations that produce mind-blowing, world-class results in the workplace are exactly the same principles and skills that produce mind-blowing, world-class results at home.

The Conversation Is the Relationship

Going hand in hand with the discovery that our lives succeed or fail one conversation at a time is a second insight, courtesy of poet and author David Whyte. During a keynote speech at TEC International's annual conference several years ago, David suggested that in the typical marriage, the young man, newly married, is often frustrated that this person with whom he intends to enjoy the rest of his life seemingly needs to talk, yet again, about the same thing they talked about last weekend. And it often has something to do with their relationship. He wonders, Why are we talking about this again? I thought we settled this. Couldn't we just have one huge conversation about our relationship and then coast for a year or two?

Apparently not, because here she is again. Eventually, if he is paying attention, it occurs to him, Whyte suggests, that "this ongoing, robust conversation he has been having with his wife is not about the relationship. The conversation *is* the relationship."

The conversation is the relationship. If the conversation stops, all of the possibilities for the relationship become smaller and all of the possibilities for the individuals in the relationship become smaller, until one day we overhear ourselves in midsentence, making *ourselves* smaller in every encounter, behaving as if we are just the space around our shoes, engaged in yet another three-minute conversation so empty of meaning it crackles.

Incremental degradation—if we compromise at work or at home; if we lower the standards about how often we talk, what we talk about, and, most important, what degree of authenticity we bring to our conversations—it's a slow and deadly slide. One company president has been known to stop candid input in its tracks with the pronouncement "Howard, I do not consider that a career-enhancing response."

Fortunately, few leaders exhibit such exaggerated violations of the general rules of communication. However, many work teams as well as couples have a list of undiscussables, issues they avoid broaching at all costs in order to preserve a modicum of peace, to preserve the relationship. In reality, the relationship steadily deteriorates for lack of the very conversations they so carefully avoid. It's difficult to raise the level if the slide has lasted over a period of years, and that's what keeps many of us stuck.

In our significant relationships, in the workplace, and in our conversations with ourselves, we'd like to tell the truth. We'd like to be able to successfully tackle the topic that's keeping us stuck or apart, but the task is too hard, we don't know how to avoid the all-too-familiar outcome of talks gone south, and besides, we've learned to live with it. Why wreck another meeting with our colleagues, another weekend with our life partner, trying to resolve the tough issues or answer the big questions? We're tired and we just want peace in the land.

The problem is, whether you are running an organization or your life, you are required to be responsive to your world. And that response often requires change. We effect change by engaging in robust conversations with ourselves and others.

Each conversation we have with our co-workers, customers, significant others, and children either enhances those relationships, flatlines them, or takes them down. Given this, what words and what level of attention do you wish to bring to your conversations with the people most important to you? Throughout the book we will explore principles and practices that will help you engage in conversations that enrich relationships, no matter how sensitive or challenging the topic.

What Is a "Fierce" Conversation?

But a "fierce" conversation? Doesn't "fierce" suggest menacing, cruel, barbarous, threatening? Sounds like raised voices, frowns, blood on the floor, no fun at all. In *Roget's Thesaurus,* however, the word *fierce* has the following synonyms: robust, intense, strong, powerful, passionate, eager, unbridled, uncurbed, untamed. In its simplest form, *a fierce conversation is one in which we come out from behind ourselves into the conversation and make it real.*

While many are afraid of "real," it is the unreal conversation that should scare us to death. Whoever said talk is cheap was mistaken. Unreal conversations are incredibly expensive for organizations and for individuals. Every organization wants to feel it's having a real conversation with its employees, its customers, its territory, and with the unknown future that is emerging around it. Each individual wants to have conversations that are somehow building his or her world of meaning.

If you are a leader, your job is to accomplish the goals of the organization. How will you do that in today's workplace? In large part, by making every conversation you have as real as possible. Today's employees consider themselves owners and investors. They own their time, their energy, and their expertise. They are willing to invest these things in support of the individuals, ideals, and goals in which they believe. Give them something real in which to believe.

What I've witnessed over and over is that when the conversation is real, the change occurs before the conversation has even ended.

Being real is not the risk. The real risk is that:

I will be known.

I will be seen.

I will be changed.

Think about it. What are the conversations you've been unable or unwilling to have—with your boss, colleague, employee, customer; with your husband, wife, parent, child; or with *yourself*—that, if you *were* able to have, might change everything?

My Own Journey

For thirteen years, I worked with corporate leaders through the auspices of TEC International, an organization dedicated to increasing the effectiveness and enhancing the lives of CEOs. Thousands of CEOs in 18 countries meet for monthly one-to-one conversations with someone like myself to focus on their businesses and lives—from budgets, strategies, acquisitions, personnel, and profitability (or the lack thereof) to faltering marriages, health issues, or kids who are upside down.

Twelve conversations over the course of a year with each CEO. Since time is a CEO's most precious commodity, it seemed essential that our time together be qualitatively different from time spent with others. Each conversation needed to accomplish something useful. My success, and that of my peers, depended on our ability to engage leaders in conversations that provoked significant change.

In the beginning, a fair number of my conversations were less than fierce. They were somewhat useful, but we remained in relatively familiar, safe territory. Some, I confess, were pathetic. No guts, no glory. I wimped out. Either I didn't have it in me that day, or I looked at the expression on my TEC member's face and took pity. I don't remember those conversations. They had no lasting impact. And I am certain my TEC members would say the same.

The fierce conversations I remember. The topics, the emotions, the expressions on our faces. It was as if, together, we created a force field by asking the questions, by saying the words out loud. Things happened as a result of those conversations.

When people asked me what I did, I told them that I ran think tanks for corporate leaders and worked with them one-to-one. That was the elevator speech. What I really did was extend an intimate invitation to my clients, that of conversation. And my job was to make each conversation as real as possible.

As my practice of robust conversations became increasingly compelling to me, I imagined that I was turning into a conversational cartographer, mapping a way toward deepening authenticity for myself and for those who wanted to join me. The CEOs with whom I worked became increasingly candid, and with that candor came a growing sense of personal freedom, vitality, and effectiveness. The most successful leaders invariably determined to engage in an ongoing, robust conversation with themselves, paying fierce attention to their work and lives, resulting in a high level of personal authenticity, ferocious integrity, emotional honesty, and a greater capacity to hold true to their vision and enroll others in it.

My colleagues worldwide asked me to conduct workshops on what I was doing, to pass along the skills needed for these conversations about which I had become so passionate. This required me to articulate for myself the approach I was developing. I led my first workshop in 1990.

In January 1999, I ran a redesigned, incredibly "fierce" workshop attended by 16 extraordinary individuals from 7 countries. In my workshops there is no role-play. No one pretends to be someone else. No one works on imaginary issues. It's all *real* play. All the participants engage in conversations as themselves, using real, current, significant issues as the focus for our practice sessions. Following one of the exercises, a colleague from Newcastle upon Tyne, England, had tears in his eyes.

"I've longed for conversations like this all my life," he said, "but I didn't know they were possible. I don't think I can settle for anything less going forward."

Attendees e-mailed others about the impact of the workshop, about how they were applying the principles and using the tools they had learned, and about the results they were enjoying with their colleagues and family members. Word spread and the demand grew. Each subsequent workshop had a waiting list and each workshop went deeper. Corporate clients invited me to work with their key executives to foster courageous dialogue within their companies.

In November 2001, I recognized that my travel schedule had gotten out of hand when I sat down in my seat at the Sydney Opera House and reached for my seat belt. But my work with clients has been worth it. Over time I recognized that we were exploring core principles, which, when embraced, dramatically changed lives . . . one conversation at a time. Fierce conversations are about moral courage, clear requests, and taking action. *Fierce* is an attitude. A way of conducting business. A way of leading. A way of life.

Many times I hear words to this effect: "Your work has profoundly improved our leadership team's ability to tackle and resolve tough challenges. The practical tools allow leaders to become fierce agents for positive change." Or this: "You've helped me engage my workforce in moving the company to a position of competitive superiority!" Or this: "A fierce conversation is like the first parachute jump from an airplane. In anticipation, you perspire and your mouth goes dry. Once you've left the plane, it's an adrenaline rush that is indescribable." Or this: "This weekend my wife and I had the best conversation we've had in ten years. It feels like falling in love all over again...."

Getting Started

Here is what I'd like you to do. Begin listening to yourself as you've never listened before.

Begin to overhear yourself avoiding the topic, changing the subject, holding back, telling little lies (and big ones), being imprecise in your language, being uninteresting even to yourself. And at least once *today*, when something inside you says, "This is an opportunity to be fierce," stop for a moment, take a deep breath, then come out from behind yourself into the conversation and make it real. Say something that is true for you. For example, my friend Ed Brown sometimes stops in midsentence and says, "What I just said isn't quite right. Let me see if I can get closer to what I really want to say." I listen intently to the next words he speaks.

When you come out from behind yourself into the conversation and make it real, whatever happens from there will happen. It could go well or it could be a little bumpy, but at least you will have taken the plunge. You will have said at least one real thing today, one thing that was real for you. And something will have been set in motion, and you will have grown from that moment. . . .

REVIEW QUESTIONS

1. What is the "accountability shuffle"? Why is it ineffective?
2. What does it mean to say, "the conversation is the relationship"?
3. Explain Scott's notion of "fierce" conversation.
4. According to Scott, what does it take to make a conversation "real"?

PROBES

1. Scott argues that similar successes and problems occur in conversations at work and conversations at home. Do you agree? If you do, what are some implications of this fact for your communicating?
2. What does Scott say about the risks of being known, being seen, and being changed? How do you respond to what she says?
3. How can the job of "mak[ing] each conversation as real as possible" actually be meaningful and productive?

Social Media, Where Interpersonal Communication Meets Mass Communication

Abdul K. Sinno, Rafic Sinno, and John Stewart

At this point of the 21st century, increasing amounts of what used to be face-to-face communication happen via social media like Facebook, Twitter, Second Life, and My Space. People who study this communication and people who use it disagree about how much of this communication is interpersonal. But its prevalence makes it important to discuss, even though, as this article notes, this kind of communicating is changing so rapidly that much of what's written about it is out of date by the time it's printed.

I co-authored this essay with two friends, a father-son team who teach social media use at Clarke University here in Dubuque, Iowa. The dad—Abdul Sinno—has been a communication scholar and teacher for over 30 years, and both he and his son Rafic know about social media as users, researchers, and teachers.

The essay begins by summarizing the research that shows how heavy use of Web-based communication technologies can affect cognitive abilities. Heavy participants in media multitasking have been shown to be better at visualizing complex spatial relationships and worse at abstract reasoning, critical thinking, problem solving, and imagination. It is clear that spending time on the Web affects how, and how well, you think.

As you evaluate the benefits and risks of extensive Web-based communication, it can help to realize how much power social media give to individuals, power that used to be limited to newspaper publishers and network television moguls. The existence and widespread use of social media make the channel or medium of communication itself the driver of important positive and negative communication effects, and this article explains how.

In addition to affecting people's fundamental cognitive abilities, social media have empowered each of us to be mass communicators—journalists, reporters, inventors, and politicians. Future developments in social media will expand these effects.

When you want to use social media to develop the kind or quality of communication that this book calls "interpersonal," it works best to use "vertical" rather than "horizontal" channels. Why? Because vertical media make it possible to develop the uniqueness that is crucial to interpersonal contacts.

MAIN IDEAS

- Contacts via social media affect the quality of our relationships and our lives.
- Heavy social media use shapes our cognitive/thinking abilities; our brains are being "massively remodeled" by our ever-intensifying use of the Web.
- Social media blur the distinction between two-person and mass communication.
- Social media empower individuals to be mass communicators.

- These effects will expand and social media uses will continue to change.
- Media literacy will become increasingly important in the schools.
- Vertical rather than horizontal social media promote interpersonal communicating.

One of our friends recently took his daughter and a group of her classmates to a concert in a nearby large city. Since they were graduating high school seniors, he treated the young women to dinner at a fancy restaurant before the concert. Right after the group was seated and before the server took their orders, each senior reached into her purse and pulled out her text messaging device. Without saying anything to anyone at the table, each began texting, and two of them at the table were texting each other. Our friend reported that he was completely excluded from this part of their interaction. Later, he told us that his daughter averages 5,000 text messages per month.

Even a few years ago, this scenario would have been unbelievable. But today, a substantial portion of the population of developed countries spends hours per day on Facebook, Twitter, Second Life, My Space, and similar sites. Digital Venturebeat reports that 234 million people age 13 and older in the United States used mobile devices in December 2009, and in the same month, Twitter processed more than a billion tweets. Social networking accounts for at least 11 percent of all time spent online in the United States.[1]

In her book, *Fierce Conversations*,[2] Susan Scott argues that the overwhelming majority of the most important understandings and decisions made between people occur one conversation at a time. Social media make these conversations ever present and ongoing. Whether with an iphone, Blackberry, ipad, or more recent device, most of us carry our social network of family, friends, and colleagues with us wherever we go. The question becomes, How all this social networking affects the quality of our communication—and thus the quality of our relationships and ultimately, the quality of our lives.

Some communication researchers and other social scientists argue that we're hurting ourselves. In late 2009, developmental psychologist Patricia Greenfield reported on dozens of studies that track how different media technologies affect cognitive abilities. Her review of these studies points out that some video games and other Web-based technologies dramatically *improve* such skills as the ability to visualize complex spatial relationships. But the process of rapid shifting among stimuli that is required by status update sites like Twitter and that is facilitated by hyperlinks *reduces* such higher-order cognitive abilities as mindfulness, abstract reasoning, reflection, critical thinking, problem solving, and imagination.[3]

Three communication researchers at Stanford confirmed these effects. They split participants in their experiments into those who do a lot of media multitasking and people who media multitask much less frequently. The heavy multitaskers were more easily distracted, had less control over their attention, and were much less able to distinguish important information from trivia.[4] Other cognitive scientists have shown that these deficiencies can become permanent, because they are evidence of actual changes in cell structure in the subjects' brains. As one reporter puts it,

> By changing our habits of mind, each new technology strengthens certain neural pathways and weakens others. The cellular alterations continue to shape the way we think even when we're not using the technology.... our brains are being 'massively remodeled' by our ever-intensifying use of the Web and related media.... What we seem to be sacrificing ... is our capacity to engage in the quieter, attentive modes of thought that underpin contemplation, reflection and introspection. The Web never encourages us to slow down. It keeps us in a state of perpetual mental locomotion.[5]

Especially given the fact that almost everybody reading this essay has been using social media sites for years, we are not going to tell you to stop. At the same time, it would be foolish to ignore the evidence that heavy media multitasking can actually reduce your abilities to concentrate, reflect, and solve problems. One solution is to learn a few important principles about social media, so you can be in a better position to understand how these technologies affect your interpersonal communicating and what you can do to maximize the positive effects and minimize the negative effects of the time you spend on these sites. This is what we offer here.

TWO-PERSON COMMUNICATION BECOMES MASS COMMUNICATION

One of the main distinctions 20th-century communication researchers made was among two-person, small-group, and mass communication. Before the World Wide Web, people connected in these three general ways. There were borderline cases, such as the meeting that got so large it became mass communication, or the video conference that included aspects of mass and two-person interactions. But generally the distinctions among two-person, group, and mass communication held, and they were used to evaluate the content that was communicated in each context. In a private, two-person conversation face-to-face or on the phone, the people involved could usually say whatever they wanted, or whatever they believed it was appropriate to say. With small groups, the stakes went up. Groups developed expectations about staying on the topic, not making inflammatory or irrelevant claims, and backing your statements with evidence. Mass media like radio, television, and newspapers were only available to some people who were empowered to put content there. Speech writers, newspaper editors, radio and television reporters or executives, and the boards of directors who controlled media outlets were the ones who controlled what was broadcasted.

Social Media Changes

Social media has changed all this. Now each individual can create and access blogs, podcasts, video, and text-based technologies that make content available to the world; content that can be easily shared across channels. Technology advances encourage even those who never spoke to speak now. You potentially have as much power as a national television broadcast station with one key difference: On the Web you can reach millions of others for free and with relatively little knowledge and skill. As this is written, three top-rated YouTube videos are Blair's Beauty Blabber, a hilarious clip of a brother and sister who are high from a visit to the dentist, and an amateur-produced musical spoof of Last Friday Night.

On social media channels, what makes content "worthy" is not determined by network television moguls but by networks of friends, viewers, and site participants who, by the click of their mouse, view a video, refer their friends to the widget of the day, promote a cause, scrutinize a company, or repost an interesting comment made by a friend. Today's top YouTube videos have been posted by individuals with great imaginations, but without any special position or title. This change in power over and control of content is one important way that the distinction between "two-person" and "mass" communication is blurred by social media.

Communication Models Change   Another way to understand the distinctive features of social media communication is to consider how it is changing the relative importance of the various parts of the communication process. Early theorizing and research hypothesized that the *communicator* was the most important link in the communication process. As the apparent instigator of the process, the "sender" was thought to be the one who determined which channel to use and what content to communicate. This understanding led in the late 1940s to the presentation by Harold Lasswell of the following model for understanding all communication:

Who → Says What → To Whom → Via Which Channel → With What Effect?[6]

This basic understanding got translated into the influential model,

Sender → Message → Receiver → Channel → Effect

But as communication research continued, it became apparent that the explanatory power of this model depended on whether it's accurate to say that the source or sender had the power and control that the model indicates. The way that researchers understood human systems was simpler back then. It seemed obvious—and it was often true—that husbands controlled communication with wives, fathers controlled communication with children, bosses with employees, superiors with subordinates, and committee chairs with committee members. In other words, hierarchy was more common then, and most people accepted it.

But soon enough, communication research found that this primary focus on the Source or Sender no longer explained what actually happens. Part of the change was cultural. Wives no longer just agreed with all the wishes of their husbands. Disenfranchised and marginalized people developed power bases in labor unions, civil and human rights organizations, and consumer groups. Once-accepted and dominant hierarchies were leveled as people developed new forms of power, and some of these hierarchies were even reversed. In politics, radical "fringe" groups gained power; in businesses, "360 degree evaluation" encouraged subordinates to evaluate superiors; and in schools, student evaluations of teachers became increasingly important. So the "Source" got displaced from the #1 position.

It also became obvious to many that most of the crucial questions about communication had to do with *outcomes*, and that attempts to communicate often produced "Effects" that were unintended by the Source or Sender. This realization helped shift the emphasis from Sender to Receiver. The 1970s saw the development of "uses and gratifications" approaches to communication that focused on analyzing receivers' communication needs and their impact on other communication elements.[7] Lasswell's original model was reconstructed to look like this:

Receiver → Sender → Channel → Message → Effects

Because much of communication is tailored to fit the receivers' needs, the uses and gratification approach or theory promoted improved understanding of many communication events. This approach worked especially well for the analysis of messages sent through such traditional media as radio, TV, newspapers, and magazines.

One of the reasons it worked is that with these traditional media, the receiver is a relatively passive recipient. Hearers, viewers, and readers do not have many choices to provide feedback or to influence the communicator's agenda, other than passively tuning away from the communication. The receiver does not have the power to change the message or answer back to the source except in the few occasions where people send a complaint or write to the editor. This power reality was even acknowledged by the U.S. Supreme Court. In the 1960s, some argued that these traditional media should be obligated to open their channels to opinions and content provided by consumers. The Supreme Court rejected the idea.[8]

Social Media Change the Model   Social media ushered in a third important development in how communication is understood. Lasswell's original model privileged the Source or Sender. Uses and gratifications theory shifted focus to the Receiver. The World Wide Web has further revolutionized the communication we experience to the point where the most accurate model starts with the Channel, which means it now looks like this:

Channel → Sender → Message → Receiver → Effect

Cell phones, e-mail, text messaging, and social media sites on the Internet make so many communication possibilities so thoroughly available to so many people, that the changes in our lives are as significant as the changes from oral to print culture—when Gutenberg invented the printing press—and from physical to electronic transmission—with the invention of the telegraph, telephone, radio, and television.

What features make social media so appealing, encompassing, and powerful? One is availability. Access to the World Wide Web is not only universal, it's free. And the devices that provide this access are relatively inexpensive and continually getting cheaper—think of simple cell phones for pennies and no charges for use of Twitter or Facebook. Websites earn money via advertising rather than subscription charges, so the more people who use a site the more valuable exposure there is for advertisers. The bigger the user base the higher the advertising revenues and the more people can join the network for free.

User-friendliness is another attractive feature. Although young people are clearly the heaviest users of social media, parents routinely learn to text their children and even grandparents and great-grandparents make use of texting, Facebook, Twitter, and blogs. The ease of use of these media allows the majority of people worldwide to use them regardless of their cultural sophistication, social status, or level of education.

These media are also individually empowering. Users can develop a unique presence, for example on their Facebook site, with their own identity, brand, and image. Each person on the social network can communicate unique content and receive responses instantly. Agendas that have in the past been set by authorities and people in power are now being set by individual users. For example, backpack reporting enables individuals to become sources for news reports that are broadcast widely. Social media have become so influential that today, most traditional media outlets have developed their own virtual presence on blogs, Twitter, and YouTube.

The Medium Is the Message/Massage/Mass Age

These developments give a new meaning to an influential 20th-century understanding of communication. In the 1960s, Canadian communication researcher Marshall McLuhan made headlines with books entitled *The Gutenberg Galaxy: The Making of Typographic Man*[9] and *The Medium Is the Massage*.[10] McLuhan's main point was that people had, up until then, overlooked the importance of the communication medium itself—whether messages were sent and received via print, face-to-face, radio, television, and so on. At the time he was writing, McLuhan was focused on the worldwide spread of television. He argued that "The new electronic interdependence re-creates the world in the image of a global village," and the "global village" metaphor played an important role in programs as varied as ecological environmentalism and the Cold War. When McLuhan wrote that "the medium is the massage," he meant that various media manipulate or "massage" human consciousness, and that this manipulation changes the ways humans think—how we define and describe problems, how we evaluate outcomes, how we think critically. McLuhan's central claim was very similar to the point the Stanford researchers make about Web multitaskers: Media use affects how we *think*.

The three of us believe that you will better understand the significance and impact of your involvement with social media if you think of it in terms suggested by McLuhan's writing. Today, we would say, *The medium is the* "*Mass Age*." By this we mean that social media have empowered each of us to be mass communicators. The arrival of the Internet created a system of highways and roads that can potentially connect any point on earth to any other point(s) or user(s). The Internet paved the way for social media vehicles and these channels in turn reshaped and redefined our communication, including our interpersonal communication. Now we have an exhaustive system that works with all the following relationship patterns:

- One to many: With social media, Angela can communicate to a group of friends and further to anybody who is interested in what she is saying.
- Many to one: Angela's group and other groups and individuals can communicate back to her.
- One to any: Angela can bypass her group to communicate to any other person or group in the world.
- Many to many: Angela is a member of her group and other groups can reciprocate communication back and forth among and between each other.

These powerful interwoven relationships have enabled people on the net to become journalists, reporters, politicians, inventors, and virtual storekeepers. In some cases, this means that people choose mass communication over face-to-face contacts. On the riverwalk last night, I (John) watched a young couple while he animatedly told her a story and she texted. The face-to-face opportunity was right there, but she chose to be online. When you become a "mass communicator," what do you gain and what do you lose?

What's Next?

Notice that right now you're using a traditional medium—the printed page—to learn about a rapidly evolving digital medium—social media. One inherent difficulty with doing this is that print can't keep up with new developments. Given the unavoidable time that it takes to produce a book, much of what's printed about digital media is out of date as soon as it appears. Recognizing this problem, we'd still like to suggest a few directions that we believe social media development will take in the future.

Shrinking Globe   We think it's inevitable that social media will keep shrinking the globe. Today those of us in the United States are a click away from China, Japan, Iran, or any other place in the world. This connectivity provides a gateway for both enhanced intercultural understanding and exchange and the proliferation of various abuses—viruses, predators, and the communication of misinformation. The dangers won't go away, but the channels will be used by

more and more people to connect with those who used to be permanent strangers. South African children will text their Canadian counterparts, Portugese
metal music fans will exchange ideas with U.S. and Brazilian fans, and political
blogs will connect people in England, Gaza, Sri Lanka, and Pakistan. People
everywhere and from all different social and economic classes will discover that
it is increasingly impossible to function in the 21st century without dealing on a
daily basis with people who are very different from you.

Usage Changes   Second, there will be continuing changes in how people use
social media. Some people will decrease their presence on a certain channel as
the novelty of the technology wears off. This happened in the recent past when
many young people shifted from e-mail to social media sites. People may also
run out of time or get too few responses from others on the same network. At
the same time, there will be more and more newcomers and they will bring more
to share. More seniors will also be joining the networks as technology becomes
easier to use. Social pressure from children and grandchildren will encourage
seniors to get on the social media bandwagon.

New Formats   New formats of social networks will evolve that integrate what
the present ones now lack. Software will be even more video-friendly as people
take advantage of opportunities to share increasingly complete, timely, and
"real" information. Linking technologies will make it increasingly easy to identify and connect with others "like you." More hot spots will be made available
by sponsors of more social gathering places.

E-books   E-books will witness a rebirth after the very near introduction of
new readers, or better yet, a net book will be offered by publishers at little or
no cost—the price will be subscribing to the service. E-book technology will
become like free printers and cell phones. Books in various languages will be
easily accessible with the click of a button. Furthermore, there will be more
reliable translations readily made available so those without second language
competencies can directly learn about various cultures. McLuhan's global village will continue to evolve.

Media Literacy   Media literacy will also finally appear in schools at every
level. Public school curricula will include more and more programming to
encourage the effective use of social media and to guide critical thinking about
it. Media developments, software, and both formal and informal educational
programming will be developed to mitigate the negative effects of extensive
media multitasking. Efforts will be made to restore critical thinking, reflective,
and imagination competencies without substantially reducing the use of social
media. This is one of the most promising directions for future development. As
people learn more about how their cognitive abilities and thinking processes are
being affected by their media use, some will make increasingly wiser and better
choices about how and where to invest their media time.

IMPLICATIONS FOR YOUR INTERPERSONAL COMMUNICATING

Remember that communication becomes more interpersonal as it moves *from* talking and listening about general ideas, stereotyped understandings, mechanical and objective facts and claims, mindless reactions, and unreflective comments *toward* listening and talking about *unique* perceptions, *unmeasureable* feelings, *responsive* choices, and thoughtful *reflections*. Some social media promote the development from impersonal to interpersonal communicating, and some social media don't.

Horizontal media are cross-sectional and comprised of status updates (for example, Twitter), short text messaging, and entertainment-based content including soft news. These are functional and useful, *and* they do not optimally promote interpersonal communicating.

Vertical media are those channels that allow participants to deeply engage in the subject matter such as blogs, dedicated websites, and subject-specific social networks like user groups, and professional and specialized discussion forums.

Horizontal media can continue to offer us relief from the demands that come from functioning in a variety of social system roles. *And* (not "but") we can also use vertical social media and other digital channels to promote interpersonal contact. Our focus can most usefully be on the four elements already summarized: uniqueness, unmeasurable elements (e.g., feelings), responses rather than reactions, and reflectiveness.

Uniqueness is the key element. We can choose the specific medium, not just because everybody is doing it, but because it works best for our needs and the people with whom we're connecting. We can bring individual insights and experiences into the content we share, rather than parroting what others have said, repeating widely shared stories, or mouthing platitudes. Remembering that each individual's experiences are unique, we can bring our own distinctive life-events into what we communicate and share our own point of view on a topic. And we can invite others to bring their uniqueness into the communication, too.

Without "wearing our hearts on our sleeves" we can also include relevant feelings with what we contribute on social media. Excitement, concern, gratitude, commitment, hesitation, eagerness, affection, support, and caution can all be a part of what we communicate. Again, the point is not to "bleed all over the screen" but to make the feeling sides of ourselves at least partly available to the people we're communicating with.

And, while we might want to keep using horizontal media for brief status updates, we can exploit opportunities to share thoughtful reflections on vertical media sites. One reason to do this is because it speaks to some of what's most human about us, which are our abilities to have perceptions about our perceptions. Unlike all other animals, humans can think about our thinking. We can decide not to say something because it might hurt the other person, be gratified because we said exactly what we meant, and wonder if we should take back or explain more fully something we just said. Each of these—the decision, the feeling of pleasure, and the questioning—reflects a perception *about* other perceptions. This is what it means to be *reflective*, and this kind of content can make communication be more interpersonal in quality.

Another reason to do this is to enhance the depth of human contact we experience. Of course we don't want to be "best friends" with everybody we contact via social media, but in-depth relationships are one of the most important pleasures and the most significant life-experiences for human beings. Vertical sites offer opportunities to establish these kinds of relationships.

CONCLUSION

Social media provide opportunities for both interpersonal communication and its opposite. The more effectively you can distinguish between these two kinds of potential, the more effective a user of social media you will be. If you're one of the people who spends more than two hours on Facebook most days, or whose iPhone logs more than 5,000 text messages a month, you owe it to yourself to make the most of these very important parts of your communication life. Recognize that, when it comes to social media, "The medium is the mass age," and that fact has important implications for what you say and how you say. Recognize, too, that you can make choices that get your uses of social media working either for you or against you. Choose wisely!

REVIEW QUESTIONS

1. Describe the apparent cognitive effects of heavy involvement in media multitasking.
2. Explain what it means to say that two-person communication has become mass communication.
3. Summarize the historical changes in our understanding of the relationships among Sender, Message, Receiver, Channel, and Effects.
4. Paraphrase: (a) "The medium is the message." (b) "The medium is the massage." (c) "The medium is the mass age."
5. Explain the differences between horizontal and vertical social media.

PROBES

1. What are some ethical implications and challenges of the fact that two-person communication has become mass communication?
2. When "the communicator" is the primary part of the process, individual choices matter most. What happens to individual choice when "the medium" is the primary part of the communication process?

3. How do social media undermine some key assumptions of capitalism?
4. How do you believe media literacy should best be taught, and at what level of school?
5. How do vertical social media promote uniqueness in communication?

NOTES

1. http://digital.venturebeat.com/2010/01/10.
2. Susan Scott, *Fierce Conversations* (New York: Viking Penguin, 2002).
3. Retrieved June 9, 2010, from http://www.sciencemag.org/cgi/content/abstract/23/5910/69.
4. Retrieved June 9, 2010, from http://news.stanford.edu/news/2009/august24/multitask-research-study-082409.html.
5. Nicholas Carr, "Does the Internet Make You Smarter or Dumber?" *Wall Street Journal,* June 5–6, 2010, pp. W1–W2.
6. Harold Lasswell, "The Structure and Function of Communication in Society" in *The Communication of Ideas,* ed. Lyman Bryson (New York: Harper & Bros., 1948), pp. 37–51.
7. Elihu Katz, "Mass Communication Research and the Study of Culture." *Studies in Public Communication* 2 (1959): 1–6.
8. Don Pember and Clay Calvert, *Mass Media Law,* 17th ed. (New York: McGraw-Hill, 2011), p. 45.
9. Marshall McLuhan, *The Gutenberg Galaxy: The Making of Typographic Man* (London: Routledge, 1962).
10. Marshall McLuhan, *The Medium is the Message* (New York: Random House, 1967).

Communication
Building Identities

Constructing Identities

John Stewart, Karen E. Zediker, and Saskia Witteborn

Now that we've defined communication and interpersonal communication, the next step is to think about the people who engage in it. For most of the past 300 years, westerners have generally understood people to be individuals—separate, singular selves. But in the last half of the 20th century, some European and American researchers rediscovered an idea that had been clear to our Greek forebears and to most members of Eastern cultures for a long time: Humans are more than singular individuals. We are relational beings, unique selves mixed from many ingredients. The readings in this chapter develop this understanding of humans *as communicators.*

I introduced this idea in the first reading of Chapter 2 when I said that communication always involves negotiating identities or selves. Every time you or I communicate with anybody, one thing we're doing is mutually working out who we are for and with each other. Identities are always in play.

One way to talk about this identity negotiation or identity management part of communication is to use the vocabulary of "co-constructing selves," which is what Karen Zediker, Saskia Witteborn, and I do in this reading. This essay comes from a basic interpersonal communication text that the three of us wrote together. We begin with some examples of how this co-construction process operates to demonstrate that it's going on all the time. We point out that, since it is a continuous process, nobody always does it perfectly or poorly. As we emphasize, there is no one best or worst way to participate in this process. There are just outcomes of how you do it, results that people may or may not want. We also make the point that this process goes on in every culture, wherever humans communicate. And the reason it's important to understand this process is that when you want to influence where your communicating is on the impersonal-interpersonal continuum explained in Chapter 2, you need to pay attention to how you're co-constructing selves.

We define identity or self as a constellation of features or labels that establish social expectations that we have of ourselves and others. Then we contrast old and new views of identities. We point out that the individualistic, Western view is very narrow and that increasing numbers of researchers and teachers are recognizing that identities are relational and multidimensional.

This multidimensionality is part of the first of the four characteristics of identities or selves that we discuss. The second is that selves are responders. No human starts behaving from ground zero, so that everything we do can be understood to be in reply or answer to something else. The third feature is that identities are developed in past and present relationships. The fourth characteristic is that identities can be both avowed and ascribed. This means that we can verbally and/or nonverbally "assert" an identity—avowal—and that others can ascribe identity features to us. This is one reason why it is important to be reflective about your communicating—because in every conversation you're not only expressing your ideas but also defining who you are.

This essay and the other readings in Chapter 3 will flesh out this basic understanding of how selves—who people are—get co-constructed in people's communicating.

MAIN IDEAS

- Identity construction is happening in almost all communication, across all cultures.
- Identity construction processes significantly affect where your communication is on the impersonal–interpersonal scale.
- Identities are constellations of socially negotiated labels that establish expectations that we have of ourselves and others.
- In the past, identity was understood as an individual, *intra*personal thing.
- Current understandings of identity as primarily social have been affected by Eastern conceptions.
- One characteristic of identities is that they are multidimensional and changing.
- Second, selves are responders; they are context dependent and developed in interaction.
- Identities are also developed in past and present relationships.
- In communication, identities are both *avowed* and *ascribed*.

WHAT IS IDENTITY OR SELF?

Notice what happens in the following conversation:

ALIA: Hi, just wanted to introduce myself. I'm Alia. I'm your new roommate. Just switched universities. Kind of sucks to move in your senior year, but well …

CHERYL: Cool. I'm Cheryl. Nice to meet you, finally. I just knew that a girl named Alia—how do you pronounce your name?—would be my new roommate, that's all. Anyways, good to meet you. Any preference in terms of where you wanna sleep?

ALIA: Not really.

CHERYL: I'm just asking because I just got back from Germany. Exchange student, you know? I was sleeping in a dorm there and was glad that my roommate let me sleep by the window. I'm kind of claustrophobic. Ha-ha. Don't worry; otherwise I'm pretty much together. Let me guess where you're from. Honestly, you don't quite look as if you were from around here.

ALIA: Well, whatdaya think?

CHERYL: Greece. Oh no, Italy.

ALIA: Naaa.

CHERYL: Spain or South America?

ALIA: Wrong again. Born in Chicago, my parents are from Iraq. Where are you from?

CHERYL: Born in Detroit and raised in Oregon.

ALIA: So you are American, too?

CHERYL: Absolutely, although it's not that important to me, really. No kidding. Could have sworn you were from Greece. My best friend in Germany looks like you, and she's Greek. Well, I feel stupid to ask this, but ... aren't you supposed to wear a scarf?

ALIA: Guess what? I am a Christian, Chaldean to be exact. Not all Arabs are Muslims, and not all Muslims are Arabs. Islam's the biggest religion in the Arab world, but there're also lots of Christians.

CHERYL: Wow. Let's talk more about that. That's exciting. I'm living with an Iraqi woman.

ALIA: Iraqi American is better. I was born here. Chicago, remember?

CHERYL: You're right, I'm sorry I went off on this cultural thing. I'm really, really glad to finally live with someone who is from another culture. I'm still in a kind of culture shock, coming back to the States from Germany. That's why I'm so glad about you.

ALIA: Sure, but first, if you don't mind, could you show me around here? I need to register before classes start.

CHERYL: Yep, no problem. I'm sorry if I talked too much. Let's start with the library.

Cheryl and Alia are constructing identities together. At first, Cheryl gives Alia a national identity that Alia does not identify with. Cheryl does this mainly because of how Alia looks. Alia is the "Iraqi woman," even though she would probably have liked to be the *person* Alia first, or the senior who is new to the university. Cheryl, on the other hand, constructs herself as a curious and outspoken young woman, a student, and someone who has been exposed to different cultures.

This conversation shows how identities or selves are outcomes of conversations and something that we do, rather than are. Cheryl and Alia move from negotiating their student identities when they talk about being a senior and an exchange student, to negotiating their national and ethnic identities, and back to negotiating their student selves again. Alia does not want to be known only as an Iraqi and an Arab. She wants Cheryl to recognize her multiple identities as a woman, a student, a Chaldean Christian, and an Iraqi American. Cheryl also emphasizes that her national identity is not that important to her. At that moment, she wants to be perceived as a knowledgeable and open person and a possible friend, and not just as an American. As you can see, identities are fluid, not static. No one wants to be put in an ethnic, national, or gender box, especially at the beginning of a relationship.

Here is another example of how identities are constructed in verbal and nonverbal talk:

JAN: Hey, how's it goin'?

HEATHER: (Silence and a scowl)

JAN: What's the matter?

HEATHER: Nothing. Forget it.

JAN: What are you so pissed about?

HEATHER: Forget it! Just drop it.

JAN: Well, all right! Pout! I don't give a damn!

Here, even though Jan and Heather are not talking about any specific object, issue, or event, they are definitely constructing identities together. In this conversation Heather's definition of herself and of Jan goes something like this:

> Right now I identify myself as independent of you (Silence. "Nothing. Forget it."). You're butting into my space, and you probably think I'm antisocial. But I've got good reasons for my anger.

On the other hand, Jan's definition of herself and of Heather is something like this:

> Right now I identify myself as friendly and concerned ("Hey, how's it goin'?" "What's the matter?"). I'm willing to stick my neck out a little, but you're obviously not interested in being civil. So there's a limit to how long I'll *stay* friendly and concerned ("Well, all right! Pout! I don't give a damn!").

We want to emphasize that nobody in these conversations is constructing identities perfectly or poorly, right or wrong. In one sense, there is no right or wrong way to participate in this process. There are just *outcomes* of how you do it, *results* that you may or may not want.

We also want to emphasize that none of the people in these conversations could avoid constructing selves. It's a process that happens whenever people communicate. Some of the most important meanings we collaboratively construct are our identities, and all communicating involves constructing identities or selves. No matter how brief or extended the contact, whether it's written or oral, mediated or face-to-face, impersonal or interpersonal, the people involved will be directly or indirectly constructing definitions of themselves and responding to the definitions offered by others. Radio talk show hosts and television newscasters are continually building identities. The person who writes a letter longhand on colorful stationery is defining him- or herself differently from the person who writes the same letter on a word processor. The person who answers the telephone, "Yeah?" is defining him- or herself differently from the one who answers, "Good morning. May I help you?"

Research on intercultural communication shows how identity construction occurs in different cultures. For instance, Bailey (2000) shows how young Dominican Americans negotiate their cultural identities by switching between Spanish and English. Speaking in Spanish indicates solidarity with their peers who are similar in cultural background. In another study, Hegde (1998) shows how immigrants from India navigate between their Indian identity and their new American identity. Saskia has also studied Arab identities and has found that people of Arab descent enact multiple national and religious identities and feel more or less strongly Arab at various times, but it really depends on the context. For instance, some people say that they call themselves Arab American mostly when they have to fill out official forms, and that they feel Arab rather than Arab American when they talk about families because family is so important in the Arab world. As Scotton (1983) summarizes, in various cultural contexts, speakers use language choices "imaginatively ... a range of options is open to them within a normative framework, and ... taking one option rather than another is the *negotiation of identities.*"

So two reasons why it's important to understand the process of identity construction are (1) that you're doing it whenever you communicate—and everybody else is, too—and (2) that the process affects who you are in relation to others. The third reason why it's important is that *your negotiation responses also affect where your communication is on the impersonal–interpersonal continuum....* Some responses just about guarantee that your communication will be impersonal. Others lead to more interpersonal communicating. So if you want to help change the quality of your contacts with your dating partner, employer, roommate, sister, or parent in either direction on the continuum, you'll probably want to learn as much as you can about this process.

Definition of Identity

Identity or self is made up of interlocking features that mark how persons behave and respond to others. Identities are constellations of labels that establish social expectations that we have of ourselves and others. These social expectations can include roles that we want or have to play in specific situations and the languages or dialects we speak and expect others to speak. When you enter a classroom in the United States, you expect your instructor to talk and behave in certain ways. For instance, most North Americans expect that a person enacting the identity of an "instructor" should normally stand in front of the class, speak in a loud and intelligible voice, have control in the classroom, and, unless it's a foreign language class, express him- or herself in some form of English. And in order to enact the role of instructor, this person needs students who enact their role. Notice how we say "enact." This is another way of emphasizing that identities are something that we *do* rather than what we *are* (Collier & Thomas, 1988; Hecht, Jackson, & Ribeau, 2003). You are not born to be a student for all of your life, but you are socialized into this identity, and it becomes salient in different times and places.

Old versus Current Views of Identity

It may sound weird to you to say that identities or selves are co-constructed in verbal and nonverbal talk. You might think of your *self* as fairly stable, identifiable, and clearly bounded. If so, you're not alone. Most people in Western cultures have been taught to think of their selves as individual containers that enclose their unique essence. As one book puts it,

> There is an individualist mode of thought, distinctive of modern Western cultures, which, though we may criticize it in part or in whole, we cannot escape. … This inescapable cultural vise has given us—or, at least, the dominant social groups in the West—a sense of themselves as distinctive, independent agents who own themselves and have relatively clear boundaries to protect in order to ensure their integrity and permit them to function more effectively in the world. (Sampson, 1993, 31)

Most members of dominant social groups in the Western world think of the boundary of the individual as the same as the boundary of the body, and that the body houses or contains the self. Common metaphors reflect this view, as when people say that a person is *"filled* with anger," "unable to *contain* her joy," *"brimming* with laughter," or "trying to get anger *out of our system"* (Lakoff 1987, 383). Some theories of psychology reinforce this view of identity or the self. Psychologists influenced by the famous therapist Sigmund Freud, for example, think of society as made up of individual selves who are each working out their inner tensions. One Freudian insisted that a student revolt against university administrators was caused by the students' unresolved conflicts with their fathers. In his view,

> protestors were taking out their inner conflicts with parental authority by acting against the authority represented by the University. It was as though there were no legitimate problems with the University; it only symbolized protestors' unresolved Oedipal conflicts with the real source of their troubles, their fathers. (Sampson, 1993, 44)

For this psychologist, selves were individual and internal.

But in the last decades of the twentieth century, the development of space travel, satellite television, and the World Wide Web; the globalization of music and business; and the end of the Cold War all helped Westerners understand that this view of the person as a bounded individual is, as one anthropologist puts it, rather "peculiar" (Geertz, 1979, 229). For centuries, people in many cultures outside the West have not been thinking this way. For example, if a North American is asked to explain why someone financially cheated another person, the North American's tendency will be to locate the cause in "the kind of person she is." A Hindu, by contrast, is more likely to offer a social explanation—"The man is unemployed. He is not in a position to give that money" (Miller, 1984, 968). This is because many members of the Hindu culture don't think of identity or the self as individual, but as social or communal. For them, identity is a function of cultural or group memberships. Or, to take another example, in a study of U.S. and Samoan child care workers, U.S. preschool teachers tended to help children socialize by developing their individuality, whereas Samoan caregivers' efforts "were directed towards helping the children learn how better to fit into their in-group" (Ochs, 1988, 199). In their broader culture, Samoans in this study also recognized the central role of other people in events that were deemed worthy of praise or compliments. So one researcher reported that when a Samoan passenger complimented a driver with language that translates, "Well done the driving," the driver typically responded, "Well done the support." "In this Samoan view, if a performance went well, it is the supporters' merit as much as the performer's" (Ochs 1988, 200). Many Japanese understand the person in a similar way. In Japan, one author notes, "The concept of a self completely independent from the environment is very foreign" (Kojima, 1984, 972). Rather, Japanese think of individuals in terms of the social context they fit into—their family, work group, and so on. The United States, Canada, Australia, Great Britain, and some other Western cultures have a strong belief in the individual self, but many European countries (e.g., Spain, Austria, and Finland) and most Asian and Latin American cultures understand identities or selves as social, relational, or group-oriented (Hofstede, 1980). (See the first reading in Chapter 11.)

It's easier to understand how identity construction works—and how to manage your own identity constructing—if you adopt what has historically been a more Eastern perspective. This doesn't mean that you have to pretend to be somebody you're not. In fact, this understanding is being accepted by communication scholars, psychologists, anthropologists, and other students of human behavior all over the world. Many of these scholars and teachers recognize that selves or identities are relational from birth, or maybe even before. They take seriously what Lev Vygotsky and George Herbert Mead, two very influential human development researchers, said several decades ago: namely, that infants are first *social* beings and only later in life learn to see themselves as *individuals*. As psychologist Edward Sampson explains,

> Both Vygotsky and Mead clearly emphasize the necessary social bases of human thinking, cognition, and mindedness. Indeed, rather than viewing the individual's mind as setting forth the terms for the social order, the reverse describes the actual event: the social process—namely, dialogue and conversation—precedes, and is the foundation for, any subsequent psychological processes that emerge. (Sampson, 1993, 103)

In short, the English terms *self* and *identity* and their meanings are only about 300 years old. Studies of history and of other cultures illustrate that the Western definition developed over the last 275 of these 300 years is very narrow. Today, this idea that selves are individual containers is being revised as communication scholars and psychologists are recognizing how much our selves are developed in communication with others. Westerners increasingly recognize that identities or selves are multidimensional and that they change in response to the people and institutions we connect with. Each of our identities has athletic, artistic, ethnic, gendered, occupational, scientific, political, economic, and religious dimensions, and all of these shift in content and importance as we move from situation to situation.

FOUR CHARACTERISTICS OF IDENTITIES OR SELVES

This understanding of identities or selves can be summarized in four primary characteristics.

1. Identities Are Multidimensional and Changing

One feature of selves is that we're complex. On the one hand, each of us is characterized by some stabilities or patterns. A person's genetic makeup is stable, and your ethnic identity also probably hasn't changed and probably won't. Someone who's known you all your life can probably identify some features you had when you were 4 or 5 years old that you still have, and as you look at old photographs of yourself, you might recognize how the identity of the person in the picture is in some ways "the same" as who you are today.

On the other hand, you are different in at least as many ways as you are the same. Think, for example, of who you were at age 9 or 10 and who you were at age 14 or 15. Adolescence is a time of *significant* change in our selves. Or, if it fits you, think of yourself before you were married & after, or your identity before and after you had children.

Some researchers broadly classify identities or selves into personal, relational, and communal features (Hecht, Jackson, & Ribeau, 2003). *Personal* identity is all the characteristics that you think make you a unique person, such as being friendly, helpful, disciplined, hard working, beautiful, and so forth. *Relational* identities are based on relationships you have with others, such as mother-daughter, teacher-student, or employer-employee. *Communal* identities are usually related to larger groups, such as ethnicities, race, religion, gender, or nationality.

2. Selves Are Responders

This point was made in Chapter 2 when we said that responsiveness is one of the five features that makes each of us a person. The main point there was to contrast responding with simply reacting. Now we want to build the meaning of this idea by noting that responding implies both *choice* (not just reacting) and *connection* with what's already happened.

To say that selves are responders is to say that we grow out of and fit into a context of actions and events that we behave-in-relation-to. On the one hand, this is just another way of saying that selves are relational or social. Remember how Alia responded to Cheryl's question about where she is from and how they both constructed their student and ethnic/national identities? They responded to each other. In one instance, Cheryl might be regarded as just reacting when she asks about Alia's absent scarf. However, in most instances, both women are responding to each other, which includes reflecting about what the other person just said. Responding means that all human action is joint action. No human starts behaving from ground zero, so that everything we do, from the very beginning, is in reply or answer to something else.

Humans begin responding from the first moment we develop any awareness, which, as we noted earlier, probably happens before birth. Every baby is born into a world of verbal and nonverbal talk, family relationships, gender patterns, ongoing activities, and social and political events. This is the sense in which no person is, "after all, the first speaker, the one who disturbs the eternal silence of the universe." Since none of us is Adam or Eve, all of our actions more or less effectively connect with or fit into the activities and language systems that surround us (Bakhtin, 1986, 69).

3. Identities Are Developed in Past and Present Relationships

The reason selves change over time is that we develop who we are in relationships with the people around us. Some of the most important parts of each person's identity are established in one's family of origin, the people with whom you spend the first five to seven years of your life. One of your parents may have consistently introduced you to new people from the time you were old enough to talk, and today you may still find it easy to make acquaintances. Or you may have moved around a lot when you were young, and today you feel secure only when you have your own "place" and you prefer to spend holidays close to home. You may treasure a wonderful relationship with your dad, or you may have had the opposite kind of experience. Your family is the role model for many types of relational, religious, or ethnic identities. For instance, you learn what it means to be a good friend or a good neighbor, a good brother or sister or mother or father, or perhaps not such a good one:

> My father is an alcoholic. He has never admitted to that fact. He and my mom used to get in lots of fights when I lived at home. The six of us kids were used as pawns in their war games. I always wondered whether or not I was responsible for his drinking. When the fights were going on, I always retreated to my room. There I felt secure. Now, I am 22, and have been married for two years. I have this affliction that, whenever the slightest thing happens, I always say I am so sorry. I am sorry when the milk is not cold, sorry that the wet towel was left in the gym bag. I just want to take the blame for everything, even things I have no control over. (Black, 1982, 9)

Many current studies about dysfunctional families emphasize how people with addictions developed the communication patterns that reinforce these addictions in their families of origin (Fuller et al., 2003). Other research focuses on how addictions affect the children or other family members of addicted persons. One review of studies about adult children of alcoholics concludes that, regardless of gender, socioeconomic group, or ethnic identity, these people develop 13 common features. For example, many adult children of alcoholics "have difficulty following a project through from beginning to end," "lie when it would be just as easy to tell the truth," "judge themselves without mercy," "take themselves very seriously," "constantly seek approval and affirmation," and "are extremely loyal, even in the face of evidence that the loyalty is undeserved" (Beatty, 1989). These books and articles illustrate how much our family of origin contributes to the response patterns that we follow in identity construction.... Past relationships contribute a great deal to the patterns that help make up our present selves.

Present relationships are also important. When you realize that a new friend really likes you, it can do great things for your self-definition. Getting a top grade from a teacher you respect can affect how you see yourself. At work, a positive performance evaluation from your supervisor or a raise can improve not only your mood and your bank account but also your perception of yourself. And again, the reverse can obviously also happen. The point is, genetic makeup does not determine your identity, and we call the communication process that produces these identities *identity construction*.

4. Identities Can Be Avowed and Ascribed

Finally, identities or selves can be ascribed and avowed. *Ascribed* means that others assign you an identity that you may or may not agree with; *avowed* means that you personally assign yourself an identity and act it out. People also try to negotiate this avowal and ascription process. Remember the conversation between Cheryl and Alia? Cheryl ascribed to Alia a somewhat stereotyped national and religious identity that Alia did not accept as her main identity in that particular situation. During the conversation they both put their student and cultural identities on the table (being from Detroit and growing up in Oregon can imply two different regional identities) and reached somewhat of an alignment on how they wanted to be perceived in this initial encounter. However, sometimes when people stereotype, they rigidly stick with their opinions about people and make them one dimensional. For instance, sometimes people talk slower when they realize that English is Saskia's second language or start immediately to talk about beer when they hear that Saskia is from Germany. It can be entertaining for a while, but then Saskia wants to be perceived as Saskia or a woman or an instructor and not only as German. Rigid ascription of identities can become a problem for the person who is ascribed the identity. This is also true for many African Americans, Latinas, or Asian Americans. People are often judged on their looks and language and not who else they are or want to be. The question of ascription and avowal will come up again when we talk about response options.

REVIEW QUESTIONS

1. Fill in the blank: "_____ appear and are constructed or worked out in verbal and nonverbal talk."
2. Identify three plausible features of the identity being offered by the person who answers the telephone with a loud "Yeah?" What are three plausible

features of the identity of the person who answers the telephone, "Good morning. May I help you?"

3. What is the difference between a reaction and a response?
4. Describe one feature of your *personal* identity. Label one feature of your *relational* identity. Describe one feature of your *communal* identity.

PROBES

1. The old view of selves is that individuality comes first, and then individuals interact to form social groups. The new view reverses this sequence. Explain how.
2. Since no person is Adam or Eve, and we are all responding to what happens around us, (a) what does this say about the claim, "He started it!" and (b) what's the most accurate way to define "creativity"?
3. What can a person do about the parts of his or her identity that were formed in past relationships? If you're the child of an alcoholic, for example, what can you do about the parts of your self that were formed by that set of experiences?
4. Does the ethnicity or culture that you primarily identify with generally view selves as individualistic or relational? How does this affect your own sense of self?
5. What past relationships most affected the development of your self? Which present relationships are having the most impact on the current development of your self?
6. If you are mainly a product of your relationships, what happens to your individual integrity?

REFERENCES

Bailey, B. (2000). Language and Negotiation of Ethnic/Racial Identity among Dominican Americans. *Language in Society, 29*: 555–582.

Bakhtin, M. M. (1986). *Speech Genres and Other Late Essays.* (Translated by V. W. McGee). Austin: University of Texas Press. (Originally published 1953.)

Beatty, M. (1989). *Beyond Codependency.* New York: Harper/Hazelden.

Black, C. 1982. *"It Will Never Happen to Me!" Children of Alcoholics as Youngsters—Adolescents—Adults.* Denver: MAC.

Collier, M. J., & Thomas, M. (1988). Cultural Identity: An interpretive perspective. In Y. Y. Kim & W. B. Gudykunst (Eds.), *Theories of intercultural communication.* Newbury Park, CA: Sage.

Fuller, B. E., Chermack, S. T., Cruise, K. A., Kirsch, E., Fitzgerald, H. E., & Zucker, R. A. (2003). Predictors of aggression across three generations among sons of alcoholics: Relationships involving grandparental and parental alcoholism, child aggression, marital aggression and parenting practices." *Journal of Studies on Alcohol, 64*: 472–484.

Geertz, C. (1979). From the native's point of view: On the nature of anthropological understanding. In P. Rabinow & W. M. Sullivan (Eds.), *Interpretive Social Science* (pp. 225–246). Berkeley: University of California Press.

Hall, B. J. (2002). *Among cultures: The challenge of communication*. New York: Harcourt College Publishers.

Hecht, M. L., Jackson II, R. L., & Ribeau, S. A. (2003). *African American communication: Exploring identity and culture*. 2nd ed. Mahwah, NJ: Erlbaum.

Hegde, R. S. (1998). A view from elsewhere: Locating difference and the politics of representation from a transnational feminist perspective. *Communication Theory, 8*: 271–297.

Hofstede, G. (1980). *Culture's consequences: International differences in work-related values*. Beverly Hills, CA: Sage.

Kojima, H. (1984). A significant stride toward the comparative study of control. *American Psychologist, 39*: 972–973.

Laing, R. D. (1961). *The self and others*. New York: Pantheon.

Laing, R. D. (1969). *The self and others*. Baltimore: Penguin Books.

Lakoff, G. (1987). *Women, fire, and dangerous things*. Chicago: University of Chicago Press.

Miller, J. G. (1984). *The development of women's sense of self*. Work in Progress, No. 12. Wellesley, MA: Stone Center Working Paper Series.

Ochs, E. (1988). *Culture and language development: Language acquisition and language socialization in a Samoan village*. Cambridge: Cambridge University Press.

Rogers, C. R. (1965). Dialogue between Martin Buber and Carl R. Rogers. In M. Friedman & R. G. Smith (Eds.), *The knowledge of man*. London: Allen and Unwin.

Sampson, E. E. (1993). *Celebrating the other: A dialogic account of human nature*. Boulder, CO: Westview.

Scotton, C. M. (1983). The negotiation of identities in conversation: A theory of markedness and code choice. *International journal of sociological linguistics, 44*: 119–125.

———

Self and Identity: Transacting a Self in Interactions with Others

Steve Duck and David T. McMahan

Steve Duck and David McMahan are communication teacher-scholars connected with the University of Iowa. Steve is a distinguished research professor and David is an award-winning teacher and consultant.

This excerpt from their interpersonal communication text begins with the important point that each of us develops our individual identity as we communicate with the people around us and encounter "powerful forces of society" such as the frown of a parent or teacher, praise from a mentor, or a bonus for doing an especially good job. The "point of this reading," they write, is that "you *do* your identity in front of audiences, and they might evaluate and comment on whether you're doing it right." This is what makes identity management such an important part of interpersonal communication.

The essay also notes that your portrayal of yourself is not entirely a matter of your own choosing; it is shaped by the social needs at the time, the social situation, the social frame, and the circumstances surrounding your performance. Your identity connects to other identities and the social situation, and it has to "make sense," somehow, in relation to them.

The essay discusses embarrassment and social predicaments in order to show how these external pressures can affect how people perform their identities. They explain how each of us works to become "an accountable self," an individual who is evaluated by others as more or less competent, moral, and likeable. They emphasize that this identity-construction process happens in everyday practices, not just special events. Greeting rituals, rules for asking questions and apologizing, norms for eye contact and touch, forms of address, and other subtle verbal and nonverbal choices all help constitute and reflect individual identities.

MAIN IDEAS

- Self or identity is a social, not an individual construction; it's not that we "are" a specific person but that we "do" our identity with others.
- Your identity choices are important, *and* you are also molded by social pressures.
- Selves are constructed or transacted in everyday practices, not just special events.
- People continually evaluate each other's identity moves to determine their moral accountability.

In keeping with this book's theme, you can't have a self without also having relationships with other people—both the personal relationships you choose and the social relationships you reject. More than that, it's impossible for a person to have a concept of self unless he or she can reflect on identity via the

From *The Basics of Communication: A Relational Perspective*. Los Angeles: Sage Publications, 2009, pp. 134–140. Reprinted with permission.

views of these other people with whom he or she has social or personal relationships. Your identity is *transacted* or constituted in part from two things: First, you take into yourself—or are reinforced for taking into yourself—the beliefs and prevailing norms of the society in which you live. Second, you are *held to account* for the identity that you project by those people you hang out with. The gang member would have lost status in the gang if he had not shot his target. As a Indiana University fan, you lose face if you don't know the score during your game with Purdue or cannot name your own team's quarterback. As a student, you are expected to know answers about the book you are reading for your class.

Let us rephrase this point: Because individuals acquire individuality through the social practices in which they exist and carry out their lives, they encounter powerful forces of society that are actually enforced on the ground by society's secret agents, their relationships with other people that affect their identities. (That "raised eyebrow" from your neighbor/instructor/team fan was actually society at work!) Your "self" is structured and enacted in relation to those people who have power over you in formal ways, like the police, but most often you encounter the institutions within a society through its secret agents: public opinion and the people you know who express opinions about moral issues of the day and give you their judgments. You, too, are one of society's secret agents, guiding what other people do and thinking just as they do....

It is important to note how the routine banality of everyday-life talk with friends who share the same values and talk about them day by day actually does something for society and helps make you who you are. Such routines reinforce people's perspectives and put events in the same sorts of predictable and routine frameworks of meaning through trivial and pedestrian communication with one another in everyday life (Wood & Duck, 2006). But—here's the point of this section, so remember it well—you *do* your identity in front of the audiences, and they might evaluate and comment on whether you're doing it right. Although we used the extreme case about the gang member as an attention grabber, the same kinds of processes are going on in interaction when you profess your undying allegiance to one football team and your supposed hatred of the opposing team. The people around you do not resent it but actually encourage you and reinforce your expression of that identity. They share it and support it. Just as the gang member accepted his identity with all its disturbing implications, so do you when you categorize the opposing team as some kind of enemy. The underlying idea—that a group of people can be treated as nothing more than depersonalized, dehumanized others—runs through team loyalty and rivalry, town versus college kids, and any other kind of stereotyping.

PERFORMATIVE SELF

So now that you know the importance of other people in influencing who you are, you are ready to move on to look more closely at the curious idea that you don't just *have* an identity; you actually *do* one. Part of an identity is not just *hav-*

ing a symbolic sense of it but doing it in the presence of other people and doing it well in their eyes. This is an extremely interesting and provocative fact about communication: Everyone *does* his or her identity for an audience, like an actor in a play. Facework is part of what happens in everyday-life communication and people have a sense of their own dignity and image—the person they want to be seen as. That is part of what gets transacted in everyday communication by the person and by others in the interaction who politely protect and preserve the person's "face." We can now restate this idea for the present chapter as being the performance of one's identity in public, the presentation of the self to people in a way that is intended to make the self look good.

Erving Goffman (1959) dealt with this particular problem and indicated the way in which momentary social forces affect identity portrayal. Goffman was particularly interested in how identity is performed in everyday life and how people manage their image in a way that makes them "look good" (Cupach & Metts, 1994). You will already have worked out for yourself that the concept of "looking good" means "looking good to *other people.*" It is therefore essentially a relational concept, but it takes you one step closer to looking at the interpersonal interaction that occurs on the ground every day. Rather than looking at society in the generalized and abstract way that George Herbert Mead did, Goffman focused on what you actually do in conversations and interactions.

...., Your portrayal of yourself is shaped by the social needs at the time, the social situation, the social frame, and the circumstances surrounding your performance. The server does not introduce herself .... to her *friends* ("Hi, I'm Roberta, and I'll be your server tonight ....") except as a joke, so her performance of the server identity is restricted to those times and places where it is called for and appropriate. Goffman differentiated a front region and back region to social performance: The front region/front stage is where your professional, proper self is performed. For example, a server is all smiles and civility in the front stage of the restaurant when talking to customers. This behavior might be different from how he or she performs in the back region/backstage (say, the restaurant kitchen) when talking with the cooks or other servers and making jokes about the customers or about being disrespectful to them. That means the performance of your identity is not sprung into action by your own free wishes but by social cues that this is the right place and time to perform your "self" in that way.

An identity is a person making sense of the world not just for him- or herself but in a way that makes sense within a context provided by others. Any identity connects to other identities. You can be friendly when you are with your friends, but you are expected to be professional when on the job and to do student identity when in class. An individual inevitably draws on knowledge that is shared in any community to which he or she belongs, so any person draws on information and knowledge that are both personal and communal. If you change from thinking of identity as about "self as character" and instead see it as "self as performer," you also must consider the importance of linguistic competence in social performance, and that includes not doing or saying embarrassing or foolish things.

EMBARRASSMENT AND PREDICAMENTS

Embarrassment is one of the big problems of social life and involves you actually performing a behavior that is inconsistent with the identity or face that you want to present. Cupach and Metts (1994; Metts, 2000) have done a large amount of research on this topic. Someone who wants to impress an interviewer but instead spills coffee on her lap will be embarrassed because her "face" of professional competence is undercut by clumsiness; someone who wants to present a "face" of being cool but who suddenly blushes or twitches will probably feel embarrassed because the nonverbal behavior contradicts the identity of being cool. In both cases, the actual *performance* of an identity (face) is undercut by a specific behavior that just does not fit that presentation of face.

People can be embarrassed by acts that undercut their **performative self,** the doing of the identity that they have claimed for themselves (such as professional competence), momentarily like this, or they can get into longer-term **predicaments** that present a greater challenge to the performative self. Think of predicaments as extended embarrassment. If you go to a job interview and your very first answer makes you look stupid, you know you are still going to have to carry on through the interview anyway, with the interviewers all thinking you are a hopeless, worthless, and unhireable idiot. You'd rather jump into a vat of boiling sulfur right now, but you cannot; you have to sit it out watching their polite smiles and feeling terrible.

Predicaments, like standing up to give a speech and realizing you brought only Page 1 of your 10 pages of notes can be a real test of character (it was for one of us authors, anyway), but predicaments test the performative self and challenge the person to live up to the claims presented in the symbolic identity that the face set up. Of course, predicaments are modified by relationships. As people become closer and more intimate, they are allowed to breach the presentation of one another's face to a greater degree than strangers may do (Metts, 2000). Part of knowing someone well is that you can cross the normal social, physical, or psychological boundaries that exist for everyone else who does not know him or her so well.

Mock put-downs are quite a common form of intimate banter in English-speaking countries but not in Eastern cultures, which suggests that the notion of face and identity is a culturally influenced one on top of everything else that influences it. However, the idea that people work together in relationships to uphold one another's face through politeness is an important one, called **teamwork** by Goffman (1971). Direct challenges to another person's competence ("You are a failure!") an openly offensive in most circumstances, although, the more intimate the relationship is, they are tolerated to a greater degree. Friends are permitted a great deal more latitude in making such comments than strangers are, and less offense is taken when a friend says such a thing than would be taken if a stranger or relatively distant and unknown colleague at work said it. Bosses may say it directly to an inferior because they have social power to break normal social rules, but it can still hurt. A worker who said it to a boss would be seen quite unambiguously as stepping outside the proper relational and hierarchical boundaries. This very fact makes a point that both context *and* relationships serve to define the sorts of communication about identity that are accepted, and vice versa. Except in live standup comedy shows where audience members attend expecting to see someone (preferably someone else) humiliated, the open attack on someone's identity management is a relational communication with great power and shock value.

SELF CONSTITUTED/TRANSACTED IN EVERYDAY PRACTICES

Although this chapter has been about personal identity, we have seen that identity is molded by the ways in which the surrounding culture influences its expression, the way that you *do* your identity and are recognized as having one. Once you recognize that your identity is not just an internal structure but also a practical performance, the relevant communication involved in "being yourself" is affected by the social norms that are in place to guide behavior in a given society. People judge your identity performance and expect you to know about the same practical world and explain or account for yourself. . . .

An important element of doing an identity in front of an audience is that you become an **accountable self,** which essentially allows your identity to be morally judged by other people. What you do can be assessed by other people as right or wrong according to existing habits of society. Any practical way of performing identity turns identity itself into a moral action—that is, identity as a way of living based on choices made about actions that a person sees as available or relevant but that others will judge and hold to account. This point moves the discussion about social construction of identity on from interaction with other people through the force of society and its value systems. Society as a whole encourages you to take certain actions (do not park next to fire hydrants, protect the elderly and the weak, be a good neighbor, recycle!).

Moral accountability... is a fancy way of saying that society as a whole makes judgments about your actions and choices and then holds you to account for the actions and choices that you make, but it also forcefully encourages you to act in particular ways and to see specific types of identity as "good" (patriot is good, traitor is bad; loyalty is good, thief is bad; open self-disclosure is good, passive aggression is bad, for example).

The identity that you thought of as your own personality, then, is not made up of your own desires and impulses but is formed, performed, and expressed within a set of social patterns and judgments built up by values and practices a community or culture through the relationships that people have with one another in it....

For all of these reasons, it makes sense to see a person's identity as a complex and compound concept that is partly based on history, memory, experiences, and interpretations by the individual, partly evoked by momentary aspects of talk (its context, the people you are with, your stage in life, your goals at the time), and partly a social creation directed by other people, society and its categories, and your relationship needs and objectives in those contexts. Your performance of the self is guided by your relationships with other people, as well as your social goals. Even your embodiment of this knowledge or your sense of self is shaped by your social practices with other people and your sense of their valuing your physical being. Your self-consciousness in their presence and the ways you deal with it also influence the presentation of yourself to other people. Although a sense of self/identity is experienced on the ground in your practical interactions with other people, you get trapped by language into reporting it abstractly as some sort of disembodied "identity," a *symbolic* representation of the little practices and styles of behavior that you actually experience in your daily interactions with other people. Once again, then, another apparently simple idea (identity, personality, self) runs into the relational influences that make the basics of communication so valuable to study.

REVIEW QUESTIONS

1. Explain what it means to say that you "do" your identity.
2. What's "facework"?
3. Explain Goffman's distinction between "front region" and "back region."
4. Extend the notion of "performative self" to define "performative contradiction."

PROBES

1. If identity is a social construction, what happens to individual integrity? How can you be true to yourself if "who you are" is socially determined or influenced?
2. Evaluate the claim that "everyday" practices are more important than special or unique events. Doesn't performance in a major event—a big game, important speech, or major project—affect identity more than subtle eye behavior or how someone greets you?

REFERENCES

Cupach, W. R., & Metts, S. (1994). *Facework.* Thousand Oaks, CA: Sage.

Goffman, E. (1959). *Behaviour in public places.* Harmondsworth, UK: Penguin.

Goffman, E. (1971). *Relations in public: Microstudies of the public order.* New York: Basic Books.

Metts, S. (2000). Face and facework: Implications for the study of personal relationships. In K. Dindia & S. W. Duck (Eds.), *Communication and personal relationships* (pp. 74–92). Chichester, UK: Wiley.

Wood, J. T., & Duck, S. W. (Eds.). (2006). *Composing relationships: Communication in everyday life.* Belmont, CA: Thomson Wadsworth.

Identity and Difficult Conversations
Douglas Stone, Bruce Patton, and Sheila Heen

This reading comes from a book called *Difficult Conversations: How to Discuss What Matters Most,* authored by three teacher-practitioners connected with the Harvard Negotiation Project. This project brings together people from Harvard's Law and Business Schools to help individuals and organizations negotiate more effectively in business and personal situations. The team has published several books that have been widely used in communication, business, social work, and law courses in several countries.

One reason these materials are influential on campuses and in workshops and seminars is that they are grounded in a solid understanding of communication. In these pages, the authors explain how identity issues, which are present whenever people communicate, can be especially challenging in difficult conversations. As they explain, a difficult conversation is "anything you find it hard to talk about. . . . When the issues at stake are important and the outcome uncertain, when we care deeply about what is being discussed or about the people with whom we are discussing it, there is potential for us to experience the conversation as difficult" (xv).

Their first point in this reading is that, even for experienced and mature professionals, identity issues can be "terrifying." Almost nothing can be more threatening than a question like, "Am I really the loyal soldier I like to think I am, or just another greedy jerk willing to betray someone for the right price?" As the authors note, problems arise when we have to face not only someone with whom we think we disagree, but also *ourselves.*

They argue that the three crucial basic identity questions are "Am I competent?" "Am I a good person?" and "Am I worthy of love?" Any one of these questions can seriously threaten our confidence, and there is no quick-and-easy fix: "Grappling with identity issues is what life and growth are all about." But there are pitfalls you can avoid.

The article talks about denial and exaggeration as two problems that can be overcome. Then they offer suggestions about how to "ground your identity," first by becoming aware of your own identity issues and then by "complexifying your identity (adopt the and stance). Their advice about "the and stance" runs parallel with what I say about the word "and" in Chapter 4.

The authors end with three "things to accept about yourself": that you will inevitably make mistakes, that your intentions are complex, and that you have contributed to the problem. Each of these helps you to cope with the identity issues that will arise, especially in difficult conversations.

MAIN IDEAS

- Identity issues can be terrifying, even for mature professionals.
- Identity issues revolve around three core issues: competence, being a good person, and being worthy of love.
- Although there is no quick fix to identity threats, it helps to avoid denial and exaggeration.
- One way to ground your identity is to become aware of your own identity issues; another is to complexify your identity.
- It's also important to remember that you will make mistakes, your intentions are complex, and you have contributed to the problem.

> I've already accepted a job elsewhere, and all that's left for me to do is tell my boss I'm leaving. I don't need any references or future business, and no one can influence my decision. And still, when I think of telling my boss, I'm *terrified*.
> —Ben, software company vice president

Viewed from the outside, Ben would seem to have nothing to fear; he holds all the cards. Even so, Ben isn't getting any sleep.

He explains: "My father worked for one company his whole life, and I always admired his loyalty. In my own life, I've tried to do the right thing, and for me a big part of that is sticking by the people around me—my parents, my wife, my children, and my colleagues. Telling my boss I'm leaving raises this loyalty issue directly. My boss was also my mentor, and has been very supportive. The whole thing is making me wonder: Am I really the loyal soldier I like to think I am, or just another greedy jerk willing to betray someone for the right price?"

DIFFICULT CONVERSATIONS THREATEN OUR IDENTITY

Ben's predicament highlights a crucial aspect of why some conversations can be so overwhelmingly difficult. Our anxiety results not just from having to face the other person, but from having to face *ourselves*. The conversation has the potential to disrupt our sense of who we are in the world, or to highlight what we hope we are but fear we are not. The conversation poses a threat to our identity—the story we tell ourselves about ourselves—and having our identity threatened can be profoundly disturbing.

From *Difficult Conversations: How to Discuss What Matters Most* by Douglas Stone, Bruce Patton, and Sheila Heen. New York: Penguin Books, 1999, 111–121.

Three Core Identities

There are probably as many identities as there are people. But three identity issues seem particularly common, and often underlie what concerns us most during difficult conversations: Am I competent? Am I a good person? Am I worthy of love?

- **Am I Competent?** "I agonized about whether to bring up the subject of my salary. Spurred on by my colleagues, I finally did. Before I could even get started, my supervisor said, 'I'm surprised you want to discuss this. The truth is, I've been disappointed by your performance this year.' I felt nauseous. Maybe I'm not the talented chemist I thought I was."
- **Am I a Good Person?** "I had intended to break up with Sandra that night. I began in a roundabout way, and as soon as she got the drift, she started to cry. It hurt me so much to see her in such pain. The hardest thing for me in life is hurting people I care about; it goes against who I am spiritually and emotionally. I just couldn't bear how I was feeling, and after a few moments I was telling her how much I loved her and that everything would work out between us."
- **Am I Worthy of Love?** "I began a conversation with my brother about the way he treats his wife. He talks down to her and I know it really bothers her. I was hugely nervous bringing it up, and my words were getting all twisted. Then he shouted, 'Who are you to tell me how to act?! You've never had a real relationship in your whole life!' After that, I could hardly breathe, let alone talk. All I could think about was how I wanted to get out of there."

Suddenly, who we thought we were when we walked into the conversation is called into question.

An Identity Quake Can Knock Us Off Balance

Internally, our Identity Conversation is in full swing: "Maybe I am mediocre," "How can I be the kind of person who causes others pain?" or "My brother's right. No woman has ever loved me." In each case, it is what this conversation seems to be saying about us that rips the ground from beneath our feet.

Getting knocked off balance can even cause you to react physically in ways that make the conversation go from difficult to impossible. Images of yourself or of the future are hardwired to your adrenal response, and shaking them up can cause an unmanageable rush of anxiety or anger, or an intense desire to get away. Well-being is replaced with depression, hope with hopelessness, efficacy with fear. And all the while you're trying to engage in the extremely delicate task of communicating clearly and effectively. Your supervisor is explaining why you're not being promoted; you're busy having your own private identity quake.

There's No Quick Fix

You can't "quake-proof" your sense of self. Grappling with identity issues is what life and growth are all about, and no amount of love or accomplishment or skill can insulate you from these challenges. Seeing your husband cry when you tell him you don't want to have another child, or hearing your coach say "Grow up" when you raise the issue of discriminatory treatment on the team, *will* test your sense of who you are in these relationships and in the world.

Not all identity challenges are earthshaking, but some will be. A difficult conversation can cause you to relinquish a cherished aspect of how you see yourself. At its most profound, this can be a loss that requires mourning just as surely as the death of a loved one. There's no use pretending there's a quick fix, or that you will never again lose your balance, or that life's toughest challenges can be overcome by mastering a few easy steps.

But there is some good news. You can improve your ability to recognize and cope with identity issues when they hit. Thinking clearly and honestly about who you are can help reduce your anxiety level during the conversation and significantly strengthen your foundation in its aftermath.

VULNERABLE IDENTITIES: THE ALL-OR-NOTHING SYNDROME

Getting better at managing the Identity Conversation starts with understanding the ways in which we make ourselves vulnerable to being knocked off balance. The biggest factor that contributes to a vulnerable identity is "all-or-nothing" thinking: I'm either competent or incompetent, good or evil, worthy of love or not.

The primary peril of all-or-nothing thinking is that it leaves our identity extremely unstable, making us hypersensitive to feedback. When faced with negative information about ourselves, all-or-nothing thinking gives us only two choices for how to manage that information, both of which cause serious problems. Either we try to deny the information that is inconsistent with our self-image, or we do the opposite: we take in the information in a way that exaggerates its importance to a crippling degree. All-or-nothing identities are about as sturdy as a two-legged stool.

Denial

Clinging to a purely positive identity leaves no place in our self-concept for negative feedback. If I think of myself as a super-competent person who never makes mistakes, then feedback suggesting that I have made a mistake presents a problem. The only way to keep my identity intact is to deny the feedback—to figure out why it's not really true, why it doesn't really matter, or why what I did wasn't actually a mistake.

Recall the chemist who asked for a raise. Her boss responded by saying, "I'm surprised you want to discuss this. The truth is, I've been disappointed by your performance this year." The chemist must now decide how to internalize this information, and what this says about her identity. The denial response might sound like this: "My boss knows business, but not chemistry. He doesn't understand how important my contributions have been. I wish I had a boss who could appreciate just how good I am."

Working to keep negative information out during a difficult conversation is like trying to swim without getting wet. If we're going to engage in difficult conversations, or in life for that matter, we're going to come up against information about ourselves that we find unpleasant. Denial requires a huge amount of psychic energy, and sooner or later the story we're telling ourselves is going to become untenable. *And the bigger the gap between what we hope is true and what we fear is true, the easier it is for us to lose our balance.*

Exaggeration

The alternative to denial is exaggeration. In all-or-nothing thinking, taking in negative feedback requires us not just to adjust our self-image, but to *flip* it. If I'm not completely competent, then I'm completely *in*competent: "Maybe I'm not as creative and special as I thought I was. I'll probably never amount to anything. Maybe I'll even get fired."

We Let Their Feedback Define Who We Are.   When we exaggerate, we act as if the other person's feedback is the *only* information we have about ourselves. We put everything up for grabs, and let what they say dictate how we see ourselves. We may turn in a hundred memos on time, but if we are criticized for being late with the 101st memo, we think to ourselves, "I can never do *anything* right." This one piece of information fills our whole identity screen.

This example may seem ridiculous, but we all think like this on occasion, and not only around dramatic or traumatic events. If the waitress gives you a funny look as she collects her tip, you're cheap. If you don't help your friends paint their house, you're selfish. If your brother says you don't visit his children enough, you're an uncaring aunt. It's easy to see why exaggeration is such a debilitating reaction.

GROUND YOUR IDENTITY

Improving your ability to manage the Identity Conversation has two steps. First, you need to become familiar with those identity issues that are important to you, so you can spot them during a conversation. Second, you need to learn to integrate new information into your identity in ways that are healthy—a step that requires you to let go of all-or-nothing thinking.

Step One: Become Aware of Your Identity Issues

Often during a difficult conversation we are not even aware that our identity is implicated. We know we feel anxious, fearful, or tentative, and that our ability to communicate skillfully has deserted us. Usually articulate, we stumble and stammer; usually empathetic, we can't stop interrupting and arguing; usually calm, we boil over with anger. But we aren't sure why. The connection to our identity is not obvious. It's easy to think, "I'm talking with my brother about how he treats his wife. What does this have to do with my identity?"

What triggers an identity quake for you may not trigger one in someone else. We each have our own particular sensitivities. To become more familiar with yours, observe whether there are patterns to what tends to knock you off balance during difficult conversations, and then ask yourself why. What about your identity feels at risk? What does this mean to you? How would it feel if what you fear were true?

It may take some digging. Consider Jimmy's story. Growing up, Jimmy developed a reputation for being emotionally distant. This posture helped protect him from all the emotional shrapnel he was exposed to in his home life. Everyone else might be quick to fly off the handle, but not Jimmy. He'd be rational to a fault.

But after years on his own, Jimmy changed. He began to see the value of acknowledging and sharing his emotions, and doing so with friends and colleagues added to the richness of his life. He wanted to reveal this change to his family, but was afraid. The patterns of who he was with them were deeply etched and, though far from perfect, were comfortable and predictable. His detachment had costs, but they were familiar costs.

He discussed his fear with a friend, who asked Jimmy some hard questions: "What are you really afraid of? What's the downside?" Jimmy's first response was that he was acting out of obligation to his family: "Someone in my family has to be the rational one. Otherwise, it will be chaos. The way things are now, everything more or less works."

All true, but Jimmy continued to consider his friend's questions and pushed himself for deeper answers. Eventually he discovered the fear that at some level he knew was there all along: "What if they reject me? What if they laugh? What if they think, 'What's gotten into him?'" Jimmy knew he'd be in for a serious identity shake-up if his parents responded badly, and he wasn't sure he wanted to risk it.

Jimmy's increased awareness of his identity concerns wasn't the end of the story. He determined he would show greater emotion around his family, and at first, the going was not smooth. There were awkward moments, and some members of his family wondered why he was acting differently. But Jimmy persisted, and in time a more genuine set of relationships replaced the old ones.

Step Two: Complexify Your Identity (Adopt the And Stance)

Once you've identified which aspects of your identity are most important to you or seem most vulnerable, you can begin to complexify your self-image. This means moving away from the false choice between "I am perfect" and "I am worthless," and trying to get as clear a picture as you can about what is actually true about you. As for everyone, what is true about you is going to be a mix of good and bad behavior, noble and less noble intentions, and wise and unwise choices you've made along the way.

For even the best and worst among us, all-or-nothing identities oversimplify the world. "I'm always there for my children." "When it comes to dating, I just have bad judgment." "I'm always a good listener." No one is *always* anything. We each exhibit a constellation of qualities, positive and negative, and constantly grapple with how to respond to the complicated situations life presents. And we don't always respond as competently or compassionately as we'd like.

Ben's fear of telling his boss that he has accepted another job is a good example of this. Is Ben loyal or is he a sellout? Both of those are simplifying labels that can't capture the complexity of the endless interactions Ben has had with the many people in his life. He has made many sacrifices for his family and many for his boss. He has worked weekends, turned down other job offers, worked hard to help the company recruit top talent. The list of things Ben has done that indicate loyalty is long indeed.

And, Ben *is* leaving his job for higher paying work elsewhere. It's reasonable for his boss to feel abandoned. That doesn't mean Ben is a bad person. It doesn't mean Ben has made a choice based on greed. He wants to put his children through college; he has been undercompensated for years and not complained.

What, then, is the bottom line on Ben? The bottom line is that there is no bottom line. Ben can feel good about many of his actions and choices, and ambivalent or regretful about others. Life is too complex for any reasonable person to feel otherwise. Indeed, a self-image that allows for complexity is healthy and robust; it provides a sturdy foundation on which to stand.

Three Things to Accept About Yourself

No doubt, there are some aspects of who you are that you will struggle with for a lifetime. When you look inside, you won't always like what you see, and you'll find that accepting those parts of yourself takes serious work. But as you move away from an all-or-nothing identity and toward a more complex view of who you are, you'll notice that it is easier to accept certain parts of yourself that have given you trouble in the past.

There are three characteristics that are particularly important to be able to accept about yourself in difficult conversations. The more easily you can admit to your own mistakes, your own mixed intentions, and your own contributions to the problem, the more balanced you will feel during the conversation, and the higher the chances it will go well.

1. You Will Make Mistakes.   If you can't admit to yourself that you sometimes make mistakes, you'll find it more difficult to understand and accept the legitimate aspects of the other person's story about what is going on.

Consider what happened between Rita and Isaiah. "It's important to me to be trustworthy—someone friends can really talk to," Rita explains. "That's part of being a good friend. Isaiah, one of my co-workers, confided in me that he was struggling with alcoholism, and I promised to keep it confidential. But I knew that a mutual friend had faced many of the same issues in the past, and so I talked with her about Isaiah's problem, to get some advice.

"Then Isaiah found out, and he was really furious. At first, I kept trying to explain that I was trying to help, and that my friend could be a valuable resource. Eventually I realized that the reason I was arguing was that I couldn't admit to myself that I had violated his trust, plain and simple. I didn't live up to my word. Once I was able to admit to myself that I made a mistake, Isaiah and I began to get somewhere in our conversation."

When you hold yourself to an all-or-nothing standard, even a small mistake can seem catastrophic and almost impossible to admit. If you are busy trying to shore up your "no mistakes, no failures" identity, you won't be able to engage in a meaningful learning conversation. And if you can't do that, you are likely to make the same mistakes again.

One reason people are reluctant to admit mistakes is that they fear being seen as weak or incompetent. Yet often, generally competent people who take the possibility of mistakes in stride are seen as confident, secure, and "big enough" not to have to be perfect, whereas those who resist acknowledging even the possibility of a mistake are seen as insecure and *lacking* confidence. No one is fooled.

2. Your Intentions Are Complex.   Sometimes we get nervous about upcoming conversations because we know that our past behavior was not always motivated by good intentions.

Consider the situation that Sally and her boyfriend, Evan, find themselves in. Sally wants to break up with Evan, but is afraid that he will accuse her of just using him to get through a lonely period. Before Sally claims that her intentions were purely positive, she should think honestly about whether they actually were. Although in the big picture Sally didn't want to hurt Evan and wasn't acting maliciously, there was at least a bit of selfishness in Sally's behavior.

By being honest with herself about the complexity of her motivations, Sally has a better chance of staying on her feet if the accusation of having bad intentions arises. And she can respond in a way that is genuine: "As I think about it, some of what you're saying makes sense. I *was* lonely, and being with you helped. I don't think that was my only reason for wanting to be with you. I did hope it would work out. There are lots of pieces to what was going on for me."

3. You Have Contributed to the Problem.   A third crucial step for grounding yourself involves assessing and taking responsibility for what you've contributed to the problem.

This is not always easy to do. Walker recently learned that his daughter Annie Mae is struggling with an eating disorder. Her college advisor called, letting Walker know that Anne Mae had checked herself into the university health clinic. Walker called to see how Annie Mae was, but couldn't seem to get past the surface exchange of "How are you doing, kiddo?" and "I'll be okay, Dad."

Walker wants to have a more genuine conversation, but he's afraid. He suspects that at least some of the issues Annie Mae is dealing with are connected to their relationship. He suspects Annie Mae thinks he was not a good father, and he fears that she might for the first time tell him so. And that prospect terrifies him.

Up until now, without knowing for sure what his daughter thinks, Walker has been able to live with the hope that he's been a good father. He'd like nothing more than for that to be true. But he suspects that the truth is more complex. After all, he was away a lot, he wasn't as supportive as he might have been, and he made promises to Annie Mae that he didn't always keep.

Walker has two options. He can try to tiptoe through the conversations with his daughter, hoping against hope that Annie Mae doesn't raise the issue of how he has contributed to their troubled relationship and her current illness. Or he can work through some of his identity issues in advance and accept in his own heart his contribution to their problems.

It won't be easy. In fact, it may be the toughest thing Walker ever does. But if he's able to accept himself and his actions for what they are, and to take responsibility for them, both in his own mind and when talking with Annie Mae, he'll probably find that over time his conversations, with his daughter become easier. And, more important, Walker will find that he no longer needs to hide. His conversations with Annie Mae won't be fraught with the potential to strike at his all-or-nothing identity as a good father. He can say to his daughter, "I wish I'd been there for you more often. I'm so sorry and sad that I wasn't," and can approach her with compassion instead of fear.

REVIEW QUESTIONS

1. What is "identity" and how is identity present in all communication?
2. What's the difference between the "core" issues of "competence" and "goodness"?
3. Explain "the all-or-nothing syndrome."
4. What parts of your own story are in the authors' description of "Jimmy"?

PROBES

1. Situation: You need to have a "difficult" conversation with a person at work who frequently leaves you off the list of recipients of important e-mails. Explain how the three core issues of "competence," "goodness," and "being worthy of love" might surface in this interaction.
2. Explain: "Grappling with identity issues is what life and growth are all about, and no amount of love or accomplishment or skill can insulate you from these challenges."
3. In Chapter 2, "Implication #5" is that "The most ordinary communication events are the most significant." Connect this idea to these authors' point, "If the waitress gives you a funny look as she collects her tip, you're cheap."
4. Explain "the and stance." Relate it to the concept of "nexting" from Chapter 2.
5. How can you acknowledge that "you have contributed to the problem" without blaming yourself for what's happening?

CHAPTER 4

Verbal and Nonverbal Contact

Verbal and Nonverbal Dimensions of Talk
John Stewart and Carole Logan

This next reading starts with its own introduction and is longer than most, so I'll make this short. These pages come from an interpersonal communication text that I co-authored with Carole Logan, a colleague who teaches communication at the University of San Diego. As you can tell from the title, the reading reverses the popular tendency to discuss verbal and nonverbal communicating in separate chapters. We explain why at the start.

This selection is broad enough in coverage to give you a fairly comprehensive introduction to both language and most nonverbal cues. We resist the "verbal/nonverbal" dichotomy by locating the main communication building blocks on a continuum or sliding scale that runs from primarily verbal (written words), to mixed (vocal pacing, pause, loudness, pitch, and silence), to primarily nonverbal (gestures, eye gaze, facial expression, touch, and space). Our goal is to encourage you to view these aspects of your communicating as holistically as you can and to notice the ways the various kinds of cues affect each other.

We briefly review the three main ways language has been discussed—as a system of symbols, an activity, and what we call a "soup." Then we discuss some features of mixed and primarily nonverbal cues. If you read both this introductory overview and the four other readings in this chapter, I think you'll have a pretty decent understanding of these parts of communication's basic ingredients.

MAIN IDEAS

- In actual communication, verbal and nonverbal elements always occur together, so it distorts both to treat them separately.
- Instead, think about a sliding scale from **primarily verbal** cues (written words) through **mixed** cues (talk speed, loudness, pitch) to **primarily nonverbal** cues (gestures, eye gaze, touch).
- The traditional approach to primarily verbal cues (language) is to treat it as a *system of symbols,* a view that is both informative and drastically oversimplified.
- A second approach treats language as an *activity;* this view is also valuable and incomplete.
- Today, language is often viewed as a "soup," a cultural surround we inhabit like a fish inhabits water. .
- The "soup" view emphasizes the important connections between language and perception—perception of nature, gender, culture, and communication itself.
- The mixed cues of "voice" or *paralinguistics* significantly affect how talk is interpreted.
- Facial expression and eye behavior are mixed cues when they help regulate conversation.
- Gestures can significantly affect how words are interpreted.
- Facial expression, eye contact and gaze, and gestures are also sometimes primarily nonverbal cues.

- Proximity is a primarily nonverbal cue; four levels of proximity or space can be culturally identified.
- Touch is also a significant primarily nonverbal cue.

Interpersonal communication texts typically devote one chapter to verbal codes and a separate one to nonverbal communication. This practice began in the late 1960s when communication researchers and teachers first discovered the importance of the nonverbal parts of communicating—eye contact, body movement, facial expression, tone of voice, touch, silence, and so on. For about 30 years, most textbooks treated each subject as significant and distinct.

But now research is focusing more and more closely on conversations as people actually experience them, and it has become obvious that you can't really separate the verbal and nonverbal parts. In the words of two researchers, "It is impossible to study either verbal or nonverbal communication as isolated structures. Rather, these systems should be regarded as a unified communication construct."[1] And as teacher and theorist Wendy Leeds-Hurwitz puts it, "In discussing communication as consisting of verbal and nonverbal modes ... we leave ourselves open to the impression that the two are somehow distinct and should be studied separately. This is not at all the case, and there is now a current body of literature devoted to rejoining the two."[2]

Interestingly, almost this same point was made at the beginning of the twentieth century by Ferdinand de Saussure, one of the founders of linguistics. Saussure said that language is like a sheet of paper, where sound makes up one side of the page and the concepts or thoughts make up the other. You can't pick up one side of the paper without picking up the other, and you can't cut one side without cutting the other. So it's best to think of them together.[3] We think the same way about the verbal and the nonverbal parts of communication; they're like the two sides of one sheet of paper.

This is actually the way they occur in human experience. For example, consider this conversation:

SCOTT: *(Smiling and nodding)* Hi, John Paul. Howzit goin'?

JOHN PAUL: *(Excited look)* Scott! *(Shaking hands)* It's good to see you! I heard you'd moved. Where've you *been*?

SCOTT: *(Smiling knowingly)* Nowhere, really. I've just been working and going to school. But Heather and I have been hanging out together quite a bit.

JOHN PAUL: *(Teasing)* Yeah, I heard that. What's the story with you two anyway?

SCOTT: *(Playful but cagey)* What do you mean "What's the story"? We just like each other, and we spend a lot of time together.

JOHN PAUL: *(Still teasing)* Yeah, like all weekend. And every afternoon. And most of the rest of the time.

"Verbal and Nonverbal Dimensions of Talk" by John Stewart and Carole Logan from Together: Communicating Interpersonally, 5th Edition. NY: McGraw-Hill, 1988. Reprinted by permission of the senior author.

SCOTT: *(Turning the tables)* Well, what about you and Bill? I've heard you two are a duo ... partners ... an item.

JOHN PAUL: *(A little shy)* Where'd you hear that? Yeah, it's pretty true. *(Brighter)* And it's kind of neat, actually. It's the first time I've felt like part of *a couple*. We might even get an apartment together. But he's got to get a job that pays more. I can't support both of us.

SCOTT: *(Friendly)* Sounds like you've got the same questions Heather and I have. But her folks are also a problem.

JOHN PAUL: *(Serious)* My mom and dad are fine. But Bill's parents don't know anything about us, and I'm trying to get him to change that. In fact, I was thinking that I'd like to talk to you about that. I also wonder how you and Heather plan to actually set up living together. But I've got to get to work now. Give me your cell number so I can give you a call, okay?

John Paul and Scott build this conversation together by using verbal and nonverbal aspects of language simultaneously. There is never a point in the talk where these two parts of communicating are separate. When Scott's intent is to be "playful," he communicates this verbally and nonverbally to John Paul. When the tone of the conversation turns "serious," John Paul communicates this through posture, facial expression, and tone of voice, as well as through the words he chooses.

This chapter emphasizes the fact that people engaged in conversation construct all verbal and nonverbal aspects of talk together. To put it in researchers' terms, utterance meaning and nonverbal meaning are not discrete and independent.[4] This is true even of words written on a page. What you might consider to be "purely verbal" written words appear in a designed typeface, on a certain weight and color of paper, and surrounded by more or less white space. All of these nonverbal elements affect how people interpret the written words of any language. Similarly, even purely nonverbal behaviors, such as gestures or eye behavior, occur in the context of some spoken or written words. One way to sort out the verbal and nonverbal aspects of language is to think in terms of a continuum or sliding scale like the following.

Primarily Verbal	**Mixed**	**Primarily Nonverbal**
written words	vocal pacing, pause, loudness, pitch, silence	gestures, eye gaze, facial expression, touch, space

Written words are classified as primarily verbal for the reasons we just gave. They appear in a nonverbal typeface surrounded by nonverbal space, but readers interpret or make meaning primarily on the basis of the words' verbal content. To the degree that you can isolate the words speakers use, they might be considered primarily verbal, too. But spoken words always come with vocal pacing, pause, loudness, pitch, and silence, and as a result these are labeled mixed. Gestures, facial expression, and so on are labeled primarily nonverbal because they can occur without words, but they are usually interpreted in the context of spoken words.

It would be possible to highlight some of the verbal parts of Scott and John Paul's conversation. Scott says, "Howzit goin'?" rather than "How is it going?" or the even more formal "It's good to see you again." He uses the general phrase "spending a lot of time together" rather than a more specific description of his and Heather's activities. For John Paul, the word "couple" is significant. The two share an understanding of what it means, in this context, to say that parents are a "problem."

We could also pinpoint some nonverbal aspects of the conversation. For example, Scott's initial tone of voice is pretty low-key, but John Paul sounds excited to see him. They touch briefly as they shake hands. Their smiles "say" several different things—"It's good to see you." "I like you." "I'm teasing." "I'm teasing back." "We've got something in common." Since they're friends, they stand fairly close together.

In order to focus on the exclusively verbal or exclusively nonverbal parts, however, we'd have to distort what actually happens in Scott and John Paul's conversation. As we've said, the verbal and nonverbal aspects of the conversation are as inseparable as the two sides of a piece of paper. So in this reading:

> We describe three approaches to *primarily verbal* cues ("language") that help clarify our reasons for combining verbal and nonverbal communication.

> We discuss how several *mixed* cues affect meaning-making and how facial expression and gestures work together with words.

> We describe the five most influential *primarily nonverbal* cues—facial expression, eye contact and gaze, space, touch, and body movement and gesture.

THREE APPROACHES TO STUDYING PRIMARILY VERBAL CUES (LANGUAGE)

1. Language Is a System of Symbols

Historically, this is the oldest point of view. From this perspective, language is a system made up of different kinds of words and the rules governing their combinations. Your grade-school teachers emphasized the systematic features of language when they helped you learn the differences among nouns, verbs, adjectives, and adverbs and the rules for making grammatical sentences. When you think of German, Mandarin Chinese, or Spanish as a "language," you're thinking of it as a language *system*. Dictionaries record a part of a language system and provide a record of, for example, word histories and new words like ROM, uplink, and downsize.

Those who study language as a system emphasize that it is a system of symbols. They develop a point made about 2,500 years ago when the Greek philosopher Aristotle began one of his major works on language this way: "Spoken words are the symbols of mental experience and written words are the symbols of spoken words."[5] As a contemporary linguist explains, "This criterion implies that for anything to be a language it must function so as to *symbolize* (represent for the organism) the not-necessarily-*here* and not-necessarily-*now*."[6] In brief, since a symbol is something that stands for something else, this approach emphasizes that units of language—words, usually—represent, or stand for, chunks or pieces of nonlinguistic reality. In the simplest terms, the word "cat" stands for the furry, purring, tail-twitching animal sitting in the corner.

One of the features of symbols that this approach also highlights is that they're *arbitrary*. This means that there is no necessary relationship between the word and the thing it symbolizes. Even though the word *five* is physically smaller than the word *three*, the quantity that *five* symbolizes is larger. So there's no necessary relationship between word (in this case, its size) and meaning. Or consider the words that people from different language communities use to symbolize a dwelling where someone lives: *casa* in Spanish, *maison* in French, and *Haus* in German. This couldn't happen unless the relationship between the word and its meaning were arbitrary.

A classic book, first published in 1923, elaborated just this point. Its authors, C. K. Ogden and I. A. Richards, diagrammed this insight with their famous "triangle of meaning" (see Figure 4–1).[7] Ogden and Richards's triangle is meant to illustrate how words are related to both thoughts and things. The word-thought relationship is direct—that's why the line is solid. For Aristotle, words stood for thoughts. The relationship between thought and thing was also more or less direct. But the word-thing relationship is arbitrary; there is no necessary relationship between the word and its referent. The dotted line across the bottom of the triangle emphasizes this point.

The main advantage of viewing language as a system of arbitrary symbols is that it alerts us to the dangers of abstractions and of the assumptions people make about what words mean by emphasizing that the *thought* or meaning associated with a word may or may not be directly related to the *thing* the word symbolizes. The clearest, most easily understood words are those that are easiest to connect with concrete reality: "this car," "my CD collection," "his blue hair." But from Ogden and Richards's point of view, people should be careful with abstract words like "safety," "style," "love," and "honesty," because the thoughts that they call up may or may not be linked to concrete realities that they symbolize. One person's writing or talk about safety may be connected with safety pins, bank vaults, or a seat belt, and because of the dotted-line relationship in the triangle,

FIGURE 4–1 Ogden and Richards's triangle of meaning.

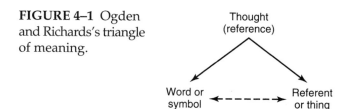

the individual to whom the person is writing or talking may not be able to tell the difference. We can also learn from this perspective that, since the relationship between words and meanings is arbitrary, we should never assume that another person means exactly what we do, even when he or she uses the same words. What does "early" mean, for example, when your mom or dad tells you to "get home early"? When your teacher says you should "get started early on your papers"? When the person you're dating feels it's too early in the relationship for sex? When you tell your roommate you want to get up early? Assumptions about identical word meaning often create communication problems.

This view of language is also drastically oversimplified, however. The triangle of meaning makes it appear that language is essentially made up of concrete nouns, labels for things in the world. It doesn't take much reflection to realize that language is much more complicated than that. Often the topic you're discussing and the ideas you want to express require abstract words, such as "love," "pride," and "homelessness." The advice to avoid these kinds of words because there are no "things" or "referents" to which they are even arbitrarily related is not very practical. And what about words like "and," "whether," "however," and "larger"? It can be really confusing to try to figure out what things these words symbolize. Even more important, we don't usually experience language as individual words, but as statements, utterances, messages, or parts of a conversation. So an approach that tries to explain living language by focusing on individual words has to be limited. All this is why it's partly true to say that language is a system of symbols, but there's much more to it than that.

2. Language Is an Activity

A second, more recent approach to the study of language views it as an activity. The most influential version of this approach began in the 1950s when several researchers showed how many utterances actually perform actions. They called these utterances "speech acts." For example, the words "I will" or "I do" in a marriage ceremony are not just symbolizing or referring to getting married. Rather, they are an important part of the activity of marrying itself. If they're not said at the right time by the right people, the marriage hasn't happened. Similarly, the words "I agree" or "Okay, it's a deal" can perform the activity of buying, selling, or contracting for work. And "Howzitgoin'?" is not about a greeting; it is the activity of greeting itself. A group of researchers called conversation analysts have shown how to extend and apply this insight about the action-performing function of language.

Conversation analysts, for instance, have identified the crucial features of many of the speech acts that people typically perform, such as promise, request, threat, offer, command, compliment, and greeting.[8] Each of these terms labels what certain utterances *do* rather than what they symbolize or say. And, these researchers point out, a given utterance won't perform this action unless it has certain features. For example, a *request* requires the speaker to ask for a preferred future behavior from the hearer, and the person who hasn't done this has not competently performed a request. A *promise* is also about a preferred future behavior, but it identifies what the speaker rather than the hearer will do.

If you understand the building blocks of each speech act, you can see why some *indirect* requests and promises will work and others won't. For example, "Are you taking your car to the game tonight?" could function as a *request* for a ride to the game, even though it does not actually identify a preferred future behavior. But it can only work as a request when the context allows both speaker and hearer to fill in the parts that the words themselves leave out. This explains how problems arise when one person fills in the blanks and another doesn't, or when one person means or hears a promise even though the crucial parts of the speech act are absent. For example, when Reggie and Kevin were discussing the game they both wanted to attend, Reggie heard Kevin's "Yeah, I'll be driving" as a *promise* to give him a ride. But Kevin meant it only as a response to Reggie's direct question. So he was surprised and a little angry when Reggie called to confirm the ride he'd "promised."

Conversation analysts have also studied several ways in which people collaborate to mutually construct some speech acts. For example, greetings, good-byes, invitations, apologies, offers, and congratulations are all speech acts that almost always require two or more conversational moves rather than just one. If one conversation partner greets the other, the expectation is that the other will respond with another greeting. If this doesn't happen, the speech act of "greeting" has only partly occurred. The same thing happens with good-byes; it takes both one person's "good-bye" *and* the other person's response. This requirement can create problems when one person means to be leaving and the other doesn't pick up on it. Similarly, an invitation is expected to be followed by an acceptance, questioning, or rejection of the invitation; an apology is expected to be followed by an acceptance or rejection, and so on. As one conversation analyst puts it:

> As we shall see, when one of these first actions has been produced, participants orient to the presence or absence of the relevant second action. There is an expectation by participants that the second action should be produced, and when it does not occur, participants behave as if it should have.[9]

Many insights into language use have been generated by people viewing it as an activity that people carry out by following certain sets of conversational rules. At the same time, the more researchers have studied communication as people actually experience it, the more they've recognized that although a great deal can be learned about the individual moves conversation partners make with their various speech acts, natural conversations almost always include unpredictable events or surprises. People improvise as much as they follow conversational rules. In other words, there is a structure to conversation, but it is less like the repetitive pattern followed by a supermarket checkout clerk and more like the loose and varied collaboration of five good musicians getting together to jam.

In summary, conversation analysts have demonstrated the value of studying language as an activity. They have shown that every time we say something, we're also doing something—that speech is a kind of action. They have catalogued many of the actions that people perform by talking and have also shown that some of these actions are produced collaboratively. But they have only been able to consider a few of the important nonverbal elements of conversation, and they have had to admit that there is almost as much improvisation as rule following. Every day people engage in greetings, good-byes, promises, threats, compliments, offers, commands, requests, and dozens of other conversation acts. But we also improvise and modify expected patterns. Finally, conversation analysts have very little to say about the crucial identity-constructing function of communication.... We believe that the most helpful approach to language is the one that includes a focus on identities.

3. Language Is a Soup

This may sound a little weird, but stay with us for a few paragraphs. This approach does include identities.

Especially in the last 30 years, many scholars have recognized the limitations of both the system and action views of language. Both of these views treat language as a tool that humans manipulate, either to arbitrarily stand for some referent or to perform an action. As we have explained, there's some truth to these views, and they can teach us some important things about language. But language is more than a tool. If it were just a tool, we could lay it aside when we didn't need it and pick up some other tool, just as we can lay aside a screwdriver and pick up a hammer. But we can't do that. As humans, we're immersed in language, like a fish is immersed in water. And this quality is what the "soup" metaphor is meant to highlight. As one writer puts it:

> In all our knowledge of ourselves and in all knowledge of the world, we are always already encompassed by the language that is our own. We grow up, and we become acquainted with [people] and in the last analysis with ourselves when we learn to speak. Learning to speak does not mean learning to use a preexistent tool for designating a world already somehow familiar to us; it means acquiring a familiarity and acquaintance with the world itself and how it confronts us.[10]

This is what it means to say that language is a soup. We're immersed in it from birth to death, just as a fish is immersed in the water in which it lives.

In fact, language experience may begin even before birth. As soon as 20 weeks after conception, the human fetus has functioning ears and is beginning to respond to sounds.[11] Its mother's voice is clearly one sound the fetus learns to identify.[12] Some pregnant couples talk to and play music for their unborn child. When the infant is born, it typically enters an environment of exclamations and greetings. Then verbal and nonverbal communication experiences fill the infant's life. Touch, eye contact, smiles, and a great deal of talk are directed to him or her. As infants develop, parents and other caregivers invite them into conversations or exclude them from conversations by providing a context for talk, by encouraging them with positive attitudes toward talk or discouraging them with negative attitudes, and by interpreting, modeling, and extending talk.[13] This process continues right up to the last tearful good-byes a person hears at death. In between, humans live more or less like nutritious morsels in a broth of language. This soup includes all the verbal and nonverbal parts of our communicative life. In fact, the theorists and researchers who treat language as a soup have begun to mean by "language" what used to be called "communication"—all the verbal and nonverbal, oral and nonoral, ways that humans make meaning together. As you might be assuming, this view of language fits most comfortably with the approach to communication outlined in Chapter 2.

Language and Perception   If this notion of language as a soup sounds a little abstract, consider one important practical implication of the fact that language is all-encompassing: Because we are immersed in language all our lives, language and perception are thoroughly interrelated.... When we perceive, we select, organize, and make meaning out of the things and events we see, hear, touch, taste, and smell. The point that language and perception are thoroughly interrelated means that everything we perceive, all the things that make up our world, is affected by the language in which we live. In the early 20th century, one version of this insight about language and perception was called the Sapir-Whorf hypothesis, for the two people who originally wrote about it, Edward Sapir and Benjamin Lee Whorf. It was summarized by Whorf in these words:

> The background linguistic system (in other words, the grammar) of each language is not merely a reproducing instrument for voicing ideas but rather is itself the shaper of ideas, the program and guide for the individual's mental activity, for his [or her] analysis of impressions.... We dissect nature along lines laid down by our native language.[14]

Thus, if you have spent enough time on boats and around the water to learn a dozen different words for water conditions, you will perceive more differences in the water than will the person who was born and raised in Cheyenne, Oklahoma City, or Calgary. That person might distinguish between *waves* and *smooth water*, but you will see and feel differences between *cats' paws, ripples, chop,* and *swells* that he or she probably won't even notice.[15] Or if you have learned important meanings for *latex, natural, lubricated,* and *spermicidal,* you can make distinctions among condoms that were impossible for the high school graduate of the 1970s or early 1980s.

A Chinese-American woman, Mandy Lam, made the point that she felt "similar to the fish that lives in an area of water where the river mixes with the ocean. I have only to travel a little further in either direction to experience the extremes." Her grandparents speak only Chinese, and she relates to them, and often to her parents and other elders, in Chinese ways. But all her premed classes are in English, and she lives in an almost completely English world at school.

As the two of us try in this [essay] to write about communication as a continuous, complex, collaborative meaning-making process, we especially notice two particular ways in which our native language limits our perceptions. The first has to do with the ways that the English language affects how people understand ongoing processes. Unlike some languages, English maintains clear distinctions between noun subjects and verb predicates, causes and effects, beginnings and ends, and this affects how native English speakers perceive communication. A surprising number of other language systems do not do this. According to one researcher, for example, Navajo speakers characteristically talk in terms of processes—uncaused, ongoing, incomplete, dynamic happenings. The word that Navajos use for wagon, for example, translates roughly as "wood rolls about hooplike."[16] The Navajo words that we would translate as "He begins to carry a stone" mean not that the actor produces an action, but that the person is simply linked with a given round object and with an already existing, continuous movement of all round objects in the universe. The English language, by contrast, requires its users to talk in terms of present, past, future, cause and effect, beginning and end. Problems arise when some things that English speakers would like to discuss just can't be expressed in these terms. To continue our example, we would like to be able to talk more clearly about the emergent, ongoing nature of communication.... But, especially since communication doesn't always obey the rules of cause and effect, the noun-plus-verb-plus-object structure of the English language makes it difficult to do this. For this topic, Navajo would probably work better than English.

The second way in which we notice that the English language affects our discussion of communication has to do with the ways English speakers perceive gender differences. One accomplishment of research encouraged by the feminist movement of the 1960s and 1970s is that people now recognize how the male bias of standard American English has contributed to the ways in which English-speaking cultures perceive women and men. The fact that, until recently, there were no female firefighters was not caused simply by the existence of the word fire*man*. It's not that simple. But research indicates that gender-biased words affect perceptions in at least three ways. They shape people's attitudes about careers that are "appropriate" for one sex but not for the other, they lead some women to believe that certain jobs and roles aren't attainable, and they contribute to the belief that men deserve higher status in society than do women.[17] This is why changes in job titles have helped open several occupations to more equal male-female participation. Consider, for example, *parking checker* instead of *metermaid*, *chair* or *chairperson* instead of *chairman*, *salesperson* instead of *salesman*, and *server* instead of *waiter* or *waitress*. We have also just about stopped referring to female physicians as woman doctors and female attorneys as lady lawyers, and it is more than a coincidence that these changes have been accompanied by significant increases in the numbers of women in these two professions.

Since the mid-1990s, both scholarly and popular books have emphasized this point about gender, language, and perception by highlighting the differences between the language worlds into which men and women are socialized in North America. Sociolinguist Deborah Tannen's book *You Just Don't Understand: Women and Men in Communication*[18] was on the best-seller list for months, and John Gray has sold millions of copies of *Men Are from Mars, Women Are from Venus*[19] and *Mars and Venus in Love.*[20] All of these books describe the ways in which women's communication differs from men's and explain how many problems between genders are influenced by these differences. Some people complain that the books reinforce the very stereotypes they're trying to reduce by generalizing about "women's communication" and "men's communication." Despite the very real danger of this oversimplification, however, there is considerable research evidence to indicate that most North American, English-speaking women and most of their male counterparts do communicate differently. In other words, carefully controlled observations of how these men and women actually talk found that there are important gender-linked patterns.

The women observed in these studies generally use communication as a primary way to establish and maintain relationships with others, whereas the men generally talk to exert control, preserve independence, and enhance status. More specifically, most of these women's communicating is characterized by seven features that are not generally found in the men's talk: an emphasis on equality, support, attention to the relationship, inclusivity, concreteness, and tentativeness, and a preference for collaborative meaning-making. Men's communicating is described in this same research as functioning to exhibit knowledge or skill, accomplish goals, assert dominance, avoid tentativeness, stay abstract rather than concrete, and minimize relationship responsiveness....[21]

To summarize, from the point of view of this soup or fish-in-water idea, language is more than a *system* we use or an *activity* we perform. It is larger than any of us; it happens to us and we are subject to it as much as we manipulate or use it.... When studied from this third perspective, language has both verbal and nonverbal aspects. Language researchers and teachers have become increasingly aware that languaging as people actually live it is less of a system or action and more of a mutual event or collaborative process. "Language" is the term these researchers and teachers use for the communicating that, as [was] said in Chapter 2, makes us who we are.

MIXED CUES: VOICE, SILENCE, FACE AND WORDS, GESTURES AND WORDS

The first section of this reading was about the primarily verbal parts of communication—the parts that are often called "language." By now, you know that language includes both verbal and nonverbal elements, but that it can still be distinguished from the "mixed" parts, which include the rate, pitch, volume, and quality of the voice; silence; facial expressions accompanying words; and gestures that accompany words. Let's consider next how these mixed cues operate.

Voice

Sometimes people overlook the fact that spoken language includes many different nonverbal vocal elements. The technical term for these cues is *paralinguistics*, and they include rate of speech, pitch variation, volume, and vocal quality. If you think about your perceptions of someone who speaks really rapidly or v-e-r-r-r-y s-l-o-o-o-w-l-y, you have a sense of how rate affects communicating. Listeners and conversation partners also make inferences about how monotone or melodic speech is, how softly or loudly someone speaks, and whether a speaker's vocal quality is resonant, squeaky, nasal, or breathy. Sometimes people manipulate these four dimensions of their voice to assist listeners in interpreting what they're saying, whether they're emphasizing various words or phrases, expressing feelings, or indicating when they're serious and when they're sarcastic or joking. In other cases, speakers don't mean to manipulate any of the four; they're "just talking normally" when people hear them as too fast, as too soft, as a monotone, or as too loud.

As these examples suggest, one of the ways people interpret others' vocal cues is to make stereotyped judgments about the speakers' personalities. It's not a good idea, but we do it nonetheless. For example, a male with a breathy voice is likely to be stereotyped as gay, or at least as young and artistic, whereas a female with the same vocal quality is usually thought of as "more feminine, prettier, more petite, more effervescent, more high-strung, and shallower."[22] Nasal voices are heard as undesirable for both males and females, and low, deep voices are perceived as being more sophisticated, more appealing, and sexier than are higher-pitched voices. People also use vocal cues to draw conclusions about the age, sex, and ethnicity of speakers they hear. What can you conclude from the fact that we use voices this way? According to Mark Knapp:

> You should be quick to challenge the cliché that vocal cues only concern how something is said—frequently they are what is said. What is said might be an attitude ("I like you" or "I'm superior to you"), it might be an emotion ... or it might be the presentation of some aspect of your personality, background, or physical features. Vocal cues will, depending on the situation and the communicators, carry a great deal of information....[23]

Silence

> With silence we express the most varied and conflicting states, sentiments, thoughts and desires. Silence is meaningful. There is the silence of fear and terror, of wonder and stupor, of pain and joy.... "Dumb silence" is a contradictory expression. Instead of describing the same thing the two terms exclude each

other; silence is not dumb and whatever is dumb is not silent. Silence is a form of communication ... dumbness, on the other hand, isolates and excludes us from all communication.[24]

The reason we classify silence as a mixed cue is that it most often becomes significant in the context of talk. As one author puts it, "A discourse without pauses [is] incomprehensible. Silence is not an interval ... but the bridge that unites sounds."[25] In other words, silence is usually noticed because of the way it relates to speaking. Examples include the failure or refusal to respond to a question, and the pregnant pause. Even the silence of the forest, prairie, mountain, lake, or bayou is most meaningful because of the way it contrasts with the noises of city crowds.

Silence is one of the least understood nonverbal behaviors, partly because people use and interpret it in so many different ways. Silence can be interpreted to mean apathy, patience, boredom, fear, sadness, love, intimacy, anger, or intimidation. We have talked with married couples who use silence as a weapon. One husband, who knew his wife hated it when he didn't talk out a problem, sometimes would refuse to talk to her for two or three days. His wife said she found this "devastating." When there are prolonged silences in group meetings, people start shifting nervously and making inferences, such as "nobody is interested," "people don't like this group," and "nobody really cares what we're doing."

But silence also works in positive ways. Beginning teachers, for example, have to learn that the silence that sometimes comes after they ask their students a question can be very fruitful. A group's silence can mean that there's a lot of thinking going on. Two close friends may also say nothing to each other just so they can share the experience of the moment. Or in an interview, silence can be a welcome opportunity for the interviewee to elaborate, return to a topic discussed earlier, or simply reorganize her or his thoughts. A friend of ours reported that the long silences he and his mother shared during the last two days of her life were some of the richest times they had spent together. Love, warmth, and sympathy are sometimes best expressed through silent facial and body movements and touch.

Facial Expression and Words

[Later in] this reading, we'll discuss facial expression as a primarily nonverbal cue. But peoples' faces also connect with words when they help to regulate utterance "turns" in conversations, and when they do, they can be considered mixed cues. The next time you're in a conversation, notice how you know when it's your turn to talk. The other person's face and eyes will almost always "tell" you. People also use faces and eyes to tell someone who approaches them either that they are welcoming the person into conversation or that they would rather be left alone.

Eye behavior is an important part of facial expression, and people use specific forms of eye behavior to accomplish several general goals in most conversations. First, we look away when we're having difficulty putting our thoughts into words. The amount of information we seem to be getting from another's eyes can be intense enough to be distracting, so if we're having trouble saying what we want to say, we look away to reduce the amount of input.

We also use eye contact to monitor feedback, to check the other's responses to the conversation. If we notice that the person is looking at us, we infer that she or he is paying attention; if we see that the person is staring into space, or over our shoulder to something or someone behind us, we draw the opposite conclusion. This phenomenon often helps make "cocktail party" conversation uncomfortably superficial. Neither conversation partner wants to be left standing alone, so both are as concerned about the next conversation as they are about the current one. As a result, both divide their looking between eye contact with the other and the search for the next partner.

Visual contact is also a primary way to indicate whose turn it is to talk. When a person tries to "catch the eye" of a server in a restaurant, the point is to open the channel, to initiate talk. And the same thing happens in conversation; I can "tell" you that it's your turn to talk by making eye contact with you. One communication researcher summarizes the typical conversation pattern in this way: "As the speaker comes to the end of an utterance or thought unit, gazing at the listener will continue as the listener assumes the speaking role; the listener will maintain gaze until the speaking role is assumed when he or she will look away. When the speaker does not yield a speaking turn by glancing at the other, the listener will probably delay a response or fail to respond...."[26] Of course, this description is accurate for some cultures and not for others. Like other non-verbal cues, the facial expressions that accompany words vary among ethnic groups, genders, social classes, and sexual preferences. Eye contact and facial expressions are so critical to regulating conversations that a speaker's elimination of either one will seriously affect the responses of the listener.

Gestures and Words

Researcher David McNeill emphasizes why gestures can be considered mixed cues by examining their connection to spoken words. In one of McNeill's articles, "So You Think Gestures Are Nonverbal?" he explains how they are not just nonverbal, because gestures and speech are part of the same language structure. As he puts it, certain "gestures are verbal. They are the overt products of the same internal processes that produce the other overt product, speech." He goes on to point out that this is another reason we have to change what we mean by "language." He writes, "We tend to consider linguistic what we can write down, and nonlinguistic, everything else...."[27] However, he says, we now know better. Language is made up of both verbal and nonverbal aspects. This is "contrary to the idea of body language, that is, a separate system of body movement and postural signals that is thought to obey its own laws and convey its own ... meanings."[28] It's misleading to talk of body language, McNeill argues, because posture and gesture are too intimately connected with the other part of language—words....

Communication researcher Janet Bavelas and her colleagues have extended McNeill's work by studying what they call interactive gestures. These are movements that are related not to the content of the conversation, but to the relationship between or among the people communicating. Interactive gestures include the listener and thus "act to maintain the conversation as a social system."[29] For example, Bavelas describes how one speaker was discussing the summer job options that would contribute the most to his career goal.

> The listener had suggested earlier that working for Canada Customs would be a good idea; the speaker, after listing several other possibilities, adds "and Customs is DEFINITELY career-oriented." As he said "Customs," the speaker moved his hand up and toward the other person (almost as if tossing something to him), with palm up, fingers slightly curled, and thumb pointing directly at the other at the peak of the movement. Our translation of this gesture is "which YOU suggested," that is, the speaker credits the other person with the idea.[30]

Other interactive gestures were translated as "Do you get what I mean?" "Would you give me the answer?" and "No, no, I'll get it myself." All of these gestures are connected not to the conversational topic, but to the other speaker. Thus, they add important social content to the conversation, content separate from what is contributed verbally. In this way, they take on part of the work of mutual meaning constructing that is normally thought to be done only by words. So these so-called nonverbal gestures are actually functioning exactly as words do to add substance to the conversation.

Bavelas and her colleagues explain the importance of this added substance when they write:

> An interesting, intrinsic problem in dialogue is that, while both partners must remain involved, only one person can talk at once. Whenever a speaker has the floor, there exists the possibility that the conversation could veer off into mono-logue. One solution to the problem … is for the speaker to involve the listener regularly. To a certain extent, the speaker can do this by verbal statements, such as "You know," "As you said," "As you know," "I'm sure you agree," etc. How-ever, the frequent use of verbal interjections and addenda would constantly disrupt the flow of content, so nonverbal means of seeking or maintaining involvement are well suited to this function....
>
> We propose that interactive gestures, for all their many specific forms and translations, form a class with the common function of including the listener and thereby counteracting the beginning of a drift toward monologue that is necessarily created every time one person has the floor.[31]

In summary, vocal rate, pitch, volume, and quality affect how people collab-oratively construct meaning in communication; this is why they can be thought of as mixed cues. Silence is another influential mixed building block. In addi-tion, many facial expressions, much eye behavior, and even many gestures work so intimately with spoken words that they should also be thought of as mixed.

PRIMARILY NONVERBAL CUES: FACE, EYE CONTACT AND GAZE, SPACE, TOUCH, MOVEMENT AND GESTURE

Although we're not going to present an exhaustive list of primarily nonverbal cues (for example, we omit appearance and dress, smells, time, and colors), we think that the following five categories will give you a broad sense of the most influential primarily nonverbal parts of your communicating.

Facial Expression

Your face is probably the most expressive part of your body and one of the most important focal points for nonverbal communicating. Most of the time, people are unaware of how much they rely on faces to give and get information. But a little reflection—or reading some of the research—can change your level of awareness. Consider, for example, how important the face is in expressing emotion. An extensive program of research has demonstrated that certain basic emotions are facially expressed in similar ways across cultures.[32] Every culture studied so far has been found to include some conventional facial expressions that people use to communicate joy or happiness, sadness, surprise, fear, anger, and disgust. There are some culture-specific rules for the display of these emotions, but they are expressed in very similar ways in most cultures.

Researchers have discovered these similarities by showing photographs of North American faces, for example, to Japanese or preliterate New Guinean observers, and then showing photographs of Japanese and New Guineans to North Americans. In most cases, members of one culture were able to identify accurately the emotions being expressed by the faces of persons from the other cultures.[33] They recognized, for example, that surprise is consistently communicated by a face with widened eyes, head tilted up, raised brow, and open mouth. Disgust is communicated with brows pulled down, wrinkled nose, and a mouth with raised upper lip and downturned corners.

Although the facial expression of emotions is similar across cultures, there are important differences in facial displays, for example, between Japanese and North Americans. Historically, Japanese have been taught to mask negative facial expressions with smiles and laughter and to display less facial emotion overall.[34] There are a number of competing ideas about why these differences exist, but regardless of the origins, differences in expression have contributed to misunderstandings between Japanese and North American businesspeople. Many Japanese still appear to be some of the least facially expressive of all cultural groups, and persons from other cultures are learning to adapt to this difference.

Eye Contact and Gaze

Although eyes are obviously a part of facial expression, gaze and eye contact are important enough to discuss separately. Eye contact appears to be one of the first behaviors that infants develop. Within a few days of birth, infants seem to recognize and attend to the caregiver's eyes. In the weeks immediately after birth, researchers have observed that simply seeing the eyes of the caregiver is enough to produce a smiling reaction.[35] Eye contact also significantly affects development. Infants who lack mutual gaze do not appear to mature perceptually and socially as rapidly as those who experience regular eye contact.[36]

If you doubt the importance of eye contact, consider the inferences you make about someone who doesn't look you in the eye "enough." What "enough" means varies from person to person, and certainly from culture to culture, but most Caucasians in the U.S. infer that the person with too little eye contact is insincere, is disinterested, lacks confidence, is trying to avoid contact, or is lying. There aren't many other possibilities. And all these inferences are negative. Generally, there are *no* positive messages conveyed by too little eye contact in white U.S. cultures....

One important function of eye gaze is to enhance the intimacy of the relationship. Especially when it is accompanied by forward lean, direct body orientation, and more gesturing, it can help promote closeness.[37] Some intimacy research has studied not sexual contact, but the kind of intimacy that increases the desire to help. Gaze has been found to increase the probability that a bystander will help a person with a medical problem or someone who has fallen.[38] But this phenomenon seems to characterize female-female contacts more than it does those involving males. As Judee Burgoon and her colleagues summarize, "Under some circumstances, prolonged gaze may serve as an affiliative cue in the form of a plea for help, while in other cases it may be seen as overly forward or aggressive behavior."[39]

Another primary function of eye behavior is to express emotions. Some of the same people who studied facial expressions have also researched how people use eyes and eyebrows to interpret the six common emotions. Generally eyes are used more than brows/forehead or lower face for the accurate perception of fear, but eyes help less for the accurate perception of anger and disgust.[40]

Feelings about others are also communicated visually. For example, if you perceive a person as being of significantly lower status than you are, the tendency will be for you to maintain considerable eye contact. On the other hand, communicators tend to look much less at high-status people. Generally, we also look more at people we like and at those who believe as we do. The obvious reason, as Albert Mehrabian explains, is that eye contact is a kind of approach behavior, and approach behaviors are connected with liking.[41] So one response to someone who is appealing is to approach by looking, and one way to avoid a person we dislike is to look away.

We also use gaze and eye behavior to make and influence credibility judgments. Several studies on persuasive effectiveness and willingness to hire a job applicant have underscored the importance of normal or nearly continuous gaze. It appears that gaze avoidance is interpreted negatively, as we mentioned above, and that it can significantly affect your chances of being perceived as credible.[42] This is why those who teach or coach people for public speaking or interview situations emphasize that speakers and interviewees should generally try to maintain eye contact 50 to 70 percent of the time. As we mentioned earlier, cultural identities affect this formula, but it is a reliable basic guideline for many North American communication situations.

The bottom line is that people give considerable weight to eye behavior and eye contact, because they apparently believe that the eyes are indeed the "windows of the soul." Especially in Western cultures, people are confident that they can spot even the most practiced liar if they can just "look the person in the eye"[43] (although detecting deception is more complicated than this, as we explain below). People are also generally impressed by the confidence and overall effectiveness of a speaker with good eye contact. But since different cultures have different estimates of what constitutes "good" eye contact, it's important not to oversimplify gaze and eye behavior and to remember that, especially because this category of nonverbal cues is given so much credence, it's important to become aware of and to learn to manage your own eye behavior.

Proximity or Space

You have probably noticed that you often feel possessive about some spaces—perhaps your room, yard, or car—and that you sometimes sit or stand very close to people with whom you're talking and at other times feel more comfortable several feet away. These feelings are related to what is known as *proxemics*, the study of the communicative effects of space or distance.

As [was] said in Chapter 2, space is one of the basic dimensions of every human's world, and the primary tension that describes this dimension is near-far. Because we all have basic human needs both for privacy (distance) and to be interdependent (nearness), one way we manage this tension is by defining and defending a *territory*. A territory is an identifiable geographic area that is occupied, controlled, and often defended by a person or group as an exclusive domain.[44] For example, for many North Americans, one's bedroom, or a particular space in a shared room, is yours whether you're in it or not, and one of the reasons you guard your right to keep it in your preferred state of neatness or disorder is to underscore the point that it's your territory. In a library, cafeteria, or other public space, people use overcoats, briefcases, newspapers, food trays, dishes, and utensils to establish a claim over "their" space, even though it's temporary.

A number of studies have identified differences between ways women and men use territory. For example, in most cultures, women are allowed less territory than are men. As Judy Pearson notes, "Few women have a particular and unviolated room in their homes while many men have dens, studies, or work areas which are off limits to others. Similarly, it appears that more men than women have particular chairs reserved for their use."[45]

Each of us also lives in our own personal space, a smaller, invisible, portable, and adjustable "bubble," which we maintain to protect ourselves from physical and emotional threats. The size of this bubble varies; how far away we sit or stand depends on our family and cultural memberships, the relationship we have with the other person, the situation or the context, and how we are feeling toward the other person at the time. Anthropologist Edward Hall says it this way:

> Some individuals never develop the public phase of their personalities and, therefore, cannot fill public spaces; they make very poor speakers or moderators. As many psychiatrists know, other people have trouble with the intimate and personal zones and cannot endure closeness to others.[46]

Within these limitations, Hall identifies four distances he observed among middle-class adults in the northeastern United States. Although the limits of each zone differ from culture to culture, something like these four types of space exist in many cultures.

Intimate Distance (Contact to 18 Inches)   This zone begins with skin contact and ranges to about a foot and a half. People usually reserve this distance for those to whom they feel emotionally close, and for comforting, protecting, caressing, or lovemaking. When forced into intimate distance with strangers—as on an elevator, for example—people tend to use other nonverbal cues to reestablish separateness. So we avoid eye contact, fold our arms, or perhaps hold a briefcase or purse in front of our body. Allowing someone to enter this zone is a sign of trust; it says we have willingly lowered our defenses. At this distance, not only touch, but also smells, body temperature, and the feel and smell of breath can be part of what we experience. Voices are usually kept at a low level to emphasize the "closed circle" established by intimates.

Personal Distance (1.5 to 4 Feet)   This is the distance preferred by most conversation partners in a public setting. Typically, subjects of personal interest and moderate involvement can be discussed at this distance. Touch is still possible, but it is limited to brief pats for emphasis and reassurance. Finer details of the other's skin, hair, eyes, and teeth are visible, but one can't discern body temperature or feel the breath.

The far range of this distance is just beyond where you can comfortably touch the other. Hall calls it the distance we can use to keep someone "at arm's length." John sometimes works as a communication consultant training people to do information-gathering interviews. In that context, he encourages the people he's training to try to work within this zone. It appears that three to four feet is far enough away not to threaten the other and yet close enough to encourage the kind of relatively candid responses that make the interviews most successful.

Social Distance (4 to 12 Feet)   More impersonal business generally is carried out at this distance. People who work together or who are attending a social gathering tend to use the closer ranges of social distance. Salespeople and customers typically are comfortable within the four- to seven-foot zone. Most people feel uncomfortable if a salesperson approaches within three feet, but five or six feet nonverbally "says," "I'm here to help but I don't want to be pushy."

At the farther ranges of this distance, eye contact becomes especially important. When a person is 10 or 11 feet away, it's easy to be uncertain about who the person is talking with until you can determine where the person is looking. This is also the distance we often use with people of significantly higher or lower status. Sitting at this distance from a superior will tend to create a much more formal conversation than might take place if one or both persons moved their chairs much closer. As a result, it can be more effective to reprimand using social distance and less effective to give praise in this zone.

Public Distance (12 to 25 Feet)   The closer range of this distance is the one commonly used by instructors and managers addressing work groups. The farthest end of this zone is usually reserved for public speeches. When communicating at this distance, voices need to be loud or electronically amplified. At the farther ranges of this distance, facial expression, movements, and gestures also need to be exaggerated in order to be meaningful.

Like many other general observations about human communication, these four distances need to be taken with a grain of salt. Several studies have shown, for example, that females sit and stand closer together than do males, and that mixed-sex pairs consistently adopt closer distances than do male-male pairs.[47] Interpersonal distance also generally increases with age from preschool and grade school through the teen years to adulthood, but this tendency is mitigated somewhat by the fact that people also tend to adopt closer distances with age peers than with those who are younger or older.[48] So people's interpretations of distance and closeness may depend not only on their cultural identity, but also on their gender and age and on the gender and age of the person with whom they're conversing.

Space is usually interpreted in the context of other nonverbal cues. For example, a Chinese-American student reported:

> [My grandfather] commands his presence with silence, limited facial expressions and lots of space between himself and others. I have never thought of jumping into his lap like Ol' St. Nick or even felt comfortable talking to him at any great length. When I do scrounge up the courage to speak to him, it is almost always to greet him or ask him to come to dinner. The speech used would have to be laden with respectful words.[49]

Touch

Touch is the most direct way that humans establish the contact that makes us who we are. "It is well documented that touch is essential to the physical, emotional, and psychological well-being of human infants and to their intellectual, social, and communication development."[50] Touch is equally important for adults, although taboos in many Western cultures make it much more difficult to accomplish. That's why some scholars believe that these cultures are "touch-starved."

Touch plays a part in just about every activity of our waking day—not just with other humans but also with objects. You may not be aware of the feel of your clothes; the chair, couch, or floor on which you're sitting, standing, or lying; or the feel of the book you're holding, the pencil or pen you're grasping, or the shoes you're wearing. But you couldn't write, walk, make a fist, smile, or comb your hair without the sense of touch. In addition, the ways in which we hold and handle such things as books, pencils, cups or glasses, and purses or briefcases can affect another person's responses to us.

Touch between persons is even more complex. Stan Jones and Elaine Yarbrough, two speech communication researchers, found that people touch to indicate positive feelings, to play, to control, as part of a greeting or departure ritual, to help accomplish a task, to combine greeting or departure with affection, and accidentally.[51] In their studies, control touches occurred most frequently, touches that were primarily interpreted to mean a request for compliance or attention getting. A spot touch with the hand to a nonvulnerable body part— hands, arms, shoulders, or upper back—frequently accompanies and emphasizes such statements as, "Move over," "Hurry up," "Stay here," "Be serious," and "Do it." A similar touch reinforces such messages as, "Listen to this," "Look at that," and "I want your attention." These touches are almost always accompanied by verbalization, and both sexes initiate these touches with almost equal frequency.

Positive affect touches were the second most frequent kind of touch Jones and Yarbrough observed. The highest number of these touches were expressions of affection. As you would expect, these occur predominantly in close relationships and include hugs, kisses, and often contacts with "vulnerable body parts"—head, neck, torso, lower back, buttocks, legs, or feet. But affection can also be communicated by touch in some business settings. Long-term work teams sometimes engage in spontaneous brief touches among team members that are interpreted as positive and supportive. On the other hand, ... sexual harassment in the workplace often consists in part of inappropriate or manipulative positive affect touching.

Research such as that of Jones and Yarbrough is important because it helps us comprehend a poorly understood, and sometimes even feared, aspect of our communicating. As Mark Knapp says:

> Some people grow up learning "not to touch" a multitude of animate and inanimate objects; they are told not to touch their own body and later not to touch the body of their dating partner; care is taken so children do not see their parents "touch" one another intimately; some parents demonstrate a noncontact norm through the use of twin beds; touching is associated with admonitions of "not nice" or "bad" and is punished accordingly—and frequent touching between father and son is thought to be something less than masculine.[52]

We know that touch is an enormously powerful kind of nonverbal communication; a very small amount of it can say a great deal. We can harness this power by becoming aware of how touch affects where our communication is on the social-cultural-interpersonal scale.

Body Movement and Gestures

The technical term for the study of movement and gesture is *kinesics*, from the Greek word for "motion." Some kinesic behaviors mean virtually the same thing whether they're performed by men or women, young or old people, and in the United States, Latin America, Europe, Australia, or Japan. For example, the head nod for agreement, shaking a fist in anger, clapping hands for approval, raising a hand for attention, yawning in boredom, rubbing hands to indicate coldness, and the thumbs-down gesture for disapproval are all interpreted similarly in at least several Western Hemisphere cultures.

Movements and gestures can also reflect the type of relationship that exists between partners or spouses. Communication researcher Mary Anne Fitzpatrick has distinguished among three general couple types who are identifiable in part by their patterns of movement and gesture. Traditionals accept conventional beliefs about relational roles, for example, about which are "the husband's" duties and which are "the wife's."[53] They value stability over spontaneity and affirm the traditional community customs that a woman should take her husband's last name when she marries, and the belief that infidelity is always inexcusable. Independent couples are at the opposite end of the ideological scale. They believe that one's relationship should not limit her or his individual freedom in any way. "The independent maintains a high level of companionship and sharing in marriage, but ... [he or she] maintains separate physical spaces to control accessibility." Separates are conventional regarding marital and family issues but also support independent values. "They may espouse one set [of values] publicly while believing another privately. The separates have significantly less companionship and sharing in their marriage."[54] One of the ways to distinguish among the three couple types is to observe their movements and gestures when they are together.

Traditionals engage in a high number of meshed movements and actions. Each partner facilitates the other partner's actions. If the woman moves toward the door, for example, the man will typically move to open it for her. Separates, on the other hand, engage in very few meshed action sequences. They are disengaged from one another. However, even though their gestures and movements don't interconnect, they are often parallel. For example, one may move toward the door while the other moves to get his or her coat. Finally, the gestures and movements of independents clash more often than they are parallel. If one moves toward the door, the other may sit down or even try to keep the door closed.

People also communicate dominance and submission posturally. A male may hook his thumbs in his belt and both females and males may stand with hands on hips in the akimbo position. When a seated person leans back with hands clasped behind her or his head, this is typically another dominance posture. When a conversational group of three is approached by a fourth person, they typically rotate their bodies out to encourage the fourth to join them or in to discourage him or her.

Forward lean is commonly interpreted as more involved and usually more positive, while "seated male and female communicators both perceived a person leaning backward and away from them as having a more negative attitude than one who was leaning forward."[55] A direct vis-à-vis posture, movement toward the other, affirmative head nods, expressive hand gestures, and stretching are all rated as "warm" behaviors, while moving away, picking one's teeth, shaking the head, and playing with hair are rated as "cold."[56] All of these descriptions illustrate how body movement and gesture make up still another important category of nonverbal behaviors.

REVIEW QUESTIONS

1. To check your understanding of the relationship between verbal and nonverbal cues, itemize six nonverbal features of the words you find in this book.
2. Explain what it means to say that words are "arbitrary symbols."
3. What's the problem with an explanation of language based on an analysis of concrete nouns?
4. What's missing, according to Stewart and Logan, from the account of language as an activity?
5. Explain the Sapir-Whorf hypothesis in your own words.
6. Give an example from your own experience of gendered (masculine/feminine) language affecting your perception of someone or something.
7. What are paralinguistics?
8. Especially in conversation, silence, this reading argues, is much more than the absence of noise. Explain.
9. Why is facial expression discussed in two separate places in this reading?
10. What are interactive gestures?
11. What makes eye behavior so important in conversations?
12. Stewart and Logan make the point that a very small amount of touch can "say" a great deal. Which other mixed and primarily nonverbal cues are similarly high in potency—where a little can go a long way?

PROBES

1. Carole and I explain some disadvantages of separate discussions of verbal and nonverbal cues. What are some advantages?
2. When does it most seem as if language is a "system"? When does this label seem least appropriate?
3. One famous author expressed something very close to the "language is a soup" idea in these words: "The limits of my language are the limits of my world." With the "soup" metaphor in mind, explain what you believe that means.
4. Carole and I repeat the claims about the differences between masculine and feminine communication styles that have been popularized by some authors. Malcom Parks's reading in Chapter 8 challenges these claims. Flip forward in the book to Chapter 8, and make a note there to discuss whether you agree with this reading or that one.

5. In your experience, which kinds of mixed and primarily nonverbal cues vary the most between or among cultures? Which kinds of cues from other cultures are the most different from your preferred patterns?
6. Give an example from your own experience of gender differences in spatial nonverbal cues.
7. Summarize three pieces of advice about your own verbal and nonverbal communicating that you drew from this reading. If you are to take seriously what's here, what three changes might you make?

NOTES

1. D. J. Higginbotham and D. E. Yoder, "Communication within Natural Conversational Interaction: Implications for Severe Communicatively Impaired Persons." *Topics in Language Disorders* 2 (1982): 4.
2. Wendy Leeds-Hurwitz, *Communication in Everyday Life* (Norwood, NJ: Ablex, 1989), p. 102.
3. Ferdinand de Saussure, *Course in General Linguistics,* ed. Charles Bally and Albert Sechehaye, trans. Roy Harris (LaSalle, IL: Open Court, 1986), pp. 66–70. After making this point, de Saussure focused his attention on the *system* of language, in order to make linguistics a "science."
4. Robert E. Sanders, "The Interconnection of Utterances and Nonverbal Displays." *Research on Language and Social Interaction* 20 (1987): 141.
5. Aristotle, "De Interpretatione," trans. E. M. Edgehill in *The Basic Works of Aristotle,* ed. Richard McKeon (New York: Random House, 1941), p. 20.
6. Charles E. Osgood, "What Is a Language?" in I. Rauch and G. F. Carr (eds.), *The Signifying Animal* (Bloomington: Indiana University Press, 1980), p. 12.
7. C. K. Ogden and I. A. Richards, *The Meaning of Meaning,* 8th ed. (New York: Harcourt Brace, 1986), p. 11. If you're interested in reading more about this view of language and its problems, see John Stewart, *Language as Articulate Contact: Toward a Post-Semiotic Philosophy of Communication* (Albany: State University of New York Press, 1995); and John Stewart (ed.), *Beyond the Symbol Model: Reflections on the Representational Nature of Language* (Albany: State University of New York Press, 1996).
8. Robert E. Nofsinger, *Everyday Conversation* (Newbury Park, CA: Sage, 1991), pp. 19–26.
9. Nofsinger, p. 51.
10. Hans-Georg Gadamer, "Man and Language," in David E. Linge (ed.), *Philosophical Hermeneutics* (Berkeley: University of California Press, 1976), pp. 62–63.
11. D. B. Chamberlain, "Consciousness at Birth: The Range of Empirical Evidence," in T. R. Verney (ed.), *Pre- and Perinatal Psychology: An Introduction* (New York: Human Sciences, 1987), pp. 70–86.

12. A. Tomatis, "Ontogenesis of the Faculty of Listening," in T. R. Verney (ed.), Pre- and Perinatal Psychology: An Introduction (New York: Human Sciences Press, 1987), pp. 23–35.

13. Beth Haslett, "Acquiring Conversational Competence." *Western Journal of Speech Communication* 48 (1984): 120.

14. John B. Carroll (ed.), *Language; Thought and Reality: Selected Writings of Benjamin Lee Whorf* (New York: Wiley, 1956), pp. 212–213.

15. For over 50 years, linguistics, anthropology, and communication textbooks have used the example of Eskimo words for snow to illustrate how language and perception are interrelated. According to this account, the importance of snow in Eskimo culture is reflected in the many terms they have for "falling snow," "drifting snow," "snow on the ground," "slushy snow," and so on. Earlier editions of this text repeated this myth. But we now know it isn't true. The myth began in 1911 when an anthropologist working in Alaska compared the different Eskimo root words for "snow on the ground," "falling snow," "drifting snow," and "a snow drift" with different English root words for a variety of forms of water (liquid, lake, river, brook, rain, dew, wave, foam, and so on). The anthropologist's comment was popularized in a 1940 article and then found its way into literally hundreds of publications that confidently asserted that Eskimos had 9, 23, 50, and even 100 words for snow. But they don't. The best available source, *A Dictionary of the West Greenlandic Eskimo Language,* gives just two: *quanik,* meaning "snow in the air," and *aput,* meaning "snow on the ground." So if you hear or read of the Eskimo-words-for-snow example, feel free to correct it. Or at least don't repeat it. See Geoffrey Pullum, "The Great Eskimo Vocabulary Hoax." *Lingua Franca* 14 (June 1990): 28–29.

16. Harry Hoijer, "Cultural Implications of Some Navajo Linguistic Categories." *Language* 27 (1951): 117.

17. J. Birere and C. Lanktree, "Sex-Role Related Effects of Sex Bias in Language." *Sex Roles* 9 (1980): 625–632; D. K. Ivy, "Who's the Boss? He, He/She, or They?" Unpublished paper, 1986; cited in D. K. Ivy and Phil Backlund, *Exploring Gender Speak: Personal Effectiveness in Gender Communication* (New York: McGraw-Hill, 1994), p. 75.

18. Deborah Tannen, *You Just Don't Understand: Women and Men in Communication* (New York: Morrow, 1990).

19. John Gray, *Men Are from Mars, Women Are from Venus* (New York: HarperCollins, 1992).

20. John Gray, *Mars and Venus in Love* (New York: HarperCollins, 1996).

21. Julia T. Wood reviews this research in *Gendered Lives: Communication, Gender, and Culture* (Belmont, CA: Wadsworth, 1994), pp. 141–145.

22. D. W. Addington, "The Relationship of Selected Vocal Characteristics to Personality Perception." *Speech Monographs* 35 (1968): 492–503.

23. Mark L. Knapp, *Essentials of Nonverbal Communication* (New York: Holt, 1980), p. 361.

24. M. F. Sciacca, *Come Si Vinci a Waterloo* (Milan: Marzorati, 1963), p. 129; quoted in Gemma Corradi Fiumara, *The Other Side of Language: A Philosophy of Listening* (London: Routledge, 1990), p. 101.

25. Sciacca, p. 26, quoted in Corradi Fiumara, p. 102.

26. Knapp, p. 298.

27. D. McNeill, "So You Think Gestures Are Nonverbal." *Psychological Review* 92 (1985): 350–371.

28. McNeill, p. 350.

29. Janet Beavin Bavelas, Nicole Chovil, Douglas A. Lawrie, and Allan Wade, "Interactive Gestures." Paper presented at the annual meeting of International Communication Association, Chicago, 1991, p. 2.

30. Bavelas, Chovil, Lawrie, and Wade, p. 7.

31. Bavelas, Chovil, Lawrie, and Wade, pp. 10–11.

32. See, for example, Paul Ekman, "Universal and Cultural Differences in Facial Expressions of Emotions," in *Nebraska Symposium on Motivation,* Vol. 19, ed. J. K. Cole (Lincoln: University of Nebraska Press, 1971), pp. 207–283; C. E. Izard, *Human Emotions* (New York: Plenum, 1977).

33. Paul Ekman, W. V. Friesen, and S. Ancoli, "Facial Signs of Emotional Experience." *Journal of Personality and Social Psychology* 39 (1980): 1125–1134; Paul Ekman and W. V. Friesen, *Unmasking the Face* (Englewood Cliffs, NJ: Prentice-Hall, 1975).

34. R. A. Miller, *Japan's Modern Myth: The Language and Beyond* (Tokyo: Weatherhill, 1982).

35. Michael Argyle and M. Cook, *Gaze and Mutual Gaze* (Cambridge, England: Cambridge University Press, 1976).

36. Janis Andersen, Peter Andersen, and J. Landgraf, "The Development of Nonverbal Communication Competence in Childhood." Paper presented at the annual meeting of the International Communication Association, Honolulu, May 1985.

37. Judee K. Burgoon, David B. Buller, and W. Gill Woodall, *Nonverbal Communication: The Unspoken Dialogue* (New York: Harper & Row, 1989), p. 438.

38. R. L. Shotland and M. P. Johnson, "Bystander Behavior and Kinesics: The Interaction between the Helper and Victim." *Environmental Psychology and Nonverbal Behavior* 2 (1978): 181–190.

39. Burgoon, Buller, and Goodall, p. 438.

40. Ekman and Friesen, *Unmasking the Face*, pp. 40–46.

41. Albert Mehrabian, *Silent Messages: Implicit Communication of Emotion and Attitudes,* 2nd ed. (New York: Random House, 1981), pp. 23–25.

42. See, for example, J. K. Burgoon, V. Manusov, P. Mineo, and J. L. Hale, "Effects of Eye Gaze on Hiring Credibility, Attraction, and Relational Message Interpretation." *Journal of Nonverbal Behavior* 9 (1985): 133–146.

43. We elaborate on the process of deception in Chapter 8. Closely related to the work on deception is research on equivocal communication. See, for example, Janet Beavin Bavelas, Alex Black, Nicole Chovil, and Jennifer Mullet, "Truths, Lies, and Equivocation," in *Equivocal Communication* (Newbury Park, CA: Sage, 1990), pp. 170–207.

44. Burgoon, Buller, and Woodall, p. 81.
45. Judy C. Pearson, *Communication in the Family* (New York: Harper & Row, 1989), p. 78.
46. Edward T. Hall, *The Hidden Dimension* (Garden City, NY: Doubleday, 1966), p. 115.
47. For example, N. M. Sussman and H. M. Rosenfeld, "Influence of Culture, Language, and Sex on Conversational Distance." *Journal of Personality and Social Psychology* 42 (1982): 66–74.
48. Burgoon, Buller, and Woodall, p. 110.
49. Mandy Lam, *Interpersonal Communication Journal,* October 19, 1996. Used with permission.
50. Burgoon, Buller, and Woodall, p. 75.
51. Unless otherwise noted, the material on touch is from Stanley E. Jones and A. Elaine Yarbrough, "A Naturalistic Study of the Meanings of Touch." *Communication Monographs* 52 (1985): 19–56.
52. Knapp, pp. 108–109.
53. Mary Anne Fitzpatrick, *Between Husbands and Wives* (Newbury Park, CA: Sage, 1988), p. 76.
54. Fitzpatrick, pp. 218–219.
55. Knapp, p. 224.
56. G. L. Clore, N. H. Wiggins, and S. Itkin, "Judging Attraction from Nonverbal Behavior: The Gain Phenomenon." *Journal of Consulting and Clinical Psychology* 43 (1975): 491–497.

Talk and Interpersonal Relationships

Steve Duck and David T. McMahan

Bridges Not Walls includes three readings by these authors because our approaches to interpersonal communication are so similar. For example, this discussion of verbal communication begins with the reminder that, "In everyday talk, words weave together seamlessly [with] ... nonverbal communication...." This is the first point that Carole Logan and I make in the reading right before this one: Although the verbal elements of interpersonal communication are usually discussed separately from the nonverbal parts, in actual practice, they occur *together*.

This discussion of the primarily verbal parts of interpersonal communication begins with the idea that each interpersonal relationship tends to be marked with words and phrases that mean something special to the people involved. Single words or phrases often remind conversation partners of funny past events or common understandings. These verbal cues can be puzzling to outsiders, which is one way to reinforce that the people who understand them have a unique relationship.

Words also reflect value judgments. "God terms" are powerful positive words and "Devil terms" elicit negative responses. In the political arena, "freedom" and "liberty" are almost universally positive in the United States, while "conservative" and "liberal" can be either God or Devil terms, depending on the context. It's important to recognize that virtually all words are value-laden; there's no such thing as purely objective or completely dispassionate language.

These authors also explain three ways that talk functions in relationships—*instrumentally, indexically,* and *essentially.* Words used *instrumentally* get something accomplished—label events, make announcements or promises, end a conversation. Words used *indexically* reflect or affect the relationship itself, like an entry in the index to a book labels a topic that's discussed on specific pages. The difference between "Please come here," and "Get over here, stupid!" is *indexical;* the first statement reflects an equal, respectful relationship and the second one shows that the relationship is one-up/one-down. Conversational hypertext is a kind of *indexical* talk. This term refers to words that point the listener to content that's not directly included in what's said. For example, "That's what the rules say," would refer the listener to a particular (unstated) set of rules. Studies show that people in close relationships often use conversational hypertext as a shorthand for shared understandings. "Jim was worried about his foot again" identifies conversation partners as friends, while, "Jim—that's my friend from high school—was worried about his foot again. He has gout and ..." would indicate that the conversation partners were not as well-acquainted.

Talk functions *essentially* when it creates and embodies relationships, as when a conversation partner says, "I've got your back," "No problem; that's what friends are for," or "I love you."

This point that talk helps create a local "culture" between people is extended in the final sections of this reading organized around the label, "ways of speaking." One distinction is between "high code" and "low code," two ways of speaking that work differently in different environments. A highly educated person might use informal, colloquial "low code" to indicate that she doesn't take herself too seriously. And a work group might stick to grammatically correct, formal "high code" when interacting with potential clients. The main point here is that words not only "carry" content, they also project a definition of the relationship that exists among speaker and listeners. Research shows that people make choices about ways of speaking in order to move closer to their listeners (convergence) or to distinguish themselves from others (divergence).

Storytelling is also a prominent form of talk. People tell stories for all sorts of reasons, and it's possible to gauge the status of relationships by listening to what stories are told, and how. We use stories to demonstrate connections with others, to entertain, to build credibility, to give a rationale for a strong feeling, and for many other reasons. We also tell stories to try to "one-up" others or, much less frequently, to indicate subservience. *Accounts* are kinds of stories that offer justifications, excuses, explanations, and apologies. Accounts are often ways we "put our spin" on what happened—indicate why we think something happened or whose fault it is. If you listen carefully to conversational talk you can figure out what *metamessages* (messages about the message—see the Tannen essay in Chapter 7) are embodied in the ways people speak.

MAIN IDEAS

- In actual talk, it's impossible to separate verbal cues from nonverbal ones. We discuss them separately, but they occur together.
- Single words or phrases often connote, or indirectly mean special things in a relationship.
- When used in actual talk, virtually all words carry more or less hidden values. No words are completely "objective."
- Talk functions in different ways: To accomplish something (*instrumentally*), to indirectly indicate the nature of the relationship (*indexically*), and to make the relationship real and talk it into being (*essentially*).
- Different "ways of speaking" build local cultures between people.
- In conversational talk, *storytelling* and the giving of *accounts* are ways people build understandings about both content—what happened, what people know, "the facts"—and relationships—who's right/wrong, with us/against us, more/less powerful, and so on.

In everyday talk, words weave together seamlessly within a context that includes nonverbal communication (NVC), or symbolic activity, such as facial expressions, hand gestures, movements, changes in posture, and pacing or timing of speech. In practice, nonverbal aspects of communication help you frame your expectations and interpretation of what someone else means. People often separate verbal and nonverbal communication into two parts: language and, the NVC system of meaning and how it connects with the words people speak (for example, how a smile frames a comment as friendly, not as hostile). Keep in mind that this split is artificial when it comes to understanding everyday life.

RELATIONSHIPS AND CONNOTATION OF WORDS

Your ability to understand people's intentions and meanings increases hugely the more personal your relationship is with them. A vast part of becoming closer to other people is getting to know them better and learning how they tick—an informal way of saying that you understand their worlds of meaning. When you know people better, you also know better than strangers what they mean when they make certain comments. Suppose Larry and one of his friends have a running joke about "tiramisu," which refers to a situation where something funny happened in a restaurant when one of them ordered tiramisu for dessert. Mentioning the word *tiramisu* is a shorthand way of saying, "This person has made a very weird response in a funny way." Larry knows that; his friend

"Talk and Interpersonal Relationships," pp. 26–47 from *The Basics of Communication: A Relational Perspective* by Steve Duck and David T. McMahan. Los Angeles: Sage, 2009. Reprinted by permission of Sage Publications.

knows that; but other people are not in on the joke. If they ever heard Larry use the word, they would never know what he meant and be completely unable to interpret any intention behind it.

In a relationship context, your assumptions, shared understandings, and forms of speech encode/transact the relationship by means of shared understanding. The understandings shared by you and your friends represent not only common understanding but also your relationship. No one else shares the exact understandings, common history, experiences, knowledge of the same people, or assumptions that you take for granted as not needing to be explained at any length.

Think for a minute about what happens when a friend from out of town comes to visit, and you go out with your in-town friends. You probably notice that the conversation is a bit more awkward even if it is still friendly: You do a bit more explaining, for example. Instead of saying, "So, De'Janee, how was the hot date?" and waiting for an answer, you throw in a conversational bracket that helps your friend from out of town understand the question. For example, you may say, "So, De'Janee, how was the hot date?" and follow it with an aside comment to the out-of-towner ("De'Janee has this hot new love interest she has a *real* crush on, and they finally went out last night").

When you talk to people, you use words that refer to your shared history and common understandings that represent your relationship or shared culture. As you talk, you monitor that knowledge and occasionally must explain to outsiders, but the very need for explanation—particularly important when you are giving a speech to an audience that does not know what you know—indicates a level of relationship, not just a level of knowledge. Relationships presume common, shared knowledge.

Although, whenever you talk, you use language (enshrouded in nonverbal communication) to denote something in the world, it is very important to recognize that there is more to talk than that. You do not just do things with words when you talk. You do things with *relationships* too, and a lot of the words you use in conversation demonstrate and transact your relationships. Therefore, over and above the differentiating that *language* does, people adopt different styles of *speaking* according to their relationship. Restaurant servers, for example, identify items strictly relevant to their task, such as broccoli, witchety grubs, and prices. Friends can refer to their previous experience together, their common history, their knowledge of particular places and times, and other experiences they both understand ("Remember when we went to Jimmie's …"). Because both of you know what is being referred to, neither of you needs to explain.

WORDS AND HIDDEN VALUES

Words differentiate the world into objects and thought units and then name them. Talk does this relationally, too: With friends, we draw on words differently than we do in work relationships, family relationships, enemy relationships, or competitive relationships.

Let's take this a little further and show how words also make value judgments and how these judgments are built into the talk that happens in relationships, and vice versa. A society or culture not only uses different words from those current in another language, obviously, but also prefers some subjects to others. For example, how do you react to the words *spider, ice cream, class test, Porsche, sour, Republican, liberty, death,* and *justice?* Communication philosopher Kenneth Burke (1966) made a distinction between **God terms** and **Devil terms** in a particular culture. God terms are powerfully evocative terms that are viewed positively in a society, and Devil terms are equally evocative terms that are viewed negatively. The obvious difference is that both are powerful, but each in a different way; terms like *justice* and *liberty,* for example, are seen very positively in U.S. society (God terms), whereas *Osama bin Laden* may be a Devil term. Depending on your political point of view, such words as *Bush* or *Rodham Clinton* may be one or the other, so you can see that God and Devil terms are not absolutes for everyone in the same society, although some terms are equivalent for everyone. The terms apply in relationships, too, because the partners in a relationship will have special references for people and events that may or may not be mentioned or topics that you know your partner is sensitive about—his or her Devil terms—and that you therefore steer away from....

We briefly indicated that symbols indicate not only what is true but also what you would like people to think, and we used the terms *presentation* and *representation* to describe this difference. At times, your speech is persuasive or preferential; it makes distinctions that you want your audience to accept as valid. Kenneth Burke's point about the value judgments built into words is very similar—namely, that your words encode your values and you see some concepts as good (communication studies) and some as bad (pedophilia). Every time you talk, you are essentially using words to argue and present your personal preferences and judgments, as well as simply describing your world. Your culture has a preference, as do you and your friends, and your communications express that in both obvious and hidden ways. Start paying more attention to those expressions of the values embedded in the words that you use to talk in your everyday lives. If you tell your instructor about your grade and say, "I think I deserved a B–, but you gave me a C+," you and the instructor both recognize that a B– is "better than" a C+ in the framework of meaning taken for granted in school. Your words are *going beyond* what they seem to be saying and are taking for granted the context, the relationship, and the culture in which the conversation occurs.

EVERYDAY LIFE TALK AND THE RELATIONSHIPS CONTEXT

Duck and Pond (1989), apart from being our favorite combination of authors' names, came up with some interesting ideas about how relationships connect with talk in everyday life. They pointed out that talk can serve three functions for relationships: It can make something happen in relationships (instrumental function), can indicate something about the relationship (indexical function), or can amount to the relationship and make it what it is, creating its essence (essential function). Although these functions might sound complicated at first, you practice each of them every day without knowing it. Let's take a closer look.

Instrumental Functions

Whenever you ask someone out for a date, to a party, to meet you for a chat or a coffee, to be your friend, or to be just a little bit more sensitive and caring, you are performing an **instrumental function of talk** in relationships. What you say reveals a goal that you have in mind for the relationship, and talk is the means or instrument by which you reveal it. Anything you say that serves the purpose of bringing something to or changing anything about the relationship is an instrumental function of talk in relationships. A proposal of marriage, a request that a relationship be put on hold, an announcement to a work group that you have been promoted and your relationship is now different, or "I never want to see you again" are all examples of the instrumental function of talk.

Indexical Functions

An **indexical function of talk** demonstrates or indicates the nature of the relationship between speakers. You index your relationship in the *way* that you talk to somebody. If you say in a sharp tone, "Come into my office; I want to see you!" you are not only being discourteous, you are indicating that you are superior to the other person and have the relational right to order him or her around. The content and relational elements of the talk occur together.

There are other ways of indexing a relationship too. Two friends talk intimately, for example, using language that they know they both understand but other people might not. Saying to your friend, "Let's meet at the LR1-VAN after I have seen Jim about his foot" contains so much coded information that anyone listening to the sentence would know you two share lots of understanding about each other's lives. You would need to explain to an outsider what the "LR1-VAN" is, who "Jim" is, and why he would be talking to you about his foot, but a close friend would not need the explanation. In your talk with other people, you constantly weave in clues about your relationships, and that is what the indexical function of talk is all about. Talk is relational, and how we use it tells people about the relationship we have with our audience.

Conversational Hypertext and Hyperlinks

We have already mentioned, without formerly naming or describing it, one form of indexical function in talk: hyperlinks. Duck (2002) noticed that lots of talk involves a kind of **conversational hypertext.** You know what hypertext is from your use of computers and the Internet, and how you talk to people works the same way. In conversation, we often use a word that suggests more about a topic and would therefore show up on a computer screen in blue, pointing you to a hyperlink. For example, you might say, "I was reading Duck and McMahan, and I learned that there are many extra messages that friends pick up in talk than I had realized before." This sentence makes perfect sense to somebody who knows what "Duck and McMahan" is, but others may not understand. On a computer, they would use their mouse to find out more about Duck and McMahan at www.sagepub.com/bocstudy, but in a conversation, they would "click" on the hypertext by asking a direct question: "What's Duck and McMahan?" Conversational hypertext, therefore, is basically the idea that all of our conversation contains coded messages that an informed listener will effortlessly understand. In relationships, the shared worlds of meaning and the overlap of perception make communication special and closer. Uninformed listeners, however, can always request that the hypertext be unpacked, expanded, or addressed directly. You and your friends talk in coded, hypertextual language all the time. Only when you encounter someone who does not understand the code do you need to further explain. In the previous example, "De'Janee" is hypertext until you have been introduced to her, and the "hot date" is hypertext until you learn that De'Janee has a new love interest. After that initial explanation, the term *hot date* might become a shared reference; even the friend from out of town now knows to what it refers. If, later in the conversation, someone starts to talk about "De'Janee's hottie," the out-of-town friend will be included in the shared knowledge, and, at that point, the group of friends will have created a new hypertext to the conversation and the relationship that even the out-of-town friend understands.

Research shows how we can tell, just from their talk, whether people know one another because of the way they treat conversational hypertext as needing no further explanation. Planalp and Garvin-Doxas (1994) reported a number of studies where they played tapes of talk to an audience and asked the listeners to say whether the people on the tape were friends. Listeners were very skilled at making this identification and could easily tell whether two conversational partners were acquainted or merely strangers. What made the difference was whether or not the talkers took information for granted or whether they explained the terms used. Said without explanation, "Jim was worried about his foot again" identified the two conversers as friends. On the other hand, the following showed them to be unacquainted: "Jim—that's my friend from high school—was worried about his foot again. He has gout and has to be careful about setting it off; it is a problem that keeps coming back. It worries him a lot, so he usually calls me when it flares up, and I have to deal with it."

Essential Functions

People very easily underestimate the extent to which talk and its nonverbal wrapping *is* a relationship. Of course, even when you are in a relationship, you and your partner do not spend every moment with each other. You experience absences, breaks, and separations: They may be relatively short (one person goes shopping), longer (a child goes to school for the day), or extended (two lovers get jobs in different parts of the country, go on vacation separately, or are involved in a commuter relationship). Because these breaks in sequence occur, there are many ways you indicate to one another that, although the interaction may be over, the relationship itself continues. For example, you might say, "See you next week," "Talk to you later," or "Next week we will be discussing the chapter on making a presentation." All of these phrases are examples of the **essential function** of talk—namely, a function of talk in making the relationship real and talking it into being by simply assuming that it exists. The above examples, talking about the continuance of the relationship beyond an upcoming absence, demonstrate that the relationship will outlast the separation.

Most of the time, however, talk creates and embodies relationships in other ways, both implicitly ("I've got you, babe") and explicitly ("You're my friend"). There can be direct talk that embodies the relationship ("I love you") or indirect talk ("What shall we do this Friday night?") that recognizes the relationship's existence but does not mention it explicitly. The essential function of talk operates in hidden ways to include more frequent coupling references to you and your partner as "we" rather than "X and I." Connection or inclusion can also be found in talk where joint planning is carried out or nicknames are used. Linguistic inclusion ("Let's ...," "we," "us"), also known as **immediacy,** is a seemingly small but nevertheless powerful way to essentialize the relationship in talk....

Ways of Speaking

In everyday conversation with people you know, other aspects of talk are worth noticing as also transacting relationships. The form or style of language through which you choose to express your thoughts carries important relational messages, and sometimes you use that knowledge as part of what you choose to say on a particular occasion. When people talk to very young children, they tend to adopt baby language; when students or employees talk with professors or supervisors, they try to sound "professional." When talking with friends, you use informal language, but in class or in conversation with your boss, your language may be a bit more complicated. Think about the difference between saying, when you're hungry, "I'm so hungry I could eat a horse" and "My state of famishment is of such a proportion that I would gladly consume the complete corporeality of a member of the species *Equus przewalski poliakov.*" The first example is written in what communication scholars call **low code,** and the second is written in **high code** (Giles, Taylor, & Bourhis, 1973). Low code is an informal and often ungrammatical way of talking; high code is a formal, grammatical, and very correct—often "official"—way of talking. You might be able to look around your lecture hall and see a sign that says something like "Consumption of food and beverages on these premises is prohibited." That is a high-code way of saying the low-code message: "Do not eat or drink here."

By now, then, you can see that not just individual words are polysemic; so is the whole structure of language and the *way in which* you speak. Let's spend some time elaborating on this so that you come to understand how it plays out in relationships with an audience, whether public or intimate.

The language you use contains more than one way of saying the same thing—a sort of stylistic polysemy. Although this may not have struck you as particularly important yet, the form of language you use to express essentially the same idea conveys its own messages about something other than the subject you're talking about. In fact, it connotes and essentializes the relationships between you and your audience, as well as conveys something about you as a person. A high form is formal, pompous, and professional; a low form is casual, welcoming, friendly, and relaxed. By choosing one form over another at a particular point of speech, you are therefore not just sending a message but doing three things: delivering *content* about a particular topic, *presenting* yourself as a particular sort of person (projecting identity), and *indexing* a particular sort of relationship to the audience. Part of your connotative meaning at a given time is always an essentializing commentary about "the state of the relationship" between the speaker and the audience, whether a large or small group or an individual. Public speakers, for example, adopt particular ways of talking depending on the group with which they strive to identify.

Just as you can set the frame, you can change it. You can choose a particular way to say something, but you may change or adapt it either to suit an audience, to see changes in feelings or in the relationship that occur during the course of the interaction. Giles and his colleagues (1973) have shown that people will change their accent, their rate of speech, and even the words they use to indicate a relational connection with the person to whom they are talking. They called this process **accommodation** and identified two types: convergence and divergence. In **convergence,** a person moves toward the style of talk used by the other speaker. For example, an adult converges when he or she uses baby talk to communicate with a child, or a brown-nosing employee converges when he or she uses the boss's company lingo style of talk. In **divergence,** exactly the opposite happens: One talker moves away from another's style of speech to make a relational point, such as establishing dislike or superiority. A good example is how computer geeks and car mechanics insist on using a lot of technical language to customers, instead of giving simple explanations that the nonexpert could understand. This form of divergence keeps the customer in a lower relational place.

The different ways of sending the same content in a message are another instance of how meaning and relationships are inextricably tied together. Talking conveys content and something about your identity. It conveys even more about your sense of the ongoing changes in your relationship with others and how it may be altered by the course of an interaction.

Narration: Telling Stories

The multilayered framing aspect of talk is especially noticeable when people tell stories. Communication scholars use the term *narrative* to cover what is involved when we say *what* people are doing and *why* they are doing it, whether talk includes funny events, tragic events, significant emotional experiences, or relational stories (meeting new people, falling in love, breaking up). You may not always notice that talk has the features of a story, but you have heard many examples—"How we met," "How my day was," and even "I couldn't do the assignment," which may not at first strike you as a story. A narrative is any organized story, report, or prepared talk that has a plot, an argument, or a theme. In a narrative, speakers do not just relate facts but also arrange the story in a way that provides an account, an explanation, or a conclusion—often one that makes the speakers look good or tells a story from their own particular point of view (i.e., when they are making their talk not only representational but also presentational).

Much of everyday life is spent telling stories about yourself and other people, whether or not they walk into bars. For example, you may tell a story about when you went into a shop and something funny or unexpected happened, or you may tell your friends how when you were working in the pizza parlor, some guy came in and couldn't, like, make his mind up about whether he wanted, like, double cheese or pepperoni, and you stood there for, like, 5 minutes while he made up his mind. Communication scholar Walter Fisher (1985) pointed out how much of human life is spent telling stories and coined the term *homo narrans* (Latin for "the person as a storyteller or narrator") to describe this tendency. Indeed, he suggested that storytelling is one of the most important human activities. Stories are also a large part of relating, so we need to spend some time exploring how people narrate and justify their action in stories.

Stories or narratives often appear to be straightforward talk, but very often they are elaborate frames, too, and can frame up excuses for your actions. For example, in the cheese and pepperoni case, the end of your story might be "I was so mad," and the details about the person making the decision are used to justify (frame) the fact that you felt irritated. People often give excuses and tell stories that help explain their actions within a set of existing frames. This section looks at how stories use, and also provide, frames for your talk to present you incidentally as a relationally responsible and attractive person (facework)....

One significant frame that sets the scene for all narratives comes from two sources: (a) the persona of the agent telling the story, making the speech, giving a toast, reporting the gossip, or talking the talk; and (b) the relationship between the speaker and the audience. Formal speakers are often introduced in ways that frame them as important for their audience by listing their rank, their accomplishments, or the reasons the audience should pay attention to them ("I am pleased to present the president of the corporation ..."; "We are very honored to have with us today the Secretary of State ..."; "Today's speaker has for a long time been a leading member of our community ..."). A formal toastmaster may wear a uniform, a priest who is speaking may wear the clothes of office, or speakers may wear business clothes to clarify their importance, professionalism, and seriousness. However, all speakers invite you to accept the important frame that they *matter* whether or not they are giving a formal presentation. The bottom line of many stories, presentations, speeches, and everyday talk really comes down to "I'm a decent person, and what I'm telling you is essentially a good idea/I did the right thing, didn't I?" You never meet anyone who does not, at root, think he or she is an essentially good person, perhaps misunderstood and undervalued but essentially decent and OK. Now you may recognize that these story "bottom lines" are not only offering justifications and accounts for acts but also using the features we have talked about in this chapter to relate the speaker and the audience. Speaking to any audience is always an act set in a relational scene....

Giving Accounts   Although narratives appear on the surface just to report (represent) events, they actually account for (present) the behaviors. **Accounts** are forms of communication that offer justifications ("I was so mad"), excuses ("I was really tired"), exonerations ("It wasn't my fault"), explanations ("... and that's how we fell in love"), accusations ("But he started it!"), and apologies ("I'm an idiot"). In short, accounts "go beyond the facts." How narratives are structured will often give a clue as to the motives of people involved or perhaps to the teller's understanding of the world. In fact, you should be noticing what you can learn about a storyteller from how he or she tells the story. Everyday communication involves different ways of narrating stories, and many give revealing insight into the thought frames of the person doing the telling.

Psychologists, communication scholars, and sociologists would talk about ... "giving an account" (Scott & Lyman, 1968), or telling a story in a way that justifies, blames, or calls for someone to account for what happened. The purpose of representational elements (or "facts") in reports can actually turn out to be presentational; that is, your description of something is not simply a report of facts but contains "spin" and therefore explains the "facts" you are reporting. For example, if you tell your friend. "I just failed a math test. It was way too hard," both of these statements appear to be facts, but one is actually an explanation for why you failed (the test was too hard) and is a personal view about the reason for your failure. It is therefore a *presentational* account and not simply a statement of fact. Your teacher may think you failed because you did not do the work, for example.

If you listen to everyday conversation, you will start to hear these sorts of framing justifications much more often now that you know what to listen for. Once you recognize their frequency, you can begin to understand something about their structure and what it tells us about communication and the implied relationship between the speaker and the audience. For example, you don't bother to justify yourself to people whose opinions you do not care about, and furthermore, you would not justify yourself to an enemy in the same way you would to a friend. You expect the friend to know more about your background and to cut you some slack. This familiarity would influence the style of your report, once again connecting talk to relationships.

Remember what we wrote at the start of this chapter: that a whole system of nonverbal communication frames what we say, too. If I say, "I love you" but grimace when I say it, that frames the words in a different way than if I smile and look all gooey when I say it.... Although we have separated talk from its real behavioral context so that you can understand features of talk itself, it never happens in practice in a way that is separated from nonverbal behavior.

REVIEW QUESTIONS

1. Explain the difference between "denotation" and "connotation."
2. Give an example of two "God terms" and two "Devil terms" in your relationship with your best friend.
3. In what ways is the *indexical* function of talk similar to the index of a book?
4. Give an example from your own experience of *conversational hypertext.*
5. What does it mean to say that "ways of speaking" construct "local cultures"?
6. Define *polysemy.*

PROBES

1. Why is it important to recognize that virtually all words carry more or less hidden values?
2. True or false: The same piece of talk can "function" instrumentally, indexically, and essentially. Explain.
3. *Conversational hypertext* and many instances of the *essential* function of talk separate listeners into the in-group—those who "get" the hypertext reference or are included in the relationship definition—and the out-group—those who don't and aren't. How can you keep these kinds of talk from alienating your listeners or making them feel excluded?
4. Identify a person you know whose storytelling portrays him or her as pretty consistently one-up. Have you been in conversation with someone whose storytelling pretty consistently portrays him or her as one-down? Comment.

REFERENCES

Burke, K. (1966). *Language as symbolic action: Essays on life, literature and method.* Berkeley: University of California Press.

Duck, S. W. (2002). Hypertest in the key of G: Three types of "history" as influences on conversational structure and flow. *Communication Theory, 12*(1), 41–62.

Duck, S. W., & Pond, K. (1989). Friends, Romans, Countrymen; lend me your retrospective data: Rhetoric and reality in personal relationships. In C. Hendrick (Ed.), *Close Relationships, 10,* 17–38. Newbury Park, CA: Sage.

Fisher, W. R. (1985). The narrative paradigm: An elaboration. *Communication Monographs, 52,* 347–367.

Giles, H., Taylor, D. M., & Bourhis, R. Y. (1973). Towards a theory of interpersonal accommodation through language use. *Language in Society, 2,* 177–192.

Planalp, S., & Garvin-Doxas, K. (1994). Using mutual knowledge in conversation: Friends as experts in each other. In S. W. Duck (Ed.), *Dynamics of relationships* (Understanding relationship processes, 4, pp. 1–26). Newbury Park, CA: Sage.

Scott, M. B., & Lyman, S. M. (1968). Accounts. *American Sociological Review, 33,* 46–62.

Two of the Most Important Words

John Stewart

This short reading focuses your attention on the ways that the words "and" and "next" function in your everyday talk. These words are important, because, as I've said before, the words we use indirectly indicate or "leak" our understandings, and these two words indirectly indicate how the speaker understands the communication process itself. In other words, "and" and "next" can be both *markers* and *triggers* of how the people using them understand communication.

Do you understand communication as a way to "get ideas across" to others? Or do you understand it as a continuous, complex, collaborative process of mutual meaning-making? You can tell in part by listening to how you use "and" and "next." Do you want to encourage yourself and others to operate with an accurate, up-to-date understanding of communication? Then try to use "and" and "next" as this essay suggests.

Your use of "and" can reflect your understanding that, when you're talking about humans communicating, there's always "more to it than that." "And" can be the opposite of the word "period," as in "That's all there is to it, period." "And" is a marker of provisionalism rather than certainty; a marker of humility rather than arrogance.

One useful exercise is to substitute the word "and" for the word "but." Why? Because "but" can cancel out everything that was said before it, while "and" keeps all the elements on the table.

"Next" can function similarly to remind people that the communication they're experiencing is continuous, unfinished, ever-unfolding. This is the same point that's made in the discussion of "nexting" in Chapter 2. Occasionally it makes good sense to think about a situation or event as closed-ended, finished, over-and-done-with. *And* (not "but"), the human world is ongoing. Each of us was born into a world of events, processes, and practices, and when we die, all of them will continue. Nobody ever utters "the first word" about any topic, and nobody ever really has "the final say" about anything. Your talk can either acknowledge this undeniable fact or ignore it.

This essay encourages you to talk out of a default orientation of open-endedness. Rather than filling your talk with statements that emphasize the "three cs" of certainty, closure, and control, see if you can approach the world as events on various trajectories, or as continually moving toward what's next.

MAIN IDEAS

- Even small words can embody or reveal speaker understandings or assumptions, and "and" and "next" often reveal how speakers understand communication.
- The word "and" can embody your recognition that communication is continuous, complex, and collaborative.
- Your use of "and" can help you avoid simplistic blaming or faultfinding and incomplete accounts of situations.
- "And" can also often usefully substitute for the word "but."
- "Next" can also reflect an understanding of communication as continuous.
- "Next" can be a marker of your default orientation about the complexity and status of the world you experience.
- When you experience a communication problem, the most functional, useful default orientation is focused on the future—what can happen *next.*

There are two primary benefits of improving your understanding of interpersonal communication and becoming more effective at it. The first is that your personal life will improve, and the second is that your business/professional life will improve.

When you understand with some sophistication how communication and interpersonal communication work, you will be better able to choose the right dating partner (or interact effectively with the person you're dating already), build a relationship smoothly and comfortably, minimize defensiveness, cope with conflict, and recognize the early signs of such serious communication problems as manipulation, harassment, deception, and verbal abuse. You will also be able to deal more gracefully with relationship endings, whether they happen because of a breakup, geographical separation, growing apart, or death. Communication is not a panacea for all of life's problems, but effective communication goes a long way to promote satisfying lives.

Your communication knowledge and skills will also benefit you at work. When your manager and the company you work for discover that you understand the complexities of human communication, and that you have listening, self-expression, questioning, facilitation, conflict management, and cross-cultural communication skills, they will see you as a problem solver. Since management can be defined as "getting things done through people" rather than "getting things done through things," effective communication is the key to effective management. People with communication and interpersonal communication knowledge and skills are assets to every organization. They provide "value-added" and ROI (return on investment). Time and again, I've seen people who improved their communication knowledge and skills get promoted to increasingly responsible and well-paid positions.

One effective way to develop these improved understandings and skills is to monitor your use of two of the most important words in the English language, "and" and "next." These words are important for two reasons: They can reflect the accuracy of your understanding of communication and they can help smooth out communication rough spots. How can such small and apparently simple words have such significant impact?

"AND" AS A MARKER AND A TRIGGER

Remember that human communication can best be understood as *the continuous, complex, collaborative process of verbal and nonverbal meaning-making*. Effective and skilled communicators understand it this way. I explained what this means in the first reading of Chapter 2. As I said there, "continuous" means partly that human communication was going on before you were born and it will continue after you die. More importantly, this term means that none of us "starts" or "finishes" any of the specific communication events we experience. We make important contributions—or refuse or fail to make them—but all our communication activities fit more or less well into an ongoing stream that was there before we were born and continues after we die. This is why we can understand each communication contribution—gesture, word, Tweet, smile—as a *response* to elements of the communication that preceded it.

The word "complex" reminds you that communication has many parts—verbal and nonverbal, cultural and psychological, historical and present parts, and so on. Nobody can keep track of every potentially important part. And it makes a huge difference whether we think we understand the situation completely or we are always remembering that more is going on than we are aware of. "Collaborative" means that no individual makes communicative meaning alone. Instead, we "co-labor" with other communicators to construct the meanings that emerge from our contact. This means that no individual controls the outcomes of any communication event. "Meaning" is what distinguishes human understanding from the kinds of understanding developed by all other animals, and the words "verbal and nonverbal" in this definition mean what's explained in this chapter.

From the perspective of your *understanding*, the word "and" can be a marker of how well you "get it" that communication has these qualities. In other words, the ways you use the word "and" in your everyday talk reflect how you understand the communication you're a part of. In this sense, "and" functions like a comma or semicolon rather than a period. Those punctuation marks indicate that the thought isn't yet finished, and the spoken or written word "and" can function similarly. "And" can also be the opposite of the word "period," as in "That's all there is to it, period." "And" is a marker of provisionalism rather than certainty;[1] it's open-ended rather than closed-ended; it's a marker of humility rather than hubris, because it can indicate that you know that there's always "more to it" than is currently on the table.

If you really understand that communication is continuous, complex, and collaborative, you won't be satisfied with such confident—and closed—pronouncements as, "It's all her fault," "We're in this fix because he didn't listen to what I said," "The people in marketing always say that," "Our personalities just clash," or "I'll never speak to her again." You will know that the situation looks like "her fault" from one perspective, *and* from her perspective it probably looks different. You will know that his "failure to listen" may be part of what put us in "this fix," *and* there's more to it than that. You'll know that marketing doesn't speak "always" with any one unified voice," *and* that even if they did, they are only one set of stakeholders. You'll know that even people with personalities that "clash" can communicate effectively. *And* you'll know that, in the real, everyday human world, a promise with "never" in it is hardly ever kept, and that even if it were, the situation would still change over time. In all of these ways—and many more—your use of the word "and" can be a *marker of your understanding* of the communication you're experiencing.

When you use the word "and" in your actual talking and listening (remember that listening involves much more than just being silent), the word can function to refine and increase the accuracy of the understanding that's being developed between you and your conversation partner(s). One way the word can do this is by substituting for the word "but." While the word "but" can take away or cancel out what comes before it, the word "and" is inclusive, additive, encompassing. The word "and" keeps all the elements being discussed on the table, in the talk between you. Consider the difference between "I love you but I wish you would change your underwear more often," and "I love you and I wish you would change your underwear more often."[2] In the first example, the "but" statement cancels out the "I love you," and in the second, the speaker's love is right there on the table along with her request about her lover's personal hygiene.

As I mentioned, "and" talk can also help keep the speaker's hubris in check, and can help construct a genuine identity of humility, because it can indicate that the speaker knows that he has not identified every important element of what's being discussed, or considered every possible reason for the problem being experienced. "I heard what she said, and I'm sure others in marketing might think differently." "I know you're really upset and I'm hoping that we can talk about this anyway." "I'm pretty certain that I don't want to go, and I know that you really want to."

So pay attention to how, and how often, the word "and" appears in your talk and writing. Try substituting it for the word "but." Try adding it to the end of pronouncements about "the way things are." Try saying it to clarify that you understand, when you express your opinion or describe how things appear to you, that there's more to it than that (others have different opinions and others see what you're seeing differently). Let this simple word be a reminder of the continuous, complex, and collaborative nature of all communication and put it in your talk so others can hear the inclusiveness, provisionalism, humility, and perspectivism that the word can help construct.

"NEXT" AS A MARKER AND A TRIGGER

These two words do some of the same work in conversation. Just as "and" can help people realize that their understandings are incomplete and reflect their own perspective, the word "next" can remind people that the communication they're experiencing really is continuous, unfinished, ever-unfolding. This point is obviously directly related to what is said about "nexting" in Chapter 2.

The term "nexting" labels a way of thinking, what some cognitive scientists would call an "orientation to" or "perspective on" what's being experienced. I know a person who prides herself on being what she calls "decisive" about some issues. She means that in some situations she is certain about her understanding and her opinion, and she has, in effect, finished thinking about that topic. Soon after I had completed a painful divorce and was not able to communicate effectively with my ex-wife, I was talking to this friend about a divorced couple I knew, each of whom had remarried, and who now got along very well with both their ex-spouse and the new partners. I expressed the hope that my ex-wife and I could reach that point. My friend declared, "That will never happen for me. I'm sorry, but I'm just not willing to even consider that." I was surprised, because her proclamation violates my basic understanding that, however communication is going at the present, it will go differently in the future. My ex-wife and I may never achieve what my divorced friends achieved. But none of us knows for sure what will happen *next* in our relationship, and when you realize that, it makes sense to be open to all kinds of future possibilities.

Is your default orientation to what you experience one that leads you to see events as divisible into finished units or always unfinished? As individually separate, or as interconnected? Are you inclined to think of a given conversation as a discrete event—asking for important information, requesting an evaluation of your work, making an apology, ending a relationship? Or do you understand each request for information to be connected with previous interactions you've had with this person and potentially connected with future ones? When you understand communication in the way I have described it here, you will be more oriented to "flow" than to separate, distinctive events.

One of the ways to track your default orientation and check your nexting is to notice the presence, in your thinking and speaking of what is sometimes called the "three cs," certainty, closure, and control. Historically, these were understood to be three of the goals and potential outcomes of the scientific method. According to many philosophers of science and practicing scientists in the 19th and 20th centuries, if you form a valid hypothesis, and then if you gather the right data, submit them to the proper quantitative analyses, and draw appropriate conclusions, you will generate valid and reliable knowledge. This knowledge was thought to be the kind that could lead to certainty about what was being studied. Certain knowledge could empower the persons holding it to control the outcomes of important processes. And the combination of certainty and control could bring the scientist to closure in her investigation. Questions get answered and each knowledge unit contributes to the inevitable progress of science. This was an early and very prominent picture of science.

Twenty-first century scientists and social scientists are much more sophisticated about what they study, whether their focus is on the natural world—physics, chemistry, biology—or the human world—psychology, communication, sociology, anthropology. Heisenberg's uncertainty principle, Godel's incompleteness theorems, chaos theory, and computational complexity theory in artificial intelligence, are just four examples of scientific developments in different fields that undercut the possibilities of certainty, closure, and control. Most contemporary scientists and social scientists understand today that, although there are definitely better and worse ways to posit hypotheses, gather data, analyze them, and draw conclusions, the best research produces findings that are highly probable and at best helpful-but-not-determinative in controlling future outcomes. And nobody expects closure, especially on the big questions. A "nexting" orientation operates similarly, with a specific focus on communication.

How can this way of understanding communication and interpersonal communication get translated into practice? One basic way is to replace fault-finding with the question, "OK, so what can happen next?" I also mentioned this in Chapter 2, and I make the point again here because it's so important. When people experience a communication problem, the natural inclination is to assess blame and assign fault. "Who forgot to check with the IT people?" "Why didn't HR do a background check?" "We lost the sale because he quoted the wrong price." "He's never on time." "This wouldn't happen if she paid her bills."

People can differ about whether it helps the situation to engage in faultfinding and blaming. Some say that it's important to assign responsibility so you can be sure the problem never happens again. *And,* even if you believe that the past can never be changed, the *only* current possibility is to take a helpful *next* step. So problem solvers, people who genuinely want to make things better, train themselves to ask, "OK, so what can happen next?" This question accepts the reality of the current situation—even if it's bad—and focuses attention on how to cope with it. This is almost always the most productive and fruitful way to begin working with any problem that's faced by an individual or a group.

Let's say that you feel misunderstood by your dating partner and you want to talk with her face-to-face, so you park in her driveway and wait for her to get home from work. When she arrives, she yells at you that you've invaded her personal space and she feels like you're "stalking" her. You try to protest that you just want to talk, but she won't have any of it. "We're through!" she shouts, as she slams her door.

You might naturally ask yourself whose fault it is that the two of you got into this fix. You might beat yourself up for forgetting to call her two nights in a row, or ignoring her while the two of you were at the recent game together. Or you might decide that it's her fault because she's upset about her mom's serious illness or stressed-out at work.

And (not "but"), if you actually want to work on this relational problem, your only focus should be on what happens next. You might decide to let there be a cooling-off period. You might decide that this is the last straw for you, and that your next move will be to confirm with her that, yes, the two of you are "through." You might write a note of apology and leave it in her mailbox. You might call a mutual friend who's helped you in the past. The point is, your fundamental orientation, if it's going to be useful, has to be focused on the future not the past.

A second way to apply a nexting way of thinking is to treat each of your personal and professional relationships developmentally. This means that you think of each relationship as moving along a trajectory, and you work to contribute to the relationship in ways that improve the relationship's progress on that trajectory. Remember that a trajectory is a curve followed by a projectile in its flight— like a baseball thrown from center field to home plate, or a basketball shot from 3-point range. Personal and professional relationships progress along analogous curves. When you're hired into a new job, for example, you're at an early stage of what you might hope is a trajectory that leads to promotion, more responsibilities, and better pay. Maybe that trajectory puts you eventually in the position of supervisor, manager, or even CEO. Or you may have little interest in advancement, and your job trajectory just goes from hiring to the time you plan to resign in 18 months. Whichever is true, you can base your communication choices on where you want to move on your trajectory. If you want to get promoted, for example, you may choose to dress for the job you want rather than the job you have. If you have different priorities, you may focus on building relationships with your co-workers rather than trying to impress your boss.

The point is, you can use the trajectory idea to decide what to do *next* either globally (Where do I want this relationship to go?) or locally (Which word is most likely to say what I mean?). Whether you're trying to cope with a specific communication problem or managing your daily communication life, you can profit from thinking about what you're doing as a series of "nexts." The reason this works is that it fits one important human reality—communication is always ongoing, unfinished, open to being redirected or redefined.

CONCLUSION

No pair of words will insure your communication success. But the words "and" and "next" can have impact that goes beyond their commonality and small size. Each of these words can be both a marker and a trigger of an accurate understanding of communication. Each can indicate or show that you are understanding communication as continuous, complex, collaborative, and unfinished, and each can also help you and your conversation partners stay on that communication trajectory.

REVIEW QUESTIONS

1. What does it mean to say that "and" and "next" can be both a "marker" and a "trigger"?
2. Explain the analogy that "and" can function as a comma or semicolon rather than a period.
3. Paraphrase the idea that "and" can reflect provisionalism and humility.
4. What are "the 3 cs"?
5. What's a "trajectory," and how is this idea used in this essay?

PROBES

1. If a person is focused on all the complexities of communication, how much danger is there that he or she will get confused or bogged down in irrelevant details? Is it ever best to keep things simple, even if some complexities are ignored?
2. Explain what it means to say that the ways a person uses "and" and "next" reflect his or her "default cognitive orientation."
3. One argument against a fault/blame orientation is that it's inaccurate; a second argument is that it's impractical. Explain each. Then respond to each argument.

NOTES

1. Jack R. Gibb, "Defensive Communication," *Journal of Communication* 11 (September 1961): 141–148.
2. Virginia Satir, "Paying Attention to Words," in Virginia Satir, *Making Contact* (Berkeley, CA: Celestial Arts, 1976).

Say What? Eight Words and Phrases to Avoid in LGBT Communication

Ben Finzel

Before you strongly agree or disagree with this short essay, please work simply to understand it. I say this because this article is written by a passionate advocate, a person making a point. Some readers will agree or disagree *politically* with what he writes, and some will reject or accept what's here on *religious* grounds. I include this reading not because of its politics or religion but because of the *communication* points that the author makes.

Finzel identifies eight words or phrases that (a) are often used in communication about gay and lesbian people and relationships, and (b) can be questioned on the grounds he presents here. In other words, this is advocacy supported by reasons, which means that whether you agree or disagree with what's being advocated, it is important to seriously consider the reasons the author gives to support his claims.

The author begins with what is by now a familiar point: Words matter. The words people use embody or "leak" the ways they understand whatever is being discussed. Just as the words "and" and "next" leak how speakers understand communication, the words "lifestyle" and "sexual preference" reveal how speakers understand sexual orientation. And the point here is not simply "political correctness." The words we speak should be chosen on the basis of accuracy and civility, not just superficial conflict avoidance.

The article is brief and Finzel's arguments are clear, so I won't repeat them here. I hope what's here can prompt some useful discussions.

MAIN IDEAS

- Words embody values and exert power, so the words we use should be as well-grounded and legitimate as possible.
- At least eight questionable words and phrases play a significant role in communication about lesbian, gay, bisexual, and transgendered (LGBT) people.
- The words "lifestyle," "sexual preference," and "choose to be gay" confuse a person's inherent, likely genetic, identity with a choice.
- "Homosexual" and "alternative" embody heteronormativity by establishing straight people as "normal" and LGBT people as "different."
- "Tolerance" positions those being tolerated as "a headache or other nuisance."
- "Special rights" makes what are arguably "normal," human rights seem unfairly preferred.
- "Friend" has become a euphemism for significant other or partner.
- Readers are encouraged to add to this list and to discuss these important ideas.

Over the years, I've written several posts about language and the words media, marketers, and other communicators use to refer to members of the LGBT community or to talk about the community itself. In March of this year (2009) I wrote a post about the Census Bureau's decision to not count LGBT people and referenced a post I wanted to write about language and words to avoid in talking with, to, or about us. At long last, here is that post I first talked about almost six months ago.

I received a good deal of comment about the Census post in March, as I did for previous posts on the topic of language. I think that's because how you talk about our community is an issue that is often fraught with tension and confusion.

Retrieved June 13, 2010 from http://www.echelonmagazine.com/index.php?id=1057

There are those well-meaning people who want to be respectful and appropriate and just don't know how. There are those folks who don't realize they're being offensive in the language they use, but would likely change if the fact were pointed out to them. And there are those folks who want to be offensive because they have a specific, negative point of view about LGBT people. This post is for all of those folks, but I suspect only the folks in the first two groups will pay attention.

Why is language important? As I said back in March (and have said previously), "language matters and words have power." What you call someone has meaning, particularly when you use language that is offensive, derogatory, or even "just" dismissive. When you seek to place LGBT people into a category of "other" or "different," you make us seem "strange," "out of the ordinary," or less than equal with other, non-LGBT people.

Even seemingly innocuous words used in a negative context can be offensive. Repeated references to "the homosexual" community and people who "choose" that "lifestyle" are really just a few steps removed from the teasing and taunting that has driven young LGBT youth to suicide and caused countless numbers of people to remain closeted for fear of what others will think of them.

It's all about what you say, what you mean, and why you're saying it. It may sound difficult to understand, but it really isn't. If a word sounds wrong in a gay and lesbian communications context, for whatever reason your common sense tells you, it probably is. But **to make it easier to determine what not to say or write and why, we've developed an initial list of eight words or phrases to avoid in LGBT communications.**

Lifestyle or "the gay lifestyle"... Referring to someone's inherent characteristics as a "lifestyle" demeans that person by referring to who they are as a person as something that is only a "way" of living that they "choose" to follow rather than an immutable characteristic of their being (such as having blue eyes). Anti-gay people and organizations refer to "the gay lifestyle" in their comments about the community and use the term in outreach efforts designed to raise money for their anti-gay attacks by raising public fears about "those people." Unfortunately, media sometimes fall into the trap of using this word or phrase and marketers have been known to use it as well, even in materials designed to attract LGBT consumers to buy a certain product or service.

Sexual preference or preference—this term brings up all kinds of conversations about whether or not LGBT people "choose" to be LGBT. By inferring that we do "choose" to be gay, anti-gay people and organizations can (often subtly) imply that we're not deserving of equality because it's just our "preference" that we're LGBT and not an immutable characteristic of our being. It's a really offensive term when used in this manner, but media and marketers still make the mistake of using the term in coverage and outreach.

Choice, choose, or "choose to be gay"—this is often the word or phrase that follows usage of the term "lifestyle" or "preference." As with the latter, using this word is a signal that we "choose" to be who we are and are therefore able to "choose" to be someone else. This kind of thinking is more than just obnoxious, it's dangerous. By telling someone that it is not okay to be who they are, you tell them that they are less than human. Words do have consequences.

Homosexual—as I've written before, the term "homosexual" is often used by anti-gay people and organizations to refer to our community with an "accepted" term. In fact, the term has been so abused that its usage now seems more clinical than contemporary and it is, to most people, a way to *slyly denigrate* our community. By referring to "the homosexual community" or the "homosexual agenda," anti-gay people and organizations attempt to make LGBT people sound like some odd/strange/uncomfortable "other" that is neither good nor acceptable.

Alternative—this term is one of the most overused in the marketers' toolkit. Used to describe things as varied as music, energy, or people, it generally means "not like the other" or "not normal." While generally viewed as less offensive than other anti-gay code words such as "preference," the term "alternative" as used in LGBT communications contexts is negative and unnecessary. Yes, we are all different, but as a gay man, I'm not an "alternative" to a straight man.

Tolerance—this term is increasingly seen as antiquated as social mores change and the general population becomes more engaged and involved with LGBT people. In the past, talking or writing about "tolerance" was fine because there was so much intolerance toward LGBT people in the world (it was an improvement at least). Now, with changes in society, the idea of "tolerating" LGBT people is becoming anachronistic. LGBT people don't want to be "tolerated" (like a headache or other nuisance), we want to be accepted for who we are. And as equal members of society, we ought to be.

Special rights—this term is frequently used by anti-gay people and organizations to position LGBT advocacy for equal rights under the law as a negative, selfish attempt to secure "special rights" that LGBT people clearly do not deserve. The right to have access to a partner during medical procedures or the right to be recognized as a married couple is not "special," it's just human. Unfortunately, this term is often included in media coverage of LGBT issues, often without any challenge to its patently false nature and anti-gay connotation.

Friend—this term is often used to refer to the partner or spouse of an LGBT person in place of the term partner or spouse. In that context, it carries the unfortunate stigma of discomfort and/or lack of respect for an LGBT person's relationship. A significant part of engaging us as individuals is based on acknowledging the people in our lives, including our partners or spouses. Far from being polite, half-acknowledging someone's relationship by referring to their significant other as a "friend," is rude and disrespectful (not to mention socially awkward).

That's it: a starting point for an important conversation. This is by no means a comprehensive list, so please add your own suggestions....

REVIEW QUESTIONS

1. Summarize the argument that sexual orientation is not a choice. Summarize the argument that sexual orientation is a choice. Include in your summaries the reasoning included by professional groups who have addressed this issue, for example, the American Medical Association, Desert Stream Ministries, and the American Psychological Association. What do you conclude?
2. Define "heteronormativity" and explain this author's position on heteronormativity.
3. What is the problem, according to this author, with being "tolerant"?

PROBES

1. Given where Mr. Finzel published this, do you think he is speaking mainly to an LGBT audience or to a heterosexual audience?
2. Draft a two paragraph response to Mr. Finzel's article that contributes to the conversation he wants to promote.

What Are the Functions of Nonverbal Communication?

Steve Duck and David T. McMahan

This brief reading rounds out the discussion of verbal and nonverbal communicating by identifying five ways nonverbal cues function in everyday talk.

The first is that nonverbal cues connect with verbal ones. As the authors note, your interpretation of words and phrases is often framed by white space, tone of voice, facial expression, gestures, and other nonverbal cues. Various nonverbal cues can *repeat* what the words say, as when you nod while saying, "Yes." They can also *substitute* for verbal cues—as when someone points rather than saying, "Over there," and they can *emphasize* the words (e.g., shouting), *moderate* or temper the certainty of the verbal message, or even *contradict* the words—as with sarcasm.

Nonverbal cues also function to regulate interaction—indicate whose turn it is to talk and when someone would like to "get a word in edgewise." Duck and McMahan give several examples of how this works.

A third function is to identify specific individuals. People do this with facial hair, body ornamentations like tattoos and piercings, and clothing. People can also distinguish others' scents—the fragrance they wear, whether they've been drinking, and whether they're a smoker.

It's probably obvious to you that another function of nonverbal cues is to provide emotional information. Your attitudes and feelings toward the other person are communicated nonverbally. Rarely does someone say, "I'm excited," "I'm impressed by you," or "Your loud voice drives me up the wall." But tone of voice, averted eyes, silence, and searching for a way to escape can make these points.

The final, and often the most important, function is to establish relational meaning. "Relational meaning" consists of the conversation partners' views of themselves in relation to the other person—whether you see yourself as older or younger, more or less competent, more or less powerful, close to or distant from the other(s). Relational meaning can be broken down into How I see myself, how I see you, how I see you seeing me, and the corresponding conclusions from you. These relational definitions are most often communicated nonverbally, with eye behavior, tone of voice, facial expression, touch, pause and timing, and so forth.

When you understand how many ways nonverbal communication functions, you can understand why it's important to be aware of it and notice how it's working.

MAIN IDEAS

- It's good to understand both the *forms* of nonverbal communication and their *functions*. *Forms* include facial expression, eye behavior, tone of voice, touch, dress, space, time and timing. *Functions* are discussed here.
- Nonverbal cues almost always significantly affect how words themselves are interpreted.
- Nonverbal cues regulate interaction—tell whose turn it is to talk.
- Individuals use various nonverbal cues to identify themselves as unique.
- Emotions are communicated mainly nonverbally.
- Relationships are also defined mainly nonverbally.

Nonverbal communication (NVC), whether static or dynamic, can affect your interactions differently, even taking you back to animal natures and the biochemistry of smell or the visual functions that work for animals (Remland, 2004). Some of these messages are communication as action in the form of unintentional leakage (for example, "smell the fear"). This leakage applies to functions of NVC that communicate your inner states or feelings, as well as indicates relational messages about liking or disliking.

INTERCONNECTS WITH VERBAL COMMUNICATION

One function of nonverbal communication involves its interconnection with verbal communication. Your interpretation of a verbal message's meaning is often framed by accompanying nonverbal elements, such as tone of voice, facial expression, and gestures.

Quite often your nonverbal communication will *repeat* your verbal communication. When you send a verbal message, you often send a corresponding nonverbal message. For example, when you say hello to someone from across the room, you might wave at the same time.

Nonverbal messages can also *substitute,* or be used in place of, verbal messages. You might wave to acknowledge someone and not say anything, but you must be very careful when substituting nonverbal for verbal messages because many cultural differences exist in the meaning of such gestures.

Nonverbal communication is often used to *emphasize* or highlight the verbal message. If you have ever gone fishing and described "the one that got away" to your friends, you have no doubt used nonverbal communication to emphasize just how big that fish really was by holding your arms out wide to indicate its gargantuan length. A verbal message can also be emphasized through your tone of voice. When you tell someone a secret, for example, you may use a hushed voice to emphasize its clandestine nature.

When nonverbal communication is used to *moderate* verbal communication, it essentially tempers the certainty of a verbal message. For instance, a doubtful tone of voice and the slight scrunching of your face and shoulders could indicate uncertainty. If your supervisor did this while saying, "I may be able to give you a raise this year," you would probably not anticipate an increase in pay. By moderating the verbal message nonverbally, your boss is letting you know there is uncertainty in that statement.

Your nonverbal communication can also *contradict* your verbal communication—sometimes intentionally, such as when you are being sarcastic. Contradiction may occur unintentionally as well—for instance, when someone charges into a room, slams the door, sits down on the couch in a huff, and, when you ask what is wrong, says, "Oh, nothing." Contradiction is not always this obvious, but even when it is more subtle, you are generally skilled at detecting it—especially when you share a close, personal relationship with the speaker. In situations of contradiction, you will be more likely to believe the person's nonverbal over verbal communication, because, as we discussed earlier, nonverbal communication is less subject to your control than is verbal communication.

REGULATES INTERACTIONS

Another function of nonverbal communication is to help regulate your interactions. Nonverbal communication informs you how you should behave and conveys how you want others to behave. Used to determine whether you should actually engage in interactions with another person, nonverbal communication helps you know when to send and when to receive verbal messages.

Regulators are nonverbal actions that indicate to others how you want them to behave or what you want them to do. A classic regulator occurs at the end of most college classes: Students begin closing their books and gathering their belongings to signal to the instructor that it is time to end class. Other regulators include shivering when you want someone to close the window or turn up the heat, a look of frustration or confusion when you need help with a problem, and a closed-off posture (arms folded, legs crossed) when you want to be left alone.

Nonverbal communication is often used to determine whether you will actually engage in conversation. If one of your friends walks past you at a rapid pace with an intense look on his or her face, it may be an indication that he or she is in a hurry or not in the mood to talk. In this case, you might avoid interacting with your friend at this time. If someone looks frustrated or confused, however, you may decide to interact with him or her because the nonverbal behavior signals a need for help.

Nonverbal communication also serves to *punctuate* how you talk to other people; it starts and ends interactions and keeps them flowing. Specifically, nonverbal communication creates a framework within which interaction happens in proper sequence. Most of the time it is perfectly effortless and unconscious, but you must *act* to get in and out of conversations: For example, you must "catch the server's eye" to start ordering in a restaurant.

You follow elaborate nonverbal rules to begin and to break off interactions. Consider what happens when you see someone walking toward you in the distance and wish to engage in conversation. Kendon and Ferber (1973) identified five basic stages in such a greeting ritual: *Sighting and recognition* occurs when you and another person first see each other. You use *distant salutation* to say hello with a wave, a flash of recognition, a smile, or a nod of acknowledgment. You may end the encounter here, but if you wish to have a conversation, you continue the greeting ritual by *lowering your head and averting your gaze (to avoid staring)* as you approach the other person, which breaks off your visual connection while you get close enough to talk and be heard. Then, in the fourth stage, *close salutation,* you most likely engage in some type of physical contact, such as a handshake, a kiss, or a hug, which brings you too close for a comfortable conversation. The fifth and final stage of greeting, therefore, involves *backing off* (e.g., taking a step back, turning to the side) to create a slightly larger space, the actual size of which is dictated by the type of relationship you share with the other person.

Nonverbal communication is also used to signal the end to an interaction. You may, for example, stop talking, start to edge away, or show other signs of departure, such as looking away from the other person more often or checking your watch. You might also step a little farther back or turn to the side.

IDENTIFIES OTHERS

Nonverbal communication also functions to identify specific individuals. Just as dogs know each other individually by smell, humans use basic olfactory recognition but can also recognize one another specifically from facial appearance. You also use such additional physical cues as muscles, beards, skin color, breasts, and the whiteness of a person's hair to identify him or her as a particular sex, age, race, or athletic ability.

Clothing, also an identifying signal, can be used to identify someone's sex (men rarely wear dresses), personality (whether they wear loud colors, sedate business attire, or punk clothing), favorite sports team, and job (police, military, security). Clothing can also identify changes in people, such as whether they have a special role today (prom outfits, wedding wear, gardening clothes), or indicate specific differences about their lives (casual Friday).

People can also distinguish others' scents: What perfume or cologne do they wear? Do they smoke? Are they drinkers? You may not comment on these kinds of clues because they are very often noticed with lower levels of awareness. If your physician smells of alcohol, however, you may well identify him or her as professionally incompetent to deal with your health concerns.

TRANSMITS EMOTIONAL INFORMATION

An additional function of nonverbal communication is to convey emotional information. When you are angry, you scowl; when you are in love, you look gooey; when you feel happy, you smile. Nonverbal communication actually allows you to convey three different kinds of emotional information.

First, NVC conveys your *attitudes about the other person* in an interaction. If your facial expression conveys anxiety, viewers assume you are frightened. If your face looks relaxed and warm, viewers assume you are comfortable. If you care about what your professor has to say, you fall silent when a lecture begins; talking in class (professors' biggest complaint about students) makes it difficult for people to hear and shows lack of respect.

Second, NVC conveys your *attitudes toward the situation.* For example, moving about while talking conveys a message of anxiety. Police officers often see fidgeting and an inability to maintain eye contact as indicators of a person's guilt.

Third, NVC conveys information about your *attitude toward yourself.* If a person is arrogant, confident, or low in self-esteem, it is expressed through nonverbal behaviors. An arrogant man may not express verbally how wonderful he sees himself, but you can tell he holds himself in high regard through his nonverbal actions, such as facial expression, tone of voice, eye contact, and body posture. If someone stands up to her full height and faces you directly, you might assume that she is confident. Conversely, if she slouches and stares at the ground, you might assume that she is shy, diffident, and insecure.

ESTABLISHES RELATIONAL MEANING
AND UNDERSTANDING

Your relationships with others guide and inform your everyday communication, and your everyday communication develops these relationships. Nonverbal communication not only regulates social interaction, it also acts as a silent *relational* regulator. Regulation of interactions serves to regulate engagement, politeness, coordination of action, and sense of pleasure in the interaction—all of which are ultimately relational in effect. The appearance of others enables you to distinguish and make judgments about them, as well as forms the basis of relational attraction. In fact, you often are attracted to people with facial and bodily features very similar to your own.

Relational meaning and understanding can be gained from all of the aforementioned functions of nonverbal communication, especially the expression of emotional information, and you will see more examples as we next work through the types of NVC. When we write about the function of nonverbal communication in the establishment of relational meaning and understanding, think specifically about how it establishes rapport, connection, engagement, responsiveness, liking, and power.

REVIEW QUESTIONS

1. Explain the difference between a nonverbal cue *emphasizing* words and *moderating* what the words say.
2. What does it mean to say that nonverbal cues can "punctuate" how you talk to other people?
3. Briefly identify examples of what Kendon and Ferber called the five basic stages of a common greeting ritual.
4. What are some nonverbal ways you *identify* yourself—dress, facial hair, and so forth.
5. In addition to the words, what nonverbal cues do you use to say, "I love you"?

PROBES

1. Which of these five functions do you believe is most important in interpersonal communication? Which creates the most problems in your communication life?
2. The authors say that nonverbal cues "transmit" or "convey" emotional information. Do you think this is accurate—is emotional information communicated by one person? Or is emotional information collaboratively constructed in most conversations?

REFERENCES

Kendon, A., & Ferber, A. (1973). A description of some human greetings. In R. P. Michael & J. H. Crook (Eds.), *Comparative ecology and behavior of primates* (pp. 591–668). New York: Academic Press.

Remland, M. S. (2004). *Nonverbal communication in everyday life* (2nd ed.). New York: Houghton Mifflin.

PART TWO

Making Meaning Together

"INHALING" AND "EXHALING"

As I noted in the Preface, the two chapters that make up Part Two are organized with the help of a breathing metaphor. At the most basic level, I use the terms *inhaling* and *exhaling* to begin to break down or organize the continuous, changing, multidimensional, often confusing process called "communicating." One commonsense, close-to-experience way to organize this overall process is to divide it up into what people take in (inhaling) and what they give out (exhaling).

You can figure out my second and most important reason for choosing this metaphor if you try to inhale without exhaling, or vice versa. These labels allow me to separate communication into two of its important parts while still emphasizing that the parts happen together. As I noted in Chapter 2, communicators are always receiving and sending at the same time. *While we're talking,* we're noticing how people are responding, and *while we're listening,* we're giving off mixed and primarily nonverbal cues.

A third reason I'm using this metaphor is that it is organic. Breathing is a part of living for most of the organisms in the world. It's vital for humans and other animals, of course, but you can also think of the fish's intake and output of water and even the plant's intake of water and output of oxygen as forms of breathing.

The fourth reason is that this metaphor organizes breathing into a process that begins with input. If somebody asks, "What are the two parts of the breathing process?" the common answer is "inhaling and exhaling," not "exhaling and inhaling." So the metaphor allows me to focus *first* on perception and listening. This reverses the historical tendency to begin one's efforts to improve communication by focusing on what one *says*. I'm convinced that listening is the often neglected but crucially important half of the listening-speaking pair, and my metaphor makes it easier to redress some of this imbalance.

No metaphor is perfect, of course, and one problem with this one is that inhaling and exhaling happen *sequentially,* while perceiving and talking take place *simultaneously.* In this sense, communication is even more dynamic than my metaphor suggests.

Chapter 5 discusses how we "take in" information and impressions about others—how we perceive individuals, relationships, and social events, and how we listen. It begins with two readings about person perception, one that reviews the process and another that discusses stereotyping. Next are two readings that focus on listening. Then Chapter 6 covers what we "give out" or "exhale." Here, two readings discuss being open, expressing thoughts and feelings, practicing self-disclosure, and speaking for yourself.

As you read these materials, remember that each of these chapters some-what artificially emphasizes one part of a process that always happens as a whole—just like the inhaling and exhaling of normal breathing. As the title of Part Two indicates, people make meaning *together,* and they do it by "inhaling" and "exhaling" *together.*

CHAPTER 5

Inhaling: Perceiving and Listening

Inhaling: Perception

John Stewart, Karen E. Zediker, and Saskia Witteborn

These next pages describe the basic processes humans use to perceive anything, as well as some of the special processes we use to perceive people. It also alerts you to five practical perception problems that can distort your communicating. The reading comes from an interpersonal communication text I wrote with two colleagues.

Our first point is that people make sense out of what we encounter by engaging three fundamental perception processes: selecting, organizing, and inferring. We do not just "soak up sense data"; rather, we actively interpret everything that we encounter, and we do this with these three moves. First, we select uses to attend to or prioritize, based not only on what's available but also on past judgments, expectations, and a variety of cultural cues. Second, we organize the cues we've selected into a whole that makes sense. And finally, we go beyond the cues to infer what they mean.

Perceptual differences can occur anywhere along this line, and so can perceptual problems. Some evidence indicates that men and women select, organize, and infer differently, as do people with different native languages.

The mental patterns that help us organize what we perceive are called *cognitive schemata*. Two kinds of schemata that especially affect communication are person prototypes and scripts. The former is a generalized representation of a "type" of person—a professor, parent, physician, or priest, for example. Stereotypes are rigid person prototypes. Scripts are generalized sequences of action—how you behave in a restaurant, for example, or how you ask someone out.

The reading also explains three processes that influence our inference making, impression formation, attribution, and stereotyping. We form impressions, in part, using implicit personality theories that shape the ways we perceive people. Attributions are explanations of other people's behavior that are based on either internal or external factors. And stereotyping is a natural process, that, while unavoidable, needs to be closely monitored.

The final section briefly discusses five perception processes that can affect where your communication is on the impersonal–interpersonal scale: fast thinking, overload avoidance, the entertainment factor, snap judgments, and attributional errors. When you've finished this reading, you should have a good general understanding of how your perception processes can affect your interpersonal communicating.

MAIN IDEAS

- Perception—of things and of people—is an active, not a passive process.
- The first active part is selection; persons attend to some available cues and not to others.
- Selection is affected by properties of the cues, for example, loudness, and by emotions and evaluations of the perceiver.

- A second active part is organizing; people arrange cues into meaningful patterns.
- Inferring is the third active part of perception; people go beyond sensory cues to assign significance and meaning to what they perceive.
- Inferences are affected by cultural assumptions, including gender patterns.
- Cognitive schemata are mental guidelines that help us process incoming cues.
- Person prototypes are schemata that provide general representations for types of persons.
- Scripts are schemata that identify sequences of actions.
- Inferences are affected by the process of impression formation—integrating observations into an overall "picture" of a person.
- Inferences are also affected by attributions, which assign a cause to a behavior. Attributions can contribute to fault/blame problems.
- Stereotyping also affects how people make inferences.
- Five perception difficulties can especially affect your interpersonal communication: fast thinking, avoiding overload, the entertainment factor, snap judgments, and attributional errors.

PREVIEW

Remember that we're using the metaphor of inhaling and exhaling to explain the receptive and expressive parts of communication.... The first point to remember is that there's much more to inhaling than the passive reception of incoming messages. Inhaling combines the two active, interpretive processes of perceiving and listening....

People make sense out of the world through their perceptual experience, and experience is affected by culture, membership in various social groups, and in fact, by every relationship a person has. Your perceptions influence and contribute to the inhaling process in profound ways. You select sensory cues, organize them mentally, and make inferences about them. One of the reasons why people select, organize, and make inferences is that each of us lives in a complex world that we have to make sense of. Three kinds of inference-making processes that people use to make sense of the world and the people in it are stereotyping, attribution, and impression formation.

PERCEPTION: AN INTERPRETIVE PROCESS

Perception can be defined as a social and cognitive process in which people assign meaning to sensory cues. People often assume that the "truth" of things exists out there somewhere in what they are seeing, hearing, touching, tasting, and smelling. For example, you know the old saying "Seeing is believing." It is tempting to think that your eyes give you a perfect picture of what is happening in your own portion of "reality." But perception takes a picture through a lens, not through a window.

Perception is shaped by the perceiving person's experience and understanding of his or her place in the world. If perception were simply a matter of accurately processing sensory cues, you would expect everybody to perceive in a fairly similar way. However, this is not how perception works; as we said, it's an active process. When we make this point, we also mean that perception is, to a considerable extent, self-initiated and voluntary, a function of each person's response choices. You are not forced to interpret cues in a certain way; you have considerable control over your perceptual processes, especially as you become come aware of them.

Perception occurs through three basic subprocesses: selection, organization, and inference making. But before these three can begin, a person has to receive information through the senses—touch, taste, smell, hearing, and sight. This information is received in the form of sensory data, or cues. A cue is the smallest perceivable "bit" of information. As soon as your outermost sensory neurons receive a cue, you begin selecting, organizing, and inferring from this information. It isn't possible to perceive anything without selecting, organizing, and inferring. So, from the start, perception is an *interpretive process*. The following brief exercise will show you that interpretation is a large part of perceiving things in the environment.

Selecting, Organizing, and Inferring

The three subprocesses of perception do not occur in any distinct, step-by-step sequence. They happen simultaneously as three inseparable events. Selection generally refers to how you pay attention to sensory cues. Organization describes the ways you construct and impose patterns or structure onto the stream of sensory cues you receive. Inferring is a label for the way you "go beyond" or interpret the cues that your senses select and organize.

Selecting   You first decide at some level of consciousness which cues to pay attention to. Sometimes it seems that you don't have a choice about whether or not to attend to certain cues—for example, a siren, a sudden bright light out of the dark, a loud scream, or a sharp pain. But most of the time people exercise a fair amount of choice about the cues they perceive.

Selection is operating when you're rushed for time in an airport looking for the ticket counter of your airline and you don't notice many details about the people around you. Your attention is focused on signs identifying airlines and listing arrivals or departures. Or, when looking for new shoes in a shopping mall, you selectively pay attention to store signs and window displays that relate to your task and typically ignore the bed and bath shop and the espresso stand. But if you suddenly become hungry, you shift your attention to anything that smells or looks like food. You can be at a noisy party and have trouble hearing another person standing less than 2 feet away, but magically overhear your name mentioned by two people gossiping at some distance. And if you are concentrating on reading this book right now, you are probably not aware

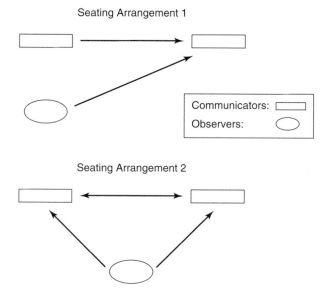

FIGURE 5–1   Diagram of Conversational Partners

of the pressure of the chair against your body or noises from the next room until reading this sentence shifts your attention to these cues.

When communicating with others, people also perceive selectively. Some research indicates that people tend to focus on whatever or whomever is easiest to attend to—the closest person, the person with the loudest voice, the person we can see most easily. For example, in a series of studies, two researchers asked subjects to observe conversations between two people and varied the seating positions of the observers (see Figure 5–1). Some observers looked directly at one of the two conversation partners but could see only the back and side of the other. When these observers were asked to rate the conversational partners on a number of scales, they found they rated the person they faced as more responsible for the topic and tone of the conversation. The observers who could see both participants equally well rated them during the same period of time as equally responsible for the tone and topics of conversation. The researchers concluded that where your attention is directed influences what you perceive. Your selective perceptions affect your judgments about the people involved (Maltz & Borker, 1982).

But the process of selection is not this simple. What you attend to is not just a response to a property of some cue—the loudest, brightest, or most visually direct. You also select cues about people based on your past judgments of them. So, if you are angry with your partner, you are far more likely to perceive all sorts of little irritating habits, just as you overlook or don't see negative characteristics in someone you love. The bottom line is that you cannot perceive all the sensory cues that are available to you. Perception is selective, and what we choose to notice affects how we respond to both things and people.

Organizing   Another way people actively participate in perception is by organizing the cues they select. You literally cannot help applying structure and stability to your world of sensations. Whenever you look at something that is vague
or ambiguous in shape or size or color, for example, you continue to focus on it
until you recognize what it is. What you are doing is arranging and rearranging
the information you have according to a series of possible patterns or forms until
the information finally makes sense to you, and you have an "Oh, so that's what
it is!" experience.

You can have this experience of perceiving patterns or structures whenever
you listen to music, too. How do you recognize your favorite songs? Research
shows that people hear something much more than note-to-note; they tend to focus on the organized *pattern* of the sounds—the melody (Fiske & Shelley, 1984). If
you've ever played the game Name That Tune, you have had the experience of suddenly recognizing not individual notes but the pattern that exists among the notes.

Once you apply a particular structure to your experience, you stabilize this
perceptual version. For example, if you've been humming a particular tune for
days, it's hard to think of how other songs sound, especially if they have somewhat similar patterns. The organization of perceptions helps you to make sense
out of whatever is occurring. You can apply the patterns or structures to very
small sensory events. Or you can develop patterns that characterize people you
know. Later on in this [essay], we'll talk about how these more complex patterns
are formed through stereotyping, the process of attribution, and impression formation. But for now, we just want to emphasize how important the way people
organize cues is to the entire process of perception and the unavoidable effects
this step has on your communication.

Inferring   To infer is to conclude, judge, or go beyond evidence. So in the
perception process, inferring means going beyond sensory cues to your own
interpretations. The inferences or judgments you make depend on the cues you
select and the ways you organize them in relation to your own assumptions,
expectations, and goals.

It might sound like inference making is a risky or even foolish process
because it means that you go beyond the "hard facts." In some ways it is dangerous, but it's also impossible not to do it. Just like selecting and organizing,
inferring is hard-wired into human sense making.... *Meaning* is a label for the
outcome of selecting, organizing, and inferring.

Our interpretations of other people and events depend on our worldviews,
past experiences, goals in life, and expectations, all of which differ from culture
to culture. Cultures are marked by the ways they answer such basic questions
as the following:

- What is the value of the individual versus the value of the group?
- How do people advance in life, by heritage or by achievement?
- How should society be organized?
- Is the nature of a human being good or evil?

- How do humans relate to each other?
- Where does meaning lie, explicitly in the language or hidden in the context? (Hall, 2002; Kluckhorn & Strodtbeck, 1961)

Many more elements can constitute a worldview of a culture, and the answers to each question lie on a continuum. In other words, worldviews are not simple; they are complex. You can value individualism, for example, when you want to make your own decisions about going to college. But you can value collectivism and the group when it comes to supporting your parents in their old age.

Worldviews influence responses to these questions and affect how people interpret cues. Saskia, for instance, was confused when she arrived on the West Coast of the United States and people smiled at her, greeted her in the streets, and talked with her on the bus. She was raised to be respectful and friendly to strangers but at the same time maintains her privacy and does not impose herself on people she does not know. It made her a little uncomfortable at first because she didn't know how to interpret certain cues she got from strangers. Was the man in the supermarket hitting on her when he smiled and asked how her day was going? Or was it just friendliness? When Saskia's parents came from Germany to visit her, her dad was impressed with "how many people she knew." He interpreted the greetings in the streets and the small talk of the checkers in the supermarket as meaning "They must know her, otherwise they wouldn't be talking to her." He was very surprised when he found out that they were strangers to Saskia. This example shows the impact of Saskia's family's worldview on their interpretations of communicative interactions.

But perceptual differences don't occur just between different ethnic or national groups—they are also gender specific. According to Malz and Borker (1982), women and men in North America interpret the same actions in conversation very differently. For example, men appear to perceive head nodding while listening as a way of indicating *agreement* with the speaker, whereas women tend to perceive head nodding as a way of signaling *that they are listening* to the speaker. For women, this is another way of indicating "I'm with you. Keep going." This difference may be at the root of a common complaint some women have about some men: "He never listens to me" (because he doesn't signal listening with head nodding) or "He's always so rational. Sometimes I just want emotional support." At the same time, frequent use of head nodding reinforces the stereotype some men have of women as unreliable because "You're always agreeing with me no matter what I say."

Socialization and biology play a role in how men and women communicate, especially when it comes to communicating emotions (Konner, 2002). Researchers say that male and female brains differ in terms of sex differences in a frontal-lobe region that is responsible for emotional reasoning. They also found that the corpus callosum, which is a mass of fibers connecting the two halves of the brain, may be larger in women's than in men's brains. If this is so, then the larger fiber mass in women's brains might help integrate the language and emotional centers better in females brains, which means that women can verbalize feelings more than men. This does not mean that they automatically do. Socialization plays another major role in how people communicate....

Now that we have explained the basic subprocesses of perception, we want to talk more about mental guidelines, or *cognitive schemata*, that help us to organize incoming information. Then we'll talk about the processes that you engage in when you make interpretations of people or things around you.

COGNITIVE SCHEMATA

In order to recognize persons and objects around us, we need mental guidelines that help us process incoming cues. These mental guidelines are called *cognitive schemata* (in the singular it's *cognitive schema*). Schemata help us to organize incoming cues about people, animals, behaviors, and objects.

Almost 80 years ago, the originator of schema theory made the point that all remembering is constructive. Rather than storing all stimuli in memory, the brain uses schemata to provide an impression of the whole. In his experiments, Bartlett (1932) used a version of the child's game Telephone, in which a message is passed along a chain of people and the story changes with each retelling. In some experiments he asked British college students to read a story from another culture, put it aside, reproduce it, and pass it on to other students. Bartlett noticed that the stories changed in systematic ways as they were passed along. This led him to suggest that in acquiring new information, humans must assimilate the new material to existing concepts or schemas. People change new information to fit their existing concepts by organizing it into previously existing mental structures. In this process, details are lost, and the knowledge fits the interpretive frames of the individual (Mayer, 1992, 230).

This explanation about how people organize new information makes sense. Saskia participated in a class where the professor played the telephone game. The students had to remember a story that included a variety of blue dragons, monks, and story characters from Asian cultures. In the end, the monks became "the dudes," the princess became a cheerleader, and the head monk a pharmacist. This does not mean that the students were careless or stupid. It means that they adapted the information to stories they had heard before. The students also ended their version of the story with "and they lived happily ever after," which did not occur in the original story but which is an ending that's very common in fairy tales that are written [in] or translated into English.

Overall, people have schemata for people, relationships, actions, and even emotions. Let's talk a little bit more about two types of these schemata: person prototypes and scripts.

Person Prototypes

A person prototype is a generalized representation of certain types of persons. It is usually based on experience and repeated personal interactions with people. Just pause and think for a moment about what *mental image* comes to your mind when you think of student, professor, lawyer, gamer, or car salesperson. Person proto-types contain information about traits and verbal and nonverbal behaviors that you believe characterize a certain type of person. What are the traits and behaviors that you associate with a professor? How about a lawyer? How about a cheerleader? And how about a homeless person? Overall, prototypes help us to orient ourselves in the world. They can help us to meet people who we think we might feel comfort-able with and can also help us to avoid dangerous situations. But they can also be misleading and can make us stereotype people. Why? Because they omit specific features. If you communicate based only on your person schemata, you will stay on the impersonal side of the communication scale described in Chapter 2.

Scripts

Scripts, which are structures dealing with certain sequences of action, are another type of cognitive schema. We all have a repertoire of scripts in our heads. They are usually based on experience and help us to know what happens next. Examples of scripts are riding the bus, greeting another person, attending a wedding, or going to a restaurant. Consider the "restaurant script" (Abelson, 1981). When people enter a restaurant, they know the different steps to go through to accomplish the goal of satisfying their hunger, having good conver-sation over a good meal, or both. This knowledge of the different steps helps us go into an almost automatic action mode so that we don't have to make decisions every single moment. So, imagine you go to a restaurant. What do you do? We guess that you would do the following in the following order: enter, be seated, order, eat, pay, tip 10 to 20 percent of the bill, and exit.

In addition, person prototypes help you to orient yourself in your restau-rant environment. Near the entrance, there will usually be a person who says, "How many?" You know that this must be a host or manager. When a person comes to your table and asks, "Are you ready to order?" wearing a certain outfit—for instance, a T-shirt with the name of the restaurant on it—you know that he or she is your server (person prototype). You also know what to expect from a server and how you are supposed to behave. You know, for instance, that the server is not supposed to yell at you, sit at your table, or spill your soda on you. The server also knows that the customer (you) is not supposed to come into the kitchen or sit on the floor when eating.

Also remember that scripts can differ in different cultures. One reason that people sometimes feel insecure when they travel is that they are not familiar with certain scripts. When Saskia is in Germany, her restaurant script looks like the following: enter the restaurant, sit down, order food and drink, eat, sit for a while after eating, call the waiter to bring the check, pay the check, leave a tip that is fair, and exit. You see that there are many similarities between the U.S. and German restaurant scripts. However, there are also differences: calling the waiter to bring the check, not leaving the money on the table, and tipping con-ventions. In Germany, the server will usually leave you alone for a while after you have dined, and it is considered rude to take away your plates immediately.

In many European countries, clearing the table right after people have eaten and putting the check on the table is interpreted as rushing the customer. So, often you have to call the waiter or waitress to bring the check. Usually you pay directly and don't leave money on the table.

Tipping conventions in U.S. and German restaurant scripts also differ. In Germany, you round up a small bill to the next dollar or, when the bill is over 10 euros, you give 10 percent or so. In the United States the standard expectation is that the tip will be around 15 percent of the bill. Knowledge about different cultural scripts for certain situations makes you a more competent communicator and can also help you to avoid embarrassment or confusion.

Person prototypes and *scripts* influence how people *organize* sensory cues. In addition, there are three processes that influence how people make *interpretations*. These processes are *impression formation, attribution,* and *stereotyping*.

COGNITIVE PROCESSES

Impression Formation

Impression formation is the complex process of integrating or synthesizing a variety of sometimes contradictory observations into a coherent overall "picture" of a person. The impression that you form is basically a combination of traits that are similar or fit together for you. When you connect a series of related interpretations about someone's behavior, you begin to develop what's called an *implicit personality theory* about the person doing the behavior. This is simply your picture (theory) of what the person's personality "must be," based on qualities or characteristics that are implied by their behavior.

In a widely cited book about person perception, three psychologists give an excellent example of how impressions form themselves into an implicit personality theory:

> Suppose you have been watching a woman at party. A lot of other people are congregated around her and you discover that she has just had a novel published. You observe her long enough to draw some tentative conclusions about her: Some of these result from attribution work; she is smart, ambitious, but particularly hard-working—conclusions you are able to draw because few people write novels and because you discover that this is her second novel and fourth published book.... You note that she is in her early 40s and reasonably attractive; her hair is a rather unnatural shade of yellow. Furthermore, she is wearing an expensive long dress. Your snap judgment is that artificial blondes who wear expensive dresses are on the frivolous side. You note that the woman is witty, and that she giggles a great deal.... Finally, you note she is consuming drinks at a rapid pace and that she has smoked several cigarettes.
>
> What have you decided? Our novelist is intelligent, ambitious, hard-working, frivolous, witty, "giggly," and nervous. Now your work really begins. How, you might ask yourself, can a person be both hard-working and frivolous? Or perhaps she is trying to create a really good impression for someone so that

her hairstyle does not so much indicate frivolousness as a concern to create a good impression.... But why would she be nervous? She's a hit, the star of the party. Maybe she is insecure (all those giggles); nervous people and people who try to create a good impression are nervous—or so you believe. Why is she insecure? (Schneider, Hastorf, & Ellsworth, 1979)

And so on. In order to give some consistency to all these observations and inferences, people work to organize the data they perceive into some coherent, stable impression. Although this impression is continually revised, it remains a global characterization of another person in which much of the original and inconsistent details get lost. So, depending on your past experience, you may conclude, for example, that the woman is very admirable but unusually nervous, a phony who's afraid of being discovered, or book smart but socially awkward.

There is now a considerable amount of communication research showing that people differ in how effectively they perceive others. For instance, researchers have discovered that stereotyping depends upon a person's mental state. If someone has high anxiety and tries to suppress stereotypic thinking, stereotyping may actually increase (Hall & Crisp, 2003). You probably have experienced this yourself. If you are traveling in a foreign country and people told you before you left to "never leave anything unattended because people steal there all the time," you may become tense and see every person around you as a potential thief.

Some people generalize and categorize more than others, and thus tend to contribute more to impersonal rather than interpersonal communication events. Their talk is *position centered* because it focuses on social roles and norms rather than the unique characteristics of individuals.

Other communicators seem better able to use the discriminatory power of perception and to note fine distinctions between one type of behavior and another. They appear to be more flexible in the perceptions they construct of others, using a higher number and more types of categories. These more sophisticated social perceivers are more likely to engage in more communication toward the right-hand end of the impersonal–interpersonal scale. These communicators are sensitive to perceptual features across a variety of different types of social situations, which makes their communication much more *person centered*. In other words, position-centered communication is nearer the left end of the continuum, and person-centered communication is nearer the right end.

Attribution

A second process of person perception is called *attribution*. When people form attributions, they devise theories or explanations about other people's behavior that provide a way of making sense out of whatever is occurring (Heider, 1958; Kelley, 1973). Often, this means assigning a cause or intention to the behavior (Kelley, 1972). For instance, a student might come late to class and the instructor might think, "That student is lazy." In the same situation a different instructor might think, "Must have been a lot of traffic today." Each of these attributions is a way for the instructor to explain or make sense of the student's behavior. The attributions also provide the instructor with some sense that he or she can predict how the student will behave in the future. When you can devise explanations for how people behave and predictions of their future behavior, you can operate with much more certainty about what is happening in a particular situation.

Notice how one of the two causes or reasons the instructor assigned to the student's behavior is anchored in this student's personality ("lazy") and the other is anchored in external factors ("traffic"). These are the response options people commonly select from: You attribute the cause of the behavior either to a character trait, mood, or disposition (*internal factors*) or to the situation (*external factors*), or to both (Heider, 1985; Rotter, 1966). When your attributions emphasize internal factors, you're more likely to interpret what happened as the person's fault or responsibility. When someone else makes mistakes, people tend to attribute the behavior to internal causes. So, for instance, imagine you're giving a presentation. You have worked hard for weeks and are very nervous. A friend has promised to come and give you mental and emotional support during the presentation. You start your presentation and realize that your friend is not there. He walks in 10 minutes late, which makes you think, "I'm not worth his time. My buddy let me down." You attribute his behavior to internal causes instead of wondering whether he got stuck in traffic.

By contrast, when people make mistakes themselves, they tend to attribute their behavior to external causes. So, when you come late to class, you might automatically offer an excuse that attributes your being late to external causes, such as "The bus didn't show up" or "My roommate had a panic attack this morning and I had to drive him to the hospital." The reason why people attribute personal mistakes to external causes is to save face and keep themselves from becoming vulnerable.

If you remember what we said about fault and blame, you'll probably get a sense of why attributions can be dangerous. Although attributions about others can help guide understanding, they also often interfere with your ability to see alternative reasons for why people behave the way they do. For instance, one researcher (Manusov, 1990) studied what happens when couples playing the game Trivial Pursuit have to make sense of their partner's obviously positive or negative nonverbal behavior. One member of each couple was recruited to act positively at one point in the game and to act negatively at another point. The study showed that couples who were happy with their relationship and each other tended to attribute positive behavior to internal causes in their partners. In contrast, unhappy couples made more external attributions. So, in this study, a person's overall attitude toward his or her partner significantly affected the attributions made about the partner's nonverbal behavior.

Stereotyping

A stereotype is defined in the *Oxford English Dictionary* (2003) as a "preconceived and oversimplified idea of the characteristics which typify a person, situation, etc.; an attitude based on such a preconception. Also, a person who appears to conform closely to the idea of a type." In other words, a stereotype is a category that people apply to other people, often based on their group membership. These categories can include gender, ethnic or national, religious, and vocational groups. Overall, stereotypes are a way that people make sense of the world and orient themselves to the people around them.

Two important dimensions of stereotypes are the following: (1) They can be positive or negative and (2) they can vary in intensity. Positive stereotypes are categorizations that evoke favorable associations, such as "Asians are good at math," "Chinese are polite," "African women are beautiful," or "African Americans are athletic." Negative stereotypes are unfavorable categorizations of a whole group of people—for example, "East Coasters are rude," "Arabs are terrorists," or "football players are lazy students." In addition to direction, stereotypes can also vary in intensity—the strength with which the stereotype is maintained. Families and peer groups affect the intensity of most people's stereotypes (Tan et al., 2001). If you continually heard when you were growing up that "foreigners" are bad because they take jobs away from native-born citizens, you are likely to believe it and may even be suspicious of foreigners.

You've undoubtedly been told many times that stereotyping is dangerous and stereotypes are bad. In many ways, this is true. Racism and sexism continue, to a considerable degree, because of stereotypes. Communication based on stereotyped perceptions of people will fall on the impersonal side of the impersonal–interpersonal continuum.

On the other hand, some stereotyping is unavoidable, and in some cases it can be helpful. When you're walking alone at night in a city, it can be legitimate and helpful to stereotype the person matching your route and your pace as a threat. The natural human tendency to categorize influences all perceptions, so it is impossible to stop stereotyping completely. You just have to be careful not to let your stereotypes become too rigid. You can do that by being aware that people sometimes put other people into boxes and by trying to see the person with his or her individual characteristics behind the stereotype.

In addition, researchers have found that communication is not always influenced by stereotypes as much as it is affected by the interaction itself (Manusov & Hedge, 1993; Manusov, Winchatz, & Manning, 1997). For instance, researchers asked how neutral, positive, and negative stereotypes about people from other cultures affect the ways in which people communicate and the judgments they make about their conversation partners. So far, they've found that stereotype-based expectancies do affect people's evaluations of their conversation partners from other cultures, but they also found that what happens during the actual conversation is more important than the stereotype. People base their judgments of others more on facial pleasantness, fluency in conversation, relaxed posture, and similar vocal cues than on the stereotypes that they bring to the interaction (Manusov, Winchatz, & Manning, 1997). This evidence indicates that even in cross-cultural conversations, where you'd think stereotypes would be most influential, these generalizations don't completely control how people respond.

PRACTICAL PERCEPTION PROBLEMS

As part of our continuing effort to blend theory and practice, we want to end this [essay] with a description of five specific difficulties that you might encounter in your perception processes. Each grows out of the complexity and culture dependence of the perception process. Each can also affect where your communication is on the impersonal–interpersonal scale.

Fast Thinking

One problem people have with the selection part of perception is that, when listening to someone, we have a great deal of spare time. In a normal conversation, native English speakers tend to speak from 115 to 130 words per minute. But normal thinking speed—if it can be quantified this way—exceeds 500 words per minute. This means that people listening to speech have a lot of extra time to get perceptually sidetracked by other cues or by their own thoughts. You might think of this perception problem as the challenge of what to do with this free time. Since it's harder to concentrate on another person's ideas than it is to focus on our own, we often take the easy way out and spend our free time thinking about our own concerns. The listening skills we describe in the next chapter clarify what else might be done with this free time.

Avoiding Overload

A second reason people sometimes tune out is to preserve some control over their environment. We are constantly bombarded with countless messages from family members, supervisors, teachers, friends, acquaintances, strangers, and the media, and if we tried to pay attention to it all, we would quickly go crazy. We can't turn off the perceptual process entirely, so we have to make decisions about the things we will attend to and the things we will let go. So sometimes we tune out to preserve our physical and emotional health. The trick is not to let the real potential of information overload force you into the habit of tuning out.

The Entertainment Factor

A third reason people sometimes fail to pay attention is that they're used to getting information in entertaining packages. Adults who grew up spending a great deal of time watching television are especially prone to expect ideas and information to come in attractive, lively, and stimulating packages with economical sound bites. If you doubt the influence of this factor, notice the way television packages the news and the way advertisers on radio, television, and in magazines present their products. Awareness of this expectation can go a long way toward reducing its impact on your perception.

In addition to these three selection problems, there are at least two types of problems that can interfere with the kind of person perception that promotes interpersonal communicating.

Snap Judgments

Snap judgments are inferences that are "usually rather immediate and do not involve complex cognitive processes" (Schneider, Hastorf, & Ellsworth, 1979, 20). They are the most limited kind of stereotype people make about others. Snap judgments are usually based on the physical characteristics of the other person and a very limited set of observations of their behavior. In the earlier description of the novelist at the cocktail party, the snap judgment is that "artificial blondes who wear expensive dresses are on the frivolous side." Snap judgments result when people evaluate whether the person they're perceiving is old or young, male or female, physically able or disabled, richly or poorly dressed, from a particular culture, and under- or overweight. Occasionally a snap judgment can be useful, such as when you're aggressively approached by a telemarketer as you're sitting down for dinner. But most of the time snap judgments are liable to distort your understanding of what the person is saying.

Attributional Errors

Earlier we explained that people make attributions to help make sense out of someone else's behavior by assigning a cause or intention to their actions. These causes or reasons for behavior get associated with the other's personality (internal factors) or something in the situation (external factors). These often lead to oversimplified conclusions about fault and blame, which ... interfere with our ability to see communication as a collaborative process. One form of distortion happens when people unequally balance internal and external factors and commit what's called the *fundamental attribution error* and the *ultimate attribution error*.

The fundamental attribution error is the mistaken tendency people have to attribute others' behaviors to internal, rather than external, causes. The ultimate attribution error assumes that, as we mentioned, people's negative behavior is caused by internal factors and that their positive behavior is caused by external factors. This means that there is a tendency to underestimate the impact of situational factors in producing another's behavior and to overestimate the role of personality factors (Kelley, 1972).

For instance, the person evaluating her *own* tendency to drive over the speed limit or be late for an appointment would be likely to attribute her actions to the situation—she is just "keeping up with traffic" or "unavoidably delayed by traffic signals and detours." But the fundamental attribution error happens when she fails to give others the benefit of this explanation and instead accounts for *their* speeding and lateness as "irresponsibility" or "carelessness."

One example of the ultimate attribution error concerns perceptions of obesity. Researchers have concluded that many people attribute obesity in other people to internal, controllable causes. Thus, those who are significantly overweight are often regarded as having no self-control and are therefore subject to blame and ridicule (Rush, 1998). Obese people are also usually viewed as unattractive, sad, depressed, and unlikable (Hiller, 1981; Triplett, 2003). Many people who think that obesity is the fault of the individual fall into the trap of the ultimate attribution error: They assign what is perceived to be negative behavior to internal personality characteristics. They also commit this error when they conclude that weight loss is caused by a good diet and the help of other people instead of asking themselves whether the weight loss also has something to do with the strong will of the person. It can help to avoid the fundamental attribution error by remembering that others' actions—just like our own—are responses to both internal and external factors.

SUMMARY

Our main point about perception is that the ways people select, organize, and make inferences about others affect the ways people communicate. Person perception by its very nature forms the basis of the "reality" you share with others every time you make contact with them. By becoming aware of the ways you perceive others, you can learn to generalize less, that is, to be more sensitive to the unique and distinctive features others make available to you as you communicate with them. Increasing your perceptual sensitivity is a major step in making the inhaling part of your communicating more effective.

Up until now, though, we've been treating the parts of perception that are considered cognitive or mental processes as occurring largely in your head. If we stayed with just this simple a picture, we would be seriously misrepresenting the way perception works. Why? Because, as we said before, listening is where the rubber of perception meets the road of communication. Listening is the concrete manifestation-in-communication of all the perceptual processes we have discussed in this chapter. When you communicate, your listening enables you to interpret (select, organize, and make inferences about) what your conversation partners are saying and doing. These perceptions change as you collaboratively build meaning....

REVIEW QUESTIONS

1. Explain what it means to say that perception is "a social and cognitive process."
2. How does a person's culture affect his or her perceiving?
3. Cognitive schemata are _____ _____ that help us to _____ incoming information.
4. This reading discusses two ways people organize information and three ways we make inferences. Label them.

5. What is an implicit personality theory?
6. What is the fundamental attribution error? What's the ultimate attribution error? How can such errors be avoided?

PROBES

1. How does this discussion of perception affect your definition of what it means to be "objective"?
2. Given the influence of person prototypes and scripts, how can you make your communicating responsive to the *particular*—as contrasted with the general—situation?
3. Explain the relationship between person-centered versus position-centered talk and impersonal versus interpersonal communicating.
4. "Perception" is a label for cognitive inhaling processes, and "listening" is a label for social inhaling processes. Explain.

REFERENCES

Abelson, R. P. (1981). Psychological status of the script concept. *American Psychologist, 36,* 715–729.

Bartlett, F. C. (1932). *Remembering: A study in experimental and social psychology.* London: Cambridge University Press.

Fiske, S. T., & Shelley, E. T. (1984). *Social cognition.* New York: Random House.

Hall, B. J. (2002). *Among cultures: The challenge of communication.* New York: Wadsworth.

Hall, N., & Crisp, R. (2003). Anxiety-induced response perseverance and stereotype change. *Current Research in Social Psychology, 8,* 242–253.

Heider, F. (1958). *The psychology of interpersonal relations.* New York: Wiley.

Kelley, H. H. (1972). Casual schemata and the attribution process. In E. E. Jones, D. E. Kanouse, H. H. Kelley, R. E. Nisbett, S. Valins, & B. Weiner (Eds.), *Attribution: Perceiving the causes of behavior.* Morristown, NJ: General Learning Press.

Kelley, H. H. (1973). The process of causal attribution. *American Psychologist, 28,* 107–128.

Kluckhorn, F. R., & Strodtbeck, F. L. (1961). *Variations in value orientations.* Evanston, IL: Row Peterson.

Konner, M. (2002). *The tangled wing: Biological constraints on the human spirit.* 2nd ed. New York: Holt, Rinehart, and Winston.

Maltz, D. N., & Borker, R. A. (1982). A cultural approach to male-female miscommunication. In J. J. Gumperz (Ed.), *Language and social identity* (pp. 196–216). Cambridge: Cambridge University Press.

Manusov, V. (1990). An application of attribution principles to nonverbal behavior in romantic dyads. *Communication Monographs, 57,* 104–118.

Manusov, V., & Hegde, R. (1993). Communicative outcomes of stereotype-based expectancies: An observational study of cross-cultural dyads. *Communication Quarterly, 41,* 338–354.

Manusov, M., Winchatz, M., & Manning, L. M. (1997). Acting out our minds: Incorporating behavior into models of stereotype-based expectancies for cross-cultural interactions. *Communication Monographs, 64,* 119–139.

Mayer, R. E. (1992). *Thinking, problem-solving, cognition.* 2nd ed. San Francisco: Freeman.

Rotter, J. B. (1966). Generalized expectancies for internal vs. external control of reinforcement. *Psychological Monographs, 80,* 609.

Rush, L. L. (1998). Affective reactions to multiple social stigmas. *Journal of Social Psychology, 138,* 421–430.

Schneider, D. J., Hastorf, A. H., & Ellsworth, P. C. (1979). *Person perception.* 2nd ed. (pp. 20–26). Reading, MA: Addison-Wesley.

It's Only Skin Deep:
Stereotyping and Totalizing Others

Julia T. Wood

Julia Wood teaches in the department of communication studies at the University of North Carolina at Chapel Hill, does research on gender and communication, and has published several interpersonal communication texts. This chapter comes from a recent book that she dedicates to enhancing its readers' understanding of "different meanings that people may attribute to what they say and do." In her book, Wood emphasizes how diversity can contribute to misunderstanding and how awareness and acceptance of diversity can help improve understanding.

As the subtitle of this selection says, this is a discussion of stereotyping, one of the most familiar and unfortunate features of the way we perceive people. As the subtitle also suggests, the key concept in this chapter is "totalizing." Wood explains that this word describes "communication that emphasizes one aspect of a person above all others." Totalizing means thinking and acting as if a single aspect of a person is the totality of that person. So calling Spike Lee a "black filmmaker" spotlights his race in a way that makes it the dominant feature that's being noticed. The same thing happens when people talk of "that short guy you dated," "a Japanese friend of mine," and "his deaf sister."

Wood makes the obvious—though important—point that totalizing has negative effects on the people who are its target. She also describes some of the effects of totalizing on the people who do it. Basically, when we engage in totalizing, we cripple our perceiving by forcing ourselves to look through blinders. As Wood puts it, "we tend to perceive others through the labels we use to describe them."

One reason people stereotype or totalize is that it's easier to deal with a one-dimensional person than someone with many different important qualities. Another reason is that several automatic human brain processes produce classifications and generalizations. It would be impossible for us constantly to notice every detail of everything available to our senses, so our brain automatically classifies what we perceive to help keep us from going nuts.

But when we perceive people, this natural process can lead us to operate on the basis of what are called "implicit personality theories" (this same idea was discussed in the previous reading). As both readings note, these are generalizations about groups of qualities that seem "obviously" to go together—like being overweight, happy, lazy, and undisciplined. Problems arise when we perceive one of these features—that a person is overweight, for example—and our implicit theory about the rest of the personality fills in other features that may or may not be parts of who the person is.

Wood discusses some of Dawn Braithwaite's research about how totalizing applies to people with disabilities. Even that term—*disabled*—is often hurtful because it makes it easier for others to reduce the amputee or the deaf or partly sighted person to the negative status of being incomplete or flawed in some vital way. You can read an article on disabled communication in Chapter 11.

Near the end of this short reading, Wood includes 10 examples of statements that often come from well-meaning people but that are usually heard by the people they're directed to as totalizing or stereotyping. This list and the other ideas in this selection should help sensitize you to whatever tendencies you have to rely on stereotypes in your communication.

MAIN IDEAS

- *Totalizing* communication is communication that emphasizes one aspect of a person above all others.
- Totalizing damages both the people who do it and the people to whom it's done.
- Stereotyping and totalizing grow out of the natural and helpful cognitive activities of classification and generalization.
- One form of totalizing defines individuals by their membership in a specific group; another reduces individuals to one aspect of their identity.
- When we think stereotypically, we expect people to conform to our perceptions of the group to which we assign them.
- When we mark an individual as an exception to his or her group, we reveal our own stereotypes.

I want to be known as a talented young filmmaker. That should be first. But the reality today is that no matter how successful you are, you're black first. (p. 92)

Those are Spike Lee's words. In an interview with Diane McDowell, reporter for *Time* magazine, the gifted filmmaker lamented the reality that most people see and respond to his blackness more than his other qualities and achievements. Sometimes, awareness of Lee's blackness overrides all other perceptions of him.

Distinguished historian John Hope Franklin made the same point in an interview with Mark McGurl, reporter for the *New York Times*. According to Franklin, many people assume that because he is an African American historian, he must study African Americans. He is often introduced as the author of 12 books on black history. In reality, Franklin points out, he is *not* a historian only of African Americans. His specialty is the history of the South and, as he notes, that history includes both whites and blacks. In fact, several of his books have focused primarily on whites in the South. Franklin has been elected president of the American Historical Association, the Organization of American Historians, and the Southern Historical Association—none of which is specifically an African American organization. Still, many people perceive his skin color above all else and they assume his ethnicity defines his work.

The misunderstanding of identity and achievement that Spike Lee and John Hope Franklin confront is not unique to people of minority races. Women report that they are often asked to serve on committees. Many times the person asking says, "We need a woman on the committee" or "We think you can provide the woman's perspective on the issues." Like Lee and Franklin, professional women may feel that all their accomplishments and abilities are erased by those who ask them to be "the woman on the committee." The language in the request communicates that all that is noticed is biological sex: She can fill the "woman slot" on the committee.

In this [reading], we focus on communication that highlights one aspect of a person—usually race, sex, sexual orientation, disability, or economic status. We discuss common instances of such communication and explore how it fosters misunderstandings and often offense.

UNDERSTANDING THE MISUNDERSTANDING

Scholars use the term *totalize* to describe communication that emphasizes one aspect of a person above all others. When someone totalizes, he or she acts as if a single facet of an individual is the totality of that person or as if that single aspect is all that's important about the person. For example, describing Spike Lee as a *black* filmmaker spotlights his race as what is worthy of attention. Calling John Hope Franklin a *black* historian emphasizes his race and obscures his professional expertise and accomplishments. Asking a professional to provide the *woman's* perspective highlights sex as the criterion for serving on committees. Referring to a person as *gay* stresses sexual orientation and obscures all the person's other qualities. Describing people as *blue collar* or *white collar* makes their class visible and everything else about them invisible.

Totalizing affects both those who do it and those who are its targets. When we feel that someone totalizes us, we are likely to be offended and resentful. We may also be hurt that we have been reduced to a single part of our identity—perhaps not the part most important to us in a particular context. These feelings create barriers to open, healthy communication and comfortable relationships.

Less obvious but no less important is the impact of totalizing on people who engage in it. Language shapes our perceptions by calling certain things to our attention. When we use language that focuses our attention on race, class, sex, or any [other] single aspect of another person, we limit our perception of that person. In other words, we tend to perceive others through the labels we use to describe them.

Kenneth Burke, a distinguished critic of language and literature, observes that language simultaneously reflects, selects, and deflects. In his book *Language as Symbolic Action,* Burke writes: "Any given terminology is a *reflection* of reality, by its very nature as a terminology it must be a *selection* of reality; and to this extent it must function also as a *deflection* of reality" (p. 45). Burke means that the words we use to reflect our perceptions select certain aspects of what we are describing while simultaneously deflecting, or neglecting, other aspects of what we are describing. When we select *woman, black, gay,* and so forth to describe people, other aspects of those people are deflected (neglected or added as an afterthought). Consequently, we may not see in others whatever our labels deflect. Thus, we are unlikely to interact with those others in their wholeness.

Most of us wouldn't intentionally reduce another person to one aspect of who he or she is, but it happens. One motive for totalizing is the desire for reducing uncertainty. We tend to be uncomfortable when we are unsure about others and situations. To ease discomfort, we often attempt to reduce our uncertainty about others and circumstances. One way to do this is to define others as belonging to a group about which we have definite ideas (although the ideas may not be accurate). It is easier to think of Spike Lee as black than to try to perceive him as a unique individual who is—among other things—male, young, a filmmaker, educated, and African American.

In the classic book *The Nature of Prejudice,* psychologist Gordon Allport observed that stereotyping and prejudice grow out of normal—not deviant or unusual—cognitive activities. Specifically, Allport identified classification and generalization as commonplace mental activities that can foster stereotypes and prejudice. One reason we use stereotypes, then, is that they reduce our uncertainty by grouping people into broad classes that obscure individual characteristics.

A second reason we stereotype is that we rely on what psychologists call implicit personality theory. Most of us have certain unspoken and perhaps unrecognized assumptions about qualities that go together in personalities. Many people assume that attractive individuals are more extroverted, intelligent, and socially skilled than less attractive individuals. Another common implicit personality theory (one that research does not support) is that people who are overweight are also lazy, undisciplined, and happy. In both examples, we attribute to others a constellation of qualities that we associate with a particular quality we have noticed.

If we meet an individual who is overweight (in our judgment), we may assume that the person meets our implicit personality theory of overweight people and is happy, lazy, and undisciplined. Our implicit personality theories may also lead us to think that a nice-looking person must be intelligent, outgoing, and socially skilled. When we rely on our implicit personality theories, we latch onto one quality of another person—often a characteristic we can see, such as race, sex, or weight—and attribute to the person other qualities that we perceive as consistent with the quality we have identified....

One form of totalizing... involves defining individuals by their membership in a specific group. Years ago sociologist Louis Wirth conducted classic studies of racial prejudice. One of his more important conclusions was that when we perceive people primarily in terms of their membership in a particular racial or ethnic group, we tend to think about them and interact with them in terms of our stereotypes of race, regardless of their unique qualities, talents, and so forth. In other words, their individuality is lost, submerged in our preconceptions of the group to which we assign them.

A second form of totalizing reduces individuals to one quality or aspect of their identities. This type of totalizing is evident in some of the language used to describe persons who have disabilities. How we perceive and label people with disabilities is the research focus of Dawn Braithwaite, a communication scholar at Arizona State University West. From interviews with persons who have disabilities, Braithwaite learned that the term *disabled person* is likely to offend. The reason is that the term suggests that their personhood is disabled—that they are somehow inadequate or diminished as persons simply because they have disabilities. One of the people Braithwaite interviewed asserted, "I am a person like anyone else" (1994, p. 151). Another interviewee said, "If anyone refers to me as an amputee, that is guaranteed to get me madder than hell! I don't deny the leg amputation, but I am me. I am a whole person" (1994, p. 151).

Individuals who have disabilities have been vocal in resisting efforts to label them *disabled*. They point out that calling them disabled emphasizes their disabilities above all else. "We're people who have disabilities. People first," a deaf student explained to me. When someone with a disability is described as disabled, we highlight what they cannot do rather than all they can do....

When we think stereotypically, we expect people to conform to our perceptions of the group to which we assign them. Sometimes, however, we meet someone who doesn't fit our stereotypes of the group to which we think he or she belongs. Have you ever said or heard the phrases "woman doctor," "male nurse," or "woman lawyer"? Notice how they call attention to the sex of the doctor, nurse, or lawyer. Have you ever heard or used the phrases "man doctor," "woman nurse," or "man lawyer"? Probably not—because it is considered normal for men to be doctors and lawyers and women to be nurses. Many people perceive it as unusual for women to practice law or medicine or men to be nurses. "Woman doctor," "male nurse," and "woman lawyer" spotlight the sex of individuals as the element worthy of notice. The phrases also reflect stereotyped views of the professional groups.

When we mark an individual as an exception to his or her group, we unknowingly reveal our own stereotypes. In fact, we may reinforce them because marking an individual who doesn't conform to the stereotype as unusual leaves our perceptions of the group unchanged. All we do is remove the "exceptional individual" from the group. Consider these statements:

White manager to black manager:	"You really are exceptional at your job." [*Translation:* Black women aren't usually successful.]
Male professional to female professional:	"You don't think like a woman." [*Translation:* Most women don't think like professionals.]
Able-bodied individual to person in wheelchair:	"I'm amazed at how well you get around." [*Translation:* I assume that people who use wheelchairs don't get out much.]
Upper-class person to working-class person:	"It's remarkable that you take college classes." [*Translation:* Most working-class people aren't interested in higher education.]
White person to African American:	"I can't believe you don't like to dance." [*Translation:* I think that all blacks dance, have rhythm.]
Heterosexual to lesbian:	"I think it's great that you have some male friends." [*Translation:* Most lesbians hate men.]
Homeowner to maid:	"You speak so articulately." [*Translation:* I assume most domestic workers don't speak well and/or aren't educated.]
White man to black man:	"I never think of you as black." [*Translation:* You don't fit my views of blacks; you're an exception to my (negative) stereotype of blacks.]
Christian to Jew:	"I'm surprised at how generous you are." [*Translation:* Most Jews are tight with money.]
African American to white person:	"You're not as stuffy as most of your people." [*Translation:* Most whites are stuffy, or up-tight, but you're not.]

Would any of the above statements be made to a member of the speaker's group? Would a heterosexual say to a heterosexual woman, "It's great that you have some male friends"? Would a white man say to another white man, "I never think of you as white"? Would a maid say to his or her employer, "You speak so articulately"? Would a white person say to another white person, "I can't believe you don't like to dance"? In each case, it's unlikely. By changing the speakers in the statements, we see how clearly the statements reflect stereotypes of groups.

Communicating that you perceive an individual as an exception to his or her group invites two dilemmas. First, it expresses your perception that the person belongs to a group about which you have preconceptions. Understandably, this may alienate the other person or make her or him defensive. The person may feel compelled to defend or redefine the group from which you have removed that individual. An African American might, for instance, say "Lots of blacks don't enjoy dancing." A working-class person might inform an upper-class person that "education has always been a priority in my family."

A second possible response to communication that marks an individual as an exception to her or his group is the effort to deny identification with the group. A professional woman may strive not to appear feminine to avoid being judged by her colleagues' negative perceptions of women. A white person may try to "talk black" or play music by black artists to prove he or she isn't like most whites. The group stereotypes—no matter how inaccurate—are left unchallenged.

Whether individuals defend or redefine their groups or separate themselves from the groups, one result is the same: The possibilities for open communication and honest relationships are compromised.

REVIEW QUESTIONS

1. Define *totalizing* in your own words, and give an example from your own experience of how totalizing can affect communication.
2. Specifically how does totalizing affect the person who *does* it?
3. Define and give an example of *implicit personality theory.*
4. Use Wood's article to explain why many female attorneys do not like to be called a "woman lawyer."
5. Explain the point Wood is making when she asks, "Would a white man say to another white man, 'I never think of you as white'?"

PROBES

1. On the first day of class, the instructor says in a genuinely pleased way, "It's great to have so many persons of color in the class." Explain how this can be heard as a totalizing statement.
2. Wood quotes Gordon Allport to make the point that stereotyping is a normal, natural activity. But if it's normal and natural, then how much sense does it make to encourage people not to do it?

3. Privately, if you prefer, or with a classmate, if you're willing, explore some of your own implicit personality theories. For example, if you're not thinking carefully about it, what qualities do you presume a person has who is (a) a teenage African-American male, (b) a female athlete, (c) a 20-something gay male, (d) a middle-aged female nurse?
4. If it's obviously true that a person does not have normal sight, hearing, intelligence, or mobility, what is the problem with referring to that person as "disabled"?
5. What's the connection between the main point made in this reading and the impersonal–interpersonal continuum discussed in Chapter 2?

REFERENCES

Allport, G. (1979). *The nature of prejudice.* Reading, MA: Addison-Wesley.
Braithwaite, D. (1994). Viewing persons with disabilities as a culture. In L. Samovar & R. Porter (Eds.), *Intercultural communication: A reader* (7th ed., pp. 148–154). Belmont, CA: Wadsworth.
Burke, K. (1966). *Language as symbolic action.* Berkeley: University of California Press.
McDowell, D. (1989, July 17). He's got to have his way. *Time,* pp. 92–94.
McGurl, M. (1990, June 3). That's history, not black history. *New York Times Book Review,* 13.
Wirth, L. (1945). The problem of minority groups. In R. Linton (Ed.), *The science of man* (pp. 347–372). New York: Columbia University Press.

Mindful Listening
Rebecca Z. Shafir

Rebecca Shafir, the author of this essay, reports that she has learned a great deal about communication and listening from Zen Buddhist philosophy. As you may know, Zen is an Eastern philosophy that was first imported into the United States in the 1960s. Since then, it has sometimes been stereotyped as silly, New Age thinking. But those who seriously study this philosophy know that it offers westerners insights and guidelines that can substantially improve our communicating.

One contribution from this and other Buddhist writings is the concept of "mindfulness." This is a label for a way of focusing your attention that can produce significant benefits. I have included this reading in order to clarify what "mindfulness" means and how it can improve your listening.

Initially, Shafir characterizes mindful listening as the ability to receive the spoken word accurately, retain information, sustain attention, attend to your own responsive speech, and encourage the speaker. She emphasizes the importance of a strong intent to assure a positive outcome—which means that mindfulness is not a permanent state, because no one has this strong positive intent all the time.

Mindfulness is the opposite of multitasking, which is a skill that many contemporary people value very highly. As Shafir writes, "Our environment with its constant bombardment of stimuli challenges your innate ability to relax and focus completely on one task at a time." This bombardment can encourage mindlessness, an orientation that prevents effective listening.

Shafir's discussion of the work of one of her Buddhist mentors, Thich Nhat Hanh, emphasizes both the simplicity and the unusualness of mindfulness. Thich Nhat Hanh describes two ways to wash the dishes. "The first is to wash the dishes in order to have clean dishes and the second is to wash the dishes in order to wash the dishes." The first is mindless, because when you wash the dishes this way, your focus is not on the present but on the future—what the dish washing will accomplish. The second is mindful because your focus is on what is currently occurring, here and now. Buddhist philosophy emphasizes the importance and value of attending to the present—being mindful.

This simple example makes it clear that many Western cultural values discourage mindfulness. North Americans are praised for our abilities to "get things done," solve problems, and build impressive structures and systems. These capabilities are undeniably productive. But this cultural emphasis on constant accomplishment can divert us from important present-tense experiences: enjoying a discovery with a child, profoundly appreciating a beautiful view, taking in the aroma of a landscape, listening closely to a friend. Zen reminds us of the complementary value of these mindful experiences. One of its slogans is "Don't just do something. Sit there!"

It is important and useful, I believe, to take this advice about mindfulness into your listening. Most of us are too busy to do this all the time. But we should at least have available to us, as one of our important communication options, the ability to listen mindfully.

MAIN IDEAS

- A good listener can be defined as one who is *mindful* of the wide spectrum of listening skills that include accurate receiving, retaining information, sustaining attention, attending to your own speech, and encouraging the person you are listening to.
- Mindful listening can be applied in many different kinds of listening, including information seeking and processing, evaluating, and therapeutic or empathic listening.
- Mindfulness is focused attention on the present; it is the opposite of mindlessness, where attention is focused on the future—what's next.
- Thich Nhat Hanh, a Zen Buddhist monk, has written useful advice about mindfulness.
- One kind of mind*less* listening involves planning what you are going to say next.
- Mindfulness can require practice to develop "one-pointed" concentration; this is the opposite of multitasking.
- Mindful listening can helpfully promote interpersonal-quality communication.

How tiresome it is to leave a performance review with the comment written in bold print: **"Your listening skills need work."** It is a déjà vu experience for many of us, one that we can easily recall from numerous early sources: our parents, scout leaders, coaches, and teachers. Since our youth these words of wisdom have come in various forms. For example: "Stop talking and pay attention," as if when we stop talking we somehow start paying attention, or more indirectly, "Maybe you should get your hearing checked." When we are told to listen up, what exactly does that mean? How do we know if we are really listening (and paying attention) or just acting like we are? How can we convince others, like the boss, that our listening skills are deserving of a promotion? Would we know a good listener if we met one? How far are we from being considered a good listener?

… If you were to poll various individuals and ask what it means to be a good listener, you would hear several versions. Here are some examples. Sales consultant Michael Leppo describes good listening as the ability to hear attentively. Michelle Lucas, a psychotherapist, says that good listening is a process of showing respect and validating a person's worth. The International Listening Association defines listening as "the process of receiving, constructing meaning from, and responding to spoken and/or nonverbal messages." Others say it is simply the ability to understand and remember what was said. Ralph G. Nichols, one of the founding fathers of listening studies, said, "Listening is an inside job—inside action on the part of the listener." This suggests that good listening is the ability to get into the shoes of the speaker in order to see his side of the issue.

… I will define a good listener as one who is *mindful* of the wide spectrum of listening skills. These include the ability to

- receive the spoken word accurately, interpret the whole message (the words, gestures, and facial expressions) in an unbiased manner;
- retain the information for future use;
- sustain attention to the spoken word at will; listening is a process that occurs *over time*;
- attend to *your* speech and be sensitive to the accuracy of the message and the possible interpretations that could be derived from it; and
- encourage a speaker to speak from his [or her] heart and expound on his or her ideas without censure. This makes your speaker feel valued and respected.

… Mindful listening is already a part of you. However, it does require a desire to listen. A desire to listen involves a curiosity for new information and a willingness to pay more respect to your speaker. If your desire is to build stronger personal and professional relationships, a degree of compassion is a basic requirement to becoming a better listener.

Mindful listening is the mind and body working together to communicate. Furthermore, it does not require two functioning ears to listen in a mindful way. Mindful listening requires you to see, hear, and feel with your whole being. To attend mindfully to the message, whether the message is spoken or signed, is to perceive as closely as possible the intent and experience of the speaker.

Mindful listening can be applied to the wide continuum of listening types:

- information processing
- information seeking
- critical or evaluative listening
- therapeutic listening
- empathetic or compassionate listening
- small-talk listening ...

MINDFULNESS: LISTENING IN THE MOMENT

Concentration is the key to performing *any* meaningful activity well. It is heartening to know that we innately possess the ability to concentrate. It does not require any special training, just frequent application. Think of an activity that requires complete, sustained attention, such as taking an important test, driving in a snowstorm, or playing chess. Your focus on these tasks is propelled by a strong intent to assure a positive outcome—to excel in school, get home safely, or choose the best move. However, the more you concentrate on the *process,* the more positive will be the outcome. Reading each test item carefully, looking for tricky wordings, and rechecking your answers increases your chance of scoring a high grade. If you were to think of nothing but getting an A, the end result would not be so positive.

On the other hand, there are activities that once required a similar level of concentration, but have now become mindless, like sweeping the floor or grocery shopping. These rote activities give the brain a chance to unwind and relax. You can think about other things and even perform other tasks simultaneously: you can eat *and* read, surf the Internet *and* listen to music. These combinations can be very enjoyable. However, you may tend to overuse this ability to multitask and misuse it when it is necessary to focus your attention on a single activity, such as listening. Our environment with its constant bombardment of stimuli challenges your innate ability to relax and focus completely on one task at a time.

Not long ago, I was in an airport with an hour wait for my plane, and I met a former high-school classmate whom I hadn't seen in more than 20 years. We decided to go across the street to a nice hotel for something to drink while we caught up on each other's lives. Outside the bar was a sign that invited us to COME IN AND RELAX. As soon as we were inside, we noticed five TVs, all tuned to different channels! In addition, there was noise from the nearby kitchen and a radio playing behind the bar. Some patrons at tables tried to maintain conversation-like activities while their eyes shifted from TV to TV. It was dizzying! It took every bit of our concentration to hear each other and even more effort to discuss anything in depth. It occurred to me that an intensely distracting environment is regarded by many people as "relaxing."

You lull yourself into a false sense of competency when you think you can make dinner, plan that sales meeting, and help your son with his homework, all at the same time. You may finish all these tasks in 30 minutes or less, but how is the quality? When you look closely, dinner was just edible, you overlooked two of the seven main points for the meeting, and your son is able to spell only six of the ten words on his vocabulary homework. Since the goal is to *finish* these tasks so that you can rush onto the next one, the results are less than satisfactory. You feel depleted and inadequate.

Such mindlessness becomes a habit and begins to creep into tasks that require your full concentration. How often do you look back at the week, the month, the year, and wonder where the time went? Many of us can't remember because most of the time we were in a fog of preoccupation with the past or planning the future. Our attention was scattered all over the place, and the quality of our actions was just good enough to get by. Substandard performance on any task results in low self-esteem and lack of fulfillment.

Eknath Easwaran, author of *Words to Live By: Inspiration for Every Day*, speaks of the dangers of mindlessness: "There is no joy in work which is hurried, which is done when we are at the mercy of pressures from outside, because such work is compulsive. All too often hurry clouds judgment. More and more, to save time, a person tends to think in terms of pat solutions and to take shortcuts and give uninspired performances."

When mindlessness teams up with personal barriers, our ability to concentrate on the message is out of reach. The antidote is to challenge those distractions and focus on the process—establishing a warm relationship with another person, seeing the other's view, and accepting it as valid whether you agree with it or not. Focus on process ensures the favorable outcome you hope for—repeat sales, cooperation from difficult people, better recall.... If, however, you still find that your barriers overpower your ability to focus, then you need to spend a bit more time thinking them through.

In my search for a practical means of improving the ability to concentrate and listen more effectively, I came across the writings of Thich Nhat Hanh, a Zen Buddhist monk. After studying his book, *The Miracle of Mindfulness,* I found that my ability to listen had become richer. The essence of Zen is to be in the present. Thich Nhat Hanh describes mindfulness as keeping your consciousness alive to the present reality. Living the present moment of any activity, paying attention to the process, lend themselves to a quality outcome.

A good way to experience mindfulness is to choose a task you typically rush through, like washing the dishes. According to Thich Nhat Hanh, "There are two ways to wash the dishes. The first is to wash the dishes in order to have clean dishes and the second is to wash the dishes in order to wash the dishes." He says that if we hurry through the dishes, thinking only about the cup of tea that awaits us, then we are not washing the dishes to wash the dishes; we are not alive during the time we are washing the dishes. In fact, we are completely incapable of realizing the miracle of life while standing at the sink. "If we can't wash the dishes," he continues, "the chances are we won't be able to drink our tea either. While drinking the cup of tea, we will only be thinking of other things, barely aware of the cup in our hands."

When you are listening to another but planning your own agenda at the same time, you are really talking to yourself and therefore not truly listening. You have escaped the present in order to be in the future. You may be physically present, but mentally you are bouncing back and forth between past events and future expectations.

Another challenge to mindful listening is that the average person speaks at a rate of 125 words per minute, yet we can process up to 500 words per minute. During that lag time, you can think about your to-do list or you can listen mindfully by using that time to summarize what the speaker has said so far or see the possibilities in what the speaker is proposing. You can also note the emphasis in his voice or the degree of concern in his gestures and facial expressions. When you are in the speaker's movie, you use your resources to be a competent, intelligent listener.

If you have difficulty putting your thoughts, judgments, and other noise aside while you are trying to get into the speaker's movie, you may need some practice staying in the present. Poor listeners have little patience for the present. Thoughts of yesterday and tomorrow are more enticing. Your barriers have little tolerance for information or ideas that are contrary or too lengthy. Impatience shows itself when you fall out of the speaker's movie or want to interrupt. . . .

Time spent listening, consulting, teaching, or working in the present can be just as memorable as those moments is your life when time appeared to stand still. When listening mindfully, however, your perception is heightened and you experience multilevel awareness. You are able to delve into what makes the speaker tick, how well his body language matches or contradicts his spoken message, his mood, energy level, and other subtle nuances. When you are fully absorbed in the speaker's movie, you are in the present; time appears to stand still. Mindful listening is not a trance or a hypnotic state. You are aware of your surroundings, but they are not a distraction.

The 1st-century Buddhist philosopher Ashvagosha gives a humorous account of mindful listening:

> If we are listening to a friend, even if a parrot flies down and perches on his head, we should not get excited, point to the parrot, and burst out, "Excuse me for interrupting, but there's parrot on your head." We should be able to concentrate so hard on what our friend is saying that we can tell this urge, "Keep quiet and don't distract me. Afterwards I'll tell him about the bird."

He goes on to describe mindfulness as "one-pointedness." This means to focus the attention completely on one task at a time. By applying this approach to your daily tasks, you can complete the same number of tasks, only with better quality, and hence, better outcomes. Many of my students tell me they are better able to prioritize activities and eliminate the time wasters. When being mindful appears daunting, remember that one minute of mindfulness makes up for many minutes of mindlessness. . . .

A similar mind–body connection was described by Mihaly Czikszentmihalyi, author of *Flow*. He defines a flow experience as the pleasant state of concentration or total absorption in a task. Those he interviewed—painters, dancers, and athletes—said that when they were in the midst of their art or hobby, their state of focused energy was like "floating" or "being carried by the flow." When you experience flow often, the quality of your life improves. The opposite of flow is mindlessness. During mindless listening, your barriers create resistance to the message; your mind is scattered....

In my listening classes, we begin to practice mindfulness in gentler doses. We begin by experiencing orange juice as I narrate. Students watch the rush of the deep orange color as the juice is poured into their cups. Together, we smell the citrus perfume and notice how our mouths begin to water. We sip and savor the tartness. We consider the work that went into producing this cup of juice and imagine the beauty of the tree from which it came. We think about the people who made it possible to get the juice to our table. This full experience endures until the last sip. As they listen and ponder the juice, it's always interesting to note that no one looks around the room; each one's gaze and mental focus are centered on the juice.

The point of the exercise is to take a simple human act, something that we typically take for granted, and make it come alive. So often we sleep through life, attributing little or no meaning to our daily activities. Imagine if you lent that same zest to sipping your coffee, conducting a meeting, or cleaning out the refrigerator; how much more satisfied would you feel at the end of the day? I can be sure my students will never again drink orange juice the old way. And if they need a mindfulness refresher, they will simply pour themselves a glass of orange juice.

Mindfulness connects us with the experience of the moment, no matter what the activity. With listening, mindfulness connects us to the listener. *Mindlessness*, on the other hand, means letting the ego-dominated self—concerns with status, past experiences, and other barriers—separate us from the listener. The mindful listener lacks this obsessive self-consciousness that interferes with the ability to concentrate. We feel happier and more positive when we are not focusing on the self....

Students ask, "Do I have to be mindful all the time? Isn't that exhausting? Doesn't it take too much time?" Ideally, to make mindfulness a habit, we should perform as many acts as possible carefully and with thought. Begin by noticing how often you act mindlessly—driving through a stoplight, leaving the house without your keys, taking down the wrong phone number. That kind of wasted energy is exhausting and time consuming. Mindfulness saves time because you think as you act. Slowing down and carrying out the task with mindfulness significantly reduces the chances of error and mishap....

Recently, a coworker who was about to leave for her vacation told me three vital points to include on an upcoming financial report. Feeling cocky (after all I was writing a book on listening!), I did not take that mindful twenty seconds to repeat what she had said or write it down. Two days later when writing the report, I was able to recall only about 90 percent of the information. To get that forgotten 10 percent, I had to spend another hour tracking down another source....

Instead of insulting yourself when mindlessness strikes, consider it a wake-up call to become mindful. Make it a point to commend yourself for the moments of mindfulness that make up your day.

Initially, it may seem like you are taking more time to carry out your tasks. You are used to doing everything in haste, so even a minute more will seem like days. Yet as your ability to concentrate improves, you will become more efficient. Tasks done mindfully are done right the first time. There is no need to recheck or redo. Mindfulness saves time.

REVIEW QUESTIONS

1. In your own words, define *mindfulness*.
2. List four specific things that you will be doing when you listen to someone mindfully. For example, describe your posture, eye behavior, and facial expression; the connection between your conversation partner's word choices and yours; and so on.
3. The average speaking rate is 125 words per minute, and we can process up to 500 words per minute. How does Shafir suggest that you use the "spare time" that is created by this difference?
4. Does Shafir believe that you should work to be mindful all the time? Explain.

PROBES

1. Do video games encourage mindfulness or mindlessness? Explain.
2. Shafir argues that "you lull yourself into a false sense of competency" when you believe that you can multitask successfully. Explain what she believes is the practical danger of multitasking. Why does she call it a "false sense of competency"?
3. Athletes and artists sometimes talk about being "in the zone" or "in the flow." What is the relationship between this experience and mindfulness?

Empathic and Dialogic Listening

John Stewart, Karen E. Zediker, and Saskia Witteborn

This reading offers a fairly extended treatment of two kinds of helpful listening. Empathic listening enables you to understand the *other* person, thoroughly and fully. Dialogic listening takes the process one step farther. Rather than focusing mainly on what the other person is thinking and feeling, dialogic listening helps the two of you—or all the people in the conversation—build meaning together. So when dialogic listening works well, everybody understands each other *and* the people involved co-create new understandings that go beyond the individuals.

Karen, Saskia, and I break emphatic listening down into three main skill sets: focusing, encouraging, and reflecting. The focusing section develops what Rebecca Shafir wrote about mindfulness. We outline four specific ways to focus on the person you're listening to.

Encouraging skills are communication moves that "pull" more talk from the other person. They are designed to help your conversation partner(s) get more of what they're thinking and feeling on the table between you. Some encouraging skills are nonverbal, and some are verbal. We offer five ways to encourage people, and we also suggest two kinds of questions that are good to avoid.

Reflecting skills enable your conversation partner(s) to understand what you have heard and understood. This enables them to clarify their meanings, where necessary, and to correct any misunderstandings. The main reflecting skill is paraphrasing.

As we note, there are no "six easy steps" or "five sure-fire techniques" for dialogic listening. It takes a different level of understanding and practice. If you have trouble with this section of the reading, you might look over the materials in Chapter 12, "Promoting Dialogue." They reinforce what's discussed here and give some additional examples.

The primary ingredient for dialogic listening is *your willingness and ability to collaboratively co-construct meaning with your conversation partner(s)*. You can't listen dialogically until you move beyond your desire to "make sure she understands you" and "get your point across." Dialogic listening begins with the understanding that "the point" needs to be what's shared among those in the conversation, not just your ideas.

The primary metaphor for dialogic listening is "sculpting mutual meanings." We refer to the situation of two people seated on either side of a potter's wheel, with their four wet hands shaping the clay on the wheel. Taken figuratively, this is what it means to "sculpt mutual meaning."

We describe four specific communication moves that can help you listen dialogically: focus on "ours," paraphrase-plus, ask for a paraphrase, and run with the metaphor. We also offer an extended example conversation that illustrates these communication moves. Our goal, here and in Chapter 12, is to encourage you and empower you to work toward creating dialogic moments in more of your communicating.

MAIN IDEAS

- Empathic listening focuses on the *other* person's thoughts and feelings.
- Empathic listening requires three skill sets: focusing, encouraging, and reflecting.
- Focusing means being mindful (see the previous reading) by aiming your posture, making appropriate eye contact, moving responsively, and making responsive sounds.

- Encouraging "pulls" talk from the other with "Say more," or "For example?" mirroring, asking clarifying and open questions, and using attentive silence.
- It helps to avoid pseudoquestions and "Why?" questions.
- Reflecting checks perceptions by paraphrasing, adding an example, and gently pursuing verbal and nonverbal inconsistencies.
- Dialogic listening focuses on meanings that are *constructed between* speaker and listener(s).
- Metaphorically, dialogic listening consists of sculpting mutual meanings.
- One skill is focusing on "ours."
- A second is to use a paraphrase-plus.
- A third is to run with the other person's metaphor(s).
- There are no guaranteed steps to achieve dialogue; it is a mutual accomplishment.

EMPATHIC LISTENING

When a person is listening empathically, he or she is receptive or sensitive to the full range of characteristics shared by the other person, but responds only with his or her own impersonal characteristics. Carl Rogers, a famous counselor who pioneered the technique of empathic listening, describes it as "entering the private perceptual world of the other and becoming thoroughly at home in it." He continued:

> It involves being sensitive, moment by moment, to the changing felt meanings which flow in this other person.... To be with another in this way means that for the time being, you lay aside your own views and values in order to enter another's world without prejudice. In some sense it means that you lay aside yourself. (Rogers, 1980, 142–143)

This kind of listening is important, for example, when you are aware that your friend needs to vent and you are willing to listen without adding anything beyond your friend's point of view. In fact, if you respond in these situations by saying, "Well, if I were you…" your friend may insist, "I don't need your advice. I want you to just *listen* to me." It can also be important to listen empathically if you've been asked to mediate a dispute. You can't function very well as a mediator until you fully understand each person's point of view, and empathic listening can help you build this understanding.

Empathic listening is also an important skill for parents, teachers, and managers. Family communication research indicates, for example, that toddlers, children, and adolescents often feel that their parents listen only from their own point of view, rather than taking the time and effort to fully understand the young person's thinking and feeling.

In order to listen empathically, it's important to develop three sets of competencies: focusing, encouraging, and reflecting skills. As with any complex process, it works best to select from among the various ways to focus, encourage, and reflect. Think of the specific skills like a salad bar—put on your plate the ones that you're comfortable with and that fit the situation you're in.

Focusing Skills

As with analytic listening, the first step is to orient your attention to the person you're listening to. This begins with an internal decision about how you are going to invest your time and energy. Here it helps to recall the distinction between *spending* time and *investing* it and to realize that empathic listening can often pay the dividends of any good investment. Then you remember that listening takes effort, and you put aside the other things you're doing to concentrate on the other person. At this point, focusing surfaces in four skills.

The first is *aiming your posture.* Turn your body so that you're facing or nearly facing the person you're listening to, and if you're seated, lean toward your conversation partner. This is a simple thing to do, and yet a variety of studies have underscored its importance. It's been demonstrated that when listeners focus their bodies this way, the people they're talking with perceive them as more "warm" and accessible and consequently they find it's easier to volunteer more information (Stiff et al., 1988).

A second part of focusing is making *natural and appropriate eye contact.* In Western cultures, when you look the other person in the eye, you are not only acutely aware of him or her, but you are also directly available to that person. Studies of nonverbal listening behavior in these cultures typically identify eye contact and forward body lean or movement toward the other as two of the most important indicators of attraction and contact (Halone & Pechioni, 2001). So, if you cannot easily make eye contact with the other person, move to a position where you can. If you're talking with children, get down on the same level by kneeling or sitting, so that they can see you looking at them.

As we've already noted, the amount and kind of eye contact that are "appropriate" depend partly on the cultural identities of the people involved. If you're talking with a person from a culture that proscribes eye contact except between intimates or from a superior to an inferior, it's important to try to honor these guidelines. If you're from one of these cultures, and your conversation partner is not, it can help to alter your own behavior in the direction of the other person's expectations as far as you comfortably can. But so long as you are operating in a generally Western communication context, it's important to work toward making eye contact 50 percent to 70 percent of the time.

The third and fourth ways to focus are to *move responsively* and to *make responsive sounds.* We've known people who believed they were listening intently when they sat staring at the other person, completely immobile, and with unchanging, deadpan expressions on their faces. There are two problems with this habit. The most obvious one is that, even though you may think you're listening well, it doesn't look like you are. Unless I see some response in your body and on your face, I'm not convinced that you're really being affected by what I'm saying. The second problem is more subtle: Actually you are not fully involved in what you're hearing until your body begins to register your involvement. So even though you might think you're focused when you're immobile and silent, you are not as focused as you will be when you start moving responsively and making responsive sounds. Since everybody's mind and body are intimately connected, the kinesthetic sensations of your body's responsiveness will actually help your mind stay focused.

By moving responsively, we mean smiling, nodding or shaking your head, moving your eyebrows, shrugging your shoulders, frowning, and so on. These actions should be prompted by, in response to, and linked up with what the other person says and does. So an effective listener isn't nodding or smiling all the time; she nods or smiles when that is responsive to what the other person is saying, and she frowns or shakes her head when that's responsive.

Responsive sounds include the "Mnnhuh," "Oh?" "Yeah...," "Ahh?" "Sure!" "Really?" [and] "Awww" utterances that audibly tell the other person you're tuned in to what he or she is saying. If you doubt the importance of responsive sounds, try being completely silent the next time you're listening over the phone. After a very short time the other person will ask something like "Are you still there?" We need sounds like these to reassure us that our hearer is actually listening.

These four skills may seem overly obvious or simplistic, but it is quite clear from a number of communication studies that people differ greatly in their ability to apply these behaviors.

Encouraging Skills

The second set of empathic listening skills is designed to "pull" more talk from the other person. More talk is obviously not always a good thing. But when you want to understand as completely as possible where another person is coming from, you need to have enough verbal and nonverbal talk to make the picture clear. As a result, we want to make six specific suggestions about how to encourage.

The first is the most direct one: As a listener, respond when appropriate with "Say more," "Keep talking," "Could you elaborate on that?" or "For example?" One situation where this response can help is when someone makes a comment that sounds fuzzy or incomplete. Frequently the listener's inclination is to try to paraphrase what's been said or to act on the information even though it's uncertain whether he or she has the materials to do so. Of course, it would be pretty ridiculous to respond to "I wonder what time it is" with "Could you say more about that?" But each time you hear a new idea, a new topic, or an important point being made, we suggest you begin your empathic listening effort at that moment not by guessing what the other person means but by asking her or him to tell you. "Say more," "Keep talking," or some similar encouragement can help.

A second encouraging skill is called *mirroring*. Mirroring means repeating a key word or phrase of the other person's with a question on your face and in your voice. "Repeating?" Yes, you just pick up on one term, for example, and feed it back with a questioning inflection and raised eyebrows, and the other person will elaborate on what he has just said. "Elaborate?" Yeah—you know, he will give an example, or restate what he said in other terms, or make some such effort to clarify the point he is making. Just as we have been doing here.

A third encouraging response is the *clarifying question.* Often this takes the form "Do you mean ... ?" or "When you say _____, do you mean _____?" You might ask the person to explain how he or she is defining a word or phrase, or you might ask for the implications of what is being said. In a job interview, for example, the interviewer might comment, "Our company is interested only in assertive people ..." and the candidate could ask, "When you say 'assertive,' what do you mean?" Tone of voice is an important part of clarifying questions. Remember, your questions are motivated by a need to understand more clearly; they are not meant to force the other person into a corner with a demand to "define your terms!"

Open questions are a fourth way to encourage. *Closed* questions call for a yes or no, single-word, or simple-sentence answer. *Open* questions just identify a topic area and encourage the other person to talk about it. So, "Who was that person I saw you with last night?" is a closed question, and "How's your love life going?" is a more open one. Open questions often begin with "What do you think about ...?" or "How do you feel about ... ?" while a closed version of a similar question might begin "Do you think ... ?" Both types of questions can be useful, but when you want to encourage, use open ones.

A fifth way to encourage is by using *attentive silence.* As we've said before, the point of empathic listening is to develop and understand the perspective of the speaker. So, stay focused and give the other person plenty of room to talk. This is frequently all a person needs to be encouraged to contribute more.

Our two final suggestions about encouraging highlight what *not* to do. Encouraging obviously involves asking questions, but not just any question. There are two types of questions that it helps to avoid. The first are what we call *pseudoquestions. Pseudo* means pretended, unreal, or fake, and a pseudo-question is a judgment or opinion pretending to be a question. "Where do you think you're going?" is not really a question, it's a pseudoquestion. In other words, if you think about how this question functions in actual conversation, you can hear how it's almost always a complaint or a judgment one person is making about the other. "Where do you think you're going?" usually says something like "Get back here!" or "I don't want you to leave." "Is it safe to drive this fast?" is another pseudoquestion; here, the hidden statement is something like "I'm scared by your driving," or "I wish you'd slow down." At times, we may use pseudoquestions to soften a more directly negative evaluation of the other person (Goodman & Esterly, 1990, 760). But often such softening attempts are confusing and add more frustration than they're worth. Our point here is that if you use them in your efforts to encourage, they can backfire. Instead of pseudoquestions, try to ask only real ones, genuine requests for information or elaboration.

A second kind of question to avoid is the one that begins with the word "Why," because these questions tend to promote defensiveness. When people hear "Why?" questions, they often believe the questioner is asking them for a rationale or an excuse. "Why did you decide to bring him to this meeting?" "Why are you turning that in now?" "Why didn't you call me?" "Why did you decide to do it that way?" Do you hear the implicit demand in these questions? The problem is that "Why?" questions often put the questioned person on the spot. They seem to call for a moral or value justification. As a result, they don't work as encouragers. In their place, try asking exactly the same question but begin it with different words. For example, try "How did you decide to ... ?" or "What are your reasons for ... ?" We believe that you will find it works better.

Reflecting Skills

This third set of skills will help you directly reflect the other person's perspective in the communication process. This is the central goal of empathic listening. There are three skills in this final set. The first is called *paraphrasing*. *A paraphrase is a restatement of the other's meaning in your own words, followed by a verification check.* This means there are four important parts to a paraphrase: (1) It's a restatement, not a question. A paraphrase doesn't start out by asking; it starts out by telling the other what you have heard. The first words of a paraphrase might be "So you believe that ..." or "In other words, you're saying that...." (2) It's a restatement of the other's *meaning*, not a repeat of the other's words. Meanings include both ideas and feelings, and the fullest paraphrase captures some of both. "So you're worried that ..." or "It sounds like you are really upset because you believe that ..." are two examples of restating feelings— "worry" and "upset." (3) A paraphrase has to be in your own words.... Translating the other's meaning into your words demonstrates that you've thought about it, that it's gone through your brain cells. (4) After the restatement, you finish a paraphrase with an opportunity for the other person to verify your understanding. You can do this very simply—just by pausing and raising your eyebrows, or asking "Right?" or "Is that it?" Paraphrasing is such a powerful communication move that, if you follow these four steps periodically in your conversations, your empathic listening effectiveness will improve significantly.

The second reflective skill is *adding an example*. You can contribute to the listening process by giving an example from your own experience that you believe illustrates his or her point. Remember that this is an effort to listen empathically, not to turn the conversation away from the other person's concerns and toward yours.

Remember that understanding is very different from agreement, and that neither the paraphrase nor adding an example requires you to agree with the other person. These listening responses are designed to promote the empathic listening process, to simply help you understand the other person's perspective.

The third and final reflecting skill also takes some finesse. The skill consists of *gently pursuing verbal and nonverbal inconsistencies.* The first step is to identify when you think they've occurred. You have to be sensitive enough to recognize when the words a person is speaking don't match the way she or he is saying them. A shouted, scowling "I'm not mad!!" is an obvious example of an inconsistency between verbal and nonverbal cues. Most of the time, though, it's much more subtle. John had a friend who declared she was not going to waste any more time being angry at her boss, and then spent the next half hour complaining about the boss's most recent actions. In other situations, facial expression and tone of voice accompanying a person's "Sure," "I don't care," "Go ahead with it," or "It doesn't make any difference to me" can reveal that the words are thin masks for disappointment, concern, or hurt feelings.

As a listener you can help move beyond surface-level meanings by gently pursuing the verbal/nonverbal inconsistencies you notice. We stress the word *gently.* When you notice an inconsistency, remember that it's your interpretation of what's going on; be willing to own it as your own. Remember, too, that if the other person also sees an inconsistency, there's a reason for its being there. He or she may not be ready or willing to admit the difference between cues at one level and cues at another. So don't use this skill as a license to clobber someone with a club made out of sidewalk psychoanalysis. Instead, just describe the inconsistency you think is there and open the door for the other person to talk about it.

For example, one group of professionals John worked with were experiencing some conflict over a proposal made by their new manager. The manager decided that the group needed to be more cohesive, so she proposed that each Friday afternoon the office close down an hour early so the workers could spend some time together informally chatting over wine and cheese. Most of the people welcomed the idea, but two resisted it. They didn't like what they saw as "forced socializing," and they resented the fact that only alcoholic drinks were being served. They didn't think it was appropriate to "drink on the job." John asked the group to discuss this issue as part of their listening training. Ann, the manager, turned to Gene, one of the two persons resisting the plan, and asked what he thought about these Friday afternoon get-togethers. Gene turned slightly away in his chair, folded his arms in front of him, looked down at the floor, and said, "Well ... it's a pretty ... good idea ..." Ann smiled and softly said, "Gene, your words tell me one thing and your body says something else." Then she was silent. After a couple of seconds, Gene relaxed his body posture, smiled, and admitted that he actually didn't like the plan very much. This began a conversation that ended up redesigning the get-togethers to respond to Gene's concerns.

The primary reason this listening response works is that nonverbal cues can "leak" implicit or hidden messages. Thus, a person's tone of voice, posture, eye behavior, and even facial expression often reveal levels of meaning that are obscured by his or her choice of words. Sensitive listeners try to respond to such inconsistencies and, as we suggest, gently pursue them.

DIALOGIC LISTENING

There is no simple recipe for dialogic listening—no "six easy steps" or "five surefire techniques." This is something that anybody who wants to can definitely do, but it requires an overall approach to communicating that's different from the stance most people ordinarily take when they listen or talk. You also need to maintain a sometimes-difficult tension or balance ... between holding your own ground and being open to the person(s) you're communicating with. The best way to get a sense of this approach and this tension is to understand a little bit about the idea of *dialogue.*

Dia-logos as Meaning-Through

The term *dialogue* is mde up of two Greek words, *dia* and *logos.* The *logos* in dia-logos is the Greek word for *meaning or understanding.* (The Greek term logos has other meanings, too. Sometimes it is translated as "logic," and at other times it comes into English as "language." But its most fundamental meaning is "meaning.") The *dia* in dia-logos means not "two" but *"through"* (Bohm, 1990). So dialogue is not restricted to two-person communicating, and it is an event where meaning emerges *through* all the participants. This is another way of saying that, in dialogue, meaning or understanding is *collaboratively constructed.* The important implication of this idea for each participant is that, when you're listening and talking dialogically, *you are not in control of what comes out of the communicating.* This point is stated clearly by Abraham Kaplan:

> When people are in [dialogue] ... the content of what is being communicated does not exist prior to and independently of that particular context. There is no message, except in a post-hoc reconstruction, which is fixed and complete beforehand. If I am really talking with you, I have nothing to say; what I say arises as you and I genuinely relate to one another. I do not know beforehand who I will be, because I am open to you just as you are open to me. (quoted in Anderson, Cissna, & Arnett, 1994)

As communication teacher Bruce Hyde points out, the main obstacle to dialogic listening is the kind of self or identity that replaces this openness to collaboration with the conviction that the ideas I utter are tightly connected with who I am. There's a big difference, Bruce notes, "between being right about something and being committed to something. Being right makes somebody else wrong; being committed has room to engage productively with other points of view." In other words, if you're committed, you might even welcome the chance to talk with someone who believes differently from the way you believe, but if you're committed to being right, there's not much room for people who don't share your position to be anything but wrong. The key difference has to do with identity. The person who's caught up in being right identifies him- or herself first as an advocate for a certain position. The person who's committed, on the other hand, identifies him- or herself first as a listener who's collaborating on, but not in control of, what comes out of the conversation. If you're going to listen dialogically, you have to be more interested in building-meaning-through than in being right. And this, Bruce writes, "in my experience is the hardest single thing you can ask of anyone." The first step toward dialogic listening is to recognize that each communication event is a ride on a tandem bicycle, and you may or may not be in the front seat.

Sculpting Mutual Meanings

To shift from the bicycle metaphor, we've found that it helps to think and talk about the nuts and bolts of dialogic listening with the help of the image of a potter's wheel (Stewart & Thomas, 1990). The sculpting mutual meanings metaphor was created by communication teacher Milt Thomas, and he uses it to suggest a concrete, graphic image of what it means to listen dialogically.

Picture yourself sitting on one side of a potter's wheel with your conversation partner across from you. As you participate (talk) together, each of you adds clay to the form on the wheel, and each uses wet fingers, thumbs, and palms to shape the finished product. Like clay, verbal and nonverbal talk is tangible and malleable; they're out there between people to hear, to record, and to shape. If I am unclear or uncertain about what I am thinking about or what I want to say, I can put something out there and you can modify its shape, ask me to add more clay, or add some of your own. Your specific shaping, which you could only have done in response to the shape I formed, may move in a direction that I would never have envisioned. The clay you add may be an idea I've thought about before—although not here or in this form—or it may be completely new to me. Sometimes these "co-sculpting" sessions will be mostly playful, with general notions tossed on the wheel and the result looking like a vaguely shaped mass. At other times, the basic shape is well defined and conversation partners spend their time on detail and refinement. Peoples' efforts, though, always produce some kind of result, and frequently it can be very gratifying. Sometimes I feel that our talk helps me understand myself better than I could have alone. At other times, we produce something that transcends anything either of us could have conceived of separately. This is because the figure we sculpt is not mine or yours but *ours*, the outcome of both of our active shapings.

So in order to enter into the sculpting process effectively, you need to remember, as we have said many times before, that the meanings that count between people are not just the ones inside somebody's head but also the ones that are constructed in conversations. With this understanding you will be willing to sit down at the potter's wheel, throw your clay on the wheel, and encourage the other person to add clay, too. Then you need to be willing to get your hands dirty, to participate in the collaborative process of molding meanings together.

As you might have guessed, in order to put this basic attitude into action, you need to practice some special kinds of focusing and encouraging.

Focus on "Ours"   We mentioned before that dialogic listening involves a crucial change from a focus on *me* or the *other* to a focus on *ours*, on what's *between* speaker(s) and listener(s). Contrast this with empathic listening, which requires you to try to experience what is "behind" another's outward communication. When you focus on ours, you don't look behind the verbal and nonverbal cues. You don't try to deduce or guess what internal state the other is experiencing. Instead, you concentrate on the meanings you and the other person are mutually creating between yourselves. Empathic listening can be helpful, as we said, but dialogic listening requires a move beyond empathy to a focus on ours.

It can make a big difference whether you are trying to identify what's going on inside the other person or whether you're focusing on building-meaning-between. When your focus is on the other's thoughts and feelings "behind" their words, you spend your time and mental energy searching for possible links between what you're seeing and hearing and what the other "must be" meaning. "Look at those crossed arms. She must be feeling angry and defensive." When you think this way, your attention is moving back and forth between what's outside, in the verbal and nonverbal talk, and what's inside the person's head. From this position, it's easy to believe that what's inside is more reliable, more important, more true, and hence more interesting than the talk on the surface.

But when you're focusing on ours, you concentrate on what's outside, not what's supposedly inside. We don't mean that you should be insensitive to the other person's feelings. In fact, you will be even more sensitive when you are focused on what's between you here and now. You concentrate on the verbal and nonverbal talk that the two (or more) of you are building together. In a sense, you take the conversation at face value; you never stop attending to *it* instead of focusing mainly on something you infer is behind it. This doesn't mean you uncritically accept everything that's said as "the whole truth and nothing but the truth." But you do realize that meaning is not just what's inside one person's head. Focusing on ours prepares you to respond and inquire in ways that make it clear that "getting to the meaning" is a mutual process.

Encouraging as Nexting   Dialogic listening also requires a special form of encouraging. Basically, instead of encouraging the other person(s) to "say more," you're encouraging him or her to respond to something you've just put on the potter's wheel in response to something he or she has just said. So your encouraging is a "nexting" move; it actively and relevantly keeps the collaborative co-construction process going.

One specific way to do this is with a *paraphrase-plus*. We've already said that a paraphrase consists of (1) a restatement, (2) of the other's meaning, (3) in your own verbal and nonverbal talk, (4) concluded with an opportunity for the other person to verify your understanding. The paraphrase-plus includes all of these elements *plus* a small but important addition.

The plus is your own response to the question "What's next?" or "Now what?" You start by remembering that the meanings you are developing are created between the two of you, and individual perspectives are only a part of that. If you stopped with just the paraphrase, you would be focusing on the *other* person exclusively instead of keeping the focus on what is happening *between* you. So, you follow your verifying or perception-checking paraphrase with whatever your good judgment tells you is your response to what the person said, and you conclude your paraphrase-plus with an invitation for the person to respond to your synthesis of his or her meaning and yours. The spirit of the paraphrase-plus is that each individual perspective is a building block for the team effort. For example, notice the three possible responses to Rita's comments.

RITA: I like having an "exclusive" relationship, and I want you to be committed to me. But I still sometimes want to go out with other people.

1. MUNEO: So even though part of you agrees with me about our plan not to date others, you're still a little uncertain about it. Right? (Paraphrase)
2. TIM: Oh, so you want me to hang around like an idiot while you go out and play social butterfly! Talk about a double standard! (Attack)
3. SCOTT: It sounds like you think there are some pluses and minuses in the kind of relationship we have now. I like it the way it is, but I don't like knowing that you aren't sure. I guess I want you to tell me some more about why you're questioning it. (Paraphrase-plus)

Muneo responds to Rita's comment with a paraphrase. This tells us that Muneo listened to Rita, but not much more. Tim makes a caricature of Rita's comment; his interpretation reflects his own uncertainty, anger, and fear. His comment is more a condemnation than a paraphrase. Scott offers a paraphrase-plus. He explains his interpretation of what Rita was saying, then he says briefly how he *responds* to her point, and then he moves the focus back between the two of them, to the middle, where both persons are present in the conversation and can work on the problem together. He does this by putting some of his own clay onto the potter's wheel. He paraphrases, but he also addresses the "What's next?" question as he interprets and responds to her comments. Then he concludes the paraphrase-plus with encouraging rather than simply verifying the accuracy of his paraphrase. When all this happens, both the paraphrase and the plus keep understanding growing between the individuals.

Another way to think about the paraphrase-plus is that you're broadening your goal beyond listening for "fidelity" or "correspondence." If you're paraphrasing for fidelity or correspondence, you're satisfied and "finished" with the task as soon as you've successfully *reproduced* "what she means." Your paraphrase is a success if it corresponds accurately to the other person's intent. We're suggesting that you go beyond correspondence to creativity, beyond reproducing to producing, to mutually constructing meanings or understandings between you.

Another skill you can use in the sculpting process is to *run with the metaphor.* You can build meaning into the conversation by extending whatever metaphors the other person has used to express her or his ideas, developing your own metaphors, and encouraging the other person to extend yours. As you probably know, metaphors are figures of speech that link two dissimilar objects or ideas in order to make a point. Besides "Communication is made up of inhaling and exhaling," "Conversation is a ride on a tandem bicycle," and "Dialogic listening is sculpting mutual meanings," "This place is a zoo," and "My vacation was a circus," all contain metaphors. As these examples illustrate, metaphors don't appear only in poetry or other literature; they are a major part of most everyday conversation. In our label for this skill, "run with the metaphor," for example, the term *run* itself is metaphoric.

This skill consists of listening for both subtle and obvious metaphors and then weaving them into your responses. We have found that when other people hear their metaphor coming back to them, they can get a very quick and clear sense of how they're being heard, and they typically can develop the thought along the lines sketched by the metaphor. For example, in a workshop he was leading, John was listening to an engineer describe part of his job, which involved going before regulatory boards and municipal committees to answer questions and make arguments for various construction projects. Part of what Phil said about his job was that it was a "game." John tried to run with the metaphor by asking, "What's the name of the game?" "Winning," Phil responded. John recognized that his question had been ambiguous, so he continued: "Okay, but what kind of game is it—is it baseball, football, soccer, chess, or what?" "It's football," Phil replied. "What position do you play?" "Fullback." "And who's the offensive line?" "All the people in the office who give me the information I take to the meetings." "Who's the coach?" "We don't have one. That's the major problem." This was a telling response. In fact, from that point on, the workshop was focused on one of the major management problems that engineering firm was having.

Here's another example of how running with the metaphor can work in conversation:

TANYA: You look a lot less happy than when I saw you this morning. What's happening?

ANN: I just got out of my second two-hour class today, and I can't believe how much I have to do. I'm really feeling squashed.

TANYA: *Squashed* like you can't come up for air, or *squashed* as in you have to do what everybody else wants and you can't pursue your own ideas?

ANN: More like I can't come up for air. Every professor seems to think his or her class is the only one I'm taking.

Again, the purpose of running with the metaphor is to build the conversation between the two of you in order to produce as full as possible a response to the issues you're talking about. In addition, the metaphors themselves reframe or give a new perspective on the topic of your conversation. A project manager who sees her- or himself as a "fullback" is going to think and behave differently from one who thinks in other metaphorical terms, like "general," "Joan of Arc," "guide," or "mother hen." And the work stress that "squashes" you is different from the pressure that "keeps you jumping like a flea on a griddle." Listen for metaphors and take advantage of their power to shape and extend ideas.

Remember our point that all these specific listening skills are like dishes in a salad bar: You don't eat everything, and at different times you select different dishes. Let's look at an extended example of a conversation that illustrates some of the listening attitudes and skills we've discussed. Sally and Julio start out at opposite sides in their opinions about the class. But first Julio, and then both he and Sally dialogically listen to each other. As a result, their interpretations of the class and the teacher change; they build a meaning that neither of them had at the beginning of the conversation. At the left margins, we've labeled some of the specific empathic and dialogic listening skills they're using.

SALLY: That class drives me up a wall.

*(open
question)*
JULIO: I thought it was going pretty well. What happened?

SALLY: She's so strict! We can't miss more than five hours of class, everything has to be submitted electronically, she won't take late papers. I'll bet she wouldn't even allow a makeup exam if I was in the hospital!

(say more)
JULIO: I didn't know she wouldn't take late papers. Where did you hear that?

SALLY: Alaysha told me that on Tuesday she tried to hand in the article analysis that was due Monday and Dr. Clinton wouldn't accept it.

*(clarifying
question)*
JULIO: Was there anything else going on? Hilary and I both turned in our journals late and she took them. I also thought the five-hour restriction and the e-mail requirement were pretty standard at this school.

(say more)
SALLY: Do you have them in other classes?

JULIO: Yeah. My geology prof allows only two days' absence and won't accept hardly any excuses.

(say more)
SALLY: Are your other profs so stiff and formal in class?

JULIO: Some are and some aren't. Clinton is a lot looser in her office. Have you ever talked to her there?

(paraphrase)
SALLY: No, I don't like the way she treated Alaysha.

JULIO: So Alaysha did the assignment like she was supposed to and Clinton wouldn't take it even though it was only one day late?

SALLY: Well, it wasn't e-mailed, but I still think it's pretty unreasonable. I haven't started the paper that's due this Friday, and I'll bet there's no way she'd accept it Monday.

*(paraphrase-
plus)*
JULIO: I know how that feels. But if you've got a good reason, I'll bet she would. She told me last term

that most of her rules come from what other profs tell her are the standards here. This school is really into developing responsibility and treating everybody like an adult. That's why I thought they required attendance and e-mailed papers. But I think Clinton is willing to listen, and she's bent the rules for me a couple of times. You've been doing fine in class, and I'd really be surprised if she turned you down.

SALLY: I didn't know that about this school; this is my first term here.

JULIO: Well, I didn't know about Alaysha, but she probably should have printed it out.

SALLY: Yeah. Well, thanks for listening—and for the information.

Remember that we do not mean to present these skills as a guaranteed step-by-step way to instant success. They are suggestions, guidelines, examples of ways you can behaviorally work the focusing, encouraging, and sculpting processes of dialogic listening. They won't work if you apply them woodenly or mechanically; you have to use them with sensitivity to the relationship and the situation.

As you begin using these skills—and this also applies to all the skills we have discussed—you may feel awkward and even phony. This is natural. It is part of learning any new skill, whether it's skiing, tennis, aerobics, or listening. Remember that the better you get with practice, the less awkward you will feel. Try not to let any initial feelings of discomfort distract you from working on specific ways to improve.

REVIEW QUESTIONS

1. Describe the basic similarities and differences between empathic and dialogic listening.
2. Focusing skills take time. How can the distinction between "spending" and "investing" time encourage you to take the time to focus?
3. What is it important *not* to do with your eye contact, movement, and sound if you want to focus effectively?
4. What's the difference between a clarifying question and an open question?
5. What's a "pseudoquestion"? Why is it dangerous?
6. What are the four parts of a paraphrase?
7. *Dia-logos* means "meaning-through." Explain.
8. Distinguish ethnocentric from cosmopolitan communicating.
9. How is "focus on ours" different from the "focusing" that is part of empathic listening?

PROBES

1. How can people cope with the natural tendency to feel that practicing new communication skills will make their communicating sound phony and artificial?
2. What are some real-world exceptions to the authors' advice about "Why?" questions?
3. What danger accompanies the "adding an example" skill?
4. How can you "gently pursue verbal/nonverbal inconsistencies" without playing "Gotcha!"?
5. Google the word "dialogue," and identify examples of what we discuss about its importance in business and public communication.
6. Give an example from your own experience where you or your conversation partner "ran with a metaphor."

REFERENCES

Anderson, R., Cissna, K. N., & Arnett, R. C. (Eds.). (1994). *The reach of dialogue: Confirmation, voice, and community.* Creskill, NJ: Hampton Press

Bohm, D. (1990). *On dialogue.* Oaji, CA: David Bohm Seminars.

Halone, K. K., & Pechioni, L. L. (2001). Relational listening: A grounded theoretical model. *Communication Reports, 14,* 59–71.

Rogers, C. R. (1980). *A way of being.* Boston: Houghton Mifflin.

Goodman, G., & Esterly, G. (1990). Questions: The most popular piece of language. In J. Stewart (Ed.), *Bridges not walls,* 5th ed. (p. 760). New York: McGraw-Hill.

Stewart, J., & Thomas, M. (1990). "Dialogic listening: Sculpting mutual meanings." In J. Stewart (Ed.), *Bridges not walls.* 6th ed. (pp. 184–202). New York: McGraw-Hill..

Stiff, J. B., Dillard, J. P., Somera, L., Kim, H., & Sleight, C. (1988). Empathy, communication, and prosocial behavior. *Communication Monographs, 55,* 198–213.

CHAPTER 6

Exhaling: Expressing and Disclosing

Being Open with and to Other People
David W. Johnson

The first half of "making meaning together" (the title of Part Two of *Bridges Not Walls*) is "inhaling," and the second half of this process involves what I'm calling "exhaling." As the metaphor indicates, this is the "output" or "sending" part of communication. The readings in this chapter explain interpersonal openness and self-expression.

This first reading is from a book called *Reaching Out: Interpersonal Effectiveness and Self-Actualization,* by David Johnson, a teacher at the University of Minnesota. He begins with the notion that all of our relationships can be classified on a continuum from open to closed. Of course, an "open" work or school relationship is different from an "open" family or intimate relationship, but in all cases, Johnson claims, openness means both being open *with* other people (disclosing yourself to them) and openness *to* others (listening to them in an accepting way). Relationships of all sorts develop as both kinds of openness increase.

With a considerable amount of social scientific research in the background, Johnson defines self-disclosure and identifies four of its important characteristics. He notes that effective disclosure focuses on the present rather than the past, includes feelings as well as facts, has both breadth and depth, and, especially in the early stages of a relationship, needs to be reciprocal. Then Johnson outlines the impact self-disclosure has on relationships and describes some of its benefits. He argues that "if you cannot reveal yourself, you cannot become close to others, and you cannot be valued by others for who you are." Clearly, there are various ways to self-disclose and various kinds of information to share. But this author makes a strong connection between disclosure and effective interpersonal communicating.

One benefit of disclosure is that it can begin and deepen your relationships, whether at work, home, or school. It can also increase your self-awareness and your understanding of yourself. Self-disclosure can provide, as Johnson puts it, "a freeing experience" and can also help you control challenging social situations. Another benefit of self-disclosure is that it can help you manage stress and adversity.

Johnson also lists eight ways to keep self-disclosures appropriate. I think each of the eight is useful. As he notes, disclosures need to be part of an ongoing relationship, not "off the wall" or "out of nowhere." They need to be focused on the people present and sensitive to others' possible distress. Disclosure ought to be intended to improve the relationship and should move to deeper levels only gradually. Johnson also usefully notes that "there are times when you will want to hide your reactions," and he explains when and why.

In the final section of this reading, Johnson talks about the connection between self-disclosure and self-presentation. He discusses how all of us help manage others' impressions of who we are, in part with our self-disclosures. He compares and contrasts the motives of "strategic self-presentation," which means efforts to shape others' impression of us, and "self-verification," which is the desire to have others perceive us as we genuinely perceive ourselves. As he notes, "self-presentation and impression management are part of everyone's life," which is why Johnson believes that the more you know about self-disclosure, the more effective you can be at this part of your communicating.

MAIN IDEAS

- Relationships can be classified on a sliding scale from "open" to "closed," where openness means both being open *with* others by disclosing and being open *to* others by listening well.
- Openness *with* another requires self-disclosure, which requires some level of self-awareness, self-acceptance, and trust.
- Self-disclosure is revealing to another person how you are responding to the present situation and giving information that helps others understand your present responses.
- Healthy relationships are built on self-disclosure.
- Self-disclosure enables you and others to get to know each other.
- Self-disclosure allows you and others to identify common goals and overlapping needs, interests, activities, and values.
- Self-disclosure is necessary to collaborate to accomplish goals.
- Self-disclosure improves the quality of relationships and allows the discloser to validate her perceptions of reality.
- Self-disclosure can increase self-awareness and be liberating.
- You can always choose what to disclose and when.
- There are at least eight principles for keeping disclosures appropriate.
- Appropriate disclosures are selective and adapted to their audiences.
- Two motives for disclosure are strategic self-presentation and self-verification.

Relationships may be classified on a continuum from open to closed. *Openness* in a relationship refers to participants' willingness to share their ideas, feelings, and reactions to the current situation. On a professional basis, relationships among collaborators who are working to achieve mutual goals tend to be quite open, while relationships among competitors who are seeking advantages over each other tend to be quite closed. On a personal level, some relationships (such as friendships) are very open, while other relationships (such as casual acquaintances) are relatively closed. The more open participants in a relationship are with each other, the more positive, constructive, and effective the relationship tends to be.

Openness has two sides. To build good relationships you must be both open *with* other people (disclosing yourself to them) and open *to* others (listening to their disclosures in an accepting way). Usually, the more that people know about you, the more likely they are to like you. Yet self-disclosure does carry a degree of risk. For just as knowing you better is likely to result in a closer relationship, sometimes it could result in people liking you less. "Familiarity breeds contempt" means that some people may learn something about you that detracts from the relationship. Because disclosing is risky, some people prefer to hide themselves from others in the belief that no reaction is better than a possible negative reaction. "Nothing ventured, nothing gained," however, means that some risk is vital to achieving any worthwhile goal. To build a meaningful relationship you have to disclose yourself to the other person and take the risk that the other person may reject rather than like you.

The other side of the coin is responding to the other person's self-disclosures. Being open to another person means showing that you are interested in how he or she feels and thinks. This does not mean prying into the intimate areas of his or her life. It means being willing to listen in an accepting way to his or her reactions to the present situation and to what you are doing and saying. Even when a person's behavior offends you, you may wish to express acceptance of the person and disagreement with the way he or she behaves.

In order for the relationship to build and develop, both individuals have to disclose and be open to other people's disclosures. Openness depends on three factors: self-awareness, self-acceptance, and trust....

OPENNESS WITH OTHER INDIVIDUALS

You are *open with* other persons when you disclose yourself to them, sharing your ideas, feelings, and reactions to the present situation, and letting other people know who you are as a person. To be open with another person you must (a) be aware of who you are, (b) accept yourself, and (c) take the risk of trusting the other person to be accepting of you. Openness thus can be described as being dependent on self-awareness (S), self-acceptance (A), and trust (T) (O = S A T). Commonly, openness is known as self-disclosure.

What Is Self-Disclosure?

Self-disclosure is revealing to another person how you perceive and are reacting to the present situation and giving any information about yourself and your past that is relevant to an understanding of your perceptions and reactions to the present. Effective self-disclosure has a number of characteristics:

1. **Self-disclosure focuses on the present, not the past.** Self-disclosure does not mean revealing intimate details of your past life. Making highly personal confessions about your past may lead to a temporary feeling of intimacy, but a relationship is built by disclosing your reactions to events you both are experiencing or to what the other person says or does. A person comes to know and understand you not through knowing your past history but through knowing how you react. Past history is helpful only if it clarifies why you are reacting in a certain way.

2. **Reactions to people and events include feelings as well as facts.** To be self-disclosing often means to share with another person how you feel about events that are occurring.
3. **Self-disclosures have two dimensions—breadth and depth.** As you get to know someone better and better, you cover more topics in your explanations (breadth) and make your explanations more personally revealing (depth).
4. **In the early stages of a relationship, self-disclosure needs to be reciprocal.** The amount of self-disclosure you engage in will influence the amount of self-disclosure the other person engages in and vice versa. The polite thing to do is to match the level of self-disclosure offered by new acquaintances, disclosing more if they do so and drawing back if their self-disclosure declines. Once a relationship is well established, strict reciprocity occurs much less frequently.

Impact of Self-Disclosure on Relationships

Healthy relationships are built on self-disclosure. A relationship grows and develops as two people become more open about themselves to each other. *If you cannot reveal yourself, you cannot become close to others, and you cannot be valued by others for who you are.* Two people who let each other know how they are reacting to situations and to each other are pulled together; two people who stay silent about their reactions and feelings stay strangers.

There are many ways in which self-disclosure initiates, builds, and maintains relationships. *First, self-disclosure enables you and other people to get to know each other.* Most relationships proceed from superficial exchanges to more intimate ones. At first, individuals disclose relatively little to another person and receive relatively little in return. When initial interactions are enjoyable or interesting, exchanges become (a) broader, involving more areas of your life, and (b) deeper, involving more important and sensitive areas. In terms of breadth, from discussing the weather and sports, as the relationship develops you may discuss a wider range of topics (such as your family, your hopes and dreams, issues at work, and so forth) and share more diverse activities (such as going to movies or plays together, going bike riding or playing tennis together, and so forth). In terms of depth, you might willingly talk with a casual acquaintance about your preferences in food and music but reserve for close friends discussions of your anxieties and personal ambitions. The longer people interact, the more topics they tend to be willing to discuss and the more personally revealing they tend to become. This does not mean that getting to know another person is a simple process of being more and more open. You do not simply disclose more and more each day. Rather, there are cycles of seeking intimacy and avoiding it. Sometimes you are candid and confiding with a friend, and other times you are restrained and distant. The development of caring and commitment in a relationship, however, results from the cumulative history of self-disclosure in the relationship.

Second, self-disclosure allows you and other individuals to identify common goals and overlapping needs, interests, activities, and values. In order to know whether a relationship with another person is desirable, you have to know what the other person wants from the relationship, what the other person is interested in, what joint activities might be available, and what the other person values. Relationships are built on common goals, interests, activities, and values. If such information is not disclosed, the relationship may end before it has a chance to begin.

Third, once common goals have been identified, self-disclosure is necessary to work together to accomplish them. Working together requires constant self-disclosure to ensure effective communication, decision making, leadership, and resolution of conflict. Joint action to achieve mutual goals cannot be effective unless collaborators are quite open in their interactions with each other.

Just as relationships are built through self-disclosure, *relationships can deteriorate for lack of self-disclosure.* Sometimes people hide their reactions from others through fear of rejection, fear of a potential or ongoing conflict, or feelings of shame and guilt. Whatever the reason, if you hide how you are reacting to the other person, your concealment can hurt the relationship, and the energy you pour into hiding is an additional stress on the relationship. Hiding your perceptions and feelings dulls your awareness of your own inner experience and decreases your ability to disclose your reactions even when it is perfectly safe and appropriate to do so. The result can be the end of the relationship. Being silent is not being strong—strength is the willingness to take a risk by disclosing yourself with the intention of building a better relationship.

Benefits of Self-Disclosure

We disclose information to another person for many reasons. *First, you begin and deepen a relationship by sharing reactions, feelings, personal information, and confidences.* This topic has already been discussed.

Second, self-disclosure improves the quality of relationships. We disclose to those we like. We like those who disclose to us. We like those to whom we have disclosed. Overall, it is through self-disclosure that caring is developed among individuals and commitment to each other is built.

Third, self-disclosure allows you to validate your perception of reality. Listeners provide useful information about social reality. The events taking place around us and the meaning of other people's behavior are often ambiguous, open to many different interpretations. By seeing how a listener reacts to your self-disclosures, you get information about the correctness and appropriateness of your views. Other people may reassure you that your reactions are "perfectly normal" or suggest that you are "blowing things out of proportion." If others have similar interpretations, we consider our perceptions to be valid. Comparing your perceptions and reactions with the reactions and perceptions of others is called *consensual validation.* Without self-disclosure, consensual validation could not take place.

Fourth, self-disclosure increases your self-awareness and clarifies your understanding of yourself. In explaining your feelings in watching a sunset or why you like a certain book, you clarify aspects of yourself to yourself. In sharing your feelings and experiences with others, you may gain greater self-understanding and self-awareness. Talking to a friend about a problem, for example, can help you clarify your thoughts about a situation. Sharing your reactions with others results in feedback from others, which contributes to a more objective perspective on your experiences.

Fifth, the expression of feelings and reactions is a freeing experience. Sometimes it helps to get emotions and reactions "off your chest." After a difficult day at work, it may release pent up feelings by telling a friend how angry you are at your boss or how unappreciated you feel. Even sharing long-term feelings of insecurity with a trusted friend may free you from such feelings. Simply being able to express your emotions is a reason for self-disclosure.

Sixth, you may disclose information about yourself or not as a means of social control. You may deliberately refrain from talking about yourself to end an interaction as quickly as possible or you may emphasize topics, beliefs, or ideas that you think will make a favorable impression on the other person.

Seventh, self-disclosing is an important part of managing stress and adversity. Communicating intimately with another person, especially in times of stress, seems to be a basic human need. By discussing your fear, you free yourself from it. By sharing your anxiety, you gain insight into ways to reduce it. By describing a problem, you see ways to solve it. The more you seek out a friend in times of adversity and discuss the situation openly, the more you will be able to deal with the stress and solve your problem.

Finally, self-disclosure fulfills a human need to be known intimately and accepted. Most people want someone to know them well and accept, appreciate, respect, and like them.

Keeping Your Self-Disclosures Appropriate

You only self-disclose when it is appropriate to do so. Just as you can disclose too little, you can also be too self-disclosing. Refusing to let anyone know anything about you keeps others away. Revealing too many of your reactions too fast may scare others away. Typically, a relationship is built gradually and develops in stages. Although you should sometimes take risks in sharing your reactions with others, you should ensure that the frequency and depth of your reactions are appropriate to the situation. When you are unsure about the appropriateness of your self-disclosures, you may wish to follow these guidelines:

1. I make sure my disclosures are not a random or isolated act but rather part of an ongoing relationship.
2. I focus my disclosures on what is going on within and between persons in the present.
3. I am sensitive to the effect a disclosure will have on the other person. Some disclosures may upset or cause considerable distress. What you want to say

may seem inappropriate to the other person. Most people become uncomfortable when the level of self-disclosure exceeds their expectations.

4. I only disclose when it has a reasonable chance of improving the relationship.
5. I continue only if my disclosures are reciprocated. When you share your reactions, you should expect disclosure in return. When it is apparent that self-disclosures will not be reciprocated, you should limit the disclosures you make.
6. I increase my disclosures when a crisis develops in the relationship.
7. I gradually move my disclosures to a deeper level. Self-disclosures may begin with the information acquaintances commonly disclose (such as talking about hobbies, sports, school, and current events) and gradually move to more personal information. As a friendship develops, the depth of disclosure increases as well. Disclosures about deep feelings and concerns are most appropriate in close, well-established relationships.
8. I keep my reactions and feelings to myself when the other person is competitive or untrustworthy. While relationships are built through self-disclosure, there are times when you will want to hide your reactions. If a person has been untrustworthy and if you know from past experience that the other person will misinterpret or overreact to your self-disclosure, you may wish to keep silent....

SELF-DISCLOSURE AND SELF-PRESENTATION

The image of myself which I try to create in my own mind that I may love myself is very different from the image which I try to create in the minds of others in order that they may love me.

—W. H. Auden

Self-disclosure is based on self-awareness, self-acceptance, and taking the risk of revealing yourself to others. Self-disclosure takes place in an ongoing social interaction in which you choose how you wish to present yourself to others. Most people are concerned about the images they present to others. The fashion industry, the cosmetic companies, diet centers, and the search for new drugs that grow hair, remove hair, whiten teeth, freshen breath, and smooth out wrinkles, all exploit our preoccupation with physical appearance. Manners, courtesy, and etiquette are all responses to concern about the impressions our behavior makes.

In *As You Like It,* William Shakespeare wrote, "All the world's a stage, and all the men and women merely players." Erving Goffman put Shakespeare's thought into social science by arguing that life can be viewed as a play in which each of us acts out certain scripted lines. Our scripts are a reflection of the social face or social identity that we want to present to others. *Self-presentation* is the process by which we try to shape what others think of us and what we think of ourselves. It is part of *impression management*—the general process by which you behave in particular ways to create a desired social image.

In presenting yourself to others, you have to recognize that there are many complex aspects of yourself. It is as if you have a number of selves that are tied to certain situations and certain groups of people with whom you interact. The self you present to your parents is usually different from the self you present to your peers. You present yourself differently to your boss, subordinates, colleagues, customers, neighbors, same-sex friends, opposite-sex friends, and strangers. When you are playing tennis, the aspect of yourself that loves physical exercise and competition may be most evident. When you attend a concert, the aspect of yourself that responds with deep emotion to classical music may be most evident. In church, your religious side may be most evident. In a singles bar, your interest in other people may be most evident. In different situations and with different people, different aspects of yourself will be relevant.

In presenting yourself to others, you have to vary your presentation to the audience. Societal norms virtually require that you present yourself in different ways to different audiences. You are expected to address someone considerably older than you differently from the way you address your peers. You are expected to address the president of the United States differently from how you address your next-door neighbor. In formal situations you are expected to act in ways different from how you would act in informal situations. Depending on the setting, the role relationship, and your previous experience with the person, you are expected to monitor your behavior and present yourself accordingly.

In presenting yourself to others, you basically have two motives: strategic self-presentation and self-verification. *Strategic self-presentation* consists of efforts to shape others' impressions in specific ways in order to gain influence, power, sympathy, or approval. Job interviews, personal ads, political campaign promises, and a defendant's appeal to a jury are examples. Your goal may be to be perceived as likable, competent, moral, dangerous, or even helpless, depending on the situation and the relationship. You communicate who you are and what you are like through your clothes, appearance, posture, eye contact, tone of voice, manners, and gestures. There are many people who believe that you will be perceived in quite different ways depending on your style of dress, manner, and cleanliness. Clothing, they believe, transmits messages about the wearer's personality, attitudes, social status, behavior, and group allegiances. People who wear clothes associated with high status tend to have more influence than those wearing low-status clothes. Somber hues (grays, dark blues, or browns) of clothing seem to communicate ambition, a taste for moderate risks and long-range planning, and a preference for tasks that have clear criteria for success and failure. Attention to clothes, posture, eye contact, tone of voice, manners, and gestures may be especially important for first impressions.

Related to strategic self-presentation are ingratiation and self-promotion. *Ingratiation* describes acts that are motivated by the desire to get along and be liked. When people want to be liked, they put their best foot forward, smile a lot, make eye contact, nod their heads, express agreement with what is said, and give compliments and favors. *Self-promotion* describes acts that are motivated by a desire to "get ahead" and be respected for one's competence. When people want to be respected for their competence, they try to impress others by talking about themselves and immodestly showing off their knowledge, status, and exploits.

The second self-presentation motive is *self-verification*—the desire to have others perceive us as we genuinely perceive ourselves. This is sometimes known as *open self-presentation,* which consists of efforts to let others see you as you believe yourself to be. People generally are quite motivated to verify their existing self-view in the eyes of others. People, for example, often selectively elicit, recall, and accept feedback that confirms their self-conceptions. This statement does not mean that they wish to fool others about who they are. People often work hard to correct others whose impressions of them are mistaken. They may want to make a good impression, but they also want others (especially their friends) to have an accurate impression, one that is consistent with their own self-concept.

Self-presentation and impression management are part of everyone's life. Some people do these things more consciously and successfully than others. People differ in their ability to present themselves appropriately and create the impression they want. The more self-monitoring you are, the more sensitive you tend to be to strategic self-presentation concerns, poised, ready, and able to modify your behavior as you move from one situation to another.

The self is an enduring aspect of human personality, an invisible "inner core" that is stable over time and slow to change. The struggle to "find yourself" or "be true to yourself" is based on this view. Yet at least part of the self is malleable, molded by life experiences and different from one situation to the next. In this sense, the self is multifaceted and has many different faces. Each of us has a private self consisting of our innermost thoughts and feelings, memories, and self-views. We also have an outer self, portrayed by the roles we play and the way we present ourselves in public. In fulfilling our social obligations and presenting ourselves to others, we base our presentations on the complexity of our personalities, the social norms specifying appropriate behavior, and the motives of revealing who we really are, verifying our views of ourselves, and creating strategic impressions.

REVIEW QUESTIONS

1. Explain the difference between being open *with* another person and being open *to* another person.
2. Explain $O = S A T$.
3. According to Johnson, what is the relationship between self-disclosure and liking?
4. List the eight possible benefits of self-disclosure.
5. Explain the relationship between self-disclosure and self-awareness.
6. Define *strategic self-presentation* and *self-verification.*

PROBES

1. Johnson argues that "in order for the relationship to build and develop, both individuals have to disclose and be open to other people's disclosures." Do you agree? Is disclosure and openness to others necessary for the development of *all* relationships? Are there any exceptions?
2. Why does self-disclosure need to be reciprocal in the early stages of a relationship? Why can it be one-sided or nonreciprocal in some later stages of a relationship?
3. Johnson notes that "there are cycles of seeking intimacy and avoiding it." Explain what he means. Why is this important to understand and practice?
4. Give an example of how self-disclosure can function as a means of social control.
5. Is there a contradiction between Johnson's preference for "openness" and his argument that self-disclosure should be "appropriate"? Doesn't appropriateness require not always being open?
6. Johnson indicates that "you have a number of selves that are tied to certain situations and certain groups of people." Do you think he believes that people also have a "core" or stable, central self? Do you?

Expression: Speak for Yourself with Clarity and Power

Douglas Stone, Bruce Patton, and Sheila Heen

This is another excerpt from the book *Difficult Conversations: How to Discuss What Matters Most* by three people connected with the Harvard Negotiation Project. I explained that project when I introduced the essay by these authors in Chapter 3.

The first short paragraph may be a little confusing, because it includes a brief summary of the rest of Stone, Patton, and Heen's book up to this point. Here's some clarification: Their book's first piece of advice for beginning a difficult conversation is to "begin from the Third Story." This means that you start not with your view or the other person's view but with a view of the situation and topic from a third person's perspective, outside both your own and the other person's points of view. Their second piece of advice is that you listen to the other person's story with a sincere desire to understand it. Their third suggestion is the topic of this reading: In order for a difficult conversation to succeed, you need to express yourself.

They point out that your goal should not be eloquence or powerful persuasion but candid and sincere explanation. Then they review some pitfalls that often undercut people's abilities to express themselves clearly. The first is the belief, held by some, that my opinion isn't worthy or valuable enough to express. It is valuable, they emphasize, just as the other person's is, too. The second pitfall is "self-sabotage," and they explain what it is and how to avoid it. Then they make essentially the same point *Bridges Not Walls* makes in Chapter 2: You are the best person to be sure that your views are present in the relationship, and even though expressing yourself can be difficult, it gives the relationship a chance to change and get stronger.

Next come some practical suggestions, the first of which is, "Start with what matters most." You should also be straightforward, saying what you mean rather than making the other person(s) guess what's important to you. The authors point out that this step often takes some reflection on your part. You need to figure out what you are really thinking and feeling, and then say it directly. They also suggest that you "avoid easing in" to your topic, starting instead with as explicit and direct a statement as you can muster.

Some of the authors' next four suggestions are stated as "don'ts" rather than "dos," but each is very useful. They advise you to keep your story as complex as the interpersonal situation actually is; as they put it, "When we try to be simple, we often end up being incomplete." Complexity can be communicated with what they call "the And stance." This advice echoes what I wrote about the word "and" in Chapter 4.

Rather than presenting your conclusions as *The* Truth, they recommend what Jack Gibb calls "provisionalism" in his essay on Defensiveness in Chapter 9. They also remind you to share where your conclusions come from and to avoid "always and never" language.

Stone, Patton, and Heen wrap up this treatment of self-expression with the suggestions that you help your conversation partner understand you by asking them to paraphrase what you've said, and to explain how they see things differently and why.

There is some good advice here. And, although the authors don't emphasize it, their advice is grounded in solid communication theory.

MAIN IDEAS

- Difficult conversations won't succeed until both or all persons clearly express themselves.
- Your overall goal should be clarity, not eloquence.
- Remember that you are entitled to be heard, just as the other person is; feel entitled and encouraged, and not obligated.
- Start with what matters most and don't make them guess what you mean.
- Include the complexity of your motives, preferences, and ideas.
- Use "Me-Me And" statements, like "I do think you are bright and talented, *and* I think you're not working hard enough."
- Present your conclusions provisionally, rather than as *The* Truth.
- Share where your conclusions come from.
- Avoid "Always" and "Never"; give the other(s) room to change.
- Ask them to paraphrase back and how they see the situation differently.

Beginning from the Third Story is a productive way to open a conversation. Listening to the other person's story with a real desire to learn what they are thinking and feeling is a crucial next step. But understanding them is

From Stone, Patton, and Heen. *Difficult Conversations: How to Discuss What Matters Most.* New York: Penguin Books, 1999, pp. 185–200.

rarely the end of the matter; the other person also needs to hear *your* story. You need to express yourself.

ORATORS NEED NOT APPLY

Expressing yourself well in a difficult conversation has nothing to do with how big your vocabulary is or how eloquent or quick-witted you are. Winston Churchill and Martin Luther King, Jr. were great orators, but in difficult conversations their powers of oration would be of no particular assistance.

In a difficult conversation your primary task is not to persuade, impress, trick, outwit, convert, or win over the other person. It is to express what you see and why you see it that way, how you feel, and maybe who you are. Self-knowledge and the belief that what you want to share is important will take you significantly further than eloquence and wit.

In the first part of this chapter we take up the issue of entitlement. To communicate with clarity and power, you must first negotiate yourself into a place where you truly believe that what you want to express is worthy of expression—a belief that your views and feelings are as important as anyone else's. Period. In the second part of the chapter, we look at how to figure out *what* you want to express and *how* you might best express it. We'll examine several common but significant expression errors, ways to avoid them, and methods for expressing yourself well.

YOU'RE ENTITLED (YES, YOU)

John, a second-year law student, was preparing to meet with a well-respected federal judge to discuss several concerns he had about his upcoming clerkship. The judge had a reputation for being a sometimes prickly and argumentative fellow, and John was anxious about losing his courage once he stepped into the judge's chambers.

John's favorite professor offered advice: "Whenever I have felt intimidated or mistreated by someone above me, I remember this—we are all equal in the eyes of God."

No More, But No Less

Regardless of our spiritual orientation, we can all benefit from the message: No matter who we are, no matter how high and mighty we fancy ourselves, or how low and unworthy we may feel, we all deserve to be treated with respect and dignity. My views and feelings are as legitimate, valuable, and important as yours—no more, but no less. For some people, that's utterly obvious. For others, it comes as important news....

Beware Self-Sabotage

Sometimes we can feel trapped between the belief that we should stand up for ourselves and a hidden feeling that we don't deserve to be heard, that we're not entitled. In this situation our unconscious mind can offer a devious—and illusory—"solution": We go through the motions of trying, but incompetently, so that in the end we fail. We wait to speak until there's not enough time to deal with our concerns. We conveniently forget our materials. All our points suddenly disappear from our head. And voilà! All of our interests are satisfied: we can feel good about trying, and secretly satisfied that we didn't succeed. This is the art of self-sabotage.

If this feels like a familiar trick in your repertoire, then you may need to pay more attention to when you are feeling ambivalent. When you sense that vaguely sick or confused feeling, imagine an enormous STOP sign to halt you in your tracks. Before proceeding, you need to engage your Identity Conversation. Why aren't you entitled? Whose voice from your past do you hear in your head telling you you're not? What would you need to feel fully entitled to speak up?

Failure to Express Yourself Keeps You Out of the Relationship

The ferry tickets to the island of Martha's Vineyard, Massachusetts, read like many transportation tickets. Perforated in the middle, the ticket carries a warning that it will be "void if detached."

We run the same risks in difficult conversations. When we fail to share what's most important to us, we detach ourselves from others and damage our relationships.

Most of us actually prefer being with someone who will speak their mind. Angela broke off her engagement because her fiancé was "too nice." He never stated a preference, never argued, never raised his voice, never asked for anything. While she appreciated his kindness, she felt something was missing: him.

If you are sometimes lonely or despondent and never share this with those close to you, then you deny them the chance to come to know a part of you. You presume that they will not respect or like or admire you as much if they knew the way you really think and feel. But it's hard to present only this sanitized version of yourself. Often, to hide parts of who we are, we end up hiding all of who we are. And so we present a front that appears lifeless and removed.

Expressing yourself can be difficult and trying, but it gives the relationship a chance to change and to become stronger. Callie, a Native American woman, did not feel particularly close to her co-workers at a tutoring program for troubled teens. Partly because they were white, she suspected they wouldn't really understand her; indeed, she often found them to be insensitive.

But one day she took a risk and shared some stories. She described how she had been called names and teased when she was younger, and how for years she yearned to be "normal." These revelations significantly changed her relationship with her colleagues, who came to have great admiration for her. Her colleagues, in turn, felt encouraged to share their own stories of feeling left out or awkward. If Callie had not shared her story, she would have deprived her colleagues of the chance to rebut a stereotype she herself harbored—that "white people don't understand and don't care." And she wouldn't have offered them the opportunity, perhaps for the first time, to understand and care about her.

A relationship takes hold and grows when both participants experience themselves and the other as being authentic. Such relationships are both more comfortable (it's more relaxing to be yourself) and nourishing to the soul ("My boss knows some of my vulnerabilities and still thinks I'm okay").

Feel Entitled, Feel Encouraged, but Don't Feel Obligated

You are entitled to express yourself. If you do not believe this to your core then you've got some work to do.

But being entitled doesn't mean you're obligated. That turns entitlement into another way to beat yourself up: "I should be saying what's on my mind, but I'm too afraid. I can't do anything right!" Expressing yourself is often extremely difficult. Finding the courage to do it is a lifelong process. If you aren't doing it as much as you'd like, it's something to work on, but not something to punish yourself about.

SPEAK THE HEART OF THE MATTER

The first step toward expressing yourself is finding your sense of entitlement to speak up; the next step is figuring out what, exactly, you want to say.

Start with What Matters Most

There's no better place to begin your story than with what is at the very heart of the matter for you: "For me, what this is really about is.... What I'm feeling is.... What is important to me is...."

Sharing what is important to you is common sense, and yet it's advice we often neglect. Consider the story of Charlie, the oldest of four brothers, who wants to improve his relationship with his youngest brother, sixteen-year-old Gage. Gage is dyslexic, which is especially tough since his older brothers all graduated near the top of their high school classes and went to college on academic scholarships. Gage struggles in school, is prone to act out, and has increasingly turned to drinking for solace.

Charlie wants to help by offering the benefit of his experience and advice: "You should definitely do the debate team. The coach is great, and it will help your college applications." And, "You know, Gage, don't overdo the drinking thing. It can really be bad news." But whatever Charlie says makes Gage feel criticized, defensive, and patronized. As a result, the two brothers have grown increasingly distant.

When we asked Charlie why the relationship is important to him, the story took a different turn. Charlie admires the way Gage works so hard to succeed. He feels bad about how he treated Gage when they were younger. And ultimately, it turns out that Charlie needs deeply to feel like a good brother, who loves and is loved in turn. As he revealed this, Charlie cried.

When Charlie finally shared these things with his brother, Gage was riveted. Charlie needed *him*. Charlie needed Gage's help in being a good brother. It proved a turning point in their relationship.

Gage would have had to be a mind reader to perceive even a hint of these meanings in Charlie's original communication. The heart of the message simply wasn't there. Nor was there a hint of the enormous depth of feelings at stake. Instead, there was a completely different message in its place: "You're a screwup who needs my help and is too dumb to ask for it."

This is unfortunately all too typical of many difficult conversations. We say the least important things, sometimes over and over again, and wonder why the other person doesn't realize what we really think and how we really feel.

As you embark upon a difficult conversation, ask yourself, "Have I said what is at the heart of the matter for me? Have I shared what is at stake?" If not, ask yourself why, and see if you can find the courage to try.

Say What You Mean: Don't Make Them Guess

One way we often skirt sharing things that are important to us is by embedding them in the subtext of the conversation rather than simply stating them outright.

Don't Rely on Subtext   Think back to the Introduction, where we discussed the dilemma of whether to engage in a conversation or to try to avoid it. One common way to manage this dilemma—especially when you're not sure you're really entitled to bring something up—is to communicate through subtext. You try to get your message across indirectly, through jokes, questions, offhand comments, or body language.

Bringing it up by not quite bringing it up seems a happy medium between avoiding and engaging. It is a way of doing neither and doing both. The problem is, to the extent you are doing both, you're doing both badly. You end up triggering all of the problems you worried you'd create by bringing it up, without getting the benefit of clearly saying what you want to say.

Imagine that you and your husband have usually spent Saturdays sleeping in, puttering around the house, walking the dog, or doing errands together. Recently, however, he has discovered golf, and has begun playing 18 holes every Saturday morning. Your Saturday regime has never been particularly important—it's not like it was a date or something—but now that it's gone, you're missing it. The two of you don't spend much time alone together during the rest of the week, and as a result, you're feeling more and more irritated with his new hobby.

You could avoid conflict altogether by simply saying nothing, though as we've seen, your unhappiness would probably still leak out in spite of yourself. Or you might try to bring it up indirectly: "Honey, there's really a lot to be done around the house this weekend." "Is golf so important that you need to play it this often?" "Honey, you are simply playing too much golf!"

None of these comments conveys what you really mean, which is: "I want to spend more time with you." Let's consider the text and subtext of what each statement is saying:

"Honey, there's really a lot to be done around the house this weekend." This comment falls short on several grounds. First, it's simply the wrong subject. Working around the house is related to but different from spending time together. Second, even if work were the issue, the statement is shared as "truth." Your husband can reply, "There's not that much to do, and we'll talk about it when I get back."

"Is golf so important that you need to play it this often?" This is a classic example of a statement masquerading as a question. It's obvious that the meaning of the comment is conveyed in the subtext. What is less obvious is what the meaning is supposed to be. Your tone conveys anger or frustration. But it's not clear what is causing the anger or what your husband is supposed to do about it. Are you angry that your husband is engaged in a meaningless sport rather than community service or household chores? Are you angry that he's not taking you along? Are you angry that you aren't spending enough time together? How would he know?

"Honey, you are simply playing too much golf!" This statement is an opinion couched as a fact. Your husband is left to wonder, "Too much golf in relation to what?" "How much golf is too much golf?" "How much would be an appropriate amount of golf?" "Even if I am playing too much golf, so what?" Of course, even if he knew the answers to these questions, he would not have received the message intended. The gap between "You are playing too much golf" and "I would like to spend more time with you" is just too great.

To do better, you need to figure out what you are really thinking and feeling, and then say it directly: "I'd like to spend more time with you, and Saturday morning was one of the few times we had to spend together. As a result, I'm finding your interest in golf irritating."

Sometimes, you'll find yourself wishing you didn't have to be explicit. You wish the other person already knew that there was a problem and would do something about it. This is a common and understandable fantasy—our ideal mate or perfect colleague should be able to read our mind and meet our needs without our having to ask. Unfortunately, such people don't exist. Over time, we may come to know better how we each think and feel, but we will never be perfect. Being disappointed that someone isn't reading our mind is one of *our* contributions to the problem.

Avoid Easing In   A related and often destructive way to communicate through subtext is what Professor Chris Argyris of Harvard Business School has called *easing in*. Easing in is where you try to soften a message by delivering it indirectly through hints and leading questions. This is all too common in performance reviews: "So, how do *you* think you've done?" "Do you think you've really done as much as you could have?" "I have the same problem, but it probably would have been a little better to.... Wouldn't you agree?"

Easing in conveys three messages: "I have a view," "This is too embarrassing to discuss directly," and "I'm not going to be straight with you." Not surprisingly, these messages increase both sides' anxiety and defensiveness. And the recipient's imagination almost always conjures up a message worse than the real one.

A better approach is to make the subject clear and discussable by stating your thoughts straight out, while also indicating, honestly, that you are interested in whether the other person sees the situation differently and, if so, how: "Based on what I know, it seems to me that you might have gotten more done. However, you know more about what happened. In what ways would you see it differently?" Then if you disagree, you can talk directly about how to test or otherwise reconcile or deal with your different views.

Don't Make Your Story Simplistic: Use the "Me-Me" And

We've all learned that for others to understand us, we need to make what we say clear and simple. Fair enough, as far as it goes. The problem is this: What's going on in our heads is often a jumble of complex thoughts, feelings, assumptions, and perceptions. When we try to be simple, we often end up being incomplete.

Imagine that you receive a memo from a co-worker that leaves you confused. You are thinking, "This memo shows incredible creativity, and at the same time is so badly organized that it makes me crazy." In your attempt to be clear, you say, "Your memo is so badly organized it makes me crazy," or worse, "Your memo makes me crazy."

You can avoid oversimplifying by using the Me-Me And. The And Stance recognizes that each of various perceptions, feelings, and assumptions is important to talk about. This is true of the other person's perceptions *and* your perceptions, the other person's feelings *and* yours. It's also true of the various perceptions, feelings, and assumptions that are going on *just inside you*. The "and" in this case is connecting two aspects of what you think or feel. And though complex, it's both clear and accurate. Me-Me And statements sound like this:

> I do think you are bright and talented, *and* I think you're not working hard enough.

> I feel badly for how rough things have been for you, *and* I'm feeling disappointed in you.

I'm upset with myself for not noticing that you were so lonely. *And* I also was having problems during that time.

I feel relieved and happy that I finally went through with the divorce—it was the right decision. *And* I do miss him sometimes.

The Me-Me And is also useful for overcoming a common obstacle to starting a difficult conversation: the fear of being misunderstood. You think your team would be the best one to take on a new client, but fear that it will sound self-serving, that you're in it only for the glory and the bonus. If this is the fear, share it along with your argument: "I have a view on this that I want to share, and I have to say that I'm nervous about doing so because I'm afraid it may sound self-serving. So if you see anything in what I say that doesn't seem legitimate, please say so and let's discuss it." Or, in a different situation, "I'm having a strong reaction here that I'd like to share, and I'm worried about feeling embarrassed if I'm not able to be clear or unemotional at first. I hope if that happens that you'll bear with me and help me stay with it until I can put it succinctly."

TELLING YOUR STORY WITH CLARITY: THREE GUIDELINES

Obviously, how you express yourself makes a difference. How you say what you want to say will determine, in part, how others respond to you, and how the conversation will go. So when you choose to share something important, you'll want to do so in a way that will maximize the chance that the other person will understand and respond productively. Clarity is the key.

1. Don't Present Your Conclusions as *The* Truth

Some aspects of difficult conversations will continue to be rough even when you communicate with great skill: sharing feelings of vulnerability, delivering bad news, learning something painful about how others see you. But presenting your story as the truth—which creates resentment, defensiveness, and leads to arguments—is a wholly avoidable disaster.

It is an easy mistake to make. It's based on an error of thought: we often experience our beliefs, opinions, and judgments as facts. When you're arguing about a favorite movie or food or sports hero, sharing judgment as the truth is fine. But in difficult conversations it doesn't wash. Facts are facts. Everything else is everything else. And you need to be scrupulously vigilant about the distinction....

Some words—like "attractive," "ugly," "good," and "bad"—carry judgments that are obvious. But be careful with words like "inappropriate," "should," or "professional." The judgments contained in these words are less obvious, but can still provoke the "Who are you to tell me?!" response. If you want to say something is "inappropriate," preface your judgment with "My view is that...." Better still, avoid these words altogether.

This is not an argument that there is no truth, or that all opinions are equally valid. It simply distinguishes opinion from fact, and allows you to have a careful discussion that leads to better understanding and better decisions rather than to defensiveness and pointless fighting.

2. Share Where Your Conclusions Come From

The first step toward clarity, then, is to share your conclusions and opinions as *your* conclusions and opinions and not as the truth. The second step is to share what's beneath your conclusions—the information you have and how you have interpreted it.

You have information about yourself that the other person has no access to. That kind of information can be important; consider sharing it. And you have life experiences that are influencing what you think and why, as well as how you feel. When you tell these stories, it puts some meat onto the bones of your views.

You and your wife argue about whether to send your daughter, Carol, to private school. Your wife says, "I really think we should do it this year. It's an important age and I know we can come up with the money." You say in response, "I think she's doing fine in public school. I think we should keep her there."

If this conversation is going to get anywhere, the two of you need to share where these conclusions come from: What specific information is in your heads? What past experiences influence how you're thinking about this? You need to share your own experience in private school—the fear you felt the first few months, the sense of never quite fitting in. How guilty you felt that your parents weren't able to buy a car because they were paying your tuition for so many years. Tell that story with all the vividness and detail that's in your head as you discuss your concerns about the decision. Nothing else you say will make sense if your wife is unaware of the experiences that inform your feelings on this subject.

3. Don't Exaggerate with "Always" and "Never": Give Them Room to Change

In the heat of the moment, it's easy to express frustration through a bit of exaggeration: "Why do you *always* criticize my clothes?" "You *never* give one word of appreciation or encouragement. The only time anyone hears anything from you is when there's something wrong!"

"Always" and "never" do a pretty good job of conveying frustration, but they have two serious drawbacks. First, it is seldom strictly accurate that someone criticizes *every* time, or that they haven't at some point said *something* positive. Using such words invites an argument over the question of frequency:

"That's not true. I said several nice things to you last year when you won the interoffice new idea competition"—a response that will most likely increase your exasperation.

"Always" and "never" also make it harder—rather than easier—for the other person to consider changing their behavior. In fact, "always" and "never" suggest that change will be difficult or impossible. The implicit message is, "What is wrong with you such that you are driven to criticize my clothes?" or even "You are obviously incapable of acting like a normal person."

A better approach is to proceed as if (however hard it may be to believe) the other person is simply unaware of the impact of their actions on you, and, being a good person, would certainly wish to change their behavior once they became aware of it. You could say something like: "When you tell me my suit reminds you of wrinkled old curtains, I feel hurt. Criticizing my clothes feels like an attack on my judgment and makes me feel incompetent." If you can also suggest what you would wish to hear instead, so much the better: "I wish I could feel more often like you believed in me. It would really feel great to hear even something as simple as, 'I think that color looks good on you.' Anything, as long as it was positive."

The key is to communicate your feelings in a way that invites and encourages the recipient to consider new ways of behaving, rather than suggesting they're a schmuck and it's too bad there's nothing they can do about it.

HELP THEM UNDERSTAND YOU

It's not easy to step into someone else's story. It's especially hard when the issues are emotionally charged or when your views are rooted in a different generation or radically dissimilar corporate culture. You'll need their help in understanding them. And they'll need your help in understanding you.

If you feel overwhelmed with anxiety when leaving your children with a babysitter, and your husband says that you should "just learn to relax," you can express your anxiety in terms he might understand: "It's like your fear of flying. You know how when I try to tell you to relax during take-off it has no impact, and in fact it makes it worse? Well this is the same sort of thing."

And recognize that different people take in information at different speeds and in different ways. For example, some people are visually oriented. For them, you may want to use visual metaphors and refer to pictures or, in a business setting, charts. Some people prefer to get their arms around the whole problem first, and can't listen to anything else you say until they do. Others like all the details up front. Pay attention to these differences.

Ask Them to Paraphrase Back

Paraphrasing the other person helps you check your understanding and helps them know you've heard. You can ask them to do the same thing for you: "Let me check to see if I'm being clear. Would you mind just playing back what you've heard me say so far?"

Ask How They See It *Differently*—and Why

Explaining your story clearly is a first step toward being understood. But don't expect instant success. Real understanding may take some back and forth. If the other person seems puzzled or unpersuaded by your story, rather than putting it more forcefully or trying to tell it in a different way, ask how *they* see it. In particular, ask how they see it *differently*.

A common tendency is to ask for agreement, perhaps because it's reassuring: "Does that make sense?" "Wouldn't you agree?" But asking the other person how they see it differently is more helpful. If you ask for agreement, people may be reluctant to share their doubts and reservations. They aren't sure whether you really want to hear them. They say, "Yes, I suppose so," but you don't know whether they're actually thinking, "Yes, in a limited, warped kind of way that's just like you." If you ask explicitly for how they see it differently, you are more likely to discover their true reaction. Then you can begin to have a real conversation.

• • •

The secret of powerful expression is recognizing that you are the ultimate authority on you. You are an expert on what you think, how you feel, and why you've come to this place. If you think it or feel it, you are entitled to say it, and no one can legitimately contradict you. You only get in trouble if you try to assert what you are *not* the final authority on—who is right, who intended what, what happened. Speak fully the range of your experience and you will be clear. Speak for yourself and you can speak with power.

REVIEW QUESTIONS

1. Describe how "self-sabotage" can cripple effective expression.
2. What does it mean to say that "failure to express yourself keeps you out of the relationship"?
3. What does it mean to "rely on subtext"?
4. Write out three "Me-Me And" statements that reflect different scenarios.
5. What do these authors advise you to use *in place of* "always" and "never"?

PROBES

1. "Speak to the heart of the matter" is simple to say and can be difficult to do. You need to pause to ask yourself what's the main issue for you, and to move away from simplistic blaming statements. Phrase some questions that you can ask yourself to identify what's "the heart of the matter" for you.

2. "Easing in" seems like a good thing to do, but these authors advise against it. Why?
3. Explain the connections between what these authors say about "and" statements and what I write about "and" and "next" in Chapter 4.
4. The final piece of advice from these authors is to complete your work of *self expression* by asking your listeners to paraphrase back and to tell how they see it differently and why. How does this advice connect to the view of communication presented in Chapter 2?

PART THREE

Relationships

One of the ways to understand the organization of *Bridges Not Walls* is to think about Part Three of the book as the place where we move from theory to practice. The four chapters in Part One defined communication and interpersonal communication, showed how selves get built and changed communicatively, and surveyed the two basic ways we make contact—verbally and nonverbally. Then the two chapters in Part Two analyzed and illustrated how people make meaning together by taking in cues via perception and listening— "inhaling"—and giving off cues via self-expression and self-disclosure—"exhaling." Now we turn to the main arenas or contexts where this communicating happens: family, friends, and intimate partners.

But if you've read the earlier chapters, you know that this theory–practice way of understanding them doesn't quite work, because they aren't all theory. Practice and theory have been woven together from the beginning, and this is an important part of studying interpersonal communication. The theories that scholars have developed are systematic descriptions of practice. In this part of the communication discipline, there are no abstract theoretical generalizations that are totally disconnected from people's lived experiences. Every theoretical principle—for example, that culture is part of all communicating, that selves are built in verbal/nonverbal talk, and that all perception involves interpretation—grows out of and can significantly affect actual practice.

So the readings in Part Three continue the marriage between theory and practice that characterizes all the materials in *Bridges Not Walls*.

CHAPTER 7

Communicating with Family and Friends

What's a Family, Anyway?

Julia T. Wood

I chose this selection because it offers a realistic description of what "family" now means, especially in the United States. These realities are different from the cultural ideal of the past *and* from what some Christian and Jewish people believe is the model prescribed in the Bible. So you may or may not believe that some contemporary forms of "family" are appropriate or desirable. There's room for a wide variety of opinions on this issue. But it's very likely that as you move through your life, you will encounter people in many different kinds of families, and Wood's comments can help your communication with these people go more smoothly.

Wood begins by contrasting the actual status of U.S. families with the myth of the traditional nuclear family—children living with a married mother and father. As she points out, the traditional picture excludes the *majority* of people living in the United States and much of the rest of the world.

Wood describes, for example, how the notion of "immediate family" is more expanded for many African Americans than for many whites. She also describes how lesbian and gay families are frequently misunderstood. She discusses some of the communication challenges faced by interracial families. And she outlines some ways members of divorced and blended families are often stereotyped.

As a member of a childless couple, Wood also talks briefly about misunderstandings that occur around families without children. She often has to field the question "Why don't you have a family?" responding with something like, "I *do* have a family—I have a husband, a sister, three nephews, and a niece." The final section in this part of the reading talks about families of choice. These are the family circles created by many gay, lesbian, bisexual, and other persons "bound together by commitment, regardless of whether there are biological or legal ties."

The second major part of this reading directly addresses the discomfort some people have about discussions of family diversity because, for example, "My church says that homosexuality is immoral [and] I can't approve of that," or "It's wrong for members of one race to adopt children of a different race." Wood argues that you can respect a family form as a legitimate choice for others without embracing the choice for yourself. She also describes how family forms change over time in any culture, and she underscores the reality of family diversity today. Wood concludes by suggesting that you can learn from observing and interacting with families different from your own. She gives an example of her own experience of learning about the relative lack of playfulness in her relationship with her partner by experiencing a family with young children.

Some of Wood's ideas are provocative. You may find yourself or some classmates resisting what she says. I hope that the group you're in will be able to discuss these responses as openly and productively as possible. I believe that the perspective on families that is offered here can provide a starting place for some fruitful thinking and talking about family communication.

MAIN IDEAS

- "Family" does not mean what it used to.
- For African Americans, families are more "extended" than for Caucasian.

- Lesbian and gay families and interracial families are frequently misunderstood.
- Divorced and blended families are challenging, and many families are childless, often by choice.
- To communicate effectively with and about 21st-century families, distinguish between personal choice and respect for others' choices.
- Recognize also that views of family change over time.
- Recognize diversity in family forms.
- Learn from differences between your family and other families.

DIFFERENT VIEWS OF WHAT FAMILY MEANS

... One of the students I advise is an African American man who is preparing for a career in marketing. Franklin is an ideal student—smart, curious about ideas, responsible in getting his work done, and serious about his studies. Not long ago, Franklin came to me visibly upset, so I invited him to sit down and tell me what was bothering him.

"My grandmother had to go in the hospital for heart surgery, so I went home to be with her." I nodded. "I missed an exam in my history class. When I got back to school, I went to see Dr. Raymond to schedule a make-up and he says he won't excuse my absence."

"Why not?" I asked. "Did he want some assurance that your grandmother really was in the hospital?"

Franklin shook his head. "No, I brought a copy of her admission form as proof. That's not the problem. He says he only excuses absences for medical problems in the student's *immediate* family."

Dr. Don Raymond, like many middle-class white people, thought of family as a mother, father (or stepmother or stepfather), and children. After all, when he was growing up, Don lived with his parents and two sisters. His other relatives did not live nearby and he saw them only once or twice a year, if that often. Now 48 years old, Don lives with his second wife and their two children, ages 12 and 15. He seldom sees his sisters and visits with his parents and in-laws only over Christmas. Aunts, uncles, and grandparents are not part of the immediate family that Don Raymond knows.

It wasn't difficult to resolve Franklin's situation. I simply called Don Raymond and talked with him about some of the typical differences between white and black family structures, and I emphasized that many African American families are more extended than those of most European Americans. Large, extended families are also common among second-generation Americans of many ethnic origins. Once Don understood that grandparents were immediate family to Franklin, he was more than willing to schedule a make-up examination.

There was nothing mean spirited or intentionally discriminatory in Don's initial refusal to schedule a make-up exam for Franklin. The problem was that he assumed—without even knowing he was making an assumption—that his definition of family was everyone's definition of family. He simply didn't understand that Franklin considered his grandmother immediate family. After all, she had raised him for the first seven years of his life, a situation not uncommon in African American families. She was more like a mother (in white terms) than a grandmother to him.

Lesbian and Gay Families

Lesbian and gay families are also frequently misunderstood. Not long ago I was having lunch with Jean and Arlene, who have been in a committed relationship for 15 years. With us were their two children, Michael and Arthur, age 6 and 8, respectively. A colleague of mine saw us in the restaurant and came over to our table to engage in small talk for a few minutes.

I offered the standard introduction: "Chuck Morris, I'd like you to meet Jean Thompson and Arlene Ross. And these are their sons, Michael and Arthur."

"Good to meet you," Chuck said. "Do you live here?"

"Yes, our home is just off Lystra Road," Arlene said. "And what about you?" Chuck asked Jean.

"Same place. The four of us are a family," she replied.

Chuck had made the mistake of assuming that the two women and the two sons constituted separate families. Once Jean clarified the relationship, Chuck understood and was not taken aback by the fact that Jean and Arlene were lesbians. Yet he was confused about the boys. "So how old were they when you got them?" he asked, assuming the boys were adopted.

"Depends on whether you count the gestation period," Jean said with a smile. She had run into this assumption before. "I carried Michael and Arlene carried Arthur."

"Oh, so they're your biological children?" he asked.

Arlene and Jean nodded.

Chuck made the mistake of assuming that lesbians (and gay men, too) can't be biological parents. Obviously they can, because sexual orientation has no bearing on a man's ability to produce viable sperm or a woman's ability to produce fertile eggs and carry a child in her womb. When we assume gay men and lesbians cannot have biological children, we conflate sexual orientation with reproductive ability.

Interracial Families

Misunderstandings also surround many interracial families. Matt and Vicky had been married for six years when they realized they weren't able to have biological children. They decided to adopt, first, James, and three years later, Sheryl. They love their son and daughter and consider themselves a close family. But, whenever they go out as a family, others subject them to stares and sometimes thoughtless comments.

"Are you baby-sitting?"

"Whose children are these?"

If you guessed that James and Sheryl are not the same race as Matt and Vicky, you're correct. The children are African American, and Matt and Vicky are European American. In recent years, two of my white friends have adopted children of other races—a young girl from China for one and a Native American girl for another. Like Matt and Vicky, they are hurt when people assume their children are not their children. Comments such as "Are you baby-sitting?" deny the families they have created.

Divorced and Blended Families

You have probably read the statistic that half of first marriages end in divorce. In addition, even more than half of second and subsequent marriages end in divorce. Divorce may end a marriage, but it doesn't end family. Instead, it changes the character and dynamics of family life.

If the former spouses had children, they are still parents, but how they parent changes. In some cases, one parent has sole custody of children and the other parent may have visiting rights. In other cases, parents agree to joint custody with each parent providing a home to children part of the time. Children experience two homes and two sets of rules, which may be inconsistent. One parent may have rigid requirements about dating, curfews, and household chores while the other parent is more relaxed.

If one or both parents remarry, families combine to create what are called blended families. Years ago *The Brady Bunch* was a popular television situation comedy. In it, two parents, each with several children, married and became a blended family. Among the Bradys, liking and comfort seemed effortless. Unlike the Bradys, many blended families find it difficult to reorganize into a functional, comfortable unit. Children may have to accommodate other children, from both former marriages and the current one, so jealousy and conflict often surface. New household rules may cause confusion, resentment, and resistance. Parents may have to accept the children's other parents and grandparents. And people outside the family may have to recognize multiple parents of children and both former and current spouses of parents.

Some children in blended families call their stepparent mother or father; other children reject that term. Similarly, some children in blended families consider their step-siblings and half-siblings brothers and sisters whereas other children don't accept those labels. When communicating with people who belong to divorced or blended families, we should be sensitive to how they perceive and name their family ties.

Families without Children

My partner and I have been married for 23 years, and we have no children. We are a family without children. I am annoyed and hurt when people ask me, as they frequently do, "Why don't you have a family?" Sometimes I reply with a question: "What do *you* mean by family?" On other occasions, I respond by saying, "I *do* have a family—I have a husband, a sister, three nephews, and a niece." I consider all six of these people my immediate family. Like other people who don't have children, I resent it when others assume that I don't have a family just because Robbie and I don't have children.

What's a Family, Anyway?

Yet another kind of family was introduced by Kathy Weston in her book, *Families We Choose*. Weston describes close friendship circles of gays and lesbians as the families they choose. For Weston, families are people who are bound together by commitment, regardless of whether there are biological or legal ties. Some biologically related people may have no commitment to each other and may refuse to interact. Siblings sometimes feel such animosity toward each other that they decide not to visit, write, call, or otherwise have contact. Some parents and children are estranged, and in extreme cases parents sometimes disown children. Biology, then, doesn't guarantee commitment.

Legal and religious procedures are also insufficient to ensure the level of commitment and caring most of us consider the crux of what a good family is. As noted earlier, current statistics indicate that approximately one-half of marriages in the United States will end in divorce. Laws that define marriage can be negated by laws that grant divorce. In a 1993 poll of the baby boom generation, only 58% of respondents said they considered it likely they would stay married to the same person for life. Pledging "until death do us part" before a magistrate or member of the clergy may create a legal marriage. It does not, however, guarantee that the people making the pledge will, in fact, be able or willing to stay together for life. These statistics show that the nature of family is neither as fixed nor as uniform as Dan Quayle suggested.

Thus, concludes Weston, it's reasonable to define family as people who elect to commit to each other in a sustained way—to have a family we choose. Their commitments may or may not be recognized by current laws or religious practices; but they are families, if by family we mean people who care about one another, organize their lives together, take care of one another, and intend to continue being together and caring for one another. This enlarged view of family pivots on the idea that people can commit to casting their fates together.

IMPROVING COMMUNICATION

When I teach about family diversity at my university, some of my students are uncomfortable. "I understand what you're saying," they often tell me, "but my church says that homosexuality is immoral. I can't approve of that." Others say, "It's wrong for members of one race to adopt children of a different race. The children will never understand their ethnic heritage. I just can't agree with interracial adoptions."

Distinguish between Personal Choice and Respect for Others' Choices

What I try to show my students is that they don't have to embrace various family forms for themselves in order to respect them as legitimate choices for other people. In other words, there's a big difference between deciding what you personally want in a family (or career or spiritual practice or education or home life) and deciding to honor the choices that others make.

We already recognize and respect varied choices in many aspects of family life. For example, some parents believe that physically punishing children is wrong; other parents believe that if you spare the rod, you spoil the child. Some parents bring up children within strong religious traditions; other parents don't introduce children to any religious or spiritual path. In some families, children have to do chores and sometimes take on jobs outside the home to earn money; children in other families get automatic allowances. Few of us would label any of these choices wrong, deviant, or antifamily. Yet we sometimes find it difficult to accept other variations among families.

Recognize That Views of Family Change

Recently I collaborated with Steve Duck, who conducts research on communication and personal relationships, to co-edit a book. It includes chapters on different kinds of families, such as cohabiting couples, long-distance relationships, gay and lesbian commitments, and African American and Hispanic families. The chapters in this book document the diversity of family forms in the United States today.

Family historian Stephanie Coontz points out that during the 300 years since Columbus landed in this hemisphere, families in the United States have taken many forms. The Iroquois lived with extended and matriarchal families, whereas the more nomadic Indian groups had small families. African American slaves saw their nuclear families wrenched apart, so they developed extended communal networks, routinely engaged in co-parenting, and took orphaned children into their homes and raised them as their own, usually without formally adopting them.

The family form idealized by Dan Quayle came late in U.S. history and sustained its status as the dominant family form for only a short period. According to Coontz, only beginning in the 1920s did the majority of working-class white people in the United States live in families that had male breadwinners and female homemakers. Today, by contrast, the majority of women work outside the home, and approximately one-half of wives who work outside the home have salaries equal to or greater than those of their husbands. The male breadwinner/female homemaker model simply doesn't describe the majority of U.S. families today.

Intact families, also part of Quayle's model, are more the exception than the rule in this country.... Nearly half of first marriages (and an even greater percentage of second marriages) end in divorce. Only 50% of children live with both their biological parents, and nearly one-quarter live with single parents, usually their mothers.

The Census Bureau's 1996 survey of 60,000 U.S. households noted several trends in families. The greatest shift is in the number of single-parent households. Between 1990 and 1995, the number of single-parent families rose by a scant 3%. In the single year 1995–1996, families headed by single mothers rose 12% as did families headed by single fathers. Some single-parent households, such as Murphy Brown's, represent choices. In other cases, single parenting is not desired or anticipated, but it becomes the only or the most acceptable option.

Recognize Diversity in Family Forms

Demographic trends in the United States clearly challenge the accuracy of any singular view of what a family is. Effective participation in current society requires us to understand that people have diverse ideas about what counts as a family and they have equally diverse ways of structuring family life. As one gay man said to me, "I don't care if straights like me and my partner or not, but I do care that they recognize I have rights to love a person and have a family just like they do." Understanding this point can help us interact effectively in two ways.

First, when we recognize the normal diversity of family forms, we can communicate more respectfully with people who have varying family structures. No longer is there a universal definition of family. Dan Quayle says single mothers are an affront to family values, but single mothers are no more or less successful in parenting than married women. Just like mothers who are married, some single mothers are devoted and effective parents, and some are not. Just like married mothers, single mothers' effectiveness depends on a variety of factors including support networks, income, education, and employment.

Most states do not recognize gay and lesbian commitments, yet the evidence suggests they can be as healthy, stable, and enduring as heterosexual unions. Even if gay and lesbian families do break up, that doesn't mean they weren't families at one time. After all, if a heterosexual couple divorces, we don't assume they were never married. Like heterosexuals, gays and lesbians can pledge a lifetime of love and loyalty; like some heterosexuals, some gays and lesbians will not realize that promise.

And what about the children of lesbian and gay parents? Child development specialist Charlotte Patterson reports that there are currently between 1 million and 5 million lesbian mothers and 1 million and 3 million gay fathers in the United States and between 6 million and 14 million children who have a gay or lesbian parent. Many states don't allow gay or lesbian partners to be legal parents, even if one partner is the biological parent. These states argue that lesbians and gays cannot raise healthy children, but this argument isn't justified, according to *New York Times* columnist Jane Gross. Based on reviewing 35 studies of children who have gay or lesbian parents, Gross concluded that these children are as well adjusted as children of heterosexual parents and that they are no more or less likely to become gay or lesbian than the children of heterosexual parents. In a separate review of research, Charlotte Patterson found that children of gay and lesbian parents and children of heterosexual parents are no different in terms of intelligence, self-concept, and moral judgment. Existing evidence shows that both heterosexuals and gays and lesbians can raise children who are healthy and happy—and both can raise poorly adjusted children who have low self-concepts.

Learn from Differences

Diverse family forms also offer an opportunity for us to consider how we form our own families and live in them. Martha Barrett interviewed same-sex couples and concluded that they tend to relate to each other on equal terms more than do heterosexual couples. Barrett suggests that gays and lesbians have something to teach the heterosexual community about equality in rights and responsibilities in intimate relationships. Similarly, interracial families may discourage us from overemphasizing race in our thinking about personal identity and family. And families in which there are children may learn from child-free families about ways to keep couple communication alive and intimate.

We can learn about others and ourselves if we are open to differences in how people form and live in families. As long as we interact only with people whose families are like ours, it's hard for us to see some of the patterns and choices we've made in our own relationships. The particular ways that we charter our families remain invisible, unseen and unseeable because they seem "normal," "the only way to be a family." Yet when we consider some of the contrasts provided by interacting with people who have families different from ours, what was invisible and taken for granted in our own relationships becomes more visible. This realization allows us to reflect on the way we've created our families. In turn, this knowledge enables us to make more informed, more thoughtful choices about the kind of family we want to have.

In other words, heterosexuals don't have to change their sexual orientation to gain insight into their own relationships by observing gay and lesbian families. A heterosexual friend of mine once told me that only through her friendship with a lesbian couple had she realized how fully she centered her life around her male partner. She chose to stay married, but she and her husband communicated about ways they could be less centered on each other and enlarge their circle of friends.

A child-free family doesn't need to have children to learn something about their own relationship from interacting with families in which children are present, I've learned a lot about my relationship with Robbie by spending time with my sister Carolyn and her husband, Leigh, and their children, Michelle and Daniel. One of the insights I've gained from visiting them is that Robbie and I didn't include much play and frolic in our relationship.

Notice I used the past tense (didn't). Watching Carolyn and Leigh play with Michelle and Daniel and then blend into playfulness with each other allowed Robbie and me to notice that the playful dimension of relating was largely missing in our interaction. When Robbie and I played with Michelle and Daniel and then with them and their parents, we revived our dormant sense of how to be playful. Since learning this, Robbie and I have become more playful, even silly at times, with each other, and this enriches our marriage. Opening ourselves to various ways of being a family allows us to enlarge our personal identities and our relationships, including our own families.

REVIEW QUESTIONS

1. What is a nuclear family? How many nuclear families do you contact regularly? How many nonnuclear families do you contact regularly?
2. Who would you say makes up your immediate family?
3. What is a blended family?
4. Given all the different kinds of family forms Wood discusses, how do you believe she would define *family*? How do you define it? What does it take, in your opinion, to have a family?
5. Fill in the blanks and discuss the significance: Between 1990 and 1995, the number of single-parent families rose by _____ percent. In the single year 1995–1996, the number of single-parent families rose by _____ percent.
6. What does the initial research indicate about children raised by gay or lesbian parents?

PROBES

1. If you feel accepting of gay and lesbian couples being parents, what do you believe are the two or three strongest arguments against or challenges to those family configurations? If you have trouble accepting gay and lesbian couples being parents, what do you believe are the two or three strongest arguments in support of those family configurations?
2. A great deal of contemporary evidence indicates that globalization is a fact of life in business, music, banking, and academia. How is globalization related to interracial families?
3. What makes stepparenting such a difficult role to perform satisfactorily?
4. Wood argues that since we already respect considerable diversity in parenting styles, it should be possible to extend this respect to nontraditional family forms. How do you respond to this argument?
5. How diverse is your experience of other families? What is one way you might be able to increase the diversity of this part of your communication experience?

REFERENCES

Barrett, M. B. (1989). *Invisible lives: The truth about millions of women-loving women.* New York: Morrow.

Card, C. (1995). *Lesbian choices.* New York: Columbia University Press.

Changes in families reach plateau, study says. (1996, November 27). *Raleigh News and Observer,* pp. 1A, 10A.

Coontz, S. (1992). *The way we never were: American families and the nostalgia trap.* New York: Basic Books.

Coontz, S. (1996, May–June). Where are the good old days? *Modern Maturity,* pp. 36–43.

Ferrante, J. (1995). *Sociology: A global perspective* (2nd ed.). Belmont, CA: Wadsworth.

Goodman, E. (1997, January 17). Adopting across racial lines. *Raleigh News and Observer,* p. 13A.

Gross, J. (1991, February 11). New challenge of youth growing up in a gay home. *New York Times,* pp. 2B, 6B.

Guttmann, J. (1993). *Divorce in psychosocial perspective: Theory and research.* Hillsdale, NJ: Lawrence Erlbaum.

Indulgent "boomers" bring an unraveling of society. (1993, October 17). *Raleigh News and Observer,* p. 6E.

Marciano, T., & Sussman, M. B. (Eds.). (1991). *Wider families.* New York: Haworth Press.

Patterson, C. (1992). Children of lesbian and gay parents. *Child Development, 63,* 83–96.

Salter, S. (1996, April 7). With this ring I thee wed, or whatever. *San Francisco Examiner,* p. B11.

Singer, B. L., & Deschamps, D. (Eds.). (1994). *Gay and lesbian stats: A pocket, guide of facts and figures.* New York: New Press.

Weston, K. (1991). *Families we choose.* New York: Columbia University Press.

Wood, J. T., & Duck, S. (Eds.). (1995). *Understanding relationship processes, 6: Understudied relationships: Off the beaten track.* Thousand Oaks, CA: Sage.

Separating Messages from Metamessages in Family Talk

Deborah Tannen

The writer of this selection is a Distinguished Professor of Linguistics at Georgetown University and the author of several best-selling books. Her work combines scholarship and readability, academic rigor and straightforward explanation. These pages come from the first chapter of a book that discusses many aspects of family communicating, including family secrets, "fighting for love," gender patterns in family talk, mothers and adult children, sibling communication, and communication among "in-laws and other strangers."

The most important point Tannen makes in this selection is the distinction between messages and metamessages. As she explains, "The *message* is the meaning of the words and sentences spoken, what anyone with a dictionary and a grammar book could figure out. . . . The *metamessage* is the meaning that is not said—at least not in so many words—but that we glean from every aspect of context: the way something is said, who is saying it, or the fact that it is said at all." Just about any two people in a situation can agree on the message. But metamessages are much more difficult to decipher and, much of the time, to interpret.

For example, in one short example of conversation that Tannen provides, a daughter asks her mother, "Am I too critical of people?" That's the message. But the mother hears the metamessage that her daughter is criticizing *her*. Metamessages are especially significant in family communication, because they often grow out of the history of the relationship, and they almost always have to do with the ways conversation partners are defining themselves and each other—for example, "I'm innocent," "Remember I'm in charge here," "You probably won't agree with this," or "If you love me, you'll say yes."

In family communication, metamessages are often negative. Speakers embed criticism in seemingly straightforward comments and questions like "Are you serving french bread?" which can mean, "Why didn't you bake dinner rolls?" Another example is "Please start your shower at seven, not seven-thirty," which can easily be interpreted as yet another complaint about the person's always being late. A paradox of family communicating is that we depend on those closest to us to see our best side, but because they are close, they also see our worst. And what they intend to be caring communication often gets expressed or interpreted as criticism.

One antidote to the problems that metamessages create is to *metacommunicate*—to talk about your ways of talking. If a family member expresses concern because he feels that his every suggestion or comment is heard as criticism, other family members are in a better position to work on this problem. He might learn to preface his comment with such meta-communicative statements as "I'm not criticizing the French bread" or, to be more direct, "I would really like it if you would make those delicious dinner rolls."

Tannen also clarifies how family communication is constantly challenged by the members' simultaneous but conflicting desires for connection and for control. Both are at the heart of a family. And ways of talking create both. "Younger siblings or children can make life wonderful or miserable for older siblings or parents by what they say—or refuse to say." If you keep in mind this simultaneous and conflicting desire, you can clarify comments and questions that might otherwise create problems. For example, "Don't start eating yet" can be heard as a control maneuver and as a connection move—and importantly, such a statement is usually both.

In a section called "Small Spark, Big Explosion," Tannen makes the point we've all experienced—what seem to be ridiculously trivial comments leading to major family disagreements. And she illustrates how metacommunication and the awareness of the twin motivations of connection and control can help.

There is more to family communication than Tannen explains here. But this reading can alert us to some troublesome elements of listening and talking with family members, and it suggests some ways to help family communication run more smoothly.

MAIN IDEAS

- The allure of family—to have someone who knows you intimately—is also what can make family communication painful.
- Family history can imbue almost everything that's said with meanings from the past.
- Family communication often embodies the principle, "I care, therefore I criticize."
- A key to dealing with hurtful family communication is to understand the distinction between *message* and *metamessage*.

- The *metamessage* is the unspoken message about the relationship between speaker and hearer; what is said by the way something is said, who says it, or the fact that it is said at all.
- Metamessages often speak louder than messages because they are about identities.
- *Metacommunication* is communication about how people are communicating—about their metamessages.
- All family communication is about connection and control.
- When you understand the double meaning of control and connection, you can cope with family metamessages.
- The paradox of family is that familiarity often breeds discomfort *and* given the enormous benefits of good family communication, it's worth the struggle to keep talking.

D o you really need another piece of cake?" Donna asks George. "You bet I do," he replies, with that edge to his voice that implies, "If I wasn't sure I needed it before, I am darned sure now."

Donna feels hamstrung. She knows that George is going to say later that he wished he hadn't had that second piece of cake.

"Why are you always watching what I eat?" George asks.

"I was just watching out for you," Donna replies. "I only say it because I love you."

Elizabeth, in her late twenties, is happy to be making Thanksgiving dinner for her extended family in her own home. Her mother, who is visiting, is helping out in the kitchen. As Elizabeth prepares the stuffing for the turkey, her mother remarks, "Oh, you put onions in the stuffing?"

Feeling suddenly as if she were sixteen years old again, Elizabeth turns on her mother and says, "*I'm* making the stuffing, Mom. Why do you have to criticize everything I do?"

"I didn't criticize," her mother replies. "I just asked a question. What's got into you? I can't even open my mouth."

The allure of family—which is, at heart, the allure of love—is to have someone who knows you so well that you don't have to explain yourself. It is the promise of someone who cares enough about you to protect you against the world of strangers who do not wish you well. Yet, by an odd and cruel twist, it is the family itself that often causes pain. Those we love are looking at us so close-up that they see all our blemishes—see them as if through a magnifying glass. Family members have innumerable opportunities to witness our faults and feel they have a right to point them out. Often their intention is to help us improve. They feel, as Donna did, "I only say it because I love you."

Family members also have a long shared history, so everything we say in a conversation today echoes with meanings from the past. If you have a tendency to be late, your parent, sibling, or spouse may say, "We have to leave at eight"—and then add, "It's really important. Don't be late. Please start your shower at seven, not seven-thirty!" These extra injunctions are demeaning and interfering, but they are based on experience. At the same time, having experienced negative judgments in the past, we develop a sixth sense to sniff out criticism in almost anything a loved one says—even an innocent question about ingredients in the stuffing. That's why Elizabeth's mother ends up feeling as if she can't even open her mouth—and Elizabeth ends up feeling criticized.

When we are children our family constitutes the world. When we grow up family members—not only our spouses but also our grown-up children and adult sisters and brothers—keep this larger-than-life aura. We overreact to their judgments because it feels as if they were handed down by the Supreme Court and are unassailable assessments of our value as human beings. We bristle because these judgments seem unjust; or because we sense a kernel of truth we would rather not face; or because we fear that if someone who knows us so well judges us harshly we must really be guilty, so we risk losing not only that person's love but everyone else's, too. Along with this heavy load of implications comes a dark resentment that a loved one is judging us at all—and has such power to wound.

... No matter what age we've reached, no matter whether our parents are alive or dead, whether we were close to them or not, there are times when theirs are the eyes through which we view ourselves, theirs the standards against which we measure ourselves when we wonder whether we have measured up. The criticism of parents carries extra weight, even when children are adults.

I CARE, THEREFORE I CRITICIZE

Some family members feel they have not only a right but an obligation to tell you when they think you're doing something wrong. A woman from Thailand recalls that when she was in her late teens and early twenties, her mother frequently had talks with her in which she tried to set her daughter straight. "At the end of each lecture," the woman says, "my mother would always tell me, 'I have to complain about you because I am your mother and I love you. Nobody else will talk to you the way I do because they don't care.'"

It sometimes seems that family members operate under the tenet "I care, therefore I criticize." To the one who is being told to do things differently, what comes through loudest and clearest is the criticism. But the one offering suggestions and judgments is usually focused on the caring. A mother, for example, was expressing concern about her daughter's boyfriend: He didn't have a serious job, he didn't seem to want one, and she didn't think he was a good prospect for marriage. The daughter protested that her mother disapproved of everyone she dated. Her mother responded indignantly, "Would you rather I didn't care?"

As family members we wonder why our parents, children, siblings, and spouses are so critical of us. But as family members we also feel frustrated because comments we make in the spirit of caring are taken as criticizing.

Both sentiments are explained by the double meaning of giving advice: a loving sign of caring, a hurtful sign of criticizing. It's impossible to say which is right; both meanings are there. Sorting out the ambiguous meanings of caring and criticizing is difficult because language works on two levels: the message and the metamessage. Separating these levels—and being aware of both—is crucial to improving communication in the family.

THE INTIMATE CRITIC: WHEN METAMESSAGES HURT

Because those closest to us have front-row seats to view our faults, we quickly react—sometimes overreact—to any hint of criticism. The result can be downright comic, as in Phyllis Richman's novel *Who's Afraid of Virginia Ham?* One scene, a conversation between the narrator and her adult daughter, Lily, shows how criticism can be the metronome providing the beat for the family theme song. The dialogue goes like this:

LILY: Am I too critical of people?
MOTHER: What people? Me?
LILY: Mamma, don't be so self-centered.
MOTHER: Lily, don't be so critical.
LILY: I knew it. You do think I'm critical. Mamma, why do you always have to find something wrong with me?

The mother then protests that it was Lily who asked if she was too critical, and now she's criticizing her mother for answering. Lily responds, "I can't follow this. Sometimes you're impossibly hard to talk to."

It turns out that Lily is upset because her boyfriend, Brian, told her she is too critical of him. She made a great effort to stop criticizing, but now she's having a hard time keeping her resolve. He gave her a sexy outfit for her birthday—it's expensive and beautiful—but the generous gift made her angry because she took it as criticism of the way she usually dresses.

In this brief exchange Richman captures the layers of meaning that can make the most well-intentioned comment or action a source of conflict and hurt among family members. Key to understanding why Lily finds the conversation so hard to follow—and her mother so hard to talk to—is separating messages from metamessages. The *message* is the meaning of the words and sentences spoken, what anyone with a dictionary and a grammar book could figure out. Two people in a conversation usually agree on what the message is. The *metamessage* is meaning that is not said—at least not in so many words—but that we glean from every aspect of context: the way something is said, who is saying it, or the fact that it is said at all.

Because they do not reside in the words themselves, metamessages are hard to deal with. Yet they are often the source of both comfort and hurt. The message (as I've said) is the word meaning while the metamessage is the heart meaning—the meaning that we react to most strongly, that triggers emotion.

When Lily asked her mother if she was too critical of people, the message was a question about Lily's own personality. But her mother responded to what she perceived as the metamessage: that Lily was feeling critical of *her.* This was probably based on experience: Her daughter had been critical of her in the past. If Lily had responded to the message alone, she would have answered, "No, not you. I was thinking of Brian." But she, too, is reacting to a metamessage—that her mother had made herself the point of a comment that was not about her mother at all. Perhaps Lily's resentment was also triggered because her mother still looms so large in her life.

The mixing up of message and metamessage also explains Lily's confused response to the gift of sexy clothing from her boyfriend. The message is the gift. But what made Lily angry was what she thought the gift implied: that Brian finds the way she usually dresses not sexy enough—and unattractive. This implication is the metamessage, and it is what made Lily critical of the gift, of Brian, and of herself. Metamessages speak louder than messages, so this is what Lily reacted to most strongly.

It's impossible to know whether Brian intended this metamessage. It's possible that he wishes Lily would dress differently; it's also possible that he likes the way she dresses just fine but simply thought this particular outfit would look good on her. That's what makes metamessages so difficult to pinpoint and talk about: They're implicit, not explicit.

When we talk about messages, we are talking about the meanings of words. But when we talk about metamessages, we are talking about relationships. And when family members react to each other's comments, it's metamessages they are usually responding to. Richman's dialogue is funny because it shows how we all get confused between messages and metamessages when we talk to those we are close to. But when it happens in the context of a relationship we care about, our reactions often lead to hurt rather than to humor.

... A key to improving relationships within the family is distinguishing the message from the metamessage, and being clear about which one you are reacting to. One way you can do this is *metacommunicating*—talking about communication.

"WHAT'S WRONG WITH FRENCH BREAD?" TRY METACOMMUNICATING

The movie *Divorce American Style* begins with Debbie Reynolds and Dick Van Dyke preparing for dinner guests—and arguing. She lodges a complaint: that all he does is criticize. He protests that he doesn't. She says she can't discuss it right then because she has to take the French bread out of the oven. He asks, "French bread?"

A simple question, right? Not even a question, just an observation. But on hearing it Debbie Reynolds turns on him, hands on hips, ready for battle: "What's wrong with French bread?" she asks, her voice full of challenge.

"Nothing," he says, all innocence. "It's just that I really like those little dinner rolls you usually make." This is like the bell that sets in motion a boxing match, which is stopped by another bell—the one at the front door announcing their guests have arrived.

Did he criticize or didn't he? On the message level, no. He simply asked a question to confirm what type of bread she was preparing. But on the metamessage level, yes. If he were satisfied with her choice of bread, he would not comment, except perhaps to compliment. Still, you might ask, So what? So what if he prefers the dinner rolls she usually makes to French bread? Why is it such a big deal? The big deal is explained by her original complaint: She feels that he is *always* criticizing—always telling her to do things differently than she chose to do them.

The big deal, in a larger sense, is a paradox of family: We depend on those closest to us to see our best side, and often they do. But because they are so close, they also see our worst side. You want the one you love to be an intimate ally who reassures you that you're doing things right, but sometimes you find instead an intimate critic who implies, time and again, that you're doing things wrong. It's the cumulative effect of minor, innocent suggestions that creates major problems. You will never work things out if you continue to talk about the message—about French bread versus dinner rolls—rather than the metamessage—the implication that your partner is dissatisfied with everything you do. (*Divorce American Style* was made in 1967; that it still rings true today is evidence of how common—and how recalcitrant—such conversational quagmires are.)

One way to approach a dilemma like this is to *metacommunicate*—to talk about ways of talking. He might *say* that he feels he can't open his mouth to make a suggestion or comment because she takes everything as criticism. She might *say* that she feels he's always dissatisfied with what she does, rather than turn on him in a challenging way. Once they both understand this dynamic, they will come up with their own ideas about how to address it. For example, he might decide to preface his question with a disclaimer: "I'm not criticizing the French bread." Or maybe he *does* want to make a request—a direct one—that she please make dinner rolls because he likes them. They might also set a limit on how many actions of hers he can question in a day. The important thing is to talk about the metamessage she is reacting to: that having too many of her actions questioned makes her feel that her partner in life has changed into an in-house inspection agent, on the lookout for wrong moves. . . .

GIVE ME CONNECTION, GIVE ME CONTROL

There is another dimension to this argument—another aspect of communication that complicates everything we say to each other but that is especially powerful in families. That is our simultaneous but conflicting desires for connection and for control. . . .

Both connection and control are at the heart of family. There is no relationship as close—and none as deeply hierarchical—as the relationship between parent and child, or between older and younger sibling. To understand what goes on when family members talk to each other, you have to understand how the forces of connection and control reflect both closeness and hierarchy in a family.

"He's like family," my mother says of someone she likes. Underlying this remark is the assumption that *family* connotes closeness, being connected to each other. We all seek connection: It makes us feel safe; it makes us feel loved. But being close means you care about what those you are close to think. Whatever you do has an impact on them, so you have to take their needs and preferences into account. This gives them power to control your actions, limiting your independence and making you feel hemmed in.

Parents and older siblings have power over children and younger siblings as a result of their age and their roles in the family. At the same time, *ways of talking create power.* Younger siblings or children can make life wonderful or miserable for older siblings or parents by what they say—or refuse to say. Some family members increase their chances of getting their way by frequently speaking up, or by speaking more loudly and more forcefully. Some increase their influence by holding their tongues, so others become more and more concerned about winning them over.

"Don't tell me what to do. Don't try to control me" are frequent protests within families. It is automatic for many of us to think in terms of power relations and to see others' incursions on our freedom as control maneuvers. We are less likely to think of them as connection maneuvers, but they often are that, too. At every moment we're struggling not only for control but also for love, approval, and involvement. What's tough is that the *same* actions and comments can be either control maneuvers or connection maneuvers—or, as in most cases, both at once.

CONTROL MANEUVER OR CONNECTION MANEUVER?

"Don't start eating yet," Louis says to Claudia as he walks out of the kitchen. "I'll be right there."

Famished, Claudia eyes the pizza before her. The aroma of tomato sauce and melted cheese is so sweet, her mouth thinks she has taken a bite. But Louis, always slow-moving, does not return, and the pizza is cooling. Claudia feels a bit like their dog Muffin when she was being trained: "Wait!" the instructor told Muffin, as the hungry dog poised pitifully beside her bowl of food. After pausing long enough to be convinced Muffin would wait forever, the trainer would say, "Okay!" Only then would Muffin fall into the food.

Was Louis intentionally taking his time in order to prove he could make Claudia wait no matter how hungry she was? Or was he just eager for them to sit down to dinner together? In other words, when he said, "Don't start eating yet," was it a control maneuver, to make her adjust to his pace and timing, or a connection maneuver, to preserve their evening ritual of sharing food? The answer is, it was both. Eating together is one of the most evocative rituals that bond individuals as a family. At the same time, the requirement that they sit down to dinner to-gether gave Louis the power to make Claudia wait. So the need for connection entailed control, and controlling each other is in itself a kind of connection.

Control and connection are intertwined, often conflicting forces that thread through everything said in a family. These dual forces explain the double mean-ing of caring and criticizing. Giving advice, suggesting changes, and making observations are signs of caring when looked at through the lens of connection. But looked at through the lens of control, they are put-downs, interfering with our desire to manage our own lives and actions, telling us to do things differ-ently than we choose to do them. That's why caring and criticizing are tied up like a knot.

The drives toward connection and toward control are the forces that underlie our reactions to metamessages. So the second step in improving communication in the family—after distinguishing between message and metamessage—is understanding the double meaning of control and connection. Once these multiple layers are sorted out and brought into focus, talking about ways of talking—metacommunicating—can help solve family problems rather than making them worse.

SMALL SPARK, BIG EXPLOSION

Given the intricacies of messages and metamessages, and of connection and control, the tiniest suggestion or correction can spark an explosion fueled by the stored energy of a history of criticism. One day, for example, Vivian was washing dishes. She tried to fix the drain cup in an open position so it would catch debris and still allow water to drain, but it kept falling into the closed position. With a mental shrug of her shoulders, she decided to leave it, since she didn't have many dishes to wash and the amount of water that would fill the sink wouldn't be that great. But a moment later her husband, Mel, hap-pened by and glanced at the sink. "You should leave the drain open," he said, "so the water can drain."

This sounds innocent enough in the telling. Vivian could have said, "I tried, but it kept slipping in, so I figured it didn't matter that much." Or she could have said, "It's irritating to feel that you're looking over my shoulder all the time, telling me to do things differently from the way I'm doing them." This was, in fact, what she was feeling—and why she experienced, in reaction to Mel's suggestion, a small eruption of anger that she had to expend effort to suppress.

Vivian was surprised at what she did say. She made up a reason and implied she had acted on purpose: "I figured it would be easier to clean the strainer if I let it drain all at once." This thought *had* occurred to her when she decided not to struggle any longer to balance the drain cup in an open position, though it wasn't true that she did it on purpose for that reason. But by justifying her actions, Vivian gave Mel the opening to argue for his method, which he did.

"The whole sink gets dirty if you let it fill up with water," Mel said. Vivian decided to let it drop and remained silent. Had she spoken up, the result would probably have been an argument.

Throughout this interchange Vivian and Mel focused on the message: When you wash the dishes, should the drain cup be open or closed? Just laying out the dilemma in these terms shows how ridiculous it is to argue about. Wars are being fought; people are dying; accident or illness could throw this family into turmoil at any moment. The position of the drain cup in the sink is not a major factor in their lives. But the conversation wasn't really about the message—the drain cup—at least not for Vivian.

Mel probably thought he was just making a suggestion about the drain cup, and in the immediate context he was. But messages always bring metamessages in tow: In the context of the history of their relationship, Mel's comment was not so much about a drain cup as it was about Vivian's ability to do things right and Mel's role as judge of her actions.

This was clear to Vivian, which is why she bristled at his comment, but it was less clear to Mel. Our field of vision is different depending on whether we're criticizing or being criticized. The critic tends to focus on the message: "I just made a suggestion. Why are you so touchy?" The one who feels criticized, however, is responding to the metamessage, which is harder to explain. If Vivian had complained, "You're always telling me how to do things," Mel would surely have felt, and might well have said, "I can't even open my mouth."

At the same time, connection and control are in play. Mel's assumption that he and Vivian are on the same team makes him feel comfortable giving her pointers. Furthermore, if a problem develops with the sink's drainage, he's the one who will have to fix it. Their lives are intertwined; that's where the connection lies. But if Vivian feels she can't even wash dishes without Mel telling her to do it differently, then it seems to her that he is trying to control her. It's as if she has a boss to answer to in her own kitchen.

Vivian might explain her reaction in terms of metamessages. Understanding and respecting her perspective, Mel might decide to limit his suggestions and corrections. Or Vivian might decide that she is overinterpreting the metamessage and make an effort to focus more on the message, taking some of Mel's suggestions and ignoring others. Once they both understand the metamessages as well as the messages they are communicating and reacting to, they can metacommunicate: talk about each other's ways of talking and how they might talk differently to avoid hurt and recriminations. . . .

THE PARADOX OF FAMILY

When I was a child I walked to elementary school along Coney Island Avenue in Brooklyn, praying that if a war came I'd be home with my family when it happened. During my childhood in the 1950s my teachers periodically surprised the class by calling out, "Take cover!" At that cry we all ducked under our desks and curled up in the way we had been taught: elbows and knees tucked in, heads down, hands clasped over our necks. With the possibility of a nuclear attack made vivid by these exercises, I walked to school in dread—not of war but of the possibility that it might strike when I was away from my family.

But there is another side to family, the one I have been exploring in this chapter. My nephew Joshua Marx, at thirteen, pointed out this paradox: "If you live with someone for too long, you notice things about them," he said. "That's the reason you don't like your parents, your brother. There's a kid I know who said about his friend, 'Wouldn't it be cool if we were brothers?' and I said, 'Then you'd hate him.'"

We look to communication as a way through the minefield of this paradox. And often talking helps. But communication itself is a minefield because of the complex workings of message and metamessage. Distinguishing messages from metamessages, and taking into account the underlying needs for connection and control, provides a basis for metacommunicating. With these insights as foundation, we can delve further into the intricacies of family talk. Given our shared and individual histories of talk in relationships, and the enormous promise of love, understanding, and listening that family holds out, it's worth the struggle to continue juggling—and talking.

REVIEW QUESTIONS

1. What's a metamessage?
2. What's metacommunication? How can metacommunication help solve problems created by metamessages?
3. "When we talk about messages, we are talking about the _____ of _____ . But when we talk about metamessages, we are talking about _____ ."
4. Explain what it means for Tannen to say "ways of talking create power."

PROBES

1. Tannen explains that one huge value of being a member of a family is that someone always "has your back"—someone who knows you so well that you don't always have to explain yourself. Yet paradoxically, family members can and do often cause pain. How can your family communication help work with this paradox?
2. Although Tannen does not make this point, other family communication writers have noted that many, if not most, metamessages are nonverbal. They are communicated by tone of voice, timing, facial expression, or touch. Review how Tannen defines metamessages. Do you think they are primarily nonverbal, primarily verbal, or both?

3. Give an example from your own experience of a piece of family communication that includes both the desire for connection and the desire for control. Explain how it might be misunderstood.

———————

Our Friends, Ourselves
Steve Duck

Steve Duck, an interpersonal communication professor at the University of Iowa, has written a number of books about how to understand and improve personal relationships. He begins this reading by explaining how "relationshipping" is a skill that each of us is taught—more or less effectively—and that we can learn to do better. He doesn't believe that building friendships is *nothing but* a mechanical process of applying certain skills, but he is convinced that skills are part of this process, just like they're part of the process of painting the *Mona Lisa*. As he suggests, the main advantage of treating relationshipping this way is that it can give you confidence in your ability to improve the ways you make and keep friends.

Duck talks about the general features that people expect friends to have and the friendship rules that people generally expect to be observed. Then he dedicates the bulk of this reading to a discussion of what he calls the "provisions" of friendships, that is, what they "provide" or do for us. He explains six reasons why we need friends: belonging and sense of reliable alliance; emotional integration and stability; opportunities for communication about ourselves; assistance and physical support; reassurance of our worth and value and opportunity to help others; and personality support.

The ideas in this reading can help you understand your friendships and can help you improve them.

MAIN IDEAS

- "Relationshipping" is the active, thoughtful, and skilled process of making relationships start, develop, and work.
- Learning to steer a relationship involves a range of abilities that must be coordinated.
- This doesn't mean that making and keeping friendships is a mechanical skill but that basic competencies are vital.
- *Features* of friendship include honesty, affection, openness, helpfulness, trust, respect, and willingness to work through problems.
- *Rules* of friendship include conversing, keeping confidences, refraining from public criticism, and repaying debts and favors.
- Friends provide at least six benefits:
  - Belonging and a sense of reliable alliance.
  - Emotional integration and stability.
  - Opportunities for communication about ourselves.
  - Assistance and physical support.

- Reassurance of our worth and value and the opportunity to help others.
- Personality support.

"Relationshipping" is actually a very complicated and prolonged process with many pitfalls and challenges. Relationships do not just happen; they have to be made—made to start, made to work, made to develop, kept in good working order and preserved from going sour. To do all this we need to be active, thoughtful and skilled. To suggest that one simply starts a friendship, courtship, romantic partnership or marriage and "off it goes" is simple-minded. It is like believing that one can drive down the street merely by turning the ignition key, sitting back and letting the car take care of itself.

On the contrary, to develop a close personal relationship (with someone who was, after all, at first a stranger to us) careful adjustment and continuous monitoring are required, along with several very sophisticated skills. Some of these are: assessing the other person's needs accurately; adopting appropriate styles of communication; indicating liking and interest by means of minute bodily activities, like eye movements and postural shifts; finding out how to satisfy mutual personality needs; adjusting our behaviour to the relationship "tango" with the other person; selecting and revealing the right sorts of information or opinion in an inviting, encouraging way in the appropriate style and circumstances; building up trust, making suitable demands; and building up commitment. In short, one must perform many complex behaviours. These necessitate proficiency in presenting ourselves efficiently, attending to the right features of the other person at the right time, and pacing the friendship properly.

Rather as learning to drive a car does, learning to steer a relationship involves a range of different abilities and these must be coordinated. Just as when, even after we have learned to drive, we need to concentrate harder each time we get into a new model, drive in an unfamiliar country or travel through unknown streets, so when entering unfamiliar relationships we have to relearn, modify or re-concentrate on the things that we do. All of us have pet stories about the strain, embarrassment and awkwardness that occurred in a first meeting with a new neighbour or a "friend of a friend": some clumsy silence, an ill-judged phrase, a difficult situation. It is in such situations that the skills of friendship are bared and tested to the limits, and where intuition is so clearly not enough.

Because it is a skill, relationshipping—even in these novel situations—is something that can be improved, refined, polished (even coached and practised) like any other skill, trained like any other, and made more fluent. It can be taken right up to the level of expertise where it all flows so skillfully and automatically that we can metaphorically focus away from the position of the relational brakes or accelerator and devise ways to drive (the relationship) courteously, skillfully, carefully, or enjoyably, so that the others in it can have a smoother ride!

Since we are not usually disposed to think of friendship and close relationships in this new kind of way, people sometimes feel irrationally resistant to doing so. "How can you represent a close personal relationship as a simple mechanical skill?" they ask. "Isn't it more mystical, more magical, more moral, less manipulative than you make it sound?" Such people seem happy to see relationships merely as pleasant, passive states: relationships just happen to us and we don't have to do anything particular—let alone do anything properly.

My answer is clear: I am not saying that friendship is all mechanical, any more than making a beautiful piece of furniture or playing an enchanting piano rhapsody or winning a sports championship is simply a mechanical exercise. But each of these activities has some mechanical elements that must be mastered before the higher-level aspects of skill can be attempted. You can't paint the *Mona Lisa* until you know something about painting figures, using a canvas, holding a brush, mixing paints, and so on. Furthermore, research backs this up. Scholars now regard "relationship work" as a process that continues right through the life of the relationship, with a constant and perpetual need for the right actions and activities at the right time to keep it all alive (for example, Baxter & Dindia, 1990)....

There are many advantages to this way of looking at relationships. It leads to a direct and useful form of practical advice for people who are unhappy with one or more of their relationships, or who are lonely or frustrated. It focuses on the things that one can do to improve relationships. It also runs counter to the common, but rather simplistic, assumption that relationships are based only on the matching of two individuals' personalities. This pervasive myth says that there is a Mr. or a Ms. Right for everyone or that friends can be defined in advance. If this were true, then we could all list the characteristics of our perfect partner—looking for a partner or being attractive to one would be like shopping for or making a checklist of things we liked. By contrast, the new approach adopted here will focus on performance, on behaviour, on the simple mistakes that people make at the various stages of friendship development.

Is it such a strange and unacceptable idea that people can be trained to adopt more satisfactory styles in relationships? Not really. Therapists, social workers, doctors, and dentists nowadays receive instruction on the ways to establish rapport with patients and how to develop a reassuring and constructive "bedside manner." We know also that insurance or car sales staff are trained in how to relate to possible customers, that airline cabin crew and the police alike receive instruction on relating to the public, and that managers are now encouraged to spend time building up good personal relationships with employees. Such emphasis on skills takes us beyond the trite commonsense advice for lonely persons to "go out and meet more people." It focuses us on the fact that relationship problems derive in part, if not on the whole, from people "doing relationships" wrongly rather than simply not getting enough opportunities to be in them.

The evidence suggests that all of us are probably missing out and not maximizing our potential for relationships. American research (Reisman, 1981) shows that people claim to have about 15 "friends" on average, although the numbers change with age (17-year-olds claim about 19, while 28-year-olds have only 12; 45-year-olds have acquired 16, while people in their sixties enjoy an average of 15). When people are asked to focus only on the relationships that are most satisfying, intimate, and close, however, the number drops dramatically to around 6 (5.6 to be precise). . . .

THE NATURE OF FRIENDSHIP

A friend of mine once defined a "friend" as someone who, seeing you drunk and about to stand up on a table and sing, would quietly take you aside to prevent you[r] doing it. This definition actually embodies quite a few of the important aspects of friendship: caring, support, loyalty, and putting high priority on the other person's interests. We shall see later in the [reading] why these are important. However, when researchers have taken a more precise look at the meaning of friendship, they have focused on two specific things: the general *features* that humans expect friends to have and the *rules* of friendship that humans expect to be observed.

There are certain features that we find particularly desirable in friends and certain characteristics that everyone believes that being a friend demands. K. E. Davis and Todd (1985) found that we regularly expect a friend to be someone who is honest and open, shows affection, tells us his or her secrets and problems, gives us help when we need it, trusts us and is also trustworthy, shares time and activities with us, treats us with respect and obviously values us, and is prepared to work through disagreements. These are things that people *expect* a friend to do for them and expect to do for the friend in return. These features constitute a quite complex picture. However, when one looks at the *rules* of friendship that people actually adhere to, then the strongest ones are rather simple (Argyle & Henderson, 1985): hold conversations; do not disclose confidences to other people; refrain from public criticism; repay debts and favours. These researchers also demonstrate that emotional support, trust, and confiding are among the rules that distinguish high-quality friendships from less close ones.

In ideal circumstances, then, a friend is an open, affectionate, trusting, helpful, reliable companion who respects our privacy, carries out interactions with all due respect to the norms of behaviour and ourselves, does not criticize us in public, and both does us favours and returns those that we do. In the real world, friendship is unlikely to live up to this ideal and we all have some range of tolerance. However, it is a *voluntary* bond between two people and the above ideals can be seen as part of an unwritten contract between them, whose violation can become the grounds for the dissolution of the relationship (Wiseman, 1986).

Another important view of friendship has been offered by Wright (1984). He too stresses the "voluntary interdependence" of friendship: it is important that people freely choose to be intertwined together in the relationship. He also places emphasis on the "person qua person" element, or the extent to which we enjoy the person for his or her own sake, rather than for the things that he or she does for us. More recent research on this idea (Lea, 1989) finds indeed that "self-referent rewards," or the way the other person makes us feel about ourselves, are just as important as these other things. The way in which the relationship helps us to feel about ourselves, and its voluntary nature, are crucial to the nature of friendship. There are good reasons why this is the case.

THE "PROVISIONS" OF FRIENDSHIP

There are several ways to start answering the large question: "Why do we need friends?" We could just decide that everyone needs intimacy, possibly as a result of dependency needs formed in childhood, just as the psychoanalysts tell us. There may be something to this, as we shall see, but there is more to the need for friendships than a need for intimacy—and there is more to the need for intimacy than we may suppose, anyway. For instance, we might want to ask how intimacy develops, how it is expressed, what else changes when it grows, and so on. We might also note the curious finding (Wheeler et al., 1983; Hays, 1989) that both men and women prefer intimate partners who are women! Indeed, Arkin and Grove (1990) show that shy men prefer to talk to women even when they are not in an intimate encounter. Not only this, but those people who talk to more women during the day have better health than those who talk to fewer women (Reis, 1986). Clearly the nature of needs for intimacy and friendship is rather intriguing and may be mediated by gender and other social contexts....

Belonging and a Sense of Reliable Alliance

In writing about loneliness and the "provisions" of relationships—what it is that they do for us—Weiss (1974) proposed that a major consequence of being in relationships is a sense of belonging and of "reliable alliance." He is touching on something very important about human experience. We all like to belong or to be accepted; even those who choose solitude want it to be the result of their own choice, not someone else's. No one wants to be an outcast, a pariah or a social reject. Indeed, the powerful effects of being made *not* to belong were long recognized as a severe punishment in Ancient Greece, where people could be ostracized and formally exiled or banished. The modern equivalent is found in the British trade union practice of "sending someone to Coventry" when they break the union rules: the person's workmates, colleagues, neighbours and associates are instructed to refuse to speak to the person about anything....

By contrast, relationships give us a sense of inclusion, a sense of being a member of a group—and, as the advertisers keep emphasizing, membership has its privileges. One of these privileges is "reliable alliance"; that is to say, the existence of a bond that can be trusted to be there for you when you need it. To [quote] a phrase, "A friend in need is a friend indeed"—or in our terms, the existence of a friendship creates a reliable alliance: one of the signs that someone is a true friend is when they help you in times of trouble.

Emotional Integration and Stability

Importantly, communities of friends provide a lot more than just a sense of belonging and reliable alliance (Weiss, 1974). They also provide necessary anchor points for opinions, beliefs, and emotional responses. Friends are benchmarks that tell us how we should react appropriately, and they correct or guide our attitudes and beliefs in both obvious and subtle ways. As an example, consider how different cultures express grief differently. In some countries it is acceptable to fall to the ground, cover oneself with dust and wail loudly; in other cultures it is completely unacceptable to show such emotion, and the emphasis falls on dignified public composure. Imagine the reaction in Britain if the Queen were to roll on the ground as a way of demonstrating grief, or in the United States if the President and First Lady attended military funerals with their faces blacked and tearing their clothes. Humans have available many different ways of demonstrating grief but they typically cope with this strong emotion in a way particularly acceptable to their own culture.

Like cultures, friends and intimates develop their own sets of shared concerns, common interests and collective problems, as well as shared meanings, common responses to life and communal emotions. Friends are often appreciated exactly because they share private understandings, private jokes, or private language. Indeed, communication researchers (Hopper et al., 1981; Bell et al., 1987) have shown that friends and lovers develop their own "personal idioms" or ways of talking about such things as feelings, sex, and bodily parts, so that they are obscure to third parties. By using a phrase with secret meaning, couples can communicate in public places about things that are private. Good examples are to be found in newspaper columns on St. Valentine's Day. What, for example, are we to make of a message I found in the local student newspaper: "Dinglet, All my dinkery forever, Love, Scrunnett"? Presumably it meant something both to the person who placed the advertisement and to the person who was the intended object of it. Be alert: the couple who announce that "We are going home to make some pancakes" may in fact be planning to have a night of passion!

Such language is just a localized version of the fact that different cultures use different dialects or languages. Equally, friends have routines of behaving or beliefs that are not shared by everyone in a particular country or culture, but for that reason they are more important in daily life. Loneliness is, and isolation can be, wretched precisely because it deprives people of such psychological benchmarks and anchor points. Lonely people lose the stability provided by the chance to compare their own reactions to life with the reactions of other people that they know, like, and respect....

So loneliness and isolation are disruptive because they deprive the person of the opportunity for comfortable comparison of opinions and attitudes with other people—of close friends. People who are parted from friends become anxious, disoriented, unhappy, and even severely destabilized emotionally; they may become still more anxious just because they feel themselves behaving erratically, or they may experience unusual mood swings. They often report sudden changes of temper and loss of control, sometimes resulting in violent outbursts; but in any case their judgment becomes erratic and unreliable, and they may become unusually vigilant, suspicious, or jumpy in the presence of other unfamiliar people.

Another function of friendship, then, a reason why we need friends, is to keep us emotionally stable and to help us see where we stand vis-à-vis other people and whether we are "doing OK." It is particularly noticeable in times of stress and crisis. I remember an occasion when all the lights [went out] in a student residence block where I was a [residence advisor]. The rational thing to do was to find a flashlight and await the restoration of power. What we all actually did was to stumble down to the common-room and chatter amongst ourselves: the need to compare our reactions to the emergency was so powerful and so universal that even the warden, a medical researcher who had doctoral degrees from both Oxford and Cambridge, did the same. Such behaviour often happens after any kind of stress or crisis, from the crowd of people who gather to swap stories after a fire or a car accident, to the nervous chatter that schoolchildren perform when the doctor comes to inject them against measles or TB....

Opportunities for Communication about Ourselves

There is a third reason why we need friends (Weiss, 1974). A centrally important need is for communication. This particular wheel was strikingly reinvented by the Quaker prison reformers several generations ago, who attempted to cut down communication between criminals in prison in order to stop them [from] educating one another about ways of committing crime. Accordingly, one of their proposals was that prisoners should be isolated from one another. What occurred was very instructive: the prisoners spent much of their time tapping out coded messages on walls and pipes, devising means of passing information to one another, and working out other clever ways of communicating. Evidently, people who are involuntarily isolated feel a need to communicate. One additional function that healthy friendships provide, then, is a place for such communication to occur—communication about anything, not just important events but also trivial stuff as well as personal, intimate details about oneself. In a study at the University of Iowa, I and my students (S. W. Duck et al., 1991) have found that most conversations with friends last very short periods of time (about three minutes on average) and deal with trivialities. They are nonetheless rated as extremely significant. They revitalize the relationship, reaffirm it and celebrate its existence, through the medium of conversation.

A mild form of this overwhelming need to communicate is to be found on railway trains, planes and long-distance buses. Here many lonely people strike up conversations—but usually monologues—which allow them to communicate to someone or to tell someone about themselves and their opinions. A striking thing about this is the intimacy of the stories that are often told. Perfect strangers can often be regaled with the life history, family details, and personal opinions of someone they have not seen before and will probably never see again. Indeed, that is probably a key part of it, for the listener who will not be seen again cannot divulge the "confession" to friends or colleagues and so damage the confessor's reputation. (In cases where it is known that the listener and confessor will meet again, as in the case of doctors and patients, priests and parishioners, counsellors and clients, or lawyers and consultants, the listeners are bound by strict professional ethical codes not to reveal what they have been told. On the train, the "ethics" are simply left to statistical chance, and the extreme improbability of the two strangers meeting one another's friends is a comfort in itself.) ...

Provision of Assistance and Physical Support

Another "provision" of relationships is simply that they offer us support, whether physical, psychological, or emotional (Hobfoll & Stokes, 1988). This section focuses on physical support and assistance, which are often as significant to us as is any other sort of support.

For example, when people lose a friend or a spouse through bereavement, they report a lack of support—they are cut off from someone who has helped them to cope with life and to adjust to its problems, tasks, and changing uncertainties. This can take one of two forms: physical support (such as help with day-to-day tasks) and psychological support (such as when someone shows that we are appreciated, or lets us know that our opinions are valued). Human beings need both of these types of support, but the types are significantly different.

This is very simply illustrated. When your friend gives you a birthday present you are supposed to accept it in a way that indicates your own unworthiness to receive it and also the kindness of the friend ("Oh you shouldn't have bothered. It really is very good of you"). In short, you repay your friend by accepting the gift as a token of friendship and by praising the friend. You "exchange" the gift for love and respect, as it were. Imagine what would happen if you repaid by giving the friend the exact value of the gift in money. The friend would certainly be insulted by the ineptness: you would have altered the nature of the social exchange and also, in so doing, the nature of the relationship, by focusing on money rather than the gift as a symbol for friendship. Indeed, Cheal (1986) has shown that gift-giving as a one-way donation is rare and gift *reciprocity* is the norm, indicating that it serves an important relational function. Gift exchange serves the symbolic function of cementing and celebrating the relationship.

There are other clear examples of this point—that the nature of the exchange or support helps to define the degree and type of relationship. For instance, many elderly people get resentful of the fact that they gradually become more and more physically dependent on other people for help in conducting the daily business of their lives. The elderly cannot reach things so easily, cannot look after themselves and are more dependent physically, while at the same time they are less able to repay their friends by doing services in return. This, then, is one reason why many people dislike or feel uneasy with old age: they resent the feeling of helpless dependency coupled with the feeling of perpetual indebtedness that can never be paid off. For many elderly people, then, the mending of a piece of furniture, the making of a fruit pie, or the knitting of a sweater can be traded off against dependency: elderly people *need to be allowed* to do things for other people as a way of demonstrating to themselves and to everyone else that they are valuable to others and can still make useful contributions to the world....

Reassurance of Our Worth and Value, and Opportunity to Help Others

People who are lonely characteristically say that no one cares about them, that they are useless, uninteresting, of low value and good for nothing. Studies of the conversation of severely depressed people invariably reveal indications that they have lost their self-respect or self-esteem (Gotlib & Hooley, 1988). In other words, they have come to see themselves as valueless, worthless, and insignificant, often because that is how they feel that everyone else sees them. Furthermore, analysis of suicide notes shows that many suicide attempts are carried out as a way of forcing some particular friend to re-evaluate the person, or to shock the friend into realizing just how much he or she really does esteem the person making the attempt. For this reason, Alfred Adler (1929) has claimed, with characteristic insight, that every suicide is always a reproach or a revenge.

One reason, then, that we appreciate friends is because of their contribution to our self-evaluation and self-esteem. Friends can do this both directly and indirectly: they may compliment us or tell us about other people's good opinions of us. Dale Carnegie's multimillion-seller book on *How to Win Friends and Influence People* stressed the positive consequences of doing this. Friends can also increase our self-esteem in other ways: by attending to what we do, listening, asking our advice, and generally acting in ways that indicate the value that they place on our opinions. However, there are less obvious and more indirect ways in which they can communicate this estimation of our value. For one thing, the fact that they choose to spend time with us rather than with someone else must show that they value our company more than the alternatives.

There is a subtler version of these points too. Just as we look to friends to provide us with all of these things, so we can get from friendship one other key benefit. Because friends trust us and depend on us, they give us the chance to help them. That gives us the opportunity to take responsibility for them, to see ourselves helping them with their lives, to give them our measured advice and consequently to feel good. Friends provide us with these possibilities of taking responsibility and nurturing other people.

Undoubtedly, these things are important in the conduct of relationships and in making them satisfactory for both partners, and it is critical that we learn to evince them effectively. However, one important point to note is that those people who are poor at doing this (e.g., people who are poor at indicating interest, or who seem to have little time for other people, or never let them help or let them give advice) will find that other people are unattracted to relationships with them. All people need indications of their estimability and need chances to nurture just as we do, and if we do not adequately provide such signs then these people will reject us—just as we would do in their position....

Personality Support

Yet there is something even more fundamental to close relationships than this. Recent research indicates that each feature mentioned above—sense of community, emotional stability, communication, provision of help, maintenance of self-esteem—in its own way serves to support and integrate the person's personality (S. W. Duck & Lea, 1982). Each of us is characterized by many thoughts, doubts, beliefs, attitudes, questions, hopes, expectations, and opinions about recurrent patterns in life. Our personalities are composed not only of our behavioural style (for example, our introversion or extraversion) but also of our thoughts, doubts, and beliefs. It is a place full of symbols, a space where we are ourselves, a system of interlocking thoughts, experiences, interpretations, expectancies, and personal meanings. Our personality would be useless to us if all of these opinions and meanings were not, by and large, supported. We would simply stop behaving if we had no trust in our thoughts or beliefs about why we should behave or how we should behave, just as we stop doing other things that we are convinced are wrong. Some schizophrenics and depressives actually do stop behaving when their thought-world falls apart: they just sit and stare.

Each of us needs to be assured regularly that our thought-worlds or symbolic spaces are sound and reliable. A friend can help us to see that we are wrong and how we can change, or that we are right about some part of our thinking. We may have vigorous discussions about different attitudes that we hold—but our friends are likely to be very similar to us in many of our attitudes and interests, so that these discussions are more probably supportive than destructive. However, we all know the anger and pain that follow a really serious disagreement with a close friend—much more unpleasant than a disagreement with an enemy. What we should deduce from all this is that we seek out as friends those people who help to support our thought-world-personality, and we feel chastened, sapped or undermined when they do not provide this support.

What sort of person best gives us the kind of personality support that I have described here? In the first instance, it is provided by people who share our way of thinking. The more of these "thought-ways" that we share with someone, the easier it is to communicate with that person: we can assume that our words and presumptions will be understood more easily by someone who is "our type" than by someone who is not—we shall not have the repetitious discomfort of perpetually explaining ourselves, our meanings, and our jokes.

Yet there is much more to it than this, although it has taken researchers a long time to sort out the confusing detail of the picture. For one thing, the type of similarity that we need to share with someone in order to communicate effectively depends on the stage that the relationship has reached. At early stages it is quite enough that acquaintances are broadly similar, but at later stages the similarity must be more intricate, precise, refined, and detailed. One of the skills of friend-making is to know what sorts of similarity to look for at which times as the relationship proceeds. General similarity of attitudes is fine at the early to middle stages, but matters much less later if the partners do not work at discovering similarities at the deeper level of the ways in which they view other people and understand their characters. Very close friends must share the same specific sorts of framework for understanding the actions, dispositions and characters of other people in general, and in specific instances of mutual acquaintance. Such similarity is rare and prized. For that reason, if for no other, it is painful and extremely significant to lose the persons who offer it.

Loss or absence of particular intimates or friends deprives us of some measure of support for our personality, and it is essential to our psychological health that we have the skill to avoid this. Losing an intimate partner or friend not only makes us die a little, it leaves floating in the air those bits of our personality that the person used to support, and can make people fall apart psychologically. Of course, this will depend on how much our personality has been supported by that partner, which particular parts are involved, how readily these parts are supported by others, how much time we have had to anticipate and adjust to the loss, and so on. But essentially the loss or absence of friends and of close, satisfying relationships does not merely cause anxiety, grief or depression; it can cause other, more severe, forms of psychological disintegration or deterioration, often with the physical and mental side-effects noted earlier. Many of the well-known psychosomatic illnesses and hysterical states are actually caused by relationship problems, although this has not been realized by as many doctors as one might expect (see Lynch, 1977). For too long the accepted medical folklore has assumed that the person's inner mental state is a given, and that it causes psychosomatic effects when it gets out of balance. It is now quite clear that the surest way to upset people's mental balance is to disturb their close relationships (Gerstein & Tesser, 1987). We need friends to keep us healthy both physically and mentally: therefore it is doubly important that we perfect the ways of gaining and keeping friends. An important first step is to recognize the different needs that each relationship can fulfill for us, and the means by which this can be achieved.

REVIEW QUESTIONS

1. Define *relationshipping*.
2. How many "satisfying, intimate, and close" relationships does the research say that people of your age typically have?
3. Duck lists four main rules that characterize friendship, according to the research. What are they?
4. Fill in the blank, explain, and tell whether you agree or disagree, and why: "Both men and women prefer intimate partners who are _____ ."
5. What does it mean to have "a sense of reliable alliance"?
6. Paraphrase and give an example from your own experience of the reality-checking function of friendships.
7. Explain what Duck means when he says that sometimes elderly people need to be allowed to do things for others.
8. According to Duck, what is the relationship between friendship networks and personal mental health? Do you agree or disagree with this claim?

PROBES

1. In what ways does Duck's example of learning to drive a car fit your experience of learning how to "do" relationships? In what ways does it not fit?
2. Test Duck's claim about the average number of "friends" reported by people of your age and the average number of "satisfying, intimate, and close" relationships. Do you find any differences among the people you know?
3. What is the function in intimate relationships of private language and personal idioms? What does the presence of these private modes of expression suggest about the similarities between friendships and cultures?
4. What explanation does Duck give for the "stranger on the train (bus, plane)" phenomenon, where your seatmate, whom you don't know, tells you intimate details of his or her life? Why does this happen?
5. How do you respond to Duck's claim that, in some important ways, birthdays are times when many people give *gifts in exchange for* respect and love?
6. Paraphrase and respond to Duck's explanation of the role of similarities in friendship relationships.

REFERENCES

Adler, A. (1929). *What your life should mean to you.* New York: Bantam.

Argyle, M., & Henderson, M. (1985). *The anatomy of relationships.* London: Methuen.

Arkin, R., & Grove, T. (1990). Shyness, sociability and patterns of everyday affiliation. *Journal of Social and Personal Relationships, 7,* 273–281.

Baxter, L. A., & Dindia, K. (1990). Marital partners' perceptions of marital maintenance strategies. *Journal of Social and Personal Relationships, 7,* 187–208.

Bell, R. A., Buerkel-Rothfuss, N., & Gore, K. (1987). "Did you bring the yarmulke for the cabbage patch kid?": The idiomatic communication of young lovers. *Human Communication Research, 14,* 47–67.

Cheal, D. J. (1986). The social dimensions of gift behaviour. *Journal of Social and Personal Relationships, 3,* 423–439.

Davis, K. E., & Todd, M. (1985). Assessing friendship: Prototypes, paradigm cases, and relationship description. In S. W. Duck & D. Perlman (Eds.), *Understanding personal relationships.* London: Sage.

Duck, W., & Lea, M. (1982). Breakdown of relationships as a threat to personal identity. In G. Breakwell (Ed.), *Threatened identities.* Chichester: Wiley.

Duck, S. W., Rutt, D. J., Hurst, M., & Strejc, H. (1991). Some evident truths about communication in everyday relationships: All communication is not created equal. *Human Communication Research, 18,* 114–129.

Gerstein, I. H., & Tesser, A. (1987). Antecedents and responses associated with loneliness. *Journal of Social and Personal Relationships, 4,* 329–363.

Gotlib, I. H., & Hooley, J. M. (1988). Depression and marital distress: Current and future directions. In S. W. Duck (Ed.) with D. F. Hay, S. E. Hobfoll, W. Ickes, & B. Montgomery, *Handbook of personal relationships.* Chichester: Wiley.

Hays, R. B. (1989). The day-to-day functioning of close versus casual friendship. *Journal of Social and Personal Relationships, 1,* 75–98.

Hobfoll, S. E., & Stokes, J. P. (1988). The process and mechanics of social support. In S. W. Duck (Ed.) with D. F. Hay, S. E. Hobfoll, W. Ickes, & B. Montgomery, *Handbook of personal relationships.* Chichester: Wiley.

Hopper, R., Knapp, M. L., & Scott, L. (1981). Couples' personal idioms: Exploring intimate talk. *Journal of Communication, 31,* 23–33.

Lea, M. (1989). Factors underlying friendship: An analysis of responses on the acquaintance description form in relation to Wright's friendship model. *Journal of Social and Personal Relationships, 6,* 275–292.

Lynch, J. J. (1977). *The broken heart: The medical consequences of loneliness.* New York: Basic Books.

Reis, H. T. (1986). Gender effects in social participation: Intimacy, loneliness, and the conduct of social interaction. In R. Gilmour & S. W. Duck (Eds.), *The emerging field of personal relationships.* Hillsdale, NJ: Lawrence Erlbaum.

Reisman, J. (1981). Adult friendships. In S. W. Duck & R. Gilmour (Eds.), *Personal relationships 2: Developing personal relationships.* London: Academic Press.

Weiss, R. S. (1974). The provisions of social relationships. In Z. Rubin (Ed.), *Doing unto others.* Englewood Cliffs, NJ: Prentice-Hall.

Wheeler, L., Reis, H. T., & Nezelek, J. (1983). Loneliness, social interaction and sex roles. *Journal of Personality and Social Psychology, 35,* 742–754.

Wiseman, J. P. (1986). Friendship: Bonds and binds in a voluntary relationship. *Journal of Social and Personal Relationships, 3,* 191–211.

Wright, P. H. (1984). Self referent motivation and the intrinsic quality of friendship. *Journal of Social and Personal Relationships, 1,* 114–130.

Relationships and Power

William Paul Young

In 2007, a small book called *The Shack* became a best-seller—over 7 million copies sold then, and many more have been sold since—even though it was a "guy-meets-God novel." Critics all over the world praised the way this book addresses the age-old question: If God is all-powerful and full of love, why doesn't God do something about the pain and evil in the world? I'll let you read the book for yourself to discover the answer to that question. I offer a short excerpt here because it says something profound about relationships.

This selection from *The Shack* makes its point about relationships via a discussion of the relationships among the three parts of what Christians have for centuries called the Trinity—Father, Son, and Holy Spirit. If you don't read theological writings—or you don't much think about Christian ideas—it might be a little strange to read some paragraphs that address these topics, especially since, in *The Shack,* God appears as three persons: a "big black woman" called "Papa"; a middle-eastern man named Jesus; and "Sarayu," the Holy

Spirit. But I hope you'll hang in there with me. As I said, many millions of people have found this book to be very much worth reading.

The central topic of this short excerpt is relationships and power. The reading is taken from the middle and near the end of *The Shack* when the central character, Mack, is getting to know his three conversation partners. The point about relationships is made clearly enough that I don't think I have to explain it here.

I do want to emphasize *why* I included this reading in this chapter. Power issues create more problems in relationships than any other single topic. Although it might be difficult for some readers to connect with a discussion about the relationships among the three parts of the Trinity, there is a model here that can actually work among humans. When Mack asks the three about the "chain of command," they laugh. Sarayu says, among other things, "We don't need power over the other because we are always looking out for the best. Hierarchy would make no sense among us. Actually, this is your problem not ours." And Papa adds, "It's one reason why experiencing true relationship is so difficult for you [humans]."

The remainder of this reading develops the idea that hierarchy is "the human paradigm" in most cultures. For example, Sarayu says, "When [humans] choose independence over relationship, you become a danger to one another. Others become objects to be manipulated . . . , and it is also used to inflict great harm." The author of *The Shack* also links this point to the larger issue about why there is so much pain and evil in the world. When it reaches this point, the reading goes beyond the focus of this chapter.

I hope you'll discover in this reading that useful ideas about communication and relationships can come from a variety of sources, including a novel about "guy meets God," and that this idea about power can affect specific relationships in your life.

MAIN IDEAS

- *How* individuals relate reveals more about their relationship than *what* they say.
- Power is an ever-present dimension of human relationships.
- When power elements define relationships, it is easier for mutual mistreatment to occur.
- Although power has become the "normal" human paradigm, it *is* possible to conceive of relationships among individuals that are not based on power or hierarchy.
- Key elements of this alternative include "graciousness," mutual concern for the best, and a concrete commitment to consistently living out of love.
- Painful human questions arise when humans "try to make sense of the world in which you live based on a very small and incomplete picture of reality."

Just then Jesus and Sarayu entered laughing through the back door, involved in their own conversation. Jesus came in dressed much as he had the day before, just jeans and a light blue button-down shirt that made his dark brown eyes stand out. Sarayu, on the other hand, was clothed in something so

"Relationships and Power" by William Paul Young from *The Shack: Where Tragedy Confronts Eternity.* Copyright © 2007. Reprinted by permission of Windblown Media.

fine and lacy that it fairly flowed at the slightest breeze or spoken word. Rainbow patterns shimmered and reshaped with her every gesture. Mack wondered if she ever completely stopped moving. He rather doubted it.

Papa leaned down to eye level with Mack. "You raise some important question, and we'll get around to them, I promise. But now let's enjoy breakfast together."

Mack nodded, again a little embarrassed as he turned his attention to the food. He was hungry anyway, and there was plenty to eat.

"Thank you for breakfast," he told Papa while Jesus and Sarayu were taking their seats.

"What?" she said in mock horror. "You aren't even going to bow your head and close your eyes?" She began walking toward the kitchen, grumbling as she went. "Task, tsk, tsk. What is the world coming to? You're welcome, honey," she said as she waved over her shoulder. She returned a moment later with still another bowl of steaming something that smelled wonderful and inviting.

They passed the food to one another, and Mack was spellbound watching and listening as Papa joined in the conversation Jesus and Sarayu were having. It had something to do with reconciling an estranged family, but it wasn't *what* they were talking about that captured Mack, it was *how* they related. He had never seen three people share with such simplicity and beauty. Each seemed totally aware of the others rather than of himself.

"So, what do you think, Mack?" Jesus asked, gesturing toward him.

"I have no idea what you're talking about," said Mack with his mouth half full of the very tasty greens. "But I love the way you do it."

"Whoa," said Papa, who had returned from the kitchen with yet another dish. "Take it easy on those greens, young man. Those things can give you the trots if you ain't careful."

"All right, I'll try to remember," Mack said as he reached for the dish in her hand. Then turning back to Jesus he added, "I love the way you treat each other. It's certainly not how I expected God to be."

"How do you mean?"

"Well, I know that you are one and all, and that there are three of you. But you respond with such graciousness to each other. Isn't one of you more the boss than the other two?"

The three looked at one another as if they had never thought of such a question.

"I mean," Mack hurried on, "I have always thought of God the Father as sort of being the boss and Jesus as the one following orders, you know, being obedient. I'm not sure how the Holy Spirit fits in exactly. He . . . I mean, she . . . uh . . ." Mack tried not to look at Sarayu as he stumbled for words. "Whatever—the Spirit always seemed kind of a . . . uh . . ."

"A free spirit?" offered Papa.

"Exactly—a free spirit, but still under the direction of the Father. Does that make sense?"

Jesus looked over at Papa, obviously trying with some difficulty to maintain the perception of a very serious exterior. "Does that make sense to you, Abba? Frankly, I haven't a clue what this man is talking about."

Papa scrunched up her face as if exerting great concentration. "Nope, I have been trying to make head or tail out of it, but sorry, he's got me lost."

"You know what I am talking about." Mack was a little frustrated. "I am talking about who's in charge. Don't you have a chain of command?"

"Chain of command? That sounds ghastly!" Jesus said.

"At least binding," Papa added as they both started laughing, and then Papa turned to Mack and sang, "Though chains be of gold, they are chains all the same."

"Now don't concern yourself with those two," Sarayu interrupted, reaching out her hand to comfort and calm him. "They're just playing with you. This is actually a subject of interest among us."

Mack nodded, relieved and a little chagrined that he had again allowed himself to lose his composure.

"Mackenzie, we have no concept of final authority among us, only unity. We are in a *circle* of relationship, not a chain of command or 'great chain of being', as your ancestors termed it. What you're seeing here is relationship without any overlay of power. We don't need power over the other because we are always looking out for the best. Hierarchy would make no sense among us. Actually, this is your problem, not ours."

"Really? How so?"

"Humans are so lost and damaged that to you it is almost incomprehensible that people could work or live together without someone being in charge."

"But every human institution that I can think of, from political to business, even down to marriage, is governed by this kind of thinking. It is the web of our social fabric," Mack asserted.

"Such a waste!" said Papa, picking up the empty dish and heading for the kitchen.

"It's one reason why experiencing true relationship is so difficult for you," Jesus added. "Once you have a hierarchy you need rules to protect and administer it, and then you need law and the enforcement of the rules, and you end up with some kind of chain of command or a system of order that destroys relationship rather than promotes it. You rarely see or experience relationship apart from power. Hierarchy imposes laws and rules and you end up missing the wonder of relationship that we intended for you."

"Well," said Mack sarcastically, sitting back in his chair, "we sure seem to have adapted pretty well to it."

Sarayu was quick to reply, "Don't confuse adaptation with intention, or seduction with reality."

"So then—uh, could you please pass me a bit more of those greens? So then we've been seduced into this preoccupation with authority?"

"In a sense, yes!" responded Papa, passing Mack the platter of greens but not letting go until he pulled twice. "I'm just looking out for you, son."

Sarayu continued, "When you chose independence over relationship, you became a danger to one another. Others became objects to be manipulated or managed for your own happiness. Authority, as you usually think of it, is merely the excuse the strong ones use to make others conform to what they want."

"Isn't it helpful in keeping people from fighting endlessly or getting hurt?"

"Sometimes. But in a selfish world it is also used to inflict great harm."

"But don't you use it to restrain evil?"

"We carefully respect your choices, so we work within your systems even while we seek to free you from them," Sarayu continued. "Creation has been taken down a very different path than we desired. In your world the value of the individual is constantly weighed against the survival of the system, whether political, economic, social, or religious—any system, actually. First one person, and then a few, and finally even many are easily sacrificed for the good and ongoing existence of that system. In one form or another this lies behind every struggle for power, every prejudice, every war, and every abuse of relationship. The 'will to power and independence' has become so ubiquitous that it is now considered *normal.*"

"It's not?"

"It *is* the human paradigm," added Papa, having returned with more food. "It is like water to fish, so prevalent that it goes unseen and unquestioned. It *is* the matrix; a diabolical scheme in which you are hopelessly trapped even while completely unaware of its existence."

Jesus picked up the conversation. "As the crowning glory of creation, you were made in our image, unencumbered by structure and free to simply 'be' in relationship with me and one another. If you had truly learned to regard one another's concerns as significant as your own, there would be no need for hierarchy."

Mack sat back in his chair, staggered by the implications of what he was hearing. "So are you telling me that whenever we humans protect ourselves with power ..."

"You are yielding to the matrix, not to us," finished Jesus.

"And now," Sarayu interjected, "we have come full circle, back to one of my initial statements: you humans are so lost and damaged that to you it is almost incomprehensible that relationship could exist apart from hierarchy. So you think that God must relate inside a hierarchy as you do. But we do not."

"But how could we ever change that? People will just use us."

"They most likely will. But we're not asking you to do it with others, Mack. We're asking you to do it with us. That's the only place it can begin. We won't use you."

"Mack," said Papa with an intensity that caused him to listen very carefully, "we want to share with you the love and joy and freedom and light that we already know within ourselves. We created you, the human, to be in face-to-face relationship with us, to join our circle of love. As difficult as it will be for you to understand, everything that has taken place is occurring exactly according to this purpose, without violating choice or will."

"How can you say that with all the pain in this world, all the wars and disasters that destroy thousands?" Mack's voice quieted to a whisper. "And what is the value in a little girl being murdered by some twisted deviant?" There it was again, the question that lay burning a hole in his soul. "You may not cause those things, but you certainly don't stop them."

"Mackenzie," Papa answered tenderly, seemingly not offended in the least by his accusation, "there are millions of reasons to allow pain and hurt and suffering rather than to eradicate them, but most of those reasons can be understood only within each person's story. I am not evil. You are the ones who embrace fear and pain and power and rights so readily in your relationships. But your choices are also not stronger than my purposes, and I will use every choice you make for the ultimate good and the most loving outcome."

"You see," explained Sarayu, "broken humans center their lives around things that seem good to them but will neither fill them nor free them. They are addicted to power, or the illusion of security that power offers. When a disaster happens, those same people will turn against the false powers they trusted. In their disappointment, either they become softened toward me or they become bolder in their independence. If you could only see how all of this ends and what we will achieve without the violation of one human will—then you would understand. One day you will."

"But the cost!" Mack was staggered. "Look at the cost—all the pain, all the suffering, everything that is so terrible and evil." He paused and looked down at the table. "And look what it has cost you. Is it worth it?"

"Yes!" came the unanimous, joyful response.

"But how can you say that?" Mack blurted. "It all sounds like the end justifies the means, that to get what you want you will go to any length, even if it costs the lives of billions of people."

"Mackenzie." It was the voice of Papa again, especially gentle and tender. "You really don't understand yet. You try to make sense of the world in which you live based on a very small and incomplete picture of reality. It is like looking at a parade through the tiny knothole of hurt, pain, self-centeredness, and power and believing you are on your own and insignificant. All of these thoughts contain powerful lies. You see pain and death as ultimate evils and God as the ultimate betrayer, or perhaps, at best, as fundamentally untrustworthy. You dictate the terms and judge my actions and find me guilty.

"The real underlying flaw in your life, Mackenzie, is that you don't think I am good. If you knew I was good and that everything—the means, the ends, and all the processes of individual lives—is all covered by my goodness, then while you might not always understand what I am doing, you would trust me. But you don't."

"I don't?" asked Mack, but it was not really a question. It was a statement of fact, and he knew it. The others seemed to know it too, and the table remained silent.

Sarayu spoke. "Mackenzie, you cannot produce trust, just as you cannot 'do' humility. It either is or is not. Trust is the fruit of a relationship in which you know you are loved. Because you do not know that I love you, you *cannot* trust me."

Again there was silence, and finally Mack looked up at Papa and spoke. "I don't know how to change that."

"You can't, not alone. But together we will watch that change take place. For now I just want you to be with me and discover that our relationship is not about performance or your having to please me. I'm not a bully, not some self-centered demanding little deity insisting on my own way. I am good, and I desire only what is best for you. You cannot find that through guilt or condemnation or coercion, only *through* a relationship of love. And I do love you...."

Together they began the walk down the dock. As they approached the shore, they slowed again. Jesus put his hand on Mack's shoulder and gently turned him until they were face-to-face.

"Mack, the world system is what it is. Institutions, systems, ideologies, and all the vain, futile efforts of humanity that go with them are everywhere, and interaction with all of it is unavoidable. But I can give you freedom to overcome any system of power in which you find yourself, be it religious, economic, social, or political. You will grow in the freedom to be inside or outside all kinds of systems and to move freely between and among them. Together, you and I can be in it and not of it."

"But so many of the people I care about seem to be both in it and of it!" Mack was thinking of his friends, church people who had expressed love to him and his family. He knew they loved Jesus, but he also knew they were sold out to religious activity and patriotism.

"Mack, I love them. And you wrongly judge many of them. For those who are both in it and of it, we must find ways to love and serve them, don't you think?" asked Jesus. "Remember, the people who know me are the ones who are free to live and love without any agenda."

"Is that what it means to be a Christian?" It sounded kind of stupid as Mack said it, but it was how he was trying to sum everything up in his mind.

"Who said anything about being a Christian? I'm not a Christian."

The idea struck Mack as odd and unexpected, and he couldn't keep himself from grinning. "No, I suppose you aren't."

They arrived at the door of the workshop. Again Jesus stopped. "Those who love me have come from every system that exists. They were Buddhists or Mormons, Baptists or Muslims; some are Democrats, some Republicans and many don't vote or are not part of any Sunday morning or religious institutions. I have followers who were murderers and many who were self-righteous. Some are bankers and bookies, Americans and Iraqis, Jews and Palestinians. I have no desire to make them Christian, but I do want to join them in their transformation into sons and daughters of my Papa, into my brothers and sisters, into my Beloved."

"Does that mean," said Mack, "that all roads will lead to you?"

"Not at all." Jesus smiled as he reached for the door handle to the shop. "Most roads don't lead anywhere. What it does mean is that I will travel any road to find you...."

REVIEW QUESTIONS

1. Briefly explain the Christian notion of the Trinity.
2. Explain the difference between a "chain of command" and a "circle of relationship."
3. Paraphrase: "When you chose independence over relationship, you became a danger to one another."
4. Explain the author's use of the term, "the matrix" in the middle of this reading. How does this relate to the classic film series of that name?

PROBES

1. Use an Internet search engine to identify why this author chose to call his Holy Spirit character, "Sarayu."
2. What's the relationship between choosing "independence" and basing relationships on power?
3. What is the short answer, in this reading, to the question, "If God is all-powerful, why does God permit pain and evil in the world?"

CHAPTER 8

Communicating with Intimate Partners

Communicating Closeness: Intimacy, Affection, and Social Support

Laura K. Guerrero, Peter A. Andersen, and Walid A. Afifi

This reading comes from an interpersonal communication textbook written by three authors associated with universities in Arizona and California. Guerrero, Andersen, and Afifi discuss how to understand, experience, and express intimacy, verbally and nonverbally. You will notice that their writing style is different from mine and that of several other authors in *Bridges Not Walls*. These writers want to emphasize description rather than prescription (describing how things work rather than giving advice) and to support every claim with references to communication research. So there are few direct suggestions, lots of citations in parentheses, and a long list of references at the end of the reading. You can use these references to dig deeper into any of the topics they discuss here. And even though the large number of citations can be distracting, it's also good to know that their claims are based on solid research evidence.

The reading begins with the reminder that intimate relationships form "the cornerstone of our lives and our emotional well-being." The authors distinguish "intimacy" from sexual involvement, especially because intimacy is a long-term feature of some relationships that includes not just passion but also trust, warmth, deep friendship, and support. They point out that the experience of intimacy is rooted in internal processes—feelings and thoughts people have for each other. They develop this point by distinguishing among love, passion, interpersonal warmth, and joy.

They point out that intimacy is expressed nonverbally and verbally through positive involvement, immediacy behaviors, and high levels of interpersonal affection. A key element of intimacy is communication about uniqueness: ". . . people develop an idiosyncratic style of communication that reflects the unique characteristics of their personalities and the relationship they share." This point echoes what's written in Chapter 2 about uniqueness as a cornerstone of interpersonal-quality communication. Three other features of intimate communication are depth, comfort with silence, time and repeated interaction, and positive feelings (they use the word "affect" for *feelings,* as in "positive affect"). Listening and understanding is also crucial to intimacy.

The final part of this excerpt discusses direct and indirect, verbal and nonverbal ways of communicating social support, because "making sacrifices for one another and providing social support are key ways of increasing intimacy. . . ." One study of nonverbal communication that they cite underscores the importance of hugs, physical closeness, empathic facial expressions, attentiveness, pats, and eye contact. Verbally, one key is that messages be "person-centered" rather than "position-centered." The reading does an especially good job of illustrating why both verbal and nonverbal communication is critical to the development and maintenance of intimacy.

MAIN IDEAS

- Intimacy is the cornerstone of our lives and our emotional well-being.
- Intimacy is not the same as sexual involvement; it necessarily includes warmth, depth, long-term commitment, sharing, and support.
- Intimacy can be communicated with positive involvement behaviors, immediacy behaviors, and high levels of interpersonal affection.
- Intimate relationships are clearly unique for the participants.
- Intimacy typically includes comfort with silence.
- Intimacy requires development over time and repeated interactions.
- Intimacy is associated with extensive positive emotions of satisfaction, affection, and joy.
- Intimate relationships include abundant listening and understanding.
- Comfort and social support are key ways of increasing intimacy.
- Social support is communicated indirectly and directly, verbally and nonverbally.

Kevin treasures his close friendships. Among his dozens of friends, two are most special. His most romantic relationship is with his girlfriend Jennifer. He says that she brightens his day. They spend a lot of time together talking, touching, comforting, and listening. They play tennis and bicycle together. Jennifer says that she has never felt the same warmth and trust with another boyfriend. Best of all, she can tell him anything, and he listens! Kevin's other close relationship is with Dan. Kevin and Dan went through high school together, ran track, played football, and were on the debate team together. Today they still take ski trips and run together, and they have great conversations about everything—business, sports, politics, and life in general. Unlike with his other male friends, Kevin can talk to Dan about anything, even Jennifer. And importantly, he can count on Dan for anything.

Intimate interactions are a special type of communication that occur in our closest relationships. These interactions transpire among close friends, within tightly knit families, in romantic relationships, and in many marriages. In everyday language, most people do not use the term *intimate* to describe their closest relationships. Instead, Kevin would be more likely to refer to his intimate relationships with Dan and Jennifer as close, friendly, warm, affectionate, cozy, caring, bonded, warmhearted, convivial, compassionate, and even loving. In fact, research shows that the most common term people use for intimate relationships is *close relationships* (Parks & Floyd, 1996). Dan and Kevin would never say they have an intimate relationship, even though by our definition they do; they would say they are "best" friends or "close" friends.

In their article on the "bright side of relational communication," Andersen and Guerrero (1998a) stated that intimate relationships are the foundation of our lives:

> Almost without exception, our relationships with friends and loved ones are the cornerstone of our lives and our emotional well-being. The warm feeling of an intimate conservation, a reassuring hug, seeing a close friend after a long absence, or sharing joy with one's family are experiences each of us has had. Indeed, the brightest side of life's experience often occurs in close intimate relationships during the exchange of warm, involving, immediate messages. (p. 303)

Kevin's close relationships with both Jennifer and Dan play vital roles in his life. Yet these two relationships are also likely to differ in important ways. If Kevin kept a diary of the behaviors that he used to communicate intimacy, affection, and social support to Dan and Jennifer, what types of behaviors would likely be similar across the two relationships? What behaviors might be more characteristic of his best friendship with Dan? Which might be reserved for his romantic relationship with Jennifer? To answer these and other questions, this reading examines the feelings, behaviors, and relationships that comprise the experience of intimacy, as well as the related experiences of affection and social support. First, we help you recognize intimacy when you see and feel it and understand its importance in your life. Second, we discuss the nonverbal and verbal behaviors that communicate intimacy, affection, social support, and comfort.

UNDERSTANDING INTIMACY

Intimacy refers to the special relational states and interactions that occur in close relationships, characterized by feelings of warmth, trust, and deep friendship. For many people, intimacy is synonymous with sexual involvement; however, that is *not* the meaning of intimacy we intend in this chapter. Sex can be intimate or impersonal, although the best sexual encounters certainly are intimate ones for most people. To use a thermal metaphor, if sexual encounters are hot, then intimate interactions are best characterized by warmth (Sternberg, 1987). And according to Sternberg (1987), "over the long term maintaining intimacy—communication, sharing, support and the like—is more important than maintaining passion" (p. 222). Thus having dinner with an old friend, going to your son's graduation, chatting with your significant other by the fireplace with a glass of wine, and telling your best friend about your new love are all intimate encounters.

These intimate encounters have a quality that is lacking in everyday interactions between strangers and acquaintances. Sternberg (1987) suggested that intimacy comprises feelings of warmth, trust, and happiness, which are present only in close relationships. Among the hundreds of people you meet at school, at work, in organizations, and through your family, acquaintances, and friends, you will build intimate relationships with only a few. Moving a relationship from impersonal to intimate is a fragile process (Andersen, 1998a). Many factors—such as cultural or personality differences, inappropriate behavior, loss of trust, lack of attraction, and lack of similarity, to mention just a few—can throw a relationship off track and prevent it from becoming a special, intimate one.

Locating intimacy is not easy; it comes in a variety of forms and contexts and can be found in feelings, interactions, and relationships (Acitelli & Duck, 1987; Andersen, 1999; Andersen et al., 2006; Prager & Roberts, 2004). However, researchers have argued that interaction plays the most central role in creating and sustaining intimacy (Andersen et al., 2006). This is because interaction is the means through which people share intimate thoughts and feelings. Intimate interaction is also the vehicle through which people develop and maintain close relationships. Intimate thoughts and feelings lead to intimate behavior; intimate behavior then leads to more thoughts and feelings of intimacy. Both the experience and the expression of intimacy enhance the quality of relationships. As Prager (2000) observed, "If intimacy is one of the most often discussed aspect of personal relationship functioning, then there are good reasons. It is predictive of the highest levels of satisfaction, love, and trust as well as the primary reward of closeness" (p. 229).

Experiencing Intimacy

The experience of intimacy is rooted in internal processes related to feelings and thoughts. The feelings two people have for each other are the foundation of intimate relationships. These feelings are variously described as warmth, love, bondedness, emotional connectedness, and affection. Andersen and Guerrero (1998a) argued that the feelings of warmth that occur in the presence of a friend, close relative, or relational partner are at the heart of intimate relationships. In marital relationships, emotional intimacy is connected to every other kind of intimacy: social, sexual, intellectual, and recreational (McCabe, 1999). These feelings may accompany a hug from a close friend, a talk with a lover, or a holiday celebration with the family. Statements that disclose one's vulnerable emotions are especially conducive to feelings of intimacy (Prager & Roberts, 2004).

Partners in close relationships feel numerous positive emotions when interacting with or thinking about each other. Guerrero and Andersen (2000) described a cluster of interpersonal emotions, including love, passion, warmth, and joy, that are related to affection. **Love** is an inherently relational emotion that is evoked in relationships and is associated with an intense desire to maintain closeness (Aron & Aron, 1986; Shaver, Morgan, & Wu, 1996). **Passion** is sometimes conceptualized as a part of love between romantic partners (Sternberg, 1986, 1988), although others see passion as encompassing feelings of attraction and sexual arousal. **Interpersonal warmth** is another inherently relational emotion that people experience as a sense of pleasantness, contentedness, and intimacy during interactions with relational partners, such as friends, lovers, and family members (Andersen & Guerrero, 1998a). Finally, **joy** (or happiness) is an interpersonal emotion because it is commonly experienced after receiving praise from others or from being the object of love, affection, and/or admiration (Schwartz & Shaver, 1987). When partners frequently experience these types of emotions in connection with each other, they tend to feel closer and be happier with their relationship (Feeney, Noller, & Roberts, 1998; Prager & Buhrmester, 1998).

Thoughts and perceptions are also an important part of the intimacy experience. Prager and Roberts (2004) argued that intimacy is experienced through shared knowledge. This knowledge is gained through mutual self-disclosure, spending time together, and observing one another's behavior. These types of interactions help people reduce uncertainty so that they can predict and explain one another's feelings and behaviors. Think about your closest friends. You probably know a lot about them (and they about you) that other people do not know. Feelings of intimacy are also enhanced when people believe that their partners understand and value them (Prager, 2000).

Expressing Intimacy

If intimate feelings are not communicated, they remain internal processes that have little effect on a relationship (Andersen et al., 2006). Self-disclosure, which includes sharing personal information about oneself and expressing feelings, is essential for intimacy to develop. Intimacy is often communicated nonverbally through **positive involvement** behaviors, which represent the intersection of involvement and positive affect (Guerrero, 2004; Prager, 2000). Involvement behaviors show that a person is interested and engaged in an interaction. Positive affect cues show that a person is experiencing affectionate emotions, such as liking, joy, warmth, or love. Positive involvement behaviors include a host of verbal and nonverbal messages that reflect intimacy and warmth. These behaviors have also been called **immediacy behaviors**—actions that signal warmth, communicate availability, decrease psychological and/or physical distance, and promote involvement (Andersen, 1985). Importantly, intimacy cannot be created or sustained if only one person expresses feelings of closeness to the other. Thus reciprocity is a critical part of intimate interaction; people must not only express intimate thoughts and feelings to each other, they must also respond positively to those expressions of intimacy.

As Andersen (1999) noted, "Immediacy behaviors are foundations by which intimate interactions and intimate relationships are created and sustained" (p. 219). However, immediacy behaviors, such as making eye contact, smiling, and using a pleasant tone of voice, are important in nonintimate relationships as well. Consequently, while immediacy behaviors are essential components of intimate relationships, they are not enough by themselves. Intimate relationships also (1) are unique, (2) contain depth, (3) exist over time in that they have a history and a future and are marked by rituals, (4) involve the exchange of very high levels of positive emotions, and (5) are characterized by high levels of listening and understanding. Intimacy is characterized by high levels of **interpersonal affection** in relationships (Floyd, 2006; Pendell, 2002). Affection, which is similar to intimacy, is characterized by liking and high regard for another and the communication of affectionate and immediate behaviors, and it is vital to mental and physical health (Pendell, 2002).

Uniqueness. Unlike many short-term relationships, interactions in intimate relationships are unique. Knapp (1983) argued that when we first meet people, our communication tends to be scripted. In other words, we use conventional language that is widely understood. However, as a relationship becomes close, Knapp suggested, two people develop an idiosyncratic style of communication that reflects the unique characteristics of their personalities and the relationship they share. A study by Hopper, Knapp, and Scott (1981) revealed that couples use unique forms of communication in their relationships. For example, one couple reported that twitching their noses signaled "You're special," while another reported that twisting their wedding rings meant "Don't you dare do or say that!" Every close relationship produces intimate interactions that have a unique flavor.

A close relationship, like Kevin and Jennifer's, is an irreplaceable and one-of-a-kind romance; it is unique. Hendrick and Hendrick (1992) maintained that intimacy "is characterized by genuineness and an absence of 'role' relationships" (p. 166). Thus, if someone can instantly replace one intimate relationship with another, it probably was not very intimate after all. But the intimate interactions individuals share with their boyfriend or girlfriend, their best friend, and their mother or father are unique. Intimate interactions use special forms of communication that individuals can share only with certain others with whom they share great trust and closeness. Think of a dark family secret, a sexual interaction you had with a relational partner, or a disclosure from a close friend about his or her sexual identity. With how many people could you share this information? Probably very few. Intimate relationships are special and relatively rare, although people often have numerous intimate interactions within their few special relationships.

Depth. Intimate interactions are deep rather than superficial connections. They are characterized by the sharing of time and space, touch, and in-depth self-disclosure not found in other relationships. Later in this chapter, we will explore some of the nonverbal and verbal behaviors that lead to deep interactions. In intimate relationships, partners "can communicate deeply and honestly … sharing innermost feelings" (Sternberg, 1987, p. 333). Self-revealing statements that convey vulnerable emotions are especially conducive to intimacy (Prager & Roberts, 2004). Self-disclosure plays a critical role in relationship development because as people become closer, they share their innermost thoughts and feelings (see Chapter 6). Only by sharing personal information, thoughts, and feelings can two people get to know each other well enough to develop a close, intimate relationship.

Comfort with Silence. Of course, self-disclosure is not the only way in which a couple can communicate depth. In the beginning stages of relationships, people often feel compelled to talk so as to prevent an awkward silence. In close relationships, however, silence can communicate comfort and connection. For example, a couple driving across town might hold hands and snuggle while listening to romantic music on the radio, and two close friends might smile and laugh together during certain scenes while watching their favorite movie (which they have seen together many times). Such interaction shows that non-verbal communication, and even silence, can indicate that two people share a deep connection with each other.

Time and Repeated Interaction.   Intimate interactions rarely arise out of thin air. They typically occur in relationships that are well developed and between people who have sustained their relationship across multiple episodes and interactions. Intimate communication occurs in interaction sequences that may unfold over months, years, and even decades. Miller, Cody, and McLaughlin (1994) illustrated this point when they explained that intimate partners share more experiences and participate together in a wider range of situations than nonintimates. Rituals such as annual birthday celebrations, anniversaries, holidays spent together, and the renewal of wedding vows help people sustain intimacy and commitment in their relationships (Braithwaite & Baxter, 1995; Werner et al., 1993). Total time spent together is also predictive of higher relational satisfaction and intimacy in both marital and dating relationships (Egland, Stelzner, Andersen, & Spitzberg, 1997; Emmers-Sommer, 2004). As Andersen (1999) stated, "Although many parents tell their children they love them, they proceed to spend time on dozens of activities while spending little time with their children. Not surprisingly, many of these children feel unloved despite their parents' words" (p. 64). Some researchers believe that quality of time is more important than quantity of time (Emmers-Sommer, 2004). This is probably true, although people have more opportunities to spend quality time together when they are in frequent contact with one another.

Positive Affect.   High levels of positive affect characterize the most fulfilling and satisfying relationships for both men and women (Prager & Buhrmester, 1998). While negative communication is common in many intimate exchanges (see Chapters 9 and 10), in general, intimacy is fostered by a higher ratio of positive to negative behaviors. Feeney et al. (1998) reviewed several studies showing that happy couples report "higher rates of positive behaviors in their daily interactions with their partners" and that "more than three-quarters of couples ... identified positive intimate behaviors as crucial to maintaining satisfaction in their relationships" (pp. 480–481). Using friendly, constructive forms of communication probably helps maintain relationships because it makes people feel good (Guerrero & Andersen, 2000). In another review of the literature, Kelly et al. (2003) observed that happy couples are not necessarily defined by the verbal content of their communication but rather by the positive emotions they "appear to be experiencing—the smiles, laughs, affection, and warmth" (p. 729). The expression of positive emotions such as love, passion, warmth, and joy is particularly important in communicating affection. Complimenting your partner, showering your partner with affection, and making sacrifices for your partner are maintenance behaviors that are likely to make your partner *feel* good and therefore strengthen the intimate bond that you share.

Listening and Understanding.   Having a partner who listens and is understanding is very important for relational satisfaction and need fulfillment (Prager & Buhrmester, 1998). In fact, one study showed that among a large set of communication variables, perceived understanding was the best predictor of relational satisfaction (Egland et al., 1997). This study also found that a listener's ability to "backchannel" (saying "uh huh" and nodding in the appropriate places), actively listen, and show nonverbal immediacy were important predictors of perceived understanding. These types of behaviors validate the partner's thoughts and feelings. People who are understanding also tend to be more emotionally supportive and sensitive to the needs of their partners. As we shall discuss later in this chapter, being emotionally supportive is a key communication skill that helps people develop and maintain intimate relationships (Burleson, 2003)....

COMFORT AND SOCIAL SUPPORT

Another important way in which people communicate intimacy and affection is by showing that they are there for relational partners in times of distress. Making sacrifices for one another and providing social support are key ways of increasing intimacy and maintaining relationships. When people have the intention of establishing intimacy with a friend, they both give and receive more social support from that friend (Sanderson et al., 2005). People feel distress in reaction to a wide variety of situations. In S. M. Jones's (2000) study of distressing events among college students, the following were most frequently described as distressing: problems in a romantic relationship, college performance (grades), friend/roommate problems, family problems, work-related stress, family illness, death, and personal illness/injury.

Indirect Ways of Communicating Comfort and Social Support

Floyd (2006) has labeled social support as an indirect but powerful means of communicating affection. Verbal behaviors, such as saying "I care about you," are direct expressions of affection. Floyd also argues that many nonverbal behaviors, such as giving someone a hug, are direct expressions of affection because they are commonly interpreted as affectionate. In contrast, many forms of social support are indirect expressions of affection because they *imply* that a person feels affection for someone. To illustrate this, Guerrero and Floyd (2006) gave the following example of providing social support to a new mother: "The relatives and friends of the young mother might ... show their affection by offering to babysit, bringing her meals, taking care of her yardwork, and sending her money to help with her financial needs" (p. 93). Although these types of actions would not directly communicate affection, they would let the young mother know that she was loved and cared for. These types of socially supportive behaviors send especially strong messages of affection even though they are indirect; they also tend to be used more commonly than direct messages in certain types of relationships, such as those between fathers and sons or male friends (Morman & Floyd, 1999). Thus you probably wouldn't be surprised to see Kevin (who is a math whiz) helping Dan with his calculus homework, but you probably would be surprised if you heard Kevin tell Dan "I love you" and then embrace him with a big hug.

Nonverbal Ways of Communicating Comfort and Social Support

Of course, many direct nonverbal behaviors communicate both affection and comfort. Although friends such as Dan and Kevin may not show much nonverbal affection to each other during their everyday interactions, during times of distress they would probably feel freer to comfort each other using behaviors such as hugs or pats on the arm. Dolin and Booth-Butterfield (1993) investigated nonverbal behaviors related to comforting by asking students how they would react nonverbally if their roommate was distressed because of a recent relational breakup. The students reported that they would use the following behaviors most frequently:

- *Hugs* (reported in 41.9% of the accounts): giving the person a whole-body hug or hugging him or her around the shoulder
- *Close proxemic distancing* (40.9%): sitting down next to the person or leaning closer
- *Facial expression* (38.7%): looking empathetic, sad, or concerned
- *Attentiveness* (37.7%): listening carefully and nodding as the person talked about the distressing event
- *Increased miscellaneous touch* (34.4%): using all forms of touch other than hugs or pats, such as holding the person's hand or stroking his or her hair
- *Pats* (26.9%): using short, repetitive movements such as patting the distressed person's arm or shoulder
- *Eye contact* (23.7%): looking directly at the distressed person, particularly while he or she is talking

In addition to these behaviors, Dolin and Booth-Butterfield (1993) found a few other nonverbal comforting strategies that were reported less often. Some students described behaviors related to weeping, such as crying with the distressed person or offering a "shoulder to cry on." Some said that they would engage in emotional distancing behavior, such as trying to remain uninvolved, getting comfortable, or fixing a cup of coffee. Presumably, these strategies would keep the individual from experiencing too negative affect while talking to the distressed person. Other students reported that they would engage in instrumental activities, such as getting the distressed person a tissue or something to eat. Still others indicated that they would show concern through warm vocal tones and empathetic gestures. For example, if the distressed person was angry, the individual in the comforting role might clench her or his fist to mirror the distressed person's anger.

Verbal Ways of Communicating Comfort and Social Support

Verbal strategies are important in the comforting process. In particular, messages that are person centered seem to help people alleviate emotional distress (Applegate, 1980; Burleson, 1982, 2003). **Person-centered messages** acknowledge, elaborate on, and validate the feelings and concerns of the distressed person. Comforting messages can be ranked as high or low in quality based on how person-centered they are (Applegate, 1980; Burleson, 1982, 1984; S. M. Jones, 2000). Highly person-centered messages help the distressed person gain a perspective on her or his feelings by placing them in a broader context. These messages also legitimize the distressed person's feelings. Suppose that Dan gets a C in his calculus exam even though he studied diligently. If Kevin used a highly person-centered message, he might say something like

> It sure must be frustrating to study hard for a test and then get a C. In fact, that really surprises me because you are smart. Don't you think you'll do better in the next test now that you know the type of questions your professor asks?

Notice that the highly person-centered response conveys understanding ("It sure must be frustrating") and support ("You are smart") while also helping the distressed person to think about the event in a different way (perhaps as a learning experience).

Moderately person-centered messages acknowledge the distressed person's feelings, but they do not help the distressed person contextualize or elaborate on her or his feelings as well as do highly person-centered messages. For example, Kevin might tell Dan, "I'll bet the test was really hard, and I'll bet most people got Cs or worse, so you shouldn't feel that bad." Or he might say, "It's only one test. You'll do better in the next one. Let's go see a good movie—that will help get your mind off this." Note that these messages provide neat, easy explanations and solutions that do not allow for much elaboration. These types of messages, which are frequently used by people in the comforter's role, provide comfort that is okay but not great.

Finally, messages that are low in person centeredness (sometimes called position-centered messages) implicitly or explicitly deny the legitimacy of the distressed person's feelings, sometimes by blaming the distressed person for the situation and other times by changing the topic or the focus. For example, Kevin might tell Dan, "It's only one test. You shouldn't make such a big deal out of it." Worse yet, he might say, "I'm sure some people got As, so you really don't have anyone to blame but yourself. I helped you as much as I could, but I guess calculus is just too hard for you to understand." Or Kevin might also start talking about himself: "I got a C in a test once too. It was a real bummer, but that's life. Hey, do you want to get some lunch or something?"

As you might suspect, several studies have shown that people who use highly person-centered messages provide the best comfort and are perceived the most positively (Burleson & Samter, 1985a, 1985b; Jones & Burleson, 1997;

Jones & Guerero, 2001). Highly person-centered messages are perceived as the most appropriate, effective, helpful, and sensitive. These messages are likely to be effective in expressing care and concern, but perhaps more important, they might help the distressed person reevaluate the situation so that the event seems less distressing (Burleson & Goldsmith, 1998; S. M. Jones, 2000).

Of course, when comforting someone, it is important to use both verbal and nonverbal strategies. Jones and Guerrero (2001) investigated whether both nonverbal intimacy behaviors and verbal person centeredness influenced the quality of comforting behavior. They trained people to enact high, moderate, and low levels of nonverbal intimacy and person centeredness and then had them listen and react to people's distressing stories. They found that both nonverbal intimacy behaviors and person centeredness had strong effects on comforting quality. When distressed people interacted with someone who used high levels of nonverbal intimacy and high levels of person centeredness, they reported feeling the best. When high person-centered messages were paired with low levels of nonverbal intimacy or, conversely, when low person-centered messages were paired with high levels of nonverbal intimacy, the overall comforting quality decreased. Not surprisingly, comforters who used low levels of both nonverbal intimacy and person centeredness were the least effective at alleviating distress. Recent studies have confirmed the importance of nonverbal intimacy and immediacy in high-quality, successful comforting (Jones, 2004; Jones & Burleson, 2003).

Thus if you want to do a good job of comforting someone, you should pay attention to both your verbal and your nonverbal behaviors. It is also important to let the distressed person talk rather than changing the topic or focusing the discussion on yourself. When people can freely disclose their distressing circumstances to others, it helps them vent their negative emotion and possibly think through and reassess the problem, which can contribute to psychological and physical well-being (Burleson & Goldsmith, 1998; Pennebaker, 1989; Pennebaker, Colder, & Sharp, 1990).

REVIEW QUESTIONS

1. Compare and contrast intimacy and sexual involvement.
2. Identify some specific internal feelings that are closely linked to intimacy.
3. What is the connection between self-disclosure and intimacy?
4. What is "reciprocity"? What is the role of reciprocity in the development and maintenance of intimacy?
5. Describe the connections between what's said about uniqueness in Chapter 2 and what these authors say about uniqueness.
6. Explain the relationship between relationship "depth" and relationship "breadth." Which is more important for intimacy?
7. Give two examples of social support that you have (a) given and (b) received in the last month.

PROBES

1. Since immediacy behaviors are essential components of many relation-ships that are not intimate, including teacher–student and supervisor–subordinate relationships, what makes immediacy behaviors different in intimate relationships?
2. This reading emphasizes the importance of internal feelings to intimacy. What is the connection between this point about the *psychology* of intimacy and the *communication* of intimacy?
3. Connect what's said here about intimacy and listening with the discussions of listening in Chapter 5.

REFERENCES

Acitelli, L. K., & Duck, S. W. (1987). Intimacy as the proverbial elephant. In D. Perlman & S. W. Duck (Eds.), *Intimate relationships: Development, dynamics, and deterioration* (pp. 297–308). Newbury Park, CA: Sage.

Andersen, P. A. (1985). Nonverbal immediacy in interpersonal communication. In A. W. Siegman & S. Feldstein (Eds.), *Multichannel integrations of nonverbal behavior* (pp. 1–36). Hillsdale, NJ: Erlbaum.

Andersen, P. A. (1998). The cognitive valence theory of intimate communication. In M. T. Palmer & G. A. Barnett (Eds.), *Progress in communication sciences: Vol. 14. Mutual influence in interpersonal communication: Theory and research in cognition, affect and behavior* (pp. 39–72). Stamford, CT: Ablex.

Andersen, P. A. (1999). *Nonverbal communication: Forms and functions.* Mountain View, CA: Mayfield.

Andersen, P. A., & Guerrero, L. K. (1998). The bright side of relational communication: Interpersonal warmth as a social emotion. In P. A. Andersen & L. K. Guerrero (Eds.), *Handbook of communication and emotion: Research, theory, applications, and contexts* (pp. 303–329). San Diego, CA: Academic Press.

Andersen, P. A., Guerrero, L. K., & Jones, S. M. (2006). Nonverbal intimacy. In V. Manusov & M. L. Patterson (Eds.), *The handbook of nonverbal communication* (pp. 259–277). Thousand Oaks, CA: Sage.

Applegate, J. L. (1980). Person-centered and position-centered teacher communication in a day care center. *Studies in Symbolic Interactionism, 3,* 59–96.

Aron, A., & Aron, E. N. (1986). *Love as the expansion of self: Understanding attraction and satisfaction.* New York: Hemisphere.

Braithwaite, D. O., & Baxter, L. A. (1995). "I do" again: The relational dialectics of renewing marriage vows. *Journal of Social and Personal Relationships, 12,* 177–198.

Burleson, B. R. (1982). The development of comforting communication skills in childhood and adolescence. *Child Development, 53,* 1578–1588.

Burleson, B. R. (1984). Comforting communication. In H. W. Sypher & J. L. Applegate (Eds.), *Communication by children and adults* (pp. 63–104). Beverly Hills, CA: Sage.

Burleson, B. R. (2003). The experience and effects of emotional support: What the study of cultural and gender differences can tell us about close relationships, emotion, and interpersonal communication. *Personal Relationships, 10,* 1–23.

Burleson, B. R., & Goldsmith, D. J. (1998). How the comforting process works: Alleviating emotional distress through conversationally induced reappraisals. In P. A. Andersen & L. K. Guerrero (Eds.), *Handbook of communication and emotion: Theory, research, contexts, and applications* (pp. 246–275). San Diego, CA: Academic Press.

Burleson, B. R., & Samter, W. (1985a). Consistencies in theoretical and naïve evaluations of comforting messages. *Communication Monographs, 52,* 104–123.

Burleson, B. R., & Samter, W. (1985b). Individual differences in the perception of comforting messages. *Central States Speech Journal, 36,* 39–50.

Dolin, D. J., & Booth-Butterfield, M. (1993). Reach out and touch someone: Analysis of nonverbal comforting responses. *Communication Quarterly, 41,* 383–393.

Egland, K. L., Stelzner, M. A., Andersen, P. A., & Spitzberg, B. H. (1997). Perceived understanding, nonverbal communication and relational satisfaction. In J. Aitken & L. Shedletsky (Eds.), *Intrapersonal communication processes* (pp. 386–395). Annandale, VA: Speech Communication Association.

Emmers-Sommer, T. M. (2004). The effect of communication quality and quantity indicators on intimacy and relational satisfaction. *Journal of Social and Personal Relationships, 21,* 399–411.

Feeney, J. A., Noller, P., & Roberts, N. (1998). Emotion, attachment and satisfaction in close relationships. In P. A. Andersen & L. K. Guerrero (Eds.), *Handbook of communication and emotion: Research, theory, applications and contexts* (pp. 273–305). San Diego, CA: Academic Press.

Floyd, K. (2006). Human affection exchange: XII. Affectionate Communication is associated with diurnal variation in salivary free cortisol. *Western Journal of Communication, 70,* 47–63.

Guerrero, L. K. (2004). Observer ratings of nonverbal involvement and immediacy. In V. Manusov (Ed.), *The sourcebook of nonverbal measures: Going beyond words* (pp. 221–235). Mahwah, NJ: Lawrence Erlbaum.

Guerrero, L. K., & Andersen, P. A. (2000). Emotion in close relationships. In C. Hendrick & S. S. Hendrick (Eds.), *Close relationships: A sourcebook* (pp. 171–183). Thousand Oaks, CA: Sage.

Guerrero, L. K., & Floyd, K. (2006). *Nonverbal communication in close relationships.* Mahway, NJ: Lawrence Erlbaum.

Hendrick, S. S., & Hendrick, C. (1992). *Liking, loving, and relating* (2nd ed.). Pacific Grove, CA: Brooks/Cole.

Hopper, M. L., Knapp, M. L., & Scott, L. (1981). Couples' personal idioms: Exploring intimate talk. *Journal of Communication, 31,* 23–33.

Jones, S. M. (2000). *Nonverbal immediacy and verbal comforting in the social process.* Unpublished doctoral dissertation. Arizona State University, Tempe.

Jones, S. M. (2004). Putting the person into person-centered and immediate emotional support: Emotional change and perceived helper competence as outcomes of comforting in helping situations. *Communication Research, 32,* 338–360.

Jones, S. M., & Burleson, B. R. (1997). The impact of situational variables on helpers' perceptions of comforting messages: An attributional analysis. *Communication Research, 24,* 530–555.

Jones, S. M., & Burleson, B. R. (2003). Effects of helper and recipient sex on the experience and outcomes of comforting messages: An experimental investigation. *Sex Roles, 48,* 1–19.

Jones, S. M., & Guerrero, L. K. (2001). The effects of nonverbal immediacy and verbal person-centeredness in the emotional support process. *Human Communication Research, 27,* 567–596.

Kelly, A. B., Fincham, F. D., & Beach, S. R. H. (2003). Communication skills in couples: A review and discussion of emerging perspectives. In J. O. Greene & B. R. Burleson (Eds.), *Handbook of communication and social skills* (pp. 723–751). Mahwah, NJ: Lawrence Erlbaum.

Knapp, M. L. (1983). Dyadic relationship development. In J. Wiemann (Ed.), *Nonverbal interaction* (pp. 179–197). Beverly Hills, CA: Sage

McCabe, M. P. (1999). The interrelationship between intimacy, relationship functioning, and sexuality among men and women in committed relationships. *Canadian Journal of Human Sexuality, 8,* 31–39.

Miller, L. C., Cody, M. J., & McLaughlin, M. L. (1994). Situations and goals as fundamental constructs in interpersonal communication research. In M. L. Knapp & G. R. Miller (Eds.), *Handbook of interpersonal communication* (pp. 162–198). Thousand Oaks, CA: Sage.

Morman, M. T., & Floyd, K. (1999). Affectionate communication between fathers and young adult sons: Individual- and relational-level correlates. *Communication Studies, 50,* 294–309.

Parks, M. R., & Floyd, K. (1996). Meanings for closeness and intimacy in friendship. *Journal of Social and Personal Relationships, 13,* 85–107.

Pendell, S. D. (2002). Affection in interpersonal relationships: Not just a fond or tender feeling. In W. B. Gudykunst (Ed.), *Communication yearbook 26* (pp. 70–115). Mahwah, NJ: Erlbaum.

Pennebaker, J. W. (1989). Confession, inhibition, and disease. In L. Berkowitz (Ed.), *Advances in experimental social psychology* (Vol. 22, pp. 211–244). San Diego, CA: Academic Press.

Pennebaker, J. W., Colder, M., & Sharp, L. K. (1990). Accelerating the coping process. *Journal of Personality and Social Psychology, 58,* 528–537.

Prager, K. J. (2000). Intimacy in personal relationships. In C. Hendrick & S. S. Hendrick (Eds.), *Close relationships: A sourcebook* (pp. 229–242). Thousand Oaks, CA: Sage.

Prager, K. J., & Buhrmester, D. (1998). Intimacy and need fulfillment in couple relationships. *Journal of Social and Personal Relationships, 15,* 435–469.

Prager, K. J., & Roberts, L. J. (2004). Deep intimate connection: Self and intimacy in couple relationships. In D. J. Mashek & Y. A. P. Aron (Eds.), *Handbook of closeness and intimacy* (pp. 43–60). Mahwah, NJ: Lawrence Erlbaum.

Sanderson, C. A., Rahm, K. B., Beigbeder, S. A., & Metts, S. (2005). The link between the pursuit of intimacy goals and satisfaction in close same-sex friendships: An examination of the underlying processes. *Journal of Social and Personal Relationships, 22,* 75–98.

Schwartz, J. C., & Shaver, P. (1987). Emotions and emotion knowledge in interpersonal relations. In W. H. Jones & D. Perlman (Eds.), *Advances in personal relationships* (pp. 197–241). Greenwich, CT: JAI Press.

Shaver, P. R., Morgan, H. J., & Wu, S. (1996). Is love a "basic" emotion? *Personal Relationships, 3,* 81–96.

Sternberg, R. J. (1986). A triangular theory of love. *Psychological Review, 93,* 119–135.

Sternberg, R. J. (1987). *The triangle of love: Intimacy, passion, commitment.* New York: Basic Books.

Sternberg, R. J. (1988). Triangulating love. In R. J. Sternberg & M. L. Barnes (Eds.), *The psychology of love* (pp. 119–138). New Haven, CT: Yale University Press.

Werner, C. M., Altman, I., Brown, B. B., & Ganat, J. (1993). Celebrations in personal relationships: A transactional/dialectical perspective. In S. Duck (Ed.), *Social context and relationships* (pp. 109–138). Newbury Park, CA: Sage.

———

Gender and Ethnic Similarities and Differences in Relational Development

Malcolm R. Parks

This reading may challenge you in a couple of ways, and, if it does, you will definitely profit from meeting the challenge. Malcolm Parks is a communication teacher and researcher who uses social scientific methods to study personal networks—the webs of family members, friends, co-workers, and others among and with whom we live our lives. Because he is a social scientist, his writing is more dense than several of the other essays in *Bridges Not Walls*. This is one challenge; you will probably have to read this selection slowly and maybe more than once.

A second challenge comes from the findings and conclusions he reports. Parks' and his colleagues' work demonstrates how much we can learn about personal relationships when we progress from studying individuals or pairs to examining interpersonal networks. This reading uses the findings of network research to seriously question two popular beliefs, one about gender differences in personal relationships ("Men are from Mars and women are from Venus") and the other about the connection between ethnicity and culture ("Blacks tend to…whereas Latinos and Asians are more…"). Parks demonstrates with ample research citations that both beliefs are oversimplified, inaccurate, and damaging.

The first section of the reading focuses on the role of gender in the development of personal relationships. Parks outlines several problems with studies that have ignored the impact of personal networks. First, he reviews some of the work that has led to oversimplified conclusions about gender differences, and then he reports some studies that challenge those findings.

Throughout the book that this reading was taken from, Parks cites six "core studies" that included sophisticated network measures. In this selection, he uses this research and other publications to probe several simplistic conclusions. He reports, for example, that "contrary to stereotype, men were just as committed to their personal relationships as women. This was true in both same-sex friendships and romantic relationships." In addition, "There was no difference in the level of support for the relationship that men and women perceived from members of their friends, their partner's friends, or their own family."

Parks wraps up this section on gender differences with these words: "In summary, significant sex differences were found on only 6 of the 21 measures…. Comparisons of women and men in relational development and social network involvement can be summarized rather simply. There are a lot more similarities than differences."

The next section of the reading debunks oversimplified beliefs about the impact of ethnic differences in personal relationships. To get a sense of the complexity of the perspective that Parks and his colleagues bring to their work, notice that the studies on ethnicity that he cites measure not only depth or intimacy of relational development but also "commitment, perceived interactive synchrony, personalized communication, predictability and understanding, and the amount of communication with the partner." In addition, the research measures five network factors: "amount of overlap between the partner's networks, the number of people the subject had met in the partner's network, how often he or she communicated with them, the amount of contact between members of the two networks, and measures of support from the subject's own network as well as the partner's network." It seems fairly clear to me that, if this research can gather valid and reliable data about all these factors, and if the data are interpreted carefully, we should be able to trust the findings more completely than we can trust the findings from research that gathers data only about individual and global factors such as satisfaction, supportiveness, or communication topic.

Parks' conclusion from his review of the ethnicity and personal relationships research is similar to his conclusion about gender and personal relationships: Women and men are a whole lot more similar than different. There are some differences in some aspects of relational development and interpersonal behavior. But, as he puts it, "Why do both lay observers and professional researchers persist in believing that gender and ethnicity will explain behavior in personal relationships when the evidence plainly suggests that they do not?"

The answer is that we are thinking too superficially, he suggests. Gender and ethnicity are visible and simple differences, and it takes considerable effort to move beyond them. "Put simply, we pay more attention to obvious factors than to more subtle factors that may take more effort to recognize." There are also readily available anecdotes about gender and ethnic stereotyping to support the oversimplified claims. "Unfortunately, ease and simplicity do not always breed accuracy."

The book that this reading is taken from, along with the specific findings cited in this excerpt, clearly demonstrate the value of considering personal network factors when trying to understand interpersonal relationships. I hope that you will carry forward what you learn in this reading to your understanding of the other materials in *Bridges Not Walls*.

MAIN IDEAS

- Many popular conceptions about gender and ethnic differences are not supported by social scientific research.
- Men have been found to be as intimate and emotionally supportive as women, for example.
- Men and women report similar levels of engagement in partners' networks and support from network members.
- "There are a lot more similarities than differences" between men and women in relational development and social network involvement.
- Interethnic and intraethnic dating relationships manifest similar levels of self-disclosure, closeness, and love.
- Ethnic differences do make understanding and interpersonal coordination somewhat more difficult.
- Social network involvement, however, does not differ greatly between interethnic and intraethnic couples.
- "Gender and the degree of ethnic similarity appear to have relatively little impact on how personal relationships develop, on how relational partners relate to each other's social networks, or on how network factors are associated with the developmental pathways of romance and friendship."
- It is oversimplified (stereotyping) to believe that gender and ethnic differences account for major differences in interpersonal behavior. People—men, women, members of ethnic minorities—are as similar as they are different.

Those wishing to understand the role of gender in the development of personal relationships immediately encounter three problems with the previous literature. First, researchers have looked for sex or gender differences in only a few of the characteristics of personal relationships and their

"Gender and Ethnic Similarities and Differences in Relational Development" by Malcolm R. Parks from *Personal Relationships and Personal Networks*, pp. 146–150, 154–158, and 165–168. Mahwah, NJ: Lawrence Erlbaum Associates, 2007. Reprinted by permission.

networks that change over time. Second, researchers have focused far more on whether males and females differ on select characteristics such as supportiveness than on the question of whether various characteristics are associated in different ways for males than for females. Finding that women typically express verbal support more often than males does not, for instance, imply that verbal support functions any differently for males and females. We must compare patterns of association and not merely average differences if we are to determine whether theoretic predictions about the process of relationship development hold equally for men and women. Finally, the terms *sex* and *gender* are often conflated. By convention, writers generally use the [first] term, sex, to refer to biologically based characteristics and the [second] term, gender, to refer to characteristics and behaviors that are acquired through cultural socialization. I have used *sex* when referring to specific, direct comparisons of male and female subjects and *gender* when referring to differences or similarities more generally. We should recognize, however, that nearly any distinction is arbitrary and misleading. As we come to understand more about the interplay of physiology and social experience, it becomes apparent that the biological and social can no longer be separated in a meaningful way. We know, for example, that differences in interaction with the physical and social environment lead to differences in the way genes are expressed, even in identical twins (Fraga et al., 2005).

Intimacy and supportiveness have been the dominant topics in research on sex in personal relationships. The most common conclusion reached in the studies and commentary on these topics is that women are more intimate, caring, and emotionally supportive than men (e.g., Bank & Hansford, 2000; Bascow & Rubenfeld, 2003; Fehr, 2004; Wood, 2000). It is also commonly argued that men and women specialize in different ways of expressing closeness or caring. Men, for example, tend toward doing favors, offering assistance, sharing activities, and other forms of behavioral or instrumental assistance as expressions of closeness; whereas women are more likely to judge how close a relationship is by its emotional expressiveness and level of personal disclosure (e.g., Maltz & Borker, 1982; Wood & Inman, 1993).

The emphasis on expressiveness and personal disclosure also emerges in studies of women's friendships (e.g., Aries & Johnson, 1983; Walker, 1994). Goodman and O'Brien (2000) gave this homage to talk when describing their longtime friendship: "We were friends; we had to talk. It was the single most important—and most obvious—connection. Talk is at the very heart of women's friendships, the core of the way women connect. It's the given, the absolute assumption of friendship" (pp. 34–35).

Whereas women's relationships emphasize closeness in talk, men's relationships emphasize "closeness in the doing" (Swain, 1989). Men express affection to their same-sex friends, but are likely to do it in more indirect ways (Floyd, 1995). The lower levels of intimacy and supportiveness assumed to characterize male relationships are usually viewed as the result of males being socialized to value emotional restraint and avoid behavior that might be viewed as a sign of homosexuality (Bank & Hansford, 2000).

The belief that men are less intimate or emotionally supportive than women has, however, come under intense criticism. Many of the most extreme claims in the popular press have been debunked (Goldsmith & Fulfs, 1999). The conclusions of several well-cited academic studies purporting to show sex differences have also been called into question (e.g., Kyratzis, 2001; MacGeorge et al., 2004). For example, common beliefs asserting that males are less supportive or that they express less concern for others have not withstood careful empirical test. Moreover, it appears that men and women have similar ideas of what being close is and that they rate the intimacy of a given interaction in similar ways (Parks & Floyd, 1996b; Reis, Senchak, & Solomon, 1985). Differences in intimacy, closeness, support, and a variety of other personal relationship characteristics tend to be inconsistent and, when they appear at all, tend to be relatively small (Aries, 1996; Canary et al., 1997; Goldsmith & Dun, 1997; MacGeorge et al., 2004; Wright, 1982).

We are therefore left without a clear set of hypotheses about the role of gender in the social contextual model. The situation is made even more difficult by the fact that there is almost no research on gender differences in the social network factors associated with relational development. We know that we need to look at gender differences and similarities, but we do not know how to place our bets.

Gender and sex differences in personal relationships may take two general forms. One is a difference between groups or means. Females may report, for example, [that] they love their partners or interact with network members more or less, on average, than males. Gender differences could also appear in how these factors are correlated; that is, feelings of closeness and frequency of interaction with the partner's network might be much more strongly correlated for women than for men. These and other possibilities are examined in the sections that follow.

Sex Differences in Relational and Network Factors

...Closeness, the amount of communication with the partner, and the level [of] commitment were assessed with 11 different measures across the core studies. Six of these contributed to closeness. Of these, significant sex differences were observed on only two. Women reported greater satisfaction with their interactions than did men. Women also reported somewhat higher levels of interpersonal solidarity. Neither of these effects was particularly large, but the effect for communication satisfaction was the larger of the two.... There were no interaction effects, so these differences applied equally to same-sex friendships and romantic relationships as well as to adolescents and young adults. No other significant differences were observed among the remaining indicators of closeness. Women and men did not differ in how much they loved their partners [or] liked their partners, how similar they felt to their partners, or how uncertain they were about the relationship. Nor did any of these indicators interact with age or relational type. That is, men and women were similar across all groups.

Two measures were used to determine the amount of interaction between relational partners. One asked respondents to indicate how many days in the previous 2 weeks they had communicated with their partners, whereas the other asked respondents to estimate the percentage of their free time they had spent with the relational partner in the previous 2 weeks. There was no sex difference in the first of these. Women, however, reported spending 11% more of their free time (48% vs. 37%) with their partners than men reported spending with theirs.

The final set of relational indicators assessed commitment to the relationship. No significant differences were found in any of the three indicators. There were no significant interactions with age or relational type. Contrary to stereotype, men were just as committed to their personal relationships as women. This was true in both same-sex friendships and romantic relationships.

…Most researchers have been concerned with the support that network members provide for individuals. Here our concern is with whether the individual perceives that friends and family in the surrounding network approve [of] or oppose the relationship. Individuals obviously cannot know for sure what network members really think. They may misjudge others' approval or opposition as well. Whatever the basis of the judgment, however, the women and men in our studies tended to report similar levels of support from network members. There was no difference in the level of support for the relationship that men and women perceived from members of their friends, their partner's friends, or their own family. Similar findings emerged in another study, although the men in that study reported that family members were more approving of their dating relationship (Sprecher & Felmlee, 2000). Interestingly, in our studies, women tended to believe that their partner's family members were somewhat more supportive. This was, however, a small difference. In general, men and women perceived similar levels of support across the network of friends and family. This was true for both adolescents and young adults and in both romantic relationships and same-sex friendships.

The next set of network factors dealt with how much contact people had with members of their partner's network. Once again, there were few sex differences. Men and women reported that they had met similar numbers of their partner's family and communicated with those whom they had met with equal regularity. Although women reported that they had met a slightly greater number of their partner's friends (5.0 vs. 4.2), there was no difference in how often they communicated with the ones they had met. These findings were consistent with previous investigations showing that men and women are equally likely to meet each other's networks, although women are somewhat more likely than men to tell friends or family about a date (Rose & Frieze, 1989, 1993). National survey data indicates that 70% to 80% of all adolescents in romantic relationships report having met their partner's parents. Females were slightly more likely to meet the partner's parents, to tell others that they were a couple, and to go out together as a couple in a group. Nonetheless, the majority of males and females engaged in these behaviors and the sex difference in the percentage of people doing each of these things is small, generally less than 10% (Carver et al., 2003).

The final pair of measures assessed the extent to which people liked the members of the partner's network. There was no difference in how much women and men liked the partner's family members. There was, however, a small difference in liking for the partner's friends. Women tended to like their partner's friends somewhat more. Although their study was limited to dating relationships, Sprecher and Femlee (2000) also found that women expressed somewhat greater liking for their boyfriend's friends than men expressed for their girlfriend's friends.

In summary, significant sex differences were found on only 6 of the 21 measures of relational development and network involvement. Although women reported higher values on all six, the magnitude of differences was rather small.... Moreover, there were no significant interactions with age or type of relationship observed in any of the analyses. Thus, both adolescent and young adult women and men reported similar levels of relational development and social network involvement in their same-sex friendships and romantic relationships....

Summary of Sex Similarities and Differences

Comparisons of women and men in relational development and social network involvement can be summarized rather simply. There are a lot more similarities than differences. Men and women differed significantly on less than one third of the measures. The few differences that were observed did not fall into a pattern, but were scattered across several different factors. Aside from the women's generally higher level of satisfaction with their interactions, the differences tended to be quite small, typically accounting for only 2% to 3% of the variance. It also appears that men and women go about developing personal relationships in much the same way. For both men and women, closeness, commitment, and the amount of communication with the partner are all positively linked to each other and to the level of support and interaction with network members. When it comes to judging how close and committed the relationship is, women appear to put somewhat more weight on meeting people in the partner's network and on the amount of interaction they have with their partners. These differences were most apparent in same-sex friendships, but even here they were relatively small. Men also placed weight on the same factors.

EXPLORING INTERETHNIC RELATIONSHIPS

The growing prevalence in relationships between people of different ethnic or racial groups affords another opportunity to test the generality of the social contextual perspective. The number of interracial marriages in the United States grew by over 1,000% between 1960 and 2002 (Bureau of the Census, 2002). Although the absolute number of interracial marriages is still small, more than one half of adults in the United States report having a family member or close friend who is involved in an interracial romantic relationship and, depending on the particular ethnic/racial combination, between one third and one half say they have dated outside their ethnic group themselves (Kaiser Family Foundation, 2001; Tucker & Mitchell-Kernan, 1995). Reliable figures are not available, but the proportion of people with interethnic friendships or workplace relationships is probably far higher.

In spite of their increasing prevalence, the mainstream literature on personal relationships has paid little attention to issues of multiethnic relationships, or to issues of culture and ethnicity in personal relationships more generally (Berscheid, 1999; Sprecher & Felmlee, 2000; Gaines & Liu, 2000). Researchers have traditionally focused on general attitudes toward interethnic relationships rather than on the relationships themselves (e.g., Fang, Sidanius, & Pratto, 1998; Todd et al., 1992). The literature at this writing contains only a handful of studies of relationship development between people of differing ethnicity or cultural background (e.g., Gaines et al., 1999; Gurung & Duong, 1999; Shibazaki & Brennan, 1998).

To overcome this limitation, I return to the study of dating relationships....Compared to our other studies, this study was intended to address a more detailed set of relational and network indicators and, most importantly, to draw a more diverse sample of young adult respondents. Just over half (51.4%) came from ethnic groups other than European American. Not counting European Americans, 11 different ethnic or racial groups were represented in the sample. Chinese/Chinese Americans, Filipinos, Korean/Korean Americans, Vietnamese/Vietnamese Americans, African Americans, and "Other" were the most common designations, each accounting for 5% or more of the sample.

Subjects who reported different ethnic backgrounds from their partners were classified as having an interethnic dating relationship. Subjects whose ethnic identification matched the ethnic identification obtained from the partner were classified as having a dating relationship within their ethnic group (intraethnic). A total of 82 relationships (38%) were classified as interethnic, while the remaining 136 relationships (62%) were classified as intraethnic. These groups were then compared, first in terms of mean differences on various indicators of relational development and network involvement, and then in terms of the associations between relational development and network factors.

Interethnic Versus Intraethnic Differences in Relational and Network Factors

The data set used for these comparisons contained 26 different measures.... The six relational development factors included depth (intimacy), commitment, perceived interactive synchrony, personalized communication, predictability and understanding, and the amount of communication with the partner. The five network factors included the amount of overlap between the partner's networks, the number of people the subject had met in the partner's network, how often he or she communicated with them, the amount of contact between members of the two networks, and measures of support from the subject's own network as well as the partner's network. Differences that did not account for at least 2% of the variance ... are excluded from the discussion to follow.

Differences and Similarities in Measures of Relational Development   Expectations for intimacy or depth of interaction in personal relationships vary considerably across cultural groups (Argyle et al., 1986; Gudykunst & Nishida, 1986; Ting-Toomey, 1991). Although love may be a cultural universal, its expression in specific relationships is nonetheless subject to substantial ethnic and cultural variation (S. Hendrick & C. Hendrick, 2000; Minatoya, 1988). Although these considerations suggest that depth and intimacy might be harder to obtain in interethnic relationships, we found no differences on our measures. Similar levels of self-disclosure, closeness, and love were reported in both types of relationships.

Those involved in interethnic and intraethnic relationships also displayed similar levels of commitment. Those in interethnic relationships rated the probability (0% to 100%) of their relationship lasting in the short term (3 months) somewhat lower than those dating members of their own ethnic group (79% vs. 88%). Otherwise, there were no significant differences between the groups. Interethnic and intraethnic daters attributed similar importance to the relationship, expressed equal willingness to work to maintain it, and thought they were equally likely to get married at some point in the future. At least one other study has also failed to find differences in commitment in interethnic and intraethnic romantic relationships (Gurung & Duong, 1999).

Differences in ethnic background should make it more difficult for relational partners to understand and anticipate each others' responses. This belief has been supported in studies of interethnic acquaintance and friendship (Gudykunst & Nishida, 1986; Gudykunst, Sodetani, & Sonoda, 1987). Studies of interethnic communication also point to differences in [the] way that interaction is structured, regulated, and contextualized (Gumperz, 1982; Philips, 1983). These differences should make it more difficult for participants in interethnic relationships to coordinate or synchronize their interactions. When these ideas were put to the test, however, the results were mixed. Interethnic romantic partners expressed slightly more uncertainty about their relationship on a scale developed by Parks and Adelman (1983), but the two groups did not differ on a scale of attributional confidence developed by Gudykunst and Nishida (1986). The results for the measures of interactive synchrony were also mixed. Significant differences were found on two of the four items used to assess this dimension of interdependence. Interethnic relationships were characterized by more frequent awkward silences and the perception that it was not as easy to talk to the dating partner. On the other hand, participants in interethnic and intraethnic relationships did not differ with regard to perceptions of how smoothly conversation flowed or how much effort was needed to communicate.

There were no significant differences in the remaining measures of relational development. Those involved in a romantic relationship with a person from a different ethnic group spent an almost identical proportion of their free time with their partners as those involved in a romantic relationship with someone from their own ethnic group (59% vs. 61%). Those involved in interethnic and intraethnic relationships also felt that their communication was personalized to the same degree. Participants in both types of relationships were equally likely to assign "special meanings" to words, to use distinctive nicknames or terms of endearment, to employ special looks or gestures, and to be able to communicate without having to be verbally explicit.

Differences and Similarities in Measures of Network Involvement   Previous research provides little guidance to those embarking on a relationship outside their ethnic group regarding how others might react. It is commonly assumed that interethnic couples will encounter hostile reactions from some, if not most, members of their social networks. To be sure, it depends on whether one is perceived as "dating up" or "dating down" in terms of social status. Nonetheless, multiracial couples often report that they are the recipient of racist comments or behaviors (Rosenblatt, Karis, & Powell, 1995). Most observers believe that social network members place enormous stress on interethnic couples. The higher divorce rate among interracial marriages is sometimes attributed in part to lack of support from network members (Gaines & Brennan, 2001). Even when network members are supportive, geographic and social segregation may make it more difficult for network members to come into contact with the partners or to provide support (Abrahamson, 1996; Tucker & Mitchell-Kernan, 1995).

Although these views might lead one [to] think that social network involvement would differ greatly for interethnic and intraethnic couples, we found little evidence that interethnic couples' social networks are structured differently or provide different levels of support. In purely structural terms, there were few differences in the level of network overlap, cross-network contact, or cross-network density. A significant difference was observed on only one of the seven measures of these dimensions. On average, participants in interethnic relationships had met about one fewer member in their partner's network of 12 frequent contacts. Interestingly, there was no difference in the number of people the partner had met in the subject's network. Generally, interethnic couples named a similar number of people as common members met a greater number of people in each other's network....Both of these correlations differed significantly from the corresponding correlations in interethnic relationships, where the amount of communication between the partners was not significantly related to either network overlap or the number of people met in the partner's networks.

GENDER AND ETHNICITY IN PERSPECTIVE

Gender and the degree of ethnic similarity appear to have relatively little impact on how personal relationships develop, on how relational partners relate to each other's social networks, or on how network factors are associated with the developmental pathways of romance and friendship. The young men and women we studied reported generally similar levels of intimacy, commitment, communication, contact with network members, and support from network members in their personal relationships. Support and communication with network members was related to perceptions of intimacy, commitment, and communication within the relationship in comparable ways for men and women. Similarly, within the limits of our sample, relationships between people of different ethnic groups were experienced in much the same way as relationships between people of the same ethnic group. There were few differences in measures of relational development, the structure of relational partners' social networks, or in the level of support they reported from network members.

This is not to say that there may not be important gender differences in other aspects of relational development or interpersonal behavior. However, rather than reinforcing the idea of difference by dwelling on the relatively minor differences, it may be more useful to ask why assumptions about gender and ethnicity play such a prominent role in the popular and academic literature on personal relationships. That is, why are we so eager to conclude that men and women experience relational life in dramatically different ways when the research shows that there are actually few differences of any magnitude? And if relationships between people of different ethnic groups develop and are experienced in much the same way as relationships between people of the same ethnic group, why do we place so much weight on ethnicity in personal relationships? Why do both lay observers and professional researchers persist in believing that gender and ethnicity will explain behavior in personal relationships when the evidence plainly suggests that they do not?

Part of the appeal of gender and ethnicity as explanations for interpersonal behavior is their visibility and simplicity. Except in rare cases, biological sex is readily discerned and almost instantly triggers a gender-based interpretative framework. Ethnic and racial differences are perhaps not so obvious, but are nonetheless more easily discerned than any number of other differences in socioeconomic background, personality, and communicative style. Because so little effort is needed to recognize these differences, we are likely to be biased in favor [of] using them as a basis for explaining behavior. Put simply, we pay more attention to obvious factors than to more subtle factors that may take more effort to recognize (Zipf, 1949). This bias is reinforced by the fact that most people can readily identify examples that appear to confirm stereotyped differences. If one is looking for evidence, for example, that men are less committed than women to personal relationships, it is usually rather easy to think of a given male who is less committed than a given female within one's own circle of acquaintance. The fact that the overall distribution of commitment levels is generally very similar for males and females does not prevent people from selecting examples of less committed men and more committed women. Armed with an example that appears to confirm their initial stereotype, most people do not search their memories further for counterexamples or engage in more sophisticated cognitive evaluations.

Explanations based on gender and ethnicity are also appealing because of their simplicity. They each draw on straightforward binaries (female vs. male; same vs. different) that draw us into uncomplicated generalizations about human nature and human groups. They take advantage of the well-documented bias toward explaining others' behavior in terms of relatively stable characteristics and dispositions rather than in terms of less enduring, but often more relevant, interactive and situational factors (e.g., Ross & Nisbett, 1991). Once relational behavior is attributed to the actor's sex or ethnicity, it is no longer necessary to consider more complex situational or relational factors. Thus people frequently rely on gender and ethnicity to explain behavior because it is easy and simple to do so.

Unfortunately ease and simplicity do not always breed accuracy. The characteristics of the situation and the unfolding structure of the interaction itself are often more informative. Moreover, it may be misleading to attribute differences to sex or ethnicity even when they appear to make a difference. Differences that are assumed to be the result of sex, for example, have often been shown to be the result of underlying power differences (e.g., Molm, 1985; Scudder & Andrews, 1995).

In many parts of the world gender is still a critical feature in the organization and experience of personal relationships. In contemporary industrialized democracies like the United States, however, sex differences are becoming less pronounced. Ironically, this may be part of the reason we are so sensitive to them. As large differences disappear, small differences take on a greater perceptual importance. Thought about in this way, scholarly debate regarding whether *sex* or *gender* is the most appropriate term is in fact evidence that sex differences are attenuating. If biological sex differences were broadly predictive, it is doubtful that we would have as much need for the concept of *gender* in personal relations. Gender is, after all, an attempt to explain what cannot be explained by biological sex alone.

This is not to say that sex differences in personal relationships no longer exist or are unimportant. Important sex differences may exist in areas beyond those examined here. Some research, for example, suggests that young women may be more likely than men to attempt to alter their parents' views of their romantic partner or relationship (Leslie, Huston, & Johnson, 1986). This sort of finding begs additional research. Are women also more likely to try to influence their friends' views? Are they generally more successful at influencing network members? Are women and men equally able to ignore contrary views of network members?

Although ethnicity remains important, often to the point of bloodshed, in many parts of the world, ethnic differences are diminishing in many other areas. The young adults who participated in our research, for example, were all associated with a university in a rather diverse coastal North American city. They were therefore part of an institution that is more or less explicitly designed to bring differing ideas and people into amicable contact as well as residents of a city with numerous opportunities and mechanisms for bringing diverse people together. Moreover, young adults of diverse backgrounds often share elements of a common popular culture. Culturally diverse forms of music are, for instance, readily incorporated into popular music that is shared with an increasingly global audience.

This notion of shared culture is underscored by the fact that most (75%) of the participants in our study on ethnic differences had been born in the United States. One might argue that some shared version of "American culture" masked differences in ethnic background. A more complete examination of this hypothesis, as well as more detailed comparison of specific ethnic or racial groups, is beyond the scope of the present work. We did, however, compare subjects who were born in the United States to those who had not been born in the United States and found no consistent pattern of difference.

The similarities between relationships between people of the same and different ethnic groups also challenge our traditional conceptions of ethnicity and culture. The traditional approach to the concept of culture is to view it as a higher order social category that summarizes and controls all aspects of a more or less defined group of people. This is the view of culture as a shared set of beliefs, values, and ways of behaving. Within this perspective, any given behavior is explained by referring it to the common corpus of which it was a part. This is still a popular approach to understanding culture, including cultures of ethnicity and gender. Unfortunately, as the results in this [essay] illustrate, it does not do a very good job of accounting for either the variation within cultural groups or the similarities across cultural groups. Nor is it the only way to view culture. By the 1970s, this traditional conceptualization of culture gave way, first, to views of culture as a historically transmitted symbol system by which people develop and express meanings for social life (e.g., Geertz, 1973), and then, to views of culture as a set of repertoires, tools, or resources that people draw on to make sense and solve the problems of daily life (Philipsen, 1992; Swidler, 2001). In the latter perspective, culture is not so much something one has as something one uses. It describes individual choices in interaction rather than consistent patterns of group difference. In sum, whether one looks to the growing cross-fertilization of cultural influences or follows recent trends in scholarly thought, it is apparent that differences in ethnicity and gender are diminishing.

In spite of this, explanations based on cultural stereotypes persist. They do so not only because they are easy, simple, and perhaps made more visible even as they grow smaller, but also because speculation about ethnic and gender differences frequently serve [a] broader social agenda. Those wishing to advance the interests of minorities, for example, often take the position that members of the group speak "in a different voice" (Gilligan, 1982). The rhetoric of difference provides a basis for a common group identity and buttresses claims for enhanced status and more just treatment. In other cases the agenda is not so much political as it is commercial. Publishers and broadcasters find a ready and lucrative market for materials that play up differences in ethnicity and gender in personal relationships. These books and movies appear to offer some insight, but all too often simply recycle and reinforce existing stereotypes. They are successful, not because they challenge our existing views, but precisely because they give us comfort, making us feel that we understood all along.

The ultimate result of these discourses of difference is to encourage us to see large differences where there are small differences and to overlook underlying similarities in personal relationships across groups. In this [essay] we have explored differences in age, relationship type, gender, and ethnic composition in personal relationships. Much remains to be done to test the generality of the theory, but it does appear that the social contextual approach can help us understand several different types of personal relationships. Although the results demonstrate that social network factors and relational factors are linked in similar ways across a variety of personal relationships, they have not adequately illuminated the more specific processes by which network and relational factors interact. The broad associations between network and relational factors examined thus far undoubtedly reflect the more particular ways in which people manage information and relationships from day to day and utterance to utterance....

REVIEW QUESTIONS

1. Parks acknowledges research that has found gender differences in intimacy, supportiveness, and expressiveness but also cites studies that "debunk" these findings. How are they "debunked"?
2. What has been the basic finding about men's and women's commitment to their personal relationships?
3. What did Parks' research reveal about differences in the level of difficulty in coordinating the actions of intraethnic versus interethnic relationships? Is it more difficult for people in an interethnic relationship to coordinate their actions?
4. Parks' discussion of interethnic relationships includes the terms "dating up" and "dating down." Explain what these terms mean.
5. One of the conclusions we can draw from Parks' discussion of interethnic relationships is that ethnicity does not equal culture. Explain what this means.

PROBES

1. Parks says that one problem with earlier gender research is that the researchers focused far more on whether males and females differed than on whether various characteristics were associated in different ways for males than for females. Explain what he means.

2. Parks reports on research about intimacy, supportiveness, expressiveness, amount of communication with one's partner, interpersonal solidarity, commitment to the relationship, support network members provide for the relationship, contacts with members of partners' networks, and liking of network members. Which of these variables do you believe gives the best picture of a relationship?

3. What practical advice emerges from Parks' review of research about inter-ethnic relationships? What does this research indicate that people in these relationships should do or not do?

4. Parks speculates that one of the reasons people may focus on gender and ethnic differences rather than similarities is that gender and ethnic markers are so visible and simple. Explain what he means.

5. There are some very important political ramifications that flow from Parks' conclusions about interethnic similarities and differences. Describe them.

REFERENCES

Abrahamson, M. (1996). *Urban enclaves: Identity and place in America.* New York: St. Martin's Press.

Argyle, M., Henderson, M., Bond, M., Izuka, Y., & Contarello, A. (1986). Cross-cultural variations in relationship rules. *International Journal of Psychology, 21,* 287–315.

Aries, E. J. (1996). *Men and women in interaction. Reconsidering the differences.* New York: Oxford University Press.

Aries, E. J., & Johnson, F. L. (1983). Close friendship in adulthood: Conversational content between same-sex friends. *Sex Roles, 9,* 1183–1196.

Bank, B. J., & Hansford, S. L. (2000). Gender and friendship: Why are men's best same-sex friendships less intimate and supportive? *Personal Relationships, 7,* 63–78.

Bascow, S. A., & Rubenfeld, K. (2003). "Troubles talk": Effects of gender and gender-typing. *Sex Roles, 48,* 183–187.

Berscheid, E. (1999). The greening of relationship science. *American Psychologist, 54,* 260–266.

Bureau of the Census. (2002). *Interracial married couples.* Retrieved January 25, 2003, from http://landview.census.gov/population/socdemo/ms-la/tabms-3.txt and http://landview.census.gov/population/socdemo/hh-fam/tabMS-3.txt

Canary, D. J., Emmers-Sommer, T. M., & Faulkner, S. (199). *Sex and gender differences in personal relationships.* New York: Guilford Press.

Carver, K., Joyner, K., & Udry, J. R. (2003). National estimates of adolescent romantic relationships. In P. Florsheim (Ed.), *Adolescent romantic relations and sexual behavior: Theory, research, and practical implications* (pp. 23–56). Mahwah, NJ: Lawrence Erlbaum Associates.

Fang, C. Y., Sidanius, J., & Pratto, F. (1998). Romance across the social status continuum: Interracial marriage and the ideological asymmetry effect. *Journal of Cross-Cultural Psychology, 29,* 290–305.

Fehr, B. A. (2004). A prototype model of intimacy interactions in same-sex friendships. In D. J. Mashek & A. Aron (Eds.), *Handbook of closeness and intimacy* (pp. 9–26). Mahwah, NJ: Lawrence Erlbaum Associates.

Floyd, K. (1995). Gender and closeness among friends and siblings. *Journal of Psychology: Interdisciplinary and Applied, 129,* 193–202.

Fraga, M. F., Ballestar, E., Paz, M. F., Ropero, S., Setien, F., Ballestar, M. L., et al. (2005). Epigenetic differences arise during the lifetime of monozygotic twins. *Proceedings of the National Academy of Sciences, 102,* 10604–10609.

Gaines, S. O., Jr., Granrose, C. S., Rios, D. I., Garcia, B. F., Youn, M. S. P., Farris, K. R., et al. (1999). Patterns of attachment and responses to accommodative dilemmas among interethnic/interracial couples. *Journal of Social and Personal Relationships, 16*(2), 275–285.

Gaines, S. O., Jr., & Liu, J. H. (2000). Multicultural/multiracial relationships. In C. Hendrick & S. Hendrick (Eds.), *Close relationships: A sourcebook* (pp. 97–108). Thousand Oaks, CA: Sage.

Goldsmith, D. J., & Dun, S. A. (1997). Sex differences and similarities in the communication of social support. *Journal of Social and Personal Relationships, 14,* 317–337.

Goldsmith, D. J., & Fulfs, P. A. (1999). "You just don't have the evidence": An Analysis of claims and evidence in Deborah Tannen's *You Just Don't Understand.* In M. E. Roloff (Ed.), *Communication yearbook 22* (pp. 1–49). Thousand Oaks, CA: Sage.

Goodman, E., & O'Brien, P. (2000). *I know just what you mean: The power of friendship in women's lives.* New York: Simon & Schuster.

Gudykunst, W. B., & Nishida, T. (1986). The influence of cultural variability on perceptions of communication behavior associated with relationship terms. *Human Communication Research, 13,* 147–166.

Gumperz, J. J. (1982). *Discourse strategies.* Cambridge, England: Cambridge University Press.

Gurung, R. A. R., & Duong, T. (1999). Mixing and matching: Assessing the concomitants of mixed-ethnic relationships. *Journal of Social and Personal Relationships, 16,* 639–657.

Hendrick, S., & Hendrick, C. (2000). Romantic love. In C. Hendrick & S. Hendrick (Eds.), *Close relationships: A sourcebook* (pp. 203–215). Thousand Oaks, CA: Sage.

Kaiser Family Foundation. (2001). *Race and ethnicity in 2001: Attitudes, perceptions and experiences.* Retrieved January 25, 2003, from http://www.kff.org/content/2001/3143/

Kyratzis, A. (2001). Children's gender indexing in language: From the separate worlds hypothesis to considerations of culture, context, and power. *Research on Language and Social Interactions, 34,* 1–13.

MacGeorge, E. L., Graves, A. R., Feng, B., Gillihan, S. J., & Burleson, B. R. (2004). The myth of gender cultures: Similarities outweigh differences in men's and women's provision of and responses to supportive communication. *Sex Roles, 50,* 143–175.

Maltz, D. N., & Borker, R. A. (1982). A cultural approach to male-female miscommunication. In J. J. Gumperz (Ed.), *Language and social identity* (pp. 196–216). Cambridge, England: Cambridge University Press.

Minatoya, L. Y. (1988). Women's attitudes and behaviors in American, Japanese, and cross-national marriages. *Journal of Multicultural Counseling and Development, 16,* 45–62.

Parks, M. R., & Adelman, M. B. (1983). Communication networks and the development of romantic relationships: An expansion of uncertainty reduction theory. *Human Communication Research, 10,* 55–79.

Parks, M. R., & Floyd, K. (1996). Meanings for closeness and intimacy in friendship. *Journal of Social and Personal Relationships, 13,* 85–107.

Philips, S. U. (1983). *The invisible culture: Communication in classroom and community on the Warm Springs Indian Reservation.* New York: Longman.

Reis, H. T., Senchak, M., & Solomon, B. (1985). Sex differences in the intimacy of social interaction: Further examination of the potential explanations. *Journal of Personality and Social Psychology, 48,* 1204–1217.

Rosenblatt, P. C., Karis, T. A., & Powell, R. D. (1995). *Multiracial couples: Black and White voices.* Thousand Oaks, CA: Sage.

Shibazaki, K., & Brennan, K. A. (1998). When birds of different feathers flock together: A preliminary comparison of intra-ethnic and inter-ethnic dating relationships. *Journal of Social and Personal Relationships, 15,* 248–256.

Sprecher, S., & Felmlee, D. (2000). Romantic partners' perceptions of social network attributes with the passage of time and relationship transitions. *Personal Relationships, 7,* 325–340.

Swain, S. (1989). Covert intimacy: Closeness in men's friendships. In B. J. Risman & P. Schwartz (Eds.), *Gender in intimate relationships* (pp. 71–86). Belmont, CA: Wadsworth.

Ting-Toomey, S. (1991). Intimacy expressions in three cultures: France, Japan, and the United States. *International Journal of Intercultural Relations, 15,* 29–46.

Todd, J., Mckinney, J. L., Harris, R., Chadderton, R., & Small, L. (1992). Attitudes toward interracial dating: Effects of age, sex, and race. *Journal of Multicultural Counseling and Development, 20,* 202–208.

Tucker, M. B., & Mitchell-Kernan, C. (1995). Social structural and psychological correlates of interethnic dating. *Journal of Social and Personal Relationships, 12,* 341–361.

Walker, K. (1994). Men, women, and friendship: What they say, what they do. *Gender and Society, 8,* 246–265.

Wood, J. T. (2000). Gender and personal relationships. In C. Hendrick & S. Hendrick (Eds.), *Close relationships: A sourcebook* (pp. 301–313). Thousand Oaks, CA: Sage.

Wood, J. T., & Inman, C. (1993). In a different mode: Recognizing male modes of closeness. *Journal of Applied Communication Research, 21,* 279–295.

Wright, P. H. (1982). Men's friendships, women's friendships and the alleged inferiority of the latter. *Sex Roles, 8,* 1–20.

What Do We Know about Gay and Lesbian Couples?

Lawrence A. Kurdek

This brief article by a psychology professor at Wright State University reviews social scientific research about characteristic features of gay and lesbian relationships. I include this article partly because the question it addresses is important in the United States, and increasingly important around the world. Data from the 2000 U.S. Census indicate that 1 in 9 households made up of unmarried partners are same-sex couples, so the topic directly addresses the experiences of a significant fraction of the U.S. population. Moreover, in 2004, as the author notes, voters in 11 states determined that marriage as a legal institution should be reserved for heterosexual couples, which implies, among other things, that Americans regard these couples as different from their straight counterparts. As the reading demonstrates, this conclusion is supported by some research and challenged by some.

This article addresses a "hot topic," and I hope that, regardless of your political or religious position on this issue, you will read it for understanding. In the 21st century, it is inevitable that you will be interacting with people from a variety of cultures in your classrooms, workplaces, and in your own family. Substantive knowledge about the research on these relationships can help increase your effectiveness as a communicator.

After his introductory comments, the author reviews research on topics of particular relevance to gay and lesbian couples. Even recent studies indicate that heterosexual couples tend to assign household labor responsibilities on the basis of biological sex. On the other hand, the studies of gay and lesbian couples indicate that "husband" and "wife" roles are not assigned in this way, that work responsibilities are negotiated extensively, and that over time, partners are likely to specialize in the household tasks they do. So in this way, the research indicates that gay and lesbian relationships are somewhat different from heterosexual ones.

Research on conflict communication indicates that same-sex couples disagree over the same issues that challenge heterosexual couples, and that same-sex couples tend to resolve conflict better than heterosexual couples, because "they perceive their worlds through similar lenses." Differences in conflict management are due to how conflict is handled, not what the conflict is about.

One of the most significant differences between couple types is in perceived social support. Gay and lesbian partners perceive low levels of support from family members and high support from friends. Relationship satisfaction between the two groups, however, is similar.

Although data are limited, there is evidence that heterosexual relationships are considerably more stable than gay and lesbian relationships. Data from Norway and Sweden are similar; lesbian couples dissolve their relationships significantly more than gay couples and heterosexual couples are significantly more stable than either.

Evidence about relationship quality indicates that, on this measure, there are few significant differences between gay and lesbian couples, on the one hand, and heterosexual couples. As Kurdek summarizes, "... the relationships of gay and lesbian partners appear to work in much the same way as the relationships of heterosexual partners do."

All these findings are tentative, because of the relative lack of research that focuses specifically on gay and lesbian couples. But these conclusions can help qualify overgeneralized claims about large-scale differences between gay/lesbian and heterosexual relationships.

MAIN IDEAS

- Controversies about same-sex relationships can be informed by available findings from social scientific research.
- The large number of U.S. households headed by same-sex partners is another reason to consider this topic.
- In some ways, for example, relationship satisfaction and quality, the two types of relationships are similar.
- In other ways, for example, division of household labor, conflict management styles, social support, and stability, there are significant differences between the two types of relationships.

In November 2004, Americans in 11 states voted on whether marriage should be legal for only heterosexual couples. The resounding message from the voters in each of these states was that marriage as a legal institution should, indeed, be reserved only for couples consisting of a man and a woman. One interpretation of voters' response to the gay-marriage issue is that most Americans regard gay and lesbian couples as being different from heterosexual couples. But what does research on gay and lesbian couples say on this matter? Does evidence support the view that gay and lesbian couples work in ways that are different from the way that heterosexual couples work? Before I examine aspects of these questions, I will address the question of the number of gay and lesbian couples in America.

HOW MANY AMERICAN GAY AND LESBIAN COUPLES ARE THERE?

Because of the stigma associated with homosexuality, many gay and lesbian persons are reluctant to disclose their sexual orientation. Consequently, there are no definitive data on the number of gay and lesbian Americans. Perhaps the best available estimates were derived by Laumann, Gagnon, Michael, and Michaels (1994), who interviewed a national sample of 1,511 men and 1,921 women. Of this sample, 4.9% of the men and 4.1% of the women reported having engaged in sexual behavior with a person of their own sex since the age of 18, 6.2% of the men and 4.4% of the women reported having been attracted to a person of their own sex, and 2.8% of the men and 1.4% of the women identified themselves with a label denoting same-sex sexuality (e.g., homosexual).

Given the difficulty in estimating the number of gay and lesbian Americans, it is not surprising that there are also no definitive data on the number of gay and lesbian American couples. However, changes in the way information about households is collected in the U.S. Census have allowed estimates of the number of households headed by a person with a same-sex partner to be obtained. Data from the Census of 2000 (Simons & O'Connell, 2003) indicate that of the 5.5 million couples who were living together but not married, about 1 in 9 were same-sex couples. Of these couples, 301,026 involved male partners and 293,365 involved female partners. Children under the age of 18 resided with 22% of the male couples and with 33% of the female couples.

Because presenting oneself publicly as gay or lesbian opens the door to discrimination and even violence, estimates of the number of gay and lesbian individuals and couples are most assuredly underestimates. Nonetheless, it is clear that, despite a generally inhospitable social climate, being part of a couple is integral to the lives of many gay men and lesbians.

TOPICS RELEVANT TO GAY AND LESBIAN COUPLES

Household Labor

One perception of partners from happy couples is that each partner does something to contribute to the overall well-being of the couple. When members of a couple live together, the extent to which they depend on each other increases, making it likely that the general issue of "Who does what?" has to be confronted. For many heterosexual couples, biological sex is one major factor that determines which roles partners assume. For example, despite major changes in the number of American women who work outside the home, wives still do the majority of household tasks (Artis & Pavalko, 2003). Given the persistence with which biological sex is used to assign roles relevant to household labor in heterosexual couples, the division of household labor for gay and lesbian couples provides one way to examine how roles in relationships get assigned independently of biological sex.

Three conclusions emerge from studies of how members of gay and lesbian couples divide household labor (e.g., Carrington, 1999). First, members of gay and lesbian couples do not assign roles for household labor such that one partner is the "husband" and the other partner is the "wife." Second, although members of gay and lesbian couples do not divide household labor in a perfectly equal manner, they are more likely than members of heterosexual couples to negotiate a balance between achieving a fair distribution of household labor and accommodating the different interests, skills, and work schedules of particular partners. This pattern of negotiation holds true even when couples have children living with them (Patterson, 2000). Third, as couples become more established, partners are likely to specialize in the household tasks they do, perhaps as one way of getting household tasks done efficiently.

Conflict

Conflict is inevitable in any relationship. In heterosexual couples, conflict is often thought to occur because of systematic differences in how men and women perceive their worlds. If this view of relationship conflict is valid, then one might expect that partners from same-sex couples would resolve conflict better than partners from heterosexual couples do because they perceive their worlds through similar lenses. Research supports this expectation.

Gottman et al. (2003) videotaped partners from gay, lesbian, and married heterosexual couples discussing problems in their relationships and then coded the emotions expressed by the partners in the course of the discussions. The researchers found that, relative to heterosexual partners, gay and lesbian partners began their discussions more positively and were more likely to maintain a positive tone throughout the course of the discussion. Findings from survey data also indicate that partners from gay and lesbian couples resolve conflict more positively than spouses from married couples do: They argue more effectively, are less likely to use a style of conflict resolution in which one partner demands and the other partner withdraws, and are more likely to suggest possible solutions and compromises (Kurdek, 2004a). Gottman et al. speculated that partners from gay and lesbian couples handle conflict more positively than spouses from heterosexual couples do because they value equality more and have fewer differences in power and status between them.

It is of note that, although partners from gay and lesbian couples tend to resolve conflict more positively than spouses from married couples do, partners from gay, lesbian, and heterosexual couples are likely to disagree over the same issues. In a study in which partners rated how frequently they fought over 20 specific issues (Kurdek, 2004b), differences between gay, lesbian, and heterosexual couples were largely nonexistent. Equally striking was the finding that partners from gay, lesbian, and heterosexual couples identified the same areas as sources of the most conflict: finances, affection, sex, being overly critical, driving style, and household tasks. Thus, differences in conflict resolution appear to be due to how conflict is handled rather than to what the conflict is about.

Perceived Support for the Relationship

Based on evidence that the level of support from members of one's social network affects the health of one's relationship, current theories about relationships (e.g., Huston, 2000) recognize that relationships develop within social contexts. Several studies have examined the extent to which members of gay and lesbian couples perceive support for their relationships (e.g., Kurdek, 2004a). Relative to spouses from heterosexual couples, partners from gay and lesbian couples are less likely to name family members as support providers and are more likely to name friends as support providers. These differences are notable because they are among the largest differences found in comparisons between heterosexual and gay or lesbian couples. The lack of family support for one's primary close relationship is often viewed as a unique stressor for gay men and lesbians and perhaps represents the overall lack of legal, social, political, economic, and religious support that gay and lesbian partners experience for their relationships. On the other hand, the high level of support that gay and lesbian partners enjoy from friends has been viewed as one way in which they compensate for the absence of institutionalized support.

Satisfaction

Nearly all available evidence indicates not only that gay men and lesbians are, on average, satisfied with their relationships, but that their level of satisfaction is at least equal to that reported by spouses from married heterosexual couples (Blumstein & Schwartz, 1983; Kurdek, 2001). Further, longitudinal data from partners from gay, lesbian, and heterosexual couples indicate that, for each type of couple, self-reported relationship quality is relatively high at the start of the relationship but decreases over time (Kurdek, 1998).

Stability

Perhaps the most important "bottom-line" question asked about gay and lesbian couples is whether their relationships last. Because survey data (see Kurdek, 2004b) indicate that between 8% and 21% of lesbian couples and between 18% and 28% of gay couples have lived together 10 or more years, it is clear that gay men and lesbians can and do build durable relationships. More detailed information on the stability of gay and lesbian relationships is limited because few studies have followed the same samples of gay and lesbian couples over time. Nonetheless, findings from three studies are relevant.

Kurdek (2004a) reported that for 126 gay couples and 101 lesbian couples assessed annually up to 12 times, 24 of the gay couples (19%) and 24 of the lesbian couples (24%) dissolved their relationships. With controls for demographic variables (e.g., length of cohabitation), the difference in the rate of dissolution for gay and lesbian couples was not significant. Over a comparable period of 11 annual assessments, 70 of 483 heterosexual married couples (15%) ended their relationships. With controls for demographic variables, the dissolution rate for heterosexual couples was significantly lower than that for either gay or lesbian couples.

In their 18-month follow-up survey of partners from 1,021 married heterosexual couples, 233 cohabiting heterosexual couples, 493 cohabiting gay couples, and 335 cohabiting lesbian couples, Blumstein and Schwartz (1983) found that 4% of the married couples, 14% of the cohabiting heterosexual couples, 13% of the cohabiting gay couples, and 18% of the cohabiting lesbian couples had dissolved their relationships. Although these authors reported no statistical comparisons, my analyses of their data indicated that, although rates of dissolution did not differ for either gay couples versus lesbian couples or for gay and lesbian couples versus cohabiting heterosexual couples, both gay and lesbian couples were more likely to dissolve their relationships than married heterosexual couples were.

Andersson, Noack, Seierstad, and Weedon-Fekjaer (2004) examined differences in the dissolution rates of gay and lesbian registered partnerships in Norway and in Sweden. Because registered partnerships were first made available in Norway in 1993 and in Sweden in 1995, dissolution rates are necessarily based on couples with legal unions of relatively short duration. For both countries, dissolution rates were significantly higher for lesbian couples than they were for gay couples. In Norway, 56 out of 497 lesbian partnerships were dissolved (11.26%) as compared to 62 out of 796 gay partnerships (7.78%). In Sweden, 117 out of 584 lesbian partnerships were dissolved (20.03%) as compared to 135 out of 942 gay partnerships (14.33%). In comparison, the percentage of dissolved heterosexual marriages in Sweden was 8%. For both countries, the higher rate of dissolution for lesbian couples than for gay couples persisted even when statistical analyses controlled for length of the partnership (which, if different between the two groups, can produce illusory differences in gay and lesbian couples' stability).

In sum, the data are too scant to warrant any conclusions about the relative stability of gay and lesbian couples. However, it is of note that Blumstein and Schwartz's (1983) data indicated that the dissolution rate for cohabiting heterosexual couples was similar to that for both cohabiting gay couples and cohabiting lesbian couples. Unlike spouses from married heterosexual couples who experience social, religious, and legal barriers to leaving their relationships, cohabiting couples—whether gay, lesbian, or heterosexual—have no such institutionalized barriers. Further, although some gay and lesbian couples raise children, the majority do not (Simons & O'Connell, 2003), thereby removing another significant barrier to dissolution. Thus, perhaps what is most impressive about gay and lesbian couples is not that they may be less stable than heterosexual married couples, but rather that they manage to endure without the benefits of institutionalized supports.

Factors Predicting Relationship Quality

One way of determining whether the relationships of gay men and lesbians work the same way the relationships of heterosexual persons do is to see if the links between variables known to be relevant to relationship functioning and relationship quality are as strong for gay and lesbian partners as they are for heterosexual married partners. The predictors of relationship quality that have been examined usually come from four classes of variables commonly used in research on relationships (e.g., Huston, 2000). These include characteristics each partner brings to the relationship (such as personality traits), how each partner views the relationship (such as level of trust), how partners behave toward each other (such as communication and conflict-resolution styles), and perceived level of support for the relationship (such as that from family members and friends).

The relevant findings are easily summarized. Nearly all studies (e.g., Kurdek, 2004a) find that the links between variables from the four classes just listed and relationship quality for gay and lesbian couples do not differ from the parallel links for heterosexual married couples. That is, the extent to which relationship quality is predicted by these four kinds of variables tends to be as strong for gay and lesbian couples as it is for heterosexual couples. Thus, despite external differences in how gay, lesbian, and heterosexual couples are constituted, the relationships of gay and lesbian partners appear to work in much the same way as the relationships of heterosexual partners do.

Based on evidence that gay and lesbian relationships are influenced by the same set of factors that influence heterosexual marriages, institutionalized support for gay and lesbian relationships might be expected to enhance the stability of these relationships just as it does for heterosexual marriages. In fact, this reasoning formed one of the bases for the American Psychological Association's passing a resolution declaring it unfair and discriminatory to deny same-sex couples legal access to civil marriage and all its attendant benefits, rights, and privileges (American Psychological Association, 2004).

ISSUES FOR FUTURE RESEARCH

Future research on gay and lesbian couples needs to address several key issues. One is sampling: Because most studies have used convenience samples of mostly white and well-educated partners, the extent to which findings generalize to the larger population of gay and lesbian couples is unknown. Problems with regard to sampling may be eased as specialized populations—such as couples with civil unions from states with open records—become identified. Another issue is research methods: Most studies on gay and lesbian couples have used self-report surveys. Future work could address some of the biases associated with self-report data by employing behavioral observations as well as peer or partner ratings.

The life course of gay and lesbian relationships is another area requiring further research. Because gay and lesbian courtship is a fairly hidden process, little is known about how gay and lesbian relationships develop from courtship to cohabitation to marriage-like unions with high commitment. Recruiting dating couples for longitudinal research, however, remains a challenge. It is also necessary to establish what variables are unique to gay and lesbian persons. Most research has used theories and methods derived from work with heterosexual couples, so little is known about how variables unique to gay and lesbian persons—such as negotiating a private and public identity as a gay or lesbian person—affect the quality of their relationships. Finally, it is necessary to learn more about the forces that help stabilize relationships. Because it is unlikely that all American gay and lesbian couples will soon have the option to marry, they will need to continue to rely on less institutionalized forces to maintain the stability of their relationships. These include psychological processes such as commitment and social processes such as level of integration into the support systems of family, friends, and co-workers.

REVIEW QUESTIONS

1. According to 2000 U.S. Census data, about how many of the 5.5 million un-married and cohabiting couples are same-sex?
2. Data indicate that heterosexual couples tend to assign household labor re-sponsibilities on the basis of gender, and gay and lesbian couples tend to assign them how?
3. The relatively low level of support-for-their-relationship that gay and lesbian couples experience from their families tends to be counterbalanced by what?
4. Does research indicate that long-term gay and lesbian relationships are com-mon or rare?

PROBES

1. How do the findings about conflict styles that are reported here support the idea that gender differences constitute cultural differences?
2. Research indicates that gay and lesbian couples experience generally as high a quality of their relationship as heterosexual couples. Comment.

REFERENCES

American Psychological Association (2004). *Resolution on sexual orientation and marriage.* Retrieved November 14, 2004 from http://www.apa.org/pi/lgbc/policy/marriage.pdf

Andersson, G., Noack, T., Seierstad, A., & Weedon-Fekjaer, H. (2004). *The demographics of same-sex "marriages" in Norway and Sweden.* Rostock, Germany: Max-Planck Institute for Demographic Research. Retrieved November 14, 2004 from http://www.demogr.mpg.de/papers/working/wp-2004-018.pdf.

Artis, J. E., & Pavalko, E. K. (2003). Explaining the decline in women's household labor: Individual change and cohort differences. *Journal of Marriage and Family, 65,* 746–761.

Blumstein, P., & Schwartz, P. (1983). *American couples: Money, work, sex.* New York: William Morrow.

Carrington, C. (1999). *No place like home: Relationships and family life among lesbians and gay men.* Chicago: University of Chicago Press.

Gottman, J. M., Levenson, R. W., Swanson, C., Swanson, K., Tyson, R., & Yoshimoto, D. (2003). Observing gay, lesbian, and heterosexual couples' relationships: Mathematical modeling of conflict interaction. *Journal of Homosexuality, 45,* 65–91.

Huston, T. L. (2000). The social ecology of marriage and other intimate unions. *Journal of Marriage and the Family, 62,* 298–320.

Kurdek, L. A. (1998). Relationship outcomes and their predictors: Longitudinal evidence from heterosexual married, gay cohabiting, and lesbian cohabiting couples. *Journal of Marriage and Family, 60,* 553–568.

Kurdek, L. A. (2001). Differences between heterosexual-nonparent couples and gay, lesbian, and heterosexual-parent couples. *Journal of Family Issues, 22,* 727–754.

Kurdek, L. A. (2004a). Are gay and lesbian cohabiting couples *really* different from heterosexual married couples? *Journal of Marriage and Family, 66,* 880–900.

Kurdek, L. A. (2004b). Gay men and lesbians: The family context. In M. Coleman & L. H. Ganong (Eds.), *Handbook of contemporary families: Considering the past, contemplating the future* (pp. 96–115). Thousand Oaks, CA: Sage.

Laumann, E. O., Gagnon, J. H., Michael, R. T., & Michaels, S. (1994). *The social organization of sexuality: Sexual practices in the United States.* Chicago: University of Chicago Press.

Patterson, C. J. (2000). Family relationships of lesbians and gay men. *Journal of Marriage and Family, 62,* 1052–1069.

Simons, T., & O'Connell, M. (2003). *Married-couple and unmarried-partner households: 2000.* Washington, DC: U.S. Census Bureau. Retrieved November 14, 2004, from http://www.census.gov/prod/2003pubs/censr-5.pdf

---

Word of Mouth Goes World of Mouth

Erik Qualman

The growing popularity of Facebook, Twitter, and other social media sites has changed the communication experiences of millions of people, and this author describes some of the ways social media use affects dating and the development of intimate relationships. He begins with the idea that all human beings have the need both to "be our own individual" and "to feel that we belong to and are accepted by a much larger social set." Today's young people are willing to give up considerable privacy in order to meet this second need, he writes, and this is part of what makes social media connections attractive.

This article raises questions about several general conclusions that people tend to make about social media. One is that people are so overloaded with tasks and information already, they can't afford to "waste their time" with Tweets and posts. Qualman argues that "wasting time on Facebook and social media actually makes you more productive." He also points out that this benefit stretches around the globe. Social media enable friendship circles to be international.

Qualman proposes that "Are you on Facebook" is the new "Can I get your phone number?" After connecting via social media, a couple's first face-to-face date can be, in effect, the fourth or fifth important contact. Meetings on social networks, he writes, are "easier than face-to-face because you avoid awkward silences, don't have to worry about who is going to pay the check, and don't experience potentially embarrassing situations (poppy seed between the teeth, anyone?)." In addition, social media sites enable you to evaluate others by checking to see how many friends the two of you have in common.

Social media also allow individuals to "take real-time inventories of their lives and help answer the age-old question, 'What am I doing with my life?'"

Qualman also notes that problems are created by heavy use of social media. Some people are even more uncomfortable speaking in public, and writing skills have eroded "from living in a 140-character world." Traditional boundaries are also often violated, as contacts can be made 24/7 and most access is free.

The bottom line is that social media have the potential for changing the ways interpersonal communication happens. This and other readings in this book provide you with ways to explain how, and to decide what to do about it.

MAIN IDEAS

- Social media use has become the most popular activity on the Web.
- One reason for its popularity is that it helps people meet their need to be accepted by a large social set.
- Social media allow you to easily stay abreast of people you want to stay connected with via casual observation.
- Social media can also make you more, rather than less, productive.
- Social media facilitate contacts across the globe.
- "Are you on Facebook?" is the new "Can I get your phone number?"
- Traditional dating can be facilitated by social media use.
- Social media allow you to assess the trajectory of your life.
- There are also downsides of social media use, including increased fear of public speaking, poor grammar and diction, and shorter attention span.

Why is there even a need for social media? In less than three years, it became the most popular activity on the Web,[1] supplanting pornography for the first time in Internet history. Even search engines weren't powerful enough to do that.

Remember several years back when the last three to four seconds of many television commercials prompted viewers to use various AOL keywords? You don't see or hear that anymore do you? What do you see? People are sending this traffic to social networks. A very prominent example of this is CBS, which sends a majority of its March Madness basketball traffic, not to its own website, but to www.facebook.com/brackets.

Why has social media's popularity been so meteoric? This rapid ascent is due in large part to its ability to help people avoid *information indigestion*. At first glance, this would seem counterintuitive because social media, in its inherent nature via status updates, microblogs, social bookmarks, video sharing, photo commenting, and so on, actually produces more content and information. Because of this increase in information, you would think that it would cause more confusion, not less. But, when we dive deeper, we can see why this is not the case.

In his groundbreaking book, *The Long Tail*, Chris Anderson eloquently describes the ability of the Internet within free markets to easily and effectively service small interest groups:

> The great thing about broadcast is that it can bring one show to millions of people with unmatchable efficiency. But it can't do the opposite—bring a million shows to one person each. Yet that is exactly what the Internet does so well. The economics of broadcast era required hit shows—big buckets—to catch huge audiences. Serving the same stream to millions of people at the same time is hugely expensive and wasteful for a distribution network optimized for point-to-point communications. Increasingly, the mass market is turning into a mass of niches.[2]

As we have seen, this is very powerful stuff. *The Long Tail* is great for individualism, however at the same time, it greatly fragments the market. Life was much simpler when we knew that all our world news would come from *Time* and *Life* magazines. Fragmentation can be a stress-inducing issue for people.

As human beings, we have the dichotomous psychological need to be our own individual, yet we also want to feel that we belong to and are accepted by a much larger social set. People are willing to keep *open running diaries* as a way to stay connected because their ultimate desire is to feel accepted.

The younger the generation, the less concerned they are about privacy.

If you can make something more relevant to me by having less privacy, well that is a small price to pay.

—Bill Tancer, General Manager, Global Research, Hitwise

Part of this lies in a yearning to have a clear understanding of what the majority of people are doing.

It was much easier to know what the majority was doing when all you had to do was tune into Casey Kasem's *American Top 40* to find out the latest and greatest in music or to flip through *Vogue* magazine to quickly grasp every fashion trend.

WHO CARES WHAT YOU ARE DOING?

Why do I care if my friend is having the most amazing peanut-butter-and-jelly sandwich? Or that someone is at her kid's dance recital? These types of questions are often posed by someone who doesn't understand social media rather than by someone who hasn't embraced social media; there is a difference. These questions are usually posed by someone who is frustrated because they don't understand what social media is about.

Heavy social media users actually don't care about every little thing happening in their friend's lives all the time. Yes, there are the exceptional few who view every post, photo, or comment. Individual users make personal choices about how they establish their settings and, more important, viewing behavior.

This is similar to a BlackBerry or iPhone where users can customize their settings so that the unit vibrates every time a message comes in or they can disable that setting and download messages on their time, thereby avoiding *crackberry* syndrome (addictive immediate response to every incoming message).

The key with social media is that it allows you to easily stay abreast of people you want to stay connected with via casual observation. Someone might argue, "well I already don't have enough time in my day, how can I possibly follow anybody else or keep those following me informed? I can't waste my time like that!" This is a fundamental misunderstanding! One of the key maxims of this book is that *wasting time on Facebook and social media actually makes you more productive.* Let's look at an example with a fictitious character dubbed Sally Supermarket.

We find Sally Supermarket at her favorite place and name-sake. It's Fourth of July weekend, so a few of the checkout lanes are much longer than normal. It's going to be roughly a 10-minute wait until she reaches the cashier. During these 10 minutes she can:

A. Flip through a magazine she has no interest in.
B. Be rude and place a call on her cell phone. Most likely annoying the others in line around her and potentially the person receiving the call as well, because it's loud in the supermarket, and she might have to hang up the call at any time.

C. Check on updates from her social media.

D. Ruminate about how upset she is that she has to wait in line for 10 minutes, which she definitely doesn't have time for.

Sally chooses option C, and here's what occurs:

- *Sally's status:* "Bummed that the supermarket is out of mayonnaise—I was planning to make my cold chicken curry salad for the annual picnic tomorrow."
- *Friend 1's status:* "Excited to be boarding a plane to DC for the weekend!"
- *Friend 2's status:* "Who knew my kids would love mandarin oranges in a can?"
- *Friend 3's status:* "I'm pregnant!"
- *Sally's daughter's status:* "Excited! Got an A on my psychology exam—off to get a Frappuccino to celebrate!"
- *Friend 4's comment:* "Sally, plain yogurt is a great substitute for mayo—use a third more curry than normal to kill the bitterness. I recommend Dannon. It's healthy too!"
- *Friend 3's status:* "Going in for first ultrasound. We've decided not to find out if the baby is a boy or a girl ahead of time."
- *Friend 5's post:* "Great video on bike decorating for the Fourth of July is found here: www.tinyurl.com/4th/."

After reading the status updates from her friends on her phone, Sally still has about four minutes before she'll be at the front of the checkout lane, so she runs to get some plain yogurt (like her friend recommended). While checking out she sees a $10 gift card for Starbucks hanging above the magazines, which she purchases with the intent of mailing it to her daughter as a surprise congratulations for doing well on her exam and to let her know she's thinking about her.

Sally will see Friend 3 tomorrow at the picnic and be able to congratulate her on her pregnancy. Staying up to date on Friend 3 means that Sally won't spend time speculating whether Friend 3 was just putting on extra weight. Sally can also avoid asking if the couple knows whether the baby will be a boy or girl because Sally already knows that they are waiting based on Friend 3's last updated social media message. Sally knows from firsthand pregnancy experience how tiring answering the "Do you know if it's a boy or girl?" question can become—if only she had social media back then!

On the way home, Sally's husband calls her.

"Hey, honey, I'm on my way home from the supermarket—how are you?"

"Struggling—Jack and I are trying to decorate his bike, but it's not looking so hot, and the crepe paper keeps tearing in the spokes."

"Not sure if this will help, but Friend 5 just bookmarked a video about bike decorating—maybe you could check it out for some ideas."

This Sally Supermarket example is a little played up for the purpose of illustration, but it certainly isn't far-fetched. This is a simple example of why social media isn't just for teenagers with too much idle time on their hands.

FOREIGN FRIENDS ARE NOT FORGOTTEN

This depiction by German-based social media user, Christoph Marcour, is a quick example of how social media can easily keep us globally connected:

> One thing I enjoy the most about social media is staying in touch with my friends in America. Before, I would occasionally travel to the United States for work; primarily to New York and Houston. I was generally very busy leading up to these trips and often didn't have time to e-mail or call my friends—all of which lived in Indianapolis. My friends from Indy also traveled for work quite a bit. So, ironically, we'd often be in the same city at the same time and not know it till months later.
>
> That doesn't happen anymore, now we have the chance to see each other once or twice a year. Because even if I'm not directly reaching out to them if I put in my status "packing for New York" or "Bummed that my flight to Houston is delayed," they see that, just as I see similar items that they are updating....[3]

"ARE YOU ON FACEBOOK?" IS THE NEW "CAN I GET YOUR PHONE NUMBER?"

The most underlying factor for this new inbox may be the seismic shift in the way people exchange information. Let's take a quick look at the evolution of dating over the past 10 years. First, people used to give out their home phone number. Then people began to give out their e-mail address instead.

At first it seemed odd to ask someone for a date over e-mail, but then it became quite natural. Then we progressed to mobile phone numbers because some people didn't have landlines anymore. Besides, it was easier to text message one another—it was less intrusive and awkward: "What are you doing tonight?"

Today with social media, when people meet, it's common for one of them to ask the other person, "Are you on hi5?" "Are you on Facebook?" or "Tu estas en Orkut?" Just as people use the word Google as a verb—google it—they are starting to use phrases like "Facebook me or send me a Tweet." People are no longer exchanging e-mails, they are exchanging each other's social media information. In many instances, people would never give out their e-mail addresses, and if they desired that type of communication, social networks have inboxes of their own that replicate and replace e-mail.

Executives are still holding hard and fast to the concept of the traditional inbox. In a survey of 180 Chief Marketing Officers of $1 billion corporations that was conducted by GfK Roper Public Affairs and Media, they found that while 70 percent were decreasing their marketing budgets, the area in which they were least likely to make cuts was e-mail.[4] You can't necessarily blame them for this type of thinking. This has been one of their best performing channels for years, and they've spent money building and managing their databases.

Now and in the future, marketers need to adjust their way of thinking because it's no longer about building out the existing database. Instead, you could be in communication with fans and consumers on someone else's database (Facebook, YouTube, Twitter, etc.). Yet, many companies fail to grasp this new concept. They build elaborate YouTube or Flicker pages, placing callouts and click actions that send the user outside the social network, often to their company website or a lead capture page. These companies still believe they need to get users into their prospecting databases in order to market to them. They are doing a disservice to their loyal fan base and in turn a disservice to themselves.

It's analogous to meeting a pretty girl in a bar and asking if she would like a drink. When she responds "yes," rather than ordering a drink from the bartender, you grab her and rush her into your car and drive her back to your place; because after all, you have beer in your fridge. This is not a sound courtship strategy, nor should companies employ comparable social media strategies in "courting" potential customers. It is best to be patient rather than to rush into things, without consumer confidence; just like in dating, you have nothing without it.

DEEP DIVE INTO DATING 101

Let's digress back to our dating scenario on social media. Social networks are fantastic for meeting new people and dating. If a girl meets a guy out on the town and they exchange names and connect within a social media network—it's a gold mine of data.

The more friends you have in common within a shared social network, the more secure you feel knowing the other person isn't some form of lunatic. Photos are helpful, especially if the night before was a bit wild and a little fuzzy. If you are listed in a network for "Star Trek Fanatics" or "Dracula Oprah" that will be even more telling about who you really are. What you do, who you work for, where you live and have lived, provides additional insight into your personality.

If all checks out fine, that first date is more like a fourth date, you aren't asking question like "Where did you go to college?" or "What are your hobbies?" It's somewhat sad, but true. You will still probably ask these questions so that it won't appear that you are a stalker or to show a polite interest, but it is a completely different dynamic than the world baby boomers, or even Generation Xers, grew up in. Social networks make it easier to stay in touch with someone new before you are at the "Let's grab a drink" stage. It's easier than face-to-face because you avoid awkward silences, don't have to worry about who is going to pay the check, and don't experience potentially embarrassing situations (poppy seed between the teeth anyone?).

Already gaining popularity on the dating side of things is leveraging the mobility of having alerts sent to your phone so that you are connected to people who are currently in your area. Going one step further, some tools recommend locations based on your mood. Instead of listing the top-10 restaurants in the SoHo area of New York, it lists the top-10 romantic restaurants or the top-20 hip, laid-back restaurants; so, if it was your first date, it wouldn't be awkward being at a place with white-glove service and dining by candlelight.

The benefits of this type of relationship building hold true from business to consumer as well. Businesses capture more information via social media about their consumers than they've ever had before. Good businesses realize that the relationship still needs to be cultivated (see the grabbing the girl from the bar analogy). Good businesses realize that it's not all about the instant win of getting someone into a database. Rather it is cultivating that relationship via social media. If it's done correctly, you will have a relationship that lasts a lifetime.

ASSESS YOUR LIFE EVERY MINUTE

The examples presented in this section stress a crucial maxim of this book. Social media allows individuals to take real-time inventories of their lives and help answer the age-old question "What am I doing with my life?"

Bill Tily, 83, says,

> I actually made a habit of physically printing out my social media updates from the previous month and going through them one by one and highlighting updates that weren't necessarily contributing to a "full" life. Over time, I reduced the amount of "waste" and actually became so cognizant of it during the actual act of updating my stats that I'd recognize in that specific moment in time what I would deem an "unfruitful activity" and cease engaging in it immediately. My life is much more fulfilling because of this! I wish these social media tools were around a long time ago![5]

Heather, a mother of three, has her own story about how social media is helping her lead a more productive life:

> I had a close friend who was married without children. One day she confided in me that she didn't know if she was ready for children. She thought she was but then she mentioned something that floored me; the conversation went something like this:
>
> "Heather, I'm just not sure that I'm up for it, I mean you are probably the most with-it person that I know and it seems like your kids are all that you can handle."
>
> To which I responded, "Yes, having kids is life-changing and presents its new challenges, but it's not as bad as people let on; for every one thing my kids do bad, they do nine things that light up my life."
>
> "Really? That's good news to hear and helps alleviate some of my concerns, but to be blunt, it's also a little surprising given the social media status updates I receive from you."
>
> I was obviously surprised to hear this revelation from one of my closest friends, and I didn't think it had much validity. So, later that day, I wanted to prove it was unwarranted. I pulled up the last several weeks of updates, which didn't take me too long since I only did one or two updates per day. There it was staring back at me in black and white; my friend was exactly

right! While my kids were the greatest joy in my life, you would never know it from reading my updates. My kids provided 90 percent of all the new wonders and happiness in my life, yet I was conveying the exact opposite in my status updates. For every one positive status update about my kids, "Lilly gives the best hugs" or "I posted Will's beautiful finger painting on the fridge," I'd post nine negative ones, "Have a massive headache from the kids nonstop screaming" or "Not sure I can handle a full day at the zoo with the kids again."

The reality of the situation shocked me, and I was fearful that there was a possibility that I was also projecting this negative attitude onto the kids. The answer to this came sooner than expected. For the next few weeks, I made a concerted effort not to post anything remotely negative on the social media platforms I used. Or at least have it reflect my reality, nine positive posts for every single negative post. Then one day, about two weeks into practicing this experience, it really hit home when my four-year-old tugged at my shirt and looked up at me with her big blue eyes and said, "Mommy, you seem a lot more happy, and I really like it."[6]

Updating your status or microblogging about what you are doing are immediate reminders of exactly that! And, if you pause, like Bill, and look back over a day, week, or month of what you posted, it is extremely enlightening because it shows you how you are spending what precious time you have.

MILLENNIALS—ALL ABOUT GIVING BACK

In 2008, Millennials (Generation Yers) showed up in record numbers to vote. In comparison, record numbers of jaded Generation Xers never stepped out to vote when they were in their early 20s, despite all the Rock the Vote hoopla on MTV at the time.[7]

In 2008, the most popular Facebook application wasn't a fancy game, music, or TV show. It was an application called "Causes" with almost 20 million active monthly uses.[8] The application was quite simple in its description: Causes lets you start and join the causes you care about. Donations to Causes can benefit over a million registered nonprofit organizations. Not surprisingly, this was a far cry from the 1980's "Me Generation." Recall that one of the popular songs of that era was Madonna's "Living in a Material World."

Generation Yers grew up in the 1980s, and after witnessing the horror that can be caused by narcissistic behavior, they wanted to do everything in their power to be the opposite of that. Their kids aren't going to grow up as latchkey kids. The social community aspect simply doesn't stop at discussing the hottest young pop star. No, Generation Y has a strong sense for making the world a better place.

While the majority of this book stresses the many positive aspects of social media, we'd be misleading if we did not highlight the downside as well. One trend we are starting to see is Generation Y and Z's difficulty with face-to-face interactions.

THE NEXT GENERATION CAN'T SPEAK

The desire and ability to meet new people has rapidly eroded so much so that humans fear public speaking more than death. This led comedian Jerry Seinfeld to quip, "According to surveys on what we fear...you are telling me that at a funeral, most people would rather be the guy in the coffin than have to stand up and give the eulogy?"[9]

Difficult and awkward subjects are much easier to deal with hiding behind instant messaging or social media comments than face-to-face.

And even written skills have eroded from living in a 140-character world.

A study by the nonprofit group that administers the SAT and other placement tests (National Commission on Writing at the College Board) found:

- 50 percent of teens surveyed say they sometimes fail to use proper capitalization and punctuation in assignments.
- 38 percent have carried over IM or e-mail shortcuts such as LOL.
- 25 percent of teens have used :) and other emoticons.
- 64 percent have used at least one of the informational elements in school.[10]

So, yes there are downsides to not having as much face-to-face interaction and that's a challenge these two generations and future generations face because technology is an intrinsic part of their lives, but the positive aspects are plentiful. They have an understanding of their place in the global community and are more creative and collaborative. They don't mind challenging the status quo—which is much different than simply not respecting it. They expect a better work–life balance, are better at prioritization and multitasking. They need more guidance in management skills, project planning, and business communication.

They are less likely to understand boundaries whether that is answering e-mail from a friend during business hours or taking e-mail from a manager at 11 PM. To them, things are just more fluid; it's not a 9-to-5 world, it's a 24/7 world, and it's up to the individual to properly balance the hours in the day. Generation Xers and Yers think it's laughable that a company would block Facebook or YouTube during work hours—you are either getting the job done or you are not getting the job done. Workers realize that if they play during the workweek they will have to work on Saturday to complete the necessary tasks. But that is a conscious decision they make.

REVIEW QUESTIONS

1. What's "information indigestion"? How does social media use help manage it?
2. What's "crackberry syndrome"?
3. How, according to this author, can status updates or microblogging contribute to the development of your self-awareness?

PROBES

1. Do you agree with Qualman that social media users are willing to give up considerable privacy in order to stay well-connected? How might this shift in privacy-priority affect communication between generations?
2. How thoroughly are you persuaded by Qualman's argument that "wasting time on Facebook and social media actually makes you more productive"?
3. Do you agree with Qualman that "Are you on Facebook?" is the new "Can I get your phone number?"?
4. Do you think that your own use of social media has made you a more effective or a less effective communicator overall?

NOTES

1. Hitwise, June 2008.
2. Chris Anderson, *The Long Tail* (New York: Hyperion, 2006), Chapter 2.
3. Christoph Marcour, personal interview.
4. "CMOs Not Ready to Embrace Social Networking Sites, Survey Shows," survey conducted by Epsilon, November 24, 2008, http://www. corporatelogo.com/hotnews/cmo-marketing-social-networking-sites. html.
5. Bill Tily, personal interview.
6. Heather Endreas, personal interview.
7. Melissa Dahl, "Youth Vote May Have Been Key in Obama's Win," msnbc. com, November 5, 2008, http://www.msnbc.msn.com/id/27525497.
8. Facebook Application Statistics.
9. Jerry Seinfeld, http://www.wittcom.com/fear_of_public_speaking.htm.
10. Anick Jesdanun, "OMG!: (It Ain't Write," AP—*New York Post*, National Commission on Writing at the College Board, April 27, 2008, http:// www.nypost.com/seven/04252008/news/nationalnews/omg_it_aint_ write_108037.htm?CMP=EMCemail_edition&DATE=04252008.

PART FOUR

Bridges Not Walls

The first three parts of this book are designed to help you understand the foundations of interpersonal communication (Part One), the ways in which people make meaning together (Part Two), and the relationships people inhabit (Part Three). Part Four focuses on interpersonal problems that people experience and how communication can help them cope with these problems.

The first chapter of Part Four describes a variety of painful communication walls—deception, betrayal, aggression, hurtful messages, defensiveness, and the manipulative use of power. Then Chapter 10 focuses on the general communication wall called conflict, offering both understandings and skills for managing conflict effectively. Next, Chapter 11 discusses how to bridge cultural differences, and Chapter 12 explains how dialogue can bring people together. The materials on dialogue bring much of the book into a full circle by returning to the approach to interpersonal communication that I outlined in Chapter 2 and showing how dialogue can work in many different settings.

As a whole, Part Four translates the practical theory and principles of the first three parts of the book into strategies for helping you cope with many of the communication difficulties that most of us experience every day.

CHAPTER 9

Coping with Communication Walls

Deception, Betrayal, and Aggression

John Stewart, Karen E. Zediker, and Saskia Witteborn

This reading discusses three of the more difficult elements of interpersonal communicating: lying, betrayal, and aggression. The reading combines insights from research into these phenomena with some practical suggestions about how to cope with them.

Karen, Saskia, and I begin by reviewing some research and some suggestions about deception or lying. We make the point that, like all forms of communication, lying is a joint action. Some people make it relatively easy for others to lie to them, and others make it desirable. This is not to "blame the victim" of deception, but only to remind communicators that it takes more than one person to lie. It is also important to realize that lying can be both intentional and unintentional. Especially when people are paying attention to social expectations and rules—which is just about all the time—it can be almost impossible to "tell the whole truth and nothing but the truth."

Next we discuss six motives for lying that emerge from some research, three of which the researchers call "positive," and three "negative," because of their likely impact on receivers. We also describe some of the most common consequences of deception. We note that the collaborative nature of deception becomes clearest when the deceived person decides to expose his or her relational partner's lies or to ignore or suppress them.

Then we summarize the viewpoint of another researcher who argues that there are no "positive" motives for lying. We ask you to consider which of these views makes most sense to you—that deception is inevitable and is sometimes a good thing, or that lying always objectifies and dehumanizes the receiver, and should be avoided whenever possible.

The second section of the reading focuses on betrayal, communication that violates trust and the expectations on which the relationship is based. We note that a very high percentage of relational and dating partners report that they have experienced betrayal, which is more common than you might think. We discuss five features of betrayal that may empower you to understand it more effectively the next time it happens to you and that may also remind you how to reduce the number of times you betray others.

The final section discusses hurtful messages, aggression, and violence. The first part pulls highlights from the next reading in this chapter, by Anita Vangelisti. Dr. Vangelisti's research identified 10 types of hurtful messages that people experience in relationships with partners, friends, and family members. In the next reading, she describes the outcomes of her research in more detail than we do here.

The section of the reading on verbal aggression defines the phenomenon and describes how it takes some of its various forms. We also offer some suggestions for dealing with the verbal aggression you experience.

The final paragraphs of this reading briefly treat psychological abuse and physical violence. These brief paragraphs certainly do not do justice to these important topics, but we hope enough is said here to empower those who suffer abuse or violence to begin to understand and cope with it. I also hope that those who inflict psychological abuse or physical violence can see from what's here that these behaviors are more common than they might have realized and that there are people who can understand them and can help.

MAIN IDEAS

- Deception—lying—is a common element of communication.
- Like all other elements, deception is a joint construction; deceiver and deceived co-construct the lie.
- Six reasons (motives) for lying have been identified: egoism, benevolence, utility, exploitation, malevolence, and regress.
- Some researchers believe that the first three motives can be positive; others argue that deception is *always* damaging to the relationship.
- Since deception is collaboratively constructed, each person's choices, for example, to ignore or confront, can affect outcomes.
- Like deception, betrayal is a common interpersonal experience.
- Betrayal is worst in the most intimate relationship, affects the betrayed most, tends to be followed by relationship termination, and is gender-influenced.
- Ten types of hurtful messages have been studied.
- Outcomes—for example, level of hurt—and next steps in the relationship are affected by responses to hurtful messages (this is one way they are co-constructed).
- Verbal aggression attacks another's self-concept.
- Once aggression occurs, the tendency is for it to escalate.
- Psychological abuse and physical violence often emerge as verbal aggression spirals out of control.
- There are no "easy fixes" for these forms of interpersonal violence, but individual choices can definitely make a difference.

DECEPTION

I've been going out with my current boyfriend for several months now and we spend most of our time together. I went home for the weekend to visit my grandmother, and when I returned a friend of ours told me that Josh was out dancing with his ex-girlfriend while I was gone. Josh had told me that he didn't want to have anything to do with her anymore, so obviously I was hurt and confused. When I saw my boyfriend this morning I asked him about his weekend, and he didn't say anything about going out. I wonder if I should ask him if he was out with her, but I really don't want to hear it if he was. But I'm not sure I can trust him until I know the truth, and if it's truth I don't want to hear, I don't know how I can trust him any more in this relationship.

You've probably heard stories like this one. Perhaps you've even told a story like this, or had one told about you. The reality and even the perception of deception can profoundly affect interpersonal relationships. In the next several paragraphs, we explore the motives or reasons for deception in interpersonal communication and identify some of the potential consequences for the relationship.

Motives for Deception

Deception can vary from blatant lies to indirect actions such as exaggerations and false implications (Hopper & Bell, 1984). Whereas most people believe that deception is intentional, it can also be unintentional, as when someone misremembers or mistakenly forgets or omits information. Like all other communication phenomena, deception is a joint action, the outcome of a collaboration between or among communicators. Some people make it relatively easy for others to lie to them when they make choices that are either gullible or overly demanding. It can be easy to lie to the person who believes almost everything he hears, for example. Authoritarian people also help create communication contexts in which lying is easier. If your parent is always on your case, demanding to know what you are doing all the time, you may be more inclined to lie in order to negotiate the tension between interdependence and autonomy. Some people decide whether or not to deceive others based on the threat of being caught. If the danger of being discovered is high, and discovery has undesirable consequences, then a person might choose not to lie.

In addition, sometimes you may know, or at least suspect, that you are not being told the truth but decide not to confront others about their deception. One of us has a friend who is a compulsive liar, and most people who know her well understand that this is part of her way of being with others. We know the verbal and nonverbal signs that accompany her deceptions, probably better than she does herself, and we choose not to "call her" on every one of her lies. Sometimes the choice to "let her lie" is made out of a desire to save time, because the issue of the lie is not central to the conversation or simply because holding her accountable for her lies would require more of an emotional investment than we'd like to make at the time. Occasionally, couples even collaborate on lies, and this is called collusion (Andersen, 1998). One partner may routinely deceive the other about infidelities, for example, and although the other suspects the truth, he or she agrees, for whatever reasons, to look the other way. In short, like all other kinds of communication, deception is strongly influenced by its context.

Communication researchers Dan O'Hair and Michael Cody (1994) identify six motives or reasons people give for lying to their relational partners. Three of the motives—*egoism, benevolence,* and *utility*—are labeled positive because they generally have positive consequences for at least one individual and appear to O'Hair and Cody to do no harm to the relationship. The other three—*exploitation, malevolence,* and *regress*—are labeled negative because their consequences do include harm to at least one person in the relationship. Egoism and exploitation are positive and negative forms of *self-related* motives, benevolence and malevolence are related to the *other,* and utility and regress have to do with the *relationship.*

Self-related motives for deception highlight what an individual can gain or retain through deception. Egoism helps to protect or promote the deceiver's self-concept. Think about times when you have stretched the truth on a job application or told someone something about yourself that was not quite true in order to be viewed in a positive light or to avoid embarrassment. Exploitation is lying with a purely selfish motive. When you pretend to be interested in someone in order to get information or to achieve some other personal goal, you have exploited the deceived. You may believe that your decision to exploit another is no different from beefing up your résumé, but arguably there is a difference in degree regarding both the effect on the relationship and the potential damage to the other person.

Benevolence and malevolence are deceptive practices that are other-focused. Benevolent lies are motivated by the desire to protect the self-esteem, safety, or general well-being of the other person. Lies told by people who were hiding Jews from the Nazis in World War II, by members of the Underground Railroad facilitating travel of runaway slaves in the U.S. Civil War era, or by networks designed to help protect wives or husbands in physically abusive relationships are all deceptions motivated by benevolence. Distorted truths or blatant lies that parents tell their children in order to protect the child's sense of worth or well-being are another kind of benevolent deception. Malevolence, on the other hand, is motivated by the desire to hurt others and may include deception designed to sabotage others or to get revenge or retaliation. The motive for benevolence may be viewed as pure even though the consequences of the deception may not be altogether productive, but malevolence has at its core negativity, and the results of malevolent deception are almost always negative for both the people involved and the relationship.

The two final motivations for deception focus on outcomes for the relationship itself. When someone employs utility as a motive for deception, the goal is to improve, enhance, escalate, or repair the relationship. In the example at the beginning of this [reading], Josh could have been trying to protect the relationship when he avoided telling his girlfriend about running into his ex while his girlfriend was out of town. Since his girlfriend was already worried about her grandmother's health, Josh may have believed that it wasn't useful to bring up a casual contact, especially when the fact that they were at the same club at the same time didn't mean much to him. Utility can also be a motivation to ignore a friend's compulsive lying. Ignoring another's deception is one way to keep the peace in a relationship, even when that stability is based on a lack of trust. Regress, on the other hand, means using a lie to damage or terminate a relationship. For instance, Jamal might tell his steady date Anna that they should go back to being "just friends" when the truth is that Jamal wants Anna to end the relationship. In this case, Jamal is manipulating Anna rather than being accountable for his own preference (O'Hair & Cody, 1994, 196).

Consequences of Deception

Most acts of deception have unintended consequences. In fact, if people carefully considered the potential ramifications of deception, they would often find that, in the long run, it would be less trouble to tell the truth. One unintended consequence is that when deception is undetected, it becomes a burden for the deceiver. In some cases people who deceive others feel a sense of autonomy, privacy, or control, but often these feelings are compromised by feelings of shame or guilt for lying to others and perhaps even anger at or contempt for the person they are lying to. Frequently, in order to maintain a falsehood, additional lies must be told to additional people. Any deception requires the deceiver to remember the details of the lie for as long as it is maintained, coordinate subsequent supporting lies, and maintain a heightened awareness of both verbal and nonverbal cues. This increased attention to one's own communication usually generates stress, which is ironic, since stress avoidance may have been the reason for the deception in the first place.

Once a deception has been detected by or revealed to a relational partner, the consequences expand and are almost universally negative. Until people discover that someone has lied to them, they generally operate from a "truth bias," that is, a basic belief that the other communicator is telling the truth. This state quickly changes to a "lie bias" once deception is revealed (O'Hair & Cody, 1994, 197). At this point, the deceived person is likely to assume that that communicator is always lying. This change in a relationship is one way that many people discover how trust is a precious commodity that, once lost, is difficult to fully regain.

The collaborative nature of deception becomes clearest when the deceived person decides to expose his or her relational partner's lies or to ignore or suppress them. Suppression may require increasingly monumental efforts, including lying to yourself about the fact that you are being lied to, accusing others of lying to you about a partner's indiscretions, and even lying to others about your relational partner's behaviors. Exposing the lie, however, means admitting to the deceiver and to others one's hurt, loss of esteem, anger, and increasing uncertainty about the future of the relationship. The deceiver who is caught and confronted by the deceived partner frequently also suffers embarrassment, guilt, and loss of credibility. Deception often increases tension, conflict, and even aggression in a relationship.

For these reasons and others, communication researcher and teacher Bill Wilmot argues that deception is *always* damaging to the other person and to the relationship. Wilmot contends that deception, by its very nature, is a self-centered act. Unlike O'Hair and Cody, Wilmot does not believe that any motives for deception are positive. Even when you convince yourself that your deception benefits the other or the relationship, Wilmot maintains that

> the recipient of the deception has no hand in deciding if it is "good" for the relationship or not—he or she is out of the loop.... Deception, even in its benign forms, is a form of information control that one exercises; you want to be the one determining the course of the relationship, so you withhold information from the partner. (Wilmot, 1995, 107–108)

If indeed the lowest common denominator in a relationship is two, an individual's choice to deceive is also a choice to short circuit the relationship by leaving the other partner out.

Whether you view deception as self or other motivated, patterns of deception are established collaboratively in relationships, and you can choose to sustain them or alter them. You do not have ultimate control over the direction of your relationships' spirals, because it always takes at least two. But your choices do contribute to sustaining, revealing, and preventing deception in your interpersonal relationships. If you are aware of a pattern of deception in an intimate relationship, we think that it would be useful for you to consider the motives for deception and the consequences of it for yourself, your partner, and the relationship. It may be that deception is a way to meet your need for privacy, control, or belonging, but there are consequences for choosing deception as a way to achieve the balance you are seeking. Whether you are the one in the relationship doing more of the deceiving, or the person who has been or is being lied to, you can start to alter the communicative pattern you've helped establish by interjecting more honesty whenever possible. Sometimes revealing a lie and working through its aftermath can lead to relationship development and growth.

We hope it is obvious that we are not advising you to be brutally honest all of the time in all of your relationships. Telling your boss that you think she has a big nose, for example, is irrelevant to the working relationship and could be considered malevolent, to say nothing of how foolish it might be if you are up for review. But when a pattern of deception is present between you and the people closest to you, it is important to identify what is going on and to restore as much of the truth as the relationship can contain. We also hope that you will at least think carefully about our point that deception is a collaboratively created phenomenon. It takes two to develop and maintain patterns of deception, and if you want to change the patterns, you'll need to make a choice to change your role in sustaining them. If you decide not to change the patterns, then at least acknowledge personal accountability for your part in them.

BETRAYAL

Deception and betrayal are closely related; in fact, some researchers see them as almost synonymous. The difference is that betrayal violates the betrayed person's expectations and can do so even when the person doing the betraying tells the truth. Researchers Walter Jones and Marsha Parsons Burdette define betrayals as "violations of trust or expectations on which the relationship is based" (Jones & Burdette, 1994, 244). Their research reveals five important features of betrayal.

First, betrayal appears to be common in interpersonal relationships. Over 90 percent of the participants in one study could easily provide stories of betrayal episodes in which they either did the betraying or were betrayed. As people move from the impersonal end of the continuum toward the interpersonal end, they tend to develop a sense of trust and commitment that grows out of mutual expectations consistently being met, even when some of these expectations remain unstated. It is not surprising, then, that any violation of expectations can be viewed as a betrayal by at least one of the partners.

Many different types of betrayal have been reported, including extramarital and extrarelational affairs, lies, revealed confidences, drinking and drugging, lack of support from a partner, ignoring a friend or partner, criticism, and gossip. Some of the most extreme forms of betrayal reported, and also the most severe, include being abused or abandoned by a parent. Unfortunately, the most painful kinds of betrayal happen in the most important relationships, probably because the expectations about communication and behavior are the highest in relationships that are most important. In relatively impersonal relationships, expectations are more socially shaped, and when social expectations are unmet, the consequences are less profound.

A second feature of betrayal is that the consequences of a betrayal incident differ significantly, depending on whether one is the betrayer or the betrayed. It may seem obvious that those who are betrayed described the relationship as having worsened in the aftermath of the betrayal incident. But it is interesting to note that those who did the betraying generally reported that the relationship had stayed the same or even improved after their betrayal.

Despite this potential optimism, the third feature is that betrayal tends to be followed by relationship termination. This obviously happens in romantic relationships and friendships, which are often referred to as relationships of choice. But even involuntary relationships, such as those between family members and co-workers, suffer serious decline following incidents of betrayal. One major reason is that betrayal involves disconfirmation of expectations, norms of interaction, and, most important, disconfirmation of the other as significant in the relationship. As Jones and Burdette (1994) explain, "The treachery is not just in the actual harm done to another, but also in the fact that betrayals threaten a major source of one's feelings of identity and well-being" (245). That source is the relationship itself. Effects of betrayal can last for a long time, and mitigation often requires help from a counselor, pastor or priest, or a trusted friend.

A fourth finding from studies of betrayal is that gender differences are prominent. Women are more likely to betray and be betrayed by other women, usually when one woman reveals a confidence or secret. Men report betraying their romantic partners more than they betray partners in any other relationship, and most often the nature of their betrayal is sexual. However, men report that they are most often betrayed by co-workers with whom they compete. Men and women also classify incidents of betrayal in significantly different ways. Men are more likely to identify only overt acts or events as betrayals, whereas women are more likely to describe a general lack of emotional support as a betrayal.

Finally, Jones and Burdette conclude that some personality traits may correlate with betrayal behavior. People who are likely to betray others also appear to be generally more jealous, suspicious, envious, and resentful of others. In addition, they tend to have more personal problems, including alcoholism or other addictions, depression, and a self-reported inability to sustain intimate relationships. These characteristics distinguish between those who are more likely to betray others, and they also identify those who are most likely to be betrayed.

Like deception, betrayal involves actions that leave at least one person out of the decision-making loop as the person doing the betraying attempts to control the destiny of the relationship on his or her own. Also like deception, betrayal diminishes trust between relational partners and damages the relationship itself.

When you notice patterns of betrayal in your relationships, it can be helpful to reflect on your expectations of the other person(s) and of the relationship(s). If you can talk to your relational partner and make some of your expectations explicit, then it may be easier for him or her to meet them. You can also discuss what expectations are most important to each of you, because even when people share mutual expectations, the value each places on any expectation can vary dramatically. When you experience incidents of betrayal, you may find it useful to get some perspective on your communication patterns from a third party and to express your feelings about the choices you have made and those that have been made for you.

HURTFUL MESSAGES, AGGRESSION, AND VIOLENCE

Aggression and violence are two additional relational problems that are influenced by power dynamics. When one party asserts control and influence over the other, patterns of hurtful messages, aggression, and violence may occur. These patterns are not simply created by the person who strikes out in anger or frustration. Like all relational patterns, these are also co-constructed. We definitely do not condone the behaviors of friends, family members, and romantic partners who berate and abuse others. At the same time, we also do not encourage friends, family members, and romantic partners who choose to accept emotional abuse. We acknowledge that sometimes people with less power—children, the elderly, a person in an unfamiliar culture—may not have many choices available. But we urge victims of abuse not to believe that their only option is to accept or reinforce the pattern.

Hurtful Messages

Hurtful messages are one of the ways that people attempt to assert power. Communication teacher and researcher Anita Vangelisti (1994 also see p. 340) identified 10 types of hurtful messages people experience in relationships with partners, friends, and family members. The people Anita questioned reported all of the following hurtful messages: *Accusations* about the other's negative behavior ("You are a liar"), *evaluations* of the other person's value as a human being ("You have got to be the most worthless son on the face of the planet"), *directives* or commands ("Just get out of my face"), *advice* ("You really ought to so something about your appearance"), *expressions of desire* ("I don't want to have anything to do with you"), *information disclosure* ("I'm really not attracted to you anymore"), *interrogating questions* ("Were you out with that no-good loser again?"), threats ("If you think you can leave me, you have another think coming"), *jokes* that put down the other ("The way you do that, you'd think your hair was blonde!"), and *lies* ("No I didn't cheat on you with her last week"). Clearly there are many ways to hurt another person, and the extent of the pain associated with each type of hurtful message depends on the context and the nature of the relationship.

In fact, the experience of hurt is also a relational phenomenon. A message that may be viewed as innocuous from a friend can be very painful when uttered by a family member or romantic partner. Vangelisti (1994) identified three factors that seem to affect how hurtful messages are interpreted: (1) the intent of the person communicating the hurtful message; (2) whether the parties shared a family or nonfamily relationship; and (3) the level of intimacy. One's overall satisfaction with a relationship also influences the extent to which relational partners emphasize hurtful messages. If a relationship is not very satisfying, people come to expect hurtful messages and pay less attention to them. Of course, as hurtful messages increase, overall satisfaction with the relationship decreases, and patterns of put-downs tend to create and maintain degenerative spirals.

When you are angry with someone or frustrated by your circumstances, consider the effects your hurtful messages may have. Many hurtful messages are difficult to repair, and although Vangelisti notes that those in intimate or family relationships may be more forgiving of them, participants in her study reported that it was difficult to forget them. Often they remembered the specific words of a message even years after they were spoken. Hurtful statements have rarely led to positive change in relationships and are often a part of relationship termination.

Verbal Aggression

Two communication researchers who spearheaded the study of verbal aggression noted that when someone uses verbal aggression they attack the self-concepts of other people (Infante & Wigley, 1986). Attacks on character, ridicule, rough teasing, and profanity are all forms of verbal aggression. In contrast to content or topic, verbally aggressive messages focus on the identity of the person being attacked. Karen recalls one verbally aggressive message that called into question her identity as a communication professional. An extended family member was frustrated when she felt out of the loop on the timing of a visit from Karen's dad, and rather than strike out at the members of the family with whom she lived, she chose to strike out at Karen by asking, "Don't you ever *use* that communication stuff you teach in your classes? What happened to all that stuff on family communication? Your family doesn't seem to be very good at it!"

As Wilmot and Hocker (2001) note, the forms that verbal aggression take can differ from relationship to relationship and culture to culture. They point out that in cultures that value individualism, verbally aggressive remarks are generally directed against a person (Carey & Mongeau, 1996). Examples might include "You are so stupid!" "You're ugly," "I wish you had never been born!" and "You are such a slob." By contrast, verbal aggression in collectivist cultures generally takes the form of attacks against the group, village, tribe, or family the person being attacked identifies with (Vissing & Baily, 1996). Examples of verbally aggressive statements toward the group may include "You Irishmen are just a bunch of drunken idiots" or "All Greeks are geeks."

In a study of verbal aggression among college-age couples, Sabourin (1995) found that aggressive partners would attack each other in escalating verbal exchanges in an attempt to gain control. Both would make escalating accusations and assertions in a pattern of domineering talk in which neither would accept the other's desire for control. As Sabourin notes, couples often found themselves stuck in escalating spirals that seemed out of control. She writes,

> The boundaries between individuals and the potential for empathy are lost. The partner is no longer experienced as a distinct individual deserving of respect but instead, as an extension of [the aggressive person]. In the process of escalating aggression, paradoxically, the power of both partners is lost to the pattern between them. (Sabourin, 1995, 281)

If you find that you are involved in battles of verbal aggression that seem to be spiraling out of control, what are some of your nexting choices? One effective way to shift away from verbal aggression is to focus on the content of the conflict rather than the character of the other person(s). Remember, verbal aggression is defined in part by the ways it attacks the character and self-concept of the other. Choosing to focus on the issue at hand rather than the identity of the other is one effective way to break degenerative spirals fueled by verbal aggression. If you and your partner do not curb your patterns of verbal aggression, you should be aware that sustained patterns of verbal aggression often lead to episodes of psychological abuse and even to patterns of violence. So, it is definitely worth it to try to intervene.

Psychological Abuse

Psychological abuse, like verbal aggression, can take a variety of forms, and what feels abusive in one relationship may not be interpreted the same way in another relationship. One researcher notes that instances of psychological abuse including the "creation of fear, isolation, economic abuse, monopolization, degradation, rigid sex-role expectations, withdrawal, [and] contingent expressions of love" are widespread enough to occur in some form in all intimate or close relationships (Marshall, 1994, 294).

In many cases, psychological abuse, like other forms of aggression and violence, is one way that relational partners assert dominance and control. The individual who chooses this form of verbal aggression is actively engaged in constructing an identity of the other that is subordinate and powerless. When, for whatever reason, their partner accepts this construction of identity, patterns of abuse are likely to continue. Students have reported that when they look back on relationships characterized by psychological abuse, they often wonder why they allowed their partner to define them as dependent when in most other contexts and relationships they were independent or interdependent people. One of the ways to respond to psychological abuse and other forms of verbal aggression is to use perception checking. You may find it helpful to solicit the perceptions of a close friend, family member, religious leader, or counselor to check your own perceptions of yourself and those features of your identity that feel imposed on you by your abusive relational partner.

Physical Violence

You might wonder why anyone would stay in a relationship that is physically violent. Part of the reason may be that, like other forms of violence in relationships, physical violence is often part of a pattern that develops over time, sometimes without the participants being fully aware that they are co-creating it. Most often, however, incidents of relational violence can be predicted by the extent to which verbal aggression and psychological abuse are occurring. Rarely do episodes of physical abuse exist in isolation. Most of the reports of physical violence in intimate relationships indicate that women are more likely to be harmed than men, but both men and women use physical violence as a tactic. Adults are more likely to use physical violence with children as discipline and as a way to assert influence and control.

Unfortunately the occurrence of physical violence as a tactic for negotiating power in a relationship is more common than you might imagine. One report suggests that in dating couples, 30–40 percent report violent incidents, including "pushing, shoving, slapping, kicking, biting, hitting with fists, hitting or trying to hit with an object, beatings, and threats/use of a weapon" (Cate & Lloyd, 1992, 97). Most of us have heard reports on the national news of children so determined to save themselves and their siblings from continued abuse by a parent that they feel their only recourse is to murder their mom or dad. Women who murder their abusive spouses have successfully used self-defense pleas to avoid life in prison for terminating abusive relationships by terminating their abusive partners.

Most people will not experience extreme forms of physical abuse in their relationships, but if you or someone you know is in an abusive or violent relationship, on either side of the situation, we hope that the information we have sketched here can help you gain a better understanding of what is happening and provide you with some choices about what to do next. Of course, the abuse will not magically disappear just because you—or others—understand that physical violence is related to verbal aggression or that physical abuse often follows a cyclical pattern of increasing tension, some precipitating event, and a physically violent act, followed by remorse and often some form of restitution. At the same time, you or the person you are trying to advise can make choices about the ways to negotiate power in your relationships so these relationships do not include violence. You may need to change the context in which the relationship is maintained, for example, by putting physical distance between you and your partner. It may also be necessary to seek outside counsel and support from a third party and to learn new patterns of communication using more productive strategies for negotiating power in the relationship. Our point is that one person can choose to alter his or her own behaviors that contribute to the patterns of communication enacted in a problematic relationship and can explore appropriate ways to use the power currencies he or she has in those relationships.

REVIEW QUESTIONS

1. Explain the difference between positive and negative motives for deception.
2. Define *truth bias* and *lie bias.*
3. Describe what some research has suggested are the personality features of frequent betrayers.
4. How does betrayal fit into the common pattern of communication in the family of an addicted person?
5. Explain the three factors that affect how hurtful messages are interpreted.
6. Paraphrase: "In the process of escalating aggression, paradoxically, the power of both partners is lost to the pattern between them."

PROBES

1. O'Hair and Cody would probably view the lies told to Nazi soldiers to protect Jews in hiding as "benevolent" and therefore positive. But Wilmot does not believe that any motives for deception can be completely positive, and he briefly explains why. What do you believe? Explain.
2. What do you think is the most negative motive for deception?
3. How do you respond to the claim that deception is collaborative?
4. The authors say that they are not advising you to be "brutally honest" in all your relationships. What are they advising?
5. What makes betrayal so interpersonally toxic?
6. What resources are available in your community for people who are experiencing physical violence in a close relationship?

REFERENCES

Andersen, P. (1998). *Nonverbal communication: Forms and functions.* New York: McGraw-Hill.

Carey, C., & Mongeau, P. (1996). Communication and violence in courtship relationships. In D. Cahn and S. Lloyd (Eds.), *Family violence from a communication perspective* (pp. 127–150). Hillsdale, NJ: Lawrence Erlbaum.

Cate, R. M., & Lloyd, S. A. (1992). *Courtship.* Thousand Oaks, CA: Sage.

Deutsch, M. (1973). Conflicts: Productive and destructive. In F. Jandt (Ed.), *Conflict resolution through communication.* New York: Harper and Row.

Emerson, R. (1962). Power-dependence relations. *American Sociological Review*, 27, 31–41.

Hopper, R., and Bell, R. A. (1984). Broadening the deception construct. *Quarterly Journal of Speech, 70*, 288–300.

Infante, D., & Wigley, C. (1986). Verbal aggressiveness: An interpersonal model & measure. *Communication Monographs, 53*, 61–69.

Jones, W. H., & Burdette, M. P. (1994). Betrayal in relationships. In A. L. Weber & J. H. Harvey (Eds.), *Perspectives on close relationships* (pp. 245–262). Boston: Allyn and Bacon.

Marshall, L. L. (1994). Physical and psychological abuse. In W. Cupach & B. Spitzberg (Eds.), *The darkside of interpersonal communication* (pp. 292–297). Hillsdale, NJ: Lawrence Erlbaum.

McGraw, P. (2003). *Relationship rescue: A seven-step strategy for reconnecting with your partner*. New York: Hyperion.

O'Hair, H. D., & Cody, M. J. (1994). Deception. In W. Cupach & B. Spitzberg (Eds.), *The dark side of interpersonal communication*. Hillsdale, NJ: Lawrence Erlbaum.

Sabourin, T. C. (1995). The role of negative Reciprocity in spouse abuse: A relational control analysis. *Journal of Applied Communication Research, 23*, 271–283.

Vangelisti, A. (1994). Messages that hurt. In W. Cupach & B. Spitzberg (Eds.), *The dark side of interpersonal communication* (pp. 61–79). Hillsdale, NJ: Lawrence Erlbaum.

Vissing, Y., & Baily, W. (1996). Parent-to-child verbal aggression." In D. Cahn & S. Lloyd (Eds.), *Family violence from a communication perspective* (pp. 85–107). Hillsdale, NJ: Lawrence Erlbaum.

Wilmot, W. W. (1995). *Relational communication*. New York: McGraw-Hill.

Wilmot, W., & Hocker, J. (2001). *Interpersonal conflict*. Boston: McGraw-Hill.

Messages That Hurt

Anita L. Vangelisti

I remember when Anita Vangelisti was an undergraduate student in my interpersonal communication class. Now she is a respected researcher and a professor at the University of Texas. This reading, which I excerpted from a considerably longer chapter, summarizes some of Anita's work on messages that hurt. It's the basis for the discussion of hurtful messages on page 347.

This selection reviews work done by others and reports on some studies Anita and her colleagues have done. As she notes, one of her early moves was to ask several hundred college students to recall a situation in which someone said something to them that hurt their feelings. From these data, she was able to identify *categories* of hurtful messages. They are summarized in Table 1 and include accusations, evaluations, threats, and lies. She also identified nine *topics* of hurtful messages, including romantic relations, sexual behavior, physical appearance, and personality traits. This early research gave Anita an overall view of the phenomenon she was studying.

One of her next moves was to explore why some messages hurt more than others. She found that informative messages hurt the worst, primarily because there seems to be little opportunity to defend oneself or repair the damage created by comments like "You aren't a priority in my life," "I decided we can only be friends," or "I'm really attracted to Julie." As you might expect, messages centering on romantic relationships were also perceived as extremely hurtful. And again, their hurtfulness is partly a function of how much the recipient can do about the message. The most hurtful messages tend to be those that we can do the least to respond to. This is one of the reasons why recipients in at least one study responded to extremely hurtful messages by withdrawing—either by crying or by verbally complying.

Anita extends her discussion of these most hurtful messages by reviewing some attributions that people make to help them cope. (For a review of attributions, look back at the reading by Karen, Saskia, and I in Chapter 5.) Sometimes people cope by providing a generous attribution about intent—"After all, she didn't *mean* to hurt my feelings." In other situations, intent is clearer, and the person receiving the message asks, "How could anyone say something like that *on purpose?*"

The mental effort expended to make sense of hurtful messages varies, as you might expect, with the closeness of the relationship. Few people invest much effort in a hurtful message from a store clerk, but a comment from one's spouse might provoke considerable work. There are exceptions to this rule, however, including the son who excuses his father's put-downs with "I guess that's what fathers are supposed to do" and the abused wife who minimizes the negative messages received from her husband.

The final section of this reading focuses on how hurtful messages affect relationships. When the message is perceived to be unintentional, the impact on the relationship tends to be negligible. When the hurt is perceived to be intentional, there is a greater impact, but this tendency is balanced by the tendency to excuse intimates. In both family and dating relationships, hurtful messages are often forgiven.

Anita's research clearly demonstrates the inaccuracy of the old adage "Sticks and stones can break my bones, but names can never hurt me." Hurt is a relational phenomenon that depends not only on what is said but when, by whom, to whom, and how seriously. But the potential of destructive words is clearly great. "Names" and other hurtful messages can cut deep.

MAIN IDEAS

- "Regardless of intentionality, context, or source, feelings of hurt are evoked by and expressed through communication."
- Research has identified 10 kinds of hurtful messages and 9 hurtful topics.
- Some messages hurt more than others because of differences in repair opportunities, breadth and depth of the relationship, and possibilities for repair success.
- It is also challenging to respond to hurtful messages because of the attributional work that has to be done—"She doesn't mean it;" "How could anyone say that on purpose?"
- Many responses to hurtful messages assert that they are unintentional. (Almost 65 percent of hurtful messages are perceived to be unintentional.)

- Hurtful messages also decrease relational closeness.
- "Words can 'hurt'—both individuals and relationships."

After my parents got divorced, my father sat down and had a long talk with me. He told me a lot of things that my mom did to hurt him and tried to explain his side of the story. I already knew most of what he said, but there was one thing that really surprised me. He said, "Your mother never really loved you as much as she did your brother or sister. . . . It was obvious from the start. You looked like me and she couldn't hide her feelings." He probably didn't mean this the way I took it, but it has bothered me ever since. I wish now he wouldn't have said it. I'm not sure why he did. I guess he was just expressing his anger.

Although most of us have used the old adage "sticks and stones may break my bones,"[1] few who study communication would argue that the impact of words on people and relationships is less than that of physical objects—whether those objects be sticks, stones, bats, or fists. Words not only "do" things when uttered (Austin, 1975), but they have the ability to hurt or harm in every bit as real a way as physical objects. A few ill-spoken words (e.g., "You're worthless," "You'll never amount to anything," "I don't love you anymore") can strongly affect individuals, interactions, and relationships.

Feeling hurt, by its nature, is a social phenomenon. Except in relatively rare circumstances, people feel hurt as a result of some interpersonal event—something they perceive was said or done by another individual. The hurtful utterance may be spoken with the best of intentions or it may be overtly aggressive. It may occur as a one-time event or it may be embedded in a long history of verbal abuse. It may be spoken by a complete stranger or by a life-long friend. Regardless of intentionality, context, or source, feelings of hurt are evoked by and expressed through communication. Although theorists of emotion and of communication have acknowledged the potential association between social interaction and the elicitation of emotions such as hurt, theoretical work has only recently begun to explain the processes that link communication and emotion (Averill, 1980; Bowers, Metts, & Duncanson, 1985; de Rivera & Grinkis, 1986; Shimanoff, 1985, 1987; Weiner, 1986).

Weiner (1986) suggested that emotions are determined, in part, by attributions. He and his colleagues have found, for example, that the attributions people make about interpersonal events distinguish whether individuals feel anger, guilt, or pity (Weiner, Graham, & Chandler, 1982). Given this, when people feel hurt, their attributions concerning the messages that initially evoked their feelings should distinguish those (hurt) feelings from other similarly "negative" emotions. Although researchers have begun to study the association between attribution and emotion, they have largely neglected the relationship between communication and attribution. Because attributions are based, in part, on individuals' observations of interpersonal events, the messages that people believe evoked their feelings of hurt are central to understanding how hurt is elicited.

The purpose of this reading is to begin to describe the social interactions that people define as hurtful....

EXAMINING MESSAGES THAT HURT

To begin to describe hurtful messages, data collected from two groups of undergraduate students were examined. The first set of data was collected from students ($N = 179$) enrolled in a large, introductory communication course. The second data set was collected approximately 1 year later and consisted of responses from individuals ($N = 183$) enrolled in one of several introductory communication courses.

Respondents were instructed to recall a situation in which someone said something to them that hurt their feelings. Then they were asked to write a "script" of the interaction as they remembered it. They were told to include what was said before the hurtful comment was made, what the comment was, and how they reacted to the comment.[2] After completing their script, participants were asked to look back on the conversation they described and to rate how hurtful it was (a high score indicated that it was "Extremely Hurtful" and a low score that it was "Not At All Hurtful").[3]

Inductive analysis (Bulmer, 1979) was used to develop a category scheme to describe the acts of speech that characterize hurtful messages.[4] With the exception of the data from five respondents (who could not recall any particularly hurtful messages), over 96 percent of the messages were codable into the typology. Definitions and examples of the categories are provided in Table 1.... The most commonly perceived hurtful messages across both data sets were accusations, evaluations, and informative messages, whereas the least common were lies and threats.

A brief perusal of these data suggested that the messages varied in terms of how hurtful they were to respondents. Interactions ranged from a former coach telling a respondent, "My, you seem to have put on a few pounds" to a physical education teacher exclaiming, "You are the worse [sic] player I've ever seen in my life!" In one case, a peer asked a respondent who was mourning her father's death, "When are you going to get over this?" In another, a respondent's stepmother told her, "You caused your grandmother's death. She died of a broken heart because you didn't show her how much you loved her." Although all of these examples were rated above the midpoint in terms of how hurtful they were to respondents, some were rated as more hurtful than others....

TABLE 1 Typology of Hurtful Message Speech Acts

Definition	Examples
Accusation: A charge of fault or offense.	"You are a liar." "You're such a hypocrite."
Evaluation: A description of value, worth, or quality.	"Well, if I met him and liked him, I would have remembered him." "Going out with you was the biggest mistake of my life."
Directive: An order, set of directions, or a command.	"Just get off my back." "Just leave me alone, why don't you!"
Advice: A suggestion for a course of action.	"Break up with her so you can have some fun." "I think we should see other people."
Expression of Desire: A statement of preference.	"I don't want him to be like you." "I don't ever want to have anything to do with you."
Information: A disclosure of information.	"You aren't a priority in my life." "Well, I'm really attracted to Julie."
Question: An inquiry or interrogation.	"Why aren't you over this [a family death] yet?"
Threat: An expression of intention to inflict some sort of punishment under certain conditions.	"If I find out you are ever with that person, *never* come home again."
Joke: A witticism or prank.	"The statement was really an ethnic joke against my ethnicity."
Lie: An untrue, deceptive statement or question.	"The worst part was when he lied about something …"

TABLE 2 Examples of Hurtful Topics

Topic	Example
Romantic Relations	"He never liked you anyway. He just used you to get back at me."
Nonromantic Relations	"You're trying too hard to be popular … you're ignoring your 'real' friends."
Sexual Behavior	"Why? Do you still want to sleep around?"
Physical Appearance	"God almighty you're fat!"
Abilities/Intelligence	"I guess it's hard for you teenage illiterates to write that stuff."
Personality Traits	"Well, I think you're selfish and spoiled!"
Self-Worth	"I don't need you anymore."
Time	"We don't do things together like we used to."
Ethnicity/Religion	"You're a stupid Jew!"

The topics addressed by hurtful messages were coded using a procedure identical to the one outlined for the coding of message type. Initial categories were generated, the data were coded, the categories were refined, and the data were recoded. Table 2 provides a list of topic categories as well as examples of each topic. Over 93 percent of the messages reported were codable into the typology.…

WHY SOME MESSAGES HURT MORE THAN OTHERS

Of the hurtful messages described, informative statements were the only speech acts that were rated extremely hurtful more often than they were rated low in hurtfulness. Informative statements, in short, were most typically seen as highly hurtful messages. Although potential explanations for this finding vary, the ability of recipients to "repair" or offer alternatives to the content of the message seems a particularly likely contributor. Whereas listeners are less likely than speakers to initiate repair (Schegloff, Jefferson, & Sacks, 1977), when accused or evaluated, recipients have the control to either overtly or covertly "defend" themselves against hurt. If the speaker does not initiate repair, the recipient may do so by offering alternatives to the accusation (e.g., accounts, excuses, justifications) and even verifying those alternatives with examples from his or her own experiences.[5] On the other hand, when informed of something, there are few such arguments available. The opportunities for recipients to repair any damage to their own face are severely limited. If, for example, a person is accused of being selfish and inconsiderate, that person can point out instances in which that has not been the case. However, if the same person is informed by a lover that the lover is "seeing someone else," there is little the person can say to counter the statement.

Like informative statements, hurtful messages (in the second data set) centering on romantic relationships were, more often than not, perceived as extremely hurtful (although this difference was significant only for the second data set, messages in the first data set were similarly distributed). Given that over 54.5 percent of the informative messages concerned romantic relationships (i.e., "I don't love you anymore," "I've been sleeping with someone else," "I decided we can only be friends"), this finding is not surprising. It is interesting, however, that participants tended to rate these relational hurts as more hurtful, whereas they tended to rate some personal or individual hurts (i.e., statements regarding self-worth) as less hurtful. One explanation for this contrast involves the potential recency of the messages concerning romantic relationships. Because the sample for this study was college students, events centering on romantic relationships may have been more recent and therefore more salient in the minds of respondents. However, this was not the case.... Furthermore, participants' ratings of hurtfulness were positively correlated with the amount of time that had passed since the hurtful event....

A second explanation is that hurtful messages focusing on relational issues, like those comprised of informative statements, may be more difficult for recipients to repair than messages that emphasize nonrelational issues. This explanation is supported by the finding (in the first data set) that hurtful messages concerning nonromantic relationships were seen as extremely hurtful more often than not. (In the second data set this difference was not significant, but the data were distributed in a similar pattern.) Because relationships involve two people, they are at once controllable and uncontrollable. Each individual has the power to influence, but neither has complete reign.

In contrast, many nonrelational issues such as time management are more controllable. Recipients may repair by excusing, justifying, or apologizing for their behavior or choices (McLaughlin, 1984). Further, because recipients have access to a great deal of information concerning their own behavior (e.g., the situational parameters they face), they may be able to rationalize their limitations by adjusting their own criteria for evaluating the behavior. Other nonrelational issues such as physical appearance and intelligence are relatively uncontrollable. Recipients therefore need not take responsibility for evaluative remarks or questions from others.

In comparison to nonrelational issues, relational issues present both recipients and speakers with a unique situation. Neither has complete control or responsibility for relational outcomes. As a result, when one partner evaluates ("You aren't going to make a very good husband") or makes an accusation ("You don't care about our friendship at all") concerning the relationship, the other is faced with a dilemma. He or she must seek a repair strategy that addresses the (relational) issue at hand without threatening the face of either partner. In many cases, these two goals are incompatible. The difficulties of dealing with such incompatible goals are reflected by the findings of a pilot study that suggest that recipients tend to react to extremely hurtful messages by withdrawing—either by crying or verbally acquiescing to their conversational partner (Vangelisti, 1989).

In addition to presenting participants with potentially difficult behavioral choices, extremely hurtful messages may also create some difficult cognitive tasks. When a loved one says something that hurts, participants may make one of at least two attributional choices. First, they may reason that the person did not intend to hurt their feelings. If this choice is made, the message may evoke feelings of hurt, but might not have a major effect on the relationship ("After all, she didn't *mean* to hurt my feelings"). Second, participants may believe that the message was intentionally hurtful. If so, they will likely have more difficulty discounting the impact of the message on the relationship ("How could anyone say something like that *on purpose?*"). In some cases, people may examine the available data to determine whether or not a message was intended to hurt. In others, the need or desire to maintain a close relationship may encourage participants to make attributions that minimize the intentionality they attach to hurtful messages.

The cognitive "effort" that individuals expend to make sense of hurtful messages should depend, in part, on the individuals' relationship with the person who uttered the message. For example, if a clerk in a department store hurts a person's feelings, that person is probably less likely to spend time contemplating the clerk's motives than if the same person was treated badly by a friend, parent, or spouse. Why? In part because people expect to be treated by intimate relational partners in relatively positive ways.

Obviously, there are exceptions to this rule. For instance, when explaining why his father said something hurtful to him, one respondent noted, "I don't understand why he always puts me down. I guess that's what fathers are supposed to do." Clearly this respondent did not expect positive feedback from his father. The rather bewildered account of his father's behavior suggests that the

hurtful message described by the respondent may have been one of many—
that it was contextualized in an ongoing stream of verbal abuse (Leffler, 1988;
Vissing, Straus, Gelles, & Harrop, 1991; Yelsma, 1992) and/or intentional verbal
aggression (Infante, Riddle, Horvath, & Tumlin, 1992; Martin & Horvath, 1992).
Another example would be a physically abused wife who comes to expect negative behavior from her spouse. Even in such extreme cases, however, researchers
have found that both the abused and the abuser use cognitive strategies to minimize the control and intentionality associated with abusive acts (Andrews, 1992;
Herbert, Silver, & Ellard, 1991; Holtzworth-Munroe, 1992). In the context of close
relationships, acts of violence are often interpreted as representing "love" rather
than more obvious emotions such as anger or rage (Cate et al., 1982; Henton et
al., 1983). In short, relational intimacy, the type of relationship people have with
those who utter hurtful messages, and the intentionality attributed to the message should affect the impact of hurtful messages on relationships....

DISCUSSING THE IMPACT OF HURTFUL MESSAGES ON RELATIONSHIPS

Although the vast majority (64.8 percent) of hurtful messages were perceived
to be unintentional, those that were seen as intentional had a significantly
greater distancing effect on the relationship. Recipients' remarks regarding
intentionality reflected their willingness to make allowances for a variety of
speaker difficulties. When asked whether the speaker intended to hurt them, recipients often made comments such as "she was mad at someone else," "he just
doesn't know how to fight," "he has a personal problem with alcohol," or "he
said it because he loves me." If speakers seemed to regret the hurtful message
(Knapp et al., 1986), or if the message was offered for the good of the recipient
(Weber & Vangelisti, 1991), the message did not have as strong an effect on the
relationship. In contrast, when recipients perceived that the message was intentionally hurtful, their remarks frequently focused on stable personality traits of
the speaker: "She's just that sort of person," "he is very cruel and unforgiving,"
"he doesn't care about anyone except himself...."

The impact of hurtful messages on relational intimacy was also affected
by ratings of relational closeness at the time the message was uttered. Ratings
of relational closeness were negatively associated with the distancing effect
of hurtful messages. Because there was not a similarly negative association
between closeness and message hurtfulness, the apparent lack of distancing in
more intimate relationships was not due to the fact that the messages hurt less.
Instead, those who were involved in intimate relationships may be more willing
to offer interpretations of the hurtful messages that are less harmful to the relationship. It is also possible that intimates have developed idiosyncratic patterns
to deal with hurtful events (Montgomery, 1988), or that they have developed
enough of a positive regard for one another that a single hurtful message does
not affect relational intimacy (Knapp, 1984).

Similar explanations may be offered for the findings concerning family relationships. Although intimacy did not significantly differentiate between family and nonfamily relationships, results indicated that hurtful messages occurring in the context of the family had less of an effect on the relationship than did those occurring in nonfamily contexts. In contrast to intimate nonfamily relationships, family associations may encourage people to deal with hurtful messages by relying on the assumption that the relationships are involuntary and therefore virtually impossible to dissolve. One respondent noted in the margin of his questionnaire that "It seems if something happens with your family … [you are] a lot more apt to forgive them." Because family members are, for all practical purposes, irreplaceable, recipients of hurtful messages may feel more obligated to absorb the blow of a hurtful message without allowing it to impact the family relationship. In addition, the variety of circumstances family members have experienced together may create a sort of "immunity" to the impact of hurtful messages. Family members' experience with other negative interpersonal events may better prepare them for the feelings of hurt that can be elicited by other members.…

In sum, the findings of this research suggest that the old adage concerning "sticks and stones" requires, at the very least, a lengthy addendum. Hurt is a socially elicited emotion (de Rivera, 1977)—people feel hurt because of the interpersonal behavior of others. Because feelings of hurt are elicited through social interaction, words can "hurt"—both individuals and relationships.

REVIEW QUESTIONS

1. Paraphrase the relationship between attributions and hurtfulness that Anita outlines in the third paragraph of this reading.
2. What is the main characteristic of a hurtful message that informs?
3. Why does Anita believe that informative hurtful messages are so painful?
4. What is Anita's theoretical explanation for the finding that recipients tend to react to extremely hurtful messages by withdrawing?
5. How does the desire to maintain a close relationship sometimes affect attributions about a hurtful message?
6. What do you make out of the finding that almost 65 percent of hurtful messages were perceived to be unintentional?

PROBES

1. If you were a participant in Anita's first study, what two examples of hurtful messages would you first recall? Label them using the categories in Table 1. Then identify the topics of these messages, as in Table 2.
2. What is the frequency of hurtful messages in your life by topic type? Which topic in Table 2 do you hear the most hurtful messages about? What is ranked second and third?

3. "Time heals all wounds," the saying goes. Yet Anita found that "participants' ratings of hurtfulness were positively correlated with the amount of time that had passed since the hurtful event." Comment on this finding.
4. Explain how, in the context of close relationships, "acts of violence are often interpreted as representing love.'"
5. Anita found in her research that the distancing effects of hurtful messages in intimate relationships were less than she expected. How does she explain this finding?

NOTES

1. Steve Duck has informed me of a German proverb that provides a more accurate representation of the association between words and feelings of hurt: "Böse Disteln stechen sehr, böse Zungen stechen mehr." A colleague from Germany, Jurgen Streeck, confirmed the translation: "Nasty thistles hurt/stick a great deal, but nasty words hurt/stick more."
2. Respondents participating in the second data collection session were also asked to indicate how long ago the hurtful message occurred.
3. To reduce demand characteristics, participants were also informed that some people may not have experienced (or may not be able to remember) the type of conversations called for by the questionnaire and that part of the research project was to assess the percentage of people who could and could not do so. Subjects were further reminded that they would receive extra credit regardless of whether or not they completed the questionnaire (see Planalp & Honeycutt, 1985).
4. Because the data were collected approximately 1 year apart, the analyses were conducted separately (also approximately 1 year apart). The initial category scheme, therefore, was primarily developed using the first data set. The second set of data was collected, in part, to demonstrate the applicability of the category scheme and to replicate the frequencies found using the first data set.
5. Work on accounts, blaming, excuses, and attributions (e.g., Cody & McLaughlin, 1988; Fincham, Beach, & Nelson, 1987; Fincham & Jaspers, 1980; Harvey, Weber, & Orbuch, 1990; Hilton, 1990; McLaughlin, Cody, & French, 1990; Weber & Vangelisti, 1991; Weiner et al., 1987) certainly supports the notion that people generate such alternatives to explain unexpected social circumstances, potentially negative behavior, or broken social contracts.

REFERENCES

Andrews, B. (1992). Attribution processes in victims of marital violence: Who do women blame and why? In J. H. Harvey, T. L. Orbuch, & A. L. Weber (Eds.), *Attributions, accounts, and close relationships* (pp. 176–193). New York: Springer-Verlag.

Austin, J. L. (1975). *How to do things with words* (2nd ed., J. O. Urmson & M. Sbisa, Eds.). Cambridge, MA: Harvard University Press.

Averill, J. R. (1980). A constructivist view of emotion. In R. Plutchik & K. Kellerman (Eds.), *Theories of emotion* (Vol. 1, pp. 305–339). New York: Academic Press.

Bowers, J. W., Metts, S. M., & Duncanson, W. T. (1985). Emotion and interpersonal communication. In M. L. Knapp & G. R. Miller (Eds.), *Handbook of interpersonal communication* (pp. 500–550). Beverly Hills, CA: Sage.

Bulmer, M. (1979). Concepts in the analysis of qualitative data. *Sociological Review, 27,* 651–677.

Cate, R. M., Henton, J. M., Koval, J., Christopher, F. S., & Lloyd, S. (1982). Premarital abuse: A social psychological perspective. *Journal of Family Issues, 3,* 79–90.

Cody, M. J., & McLaughlin, M. L. (1988). Accounts on trial: Oral arguments in traffic court. In C. Antake (Ed.), *Analyzing everyday explanation: A casebook of methods* (pp. 113–126). London: Sage.

de Rivera, J. (1977). *A structural theory of the emotions.* New York: International Universities Press.

de Rivera, J., & Grinkis, C. (1986). Emotions in social relationships. *Motivation and Emotion, 10,* 351–369.

Fincham, F. D., Beach, S., & Nelson, G. (1987). Attribution processes in distressed and nondistressed couples: III. Casual and responsibility attributions for spouse behavior. *Cognitive Therapy and Research, 11,* 77–86.

Fincham, F. D., & Jaspers, J. M. (1980). Attribution of responsibility: From man the scientist to man as lawyer. In L. Berkowitz (Ed.), *Advances in experimental social psychology* (Vol. 13, pp. 82–139). New York: Academic Press.

Harvey, J. H., Weber, A. L., & Orbuch, T. L. (1990). *Interpersonal accounts.* Oxford: Blackwell.

Henton, J. M., Cate, R. M., Koval, J., Lloyd, S., & Christopher, F. S. (1983). Romance and violence in dating relationships. *Journal of Family Issues, 4,* 467–482.

Herbert, T. B., Silver, R. C., & Ellard, J. H. (1991). Coping with an abusive relationship: I. How and why do women stay? *Journal of Marriage and the Family, 53,* 311–325.

Hilton, D. J. (1990). Conversational processes and causal explanation. *Psychological Bulletin, 107,* 65–81.

Holtzworth-Munroe, A. (1992). Attributions and maritally violent men: The role of cognitions in marital violence. In J. H. Harvery, T. L. Orbuch, & A. L. Weber (Eds.), *Attributions, accounts, and close relationships* (pp. 165–175). New York: Springer-Verlag.

Infante, D. A., Riddle, B. L., Horvath, C. L., & Tumlin, S. A. (1992). Verbal aggressiveness: Messages and reasons. *Communication Quarterly, 40,* 116–126.

Knapp, M. L. (1984). *Interpersonal communication and human relationships.* Boston: Allyn & Bacon.

Knapp, M. L., Stafford, L., & Daly, J. A. (1986). Regrettable messages: Things people wish they hadn't said. *Journal of Communication, 36,* 40–58.

Leffler, A. (1988). *Verbal abuse and psychological unavailability scales and relationship to self-esteem.* Paper presented at the annual meeting of the American Psychological Association, Atlanta, GA.

Martin, M. M., & Horvath, C. L. (1992, November). *Messages that hurt: What people think and feel about verbally aggressive messages.* Paper presented at the annual meeting of the Speech Communication Association, Chicago, IL.

McLaughlin, M. L. (1984). *Conversation: How talk is organized.* Beverly Hills, CA: Sage.

McLaughlin, M. L., Cody, M. J., & French, K. (1990). Account-giving and the attribution of responsibility: Impressions of traffic offenders. In M. J. Cody & M. L. McLaughlin (Eds.), *The psychology of tactical communication* (pp. 244–267). Clevedon, England: Multilingual Matters.

Montgomery, B. M. (1988). Quality communication in personal relationships. In S. W. Duck (Ed.), *Handbook of personal relationships* (pp. 343–359). New York: Wiley.

Planalp, S., & Honeycutt, J. M. (1985). Events that increase uncertainty in personal relationships. *Human Communication Research, 11,* 593–604.

Schegloff, E. A., Jefferson, G., & Sacks, H. (1977). The preference for self-correction in the organization of repair in conversation. *Language, 53,* 361–382.

Shimanoff, S. B. (1985). Rules governing the verbal expression of emotion between married couples. *Western Journal of Speech Communication, 49,* 147–165.

Shimanoff, S. B. (1987). Types of emotional disclosures and request compliance between spouses. *Communication Monographs, 54,* 85–100.

Vangelisti, A. L. (1989, November). *Messages that hurt: Perceptions of and reactions to hurtful messages in relationships.* Paper presented at the meeting of the Speech Communication Association, San Francisco, CA.

Vissing, Y. M., Straus, M. A., Gelles, R. J., & Harrop, J. W. (1991). Verbal aggression by parents and psychosocial problems of children. *Child Abuse and Neglect, 15,* 223–238.

Weber, D. J., & Vangelisti, A. L. (1991). "Because I love you": The use of tactical attributions in conversation. *Human Communication Research, 17,* 606–624.

Weiner, B. (1986). *An attributional theory of motivation and emotion.* New York: Springer-Verlag.

Weiner, B., Amirkhan, J., Folkes, V. S., & Verette, J. A. (1987). An attributional analysis of excuse giving: Studies of a naïve theory of emotion. *Journal of Personality and Social Psychology, 52,* 316–324.

Weiner, B., Graham, S., & Chandler, C. C. (1982). Pity, anger, and guilt: An attributional analysis. *Personality and Social Psychology Bulletin, 8,* 225–232.

Yelsma, P. (1992, July). *Affective orientations associated with couples' verbal abusiveness.* Paper presented at the bi-annual meeting of the International Society for the Study of Personal Relationships, Orono, ME.

Defensive Communication

Jack R. Gibb

The next selection, a classic article by communication consultant Jack Gibb, describes how defensiveness happens and what you can do to build a supportive rather than a defensive communication climate. Although it is old, this essay contains an elegant description of a very important and prevalent communication "wall."

As Gibb points out, when you anticipate or perceive that you are threatened by a person or a situation, you will usually react defensively, and so will the other persons involved. When any combination of the six "defensiveness-producing" elements is present, a spiral usually begins, a spiral that starts with a little discomfort and often escalates into all-out conflict.

But, Gibb notes, you can also start a spiral in the other direction. The more supportive you can be, the less other people are likely to read into the situation distorted reactions created by their own defensiveness. So when you can manifest any combination of the six alternative attitudes and skills, you can help reduce the defensiveness that's present. You don't have to give up or give in. You just have to stop trying so hard to demean, control, and impose your hard-and-fast superiority on others.

This essay was written before authors understood that it's inappropriate to refer to people in general as "he" and "him." I hope you'll be able to read beyond this feature of the language for Gibb's excellent ideas. Defensiveness is a common communication "wall," and there are some helpful actions you can take to bridge it.

MAIN IDEAS

- Defensiveness emerges when an individual perceives or anticipates threat; it is focused on protecting one's self.
- Defensiveness undermines effective communication.
- Six elements in the communication climate promote defensiveness: evaluation, control, strategy, neutrality, superiority, and certainty.
- In order to reduce defensiveness, communicators should integrate into their verbal and nonverbal talk six alternative aspects of the communication climate: description, problem orientation, spontaneity, empathy, equality, and provisionalism.

One way to understand communication is to view it as a people process rather than as a language process. If one is to make fundamental improvement in communication, he must make changes in interpersonal relationships. One possible type of alteration—and the one with which this paper is concerned—is that of reducing the degree of defensiveness.

"Defensive Communications" by Jack Gibb from *Journal of Communication*, September 1961, Vol. 11, No. 13, pp. 141–148. Reprinted by permission of Blackwell Publishing Ltd.

DEFINITION AND SIGNIFICANCE

Defensive behavior is defined as that behavior which occurs when an individual perceives threat or anticipates threat in the group. The person who behaves defensively, even though he also gives some attention to the common task, devotes an appreciable portion of his energy to defending himself. Besides talking about the topic, he thinks about how he appears to others, how he may be seen more favorably, how he may win, dominate, impress, or escape punishment, and/or how he may avoid or mitigate a perceived or an anticipated attack.

Such inner feelings and outward acts tend to create similarly defensive postures in others; and, if unchecked, the ensuing circular response becomes increasingly destructive. Defensive behavior, in short, engenders defensive listening, and this in turn produces postural, facial, and verbal cues which raise the defense level of the original communicator.

Defense arousal prevents the listener from concentrating upon the message. Not only do defensive communicators send off multiple value, motive, and affect cues, but also defensive recipients distort what they receive. As a person becomes more and more defensive, he becomes less and less able to perceive accurately the motives, the values, and the emotions of the sender. The writer's analyses of tape recorded discussions revealed that increases in defensive behavior were correlated positively with losses in efficiency in communication.[1] Specifically, distortions became greater when defensive states existed in the groups.

The converse, moreover, also is true. The more "supportive" or defense reductive the climate the less the receiver reads into the communication distorted loadings which arise from projections of his own anxieties, motives, and concerns. As defenses are reduced, the receivers become better able to concentrate upon the structure, the content, and the cognitive meanings of the message.

CATEGORIES OF DEFENSIVE AND SUPPORTIVE COMMUNICATION

In working over an 8-year period with recordings of discussions occurring in varied settings, the writer developed the six pairs of defensive and supportive categories presented in Table 1. Behavior which a listener perceives as possessing any of the characteristics listed in the left-hand column arouses

TABLE 1 Categories of Behavior Characteristic of Supportive and Defensive Climates in Small Groups

Defensive Climates	Supportive Climates
1. Evaluation	1. Description
2. Control	2. Problem orientation
3. Strategy	3. Spontaneity
4. Neutrality	4. Empathy
5. Superiority	5. Equality
6. Certainty	6. Provisionalism

defensiveness, whereas that which he interprets as having any of the qualities designated as supportive reduces defensive feelings. The degree to which these reactions occur depends upon the personal level of defensiveness and upon the general climate in the group at the time.[2]

Evaluation and Description

Speech or other behavior which appears evaluative increases defensiveness. If by expression, manner of speech, tone of voice, or verbal content the sender seems to be evaluating or judging the listener, then the receiver goes on guard. Of course, other factors may inhibit the reaction. If the listener thought that the speaker regarded him as an equal and was being open and spontaneous, for example, the evaluativeness in a message would be neutralized and perhaps not even perceived. This same principle applies equally to the other five categories of potentially defense-producing climates. The six sets are interactive.

Because our attitudes toward other persons are frequently, and often necessarily, evaluative, expressions which the defensive person will regard as nonjudgmental are hard to frame. Even the simplest question usually conveys the answer that the sender wishes or implies the response that would fit into his value system. A mother, for example, immediately following an earth tremor that shook the house, sought for her small son with the question: "Bobby, where are you?" The timid and plaintive "Mommy, I didn't do it" indicated how Bobby's chronic mild defensiveness predisposed him to react with a projection of his own guilt and in the context of his chronic assumption that questions are full of accusation.

Anyone who has attempted to train professionals to use information-seeking speech with neutral affect appreciates how difficult it is to teach a person to say even the simple "who did that?" without being seen as accusing. Speech is so frequently judgmental that there is a reality base for the defensive interpretations which are so common.

When insecure, group members are particularly likely to place blame, to see others as fitting into categories of good or bad, to make moral judgments of their colleagues, and to question the value, motive, and affect loadings of the speech which they hear. Since value loadings imply a judgment of others, a belief that the standards of the speaker differ from his own causes the listener to become defensive.

Descriptive speech, in contrast to that which is evaluative, tends to arouse a minimum of uneasiness. Speech acts which the listener perceives as genuine requests for information or as material with neutral loadings is descriptive. Specifically, presentations of feelings, events, perceptions, or processes which do not ask or imply that the receiver change behavior or attitude are minimally defense producing. The difficulty in avoiding overtone is illustrated by the problems of news reporters in writing stories about unions, communists, Blacks, and religious activities without tipping off the "party" line of the newspaper. One can often tell from the opening words in a news article which side the newspaper's editorial policy favors.

Control and Problem Orientation

Speech which is used to control the listener evokes resistance. In most of our social intercourse someone is trying to do something to someone else—to change an attitude, to influence behavior, or to restrict the field of activity. The degree to which attempts to control produce defensiveness depends upon the openness of the effort, for a suspicion that hidden motives exist heightens resistance. For this reason attempts of nondirective therapists and progressive educators to refrain from imposing a set of values, a point of view, or a problem solution upon the receivers meet with many barriers. Since the norm is control, noncontrollers must earn the perceptions that their efforts have no hidden motives. A bombardment of persuasive "messages" in the fields of politics, education, special causes, advertising, religion, medicine, industrial relations, and guidance has bred cynical and paranoidal responses in listeners.

Implicit in all attempts to alter another person is the assumption by the change agent that the person to be altered is inadequate. That the speaker secretly views the listener as ignorant, unable to make his own decisions, uninformed, immature, unwise, or possessed of wrong or inadequate attitudes is a subconscious perception which gives the latter a valid base for defensive reactions.

Methods of control are many and varied. Legalistic insistence on detail, restrictive regulations and policies, conformity norms, and all laws are among the methods. Gestures, facial expressions, other forms of nonverbal communication, and even such simple acts as holding a door open in a particular manner are means of imposing one's will upon another and hence are potential sources of resistance.

Problem orientation, on the other hand, is the antithesis of persuasion. When the sender communicates a desire to collaborate in defining a mutual problem and in seeking its solution, he tends to create the same problem orientation in the listener; and, of greater importance, he implies that he has no predetermined solution, attitude, or method to impose. Such behavior is permissive in that it allows the receiver to set his own goals, make his own decisions, and evaluate his own progress—or to share with the sender in doing so. The exact methods of attaining permissiveness are not known, but they must involve a constellation of cues and they certainly go beyond mere verbal assurances that the communicator has no hidden desires to exercise control.

Strategy and Spontaneity

When the sender is perceived as engaged in a stratagem involving ambiguous and multiple motivations, the receiver becomes defensive. No one wishes to be a guinea pig, a role player, or an impressed actor, and no one likes to be the victim of some hidden motivation. That which is concealed, also, may appear larger than it really is with the degree of defensiveness of the listener determining the perceived size of the suppressed element. The intense reaction of the reading audience to the material in *Hidden Persuaders* indicates the prevalence of defensive reactions to multiple motivations behind strategy. Group members who are seen as "taking a role," as feigning emotion, as toying with their colleagues, as withholding information, or as having special sources of data are especially resented. One participant once complained that another was "using a listening technique" on him!

A large part of the adverse reaction to much of the so-called human relations training is a feeling against what are perceived as gimmicks and tricks to fool or to "involve" people, to make a person think he is making his own decision, or to make the listener feel that the sender is genuinely interested in him as a person. Particularly violent reactions occur when it appears that someone is trying to make a stratagem appear spontaneous. One person has reported a boss who incurred resentment by habitually using the gimmick of "spontaneously" looking at his watch and saying, "My gosh, look at the time—I must run to an appointment." The belief was that the boss would create less irritation by honestly asking to be excused.

Similarly, the deliberate assumption of guilelessness and natural simplicity is especially resented. Monitoring the tapes of feedback and evaluation sessions in training groups indicates the surprising extent to which members perceive the strategies of their colleagues. This perceptual clarity may be quite shocking to the strategist, who usually feels that he had cleverly hidden the motivational aura around the "gimmick."

This aversion to deceit may account for one's resistance to politicians who are suspected of behind-the-scenes planning to get his vote, to psychologists whose listening apparently is motivated by more than the manifest or content-level interest in his behavior, or to the sophisticated, smooth, or clever person whose "oneupmanship" is marked with guile. In training groups the role-flexible person frequently is resented because his changes in behavior are perceived as strategic maneuvers.

In contrast, behavior which appears to be spontaneous and free of deception is defense reductive. If the communicator is seen as having a clean id, as having uncomplicated motivations, as being straightforward and honest, and as behaving spontaneously in response to the situation, he is likely to arouse minimal defense.

Neutrality and Empathy

When neutrality in speech appears to the listener to indicate a lack of concern for his welfare, he becomes defensive. Group members usually desire to be perceived as valued persons, as individuals of special worth, and as objects of concern and affection. The clinical, detached, person-is-an-object-of-study attitude on the part of many psychologist-trainers is resented by group members. Speech with low affect that communicates little warmth or caring is in such contrast with the affect-laden speech in social situations that it sometimes communicates rejection.

Communication that conveys empathy for the feelings and respect for the worth of the listener, however, is particularly supportive and defense reductive. Reassurance results when a message indicates that the speaker identifies himself with the listener's problems, shares his feelings, and accepts his emotional reactions at face value. Abortive efforts to deny the legitimacy of the receiver's emotions by assuring the receiver that he need not feel bad, that he should not feel rejected, or that he is overly anxious, though often intended as support giving, may impress the listener as lack of acceptance. The combination of understanding and empathizing with the other person's emotions with no accompanying effort to change him apparently is supportive at a high level.

The importance of gestural behavioral cues in communicating empathy should be mentioned. Apparently spontaneous facial and bodily evidences of concern are often interpreted as especially valid evidence of deep-level acceptance.

Superiority and Equality

When a person communicates to another that he feels superior in position, power, wealth, intellectual ability, physical characteristics, or other ways, he arouses defensiveness. Here, as with the other sources of disturbance, whatever arouses feelings of inadequacy causes the listener to center upon the affect loading of the statement rather than upon the cognitive elements. The receiver then reacts by not hearing the message, by forgetting it, by competing with the sender, or by becoming jealous of him.

The person who is perceived as feeling superior communicates that he is not willing to enter into a shared problem-solving relationship, that he probably does not desire feedback, that he does not require help, and/or that he will be likely to try to reduce the power, the status, or the worth of the receiver.

Many ways exist for creating the atmosphere that the sender feels himself equal to the listener. Defenses are reduced when one perceives the sender as being willing to enter into participative planning with mutual trust and respect. Differences in talent, ability, worth, appearance, status, and power often exist, but the low defense communicator seems to attach little importance to these distinctions.

Certainty and Provisionalism

The effects of dogmatism in producing defensiveness are well known. Those who seem to know the answers, to require no additional data, and to regard themselves as teachers rather than as co-workers tend to put others on guard. Moreover, in the writer's experiment, listeners often perceived manifest expressions of certainty as connoting inward feelings of inferiority. They saw the dogmatic individual as needing to be right, as wanting to win an argument rather than solve a problem, and as seeing his ideas as truths to be defended. This kind of behavior often was associated with acts which others regarded as attempts to exercise control. People who were right seemed to have low tolerance for members who were "wrong"—i.e., who did not agree with the sender.

One reduces the defensiveness of the listener when he communicates that he is willing to experiment with his own behavior, attitudes, and ideas. The person who appears to be taking provisional attitudes, to be investigating issues rather than taking sides on them, to be problem solving rather than debating, and to be willing to experiment and explore tends to communicate that the listener may have some control over the shared quest or the investigation of the ideas. If a person is genuinely searching for information and data, he does not resent help or company along the way.

CONCLUSION

The implications of the above material for the parent, the teacher, the manager, the administrator, or the therapist are fairly obvious. Arousing defensiveness interferes with communication and thus makes it difficult—and sometimes impossible—for anyone to convey ideas clearly and to move effectively toward the solution of therapeutic, educational, or managerial problems.

REVIEW QUESTIONS

1. How does Gibb define *defensiveness?*
2. What does defensiveness defend? What does supportiveness support?
3. How can description accomplish the same purpose as evaluation?
4. Based on what you've already read about empathy in Chapter 5, how is neutrality the opposite of empathy?

PROBES

1. Does Gibb see defensiveness as a relational thing—something that's created *between* persons—or does he see it as something one person or group creates and forces on another person or group?
2. Gibb cautions us about the negative effects of evaluation. But is it possible actually to be non-evaluative? Or is that what Gibb is asking us to do?
3. Although most of Gibb's examples use verbal cues, each of the categories of defensiveness and supportiveness is also communicated nonverbally. Can you identify how you nonverbally communicate evaluation? Control? Strategy? Superiority? Spontaneity? Empathy? Equality?
4. Self-disclosing is one way to communicate spontaneity. Can you identify communication behaviors that help create the other kinds of supportive climate?
5. Which categories of defensive behavior are most present in your relationship with your lover or spouse? Your employer? Your parents? Which categories of supportive behavior characterize those relationships?

NOTES

1. J. R. Gibb, "Defense Level and Influence Potential in Small Groups," *Leadership and Interpersonal Behavior,* ed. L. Petrullo and B. M. Bass (New York: Holt, Rinehart and Winston, 1961), pp. 66–81.

2. J. R. Gibb, "Sociopsychological Processes of Group Instruction," *The Dynamics of Instructional Groups,* ed. N. B. Henry (Fifty-ninth Yearbook of the National Society of the Study of Education, Part II, 1960), pp. 115–135.

Power: The Structure of Conflict
William W. Wilmot and Joyce L. Hocker

This excerpt from the book *Interpersonal Conflict* explains how power works in conflict situations and how you can manage it. The authors have years of practical experience helping individuals and groups deal with conflict, and *Interpersonal Conflict* has been one of the most trusted conflict texts for years.

After defining power, Wilmot and Hocker explain two different orientations toward power, one that increases difficulties and another that can help resolve conflicts. The first is an "either/or" orientation to power that is common in news stories and the understandings of the person-on-the-street. In what the authors call a "distressed system," power concerns outrank concerns about rights and interests. In an effective system, by contrast, interests are primary, rights are important, and power plays a smaller role.

An effective and ethical system for exercising power is found in the second "both/and" way. This means that parties understand that everyone involved has some power and that, if the focus stays on harmony and cooperation, power relationships can be worked out. This both/and orientation is common in Japanese and Javanese cultures, it is often the first choice of women in Western cultures, and it is consistent with my discussion of "And" in Chapter 4. Another term for this orientation is "relational," and in the next section of the reading Wilmot and Hocker develop a relational theory of power.

The starting point of this theory is that power happens between people. One person does not "have" power on his or her own; he or she has power only *in relation to* other people, certain topics, particular times, certain contexts, and so on.

From this relational perspective, individuals possess various power currencies, and Wilmot and Hocker discuss four of them that spell the word RICE. *R* is for resource control, which is the power to control rewards or punishments. *I* stands for interpersonal linkages, the power to connect people to accomplish goals. A third currency is Communication skills—persuasive ability, listening skills, leadership skills, and the ability to communicate caring and warmth. All these skills generate power in various contexts. The fourth power currency is *E*xpertise—special knowledge, skills, and talents that are useful for certain tasks. As Wilmot and Hocker summarize, it helps to understand the power currencies available to you and other parties in a conflict because all can move from believing that they have no choice but to respond in a given way to understanding that everyone has some power.

Next, Wilmot and Hocker discuss how calm persistence can help lower-power people deal with powerful institutions or authorities. They offer four specific ways that lower-power people can cope with conflict situations.

The final section of the reading focuses on metacommunication (see Deborah Tannen's essay in Chapter 7). By talking explicitly about the importance and value of the relationship or by deciding in advance how the parties will handle their conflicts, power difficulties can be avoided.

Wilmot and Hocker conclude by explaining what they call the "paradox of power." To be effective, people need to take advantage of opportunities and use resources at their disposal, but within an ongoing relationship, maximizing individual power is counterproductive for everyone involved. So the paradox is that each of us needs some power, but if we have too much, communication will be difficult. Each conflict partner's goal should be to balance the power that exists between or among the parties so that power facilitates rather than prevents interpersonal communication.

MAIN IDEAS

- Power is a pervasive and often damaging element of all interpersonal relationships.
- An "either/or" view of power distorts its impact on a distressed relational system (family, couple, work group).
- A focus on rights and/or interests rather than on power can help a system become or stay balanced.
- Experiences in non–U.S. cultures reveal the benefits of a "both/and" view of power.
- Constructive conflict management requires relational (both/and) communication theory and practice (see earlier discussions of "and" and "next").
- Relational theory emphasizes that power is not simply "owned" but is given and received; it is "a product of the social relationship in which certain qualities become important and valuable to others."
- Four individual power currencies contribute to relational power: resource control, interpersonal linkages, communication skills, and expertise (RICE).
- Lower-power people in a conflict often can gain more equal power by calmly persisting in their requests.
- Four specific communication moves can help low-power people: speaking up with strengths and weaknesses; making beliefs, values, and priorities clear; staying emotionally connected; and stating differences while allowing others to do the same.
- Higher-power people can also help empower lower-power people.
- Metacommunication can also help balance power by transcending the win/lose structure.

WHAT IS POWER?

In interpersonal and all other conflicts, perceptions of power are at the heart of any analysis. Hundreds of definitions of power tend to fall into three camps. Power is seen as (1) *distributive* (either/or), (2) *integrative* (both/and), or (3) *designated* (power to a certain relationship). *Distributive* definitions of power stress that "with force, control, pressure or aggression, one individual is able to carry his or her objective over the resistance of another and thus gain power" (Dahl 1957, 3). Distributive approaches focus on power over or power against the other party.

Integrative definitions of power highlight power *with* the other. Integrative views stress "joining forces with someone else to achieve mutually acceptable goals" (Lilly 1989, 281). Integrative definitions focus on "both/and"—both parties have to achieve something in the relationship. As we shall see, it is not what outsiders say about power, but the views the conflict parties have that determine the outcomes of their conflicts.

Designated power "gives" power to a certain relationship, rather than power being held by individuals or even teams. In designated power, people confer power on a marriage, a work group, a family, or a group of friends with whom one is in relationship....

ORIENTATIONS TO POWER

When a dispute occurs between two people, they often talk about power, and their perspectives on how it operates will predispose them to engage in certain communicative moves. People feel passionately about power—who has it, who ought to have more or less, how people misuse power, and how justified they feel in trying to gain more power for themselves. This orientation toward power seems to be true for many reasons.

We each need enough power to live the life we want. We want to influence events that matter to us. We want to have our voices heard, and make a difference. We want to protect ourselves against perceived harm. We want to hold in high esteem ourselves and those we care about. We do not want to be victimized, misused, or demeaned. No one can escape feeling the effects of power—whether we have too much or too little, or someone else has too much or too little.

When people struggle with each other, they almost never agree on anything having to do with power. For example, if you are a student intern in a real estate firm and you feel that brokers have all the power, you are likely to keep silent even when you disagree—giving the impression that you agree when you don't. If, on the other hand, you feel that both you and the brokers have sources of power, you will be more likely to engage in discussion to work through issues. As an intern, you may have sources of power such as a different set of acquaintances, free time on weekends when the brokers are involved with their families but need to work, or a fresh outlook and a desire to learn. If you think of yourself, however, as "just a lowly intern," you may miss many opportunities to be a team member because you have assessed your power incorrectly....

Either/Or Power

When you examine typical newspaper stories about power, you read about the either/or (distributive) notions of power. In fact, it is difficult to even find examples of any other orientation toward power in the popular press. Many people think that power is only "force"—pushing others around against their will. When you examine nations using military might against other nations, you see either/or power in operation.

Once a relationship begins to go downhill, concerns with power increase. As any relationship deteriorates, the parties shift to a more overt focus on power—and this shift is reflected in their discourse (Beck, 1988). In fact, a characteristic of destructive power is that parties start thinking and talking about power. Almost no one thinks that he or she has more power than the other power, at least when emotions run very high. We think the other has more power, which then justifies dirty tricks and our own attempt to gain more power. We often see ourselves as blameless victims of the other's abuse of power. When partners are caught in this destructive cycle of either/or power, their communicative interactions show a lot of "one up" responses, or attempts to demonstrate conversational power over each other (Sabourin & Stamp, 1995). Partners might say, "She is just trying to control me," or "I'm not going to let him push me around." People, whether married couples or work colleagues, try to "keep score"—watching the "points" they have vis-à-vis the other party (Ross & Holmberg, 1992). When partners develop an overt concern with power, their struggles over power are directly related to relationship satisfaction (Kurdek, 1994). Figure 1 demonstrates how concerns rank in a distressed relationship.

As Ury, Brett, and Goldberg (1988) so aptly note, the focus for a dispute becomes power—who has the right to move the other. The teenager who says, "You can't boss me around," the spouse who shouts, "Just who do you think you are?" and the co-worker who states, "Well, we'll see who the boss is around here!" are all highlighting power and giving it center stage in the dispute. These struggles often escalate. Dissatisfied couples are more than three times as likely to escalate episodes and focus on power than satisfied couples (Alberts & Driscoll, 1992).... We are not suggesting that power shouldn't be an issue. Rather, we suggest that when power itself becomes the main focus of thinking and discussion, parties are likely to be involved in an escalating power struggle, and may well have temporarily lost sight of interests and solutions.

Notice in Figure 1 that disputes also involve "rights" and "interests." Rights, similar to our idea of core concerns, include not being discriminated against,

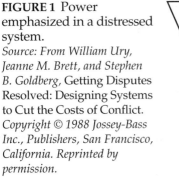

FIGURE 1 Power emphasized in a distressed system.
Source: From William Ury, Jeanne M. Brett, and Stephen B. Goldberg, Getting Disputes Resolved: Designing Systems to Cut the Costs of Conflict. *Copyright © 1988 Jossey-Bass Inc., Publishers, San Francisco, California. Reprinted by permission.*

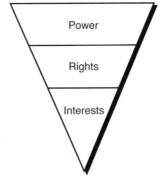

being free from physical harm, and other constitutional and legal guarantees we have as citizens. Sometimes it is more appropriate that disputes get settled on the basis of rights rather than power or interests. For example, if the famous *Brown* v. *Board of Education* case in 1954 outlawing segregation in public schools had been settled on the basis of power, it would have resulted in a struggle in the streets. If, on the other hand, it had been settled on the basis of interests, Brown might have negotiated her way into school, but the country's social policy would not have changed. When we solve a dispute based on interests, the goals and desires of the parties are the key elements. For instance, if you don't want your teenage son to use the car, you can (1) tell him it is not OK as long as you pay the bills in the house (power); (2) let him know that you own the car and have all the rights to its use (rights); or (3) let him know that you are dissatisfied with how he drives, and until you are convinced he will be safe, you will not lend the car (interests). Thus, disputes can occur on any one of the three levels. When power becomes the only personal goal, the dispute is harder to resolve.

Figure 2 illustrates an effective system in which the emphasis is on interests with rights and power playing smaller but still important roles. As you can see by comparing Figure 1 with Figure 2, an overemphasis on power is symptomatic of a distressed system.

Both/And Power

Two alternatives to viewing disputes as power struggles can help us out of the distributive power dilemma. Boulding (1989) notes that "the great fallacy, especially of political thinking in regard to power, is to elevate threat power to the position of dominance" (10). Interpersonal relationships reflect the same fallacy—many people just can't envision power in terms other than "either/or," or "win/lose." Yet a study of the dynamics of successful disputes and ongoing relationships reveals that power functions on a broader basis than either/or thinking. Disputes become power struggles if the parties allow them to be defined as such. If we think of power "merely in terms of threat, we will get nowhere" (250). Conceptually, the alternative to framing disputes as power struggles is to place power in a position subordinate to rights and needs.

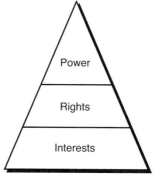

FIGURE 2 Power deemphasized in an effective system.
Source: From William Ury, Jeanne M. Brett, and Stephen B. Goldberg, Getting Disputes Resolved: Designing Systems to Cut the Costs of Conflict. *Copyright © 1988 Jossey-Bass Inc., Publishers, San Francisco, California. Reprinted by permission.*

To help us understand the cultural basis of our assumptions, Augsburger (1992) details the lack of verbal fighting in some other cultures. In these cultures, power is activated as both/and or designated power, discussed in the next section. In Japanese and Javanese cultures, for instance, to name two obvious examples, harmony and cooperation are basic values, and verbal contradiction is not the automatic first choice in conflict. A more accepted process is to affirm the strengths of each other's position, let them stand without attack, and then join in exploring other options. Both parties search for superior options (59).

Both/and power is often the first choice of women in our culture. Researchers at the Stone Center at Wellesley have spent two decades explicating "relational theory" in an attempt to balance the traditional male orientation that permeates U.S. culture. In their view, relational theory is a belief system that describes how growth and effectiveness occur (Fletcher, 1999). Masculine theories, which until the last 20 years or so have been accepted as the only psychologically sound theories, often assumed that maturity and competence depend on autonomy, or separation from constraints, other people, and group identity. Boys, for instance, learn to relate to power through games and competition more than girls do. Boys learn to be comfortable with the hierarchy of teams, captains, coaches, and bosses. Girls learn to play with less focus on hierarchy. Many girls' games are cooperative in nature, with girls taking roles to play out, after discussing together what to do. As Heim and Galant (1993) notes, "There's no boss in dolls." For boys, conflict means competition, which often enhances relationships. For girls, competition is often painful and damages relationships. Girls often prefer to look for a win/win situation (Heim & Galant, 1993, 27).

Relational theory and practice offer the idea that maturity and competence depend on growth-in-connection and mutuality. The ability to develop relationally depends on mutual empathy, mutual empowerment, responsibility to both oneself and others, and the ability to experience and express emotion, to experience and learn from vulnerability, to participate in the development of another, and to enhance each other's efforts (Fletcher, 1999; Jordan et al., 1991). This approach does not need to be seen strictly as a female approach. Many effective forms of conflict resolution depend on a relational approach. Some situations in which power is heavily unbalanced also require a level of competition and assertiveness that does not come naturally for many women. If competition remains the dominant approach, however, constructive conflict resolution is unlikely to occur, except temporarily....

A RELATIONAL THEORY OF POWER

A common perception is that power is an attribute of a person. If you say, "Lynn is a powerful person," you may, if she is your friend, be referring to such attributes as verbal facility, intelligence, compassion, warmth, and understanding. Or you may refer to a politician as powerful, alluding to her ability to make deals, call in favors, remember names and faces, and understand complex economic issues. In interpersonal relationships, however, excluding situations of unequal physical power and use of violence, power is a property of the social relationship rather than a quality of the individual. Lynn, for instance, has power with her friends because she has qualities they value. When she suggests something to do, like going on an annual women's backpacking trip, her friends try to clear their calendars because they like her, have fun with her, and feel understood by her. Lynn has a way of making a group feel cohesive and at ease. But if an acquaintance hated backpacking, did not like some of the other people going on the trip, and was irritated at Lynn because of a misunderstanding that had not yet been cleared up, Lynn's power with the irritated acquaintance would lessen considerably.

Similarly, if a politician did not show any interest in a bill that a human rights group was trying to get on the table in their state legislature and, furthermore, if the politician were a congresswoman representing another state, the congresswoman would have little power with the human rights group. Would she still be "a powerful person"? She would be to her constituents but not to the interest group in question.

Power is not owned by an individual but is a product of the social relationship in which certain qualities become important and valuable to others (King, 1987; Rogers, 1974; Harsanyi, 1962a; Deutsch, 1958; Dahl, 1957; Soloman, 1960). Deutsch (1973) states the case well: "Power is a relational concept; it does not reside in the individual but rather in the relationship of the person to his environment. Thus, the power of an agent in a given situation is determined by the characteristics of the situation" (15). Rather than residing in people, "power is always interpersonal" (May, 1972, 23). In the strictest sense, except when violence and physical coercion are used, power is given from one party to another in a conflict. Power can be taken away when the situation changes. Power dynamics are fluid, changing, and dependent on the specific situation. Each person in a conflict has some degree of power, though one party may have more compared to the other, and the power can shift during a conflict....

INDIVIDUAL POWER CURRENCIES

You may have had the experience of traveling in a foreign country and trying to adapt to the use of different currencies. Drachmas, used in Greece, are worthless in India, where rupees are used to buy items of value. A pocketful of rupees is worthless in France unless you exchange it for the local currency. Just as money depends on the context in which it is to be spent (the country), your power currencies depend on how much your particular resources are valued by the other persons in your relationships (Rodman, 1967, 1972). You may have a vast amount of expertise in the rules of basketball, but if your fraternity needs an intramural football coach, you will not be valued as much as you would be if they needed a basketball coach.

Power depends on having currencies that other people need. In the same manner, if other people possess currencies you value, such as the ability to edit a term paper or the possession of a car, they potentially maintain some degree of power over you in your relationships with them. Conflict is often confusing because people try to spend currency that is not valued in a particular relationship....

R

Resource control: Often comes with one's formal position in an organization or group. An example is the controlling of rewards or punishments such as salary, number of hours worked, or firing. Parents control resources such as money, freedom, cars, and privacy for teenagers.

I

Interpersonal linkages: Your position in the larger system, such as being central to communication exchange. If you are a liaison person between two factions, serve as a bridge between two groups that would otherwise not have information about each other, or have a network of friends who like each other, you have linkage currencies.

C

Communication skills: Conversational skills, persuasive ability, listening skills, group leadership skills, the ability to communicate caring and warmth, and the ability to form close bonds with others all contribute to interpersonal power. All people need to be related to others, to matter to others, and to be understood by others. Those who communicate well gain value and thus interpersonal power.

E

Expertise: Special knowledge, skills, and talents that are useful for the task at hand. Being an expert in a content area such as budget analysis, a process area such as decision-making methods, or a relational area such as decoding nonverbal cues may give you power when others need your expertise.

Resource control often results from attaining a formal position that brings resources to you. The president of the United States, regardless of personal qualities, will always have some resources that go along with the job. Leadership and position, by their very nature, place a person in a situation in which others are dependent upon him or her, thus bringing ready-made power. Whatever your position—secretary, boss, chairperson, teacher, manager, or volunteer—you will be in a position to control resources that others desire. Many resources are economic in nature, such as money, gifts, and material possessions (Warner, Lee,

& Lee, 1986). Many people try to be close and supportive to those around them by buying gifts. They trade on economic currencies in order to obtain intimacy currencies from others. Their gifts are not always valued enough to bring them what they want, however. Not surprisingly, people who give gifts to each other often try to work out an agreement, probably implicitly, about the amount of money that can be spent to keep the dependence (and power) equal. If an inordinate amount of money is spent by one person, then typically the other person feels overly indebted. As Blau (1964) writes, "A person who gives others valuable gifts or renders them important services makes a claim for superior status by obligating them to himself" (108). People with little money usually have limited access to these forms of power. College graduates who cannot find jobs must remain financially dependent on parents, thus limiting independence on both sides. Elderly people whose savings shrink due to inflation lose power; mothers with children and no means of support lose most of their choices about independence, thus losing most of their potential power. Economic currencies are not the only important type of power currency, but they operate in small, personal conflicts as well as in larger social conflicts.

Another cluster of power currencies comes from one's *interpersonal linkages*, a set of currencies that depend on your interpersonal contacts and network of friends and supporters. People often obtain power based on whom they know and with whom they associate. For instance, if you have a good friend who has a mountain cabin you can share with others, then you have attained some power (if your family or friends want to go to the cabin) because of your ability to obtain things through other people. Young children try to trade on their linkage currencies when they say such things as "My Uncle Ben is a park ranger, and he will give us a tour of the park."

Interpersonal linkages help one attain power through coalition formation. Whenever you band together with another (such as a good friend) to gain some sense of strength, this coalition can be a form of power (Van de Vliert, 1981). The small boy who says, "You better not hit me, because if you do, my big sister will beat you up" understands the potential value of coalitions.... Interpersonal linkages are a source of power when people check out their network for what classes to take, where jobs might be available, where rentals might be found, and other kinds of information. "Who you know" is often a source of power.

One's *communication skills* also serve as potential power currencies. If you can lead a group in a decision-making process, speak persuasively, write a news release for your organization, serve as an informal mediator between people who are angry with each other, or use tact in asking for what you want, you will gain power because of your communication skills. Many times, students who have developed their communication skills are employed upon graduation because of their skills. Employers are willing to teach technical and specialized skills later. Conversationally, your skills make a considerable difference, too. As Millar and Rogers (1988) demonstrated, when others allow us to dominate the conversation we have attained a source of power. Likewise, if you can facilitate the social process of a group, serve as the fun-loving joker in the family, or get conversations started at work, others typically will value you. It is not only the qualities, per se, that bring power but that these currencies are valued by others.

Communication skills also include the ability to form bonds with others through love, sex, caring, nurturing, understanding, empathic listening, warmth, attention, and other characteristics of intimate relationships. If a father provides genuine warmth and understanding to his teenage daughter who is going through a tough time at school, his support is a currency for him in their father-daughter relationship....

Expertise currencies are involved when a person has some special skill or knowledge that someone else values. The worker who is the only one who can operate the boiler at a large lumber mill has power because the expertise is badly needed. The medical doctor who specializes in a particular area has expertise power because her information and skills are needed by others. Almost all professions develop specialized expertise valued by others, which serves as a basis of power for people in the profession. Family members develop expertise in certain areas that others within the family come to depend on, such as cooking, repairing the car, or babysitting.

We limit our own power by developing some currencies at the expense of others. For example, women have traditionally been most comfortable using power to bond with others (Miller, 1991), providing more warmth and affection than men do (Johnson, 1976). If this particular communication skill is developed at the expense of the ability to clarify a group discussion, a woman unnecessarily limits her power potential. The person who trades on currencies of interpersonal linkages, such as access to the boss, may neglect the development of expertise. The person who gains power by controlling resources, such as money or sex, may neglect the development of communication skills, resulting in a relationship based on coercive instead of shared power; withdrawing warmth in intimate relationships too often substitutes for good communication skills. A worker who focuses on the development of expertise in computer programming and systems analysis may ignore the power that can be developed through interpersonal linkages, thus furthering a tendency toward isolation in the organization. The most effective conflict participant develops several forms of power currencies and knows when to activate the different forms of power. A repertoire of currencies is a better base for sharing power than exclusive reliance on one form of power, which too often leads to misuse of that power.

Clarifying the currencies available to you and the other parties in a conflict helps in the conflict analysis. People are often unaware of their own sources of productive power, just as they do not understand their own dependence on others. Desperation and low-power tactics often arise from the feeling that one has no choice, that no power is available. Analyze your power currencies when you find yourself saying, "I have no choice." Usually, you are overlooking potential sources of power....

The Power of Calm Persistence

Lower-power people in a conflict often can gain more equal power by persisting in their requests. Substantive change, when power is unequal, seldom comes about through intense, angry confrontation. Rather, change results from careful thinking and from planning for small, manageable moves based on a solid understanding of the problem (Lerner, 1989, 15). When intensity is high, people react rather than observe and think. We overfocus on the other instead of an analysis of the problem, and we move toward polarization. Lower-power parties cannot afford to blow up. One source of power the lower-power person has, however, is careful, calm analysis that directs attention to the problem. If lower-power people have patience and avoid giving up out of frustration, they gain "nuisance value," and the higher-power person or group often listens and collaborates just to get them to go away. Persuasive skills become crucial. The low-power person must analyze the rhetorical situation well, taking into account what will be judged appropriate, effective, credible, and practical....

Some suggestions for dealing with large, impersonal institutions are as follows:

- Identify the individuals on the phone by name and ask for them when you call back.
- Stay pleasant and calm. State clearly what you want, and ask for help in solving the problem.
- Follow the rules even if you think they are ridiculous. If they want five copies of a form, typed and folded a certain way, give it to them. Then point out that you have followed the rules and expect results.
- Write simple, clear memos summarizing what you want, what you have done, and when you expect a response.
- Tell them all the steps you took to try to get a response from them.
- Avoid taking out your frustration on low-power individuals in the organization. They may respond with "I'm just following the rules," avoiding personal responsibility—and who could blame them? Instead, be courteous and ask for help. Humor always helps if it is not at someone else's expense....

Rather than remaining in self-defeating spirals, Lerner (1989, 35) suggests that people in low-power positions adopt the following moves:

- *Speak up and present a balanced picture of strengths as well as weaknesses.* One might say, "It's true that I am afraid to ask my boss for a raise, even though you want me to. But I earn a steady paycheck and budget and plan well for our family. I want some credit for what I do already contribute."
- *Make clear what one's beliefs, values, and priorities are, and then keep one's behavior congruent with these.* An entry-level accountant in a large firm was asked by the comptroller to falsify taxable deductions, hiding some of the benefits given to employees. The accountant, just out of school and a single parent, said, "When you hired me I said I was committed to doing good work and

being an honest accountant. What you are asking me to do is against the code of ethics and could result in my losing my license. I can't afford to take that risk. I'm sure you'll understand my position."

- *Stay emotionally connected to significant others even when things get intense.* It takes courage for a low-power person to let another person affect him or her. One teenage son was furious and hurt when his father decided to remarry, since the son did not like the wife-to-be at all and felt disloyal to his mother. After some tough thinking, he decided to tell his father honestly how he felt, what he did not like, and what he feared about the new marriage instead of taking another way out, such as angrily leaving his father's house to live with his mother in another state. This conversation balanced the power between father and son in an entirely new way.

- *State differences, and allow others to do the same.* The easiest, but often not the best, way for a low-power person to manage conflict is to avoid engagement. Again, courage is required to bring up differences when a power imbalance is in place. Brad, a college freshman, worked at a fast-food place during school. He was unhappy because the manager kept hiring unqualified people (without checking their references) and then expected Brad to train them and provide supervision, even though Brad was barely making more than minimum wage. Finally Brad told the manager, "I have a different way of looking at whom you should hire. I try to do a good job for you, but I have to try to work with people who have no experience and maybe don't have the personality to pitch in and work hard as part of the team. Would you consider letting me sit in on interviews and look over applications?" The manager was pleased with Brad's initiative and said yes.

Empowerment of Low-Power People by High-Power People

Sometimes it is clearly to the advantage of higher-power groups or individuals to purposely enhance the power of lower-power groups or individuals. Without this restructuring of power, working or intimate relationships may end or rigidify into bitter, silent, passive aggressive, and unsatisfactory entanglements. Currencies valued by higher-power people can be developed by lower-power people if they are allowed more training, more decision-making power, or more freedom. For instance, in one social service agency, Sharon was not doing well at directing a grant-funded program on finding housing for homeless people. Jan, the director of the agency, realized that Sharon was a good fund-raiser but not a good program director. By switching Sharon's job description, the agency gained a good employee instead of continuing a series of negative job evaluations that would have resulted in Sharon's eventual termination....

Metacommunication

Another way to balance power is to transcend the win/lose structure by jointly working to preserve the relationship during conflict. By metacommunicating during or before conflicts (talking about the relationship or about how the parties will handle their conflicts), the parties can agree about behaviors that will not be allowed (such as leaving during a fight).

Metacommunication focuses the parties on the process of their communication with each other. They talk about their communication, and if that fails, they can agree to bring in outside mediators or counselors. They can agree that whenever a serious imbalance occurs, the high-power party will work actively with the low-power party to alter the balance in a meaningful way. Usually romantic partners, friends, family members, and work partners can accomplish such joint moves if they agree that the maximization of individual power, left unrestrained, will destroy the relationship. They see that individual power is based relationally, that dependence begets power, and that successful relationships necessitate a balancing of dependencies and therefore of power. The lack of a balanced arrangement is a signal to reinvest in the relationship rather than a clue that the relationship is over. The person temporarily weaker in the relationship can draw on the relationship currencies, as if the relationship were a bank and the currencies were savings. The weaker party can claim extra time, space, money, training, empathy, or other special considerations until the power is brought back into an approximation of balance. . . .

Most of us are caught in a paradox of power. To be effective people, we need to maximize our abilities, take advantage of opportunities, and use resources at our disposal so we can lead the kind of lives we desire. Yet within the confines of an ongoing relationship, *maximization of individual power is counterproductive* for both the higher-power and lower-power parties. The unrestrained maximization of individual power leads to damaged relations, destructive moves, more destructive countermoves, and the eventual ending of the relationship. Since people are going to take steps to balance power—destructively if no other means are available—we can better manage conflict by working to balance power in productive and creative ways. Equity in power reduces violence and enables all participants to continue working for the good of all parties, even in conflict.

REVIEW QUESTIONS

1. Distinguish among *distributive, integrative,* and *designated* power. Give an example of each.
2. If people are talking about how little power they have in a conflict, this can be a sign that the system they're in is what Wilmot and Hocker call "distressed." Explain.

3. How are the comments about "both/and" power related to discussions of "and" and "next" in Chapters 2 and 3?
4. "Power is not owned by an individual but is a product of the social relationship in which certain qualities become important and valuable to others." Explain.
5. Define resource control, interpersonal linkages, communication skills, and expertise as aspects of a person's power.
6. Paraphrase Wilmot and Hocker's advice to the low-power person in a conflict.
7. Define *metacommunication*.
8. Explain the "paradox of power."

PROBES

1. Wilmot and Hocker's idea of both/and power sounds good, but it may be naïve. If you are in a conflict with someone who sees power only as either/or, how can you change his or her orientation?
2. Recall a specific conflict that you have experienced in the past few weeks. Analyze your power in this conflict in R-I-C-E terms. What resource control did you have? What interpersonal linkages were important? What communication skills gave you power in this situation? What expertise did you have? How are the outcomes of that event related to the power that you had?
3. Give an example of how metacommunication can help balance power in an interpersonal conflict.

REFERENCES

Alberts, J., & Driscoll, G. (1992). Containment versus escalation: The trajectory of couples' conversational complaints. *Western Journal of Communication, 56,* 394–412.

Augsburger, D. W. (1992). *Conflict mediation across cultures: Pathways and patterns.* Louisville, KY: Westminster/John Knox Press.

Beck, A. T. (1988). *Love is never enough.* New York: Harper & Row.

Blau, P. M. (1964). *Exchange and power in social life.* New York: John Wiley & Sons.

Boulding, K. (1989). *Three faces of power.* Newbury Park, CA: Sage Publications.

Dahl, R. A. (1957). The concept of power. *Behavioral Science, 2,* 201–215.

Deutsch, M. (1949). A theory of competition and cooperation. *Human Relations, 2,* 129–151.

Deutsch, M. (1958). Trust and suspicion. *Journal of Conflict Resolution, 2,* 265–279.

Deutsch, M. (1973). Conflicts: Productive and destructive. In F. E. Jandt (Ed.), *Conflict resolution through communication.* New York: Harper & Row.

Fletcher, J. (1999). *Disappearing acts: Gender, power, and relational practice at work.* Cambridge: MIT Press.

Heim, P., & Galant, S. K. (1993). *Smashing the glass ceiling: Tactics for women who want to win in business.* New York: Simon & Schuster.

Johnson, P. (1976). Women and power: Toward a theory of effectiveness. *Journal of Social Issues, 32,* 99–110.

Jordan, J., Kaplan, S., Miller, J., Stiver, I., & Surrey, J. (1991). *Women's growth in connection.* New York: Guilford Press.

King, A. (1987). *Power and communication.* Prospect Heights, IL.: Waveland Press.

Kurdek, L. A. (1994). Areas of conflict for gay, lesbian, and heterosexual couples: What couples argue about influences relationship satisfaction. *Journal of Marriage and the Family, 56,* 923–935.

Lerner, H. G. (1989). *The dance of intimacy.* New York: Harper & Row.

Lilly, E. R. (1989). The determinants of organizational power styles. *Educational Review, 41,* 281–293.

May, R. (1972). *Power and innocence: A search for the sources of violence.* New York: Dell Publishing.

Millar, F. E., & Rogers, L. E. (1987). Relational dimensions of interpersonal dynamics. In M. D. Roloff & Miller, G. R. (Eds.), *Interpersonal processes: New directions in communication research* (Vol. 14, pp. 117–139). *Sage Annual Reviews of Communication Research.* Newbury Park, CA: Sage Publications.

Millar, F. E., & Rogers, L. E. (1988). Power dynamics in marital relationships. In O. Noller & Fitzpatrick M. A. (Eds.). *Perspectives on marital interaction,* (pp. 78–97). Clevedon, UK: Multilingual Matters.

Miller, J. B. (1986). What do we mean by relationships? In *Work in progress.* Stone Center Working Paper Series, no. 22. Wellesley, MA: Stone Center, Wellesley College.

Miller, J. B. (1991). Women's and men's scripts for interpersonal conflict. *Psychology of Women Quarterly, 15,* 15–29.

Rodman, H. (1967). Marital power in France, Greece, Yugoslavia, and the United States: A cross-national discussion. *Journal of Marriage and the Family, 29,* 320–325.

Rodman, H. (1972). Marital power and the theory of resources in cultural context. *Journal of Comparative Family Studies, 3,* 50–69.

Rogers, M. F. (1974). Instrumental and infra-resources: The bases of power. *American Journal of Sociology, 79,* 1418–1433.

Ross, M., & Holmberg, D. (1992). Are wives' memories for events in relationships more vivid than their husbands' memories? *Journal of Social and Personal Relationships, 9,* 585–604.

Sabourin, T. C., & Stamp, G. H. (1995). Communication and the experience of dialectical tensions in family life: An examination of abusive and nonabusive families. *Communication Monographs, 62,* 213–242.

Soloman, L. (1960). The influence of some types of power relationships and game strategies upon the development of interpersonal trust. *Journal of Abnormal and Social Psychology, 61,* 223–230.

Ury, W., J. Brett, & Goldberg, S. (1988). *Getting disputes resolved.* San Francisco, CA: Jossey-Bass.

Van de Vliert, E. (1981). Siding and other reactions to a conflict. *Journal of Conflict Resolution, 25(3)*, 495–520.

Warner, R. L., Lee, G. R. & Lee, J. (1986). Social organization, spousal resources, and marital power: A cross-cultural study. *Journal of Marriage and the Family, 48*, 121–128.

Verbal Aggression Interventions: What Should Be Done?

Charles J. Wigley III

Verbal aggression is communication that attacks another person's self-concept. As the readings in Chapter 4 point out, this behavior should be called *communicative* aggression, not "verbal" aggression, because it necessarily involves both verbal and nonverbal elements. This idea is assumed in this article, even though it isn't highlighted.

Since this article originally appeared in a scholarly journal, it is filled with references to previous research. I hope you can read around the references to get the important ideas that are explained here.

The author's first point is that aggression is different from "argumentativeness." The former is constructive and the latter is highly destructive. For one thing, whereas communication that attacks people's self-concept may not always lead to physical violence, its presence may be essential to physical violence. On the other hand, the willingness and ability to argue, to present a case to support an opinion—even a strong one—is helpful in many relationships. And the key link between the two is that training in arguing can help reduce verbal aggression because "it offers a behavioral substitute" that relies "on critical thinking rather than emotional initiative or response."

Wigley reviews some literature that indicates that one of the most important causes of communicative aggression is lack of argumentation skills. It follows that people who *have* argumentative skills will be less likely to engage in communicative aggression, because they have other options available to them. The best way to teach these skills is via a training program that involves "the dense practice of argument" as a set of *dialogic* skills. "Dialogic" here means that these skills have to be learned and applied in partnership with other communicators—what Chapter 2 of *Bridges Not Walls* calls "co-laboratively."

The article outlines a five-part model of effective arguing that consists of (1) stating the controversy in propositional form, (2) analyzing the proposition and inventing arguments, (3) advocating and defending one's own position, (4) attacking the position of others, and (5) managing interpersonal relations during the argument. The main skills involved in (5), which is the focus of *Bridges Not Walls,* is (a) being able to disagree with another person while confirming his or her personal competence, and (b) engaging in paraphrasing and other similar communication behaviors.

The last section of this reading reviews the benefits that might flow from efforts to teach argument skills in order to reduce communicative aggression. Education in group settings works best, because of the need to practice the new skills in a "dialogic" situation. And these principles can and should be taught especially in populations known to engage in aggression, such as prisoners, business executives, and laborers.

MAIN IDEAS

- Verbal or communicative aggression is communication that attacks another person's self-concept.
- Argumentativeness is the ability to engage effectively in argument.
- Argumentativeness is often very constructive whereas verbal aggressiveness is destructive.
- One significant cause of communicative aggression is lack of skill in arguing.
- One way communicative aggression can be reduced is to teach people how to argue effectively.
- Effective argument consists of five key skills: stating the controversy, analysis and invention of arguments, advocating and defending one's own position, attacking the other position, and managing interpersonal relations during an argument.
- The fifth skill can be most difficult and consists mainly of being able to disagree while confirming the other's personal competence and being able to engage in perspective-taking behaviors.
- More instruction in making arguments could significantly reduce the occurrence of communicative aggression.

Verbal aggressiveness refers to a personality characteristic involving one's tendency to attack the self-concept of others (see Infante & Rancer, 1982; Infante & Wigley, 1986), whereas verbal aggression is not a personality characteristic but, rather, the behavior of engaging in aggression (Infante, 1995). Just as persons might not laugh at a joke that they think is funny, others might restrain themselves from aggressive communication behavior, even when they really feel like "lashing out!" Thus, verbal aggressiveness is a tendency (i.e., a trait), whereas verbal aggression is a manifestation of that tendency (i.e., a behavior). The focus here is on reducing verbal aggression (i.e., the behavior), even when the communicative exchange involves participants with high levels of the trait of verbal aggressiveness. Parallel to this conceptual structure is the distinction between argumentativeness (which is a trait) and arguing (which is the behavior of speaking arguments). . . .

Comprehensive reviews of studies of argumentativeness and verbal aggressiveness (Infante, 1987 [both variables]; Infante & Rancer, 1996 [both variables]:

"Verbal Aggression Interventions: What Can Be Done?" by Charles J. Wigley III from *Communication Monographs,* Vol. 75, No. 4 (December 2008), pp. 339–350. Reprinted with permission of *Communication Monographs.*

Rancer, 1998 [argumentativeness]; Rancer & Avtgis, 2006 [both variables]; Wigley, 1998 [verbal aggressiveness]) resound with a central message, to use the words of Infante and Rancer (1996, p. 327), "Argumentativeness is constructive, whereas verbal aggressiveness is destructive." Research across multiple contexts indicates the highly destructive nature of verbal aggression (see Rancer & Avtgis, 2006). Consider one of those contexts: research in marital settings reveals that violent marriages have more incidents of verbal aggression than nonviolent marriages (Infante, Chandler, & Rudd, 1989; Sabourin, Infante, & Rudd, 1993) and that people in violent marriages perceive higher levels of verbal aggression than couples in nonviolent marriages (Infante et al., 1990). It can be argued that verbal aggression is a precursor of violence (see Roloff, 1996, for an explanation of catalyst hypothesis; see also, Burman, John, & Margolin, 1992) and that, even if verbal aggression does not cause physical violence, its presence may be essential to physical violence (an interesting literature review considering issues of jealousy, battery, self-defense, and violent criminals may be found in Wilkinson and Hamerschlag, 2004). As Rancer and Avtgis explain (2006, p. 96), "relationships in which verbal aggression is present will not necessarily lead to physically aggressive behavior; however, where physical aggression is present in marital relationships, verbal aggression is almost always present." Conversely, there is little evidence suggesting that arguing, itself, is bad and at least some studies have found that high levels of argument between spouses does not necessarily lead to relationship deterioration (Fitzpatrick, 1988; Gottman, 1994). . . .

Society's problem of "verbal aggressiveness" is in its behavioral manifestation (i. e., verbal aggression). Even if the personality characteristic (described by Infante & Wigley, 1986) is an individual difference that is inherited (Beatty & McCroskey, 1997; see Horvath, 1995), it is expression of that tendency as actual verbal aggression that creates the problem. Verbal aggression might be harmful to the target of aggression (e.g., hurt feelings), to the aggressor (e.g., feelings of guilt), to the observer of aggression (e.g., learning more violent methods), and to the relationships among the parties involved (e.g., diminished levels of mutual attraction). Unlike verbal aggressiveness, which might be an inherited individual difference, verbal aggression (an act of speaking or sending) is the result of volition (Infante, 1995). Accordingly, efforts to make alternatives to verbal aggression attractive to a speaker might result in less verbal aggression.

The role communication scholars might play in reducing verbal aggression is endorsed by Infante (1995, p. 51), "An appropriate and convenient place to begin this undertaking [of trying to control verbal aggression] is in the communication classroom where, once developed and refined, progress can be adapted and expanded to other areas of society." One approach to controlling verbal aggression is training in arguing. The idea is that training in arguing will aid in reducing verbal aggression because it offers a behavioral substitute of rhetoric relying on critical thinking rather than emotional initiative or response. The next section offers research suggesting a causal link between communication training and enhanced critical thinking (and, thereby, arguably, a reduction in verbal aggression).

WHAT POTENTIAL CAUSES EXIST FOR
THIS PROBLEM?

Could an argumentative skill deficiency be a leading cause of verbal aggression (see Infante et al., 1984)? For some time, it has been thought that enhancing one's critical thinking skills would lead to other positive effects, especially on individuals' communication traits, and it has long been thought that individuals' levels of verbal aggression would decrease as the result of training in argumentation. Why? Although there may be a genetic basis for verbal aggressiveness (Beatty & McCroskey, 1997), it has long been believed that there are four nongenetic possible causes for aggression: (1) argumentative skill deficiency [hereafter ASD], (2) psychopathological basis, (3) disdain toward target of aggression, and (4) social learning (Infante et al., 1984). Other causes may exist, such as chemical influences (e.g., medicines or alcohol; Wigley, 2006), but the five causes indicated, including genetics, seem most likely....

A number of investigators have put forth the proposition that skills training in arguing will provide the arguer with a superior path to verbal victory in contrast with using verbal aggression. It is also possible, however, that an aggressive individual will simply add arguing skills to his or her arsenal of verbal weapons. Contrary to the belief that improved arguing skills might lead to less verbal aggression, it might be the case that improving arguing skills has no direct affect on verbal aggression, or, perhaps, it results in more aggression because the individual's confidence in dealing with confrontation has been enhanced by the skills training. Does argumentative skill training enhance critical thinking and reduce the amount of verbal aggression (i. e., an irrational behavior)?

Allen, Berkowitz, Hunt, and Loudon (1999) completed a meta-analysis of the role of skills training classes in communication (including argumentation, debate, discussion, public speaking) and competitive forensics (including debate, discussion and individual events) on critical thinking. They alluded to Garside's (1996) definition of critical thinking, i.e., thinking that is "clear, precise, accurate, relevant, logical, consistent" and that, as well, looks for sufficient evidence to warrant a claim, that monitors the state of "existing information" to assess strengths and weaknesses, and that is unbiased....

The empirical evidence provides strong support for the conclusion that communication skills training enhances critical thinking skills, especially training in argumentation....

Clearly, social interaction ... involves communication to a very great extent. Enhancing communication skills through training is likely to lead to more social interaction, more self-correction of thinking, and improved critical thinking. Kuhn (2005) emphasized that, in educational settings, communication must be something other than mere "consecutive self expression" (p. 124) because "... the central purpose of the [classroom discussion] activity is to develop students' argument skills." Kuhn further noted "... that these skills are, in essence, dialogic." The model offered by Kuhn depends not on formal teaching of, e.g., deliberative forms (e.g., stock issues analysis) but, rather, the "dense practice of argument" (p. 151) so that students can learn to value arguing and, accordingly, develop arguing (and thinking) skills. Of course, a number of other scholars have designed skills training programs for the objective of enhancing critical thinking skills. Do these programs lead to less frequent utilization of verbal aggression? The next section looks at these solutions.

HOW MIGHT THE PROBLEM BE ADDRESSED?

Generally, the reported approaches to reducing aggression through training can be distinguished in at least one key regard: Some programs place emphasis on educating trainees about the harmful nature of aggression, whereas others place emphasis on developing affirming communication skills. Although no program should be singled out as exclusively relying on "educating about aggression" or "developing affirming repertoires," the research reported seems to suggest that training in constructive communication behaviors (i.e., what *to* say) might be more valuable than training against destructive communication behaviors (i.e., what *not* to say). For example, Infante has long maintained the great value of knowing when to "let go" of an argument in order to maintain personal relationships (Infante, 1988) and the value of affirming communication as part of excellent interpersonal communication. He has, as well, underscored the pitfalls of aggression....

Infante (1988, pp. 10–12) offered a five-part model (hereafter noted as FPM) for teaching or nonscholastic "self-study," including (1) "stating the controversy in propositional form," (2) analyze the proposition and invent arguments, (3) advocate and defend one's own position, (4) attack the positions of others, and (5) "managing interpersonal relations during an argument." Infante offered the "Inventional system" for generating arguments. In this system, the arguer uses questions to discover argumentative grounds for problem, blame, solution, and consequences. The final sentence of the book describes Infante's belief about readers mastering the book (p. 141): "You will possess a preference for rational discourse." It is clear that the implied alternative to rational discourse was verbal aggression....

Infante's advisee, Rancer (1979), wrote the first doctoral dissertation on argumentativeness. Rancer, Whitecap, Kosberg, and Avtgis (1997) went on to develop a skills training program for seventh and eighth graders based on Infante's Inventional System. Using initial letters of the words "problem, blame, solutions, consequences" as a mnemonic device, Rancer and his colleagues taught adolescents to choose from an "arguing menu" consisting of peanut butter and soda crackers. Subsets for these four categories, as well, were associated with food. After receiving one week of training, results demonstrated an increase in trait argumentativeness scores. A follow-up investigation completed seven months to one year later (Rancer et al., 2000) revealed that the scores remained at the high levels. Thus, the training in arguing (using a modification of the Inventional System) had immediate results and consequences. Surprisingly, however, a secondary effect occurred. Verbal aggressiveness scores increased significantly after the one week of training and, notably, the increase in scores continued after the immediate post-test (i.e., verbal aggressiveness scores significantly increased from the immediate post-training measurement to the measurement approximately seven months to one year later). This unintended effect for verbal aggressiveness is explained by the authors as having a number of possible causes (see Meyer et al., 2004, for an interesting description of an adolescent control group that appeared to experience a significant increase in verbal aggression). Notably, Rancer et al. (2000) suggest that one way to alter their training program would be to place increased emphasis on Infante's "manag[e] interpersonal relations during an argument." A training program designed to improve students' critical thinking while also managing interpersonal conflict was developed by Johnson and Johnson (1989)....

Johnson and Johnson identified two key skills for managing controversies constructively: (1) being "able to *disagree with each other's ideas while confirming each other's personal competence*" (p. 102, emphasis in original) and (2) engaging in perspective-taking behaviors (e.g., paraphrasing). Specifically, although not identifying argumentative skill deficiency as a construct, they indicated that "the abilities to gather, organize, and express information, to challenge and disagree, and to engage in reason logically are essential for the constructive management of controversies" (p. 102).

The Johnson brothers designed a program to train students in managing controversy constructively, the "Teaching Students to be Peacemaker Program" [hereafter Peacemaker]. Peacemaker was based (Johnson & Johnson, 2001) on research investigating communication, conflict resolution, constructive conflict, integrative negotiations, and perspective....

Peacemaker trains through five steps: (1) learning to identify conflict, (2) understanding how to negotiate integrative agreements, (3) studying mediation techniques, (4) practicing mediation in the classroom setting, and (5) learning to enhance negotiation and mediation skills. The Johnsons (2001) executed a meta-analysis on 17 studies completed by them during a 12-year time span (1988–2000)....

The results of the analysis supported the conclusion that students can be trained to manage conflict constructively, maintain interpersonal respect, and use less verbal aggression. Hample (2003) describes the communication training in Peacemaker as consonant with constructive interpersonal conflict management. Hample highlights (2003, p. 452) the potential consequences of such training including, *inter alia*, a favorable communication climate, "assertiveness without verbal aggression," and improved perspective taking. The next section summarizes the minimal negative results and consequences that would be incurred, while receiving considerable benefits, from intervention.

WHAT SPECIAL BENEFITS MIGHT FLOW FROM NEW APPROACHES TO SOLVING THE PROBLEM?

Hample (2003) underscores that any intervention or interventions attempting to (1) increase levels of argumentativeness to reduce aggression, or (2) reduce verbal aggression to enhance argumentativeness, will have to be implemented separately, or, minimally, as one program with "two separate emphases" (p. 451). The current empirical evidence suggests that the FPM offered by Infante, with its fifth point "manag[e] interpersonal relations during an argument" could be used with a Peacemaker style program. Because (1) the meta-analysis of Allen et al. (1999) demonstrated that virtually any communication skills instruction can enhance critical thinking skills; (2) the Rancer et al. (1997, 2000) research showed that a modified FPM offered by Infante (1988) can be used to enhance arguing (and, therefore, critical thinking) skills; and (3) the two Johnson and Johnson (1989, 2001) meta-analyses demonstrate that a Peacemaker style program of training individuals to communicate in a respectful, nonaggressive way, with others (i.e., without verbal aggression) can be implemented over a fairly short time period, it seems reasonable to argue for the position that verbal aggression interventions are warranted. Offering the Inventional System alone might result in increased aggression. Even basic communication training, such as that employed by Weldon (2000) (but without an emphasis on peer mediation), seemed to result in increased argumentativeness and verbal aggressiveness scores among adolescents. Conversely, offering a version of Peacemaker alone might enhance social relationships, reduce conflict, and yet not result in greater levels of critical thinking. Using the FPM of Infante with the Inventional System (for Part 2) and adaptation of Peacemaker (for Part 5) would likely avoid the negative consequences of less developed programs while enhancing argumentative skills, enhancing critical thinking skills, and reducing verbal aggression. Such interventionist activity would have, based on the last 40 years of research findings, substantially positive results (even if we have not fully parceled out the causes of verbal aggression). The agency for such an intervention might be self-study, but given the complexity of the issues and the proven success of communication skills training and of Peacemaker training in school settings, formal intervention by schools seems warranted. At the very least, Kuhn's (1991, 2005) call for greater emphasis on dialogic argument over controversial issues within classrooms is justified when one also considers training students to, in Infante's (1988, p. 12) words, "manag[e] their interpersonal relations during an argument." The proposed intervention activity could take place in grade schools, high schools, and colleges. Johnson and Johnson's Peacemaker program demonstrates that young learners can understand the concepts and recall the key information concerning effective interpersonal negotiations with others.

The fact that the issues of intervention (to reduce verbal aggressiveness while trying to develop arguing skills) have been with us for at least 40 years suggests that taking immediate steps will not be premature. Even 30 years ago, Johnson and Johnson (1979) explained that teachers seeking to "promote constructive controversy" should "… teach perspective-taking and confirmation skills to students, and emphasize rational argument" (p. 62). The research findings during the last three decades in communication and education support taking action. The next step for communication scholars is to adapt the training models to their own curricular settings. Such adaptations will need to have clearly stated objectives (e.g., to enhance critical thinking while reducing aggression, to increase dialogic argument while reducing aggression) and should include measurement schemes to carefully assess their favorable (critical thinking) and unfavorable (verbal aggression) short-term results and long-term consequences. Some curricular changes might involve adding skills components focusing on (1) "What to say to maintain relationships" within argumentation and debate courses, (2) experiences in Kuhn's dialogic argument within interpersonal or small group communication courses, or, for example, (3) developing supportive communication climates within interviewing courses. Some educators have taken such steps in their classrooms. Others may wish to intervene in settings with populations known to engage in aggression, such as prisoners (e.g., teaching how to express demands in a positive fashion), business executives (e.g., that the maxim "Praise in public, criticize in private" should be abandoned in favor of "Praise in public, praise even more in private"), and laborers (e.g., not only how to be accepting of others, but how to welcome others verbally). Although most of the existing research has been based on schoolchildren and college students, there is no good reason stated in the literature as to why intervention should not work in other groups (college students are people, too!). The research reported in this essay strongly supports the conclusion that reducing verbal aggression through well-designed interventions (as described) can lead to an improved quality of life.

REVIEW QUESTIONS

1. Distinguish verbal/communicative aggression from argumentativeness.
2. Explain the four main nongenetic possible causes for aggression.
3. Explain the five-part model for effective arguing.
4. Review the two main skills for managing interpersonal relations during an argument.
5. What is "the Peacemaker program"?

PROBES

1. Verbal/communicative aggression in marital relationships is bad, *and* high levels of argument between spouses does not necessarily lead to relationship deterioration—in other words, arguing can be good. Explain.

2. According to this article, why is argument skills training likely to reduce verbal/communicative aggression?
3. What chapters in *Bridges Not Walls* include material that can help train people to engage in constructive argument effectively? Explain.

REFERENCES

Allen, M., Berkowitz, S., Hunt, S., & Loudon, A. (1999). A meta-analysis of the impact of forensics and communication education on critical thinking. *Communication Education, 48,* 18–30.

Beatty, M. J., & McCroskey, J. C. (1997, May). *It's in our nature: Verbal aggressiveness as temperamental expression.* Paper presented at the annual convention of the International Communication Association, Montreal, Canada.

Burman, B., John, R. S., & Margolin, G. (1992). Observed patterns of conflict in violent, nonviolent, and nondistressed couples. *Behavioral Assessment, 14,* 15–37.

Fitzpatrick, M. A. (1988). *Between husbands and wives: Communication in marriage.* Newbury Park, CA: Sage.

Garside, C. (1996). Look who's talking: A comparison of lecture and group discussion teaching strategies in developing critical thinking skills. *Communication Education, 45,* 212–227.

Gottman, J. M. (1994). *What predicts divorce? The relationship between marital processes and marital outcomes.* Mahwah, NJ: Lawrence Erlbaum Associates, Inc.

Hample, D. (2003). Arguing skill. In J. O. Greene & B. R. Burleson (Eds.), *Handbook of communication and social interaction skills* (pp. 439–477). Mahwah, NJ: Lawrence Erlbaum Associates, Inc.

Horvath, C. W. (1995). Biological origins of communicator style. *Communication Quarterly, 43,* 394–407.

Infante, D. A. (1987). Aggressiveness. In J. C. McCroskey & J. A. Daly (Eds.), *Personality and interpersonal communication* (pp. 157–192). Beverly Hills, CA: Sage.

Infante, D. A. (1988). *Arguing constructively.* Prospect Heights, IL: Waveland Press.

Infante, D. A. (1995). Teaching students to understand and control verbal aggression. *Communication Education, 44,* 51–63.

Infante, D. A., Chandler, T. A., & Rudd, J. E. (1989). Test of an argumentative skill deficiency model of interspousal violence. *Communication Monographs, 56,* 163–177.

Infante, D. A., Chandler, T. A., Rudd, J. E., & Shannon, E. A. (1990). Verbal aggression in violent and nonviolent marital disputes. *Communication Quarterly, 38,* 361–371.

Infante, D. A., & Rancer, A. S. (1982). A conceptualization and measure of argumentativeness. *Journal of Personality Assessment, 46,* 72–80.

Infante, D. A., & Rancer, A. S. (1996). Argumentativeness and verbal aggressiveness: A review of recent theory and research. In B. R. Burleson (Ed.), *Communication yearbook 19* (pp. 319–351). Thousand Oaks, CA: Sage.

Infante, D. A., Trebing, D. J., Shepherd, P. E., & Seeds, D. E. (1984). The relationship of argumentativeness to verbal aggression. *Southern Speech Communication Journal, 50,* 67–77.

Infante, D. A., & Wigley, C. J., III. (1986). Verbal aggressiveness: An interpersonal model and measure. *Communication Monographs, 53,* 61–69.

Johnson, D. W., & Johnson, R. T. (1979). Conflict in the classroom: Controversy and learning. *Review of Educational Research, 49,* 51–70.

Johnson, D. W., & Johnson, R. T. (1989). *Cooperation and competition: Theory and research.* Edina, MN: Interaction Book.

Johnson, D. W., & Johnson, R. T. (2001, April). *Teaching students to be peacemakers: A meta-analysis.* Paper presented at the annual meeting of the American Educational Research Association, Seattle, WA. (ERIC Document Reproduction Service No. ED460178.)

Kuhn, D. (1991). *The skills of argument.* Cambridge, MA: Cambridge University Press.

Kuhn, D. (2005). *Education for thinking.* Cambridge, MA: Harvard University Press.

Meyer, G., Roberto, A. J., Boster, F. J., & Roberto, H. L. (2004). Assessing the Get Real about Violence® curriculum: Process and outcome evaluation results and implications. *Health Communication, 16,* 451–474.

Rancer, A. S. (1979). *An examination of the impact of selected interpersonal and situational variables on argumentativeness.* Unpublished doctoral dissertation, Kent State University, OH.

Rancer, A. S. (1998). Argumentativeness. In J. C. McCroskey, J. A. Daly, M. M. Martin, & M. J. Beatty (Eds.), *Communication and personality: Trait perspectives* (pp. 149–170). Cresskill, NJ: Hampton.

Rancer, A. S., & Avtgis, T. A. (2006). *Argumentative and aggressive communication: Theory, research, and application.* Thousand Oaks, CA: Sage.

Rancer, A. S., Avtgis, T. A., Kosberg, R. L., & Whitecap, V. G. (2000). A longitudinal assessment of trait argumentativeness and verbal aggressiveness between seventh and eighth grades. *Communication Education, 49,* 114–119.

Rancer, A. S., Whitecap, V. G., Kosberg, R. L., & Avtgis, T. A. (1997). Testing the efficacy of a communication training program to increase argumentativeness and argumentative behavior in adolescents. *Communication Education, 46,* 273–286.

Roloff, M. E. (1996). The catalyst hypothesis: Conditions under which coercive communication leads to physical aggression. In D. D. Cahn & S. A. Lloyd (Eds.), *Family violence from a communication perspective* (pp. 20–36). Thousand Oaks, CA: Sage.

Sabourin, T. C., Infante, D. A., & Rudd, J. E. (1993). Verbal aggression in marriages: A comparison of violent, distressed but nonviolent, and nondistressed couples. *Human Communication Research, 20,* 245–267.

Weldon, R. A. (2000, November). *Assessing the effectiveness of basic interpersonal communication training in a sixth grade population using measures of argumentativeness and verbal aggressiveness.* Paper presented at the annual meeting of the National Communication Association, Seattle, WA. (ERIC Document Reproduction Service No. ED447538.)

Wigley, C. J., III. (1998). Verbal aggressiveness. In J. C. McCroskey, J. A. Daly, M. M. Martin, & M. J. Beatty (Eds.), *Communication and personality: Trait perspectives* (pp. 191–214). Cresskill, NJ: Hampton.

Wigley, C. J., III. (2006). Section of the research contributions. In A. S. Rancer & T. A. Avtgis (Eds.), *Argumentative and aggressive communication: Theory, research, and application* (pp. 243–244). Thousand Oaks, CA: Sage.

Wilkinson, D. L., & Hamerschlag, S. J. (2004). Situational determinants in intimate partner violence. *Aggression and Violent Behavior, 10,* 333–361.

CHAPTER 10

Conflict: Turning Walls into Bridges

Conflict and Interaction

Joseph P. Folger, Marshall Scott Poole,
and Randall K. Stutman

One of the places where it is most challenging and most important to turn communication walls into bridges is in conflict. Although conflict is a natural and normal part of every work, family, roommate, and dating relationship, few people enjoy it, and even fewer believe that they manage it well. This chapter collects some of the best advice from eight people who can help each of us "do" conflict better.

The first reading comes from a conflict management textbook written by three communication teachers. It lays out some of the basic ideas that I think are important to understand if you're going to approach conflict constructively and effectively.

The authors begin with a "textbook case" that illustrates both the bad side and the potentially good side of conflict. Although they don't emphasize this point, the case shows how your view of conflict can strongly affect the ways you deal with it. For example, many people view conflict as always painful. From this point of view, unless you enjoy being blamed, put down, and shouted at, it's hard to be positive about conflicts. But as the case study shows, there are actually some benefits to conflict. So the first step toward handling conflict effectively is to be open to the positive values of conflict so you can, as these authors suggest, analyze "both the specific behaviors and interaction patterns involved in conflict and the forces that influence these patterns."

Folger, Poole, and Stutman define *conflict* as "the interaction of interdependent people who perceive incompatible goals and interference from each other in achieving those goals." This means that struggles inside one person's head are not "conflict" as it's defined here. Conflict always involves communication. The definition also emphasizes that conflict doesn't happen unless the people involved are interdependent.

The central section of this reading distinguishes productive from destructive conflict interaction. One difference is that productive conflicts are *realistic,* which means that they focus on substantive problems the parties can potentially solve, while *nonrealistic* conflicts are mainly expressions of aggression designed to defeat or hurt the other. Productive conflict attitudes and behaviors are also *flexible,* while destructive ones are *inflexible.* In addition, productive conflict management is grounded in the belief that all parties can realize at least some of their goals, while destructive conflict is thoroughly win/lose. Finally, productive conflict happens when the parties are committed to working through their differences, rather than either avoiding them or simply favoring one position over the other.

In the final section, the authors develop the idea that every move made in a conflict affects the other parties and that this is why conflicts often degenerate into destructive cycles or patterns. These cycles can only be understood as unified wholes, and they can often be self-reinforcing. This means that, if you want to manage conflict effectively, you have to (1) look for the cycles, and (2) be willing and able to take unilateral action to break the destructive pattern. Subsequent readings in this chapter suggest what you can do *after* this to handle conflicts more effectively.

MAIN IDEAS

- In order to manage conflict effectively, start by recognizing that it can be beneficial.
- A case study demonstrates that benefits can include getting feelings into the open, the opportunity to challenge and support others, collaborative problem analysis, and growth in a group's interpersonal trust.
- Conflict is defined as the interaction of interdependent people who perceive incompatible goals and interference from each other in achieving those goals.
- The most important feature of conflict is that it is based in interaction. It occurs *between* people not "inside someone's head."
- If people are not interdependent, they won't engage in conflict; they'll just ignore each other. Acknowledging interdependence is a first step toward managing conflict well.
- It's important also to identify incompatible goals and interference in reaching goals.
- Conflicts are also "characterized by a mixture of incentives to cooperate and to compete."
- Productive conflict interaction is *realistic,* that is, based on disagreements over means or ends rather than having as its sole end "to defeat or hurt the other" (*unrealistic*).
- Productive conflict interaction depends on flexibility.
- Productive conflict interaction is guided by the belief that all parties can attain important goals.
- Productive conflict interaction can be competitive.
- Conflict occurs as a behavioral cycle or pattern of initiation-response-counterresponse.
- The key to productive conflict interaction is to develop constructive patterns rather than destructive ones.

THE POTENTIAL OF CONFLICT INTERACTION

It is often said that conflict can be beneficial. Trainers, counselors, consultants, and authors of conflict textbooks point to the potential positive functions of conflict: conflicts allow important issues to be aired; they produce new and creative ideas; they release built-up tension; they can strengthen relationships; they can cause groups and organizations to reevaluate and clarify goals and missions; and they can also stimulate social change to eliminate inequities and injustice. These advantages, and others, are raised to justify conflict as a normal, healthy occurrence and to stress the importance of understanding and handling it properly.

But why must such an argument be made? Everyone has been in conflicts, and almost everyone would readily acknowledge at least some benefits. Why then do social scientists, popular authors, and consultants persist in attempting to persuade us of something we already know? Perhaps the answer can be found by studying an actual conflict. The twists and turns of a specific case often reveal why negative views of conflict persist. Consider the fairly typical case study of a conflict in a small work group in Case 1.A.

Case 1.A   The Women's Hotline Case

Imagine yourself as a staff member in this organization:
    How would you react as this conflict unfolded?
    What is it about this particular conflict that makes it seem difficult to face—let alone solve?

Women's Hotline is a rape and domestic crisis center in a medium-sized city; the center employs seven full- and part-time workers. The workers, all women, formed a cohesive unit and made all important decisions as a group; there were no formal supervisors. The hotline had started as a voluntary organization and had grown by capturing local and federal funds. The group remained proud of its roots in a democratic, feminist tradition.

The atmosphere at the hotline was rather informal. The staff saw each other as friends, but there was an implicit understanding that people should not have to take responsibility for each other's cases. Since the hotline's work was draining, having to handle each other's worries could create an unbearable strain. This norm encouraged workers to work on their own and keep problems to themselves.

The conflict arose when Diane, a new counselor who had only six months' experience, was involved in a very disturbing incident. One of her clients was killed by a man who had previously raped her. Diane had trouble dealing with this incident. She felt guilty about it; she questioned her own ability and asked herself whether she might have been able to prevent this tragedy. In the months following, Diane had increasing difficulty in coping with her feelings and began to feel that her co-workers were not giving her the support she needed. Diane had no supervisor to turn to, and, although her friends outside the hotline were helpful, she did not believe they could understand the pressure as well as her co-workers.

Since the murder, Diane had not been able to work to full capacity, and she began to notice some resentment from the other counselors. She felt the other staff were more concerned about whether she was adding to their workloads than whether she was recovering from the traumatic incident. Although Diane did not realize it at the time, most of the staff felt she had been slow to take on responsibilities even before her client was killed. They thought Diane had generally asked for more help than other staff members and that these requests were adding to their own responsibilities. No one was willing to tell Diane about these feelings after the incident, because they realized she was very disturbed. After six months, Diane believed she could no longer continue to work effectively. She felt pressure from the others at the center, and she was still shaken by the tragedy. She requested two weeks off with pay to get away from the work situation for a while, to reduce the stress she felt, and to come back with renewed energy. The staff, feeling that Diane was slacking off, denied this request. They responded by outlining, in writing, what they saw as the responsibilities of a full-time staff worker. Diane was angry when she realized her request had been denied, and she decided to file a formal work grievance.

Diane and the staff felt bad about having to resort to such a formal, adversarial procedure. No staff member had ever filed a work grievance, and the group was embarrassed by its inability to deal with the problem on a more informal basis. These feelings created additional tension between Diane and the staff.

Discussion Questions

- *Can you foresee any benefits to this conflict?*
- *Is it possible to foresee whether a conflict will move in a constructive or destructive direction?*
- *What cues would lead you to believe that conflict is going to be productive?*

The situation at the Women's Hotline has several features in common with destructive conflicts, and might easily turn in a destructive direction. **First, the situation is tense and threatening.** The weeks during which the incident evolved were an extremely difficult time for the workers. Even for "old hands" at negotiation, conflicts are often unpleasant and frightening. **Second, participants are experiencing a great deal of uncertainty.** They are unable to understand many aspects of the conflict and how their behavior affects it. Conflicts are confusing; actions can have consequences quite different from those intended because the situation is more complicated than assumed. Diane did not know her co-workers thought she was slacking even before the tragedy. When she asked for time off, she was therefore surprised at their refusal, and her own angry reaction nearly started a major battle. **Third, the situation is extremely fragile.** The conflict may evolve in very different ways depending on the behavior of just a single worker. If, for example, the staff chooses to fire Diane, the conflict might be squelched, or it might fester and undermine relationships among the remaining members. If, on the other hand, Diane wins allies, the staff might split over the issue and ultimately dissolve the hotline. As the case continues below, observe staff members' behavior and their method of dealing with this tense and unfamiliar situation.

Case 1.B   The Women's Hotline Case, Continued

Imagine yourself in the midst of this conflict:
What would you recommend this group do to promote a constructive outcome to this conflict?

The staff committee who received Diane's grievance suggested that they could handle the problem in a less formal way if both Diane and the staff agreed to accept a neutral third-party mediator. Everyone agreed that this suggestion had promise, and a third party was invited to a meeting where the entire staff would address the issue.

At this meeting, the group faced a difficult task. Each member offered reactions they had been unwilling to express previously. The staff made several pointed criticisms of Diane's overall performance. Diane expressed doubts about the staff's willingness to help new workers or to give support when it was requested. Although this discussion was often tense, it was well directed. At the outset of the meeting, Diane withdrew her formal complaint. This action changed the definition of the problem from the immediate work grievance to the question of what levels of support were required for various people to work effectively in this difficult and emotionally draining setting. Staff members shared doubts and fears about their own inadequacies as counselors and agreed that something less than perfection was acceptable. The group recognized that a collective inertia had developed and that they had consistently avoided giving others the support needed to deal with difficult rape cases. They acknowledged, however, the constraints on each woman's time; each worker could handle only a limited amount of stress. The group recognized that some level of mutual support was essential and felt they had fallen below that level over the past year and a half. One member suggested that any staff person should be able to ask for a "debriefing contract" whenever they felt they needed help or support. These contracts would allow someone to ask for ten minutes of another person's time to hear about a particularly disturbing issue or case. The group members adopted this suggestion because they saw it could allow members to seek help without overburdening each other. The person who was asked to listen could assist and give needed support without feeling that she had to "fix" another worker's problem. Diane continued to work at the center and found that her abilities and confidence increased as the group provided the support she needed.

Discussion Questions

- *In what ways did the parties in this conflict show "good faith"?*
- *Is "good faith" participation a necessary prerequisite to constructive conflict resolution?*

This is a "textbook" case in effective conflict management because it resulted in a solution that all parties accepted. The members of this group walked a tightrope throughout the conflict, yet they managed to avoid a fall. The tension, unpleasantness, uncertainty, and fragility of conflict situations make them hard to face. Because these problems make it difficult to deal with issues in a constructive way, conflicts are often terminated by force, by uncomfortable suppression of the issues, or by exhaustion after a prolonged fight—all outcomes that leave at least one party dissatisfied. Entering a conflict is often like making a bet against the odds: you can win big if it turns out well, but so many things can go wrong that few people are willing to chance it. It is no wonder that many writers feel a need to reassure us. They feel compelled to remind us of the positive outcomes of conflict because all too often the destructive results are all that people remember.

The key to working through conflict is not to minimize its disadvantages, or even to emphasize its positive functions, but to accept both and to try to understand how conflicts move in destructive or productive directions. Such an understanding requires a conception of conflict that calls for a careful **analysis of both the specific behaviors and interaction patterns involved in conflict and the forces that influence these patterns.** Moreover, we can only grasp the fragility of conflicts and the effects that tension and misunderstandings have in their development if we work at the level at which conflicts unfold—specific interactions among the parties.

DEFINITION OF CONFLICT

Conflict is the interaction of interdependent people who perceive incompatible goals and interference from each other in achieving those goals (Hocker & Wilmot, 1985). This definition has the advantage of providing a much clearer focus than definitions that view conflict simply as disagreement, as competition, or as the presence of incompatible interests (Fink, 1968). **The most important feature of conflict is that it is based in interaction.** Conflicts are constituted and sustained by the behaviors of the parties involved and their reactions to one another. Conflict interaction takes many forms, and each form presents special problems and requires special handling. The most familiar type of conflict interaction is marked by shouting matches or open competition in which each party tries to defeat the other. But conflicts can also be more subtle. Often people react to conflict by suppressing it. They interact in ways that allow them to avoid confrontation, either because they are afraid of possible changes the conflict may bring about or because the issue "isn't worth fighting over." This response is as much a part of the conflict process as the open struggles commonly associated with conflict. This book deals with the whole range of responses to conflict and how those responses affect the development of conflicts. Conflicts can best be understood and managed by concentrating on specific behavioral patterns and the forces shaping them.

People in conflict perceive that they have incompatible goals or interests and that others are a source of interference in achieving their goals. The key word here is "perceive." Regardless of whether goals are actually incompatible or if the parties believe them to be incompatible, conditions are ripe for conflict. Regardless of whether an employee really stands in the way of a co-worker or whether the co-worker interprets the employee's behavior as interference, the co-worker may move against the employee or feel compelled to skirt certain issues. Thus, the parties' interpretations and beliefs play a key role in conflicts. This does not mean that goals are always conscious as conflict develops. People can act without a clear sense of what their goals or interests are (Coser, 1961). Sometimes people find themselves in strained interactions but are unsure how they got there. They realize afterward what their implicit goals were and how their goals were incompatible with those held by others (Hawes & Smith, 1973). Communication looms large because of its importance in shaping and maintaining the perceptions that guide conflict behavior.

Indeed, communication problems are sometimes the cause of conflicts. Tension or irritation can result from misunderstandings that occur when people interact with very different communication styles (Tannen, 1986, Grimshaw, 1990). One person's inquisitive style may be perceived by someone else as intrusive and rude. One person's attempt to avoid stepping on another's toes may be perceived by someone else as distant and cold. Style differences create difficult problems that are often related to differences in cultural backgrounds (Kochman, 1981, Dubinskas, 1992). However, the old adage "most conflicts are actually communication problems" is not always true. The vast majority of conflicts would not exist without some real difference of interest. This difference may be hard to uncover, it may be redefined over time, and occasionally it may be trivial, but it is there nonetheless. Communication processes can cause conflicts and can easily exacerbate them, but they are rarely the sole source of the difficulty.

Conflict interaction is colored by the interdependence of the parties. For a conflict to arise, the behavior of one or both parties must have consequences for the other. Therefore, by definition, the parties involved in conflict are interdependent. The conflict at the hotline would not have occurred if Diane's behavior had not irritated the other workers and if their response had not threatened Diane's position. Furthermore, any action taken in response to the conflict affects both sides. The decision to institute a "debriefing contract" required considerable change by everyone. If Diane had been fired, that too would have affected the other workers; they would have had to "cover" Diane's cases and come to terms with themselves as co-workers who could be accused of being unresponsive or insensitive.

But interdependence implies more than this: when parties are interdependent they can potentially aid or interfere with each other. **For this reason, conflicts are always characterized by a mixture of incentives to cooperate and to compete.** Any comment during conflict interaction can be seen either as an attempt to advance the speaker's own interest or as an attempt to promote a good outcome for all involved. A party may believe that having their own point accepted is more important, at least for the moment, than proposing a mutually beneficial outcome. When Diane asked for two weeks off, she was probably thinking not of the group's best interest but of her own needs. In other cases, a participant may advance a proposal designed to benefit everyone, as when the staff member suggested the "debriefing contract." In still other instances, a participant may offer a comment with a cooperative intent, but others may interpret it as one that advances individual interests. Regardless of whether the competitive motive is intended by the speaker or assigned by other members, the interaction unfolds from that point under the assumption that the speaker may value only his or her own interests. Subsequent interaction is further likely to undermine incentives to cooperate and is also likely to weaken members' recognition of their own interdependence. The balance of incentives to compete or cooperate is important in determining the direction the conflict interaction takes.

ARENAS OF CONFLICT INTERACTION

Conflict occurs in almost all social settings. Most people learn at a very young age that conflicts arise in families, playgrounds, classrooms, Little League fields, ballet centers, scout troops, and cheerleading teams. Even as relationships become more complex and people become involved in more diverse and public settings, conflicts remain remarkably similar to those experienced in childhood. (Indeed, some argue that early experiences shape involvement in conflict throughout our lives.) Adults encounter conflict in casual work relationships and emotionally intense, intimate relationships as well as in close friendships or in political rivalries. Conflict is encountered in decision-making groups, small businesses, large corporations, church organizations, and doctors' offices. Given the diversity of conflicts typically encountered, what often is of most concern is how much is at stake in any conflict. Conflicts are assessed as pedestrian or profound, trivial or tremendous, or as major or minor maelstroms. The estimate of the significance of any conflict often influences the time and effort invested in strategizing or in developing safeguards or fallbacks....

Forms of interaction are patterns of actions and reactions or moves and countermoves that parties engage in during a conflict. Violent exchanges are a form of interaction that can occur in interpersonal, intragroup, or intergroup conflicts. Similarly, negotiation is a form of interaction in which parties engage in any of these settings. Negotiation, sometimes referred to as bargaining, occurs when parties agree to explicit or implicit rules for exchanging proposals or concessions to reach a mutual agreement (Pruitt, 1981; Putnam & Poole, 1987). People often think of negotiation as a separate arena because labor-management negotiations are the most prominent example of negotiations in most people's minds. However, negotiations can occur in any of the arenas. Husbands and wives can negotiate their divorce agreements, a professor and student can negotiate a grade, environmental groups can negotiate a land-use policy, or neighborhood groups can negotiate historical preservation standards.

There are other insights, besides those centering on forms of interaction, that apply to all the arenas of conflict covered in this book. For example, most conflicts are concerned with power because power is integral to all forms of interdependence among people. How conflict influences relationships and how climate is central to the way conflict unfolds will also be examined.

PRODUCTIVE AND DESTRUCTIVE CONFLICT INTERACTION

As previously noted, people often associate conflict with negative outcomes. However, there are times when conflicts must be addressed regardless of the apprehension they create. When differences exist and the issues are important, suppression of conflict is often more dangerous than facing it. The psychologist Irving Janis points to a number of famous political disasters, such as the Bay of Pigs invasion and the failure to anticipate the Japanese attack on Pearl Harbor, where poor decisions can be traced to the repression of conflict by key decision-making groups (Janis, 1972). The critical question is: What forms of conflict interaction will yield the obvious benefits without tearing a relationship, a group, or an organization apart?

Years ago the sociologist Lewis Coser (1956) distinguished realistic from nonrealistic conflicts. **Realistic conflicts are conflicts based in disagreements over the means to an end or over the ends themselves.** In realistic conflicts, the interaction focuses on the substantive issues the participants must address to resolve their underlying incompatibilities. **Nonrealistic conflicts are expressions of aggression in which the sole end is to defeat or hurt the other.** Participants in nonrealistic conflicts serve their own interests by undercutting those of the other party. Coser argues that because nonrealistic conflicts are oriented toward the expression of aggression, force and coercion are the means for resolving these disputes. Realistic conflicts, on the other hand, foster a wide range of resolution techniques—force, negotiation, persuasion, even voting—because they are oriented toward the resolution of some substantive problem. Although Coser's analysis is somewhat of an oversimplification, it is insightful and suggests important contrasts between productive and destructive conflict interaction (Deutsch, 1973). What criteria could be used to evaluate whether a conflict is productive? **In large part, productive conflict interaction depends on flexibility.** In constructive conflicts, members engage in a wide variety of behaviors ranging from coercion and threat to negotiation, joking, and relaxation to reach an acceptable solution. **In contrast, parties in destructive conflicts are likely to be much less flexible because their goal is more narrowly defined: they are trying to defeat each other.** Destructive conflict interaction is likely to have protracted, uncontrolled escalation cycles or prolonged attempts to avoid issues. In productive conflict, on the other hand, the interaction in the group will change direction often. Short cycles of escalation, de-escalation, avoidance, and constructive work on the issue are likely to occur as the participants attempt to manage the conflict.

Consider the hotline case. The group exhibited a wide range of interaction styles, from the threat of a grievance to the cooperative attempt to reach a mutually satisfactory solution. Even though Diane and the members engaged in hostile or threatening interaction, they did not persist in this mode, and when the conflict threatened to escalate, they called in a third party. The conflict showed all the hallmarks of productive interaction. In a destructive conflict the members might have responded to Diane's grievance by suspending her, and Diane might have retaliated by suing or by attempting to discredit the center in the local newspaper. Her retaliation would have hardened others' positions and they might have fired her, leading to further retaliation. Alternatively, the hotline conflict might have ended in destructive avoidance. Diane might have hidden her problem, and the other members might have consciously or unconsciously abetted her by changing the subject when the murder came up or by avoiding talking to her at all. Diane's problem would probably have grown worse, and she might have had to quit. The center would then revert back to "normal" until the same problem surfaced again. While the damage done by destructive avoidance is much less serious in this case than that done by destructive escalation, it is still considerable: the hotline loses a good worker, and the seeds of future losses remain. In both cases, it is not the behaviors themselves that are destructive—neither avoidance nor hostile arguments are harmful in themselves—but rather the inflexibility of the parties that locks them into escalation or avoidance cycles.

In productive conflicts, interaction is guided by the belief that all factions can attain important goals (Deutsch, 1973). The interaction reflects a sustained effort to bridge the apparent incompatibility of positions. This effort is in marked contrast to destructive conflicts where the interaction is premised on participants' belief that one side must win and the other must lose. **Productive conflict interaction results in a solution satisfactory to all and produces a general feeling that the parties have gained something** (for example, a new idea, greater clarity of others' positions, or a stronger sense of solidarity). In some cases, the win-lose orientation of destructive conflict stems from fear of losing. People attempt to defeat alternative proposals because they believe that if their positions are not accepted they will lose resources, self-esteem, or the respect of others. In other cases, win-lose interaction is sparked, not by competitive motives, but by the parties' fear of working through a difficult conflict. Groups that rely on voting to reach decisions often call for a vote when discussion becomes heated and the members do not see any other immediate way out of a hostile and threatening situation. Any further attempt to discuss the alternatives or to pursue the reasons behind people's positions seems risky. A vote can put a quick end to threatening interaction, but it also induces a win-lose orientation that can easily trigger destructive cycles. Members whose proposal is rejected must resist a natural tendency to be less committed to the chosen solution and may try to "even the score" in future conflicts. **Productive conflict interaction is sometimes competitive; both parties must stand up for their own positions and strive for perceived understanding if a representative outcome is to be attained** (Cahn, 1990). A great deal of tension and hostility may result as people struggle with the conflict. Although parties in productive conflicts hold strongly to their positions, they are also open to movement when convinced that such movement will result in the best decision. The need to preserve power, save face, or make the opponent look bad does not stand in the way of change. In destructive conflict, parties often become polarized, and the defense of a non-negotiable position becomes more important than working out a viable solution. This description of productive and destructive conflict interaction is obviously an idealization. It is rare that a conflict exhibits all the constructive or destructive qualities just mentioned; indeed, many conflicts exhibit both productive and destructive interaction. However, better conflict management will result if parties can sustain productive conflict interaction patterns.

CONFLICT AS INTERACTIVE BEHAVIOR

Conflict is, by nature, interactive. It is never wholly under one person's control (Kriesberg, 1973). The other party's reactions and the person's anticipation of the other's response are extremely important. **Any comment made during a conflict is made with some awareness or prediction about the likely response it will elicit.** This predictive basis for any move in interaction creates a strong tendency for conflict interaction to become cyclic or repetitive. Suppose Robert criticizes Susan, an employee under his supervision, for her decreasing productivity. Susan may accept the criticism and explain why her production is down, thus reducing the conflict and moving toward a solution. Susan may also shout back and sulk, inviting escalation, or she may choose to say nothing and avoid the conflict, resulting in no improvement in the situation. Once Robert has spoken to Susan and she has responded, the situation is no longer totally under Robert's control: his next behavior will be a response to Susan's reaction. Robert's behavior, and its subsequent meaning to Susan, is dependent on the interchange between them. **A behavioral cycle of initiation-response—counterresponse results from the conflict interchange. This cycle cannot be understood by breaking it into its parts, into the individual behaviors of Robert and Susan.** It is more complex than the individual behaviors and, in a real sense, has a "life" of its own. The cycle can be self-reinforcing, if, for example, Susan shouts back at Robert, Robert tries to discipline her, Susan becomes more recalcitrant, and so on, in an escalating spiral. The cycle could also limit itself if Robert responds to Susan's shouting with an attempt to calm her and listen to her side of the story. Conflict interaction cycles acquire a momentum of their own. They tend in a definite direction—toward escalation, toward avoidance and suppression, or toward productive work on the conflict. The situation becomes even more complex when we remember that Robert formulated his criticism on the basis of his previous experience with Susan. That is, Robert's move is based on his perception of Susan's likely response. In the same way, Susan's response is based not only on Robert's criticism, but on her estimate of Robert's likely reaction to her response. Usually such estimations are "intuitive"—that is, they are not conscious—but sometimes parties do plot them out ("If I shout at Robert, he'll back down and maybe I won't have to deal with this"). They are always based on the parties' perceptions of each other, on whatever theories or beliefs each holds about the other's reactions. Because these estimates are only intuitive predictions, they may be wrong to some extent. The estimates will be revised as the conflict unfolds, and this revision will largely determine what direction the conflict takes. The most striking thing about this predictive process is the extraordinary difficulties it poses for attempts to understand the parties' thinking. When Susan responds to Robert on the basis of her prediction of Robert's answer, from the outside we see Susan making an estimate of Robert's estimate of what she means by her response. If Robert reflects on Susan's intention before answering, we observe Robert's estimate of Susan's estimate of his estimate of what Susan meant. This string of estimates can increase without bounds if one tries to pin down the originating point, and after a while the prospect is just as dizzying as a hall of mirrors.

Several studies of arms races (Richardson, 1960, North, Brody, & Holsti, 1963) and of marital relations (Watzlawick, Beavin, & Jackson, 1967; Rubin, 1983; Scarf, 1987) and employee-supervisor interactions (Brown 1983) have shown how this spiral of predictions poses a critical problem in conflicts. If the parties do not take the spiral into account, they run the risk of miscalculation. However, it is impossible to calculate all the possibilities. At best, people have extremely limited knowledge of the implications their actions hold for others, and their ability to manage conflicts is therefore severely curtailed. Not only are parties' behaviors inherently interwoven in conflicts, but their thinking and anticipations are as well. The key question ... is: **How does conflict interaction develop destructive patterns—radical escalation, prolonged or inappropriate avoidance of conflict issues, inflexibility—rather than constructive patterns leading to productive conflict management?**

REVIEW QUESTIONS

1. Describe what the authors mean when they say that the case study about Diane and her co-workers shows how conflict situations are tense and threatening, uncertain and fragile.
2. Explain what is significant about each of the following terms in the authors' definition of conflict: *interaction, interdependent, incompatible goals, interference.*
3. Why do the authors disagree with the old adage "Most conflicts are actually communication problems"?
4. Distinguish between realistic and nonrealistic conflict.

PROBES

1. As you read the case study about Diane and her co-workers, what single feature of the situation strikes you as the most important positive move that was made? In other words, what one thing most helped resolve this conflict productively?
2. Give an example from your own experience of the difference between a realistic and a nonrealistic conflict.
3. At one point the authors argue about the wisdom of resolving a conflict by voting. (a) What is their rationale for discouraging voting? (b) How do you respond; that is, do you agree or disagree, and why?
4. The authors end this excerpt with "the key question" of how conflicts develop destructive patterns. After you've read the other four readings in this chapter, what is your response to this key question?

REFERENCES

Brown, L. D. (1983). *Managing conflict at organizational interfaces.* Reading, MA: Addison-Wesley.

Cahn, D. 1990. *Intimates in conflict: A communication perspective.* Hillsdale, NJ: Lawrence Erlbaum.

Coser, L. (1956). *The functions of social conflict.* New York: Free Press.

Coser, L. (1961). The termination of conflict. *Journal of Conflict Resolution, 5,* 347–353.

Deutsch, M. (1973). *The resolution of conflict.* New Haven, CT: Yale University Press.

Dubinskas, F. (1992). Culture and conflict: The cultural roots of discord. In D. M. Kolb & J. M. Bartunek, (Eds.), *Hidden conflict in organizations* (pp. 187–208). Newbury Park, CA: Sage.

Fink, C. F. (1968). Some conceptual difficulties in the theory of social conflict. *Journal of Conflict Resolution, 12,* 412–460.

Grimshaw, A. D. (Ed.) (1990). *Conflict talk: Sociolinguistic investigations of arguments in conversations.* Cambridge: Cambridge University Press.

Hawes, L., & Smith, D. H. (1973). A critique of assumptions underlying the study of communication in conflict. *Quarterly Journal of Speech, 59,* 423–435.

Hocker, J. L., & Wilmot, W. W. (1985). *Interpersonal conflict.* Dubuque, IA: Wm. C. Brown.

Janis, I. (1972). *Victims of groupthink.* Boston: Houghton Mifflin.

Kochman, T. (1981). *Black and white styles in conflict.* Chicago: University of Chicago Press.

Kriesberg, L. (1973). *The sociology of social conflicts.* Englewood Cliffs, NJ: Prentice-Hall.

North, R. C., Brody, R. A., & Holsti, O. (1963). Some empirical data on the conflict spiral. *Peace Research Society: Papers I.* Chicago Conference: 1–14.

Pruitt, D. G. (1981). *Negotiating behavior.* New York: Academic Press.

Putnam, L., & Poole, M. S. (1987). Conflict and negotiation. In F. Jablin, L. Putnam, K. Roberts, & L. Porter (Eds.), *Handbook of organizational communication:* (pp. 549–599). Beverly Hills, CA: Sage.

Richardson, L. F. (1960). *Arms and insecurity.* Pittsburgh: Boxwood Press.

Roloff, M. E. (1987). Communication and conflict. In C. Berger & S. H. Chaffee, (Eds.), *Handbook of communication science* (pp. 484–534). Beverly Hills, CA: Sage.

Rubin, L. (1983). *Intimate strangers.* New York: Harper and Row.

Scarf, M. (1987). *Intimate partners: Patterns in love and marriage.* New York: Ballantine.

Tannen, D. (1986). *That's not what I meant.* New York: William Morrow.

Watzlawick, P., Beavin, J. H., & Jackson, D. D. (1967). *Pragmatics of human communication.* New York: Norton.

Communication Spirals, Paradoxes, and Conundrums

William W. Wilmot

Bill Wilmot is an interpersonal communication and conflict management teacher and a mediator who helps people in conflict all over North America. As these excerpts from his book *Relational Communication* illustrate, he has an unusually sharp sense of the complexities of interpersonal relationships. This reading combines Bill's discussion of communication spirals and his ideas about paradoxes and conundrums (relationship puzzles). It offers some helpful advice about how to turn these particular communication walls into bridges.

The first section explains that a "communication spiral" happens when "the actions of each person in a relationship magnify those of the other." Wilmot gives several examples of both positive and negative spirals that can happen in family, work, and dating relationships. He emphasizes that spirals can be powerful because they pick up a momentum that feeds back on itself. This means that closeness and harmony can create more of the same, and that bitterness and hostility can operate the same way. He lists seven features of a communication spiral and then goes into some detail about generative and degenerative spirals.

Wilmot follows this analysis of spirals with five concrete suggestions about how to alter degenerative ones. The first is deceptively simple sounding: "Do what comes unnaturally." Spirals are relational phenomena, which is to say that they are fed by both (or all) the parties in a relationship. Change is impossible so long as things continue as they have. At least one party has to "do what comes unnaturally."

A second suggestion is to use third parties—friends, counselors, relatives, clergy, or others whom you trust. A third suggestion is to reaffirm your relational goals. It can often help for people in a spiral to remind themselves and each other about the commitment they have to the relationship. This is a form of suggestion number four, "metacommunicating." This just means that you communicate about your communicating. You talk about the relationship and whatever has led to the degenerating series of actions.

The final two suggestions are that you try spending less time with the person and consider changing the external situation. Sometimes these moves will also break troublesome patterns.

The section of this reading on paradoxes and conundrums consists of brief discussions of 12 two-directional pulls that many people experience in their relationships. It can be reassuring to read that others feel some of the same tensions you do, and Wilmot also includes some suggestions about how to cope with these relational puzzles.

The first is that people want contradictory things in relationships: freedom and closeness, stability and excitement. It can be helpful to recognize that this is normal, and not necessarily problematic. A second is that both "objective" third-person observations and "subjective" insider observations about a relationship are fraught with errors. It's important to get both perspectives and not to believe that either provides "the Truth" about the relationship.

Paradox 3 is that if you leave relationships completely alone, they'll probably dissolve, and if you try to force them to happen, you can destroy them. It works best to stay in the middle of this tension. Number four is the tension between expecting a relationship to generate happiness when its purpose may be the sense of wholeness that comes from the inherently unstable dialectical encounter between two people. The fifth paradox is that we get the most pleasure *and* the most pain from our closest relationships.

Wilmot also discusses some paradoxes about the connection between "the self" and "the relationship" and the fact that "relationships can serve as springboards for growth or just toss you higher so you land harder." Number nine reminds us how changes in any part or level of a relationship reverberate to other levels. The tenth sketches the power inherent in and the problems created by relationship labels. And the last two emphasize the ever-changing, emergent quality of relationships.

By the time you complete this reading, you should have an appreciation for the sometimes startling complexity of the relationships you are a part of.

MAIN IDEAS

- Because communication is relational (co-laborative), actions of each person magnify those of the other, positively or negatively; this is a "spiral."
- Spirals tend to pick up momentum that feeds back on itself; generative spirals do this productively and degenerative spirals do this destructively.
- There are seven features of both kinds of spirals: synergy, individual contributions, symmetrical or complementary pattern, generative or degenerative quality, acceleration, changability, and impact on relationships.
- Relationships can be developed when generative spirals are encouraged.
- Six ways to alter degenerative spirals include doing what comes unnaturally, using third parties, reaffirming your relational goals, metacommunicating, spending more or less time with the person, and changing the external situation.
- Twelve pulls-in-two-directions (paradoxes and conundrums) make effective interpersonal communication challenging.
- For example, all people want both freedom and closeness.
- Left alone, relationships change, and when we try to force them, we can destroy them.
- The more intimacy and closeness we desire, the more risk is required.
- Self is produced in relationships and relationships are produced by two or more selves.
- Relationships can be managed by changing both internal and external elements.
- We can't fully understand a relationship without concepts, and abstract concepts distort living relationships.
- Generally, it helps to acknowledge the complexity of relationship so you aren't surprised when you experience problems.

A communication spiral occurs when the actions of each person in a relationship magnify those of the other. Communication spirals are evident almost everywhere, happening between humans, between us and other species, and among other species as well. A human-animal illustration should clarify the essential nature of spirals. My son Jason at age 3 saw a sleek, shiny cat. With the reckless abandonment of a child his age, he rushed at the cat to pet it. The wise cat, seeing potential death, moved out of Jason's reach. Not to be outdone, Jason tried harder. The cat moved farther away. Jason started running after the cat. The cat, no dummy about life, ran too. In a short 10 seconds from the initial lunge at the cat, Jason and the cat were running at full tilt. Luckily, the cat was faster and survived to run another day. Similarly, spirals occur in many contexts:

- A child disobeys the parent, the parent acts more punitively and harshly, and the child becomes even more unruly.
- A parent and 22-year-old son embark on a foreign adventure for 2 months—just the two of them. As the trip draws to a close, they both note on the plane ride home how close they feel to one another, and how easy their communication has become.
- An employee may be quiet and not forthcoming to the supervisor, the supervisor puts pressure on him to talk, and he becomes even more silent.
- Two guys are sitting in a bar; one accidentally touches the other, the first pushes him, an insult is uttered, and within a minute the two are fighting in the street.
- A supervisor is dissatisfied with an employee's performance but doesn't tell the employee. The employee is complaining to others about the supervisor. Both the employee and supervisor keep doing more of the same—the employee withdrawing and talking to others, the supervisor getting more annoyed and not telling the employee. Then 6 months later during the performance appraisal, the supervisor says, "We are reorganizing the office, and you won't be needed anymore."
- Two close friends buy a cabin midway between their two towns. Each time they go to the cabin, their relationship is reinforced, and not only do they ski better, they enjoy one another's company more.
- Two romantic partners feel that the other is pulling away. So each shares less, harbors grudges, and spends less time with the other, until there is a fight during which they end the relationship.
- Two opposite-sex friends spend a lot of time with one another. As they spend more time, they exclude others and feel closer and closer. It gets to the point that they don't want to begin other friendships because this one is so fulfilling.

All spirals, whether building in a positive or negative direction, tend to pick up a momentum that feeds back on itself—closeness and harmony build more closeness and harmony; misunderstanding and dissatisfaction create more misunderstanding and dissatisfaction. The responses produce a lock-step effect in relationships (Leary, 1955; Kurdek, 1991). Quality relationships, like close friendships, develop an "end in themselves"—quality—and become self-sustaining (Rose & Serafica, 1986).

"Communication Spirals, Paradoxes, and Conundrums" by William Wilmot from *Relational Communication*, 4th edition. Reprinted by permission of William Wilmot.

FIGURE 1   A communication
spiral.

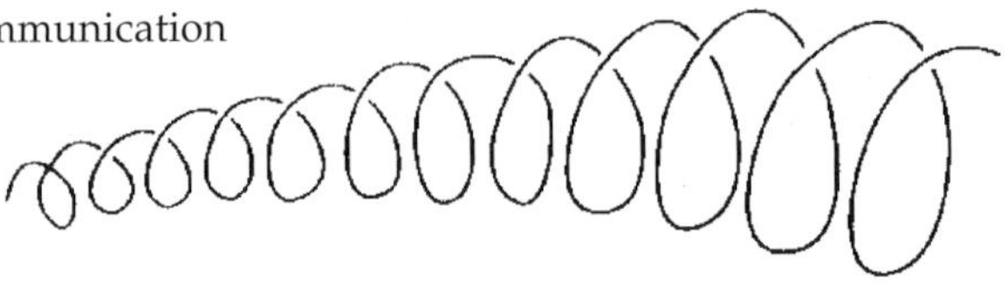

Communication spirals, whether they head in positive or negative directions, are characterized by these elements:

1. The participants' meanings intertwine in such a way that each person's behavior accelerates the dynamism of the relationship. The relational synergy
   builds upon itself in a continuously accelerating manner.
2. *Each* person's actions contribute to the overall dynamic. Whether you talk,
   retreat, engage, reinvest, or disinvest in the relationship, your communication (or lack of communication) directly impacts the other person, and vice
   versa. Each person reacts to the other (Kurdek, 1991).
3. Bateson (1972, 1979) noted long ago that spirals manifest either (1) *sym-*
   metrical communication moves or (2) *complementary* communication moves.
   In symmetrical spirals, as Person One does "more of the same" Person Two
   also does "more of the same"—for example, two people shouting at each
   other. In complementary spirals, as Person One does "more of the same"
   Person Two does "more of the opposite"—Person A shouts and Person B
   withdraws in silence (Wilden, 1980).
4. At any given period of time, a spiral is contributing to the relationship in
   either generative or degenerative ways. Generative spirals promote positive
   feelings about the relationship and more closeness; degenerative spirals
   induce negative feelings about the relationship and more distance.
5. Both generative and degenerative spirals tend to continue accelerating until
   the participants check the movement by some action.
6. Spirals can be changed, their pace quickened or slowed, or the direction
   reversed by the participants' actions.
7. Based on the communication spirals that unfold, relationships expand,
   wither, and repeat patterns of close-far.

A diagram of the nature of spirals in Figure 1 shows how the dynamics of
the communication for both persons tend to increase over time. Notice how the
cycles get larger and larger across time—which is the nature of all communication spirals.

Generative Spirals

When communicative behaviors interlock to produce more positive feelings
about the relationship, the participants are in a *generative spiral*. For instance,
the teacher who can be open and accepting of students often experiences
such spirals. Searching for the positive in a student and rewarding him or her

appropriately can open a student up for teacher influence. The more genuinely the teacher relates to the student, the better the student performs; the higher the quality of his or her performance, the more positive the teacher becomes.

Generative spirals are obviously not limited to teacher-student relationships. A highly motivated worker illustrates the same ever-widening nature of spirals. As one improves working conditions, the worker's motivation increases, which cycles back and makes for an even better climate, which increases....

In generative spirals, the perceptions of the partners become more productive and their mutual adjustments continue to build. In romantic couples, "love generates more love, growth more growth, and knowledge more knowledge" (O'Neill & O'Neill, 1972). The favorableness builds upon itself. Trust and understanding cycle back to create more trust and understanding. The relationship is precisely like a spiral—ever-widening.

We all experience generative spirals. The student who begins doing work of a high caliber earns better grades, becomes self-motivated, and enters a generative spiral. Each piece of work brings a reward (good grades or praise) that further encourages him or her to feats of excellence. And if conditions are favorable, the spiral can continue. Teachers who retrain and become more knowledgeable discover that they have more to offer students. The excited students, in turn, reinforce the teachers' desire to work hard so they can feel even better about their profession. In generative spirals, the actions of each individual [supply] a multiplier effect in reinforcement. The better you do, the more worthwhile you feel; the more worthwhile you feel, the better you do. The effects of a simple action reverberate throughout the system. An unexpected tenderness from your loved one, for instance, will not stop there. It will recycle back to you and probably come from you again in increased dosage. A good relationship with your supervisor promotes you to want to please more, and the supervisor, seeing your increased involvement, gives even more recognition to you.

Degenerative Spirals

Degenerative spirals are mirror images of generative spirals; the process is identical, but the results are opposite. In a degenerative spiral misunderstanding and discord create more and more relationship damage. As with generative spirals, degenerative spirals take many forms.

The inability to reach out and develop meaningful relationships is often compounded. The person who has reduced interest in others and does not form effective relationships suffers a lower self-esteem (because self-esteem is socially derived), which in turn cycles back and produces less interest in others. "The process is cyclical and degenerative" (Ziller, 1973). Or if one is afraid to love others, he or she shuns people, which in turn makes it more difficult to love. Also, such degenerative spirals often happen to people with regard to their sense of worth concerning work. People who have not established themselves in their profession but have been in the profession for a number of years may get caught in a spiral. They may spend time trying to appear busy, talking about others, or using various techniques to establish some sense of worth. Behavior that can change the spiral—working hard or retraining—are those least likely to occur. It is a self-fulfilling prophecy with a boost—it gets worse and worse. With each new gamut or ploy perfected (acquiring a new hobby, joining numerous social gatherings, etc.), the performance issues become further submerged.

A simple example of a degenerative spiral is the case of a lonely person. Lonely people tend to be less involved, less expressive, and less motivated in interactions. As a result, their partners in the conversation see the lonely person as uninvolved and less competent, and are less likely to initiate and maintain conversations with them. As a result, lonely people become further isolated from the social networks needed to break the cycle (Spitzberg & Canary, 1985).

Degenerative cycles are readily apparent when a relationship begins disintegrating. When distrust feeds distrust, defensiveness soars and the relationship worsens, and such "runaway relationships" become destructive for all concerned. In a "gruesome twosome," for instance, the two participants maintain a close, negative relationship. Each person receives fewer gratifications from the relationship, yet they maintain the attachment by mutual exploitation (Scheflen, 1960). When the relationship prevents one or both partners from gratifying normal needs, but the relationship is maintained, the twosome is caught in a degenerative spiral. Recent marital research demonstrates that, as love declines, negative conflict increases—a clear degenerative spiral (Lloyd & Cate, 1985).

Degenerative spirals, like generative spirals, occur in a variety of forms. A typical case involves the breakup of a significant relationship such as marriage. During a quarreling session one evening the husband says to the wife, "If you had not gone and gotten involved in an outside relationship with another man, our marriage could have made it. You just drained too much energy from us for our marriage to work." The wife responds by saying, "Yes, and had you given me the attention and care I longed for, I wouldn't have had an outside relationship." The infinite regress continues, each of them finding fault with why the other caused the termination of the marriage. The spiraling nature is clear. The more the wife retreats to an outside relationship, the less chance she has of having her needs met in the marriage. And the more the husband avoids giving her what she wants in the relationship, the more she will be influenced to seek outside relationships. One of the most common negative spirals between wives and husbands occurs when (1) the husband withdraws emotionally and (2) the wife expresses dissatisfaction to the husband (Segrin & Fitzpatrick, 1992).

Degenerative spirals are not limited to romantic relationships—they occur in all types. Parents and children often get caught up in spirals that create a dysfunctional system. The more dependent the child is on the parent, the more responsible and overburdened the parent is. And the more the parent takes responsibility for the child, the more this promotes dependence on the part of the child. It works like this: "One's actions toward other people generally effect a mirror duplication or a counter-measure from the other. This in turn tends to strengthen one's original action" (Leary, 1955)....

Altering Degenerative Spirals

Spirals, obviously, do change, with people going in and out of generative and degenerative spirals over the course of a relationship. And, as a relationship participant, you can have [an] impact on the nature of the spirals—even altering degenerative spirals once they start. There are specific choices you can make that can alter the direction a relationship is flowing.

First, alter your usual response—do what comes unnaturally. For example, if you are in a relationship where you and the other tend to escalate, [and] call each other names, you can stop the spiral by simply not allowing yourself to use negative language. Or, you can say, "This will just lead to a shouting match. I'm going to take a walk and talk with you when I come back," then exit from the normally hostile situation. Or say you have a roommate who is not very talkative and over the past 2 months you have tried to draw him out. You see that the more you talk, the more he retreats and the less he talks. Doing "more of the same" does not work, so do "less of the same." Don't act on the natural inclination to talk when he is silent; in fact, talk less and outwait him. Similarly, if you are often quiet in a group of four friends, people adapt to that by sometimes leaving you out of the decisions. Then, for the first time, begin to tell them what you would like to do. Change the patterns, and you change the spiral.

Wilmot and Stevens (1994) interviewed over 100 people who had "gone through a period of decline," and then improved their romantic, friendship, and family relationships—basically pulling out of a degenerative spiral. When asked what they did to "turn it around," it was found that a potent way of altering the patterns was to change behavior. The changes of behavior, of course, took many forms, given the particular type of relationship spiral that had occurred. Some people became more independent, some gave more "space" to the other, others changed locations or moved, and still others sacrificed for the partner or spent more time together. But the basic principle is the same—when in a degenerating or escalating set of communication patterns, change!

One last anecdote about changing patterns. I know one parent whose 11-year-old daughter was getting low grades in school. The parent had been a superb student, and the daughter, in the past, had done well. But, in the middle of the school year, the daughter started getting lower and lower grades. As the grades went down, the parent's criticism went up. Pretty soon, both the girl's grades and the mother-daughter relationship were in the cellar! After some help from an outsider, the mother took a vow to *not* talk anymore about grades, regardless of what happened. It was very difficult, for each evening the two had been arguing about grades; grades had become the focal point of the entire relationship. It only took 2 weeks, and the daughter's grades made dramatic jumps. The mother, who found "giving up" very difficult, had taken her negative part out of the communication system—and it changed.

One final note on changing your behavior. The people in the Wilmot and Stevens (1994) study noted that "persistence" was one important key to bringing about a change in the relationship. If the parent above had only stopped her criticism for one night, as soon as she resumed it, off the spiral would have gone again. The other person will be suspicious of your change at first, probably question[ing] your motives and [having] other negative interpretations. But if you are persistent in bringing the change, it will have effects on the other person, for his or her communication patterns are interlocked with yours.

Second, you can use third parties constructively. Friends, counselors, relatives, clergy, and others can sometimes provide a different perspective for you to begin to open up a degenerative system for change. Third parties can often make specific suggestions that will break the pattern of interlocking, mutually destructive behaviors that keep adding fuel to the degenerating relationship. In one case, a husband and wife went to a marriage counselor because they had come to a standoff. He was tired of her demands to always talk to her and pay attention. She was tired of his demands for more frequent sexual activity. As a result, they became entrapped in a degenerative spiral—he talked less, and she avoided situations of physical intimacy. Upon seeing the counselor, they both realized that they were getting nowhere fast. Each was trying to get the other to change first. With the help of the counselor, they renegotiated their relationship, and each began giving a little bit. Over a period of a few days they found themselves coming out of the degenerating patterns.

Third, you can reaffirm your relational goals. Often when people get stuck in negative patterns of interaction, the other automatically assumes you want to "jump ship." If you are in a downward spiral, whether with your parents, boss, lover, child, or friend, reaffirming what you each have to gain from the relationship can promote efforts to get it back. The couple who saw the counselor found that they both had an important goal to stay together—for if either one had "won" the fight and lost the relationship, neither would have gotten what he or she wanted. Relational reaffirmation can help you focus on all the things you can do to get the relationship back to a more positive phase. Good relationships take energy to sustain; similarly, making a commitment to the relationship obvious to the other will help pull you out of the debilitating negative patterns.

Fourth, you can alter a spiral by metacommunicating. Wilmot and Stevens's (1994) respondents reported having a "Big Relationship Talk"—talking about the relationship and what had led to the degenerating series of actions. When you comment on what you see happening, it can open up the spiral itself for discussion. One can say, "Our relationship seems to be slipping—I find myself criticizing you, and you seem to be avoiding me, and it looks like it is getting worse. What can we do to turn it around?" Such metacommunication, whether pointed to the conversational episodes or the overall relationship patterns, can set the stage for productive conflict management and give participants a sense of a control over the relationship dynamics. Metacommunication, especially when coupled with a reaffirmation of your relational goals ("I don't want us to be unhappy, I want us to both like being together, but we seem to ... "), can alter the destructive forces in a relationship. And, of course, you can use metacommunication in any type of relationship, such as on the job. J. P., for example, says, "Sally, it seems to me like our work enthusiasm is slipping away. What might we do to get that sense of fun back like we had about 6 months ago?"

Fifth, try to spend more or less time with the person. If you are on the "outs" with your co-workers, you could begin to spend more time with them—go to lunch, have coffee, take short strolls together. It is amazing what kinds of large changes can be purchased with just a small amount of time. Likewise, relationships often suffer because the people spend more time together than they can productively handle. So Tom always goes on a 3-day fishing trip with me in the summer as a way to both get more distance and independence in his marriage (and, coincidentally, to reaffirm our relationship with one another). Getting more distance and independence can bring you back refreshed and ready to relate again. Interestingly, Wilmot and Stevens (1994) found such "independence" moves an important way to alter a degenerating spiral.

Finally, we all recognize that changing an external situation can alter a degenerating relationship. One parent has a son who got into an ongoing battle with the principal of the junior high school. The feud went on for months, with the principal (according to the mother) tormenting her boy and the boy retaliating by being mischievous. The mutually destructive actions were arrested only when the boy switched schools. He (and the principal) had a chance to start over, not contaminated by the previous interlocking patterns.

Another way to change the external situation is to stay in the presence of the other person but move to a new environment. Many married couples have gone for extended vacations in order to give themselves time to work out new solutions to relationship problems. If the relationship is important to you and you want to preserve it, effort expended to help the relationship reach productive periods is time well spent. Retreats, for business partners, romantic partners, and friends, can allow an infusion of fresh energy into a declining relationship. Because once the degenerative phases are reached, the behaviors of each person tend to be mutually reinforcing and damaging. Each person can blame the other and claim his or her own innocence, but that will not alter the degeneration. It sometimes takes long, hard work to alter a negative spiral, and it may be successful if both put in some effort. But as every counselor knows from experience, one person alone can usually not change the relationship. If that person makes changes, and the other reciprocates, you have a chance to turn the spiral around.

Woody Allen captured the essence of relational change when he said, "Relationships are like a shark. They either move forward, or they die." Our relationships are dynamic, always moving and changing either toward or away from improvement. Participants' behaviors interlock so that each one's behavior influences the others, and the mutually conjoined behaviors intensify the other's reactions.

People look at their relationships using different time frames. Some people tend to only look at the macro perspective, charting the changes in yearly units such as "do I feel as good about my job today as I did a year ago." A relationship may not look any different today than it did yesterday, but over a year's time, you can see either overall improvement or disintegration. The long-term spirals are identified by comparing the relationship to a much earlier state.

Other times one may process and categorize a relationship on an hour-by-hour basis. For example, when Jan's romantic partner announced that she wanted to "call it off," Jan spent the next 2 weeks thinking about the relationship, talking to her partner, and doing endless processing of all the changes coming her way. Rapid relational change, especially if it is unexpected, can cause intense processing of the relationship, sometimes to the point of overload. Those who suffer from an unexpected firing, termination of a romance, or disinheritance from the family find themselves processing at a depth they didn't think possible.

What is important, is to begin to sensitize yourself to the ebbs and flows inherent in all relationships, so you can make informed choices. Becoming attuned to the nature of communication spirals can increase your understanding of these processes.

TANGLES IN THE WEB: PARADOXES AND CONUNDRUMS

As you go through life, whether you are 18 or 80, the experience and understanding of your relationships is not a linear, step-by-step process. Like relationships themselves, our understanding is imperfect, and it is easy to overestimate how much we know. Relationships are elusive.

There are some relational paradoxes (statements that are both true but contradict one another) (Wilmot, 1987) and conundrums—puzzlements and elements that are inherently unsolvable. Here are a few of them.

1. We want contradictory things in relationships: freedom and closeness, openness to talk yet protection, stability and excitement. These dialectic tensions seem to be present in all relationships.

In many romantic relationships we want both freedom and connection, excitement and stability. In the family context we often want the others to accept who we are, yet we spend inordinate amounts of time centering on how we can change them. We talk openly about the importance of "communication" in relationships, but it appears to be more of a cultural belief than an actual fact (Wilmot & Stevens, 1994; Parks, 1982). Maybe we can begin to celebrate the tension inherent in all relationships rather than trying to solve the contradictory needs, flowing with the needs as they change back and forth.

2. Both insider and outsider views of relationships are fraught with errors.

Outsiders to relationships can more accurately observe our actual communication behavior but are less accurate than we are at specifying the *meaning* of those behaviors within this particular relationship. When you, as an outsider, look at someone else's relationship, your judgments can be a good projective test for what you personally believe is the "key" to success. Think of a marriage you know that you would describe as high quality. To what would you attribute it?

- hard work
- good match on background characteristics
- being raised in nondysfunctional families
- luck
- how well they communicate with one another
- a fine match on introversion/extroversion
- similar religious affiliations
- the support of their networks of family and friends
- both being raised in the same part of the country
- the length of time they have been together
- their ability to raise children successfully
- their mutual respect and compassion
- their intelligence
- their warmth and expressiveness
- their similar life struggles
- their commitment to one another
- their clarity about how to perform their roles
- their overriding love of one another
- their supportive friends
- similar hobbies and pastimes
- being at the same level of attractiveness

Outsiders, looking at someone else's relationship, tend to rely on external or situational factors in making their guesses (Burgoon & Newton, 1991). And we tend to evaluate others a bit more harshly than they do themselves, with us seeing the limitations of one or both of the partners: "I can't believe she stays married to him—he is so boring in public." When looking at someone's communication behavior, outsiders judge conversations less favorably than do those on the inside (Street, Mulac, & Wiemann, 1988). Outsiders generate faulty hypotheses about the intentions of the communicators—"she did that because she wants to control him" (Stafford, Waldron, & Infield, 1989). When we observe others' communication, we compensate for lack of information about their internal states by using our own personal theories—our "implicit personality theories" (Stafford, Waldron, & Infield, 1989). As an outsider, our observations are fraught with errors and overinterpretations, sort of "what we get is what we see," with most of it coming from us.

As insiders, our views aren't any less biased; we just tend to focus on different aspects (Dillard, 1987; Sillars & Scott, 1983). For example, insiders to marital relationships tend to overestimate their similarity and act with confidence on their views of the other. Yet the perceptions are not objectively accurate. Therefore, *all* views of relationships are inherently distorted—outsiders and insiders alike. Researchers and book writers (including this one) are themselves influenced by their own needs and perspectives, often looking for some order in the midst of considerable chaos.

3. Relationships are problematic—if we don't do anything about their natural dynamic, they may atrophy. If we try to force them, to "make them happen," we may destroy their essential nature.

The natural forces on relationships, marriage partners having to earn a living and nurture children, friends moving away from one another, tend to move most in the direction of decreased quality over time. In a sense, it is as if there is an energy in relationships that, if you don't continually reinvest in it, will cause the relationship to atrophy. Yet, on the other hand, we need to not try to "force" relationships. It is a rare individual in this culture who can command himself or herself to "love" someone else. The question of how to enhance a long-term relationship—whether family, romantic, or friend—looms large for all of us.... It is clear that, so far, there are no guarantees in relationships.

4. Committed relationships, such as marriage, may bring us much unhappiness because we think their purpose is happiness generation. Maybe their purpose is wholeness, grounded in the dialectical encounter between mates (Guggenbuhl-Craig, 1977).

In North America and most Western cultures, people choose marriage partners and friends for what they do for us—make us happy, excite us sexually, provide a sense of fun and connection. Yet ... , maybe this "what does it do for me" sets us up for disappointment and failure. From a spiritual perspective, one could say that our relationships, while started to "make us happy," have a more difficult and nobler purpose—to allow us to be challenged, to grow, and to change. Lifetime friends, for example, may serve the function of helping us correct ourselves when we get out of line in public. Romantic partners will set the stage for our unresolved issues of life and eccentricity to flourish, and see their downside. Family members will test our commitment, resilience and love, and if we move through that test we can emerge on a higher plane of relatedness.

5. The more intimacy and closeness we want, the more risk we face in the relationship. The greatest pleasure *and* pain come from those to whom we are the closest. Relationships bring both joy and suffering.

The very relationships people spend so much time processing—romantic, family, and friendship—are the ones to bring both the extremes of joy and pain. The less close relationships, while they can bring stability and meaning into life, may not address some of our deepest needs. Risk and reward seem to be opposite sides of the same coin.

6. We often see the "self" as concrete and findable. Yet relationships are no less "real" than an individual self is.

In our culture, we take, as has been noted many times, the "self" as individual, disconnected, separate, and findable. We put the locus of most things into the self—discussing "self-esteem" and "personality" as if they were real things and not abstract concepts. Relationships are neither more nor less figments of our concepts than are our selves—but we don't tend to see it that way in this culture. It is important to note that our selves do have a conventional reality—there is a person standing there. Yet upon close examination, the "self" cannot be found. Is your brain your self? Your torso? Your legs? Your emotions? We impose the concept of "self" onto the physical and emotional aspects and stop our analysis. Relationships, while not physically represented, are no less real than are our selves. We talk about relationships, and their "reality," upon examination, is just as findable (and no less so) [as] that of the self.

7. Self is produced in relationship to others; relationships are produced from two selves.

… It has been argued that we originate and live in-relation; we co-create our selves in relation to one another. And relationships are produced from the two persons who have a communication connection. Self and other produce, and are produced by, relationship. And self is more fruitfully viewed as "with the ecological system" rather than as the center of one's world (Broome, 1991, p. 375).

8. The greatest individual growth, and the greatest derailment of individual growth, comes from the hurt and disappointment of relationships gone awry. Relationships can serve as springboards for growth or just toss you higher so you land harder.

When we face the natural traumas of life, our response determines the outcome. Trauma can bring transformation or derailment. Some people are broken when a relationship terminates, for example, or when an important person dies. Others, through grieving and slowly transforming themselves, reopen to relationships and life, reconnecting anew and building better relationships in the future.

9. We can solve problems in relationships by (1) internal, personal change; and (2) changing the external, communication connection between the two. Change at any one level reverberates to the other level, for both us and the other person.

Like the chicken and the egg, which comes first—you or relationship? And if you have difficulties, do you "get your stuff together" and then reenter other relationships, or do you begin other relationships so you can become stronger? Both routes are used, and both can work. If you undergo change, it will reverberate in all your relationships: the boundaries are permeable. If your relationship changes, it will alter you; the influence always flows both ways.

10. We can't fully understand our relationships without concepts, and as soon as we use an abstract notion we impose its limitations on what we are seeing. Labels are essential and limiting, and cannot capture an ever-changing reality. As Wilden says, "all theories of relationship require a certain artificial closure" (Wilden, 1980, p. 114).

We can't really proceed with understanding without labels, and when you introduce your "boyfriend" to your family, it gives them a clue about the relationship. Yet when you use the label, it restricts both your and the other's views of that relationship. Each relationship contains many complex and contradictory elements, and it cannot be accurately captured by "boyfriend." Further, there is always "label lag"—the relationship changes, and the label stays the same. A "married couple" of 6 months will be very different than that very same couple at 6 years or 6 decades, yet they are still referred to as married. All concepts and labels are limiting and constricting—and essential.

11. General conclusions about gender, culture, and relationships may not apply at all to your particular relationships.

One of the problems in talking about "gender" or "cultural" effects is that we are always talking about groupings that help us "understand" on an abstract level. But your particular relationship may not reflect the general norms at all. Just like a theory of gravity cannot tell you about when a particular apple will fall from a tree, studying relational dynamics will not tell you about what will happen in your relationship. When studies on gender, for example, show that females are more expressive than males, what do you do if the woman in a cross-sex romantic relationship is the less expressive of the two? It is probably better to focus on the central issue—expressiveness, and the match or mismatch between the partners—rather than trying to reflect the general norm. Similarly, the finding that gay males have more partners than lesbians or heterosexuals does not mean that a gay man cannot live a life of commitment to another.

12. Learning about relationships occurs before, during, and after the relationship is a findable event.

Our perspectives on our relationships do not end—they only change. Just think for a moment about how you interpret events that happened to you in your childhood. As you move through time you will reinterpret them many times, focusing on different aspects, and seeing them in a different light. Likewise, the friendship that you used to see as a barometer of yourself may be later seen as not helping you at all at a stage of life. A devastating romantic termination may be seen later as the "best thing that ever happened to me." While many of us do not seek difficulties, most of us say, in retrospect, that it is what produced the learning so essential to the next stage of our life. I was once talking to a fellow on a flight from Helsinki, Finland, to Boston. He was in a long-distance relationship with a Finnish woman, and he lived in Boston, and here is what he said. "I did fatherhood and marriage, so I guess I'm doing this for awhile"—making retrospective sense of his relationship that was allowing him to collect considerable frequent flyer miles!

REVIEW QUESTIONS

1. Define *communication spiral.*
2. According to this reading, what is necessary in order to stop a spiral?

3. What's the difference between a generative and a degenerative spiral?
4. What does Wilmot and Stevens's research indicate about the role of persistence in altering a degenerative spiral?
5. What is metacommunicating?
6. What is a dialectic tension in a relationship?
7. What are the specific problems Wilmot identifies with both insider and outsider views of a relationship?

PROBES

1. Explain what Wilmot means when he says that, in a spiral, "each person's behavior accelerates the dynamism of the relationship." Give an example that includes a positive dynamism and one that includes a negative dynamism.
2. Could a spiral that appears to be generative to some member(s) of a relationship appear to be degenerative to others? Explain.
3. What is one generative spiral in your communication experience that you could *enhance*? What is one degenerative spiral in your communication experience that you could *break*?
4. Wilmot suggests that one of the ways you can "do what comes unnaturally" is to stop trying to make things better. Explain why this might work.
5. Wilmot suggests that you might change an external situation in order to alter a degenerating spiral. This could include changing locations—your home, work, or school. But some people also emphasize that "Wherever you go, there you are," which is to say that you need to change your attitude or approach, not your location. What do you think works best?
6. Do you believe that the main purpose of a long-term relationship like a marriage is happiness generation, or what Wilmot calls "wholeness, grounded in the dialectical encounter between mates"?
7. What is the relationship between Wilmot's brief discussion of the self in paradoxes 6 and 7 and Stewart, Zediker, and Witteborn's discussion of the self in Chapter 3?
8. Identify one general conclusion about gender, culture, and relationships that does *not* apply to one of your relationships.

REFERENCES

Bateson, G. (1972). *Steps to an ecology of mind*. New York: Ballantine Books.
Bateson, G. (1979). *Mind and nature: A necessary unity*. New York: Bantam Books.
Broome, B. J. (1991). Building shared meaning: Implications of a relational approach to empathy for teaching intercultural communication. *Communication Education, 40,* 235–249.

Burgoon, J. K., & Newton, D. A. (1991). Applying a social meaning model to relational message interpretations of conversational involvement: Comparing observer and participant perspectives. *Southern Communication Journal, 56,* 96–113.

Dillard, J. P. (1987). Close relationships at work: Perceptions of the motives and performance of relational participants. *Journal of Social and Personal Relationships, 4,* 179–193.

Guggenbuhl-Craig, A. (1977). *Marriage dead or alive.* Murray Stein (trans.). Dallas, TX: Spring Publications.

Kurdek, L. A. (1991). Marital stability and changes in marital quality in newlywed couples: A test of the contextual model. *Journal of Social and Personal Relationships, 5,* 201–221.

Leary, T. (1955). The theory and measurement methodology of interpersonal communication. *Psychiatry, 18,* 147–161.

Lloyd, S. A., & Cate, R. M. (1985). The developmental course of conflict in dissolution of premarital relationships. *Journal of Social and Personal Relationships, 2,* 179–194.

O'Neill, N., & O'Neill, G. (1972). *Open marriage.* New York: M. Evans.

Parks, M. R. (1982). Ideology in interpersonal communication: Off the couch and into the world. In M. Burgoon, (Ed.), *Communication yearbook 5* (pp. 79–107). New Brunswick, NJ: International Communication Association/Transaction Books.

Rose, S., & Serafica, F. C. (1986). Keeping and ending casual, close and best friendships. *Journal of Social and Personal Relationships, 3,* 275–288.

Scheflen, A. (1960). Communication and regulation in psychotherapy. *Psychiatry, 26,* 126–136.

Segrin, C., & Fitzpatrick, M. A. (1992). Depression and verbal aggressiveness in different marital types. *Communication Studies, 43,* 79–91.

Sillars, A. L., & Scott, M. D. (1983). Interpersonal perception between intimates: An integrative review. *Human Communication Research, 10,* 153–176.

Spitzberg, B. H., & Canary, D. J. (1985). Loneliness and relationally competent communication. *Journal of Social and Personal Relationships, 2,* 387–402.

Stafford, L., Waldron, V. R., & Infield, L. L. (1989). Actor-observer differences in conversational memory. *Human Communication Research, 15,* 590–611.

Street, R. L., Jr., Mulac, A., & Wiemann, J. M. (1988). Speech evaluation differences as a function of perspective (participant versus observer) and presentational medium. *Human Communication Research, 14,* 333–363.

Wilden, A. (1980). *System and structure: Essays on communication and exchange,* 2nd ed. London: Tavistock Publications.

Wilmot, W. W. (1987). *Dyadic communication.* New York: Random House.

Wilmot, W. W., & Stevens, D. C. (1994). Relationship rejuvenation: Arresting decline in personal relationships. In R. Conville (Ed.), *Communication and structure.* Philadelphia, PA: Ablex, pp. 103–124.

Ziller, R. C. (1973). *The social self.* New York: Pergamon Press.

Handling the Break-Up of Relationships
Steve Duck

Like the previous reading by Wilmot, this one analyzes how relationships get into trouble and how they might be rescued. Steve Duck is a Brit, which is why you'll find the word "whilst" and the spelling "behaviour" here. For a number of years, he's been a distinguished interpersonal communication teacher and researcher at the University of Iowa. This excerpt from his book *Human Relationships* provides a way to understand how personal relationships come apart and how they can sometimes be put back together.

Duck explains the four typical phases that people go through when breaking up. The first is "intrapsychic" or internal, and consists of at least one member of the relationship brooding about his or her partner. The second phase is called "dyadic" because it's the time when the two partners (the dyad) talk with each other about breaking up. This leads, usually rapidly, to the third step, a "social" phase when they tell other people and seek their support. The final phase is called "grave-dressing," because it consists of communication that tries to "bury the relationship good and proper." During this phase, the people involved create an account of the relationship's history and demise. This account gives the partners and others a way to make sense out of what happened.

One benefit of this model is that it suggests what relational partners might do if they want to "put the relationship right" or rebuild it. You obviously can't just reverse the steps of the break-up, because memories of the old relationship and its demise are necessarily going to be involved in any new relationship that's developed. But the model does identify what people can do at the different stages or phases of dissolution. So, for example, Duck notes that if the relationship is at the intrapsychic phase of dissolution, then "repair should aim to reestablish liking for the partner rather than to correct behavioural faults in ourselves or our nonverbal behaviour." Other strategies are appropriate at other phases of a break-up. As Duck concludes, "Different parts of the story need to be addressed at different phases of breakdown."

MAIN IDEAS

- Most break-ups go through a pattern of four phases: intrapsychic, dyadic, social, and grave-dressing.
- The intrapsychic stage consists of reaching a threshold of dissatisfaction that leads you to do something decisive about a relational problem.
- The dyadic phase makes the process social by confronting one's partner.
- The social phase involves publicizing the relationship distress, getting support from others, and perhaps obtaining third-party intervention.
- The grave-dressing phase includes self-justification and marketing one's own version of the break-up.
- Understanding these phases can help you cope with relationship break-up.

By far the most common experience of negative things in relationships is the management of minor irritations and trivial hassles that arise day to day in relationships of all kinds (Duck & Wood, 1995). The rosy picture of relational progress is thus only part of the truth (and Cupach & Spitzberg, 1994, devote a whole book to the dark side). For instance, why have researchers just focused on love and overlooked needling, bitching, boredom, complaints, harassment, and enemyships (Duck, 1994)? Why do we know more about romantic relationships than we do about troublesome relationships? Things often go wrong in relationships in all sorts of ways and cause a lot of pain when they do, some of it intentionally hurtful (Vangelisti, 1994). Sometimes it is Big Stuff and leads to break-up of the relationship, but most of the time it is relatively trivial and leads to nothing except hurt feelings and the conflicts involved in *managing* the occurrence. How does it happen?

WHEN THINGS GO WRONG

There are several parts to acquaintance, and so we should expect there to be several parts to the undoing of acquaintance during relational dissolution. This is partly because relationships exist in time and usually take time to fall apart, so that at different times different processes are taking a role in the dissolution. It is also because, like a motor car, a relationship can have accidents for many reasons, whether the "driver's" fault, mechanical failure or the actions of other road users. Thus, in a relationship, one or both partners might be hopeless at relating; or the structure and mechanics of the relationship may be wrong, even though both partners are socially competent in other settings; or outside influences can upset it. All of these possibilities have been explored (Baxter, 1984; Duck, 1982; Orbuch, 1992). However, I am going to focus on my own approach to these issues and refer you elsewhere for details of the other work. . . .

The essence of my approach to relational dissolution is that there are several different phases, each with a characteristic style and concern (Duck, 1982). Thus, as shown in Figure 1, the first phase is a breakdown phase where partners (or one partner only) become(s) distressed at the way the relationship is conducted. This generates an *intrapsychic phase* characterized by a brooding focus on the relationship and on the partner. Nothing is said to the partner at this point: the agony is either private or shared only with a diary or with relatively anonymous other persons (bar servers, hairdressers, passengers on the bus) who will not tell the partner about the complaint. Just before exit from this phase, people move up the scale of confidants so that they start to complain to their close friends, but do not yet present their partner with the full extent of their distress or doubts about the future of the relationship.

Once we decide to do something about a relational problem we have to deal with the difficulties of facing up to the partner. Implicit—and probably wrongly

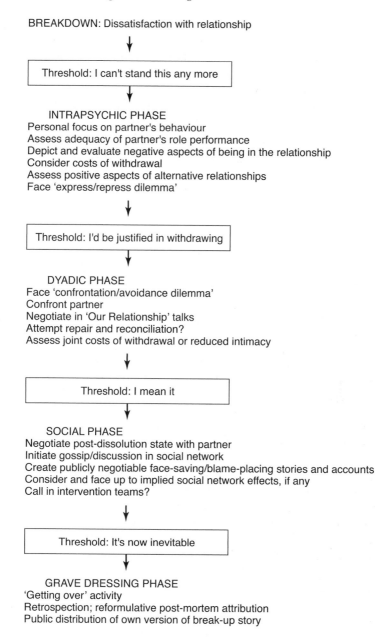

BREAKDOWN: Dissatisfaction with relationship

Threshold: I can't stand this any more

INTRAPSYCHIC PHASE
Personal focus on partner's behaviour
Assess adequacy of partner's role performance
Depict and evaluate negative aspects of being in the relationship
Consider costs of withdrawal
Assess positive aspects of alternative relationships
Face 'express/repress dilemma'

Threshold: I'd be justified in withdrawing

DYADIC PHASE
Face 'confrontation/avoidance dilemma'
Confront partner
Negotiate in 'Our Relationship' talks
Attempt repair and reconciliation?
Assess joint costs of withdrawal or reduced intimacy

Threshold: I mean it

SOCIAL PHASE
Negotiate post-dissolution state with partner
Initiate gossip/discussion in social network
Create publicly negotiable face-saving/blame-placing stories and accounts
Consider and face up to implied social network effects, if any
Call in intervention teams?

Threshold: It's now inevitable

GRAVE DRESSING PHASE
'Getting over' activity
Retrospection; reformulative post-mortem attribution
Public distribution of own version of break-up story

FIGURE 1   A sketch of the main phases of dissolving personal relationships.
Source: Reprinted from Duck (1982a; 16) "A topography of relationship disengagement of dissolution," in S. W. Duck (ed.), Personal Relationships 4: Dissolving Personal Relationships. *London: Academic Press. Reproduced by permission.*

implicit—in my 1982 model was the belief that partners would tell one another about their feelings and try to do something about them. Both Lee (1984) and Baxter (1984) show that people often leave relationships without telling their partner, or else by fudging their exits. For instance, they may say: "I'll call you" and then not do it; or "Let's keep in touch" and never contact the partner; or "Let's not be lovers but stay as friends" and then have hardly any contact in the future (Metts et al., 1989). Given that my assumption is partly wrong, it nevertheless assumes that partners in formal relationships like marriage will have to face up to their partner, whilst partners in other relationships may or may not do so. The *dyadic phase* is the phase when partners try to confront and talk through their feelings about the relationship and decide how to sort out the future. Assuming that they decide to break up (and even my 1982 model was quite clear that they may decide *not* to do that), they then move rapidly to a *social phase* when they have to tell other people about their decision and enlist some social support for their side of the debate. It is no good just leaving a relationship: we seek other people to agree with our decision or to prop us up and support what we have done. Other people can support us in ways such as being sympathetic and generally understanding. More important, they can side with our version of events and our version of the partner's and the relationship's faults ("I always thought he/she was no good," "I could never understand how you two could get along—you never seemed right for each other"). This is the *grave-dressing* phase: once the relationship is dead we have to bury it "good and proper"—with a tombstone saying how it was born, what it was like and why it died. We have to create an account of the relationship's history and, as it were, put that somewhere so that other people can see it and, we hope, accept it. In this phase, people may strategically reinterpret their view of their partner, for example by shifting from the view of the person as "exciting" to being "dangerously unpredictable" or from being "attractively reliable" to being "boring"—exactly the same features of the person are observed, but they are given different *labels* more suited to one's present feelings about the person (Felmlee, 1995).

In breakdown of relationships as elsewhere in life, gossip plays a key role. Here it works in the social and grave-dressing phases and in a dissolving relationship we actively seek the support of members of our social networks and do so by gossiping about our partners (La Gaipa, 1982). In some instances, we look for "arbitrators" who will help to bring us back together with our partner. In other cases, we just want someone to back up and spread around our own version of the break-up and its causes. A crucial point made by La Gaipa (1982) is that every person who leaves a relationship has to leave with "social credit" intact for future use: that is, we cannot just get out of a relationship but we have to leave in such a way that we are not disgraced and debarred from future relationships. We must leave with a reputation for having been let down or faced with unreasonable odds or an unreasonable partner. It is socially acceptable to say "I left because we tried hard to make it work but it wouldn't." It is not socially acceptable to leave a relationship with the cheery but unpalatable admission:

"Well basically I'm a jilt and I got bored dangling my partner on a string so I just broke the whole thing off when it suited me." That statement could destroy one's future credit for new relationships.

Accounts often serve the purpose of beginning the "getting over" activity that is essential to complete the dissolution (Weber, 1983). A large part of this involves selecting an account of dissolution that refers to a fault in the partner or relationship that pre-existed the split or was even present all along (Weber, 1983). This is the "I always thought she/he was a bit of a risk to get involved with, but I did it anyway, more fool me" story that we have all used from time to time.

However, accounts also serve another purpose: The creation of a publicly acceptable story is essential to getting over the loss of a relationship (McCall, 1982). It is insufficient having a story that we alone accept: Others must also endorse it. As McCall (1982) astutely observed, part of the success of good counsellors consists in their ability to construct such stories for persons in distress about relational loss.

PUTTING IT RIGHT

If two people wanted to put a relationship right, then they could decide to try and make it "redevelop"; that is, they could assume that repairing a relationship is just like acquaintance, and go through the same processes in order to regain the previous level of intimacy. This means that we have to assume that break-up of relationships is the reverse of acquaintance, and that to repair it, all we have to do is "rewind" it. This makes some sense: developing relationships grow in intimacy whereas breaking ones decline in intimacy so perhaps we should just try to rewind the intimacy level.

However, in other ways this idea does not work. For instance, in acquaintance we get to know more about a person but in breakdown we cannot get to know less, we must just reinterpret what we already know and put it into a different framework, model, or interpretation ("Yes, he's always been kind, but then he was always after something").

I think that we need to base our ideas about repair not on our model of acquaintance but on a broader model of breakdown of relationships that takes account of principles governing formation of relationships in general. Research on relationships has begun to help us understand what precisely happens when things go wrong. By emphasizing processes of breakdown of relationships and processes of acquaintance, we have the chance now to see that there are also processes of repair. These processes do, however, address different aspects of relationships in trouble. This, I believe, also gives us the chance to be more helpful in putting things right. Bear in mind the model just covered, as you look at Figure 2, and you will see that it is based on proposals made earlier. There are

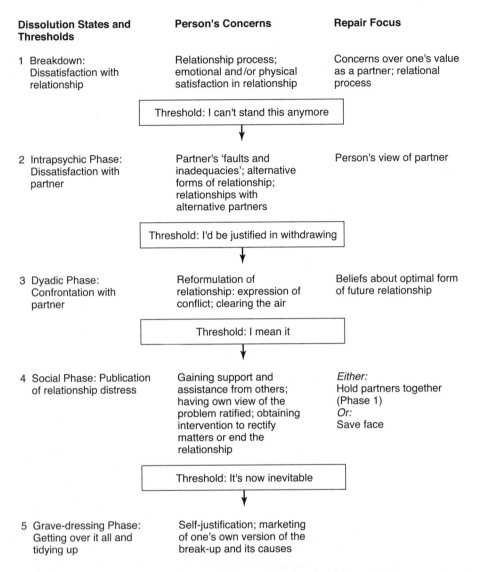

FIGURE 2   A sketch of the main concerns at different phases of dissolution.
Source: Reprinted from Duck (1984, 169) "A perspective on the repair of relationships: Repair of what when?", in S. W. Duck (ed.), Personal Relationships 5: Repairing Personal Relationships. *London: Academic Press. Reproduced by permission.*

phases to repair of relationships, and some styles work at some times and not at others (Duck, 1984).

    If the relationship is at the intrapsychic phase of dissolution, for instance, then repair should aim to reestablish liking for the partner rather than to correct behavioural faults in ourselves or our nonverbal behaviour, for instance. These latter may be more suitable if persons are in the breakdown phase instead. Liking for the partner can be reestablished or aided by means such as keeping a record, mental or physical, of the positive or pleasing behaviour of our partner rather than listing the negatives and dwelling on them in isolation (Bandura, 1977). Other methods involve redirection of attributions, that is, attempting to use more varied, and perhaps more favourable, explanations for the partner's behaviour—in brief, to make greater efforts to understand the reasons that our partner may give for what is happening in the relationship.

At other phases of dissolution, different strategies of repair are appropriate, according to this model. For instance, at the social phase, persons outside the relationship have to decide whether it is better to try to patch everything up or whether it may serve everyone's best interests to help the partners to get out of the relationship. Figure 2 thus indicates that the choice of strategies is between pressing the partners to stay together or helping them to save face by backing up their separate versions of the break-up. An extra possibility would be to create a story that is acceptable to both of them, such as "It was an unworkable relationship ... and that is nobody's fault."

Essentially, this model proposes only three things: relationships are made up of many parts and processes, some of which "clock in" at some points in the relationship's life and some at others; relationships can go wrong in a variety of ways; repairing of disrupted relationships will be most effective when it addresses the concerns that are most important to us at the phase of dissolution of relationships which we have reached.

The ways we change our "stories" about a relationship provide important psychological data, and they indicate the dynamic nature of the help that outsiders have to give to relationships in trouble. Different parts of the story need to be addressed at different phases of breakdown. Is one and the same kind of intervention appropriate at all stages of a relationship's decline? Probably not. It makes more sense to look for the relative appropriateness of different intervention techniques as those dynamics unfold. There are few "scripts" for handling break-up of relationships and many intriguing research questions surround the actual processes by which people extricate themselves (or can be helped to extricate themselves) from unwanted relationships. For example, Miller and Parks (1982) look at relationship dissolution as an influence process and show that different strategies for changing attitudes can help in dissolution. It is now a major aim in the personal relationships field to explain dissolution and repair of relationships.

REVIEW QUESTIONS

1. Define *intrapsychic, dyadic, social,* and *grave-dressing.*
2. According to Duck, what role does gossip have in the breaking-up process?
3. What are "accounts," and how do they function in the breaking-up process?
4. Why isn't the rebuilding process just the reverse of the breaking-up process?

PROBES

1. Sometimes romantic partners—especially if they're married—do try to work through their serious problems, but often the problems are so painful that they move directly from brooding to themselves to discussing with friends. How prevalent and how important do you think Duck's "dyadic" phase actually is?
2. Duck doesn't discuss the "threshold" parts of the two figures in this reading. What are they, and what is their significance?
3. Sometimes break-ups happen because of poor communication. Do you believe that a relationship ever ends because of *good* communication? Explain.

REFERENCES

Bandura, A. (1977). *Social learning theory.* Englewood Cliffs, NJ: Prentice-Hall.

Baxter, L. A. (1984). Trajectories of relationship disengagement. *Journal of Social and Personal Relationships, 1:* 29–48.

Cupach, W. R., & Spitzberg, B. Y. (1994). *The darkside of interpersonal communication.* Hillsdale, NJ: Erlbaum.

Duck, S. (1982). A topography of relationship disengagement and dissolution, In S. W. Duck (Ed.), *Personal relationships 4: Dissolving personal relationships.* London: Academic Press.

Duck, S. W. (1984). A perspective on the repair of personal relationships: Repair of what, when? In S. W. Duck (Ed.), *Personal relationships 5: repairing personal relationships.* London: Academic Press.

Duck, S. W. (1994). Stratagems, spoils, and a serpent's tooth: On the delights and dilemmas of personal relationships. In W. Cupach & B. H. Spitzberg (Eds.), *The darkside of interpersonal relationships.* Hillsdale, NJ: Erlbaum.

Duck, S. W., & Wood, J. T. (Eds.) (1995). *Confronting relationship challenges, Vol. 5. understanding relationship processes.* Thousand Oaks, CA: Sage.

Felmlee, D. H. (1995). Fatal attractions: Affection and disaffection in intimate relationships. *Journal of Social and Personal Relationships. 12,* 295–311.

La Gaipa, J. J. (1982). Rituals of disengagement. In S. W. Duck (Ed.), *Personal relationships 4: Dissolving personal relationships.* London: Academic Press.

Lee, L. (1984). Sequences in separation: A framework for investigating the endings of personal (romantic) relationships. *Journal of Social and Personal Relationships, 1,* 49–74.

McCall, G. J. (1982). Becoming unrelated: The management of bond dissolution. In S. W. Duck (Ed.), *Personal relationships 4: Dissolving personal relationships.* London: Academic Press.

Metts, S., Cupach, W., & Bejlovec, R. A. (1989). "I love you too much to ever start liking you": Redefining romantic relationships. *Journal of Social and Personal Relationships, 6,* 259–274.

Miller, G. R., & Parks, M. R. (1982). Communication in dissolving relationships. In S. W. Duck (Ed.), *Personal relationships 4: Dissolving personal relationships.* London: Academic Press.

Orbuch, T. L. (Ed.) (1992). *Relationship loss.* New York: Springer-Verlag.

Vangelisti, A. (1994). Messages that hurt. In W. R. Cupach & B. H. Spitzberg (Eds.), *The darkside of interpersonal communication* (pp. 53–82). New York: Guilford.

Weber, A. (1983). The breakdown of relationships. Paper presented to Conference on Social Interaction and Relationships, Nags Head, North Carolina, May.

I Hear You, and I Have a Different Perspective

Susan M. Campbell

This reading offers a simple but powerful suggestion for helping to turn a communication wall into a bridge. For some readers, it might have been enough simply to bullet this statement—"I hear you, and I have a different perspective"—and leave it up to you to apply it. But as Campbell unpacks the statement, I think you'll get a sense of why it works, and how.

Like most self-help materials, this is filled with examples taken from the author's experience with students and clients. I hope these give you a concrete sense of why this statement can help get a conflict unstuck.

One reason is that the statement doesn't put any conflict party "in the wrong." It embodies the fact that two people have different perspectives, without fault finding or blaming. It also helps build trust by putting beliefs and conclusions on the table, where both parties can reflect on them. In addition, you can enhance your trust in yourself because you move beyond assuming that "you'll lose yourself if you become open to the other's views." As Campbell emphasizes, "If you cannot get to the point where you can sincerely speak [these] words . . . you will never be a very good negotiator." Holding differences is an advanced communication skill, and an important one.

Another communication skill that this statement evidences is what Campbell calls "the ability to shift into a bigger mind." Especially when two people have a problem, each often brings a perspective that is anchored in her or his own preferences, expectations, assumptions, and style. There is nothing inherently wrong with this—in Chapter 12 Karen Zediker and I call this "holding your own ground." But as we also indicate there, if conflict is to be managed, this perspective needs to be broadened to include the other parties. As Campbell puts it, "Using the phrase 'I hear you, and . . .' affirms the reality and validity of both views, while at the same time giving partners a structure for containing the pain that the difference causes." This is an important point. The broader perspective that this statement offers can function to acknowledge both the difference and the pain, and it does so in a way that allows both parties to continue the conversation.

This one statement is not a panacea; it won't eliminate or manage all the conflict in your life. But it can help enhance your conflict communicating.

MAIN IDEAS

- Conflict can be scary, and it can often help to use the key phrase, "I hear you, and I have a different perspective."
- This phrase can reduce the stress of the person speaking it.
- The phrase can also enhance trust of both speaker and hearer.
- The phrase moves you to "shift into a bigger mind," that is, approach the conflict from what Stone, Patton, and Heen call "The Third Story" (Chapter 6) and to take what Folger, Scott, and Poole call a "both/and perspective."
- The phrase can also help foster presence.

> *I hear that you want to spend the weekend with your parents, and I'd prefer that we spend a romantic weekend alone.*
> *I hear you saying you want to get a new truck, and I'm afraid we won't be able to make the payments.*
> *I hear that you want to start being sexually open to other lovers, and I still want to be monogamous.*
> *I hear you saying you think we should forbid Suzie from going out with boys until she is 16, and I'm afraid she'll just do it behind our backs.*

It can be scary when someone you care about disagrees with you. Most of us prefer harmony to conflict. But if you've ever been in an emotionally engaging relationship, you probably realize that life without conflict is an impossible dream. No two people are going to want exactly the same thing at all times.

The good news is that it is possible to embrace your differences in a way that doesn't threaten your connection and in fact deepens it. Using the key phrase "I hear you, and I have a different perspective" will help you learn to honor both people's values, needs, or positions simultaneously.

Ron felt panicky every time his wife Rose stated an opinion that differed from his. As CEO of a very successful midsize company, he wasn't used to feeling intimidated by disagreement, but with Rose it felt different. In his work life, he was used to telling people what he wanted and having them agree. Noting the discrepancy between how he felt at home and at work he couldn't help but wonder, "Have I always been afraid of conflict? Is that why I made sure I got to the top of the corporate ladder?" With this question in mind, he sought the help of a Getting Real coach, hoping to learn more about practicing the truth skill "Holding Differences."

During coaching sessions he found that he had always operated on the assumption that in a conflict situation, you have basically two choices: you get others to agree with you or you give in. It never occurred to him that he might hold in mind two seemingly opposing views—that he could listen openly to someone who disagreed with him without this threatening his own viewpoint. To help him get a felt experience of this new insight, I asked him to invite Rose into a session with us.

At the time of our session, he and Rose were in disagreement about how to handle the fact that their 25-year-old son, Peter, was still living at home, didn't have a job, and didn't seem motivated to live independently from his parents. Rose thought they should tell Peter that he could no longer live with them; they would let him stay one more month, and then he was out. Ron felt worried that Peter would wind up on the streets selling drugs. As their coach, it was not my intent to solve the problem about Peter so much as to give them tools to resolve this conflict as well as future conflicts.

I asked Rose to state her position and then asked Ron to respond using the phrase "I hear you, and I have a different perspective." Here's how that went:

ROSE: I am not willing to have Peter around anymore. I'm ready to tell him he has to leave our home.

RON: I hear you saying that you're ready to ask Peter to leave, and I have a different feeling about this.

Ron's words sounded strained and unconvincing, but it was a good start. I asked Rose to state another opinion so Ron could get more practice holding differences:

ROSE: I think he'll get a job if he has to. I don't think he'll wind up living out of a shopping cart.

RON: I hear that you think he'll get himself a job if he has to, and I have a different prediction.

After a few more such practice rounds, I asked Ron to elaborate on his disagreement with Rose's position. So in addition to using the one-sentence "I hear you, and I have a different perspective," he was encouraged to expand on his initial statement, as in, "I'm afraid he'll resort to selling drugs. That's even worse than the shopping cart scenario."

He found it much less stressful to do this now that he had the idea that it was really okay to have a different view. He told us that using this key phrase was helping him feel less threatened by the fact that he and Rose disagreed. It showed him that their differences were not about one person being right and one being wrong. And the biggest insight of all was his discovery that as his fear of conflict lessened, his ability to be present with Rose increased. He was no longer defensive and guarded around her. Rose felt the shift and told him it helped her trust him more: "Now I'm not so worried that you're just trying to avoid a confrontation with Peter by taking the position you have taken. Before we learned this communication skill, I couldn't trust what you said about anything if it involved disagreeing with me. Now, I trust that you'll let me know how you really feel."

HOLDING DIFFERENCES SUPPORTS MUTUAL TRUST

The ability to be present to yourself and to another at the same time builds trust: it builds self-trust because you're no longer assuming that you'll lose yourself if you become open to the other's views; and it helps others trust you because they can sense that while you're really showing up for yourself, you care about their views as well.

If you cannot get to the point where you can sincerely speak the words "I hear you, and ... ," you will never be a very good negotiator. All relationships require frequent negotiations of one sort or another. People see things differently and want different things. It's a fact of life. And if you want your relationships to work, people need to feel that you are not just out for yourself, but that you care about their needs and views. Of course, you cannot allow yourself to be truly open to another's view if you're in fear of losing touch with your own. That's why this key phrase is so important. Holding differences is a rather advanced communication skill. But it is one that is going to become more and more useful as the world becomes more diverse, interconnected, and complex....

SHE WANTS TO TALK NOW AND
HE WANTS TO DO IT LATER

Here's a tough situation that many couples experience: One of you wants to talk about the argument you just had right away so you can get it resolved. The other needs time to cool down or collect himself. If you're the one who wants to do it now, you probably feel a fair degree of urgency. Can you imagine putting out your request, hearing the other say, "Not now," and responding with, "I hear you say you don't want to talk about it now, and I feel strongly that I want to do it right away"? Can you imagine how that might shift your consciousness from pain over your own frustration to holding a larger perspective—the pain of feeling this difference between you?

The ability to shift into a bigger mind is a very advanced relationship skill. You are not in any way abandoning your own needs. What you are doing is including *more* in your point of view. Holding a more expanded point of view fosters a deeper sense of connection with others. It also supports a higher level of creative problem solving—because it promotes cooperation instead of competitiveness. When two people have a problem, the best, most lasting and viable solution is the one that grows out of both people's participation. Using the phrase "I hear you, and ..." affirms the reality and validity of both views, while at the same time giving partners a structure for containing the pain that the difference causes. When you use this statement, it shows your partner that you are feeling pain over the discrepancy between his wants and your own. It connects you with his pain about that very same discrepancy. So, in essence, it is a shared experience of pain. Shared pain about something significant can bring partners closer together—even as they mourn the fact of their differences.

This statement also helps partners feel seen and heard. When partners feel seen, heard, and moved by the other, new creative energy gets released that had been tied up in the conflict. Using this key statement affirms that there is space for two points of view, not just one, in this relationship. This makes the relationship feel more spacious.

HOW THIS STATEMENT FOSTERS PRESENCE

Any time you are attached to getting your own way, you're probably in a state of fear. When your mind is on some feared future outcome, you're not present. This key phrase helps you get present by embracing the reality that you and your partner have differing perceptions or needs. It helps you consider and attend to more of the total reality of your current situation. The ability to see and feel more, without shutting down around the things you wish were not so, brings you more present. It's like affirming that you have the capacity to hold a view of your differences that is inclusive of both partners' needs.

REVIEW QUESTIONS

1. Explain what Campbell means when she says that this phrase is a way to "embrace your differences" without "threatening your connection."
2. Explain how this key phrase can move a conversation from "either/or" to "both/and."
3. Describe how this phrase can help build self-trust and trust between conflict partners.
4. Explain what Campbell means when she writes that this phrase "fosters presence."

PROBES

1. Campbell argues that this phrase can permit the kind of elaboration Ron made when he said, "I'm afraid he'll resort to selling drugs." What's the connection between this statement and the communication move that Ron made next?
2. Why is the "presence" that Campbell discusses at the end of this reading important?

How to Resolve Issues Unmemorably
Hugh and Gayle Prather

This reading offers a fairly complete outline of how to think about and prepare for a productive, rather than a destructive, conflict with a loved one. The authors begin with an example of a typical everyday conflict that reveals how many issues are often buried in an argument between friends or intimates. It starts as an argument about the cat window and lasts only a couple of minutes, but the Prathers identify 17 separate issues that get raised. No wonder arguments like this create more problems than they solve!

The next important point that's made in this reading is that discussions like the one about the cat window "create the relationship's terrain." In other words, the way these discussions are carried out defines the quality of the couple's relationship.

With their tongues firmly planted in their cheeks, the Prathers then offer seven "magic rules for ruining any discussion." You can probably recognize some of your favorite fighting moves in this list—I know I do. The point of the list is to contrast the main features of productive and destructive conflict.

Then the authors urge you to recognize that when you are in a conflict with a person you're close to, "to agree is not the purpose." Rather, "the only allowable purpose" for this kind of discussion "is to bring you and your partner closer." This, it seems to me, is a profoundly simple but important idea. It challenges one primary assumption most of us carry into our conflicts with people we care about: that the point is to get my way, be sure the other knows how I feel, or make the other feel bad. What might happen if couples could actually internalize this idea: that the real point of our argument is to get closer?

The rest of this reading builds on this foundation. The Prathers offer five steps for preparing to argue. All of these guidelines make good sense and, taken together, as I mentioned earlier, they provide a fairly comprehensive outline of how to prepare to "do" conflict well.

As I read some sections of their essay, I am a little frustrated by what can sound like oversimplification and naïveté. The really tough arguments are much more intense and difficult than these two authors seem to realize. But when I look again at their advice, I recognize that they understand well enough how gut-wrenching a fight with a loved one can be. They are simply convinced, as have been a great many wise people over the ages, that returning anger for anger doesn't help. Ultimately, love, which in this case means the often unromantic commitment to a relationship, is stronger than defensiveness and bitterness.

MAIN IDEAS

- Like an uncleaned carpet that can triple in weight, a relationship with unresolved issues can collapse under its own weight.
- In long-term relationships, arguments often bring to the surface multiple unresolved issues—17 in the example.
- Long-term relationships are shaped by the *ways* the partners deal with conflict. The *process* (how the parties disagree) is clearly the *product* (the shape of the relationship).
- Work to avoid the seven "magic rules for ruining any discussion."

- The purpose of conflict with an intimate is *not* "to agree" but "to bring you and your partner closer."
- Follow five steps in preparing to argue: determine that the issue is a present one; consider letting it go; consider whether this is the right time; be certain that communication, not winning, is your aim; and remind yourself that the problem is the relationship's and not your partner's.

UNFINISHED ARGUMENTS ACCUMULATE

It's not that issues don't get resolved. Indeed they are settled but settled like ketchup settles into a carpet. An uncleaned carpet can triple in weight within five years, and most relationships get so laden with undigested arguments that they collapse into a dull, angry stupor and cease to move toward their original goal.

"Albert, you've just got to install the cat window. I woke up again at 3 A.M. with Runnymede standing on my chest staring at me. I'm not getting enough alpha sleep."

"Sorry about that, Paula. I'll get to it this weekend."

"But Albert, you've been saying that for a month."

"Well, you know, honey, we could just put the cat out at night like everyone else."

"Oh, sure, and then what if he needed to get in? What if something was after him? What then?"

"What difference will the cat window make? He can still stay out all night if he wants to."

"Yes, Albert, but he can *also* get in if he *needs* to. You know, if you're not going to be a responsible pet owner, you shouldn't have a pet."

"Now there's a thought."

"I see. And I guess you don't mind breaking Gigi's heart."

"That's another thing, Paula, her name is Virginia, not Gigi. Why do we have to have a cat named Runnymede and a daughter named Gigi? Besides, I'll buy her a nice stuffed Garfield after the cat is comfortably settled in at the animal shelter."

"You know, Albert, this conversation is opening my eyes to something I've felt for a very long time."

"What's that, Paula?"

"You only care about mixed soccer. Since joining that team with the silly name you haven't been playing horsey with Gigi and you haven't been scratching Runnymede under the chin where he can't lick. You certainly pretended to like Runnymede well enough when we were dating."

"You were the one who insisted I join the team. You were the one who said it would be good for me to 'get out of the house for a change.' I like the cat. I love my daughter. But I don't want to spend my Saturdays ruining a window with a perfectly good view."

"I guess you don't really care about me either, Albert. And you can stand there calmly peeling your Snickers while wanting Runnymede to be gassed. If I didn't know how much emotion you devote to *mixed* soccer I would say you have become psychotically insensitive and unfeeling. Perhaps you should seek help."

Here Albert, proving that he is neither insensitive nor unfeeling, flings his Snickers at the window in question, grabs his soccer gear, and storms from the house, where in an afternoon match playing goalie for the Yuma Yuccas he fractures the middle three phalanges in his right hand, thus ending the question of installing anything.

EACH NEW ISSUE RESURRECTS THE OLD

We wish we could say that this dialogue was a transcript but it is a composite. If we reprinted verbatim some of the typical arguments we have heard during counseling, they would be dismissed as overwrought fiction. The large number of digressions seen here is actually commonplace and illustrates the typical residue of unsettled questions found in most long-term relationships. The difference between this and the average disagreement is that some of these words might have been thought but left unspoken. Yet the feeling of estrangement by the end of the argument would have been the same.

On this Saturday morning Paula is upset because her sleep continues to be interrupted by the cat asking to be put out. That is the sum of the issue. If the couple had sat down together instead of using the problem as a means of separating still further, they could easily have solved this one difficulty in any of a hundred different mutually acceptable ways. But a hive of older discord lies just beneath their awareness, and therefore settling just one problem in peace is harder than it would seem.

The cry of unresolved issues is strong and persistent. Any couple will feel their failure to have joined. They yearn to bridge the old gaps and fear the potential of further separation more than they welcome the opportunity to reverse the process. To bring up former differences during a discussion is not blameworthy, it is in fact a call for help, but it is mistimed.

Without realizing it—because most arguments are conducted with no deep awareness—Albert and Paula allude to 17 other issues, none of which had to be brought up to solve *this* problem. In the order they appear, here are the questions they have left unanswered in the past, a small fraction of the total residue if you consider all the others that will be mentioned in future arguments: (1) Why has Albert's promise gone unfulfilled for a month? (2) Should the cat be left out overnight? (3) Is Albert irresponsible? (4) Should the family continue having this pet? (5) Is Albert insensitive to his daughter? (6) Should Paula continue calling Virginia "Gigi"? (7) Should the cat be renamed? (8) Would a stuffed animal sufficiently compensate? (9) Is mixed soccer affecting Albert's attitude toward his daughter and pet? (10) Does the team have a silly name? (11) Is Albert being sufficiently attentive to Paula or has he changed in some fundamental way? (12) Does Paula want Albert around the house? (13) How important is the window view to Albert's happiness? (14) Does Albert still love Paula? (15) Should Albert eat Snickers? (16) Is Albert's contact with other women on Saturdays the root cause of his, in Paula's view, wavering commitment to his family? (17) Does Albert have serious psychological problems?

As can be seen here, it is not easy for most couples to concentrate on a single issue. Nevertheless it is certainly possible and, in itself, to practice doing so will begin giving them a new kind of evidence: that within this relationship there are still grounds for unity and happiness. If one of the partners deviates from this guideline, the other should not make still another issue of this or get caught up in the irrelevant point raised, but should see instead the real desire behind the digression and treat it gently and answer it with love.

DISCUSSIONS CREATE THE RELATIONSHIP'S TERRAIN

… To resolve issues in the usual way is as damaging to a relationship as not resolving them at all, because the gap is not truly bridged and the unsuccessful attempt merely adds more weight to the couple's doubts about each other. In the argument over the cat window, Paula's concern about the health of her marriage surfaces, a question of far greater importance to her than how she will manage to get more sleep, and yet without fully realizing it she exacerbates this larger problem and works against her own interests. By arguing in the manner they did, this couple, as do most, merely manufactured new issues between them. Albert probably did not mean to take that hard a stand on getting rid of the cat—he may actually have wanted to keep it. And Paula did not have real doubts about Albert's mental health.

The past that drives so many relationships into the ground is built piece by piece, smallness fitted to smallness, selfishness answered with selfishness. Yet the process is largely unconscious. Each couple quickly settles into a few sad methods of conducting arguments, but seldom is the means they use thought through or the results closely examined. One person nags, the other relents. One person reasons, the other becomes silent. One person flares, the other backs down. One person cajoles, the other gives in. But where are the joy and grandeur, where is the friendship that was supposed to flourish, the companionship that through the years was to fuse an invulnerable bond, a solace and a blessing at the close of life? Instead there is a bitter and widening wedge between the two, and even the briefest of discussions contains a hundred dark echoes from the past.

No matter how entrenched are our patterns of problem solving, they can be stepped away from easily once we see that they do not serve our interests.

The only interest served in most discussions is to be right. But, truly, how deep is this? Do we actually want to make our partner wrong, to defeat a friend, and slowly to defeat a friendship? It certainly may feel that way. Caught up once again in the emotions of a disagreement, we stride doggedly toward our usual means of concluding every argument: adamant silence, crushing logic, patronizing practicality, collapsed crying, quelling anger, martyred acquiescence, loveless humor, sulking retreat.

These postures and a thousand more are attempts to prove a point other than love, and as with all endeavors to show up one's partner, the friendship itself is the victim, because the friendship becomes a mere tool, a means of making the other person feel guilty. The love our partner has for us is now seen as leverage, and in our quiet or noisy way we set about making the relationship a shambles, not realizing that we ourselves are part of the wreckage.

THE MAGIC RULES FOR RUINING ANY DISCUSSION

… The dialogue with which we began this [reading] incorporates a few of but not all the rules for disastrous communication—yet only one or two are needed to neutralize the best of intentions. Follow these guidelines, even a little sloppily, and you are guaranteed a miserable time:

1. *Bring the matter up when at least one of you is angry.*
   Variations: Bring it up when nothing can be done about it (in the middle of the night; right before guests are due; when one of you is in the shower). Bring it up when concentration is impossible (while driving to a meeting with the IRS; while watching the one TV program you both agree on; while your spouse is balancing the checkbook).
2. *Be as personal as possible when setting forth the problem.*
   Variations: Know the answer before you ask the question. While describing the issue, use an accusatory tone. Begin by implying who, as usual, is to blame.
3. *Concentrate on getting what you want.*
   Variations: Overwhelm your partner's position before he or she can muster a defense (be very emotional; call in past favors; be impeccably reasonable). Impress on your partner what you need and what he or she must do without. If you begin losing ground, jockey for position.
4. *Instead of listening, think only of what you will say next.*
   Variations: Do other things while your partner is talking. Forget where your partner left off. In other words, listen with all the interest you would give a bathroom exhaust fan.
5. *Correct anything your partner says about you.*
   Variations: Each time your partner gives an example of your behavior, cite a worse example of his or hers. Repeat "That's not what I said" often. Do not accept anything your partner says at face value (point out exceptions; point out inaccuracies in facts and in grammar).

6. *Mention anything from the past that has a chance of making your partner defensive.*
   Variations: Make allusions to your partner's sexual performance. Remind
   your husband of his mother's faults. Compare what your wife does to what
   other women do, and after she complains, say, "I didn't mean it that way."
7. *End by saying something that will never be forgotten.*
   Variations: Do something that proves you are a madman. Let your parting
   display proclaim that no exposure of your partner could be amply revealing, no characterization too profane, no consequence sufficiently wretched.
   At least leave the impression you are a little put out.

TO AGREE IS NOT THE PURPOSE

All couples believe they know how to hold a discussion, and yet it is not an
exaggeration to say that in most long-term relationships there has rarely been
one wholly successful argument. Obviously they are filled with disagreements
that end in agreements, but when these are examined, it can be seen that at least a
small patch of reservation had to be overlooked in order for accord to be reached.

We believe this is simply how differences are settled, and so even though
we sense that our partner is still in conflict, we barge ahead with our newly
won concession, thinking the bad moment will pass. Later it becomes painfully
clear that it has not and we judge our partner irresolute. Or if we are the one
who complied, we count our little sacrifice dear and wait for reparation—which
never comes or is never quite adequate, and we cannot understand why our
partner feels such little gratitude.

The aim of most arguments is to reach outward agreement. Until that is
replaced with a desire for friendship, varying degrees of alienation will be the
only lasting outcome. Couples quickly develop a sense of helplessness over the
pattern that their discussions have fallen into. They believe they are sincerely
attempting to break out of it and are simply failing. They try different responses,
going from shouting to silence, from interminable talking to walking out of the
room, from considering each point raised to sticking tenaciously to one point,
but nothing they do seems to alter the usual unhappy ending.

There is no behavioral formula to reversing the habitual course of an
argument. It requires a shift in attitude, not in actions, even though actions will
modify in the process. No more is needed than one partner's absolute clarity
about the purpose of the argument. This is not easy but it is simple. Therefore
let us look again at what the aim should be....

The only allowable purpose for a discussion is to bring you and your
partner closer. Minds must come together to decide instead of backing away in
order to apply pressure. How is this possible, given the fact that you and your
partner are deeply selfish? Fortunately, the selfishness is compartmentalized
and your hearts remain unaffected. You need not eliminate it; merely bypass it
because you recognize that it is not in your interests to be selfish. To the ego, this
concept is insane because it sees no value in love. But love is in your interests

because you *are* love, or at least part of you is, and thus each discussion is a way of moving into your real self.

A little time is obviously needed to see one's true interests. If you rush into a discussion you will operate from your insensitivity by habit and aim for a prize your heart cares nothing about. Do not kid yourself. You *do* know whether the discussion is ending with the two of you feeling closer. The selfish part of your mind will tell you that the little sadness and sense of distance you may now feel was a small price to pay for the concession you won or the point you made. Or it will argue that it was all unavoidable. This may happen many times before you begin reversing your ordinary way of participating. This transition is an important stage of growth and entails looking more and more carefully at self-ish impulses and their aftermath. Is how you feel really worth it? Was the way it went truly unavoidable?

Thus you will come to see the result you want, and this deeper recognition will begin to eclipse your pettiness in the midst of an argument. Gradually you will catch the mistakes sooner, and eventually you will learn to avoid them from the start. For you *do* want these times of deciding to warm your hearts and lighten your steps. So persist in the guidelines we will give, and these little defeats to your relationship will slowly give way to friendship.

We are so used to thinking of a discussion as a symbol of separation that it can often be helpful to change its form enough that something new will appear to be happening and thus the old mindset is undercut. To take the usual process, break it into steps and put them in order is usually all that is needed to accomplish this.

An issue could be said to pass through five stages in reaching resolution. First, it must be thought of by at least one of the partners as an issue. Second, a moment is chosen to bring the matter up. Third, a decision is made as to the manner in which it will be presented. Fourth, there is an exchange of thoughts and feelings. And fifth, the discussion is concluded.

Most couples give very little thought to the first three stages. They simply find themselves in the thick of a so-called spontaneous argument and no one is certain at what point it began. Obviously you must become more conscious of the subjects you bring up so carelessly. Any sign of fear over what you are about to say is a very useful indicator. If you see you have a question about whether to say it, let this be your cue to break these preliminary choices into conscious steps. Do not begrudge the time; remember instead how strongly you want to begin building a real friendship.

FIVE STEPS IN PREPARING TO ARGUE

First, you might ask yourself if the issue you are thinking of is actually a pres-ent issue or merely one you have been reminded of. In other words, be certain this is currently a problem and not one the relationship may already be on its way to solving. Many people habitually rake over their marriage for signs of imperfection and naturally they find a great many, but it can be far more dis-rupting to friendship to be constantly questioning and comparing than to wait to see if the problem continues in any severe way. Meanwhile, enjoy what is already between you without telling yourself what this is....

If the issue is unquestionably a present one, the second step you might try is to let go of it. Letting go is not "better," but it is an option that current values tend to underrate. However, it must be accomplished thoroughly and honestly or the issue will grow like mold in a dark unseen place. If it is done consciously dismissal is not denial. Essentially it entails examining in detail what you do not like and then making a deliberate effort to identify with another part of you that never "takes issue" with any living thing, that is still and at ease, that acts only from peace....

If a couple espouses world energy consciousness or is on a tight budget, for one of the partners to habitually leave the hot water running, not turn off lights, or keep the refrigerator door open may be grating or even shocking to the other partner. Yet the spectacle of someone wasting energy and money is *not* grating or shocking. The interpretation we assign it, and not the act itself, determines the emotions we feel. Jordan, age two, is "shockingly irresponsible." He has even been known (yesterday, in fact) to flush a toilet five times in a row and then run to tell his big brother about the accomplishment. "John, I flush, I flush!" "That's nice." said John, blatantly contributing to the delinquency of a minor. The reason Jordan didn't tell his father (who is the family's conscience in these matters) was that he was the very one who kept showing him how it was done, thereby encouraging him to waste over 15 gallons of water (plus 6 more his father used researching that figure)....

So here we have four reactions issuing from four interpretations: pride from the father, support from the 7-year-old, excitement from the 2-year-old and, having no originality, curiosity from the cat. Clearly no uniform effect was produced by an external and unreachable cause. How then might you let go of your reaction to your spouse's wasteful habits in lieu of bringing it up one more time? Certainly you would not try dishonestly to convince yourself that the practice was not costing money or energy. Or that it did not really matter to you. Neither would you attempt to assign some motive to your partner's acts that you did not believe, such as not knowing any better or really trying hard but being unable to stop. Dishonesty does not end an unhappy line of thought. That is why reinterpretation is generally not effective....

If in your moment of consideration you are able to see these facts deeply enough, you may open your eyes to your partner's innocence and no longer feel compelled to understand why he or she does these things. But if after making the attempt to free your mind you see that you have not let the issue go, then perhaps to bring it up would be the preferable course, for undoubtedly that is better than storing anger or fear....

The third step is to consider if this is the time. If you feel an urge to bring it up quickly, be very alert to anger. Your heart is willing to wait but your ego is not, especially if it senses an opportunity to strike back. The ego is merely our love of misery, of withdrawal and loneliness, and it can feel like our own deep impulse even though it exists on the most superficial level of the mind.

For too long now our relationships have been jerked around by our own lack of awareness. There is more to your mind than selfishness. So be still a moment and let peace arise from you. Is this the time? A simple question. There need not be great soul-searching and hand-wringing over it. If your partner has just done something and this is the issue, clearly he or she is likely to be more defensive if instantly called on it. If your partner is not in a particularly happy frame of mind, is hostile, worried or depressed, a more receptive state will surely come and nothing is lost by waiting. Is this the time? Merely look and know the answer. The urge to attack when you are angry is very strong, but if you will allow yourself time to reflect on your genuine feelings, this will do more to relieve your frustration.

The fourth step is to be certain that communication is your aim. Trying to get someone to change is not communication because you have already decided what change is needed. Your partner is therefore left with nothing to say and will definitely feel your unwillingness to consider, to listen, to appreciate. So before you speak take time to hear your heart.

You are not two advocates arguing a case. You are interested in joining, not in prevailing. You are like the directors of a business you both love coming together to help it over a difficult situation. You don't care from whose lips the solution comes. You welcome the *answer.* To this end what are you willing to do if your partner becomes defensive? Are you prepared, and have you prepared, to carry through your love of the relationship? ...

The final point to consider is whether you are clear that the problem is the relationship's and not your partner's. In our example the problem was not Paula's, because her lack of sleep was affecting Albert also. One person's jealousy, appetite, hypersensitivity, frigidity, phobia, or any other characteristic that has become an issue cannot successfully be viewed as more one's responsibility than the other's because friendship is always a mutual sharing of all burdens....

You must understand that unless you make a specific effort to see through the fallacy, you *will* go into a discussion thinking one of you is more to blame than the other, and this will make it very hard to listen and be open. Learn to treat every issue as an impersonal and neutral enemy and to close ranks against it. An addiction, for example, can be viewed as you would a hurricane or a deluge—you need each other's help to survive the storm. Our dog, Sunny Sunshine Pumpkin Prather (whose very name is a masterpiece of family compromise), gets sprayed by a skunk about once a month and the smell is everyone's problem. What good would it do to blame the dog? And yet we have seen other families get angry at their dog "for being so stupid...."

These preliminary steps, which should only take an instant or two to complete, will at least make it possible for a discussion to begin with some chance of success. Now you are ready for a *real* argument, one in which your minds can join rather than separate.

REVIEW QUESTIONS

1. What point are the Prathers making by listing 17 issues that were brought up in the argument between Albert and Paula?
2. What do the authors mean when they say that discussions "create the relationship's terrain"?
3. Paraphrase this statement: "The only allowable purpose for a discussion is to bring you and your partner closer." Do you agree or disagree with it? Explain.
4. What do the authors mean when they say that you should "learn to treat every issue as an impersonal and neutral enemy and to close ranks against it"?
5. What keeps the "protect your gains" step from being selfish?

PROBES

1. What alternative do the authors offer to "being right" in a conflict?
2. What general principle or principles are violated by the seven "magic rules for ruining any discussion"? In other words, what general attitudes make these moves destructive?
3. Which of the five steps for preparing to argue do you *least* often follow? What does that fact tell you about your way of "doing" conflict?
4. A fundamental, perhaps even a radically different, perspective or point of view is behind just about everything the Prathers say about "resolving issues unmemorably." By "different," I mean different from the attitude we normally carry into a conflict. How would you describe this alternative point of view or perspective?

CHAPTER 11

Bridging Cultural Differences

The Individual and the Collective in Society
Geert Hofstede and Gert Jan Hofstede

This chapter on "Bridging Cultural Differences" begins with this rather long reading by two highly regarded intercultural communication scholar-teachers. Their primary contribution to global understanding has been to distinguish between *individualist* and *collectivist* cultures, and to explain how this fundamental distinction affects every intercultural or cross-cultural contact. Importantly, in the 21st century, individualist countries are primarily wealthy and most collectivist countries are poor.

The authors acknowledge that "power distance" is another global dimension of national cultures (see readings in Chapters 7 and 10), but their emphasis here is on individualism versus collectivism. To clarify the distinction, they note that people in clearly individualist cultures prefer to work at jobs that leave personal time for family life, offer freedom to adopt your own approach to the job, and provide challenges that lead to a personal sense of accomplishment. People in clearly collectivist cultures want jobs that provide training opportunities, have good physical working conditions, and fully use their skills. Obviously, an individualist working in a collectivist culture is likely to experience difficulties, and vice versa. Later in the article they link their distinction to the difference between *high-context* communication and *low-context* communication. High-context communication depends on the environment for interpretation (past history, physical setting, time of day, etc.); this kind of communication is frequent in collectivist cultures. Low-context communication puts the most important information in the explicit code (e.g., the words that are spoken), rather than the context, and this is common in individualist cultures.

The main parts of this essay explain how individualism and collectivism work in the family and in schools. For example, some African (collectivist) students report that, before coming to northern Europe to study, they had never been alone in a room for any sizable length of time, and northern European students returning from internships in Peru or Malaysia complained that they were never left alone by their hosts. Speaking one's mind and telling the truth about feelings is valued in individualist cultures, whereas children in collectivist cultures learn that opinions are held by groups, not individuals. Silence is often considered abnormal in individualist cultures; social conversation is compulsory. But in a collectivist culture, silence is often valued and practiced, because the fact of being together is considered "emotionally sufficient." And while collectivist cultures emphasize the importance of the socially established construct, "face," and especially the dangers of "losing face," the counterpart in individualist cultures is "self-respect."

As you would expect, marriage partner selection differs between these two types of cultures. Single people in both types of cultures desire mutual love, kindness, emotional stability, intelligence, and health. But in collectivist cultures, men preferred future brides to be younger and they put more stress on wealth, industriousness, and chastity. Women in collectivist countries want their grooms to be older and wealthier, but they de-emphasized industriousness and chastity. In addition, considerations other than love are much more important in collectivist societies than in individualist ones.

Table 3 summarizes key differences between the two kinds of cultures in language, personality, and behavior. These differences are reinforced in the schools. In the individualist classroom, for example, group formation is much more ad hoc and confrontations and open discussion are often expected. In the collectivist classroom, the virtues of harmony and face-maintenance are primary.

Fundamental ideas, for example, conceptions of human nature, also differ between the two kinds of cultures. In the individualist culture of the United States, the goal of "self-actualization" governs personal growth efforts. In a collectivist culture, the primary element to be actualized is not the self but the interest and honor of the group, which may very well require self-effacement by individuals.

At the end of this reading, the authors point out that, to the degree that this distinction is accurate, it calls into question many conclusions of both traditional psychology and traditional economics. Both social sciences are based on Western individualist thinking, even though their ideas are often presented as universal and global.

Like any global understanding or theory, this one can be criticized. Problems arise, for example, when "culture" is equated with "nationality." The theory is also very general; some cultures—the authors give Japan as an example—contain elements of both individualism and collectivism. In addition, it can be misleading to focus the analysis of culture on any one dimension. But many scholars and students across dozens of disciplines and around the world have found the Hofstedes's distinction informative and explanatory. I encourage you to discuss with others how the individualism/collectivism distinction can help inform your communication with people from cultures other than your own.

MAIN IDEAS

- One helpful way to distinguish among cultures is in terms of individualism and collectivism.
- Individualist cultures privilege the interests of the individual and collectivist cultures privilege the interests of the group.
- Survey data indicate that almost all strongly individualist countries are wealthy and almost all strongly collectivist countries are poor.
- The distinction is first learned in one's family of origin and it affects expectations about, and behavior in, all family relationships.
- A parallel distinction is between *high-context* and *low-context* communication; the former tends to occur in collectivist and the latter in individualist cultures.
- The individualist/collectivist distinction can be observed in the way schools are organized and managed in both kinds of cultures.
- These cultural differences are manifested in many different dimensions of communication.
- Individualism and collectivism also surface in the fundamental ideas that mark a culture, for example, about human nature and values.

The vast majority of people in our world live in societies in which the interest of the group prevails over the interest of the individual. We will call these societies *collectivist*, a word that to some readers may have political connotations, although the word is not being used in any political sense here. It does not refer to the power of the state over the individual but to the *power of the group*. The first group in our lives is always the family into which we are born. Family structures, however, differ between societies.

In most collectivist societies, the "family" within which the child grows up consists of a number of people living closely together: not just the parents and other children, but, for example, grandparents, uncles, aunts, servants, or other housemates. This is known in cultural anthropology as the *extended family*. When children grow up, they learn to think of themselves as part of a "we" group, a relationship that is not voluntary but is given by nature. The "we" group is distinct from other people in society who belong to "they" groups, of which there are many. The "we" group (or *in-group*) is the major source of one's identity and the only secure protection one has against the hardships of life. Therefore one owes lifelong loyalty to one's in-group, and breaking this loyalty is one of the worst things a person can do. Between the person and the in-group a mutual dependence relationship develops that is both practical and psychological.

A minority of people in our world live in societies in which the interests of the individual prevail over the interests of the group, societies that we will call *individualist*. In these, most children are born into families consisting of two parents and, possibly, other children; in some societies there is an increasing share of one-parent families. Other relatives live elsewhere and are rarely seen. This type is the *nuclear family* (from the Latin *nucleus*, meaning "core"). Children from such families, as they grow up, soon learn to think of themselves as "I." This "I," their personal identity, is distinct from other people's "I"s, and these others are classified not to their group membership but according to individual characteristics. Playmates, for example, are chosen on the basis of personal preferences. The purpose of education is to enable children to stand on their own feet. Children are expected to leave the parental home as soon as this has been achieved. Not infrequently, children, after having left home, reduce relationships with their parents to a minimum or break them off altogether. Neither practically nor psychologically is the healthy person in this type of society supposed to be dependent on a group.

MEASURING THE DEGREE OF INDIVIDUALISM IN SOCIETY

Extreme collectivism and extreme individualism can be considered the opposite poles of a second global dimension of national cultures, after power distance....

From *Cultures and Organizations: Software of the Mind* by Geert Hofstede and Gert Jan Hofstede. New York: McGraw-Hill, 2005. Reprinted by permission.

The new dimension is defined as follows. *Individualism* pertains to *societies in which the ties between individuals are loose: everyone is expected to look after himself or herself and his or her immediate family. Collectivism* as its opposite pertains to *societies in which people from birth onward are integrated into strong, cohesive in-groups, which throughout people's lifetimes continue to protect them in exchange for unquestioning loyalty....* The dimension to be identified with individualism versus collectivism was most strongly associated with the relative importance attached to the following work goal items:

For the individualist pole

1. **Personal time:** have a job that leaves sufficient time for your personal or family life.
2. **Freedom:** have considerable freedom to adopt your own approach to the job.
3. **Challenge:** have challenging work to do—work from which you can get a personal sense of accomplishment.

For the opposite, collectivist, pole

4. **Training:** have training opportunities (to improve your skills or learn new skills).
5. **Physical conditions:** have good physical working conditions (good ventilation and lighting, adequate work space, etc.).
6. **Use of skills:** fully use your skills and abilities on the job....

It is not difficult to identify the importance of personal time, freedom, and (personal) challenge with individualism: they all stress the employee's independence from the organization. The work goals at the opposite pole—training, physical conditions, and skills being used on the job—refer to things the organization does for the employee and in this way stress the employee's dependence on the organization that fits with collectivism. Another link in the relationship is that, as will be shown, individualist countries tend to be rich and collectivist countries poor. In rich countries training, physical conditions, and the use of skills may be taken for granted, which makes them relatively unimportant as work goals. In poor countries these things cannot at all be taken for granted: they are essential in distinguishing a good job from a bad one, which makes them quite important among one's work goals....

Table 1 confirms that nearly all wealthy countries score high on IDV while nearly all poor countries score low. There is a strong relationship between a country's national wealth and the degree of individualism in its culture.

INDIVIDUALISM AND COLLECTIVISM IN THE FAMILY

...The relationship between the individual and the group, like other basic elements of human culture, is first learned in the family setting. The fact that Japan scores about halfway in Table 1 (with a rank of 33–35 and an IDV of 46) can at

TABLE 1 Individualism Index (IDV) Values for 74 Countries and Regions

Country/Region	Score	Rank	Country/Region	Score	Rank
United States	91	1	**Finland**	63	21
Australia	90	2	Estonia	60	22–24
Great Britain	89	3	Luxembourg	60	22–24
Canada total	80	4–6	Poland	60	22–24
Hungary	80	4–6	Malta	59	25
Netherlands	80	4–6	Czech Republic	58	26
New Zealand	79	7	**Austria**	55	27
Belgium Flemish	78	8	**Israel**	54	28
Italy	76	9	Slovakia	52	29
Denmark	74	10	**Spain**	51	30
Canada Quebec	73	11	**India**	48	31
Belgium Walloon	72	12	Suriname	47	32
France	71	13–14	**Argentina**	46	33–35
Sweden	71	13–14	**Japan**	46	33–35
Ireland	70	15	Morocco	46	33–35
Norway	69	16–17	**Iran**	41	36
Switzerland German	69	16–17	**Jamaica**	39	37–38
Germany	67	18	Russia	39	37–38
South Africa[1]	65	19	**Arab countries**	38	39–40
Switzerland French	64	20	**Brazil**	38	39–40
Turkey	37	41	**Singapore**	20	56–61
Uruguay	36	42	**Thailand**	20	56–61
Greece	35	43	Vietnam	20	56–61
Croatia	33	44	**West Africa**	20	56–61
Philippines	32	45	**Salvador**	19	62
Bulgaria	30	46–48	**Korea (South)**	18	63
Mexico	30	46–48	**Taiwan**	17	64
Romania	30	46–48	**Peru**	16	65–66
East Africa	27	49–51	Trinidad	16	65–66
Portugal	27	49–51	**Costa Rica**	15	67
Slovenia	27	49–51	**Indonesia**	14	68–69
Malaysia	26	52	**Pakistan**	14	68–69
Hong Kong	25	53–54	**Colombia**	13	70
Serbia	25	53–54	**Venezuela**	12	71
Chile	23	55	**Panama**	11	72
Bangladesh	20	56–61	**Ecuador**	8	73
China	20	56–61	**Guatemala**	6	74

Scores for countries or regions in **bold type** were calculated from the IBM database. Scores for other countries or regions were based on replications or estimates.

[1] The data were from whites only.

least be partly understood from the fact that in the traditional Japanese family, only the oldest son continued to live with his parents, thus creating a lineal structure somewhere in between nuclear and extended.

The child who grows up among a number of elders, peers, and juniors learns naturally to conceive of him- or herself as part of a "we," much more so than does the nuclear family child. A child of an extended family is seldom alone, whether during the day or at night. An African student who came to Belgium for a university study told us that this was the first time in her life she had ever been alone in a room for any sizable length of time. Conversely, northern European students returning from internships in Peru or Malaysia complained that they were never left alone by their hosts.

In a situation of intense and continuous social contact, the maintenance of harmony with one's social environment becomes a key virtue that extends to other spheres beyond the family. In most collectivist cultures, direct confrontation of another person is considered rude and undesirable. The word *no* is seldom used, because saying "no" *is* a confrontation; "you may be right" or "we will think about it" are examples of polite ways of turning down a request. In the same vein, the word *yes* should not necessarily be seen as an approval, but as maintenance of the line of communication; "yes, I heard you" is the meaning it has in Japan.

In individualist cultures, on the other hand, speaking one's mind is a virtue. Telling the truth about how one feels is a characteristic of a sincere and honest person. Confrontation can be salutary; a clash of opinions is believed to lead to a higher truth. The effect of communications on other people should be taken into account, but it does not, as a rule, justify changing the facts. Adult individuals should be able to take direct feedback constructively. In the family, children are told one should always tell the truth, even if it hurts. Coping with conflict is a normal part of living together as a family.

... In the collectivist family, children learn to take their bearings from others when it comes to opinions. Personal opinions do not exist—they are predetermined by the group. If a new issue comes up on which there is no established group opinion, some kind of family conference is necessary before an opinion can be given. A child who repeatedly voices opinions deviating from what is collectively felt is considered to have a bad character. In the individualist family, on the contrary, children are expected and encouraged to develop opinions of their own, and a child who always only reflects the opinions of others is considered to have a weak character. The behavior corresponding with a desirable character depends on the cultural environment.

The loyalty to the group that is an essential element of the collectivist family also means that resources are shared. If one member of an extended family of twenty persons has a paid job and the others do not, the earning member is supposed to share his or her income in order to help feed the entire family. On the basis of this principle, a family may collectively cover the expenses for sending one member to get a higher education, expecting that when this member subsequently gets a well-paid job, the income will also be shared.

In individualist cultures parents will be proud if children at an early age take small jobs in order to earn pocket money of their own, which they alone can decide how to spend. In the Netherlands as in many other individualist western European countries, the government contributes substantially to the living expenses of students. In the 1980s the system was changed from an allowance to the parents to an allowance directly to the students themselves, which stressed their independence. Boys and girls were now treated as independent economic actors from age eighteen onward. In the United States it is quite normal for students to pay for their own studies by getting temporary jobs and personal loans; without government support they, too, are less dependent on their parents and not at all on more distant relatives.

Obligations to the family in a collectivist society are not only financial but also ritual. Family celebrations like baptisms, marriages, and, especially, funerals are extremely important and should not be missed. Expatriate managers from individualist societies are often surprised by the family reasons given by employees from a collectivist host society who apply for a special leave; the expatriates think they are being fooled, but most likely the reasons are authentic.

In an individualist culture when people meet they feel a need to communicate verbally. Silence is considered abnormal. Social conversations can be depressingly banal, but they are compulsory. In a collectivist culture the fact of being together is emotionally sufficient; there is no compulsion to talk unless there is information to be transferred. Raden Mas Hadjiwibowo, an Indonesian businessman from a Javanese noble family, recalled the family visits from his youth in the 1930s as follows:

> Visits among Javanese family members needed no previous appointment. Actually that could easily be done, for although the telephone had not come into common use yet, one could always send a servant with a letter asking for an appointment. But it was not done, it never occurred to one that a visit would not suit the other party. It was always convenient. Unexpected visitors did not exist. The door was (and still is) always open.
>
> The visitors were welcomed with joyful courtesy and would be asked to take a seat. The host and hostess hurriedly withdrew to change into more suitable attire than their workaday clothes. Without asking, a servant brought in coffee or tea. Cookies were offered, while in the meantime the host and hostess had joined the party.
>
> There we sat, but nobody spoke. We were not embarrassed by this silence; nobody felt nervous about it. Every now and then, thoughts and news were exchanged. But this was not really necessary. We enjoyed being together, seeing each other again. After the first exchange of news, any other communication was utterly redundant. If one did not have anything to say, there was no need to recite platitudes. After an hour or so, the guests would ask permission to leave. With mutual feelings of satisfaction, we parted. In smaller towns on the island of Java life is still like this.[1]

U.S. anthropologist and popular author Edward T. Hall distinguished cultures on the basis of their way of communicating along a dimension from high-context to low-context.[2] A *high-context* communication is one in which little has to be said or written because most of the information is either in the physical environment or supposed to be known by the persons involved, while very little is in the coded, explicit part of the message. This type of communication is frequent in collectivist cultures; Hadjiwibowo's family visit is a case example. A *low-context* communication is one in which the mass of information is vested in the explicit code, which is typical for individualist cultures. Many things that in collectivist cultures are self-evident must be said explicitly in individualist cultures. American business contracts are much longer than Japanese business contracts.

Next to harmony another important concept in connection with the collectivist family is *shame*. Individualist societies have been described as *guilt* cultures: persons who infringe upon the rules of society will often feel guilty, ridden by an individually developed conscience that functions as a private inner pilot. Collectivist societies, on the contrary, are shame cultures: persons belonging to a group from which a member has infringed upon the rules of society will feel ashamed, based on a sense of collective obligation. Shame is social in nature, guilt individual; whether shame is felt depends on if the infringement has become known by others. This becoming known is more of a source of shame than the infringement itself. Such is not the case for guilt, which is felt whether or not the misdeed is known by others.

One more concept bred in the collectivist family is *face*. "Losing face," in the sense of being humiliated, is an expression that penetrated into the English language from the Chinese; the English had no equivalent for it. David Yau-Fai Ho, a Hong Kong social scientist, defined it as follows: "Face is lost when the individual, either through his action or that of people closely related to him, fails to meet essential requirements placed upon him by virtue of the social position he occupies."[3] The Chinese also speak of "giving someone face," in the sense of honor or prestige. Basically, *face* describes the proper relationship with one's social environment, which is as essential to a person (and that person's family) as the front part of his or her head. The importance of face is the consequence of living in a society very conscious of social contexts. The languages of other collectivist cultures have words with more or less similar meanings. In Greece, for example, there is a word *philotimo*; Harry Triandis, a Greek-American psychologist, has written:

> A person is *philotimos* to the extent in which he conforms to the norms and values of his in-group. These include a variety of sacrifices that are appropriate for members of one's family, friends, and others who are "concerned with one's welfare"; for example, for a man to delay marriage until his sisters have married and have been provided with a proper dowry is part of the normative expectations of traditional rural Greeks as well as rural Indians (and many of the people in between).[4]

In the individualist society the counterpart characteristic is self-respect, but this again is defined from the point of view of the individual, whereas face and *philotimo* are defined from the point of view of the social environment.

Collectivist societies usually have ways of creating family-like ties with persons who are not biological relatives but who are socially integrated into one's in-group. In Latin America, for example, this can be done via the institution of *compadres* and *comadres* who are treated as relatives even if they are not. In Japan younger sons in past times became apprentices to crafts masters through a form of adoption. Similar customs existed in medieval central Europe.

Because families are so important in a collectivist society, selection of marriage partners is a crucial event, not only for the partners but also for both their families. U.S. psychologist David Buss coordinated a survey study of criteria for selecting a potential marriage partner.[5] His respondents were almost ten thousand young women and men, with an average age of twenty-three, from thirty-seven countries. Universally desired characteristics for both future brides and future grooms were mutual love, kindness, emotional stability, intelligence, and health. Other characteristics varied between brides and grooms and across countries. Country differences were primarily related to individualism. In collectivist countries, men preferred future brides to be younger, and they put more stress on brides being wealthy, industrious, and chaste. Women in collectivist countries wanted their future grooms to be older and wealthier, but the groom's industriousness to them played a smaller role, and the groom's chastity none at all.

The men's desire for chastity in brides, however, depended even more on the countries' poverty than on their collectivism. This can be explained as follows: increasing affluence provides women with more educational opportunities (in any society, when education becomes first available, parents give priority to boys who are not needed around the house). With affluence, girls start to move around more freely and get more opportunities for meeting boys. It also gives people more living space and more privacy. Medical care and information improve, including know-how about contraception. Young people get more opportunities for sexual exploration, and sexual norms adapt to this situation.

The stress on the brides' industriousness, wealth, and chastity in collectivist societies is a consequence of the fact that marriage in such a society is a contract between families rather than between individuals. Industriousness, wealth, and chastity are the aspects that families can observe. In many collectivist societies, marriages are arranged by a broker, and the bride and groom may have little say in the choice of their partner; sometimes they are not even supposed to meet before the wedding day. This does not mean that such marriages are less happy. Research in India has shown more marital satisfaction in arranged marriages than in love marriages and more in Indian love marriages than in American marriages. While cultural individualism fosters the valuing of romantic love, certain aspects of individualism at the psychological level make developing intimacy problematic.[6] In a survey about the role of love in marriage, answered by female and male undergraduate students in eleven countries, one question ran: "If a man (woman) had all the other qualities you desired, would you marry this person if you were not in love with him (her)?" The answers varied with the degree of individualism in the eleven societies, from 4 percent "yes" and 86 percent "no" in the United States to 50 percent "yes" and 39 percent "no" in Pakistan. In collectivist societies, considerations other than love weigh heavily in marriage.

Tables 2 and 3 summarize the key differences between collectivist and individualist societies described so far.

TABLE 2 Key Differences between Collectivist and Individualist Societies: General Norm and Family

Collectivist	Individualist
People are born into extended families or other in-groups that continue protecting them in exchange for loyalty.	Everyone grows up to look after him or herself and his or her immediate (nuclear) family only.
Children learn to think in terms of "we."	Children learn to think in terms of "I."
Harmony should always be maintained and direct confrontations avoided.	Speaking one's mind is a characteristic of an honest person.
Friendships are predetermined.	Friendships are voluntary and should be fostered.
Resources should be shared with relatives.	Individual ownership of resources, even for children.
High-context communication prevails.	Low-context communication prevails.
Trespassing leads to shame and loss of face for self and group.	Trespassing leads to guilt and loss of self-respect.
Brides should be young, industrious, and chaste; bridegrooms should be older.	Criteria for marriage partner are not predetermined.

INDIVIDUALISM AND COLLECTIVISM AT SCHOOL

The relationship between the individual and the group that has been established in a child's consciousness during his or her early years in the family is further developed and reinforced at school. This is clearly visible in classroom behavior. In the context of development assistance, it often happens that teachers from a more individualist culture move to a more collectivist environment. A typical complaint from such teachers is that students do not speak up, not even when the teacher puts a question to the class. For the student who conceives of him- or herself as part of a group, it is illogical to speak up without being sanctioned by the group to do so. If the teacher wants students to speak up, the teacher should address a particular student personally.

Students in a collectivist culture will also hesitate to speak up in larger groups without a teacher present, especially if these are partly composed of relative strangers, or out-group members. This hesitation decreases in smaller groups. In a large, collectivist or culturally heterogeneous class, creating small subgroups is a way to increase student participation. For example, students can be asked to turn around in their seats and discuss a question for five minutes in groups of three or four. Each group is asked to appoint a spokesperson. In this way individual answers become group answers, and those who speak up do so in the name of their group. Often in subsequent exercises the students will spontaneously rotate the spokesperson role.

In the collectivist society in-group–out-group distinctions springing from the family sphere will continue at school, so that students from different ethnic or clan backgrounds often form subgroups in class. In an individualist society the

TABLE 3 Key Differences between Collectivist and Individualist Societies: Language, Personality, and Behavior

Collectivist	Individualist
Use of the word *I* is avoided.	Use of the word *I* is encouraged.
Interdependent self.	Independent self.
On personality tests, people score more introvert.	On personality tests, people score more extrovert.
Showing sadness is encouraged, and happiness discouraged.	Showing happiness is encouraged, and sadness discouraged.
Slower walking speed.	Faster walking speed.
Consumption patterns show dependence on others.	Consumption patterns show self-supporting lifestyles.
Social network is the primary source of information.	Media is the primary source of information.
A smaller share of both private and public income is spent on health care.	A larger share of both private and public income is spent on health care.
Disabled persons are a shame on the family and should be kept out of sight.	Disabled persons should participate as much as possible in normal day-to-day activities.

assignment of joint tasks leads more easily to the formation of new groups than in a collectivist society. In the latter, students from the same ethnic or family background as the teacher or other school officials will expect preferential treatment on this basis. In an individualist society this would be considered nepotism and intensely immoral, but in a collectivist environment it is immoral *not* to treat one's in-group members better than others.

In the collectivist classroom the virtues of harmony and maintaining face reign supreme. Confrontations and conflicts should be avoided or at least formulated so as not to hurt anyone; students should not lose face if this can be avoided. Shaming (that is, invoking the group's honor) is an effective way of correcting offenders: they will be put in order by their in-group members. At all times, the teacher is dealing with the student as part of an in-group, never as an isolated individual.

In the individualist classroom, of course, students expect to be treated as individuals and impartially, regardless of their background. Group formation among students is much more ad hoc, according to the task or to particular friendships and skills. Confrontations and open discussion of conflicts are often considered salutary, and face-consciousness is weak or nonexistent.

The purpose of education is perceived differently between the individualist and the collectivist society. In the former it aims at preparing the individual for a place in a society of other individuals. This means learning to cope with new, unknown, unforeseen situations. There is a basically positive attitude toward what is new. The purpose of learning is less to know how to do as to know *how to learn*. The assumption is that learning in life never ends; even after school and university it will continue (for example, through post-academic courses).

The individualist society in its schools tries to provide the competencies necessary for "modern man."

In the collectivist society there is a stress on adaptation to the skills and virtues necessary to be an acceptable group member. This leads to a premium on the products of tradition. Learning is more often seen as a one-time process, reserved for only the young, who have to learn *how to do* things in order to participate in society. It is an extended rite of passage.

The role of diplomas or certificates as a result of successful completion of a study is also different between the two poles of the individualism-collectivism dimension. In the individualist society the diploma improves the holder's economic worth but also his or her self-respect: it provides a sense of achievement. In the collectivist society a diploma is an honor to the holder (and his or her in-group) and entitles the holder to associate with members of higher-status groups—for example, to get a more attractive marriage partner. It is to a certain extent "a ticket to a ride." The social acceptance that comes with the diploma is more important than the individual self-respect that comes with mastering a subject, so that in collectivist societies the temptation is stronger to obtain diplomas in some irregular way, such as on the black market....

INDIVIDUALISM, COLLECTIVISM, AND IDEAS

Individualist societies not only practice individualism but they also consider it superior to other forms of mental software. Most Americans feel that individualism is good and at the root of their country's greatness. On the other hand, the late chairman Mao Zedong of China identified individualism as evil. He found individualism and liberalism responsible for selfishness and aversion to discipline; they led people to placing personal interests above those of the group or simply to devoting too much attention to their own things. In Table 1 places with a predominantly Chinese population all score very low on IDV (Hong Kong 25, mainland China 20, Singapore 20, Taiwan 17)....

The degree of individualism or collectivism of a society affects the conceptions of human nature produced in that society. In the United States the ideas of Abraham Maslow about human motivation have been and are still quite influential, in particular for the training of management students and practitioners. Maslow's famous "hierarchy of human needs" states that human needs can be ordered in a hierarchy from lower to higher, as follows: physiological, safety and security, belongingness, esteem, and self-actualization.[7] In order for a higher need to appear, it is necessary that the lower needs have been satisfied up to a certain extent. A starving person, one whose physiological needs are not at all satisfied, will not be motivated by anything else than the quest for food, and so forth. The top of Maslow's hierarchy, often pictured as a pyramid, is taken by the motive of *self-actualization:* realizing to the fullest possible extent the creative potential present within the individual. This means doing one's own thing. It goes without saying that this can only be the supreme motivation in an individualist society. In a collectivist culture what will be actualized is the interest and honor of the in-group, which may very well ask for self-effacement from many of the in-group members. The interpreter for a group of young Americans visiting China in the late 1970s found the idea of "doing your own thing" untranslatable into Chinese. Harmony and consensus are more attractive ultimate goals for such societies than individual self-actualization.

Since *Culture's Consequences* first appeared in 1980, the individualism-collectivism dimension has gained great popularity among psychologists, especially those from the economically emerging Asian nations. The dimension implies that traditional psychology is as little a universal science as traditional economics: it is a product of Western thinking, caught in individualist assumptions. When these are replaced by more collectivist assumptions, another psychology emerges that differs in important respects. For example, individualist psychology is obviously universalist, opposing the "ego" to any "other." In collectivist psychology the ego is inseparable from its social context. People in collectivist societies make particularist distinctions: the in-group, which includes the ego, is opposed to all out-groups. This means that the results of psychological experiments in a collectivist society depend on whether participants belong to the same in-group or not....

THE FUTURE OF INDIVIDUALISM AND COLLECTIVISM

The deep roots of national cultures make it likely that individualism-collectivism differences, like power distance differences, will survive for a long time into the future. Yet if there is to be any convergence among national cultures it should be on this dimension. The strong relationship between national wealth and individualism is undeniable, with the arrow of causality directed, as shown earlier, from wealth to individualism. Countries having achieved fast economic development have experienced a shift toward individualism. Japan is an example: the Japanese press regularly publishes stories of breaches of traditional family solidarity. Care for the aged in the past was considered a task for the Japanese family, but provisions by the state have become necessary for cases where the family stops fulfilling its traditional duties.

Nevertheless, even at a level of per capita income equal to or larger than Western countries, Japanese society has conserved distinctive collectivist elements in its family, school, and work spheres. Between Western countries like Britain, Sweden, and Germany, in spite of a noticeable convergence toward individualism under the influence of common economic development, relationships between the individual and the group continue to differ. The cultures shift, but they shift together, so that their relative positions remain intact, and there is no reason why differences between them should disappear.

As far as the poor countries of the world are concerned, they cannot be expected to become more individualist as long as they remain poor. And if differences in wealth between rich and poor countries continue to increase (as in many instances they do), gaps on the individualism-collectivism dimension can only increase further.

REVIEW QUESTIONS

1. Define "individualism" and "collectivism."
2. Describe the relationship between this primary distinction and the relative wealth of a culture.
3. List at least six specific communication behaviors that differ according to whether the culture is individualist or collectivist. For example, the use of personal pronouns, conflict management strategies, occurrence of silence, and expressions of emotion.
4. What is "face," and why is "losing face" a primary concern in collectivist cultures?
5. What is the individualist culture's counterpart characteristic to "face"? Explain.
6. Describe three differences between bride- and groom-selection in individualist and collectivist cultures.
7. Describe how small group instruction works differently in individualist and collectivist schools.

PROBES

1. What problems arise from the Hofstedes's decision to collect data by country (governmental entity)? What happens when "culture" is equated with "nationality"?
2. Describe the relationship between the individualist/collectivist distinction and E. T. Hall's high/low context distinction.
3. Identify three elements of your own cultural identity—for example, gender, age, and ethnicity. Then describe individualist and collectivist elements of each. Which are more prominent—the individualist ones or the collectivist ones? Would you describe yourself culturally as primarily individualist or collectivist?

NOTES

1. From a speech by R. M. Hadjiwibowo to Semafor Senior Management College, the Netherlands, September 1983. Translation from the Dutch by Geert Hofstede with suggestions from the author.
2. Edward T. Hall, *Beyond Culture* (Garden City, NY: Doubleday Anchor Books, 1976).
3. David Yau-Fai Ho, "On the Concept of Face." *American Journal of Sociology* 81 (1986): 867–884.
4. Harry C. Triandis, *The Analysis of Subjective Culture* (New York: Wiley Interscience, 1972), p. 38.

5. David M. Buss, D. M., "Sex Differences in Human Mate Preferences: Evolutionary Hypotheses Tested in 37 Cultures." *Behavioral and Brain Sciences* 12 (1989): 1–49; and David M. Buss et al., "International Preferences in Selecting Mates." *Journal of Cross-Cultural Psychology* 21 (1990): 5–47.
6. Paul Yelsma and Kuriakose Athappilly, "Marital Satisfaction and Communication Practices: Comparisons among Indian and American Couples." *Journal of Comparative Family Studies* 19 (1988): 37–54; Karen K. Dion and Kenneth L. Dion, "Individualistic and Collectivistic Perspectives on Gender and the Cultural Context of Love and Intimacy." *Journal of Social Issues* 49 (1993): 53–69; and Geert Hofstede, *Culture's Consequences: International Differences in Work-Related Values,* abridged ed. (Beverly Hills, CA: Sage, 1984).
7. Abraham H. Maslow, *Motivation and Personality,* 2nd ed. (New York: Harper & Row, 1970).

Building Relationships with Diverse Others

David W. Johnson

For more than 25 years, educational psychologist David Johnson has been helping teachers and schools in North America, Central America, Europe, Africa, Asia, the Middle East, and the Pacific Rim take advantage of the benefits of collaborative and cooperative learning. One of the fruits of his labor is his book *Reaching Out: Interpersonal Effectiveness and Self-Actualization,* from which I've taken the next reading. This is a basic introduction to the attitudes and skills of connecting with people who are different from you.

Johnson begins with the point that although globalization is making diversity among acquaintances, classmates, co-workers, and neighbors increasingly inevitable, it is in some ways not "natural" for humans to want to get along with diverse others. For 200,000 years, as he puts it, humans lived in small hunting-and-gathering groups, interacting infrequently with others. But today we are regularly thrown together with cultural strangers. Both men and women in what have traditionally been single-sex jobs (firefighter, nurse, mail carrier, parking checker) are having to team with opposite-sex colleagues. Older and younger workers are forced to collaborate, and blacks, Latinos, Asians, whites, Arabs, Pacific Islanders, and members of other ethnic groups are thrown together with those with different, and sometimes competing, identities.

The chapter this reading was taken from explains six steps for building relationships with diverse peers, and this excerpt discusses four of the six: Accept yourself, lower barriers, recognize that diversity is a valuable resource, and work to clarify misunderstandings. The first step echoes some of what is in the readings about self-awareness in Chapter 3. Johnson encourages you to reflect on your own identity, which can be subdivided into your self-schema, gender identity, and ethnic identity, as a first step toward connecting with people different from you.

Then he offers some suggestions about lowering three barriers: prejudice, the tendency to blame the victim, and cultural conflict. Prejudice—manifested in ethnocentrism, stereotyping, or discrimination—can be a major hurdle, and Johnson explains four specific ways to overcome it. Blaming the victim occurs when people "attribute the cause of discrimination or misfortune to the personal characteristics and actions of the victim." In this section, Johnson reviews some of the information about external and internal attributions that is discussed in the first reading in Chapter 5, and shows how careful attributions can enhance your experience. Culture clash is the third barrier Johnson explains.

The next section of the reading explains some specific ways in which diversity can be openly recognized and genuinely valued. Johnson suggests four steps that can help lead toward profitable collaboration among diverse people.

The final section of this reading highlights the importance of clarifying miscommunications. Johnson could have said a great deal more here than he does, but this section does remind us of how language sensitivity and a developed awareness of stylistic differences among diverse communicators can help people deal effectively with those who are different from themselves. Johnson ends this section with seven specific suggestions; the first is "Use all the communication skills discussed in this book." Even though "this book" he was talking about was *Reaching Out,* you can interpret it as a reference to *Bridges Not Walls.* As Johnson recognizes, the skills developed in all 12 chapters of *this* book can be brought to bear on the project of improving relationships among diverse people.

You may have already thought through the ideas that Johnson discusses here. But if you haven't (or if you have and would still appreciate a reminder), this is an excellent introduction to the frame of mind and some specific skills needed to bridge differences between you and people you might initially think of as "strangers."

MAIN IDEAS

- Globalization is challenging partly because it's new; for 200,000 years humans only had to interact with people like themselves; now we interact with people different from ourselves every day.
- In order to build relationships with diverse peers, you must (a) accept yourself, (b) lower barriers to building relationships with diverse peers, (c) recognize that diversity exists and is a valuable resource, and (d) clarify misunderstandings.
- Self-awareness and self-acceptance are required first steps.
- Barriers that must be lowered include prejudice, the tendency to blame the victim, and cultural conflict.
- The third key step is to recognize and value diversity for the benefits it can provide.
- The fourth step is to clarify communication by using all the understandings and skills discussed in this book. Language sensitivity and awareness of stylistic differences are especially important.

INTRODUCTION

We live in one world. The problems that face each person, each community, each country cannot be solved without global cooperation and joint action.

Economically, for example, there has been a globalization of business reflected in the increase in multinational companies, coproduction agreements, and offshore operations. As globalization becomes the norm, more and more companies must translate their local and national perspectives into a world view. Companies that are staffed by individuals skilled in building relationships with diverse peers have an advantage in the global market.

Interacting effectively with peers from different cultures, ethnic groups, social classes, and historical backgrounds does not come naturally. For 200,000 years humans lived in small hunting and gathering groups, interacting only infrequently with other nearby small groups. Today we are required to communicate effectively with people cross-culturally, through the generations, among races, between genders, and across those subtle but pervasive barriers of class. No wonder this feels uncomfortable—we have never been required to do it before!

Diversity among your acquaintances, classmates, co-workers, neighbors, and friends is increasingly inevitable. North America, Europe, and many other parts of the world are becoming more and more diverse in terms of culture, ethnicity, religion, age, physical qualities, and gender. You will be expected to interact effectively with people with a wide variety of characteristics and from a wide variety of backgrounds. In order to build relationships with diverse peers, you must

1. Accept yourself.
2. Lower the barriers to building relationships with diverse peers.
3. Recognize that diversity exists and is a valuable resource....
4. Clarify misunderstandings.

ACCEPTING YOURSELF

If I am not for myself, who will be for me? But if I am only for myself, what am I?

—The Talmud

Two basic human needs are to

1. Join with others in a cooperative effort to achieve something great.
2. Be a unique and separate individual who is valued and respected in one's own right.

In order to meet this second need, you must accept yourself as you are and build a distinct image of yourself as a certain kind of person who has an identity differentiated and discernible from others. The greater your self-acceptance, the more stable and integrated your personal identity. Building a coherent, stable, and integrated identity that summarizes who you are as a separate, autonomous, and unique individual is the first step in building constructive relationships with diverse peers.

The Person You Think You Are

What kind of person are you? How would you describe yourself to someone who does not know you? Would your description be disjointed and contradictory, or would it be organized and consistent? Would it change from day to day, or would it stay the same over a period of years? Do you like yourself, or do you feel a basic sense of shame and contempt when you think of yourself? We all need a strong and integrated sense of personal identity that serves as an anchor in life.

Early philosophers advised us to "know thyself" and poets have told us, "To thine own self be true." We have taken their advice. Hundreds of books have been written dealing with how to get to know yourself and the *Oxford English Dictionary* lists more than 100 words that focus on the self, from *self-abasement* to *self-wisdom*. When you form a conception of who you are as a person you have an identity.

Your *identity* is a consistent set of attitudes that defines who you are. It is a subjective self-image that is a type of cognitive structure called a self-schema. A *self-schema* is a generalization about the self, derived from past experience, that organizes and guides your understanding of the information you learn about yourself from interacting with others. You have multiple schemas, multiple identities, and multiple selves. They include your view of your physical characteristics (height, weight, sex, hair and eye color, general appearance), your social roles (student or teacher, child or parent, employee or employer), the activities you engage in (playing the piano, dancing, reading), your abilities (skills, achievements), your attitudes and interests (liking rock and roll, favoring equal rights for females), and your general personality traits (extrovert or introvert, impulsive or reflective, sensible or scatterbrained). Your *gender identity* is your fundamental sense of your maleness or femaleness. Your *ethnic identity* is your sense of belonging to one particular ethnic group. Your identity consists not only of various self-schemas that you currently possess but of selves that you would like to be or that you imagine you might be. These potential selves include ideals that you would like to attain and standards that you feel you should meet (the "ought" self). They can originate from your own thoughts or from the messages of others.

Each of your self-schemas is viewed as being positive or negative. You generally look at yourself in an evaluative way, approving or disapproving of your behavior and characteristics. Your self-schemas are arranged in a hierarchy. The more important an identity is, or the higher it stands in the hierarchy, the more likely it is to influence your choices and your behavior.

To cope with stress you need more than one self. The diversity and complexity of the identity reduces the stress you experience. Self-complexity provides a buffer against stressful events. If you have only one or two major self-schemas, any negative event is going to have an impact on most aspects of your identity. The woman who sees herself primarily as a wife, for example, is likely to be devastated if her husband says he wants an immediate divorce. In contrast, the individual who has a more complex representation of self may be more protected from negative events that primarily involve only one or two of several roles. The woman who sees herself not only as wife, but also as a mother, lawyer, friend, and tennis player will have other roles to fall back on when impending divorce threatens her role of spouse. People with more complex identities are less prone to depression and illness; they also experience less severe mood swings following success or failure in one particular area of performance....

Some of the Benefits of Self-Acceptance

There is a common saying that goes, "I can't be right for someone else if I'm not right for me!" *Self-acceptance* is a high regard for yourself or, conversely, a lack of cynicism about yourself. There are a number of benefits to accepting yourself as you are, and a relationship exists among self-acceptance, self-disclosure, and being accepted by others. The more self-accepting you are, the greater your self-disclosure tends to be. The greater your self-disclosure, the more others accept you. And the more others accept you, the more you accept yourself. A high level of self-acceptance, furthermore, is reflected in psychological health. Psychologically healthy people see themselves as being liked, capable, worthy, and acceptable to other peoples. All of these perceptions are based on self-acceptance. Considerable evidence abounds that self-acceptance and acceptance of others are related. If you think well of yourself you tend to think well of others. You also tend to assume that others will like you, an expectation that often becomes a self-fulfilling prophecy.

DIFFICULTIES WITH DIVERSITY

Once you are accepting of yourself, you are in a position to be accepting of others. There are, however, a number of barriers to accepting diverse peers. They include prejudice, the tendency to blame the victim, and cultural conflict.

Prejudice

To know one's self is wisdom, but to know one's neighbor is genius.

—*Minna Antrim (author)*

Building relationships with diverse peers is not easy. The first barrier is prejudice. Prejudice, stereotyping, and discrimination begin with categorizing. In order to understand other people and yourself, categories must be used. *Categorizing* is a basic human cognitive process of conceptualizing objects and people as members of groups. We categorize people on the basis of *inherited traits* (culture, sex, ethnic membership, physical features) or *acquired traits* (education, occupation, lifestyle, customs). Categorizing and generalizing are often helpful in processing information and making decisions. At times, however, they malfunction and result in stereotyping and prejudice.

To be prejudiced means to prejudge. *Prejudice* can be defined as an unjustified negative attitude toward a person based solely on that individual's membership in a particular group. Prejudices are judgments made about others that establish a superiority/inferiority belief system. If one person dislikes another simply because that other person is a member of an ethnic group, sex, or religion, that is prejudice.

One common form of prejudice is ethnocentrism. *Ethnocentrism* is the tendency to regard our own ethnic group, culture, or nation as better or more correct than others. The word is derived from *ethnic,* meaning a group united by similar customs, characteristics, race, or other common factors, and *center.* When ethnocentrism is present, the standards and values of our culture are used as a yardstick to measure the worth of other ethnic groups. Ethnocentrism is often perpetuated by *cultural conditioning.* As children we are raised to fit into a particular culture. We are conditioned to respond to various situations as we see others in our culture react.

Prejudices are often associated with stereotypes. A *stereotype* is a set of beliefs about the characteristics of the people in a group that is applied to almost all members of that group. Typically, stereotypes are widely held beliefs within a group and focus on what other cultural and ethnic groups, or socioeconomic classes are "really like." Women have been stereotyped as more emotional than men. Men have been stereotyped as more competitive than women. Tall, dark, and handsome men have been stereotyped as mysterious. Stereotypes distort and exaggerate in ways that support an underlying prejudice or fundamental bias against members of other groups. Stereotypes are resistant to change because people believe information that confirms their stereotypes more readily than evidence that challenges them. Stereotypes almost always have a detrimental effect on those targeted, interfering with the victim's ability to be productive and live a high quality life.

Stereotypes reflect an *illusionary correlation* between two unrelated factors, such as being poor and lazy. Negative traits are easy to acquire and hard to lose. When you meet one poor person who is lazy you may tend to see all poor people as lazy. From then on, any poor person who is not hard at work the moment you notice him or her may be perceived to be lazy. Our prejudiced stereotype of poor people being lazy is protected in three ways. Our prejudice makes us notice the negative traits we ascribe to the groups we are prejudiced against. We tend to have a *false consensus bias* by believing that most other people share our stereotypes (i.e., see poor people as being lazy). We tend to see our own behavior and judgments as quite common and appropriate, and to view alternative responses as uncommon and often inappropriate. Finally, we often develop a rationale and explanation to justify our stereotypes and prejudices.

When prejudice is put into action, it is discrimination. *Discrimination* is an action taken to harm a group or any of its members. It is a negative, often aggressive action aimed at the target of prejudice. Discrimination is aimed at denying members of the targeted groups treatment and opportunities equal to those afforded to the dominant group. When discrimination is based on race or sex, it is referred to as racism or sexism.

Diversity among people can either be a valued resource generating energy, vitality, and creativity, or it can be a source of prejudice, stereotyping, and discrimination. To reduce your prejudices and use of stereotypes, these steps may be helpful:

1. Admit that you have prejudices (everyone does, you are no exception) and commit yourself to reducing them.
2. Identify the stereotypes that reflect your prejudices and modify them.
3. Identify the actions that reflect your prejudices and modify them.
4. Seek feedback from diverse friends and colleagues about how well you are communicating respect for and valuing of diversity.

Blaming the Victim

It is commonly believed that the world is a just place where people generally get what they deserve. If we win the lottery, it must be because we are nice people who deserve some good luck. If we are robbed, it must be because we are careless and want to be punished for past misdeeds. Any person who is mugged in a dark alley while carrying a great deal of cash may be seen as asking to be robbed. Most people tend to believe that they deserve what happens to them. Most people also believe that others also get what they deserve in the world. It is all too easy to forget that victims do not have the benefit of hindsight to guide their actions.

When someone is a victim of prejudice, stereotyping, and discrimination, all too often they are seen as doing *something* wrong. *Blaming the victim* occurs when we attribute the cause of discrimination or misfortune to the personal characteristics and actions of the victim. The situation is examined for potential causes that will enable us to maintain our belief in a just world. If the victim can be blamed for causing the discrimination, then we can believe that the future is predictable and controllable because we will get what we deserve.

Blaming the victim occurs as we try to attribute a cause to events. We constantly interpret the meaning of our behavior and events that occur in our lives. Many times we want to figure out *why* we acted in a particular way or why a certain outcome occurred. If we get angry when someone infers we are stupid, but we could care less when someone calls us clumsy, we want to know why we are so sensitive about our intelligence. When we are standing on a street corner after a rainstorm and a car splashes us with water, we want to know whether it was caused by our carelessness, the driver's meanness, or just bad luck. This process of explaining or inferring the causes of events has been termed *causal attribution.* An attribution is an inference drawn about the causes of a behavior or event....

In trying to understand why a behavior or event occurred, we generally choose to attribute causes either to

1. Internal, personal factors (such as effort and ability)
2. External, situational factors (such as luck or the behavior/personality of other people)

For example, if you do well on a test, you can attribute it to your hard work and great intelligence (an internal attribution) or to the fact that the test was incredibly easy (an external attribution). When a friend drops out of school, you can attribute it to a lack of motivation (an internal attribution) or lack of money (an external attribution).

People make causal attributions to explain their successes and failures. These are *self-serving* attributions, designed to permit us to take credit for positive outcomes and to avoid blame for negative ones. We have a systematic tendency to claim our successes are due to our ability and efforts while our failures are due to bad luck, evil people, or a lack of effort. We also have a systematic tendency to claim responsibility for the success of group efforts ("It was all my idea in the first place and I did most of the work") and avoid responsibility for group failures ("If the other members had tried harder, this would not have happened")....

Attributing the causes of others' failure and misfortune to their actions rather than to prejudice and discrimination can be a barrier to building constructive relationships with diverse peers. Bad things do happen to good people. Racism does exist. Innocent bystanders do get shot. It is usually a good idea to suspend any tendency to blame the victim when interacting with diverse peers.

Culture Clash

Another common barrier to building relationships with diverse peers is cultural clashes. A *culture clash* is a conflict over basic values that occurs among individuals from different cultures. The most common form is members of minority groups' questioning the values of the majority. Common reactions by majority group members when their values are being questioned are feeling:

1. *Threatened:* Their responses include avoidance, denial, and defensiveness.
2. *Confused:* Their responses include seeking more information in an attempt to redefine the problem.
3. *Enhanced:* Their responses include heightened anticipation, awareness, and positive actions that lead to solving the problem.

Many cultural clashes develop from threatening, to confusing, to enhancing. Once they are enhancing, they are no longer a barrier.

As prejudice, stereotyping, and discrimination are reduced, the tendency to blame the victim is avoided, and cultural clashes become enhancing, the stage is set for recognizing and valuing diversity.

RECOGNIZING AND VALUING DIVERSITY

In order to actualize the positive potential of diversity, you must recognize that diversity exists and then learn to value and respect fundamental differences among people. This is especially true in countries in which widely diverse groups of people live. The United States, for example, is a nation of many cultures, races, languages, and religions. In the last eight years alone, over 7.8 million people journeying from over 150 different countries and speaking dozens of different languages made the United States their new home. America's pluralism and diversity has many positive values, such as being a source of energy and creativity that increases the vitality of American society. Diversity among collaborators has been found to contribute to achievement and productivity, creative problem solving, growth in cognitive and moral reasoning, perspective-taking ability, and general sophistication in interacting and working with peers from a variety of cultural and ethnic backgrounds (Johnson & Johnson, 1989).

Within a relationship, a community, an organization, a society, or a world, the goal is not to assimilate all groups so that everyone is alike. The goal is to work together to achieve mutual goals while recognizing cultural diversity and learning to value and respect fundamental differences while working together to achieve mutual goals. Creating a *unum* from *pluribus* is done in basically four steps. *First, you develop an appreciation for your own religious, ethnic, or cultural background.* Your identification with the culture and homeland of your ancestors must be recognized and valued. The assumption is that respect for your cultural heritage will translate into self-respect.

Second, you develop an appreciation and respect for the religious, ethnic, and cultural backgrounds of others. A critical aspect of developing an ethnic and cultural identity is whether ethnocentricity is inherent in your definition of yourself. An in-group identity must be developed in a way that does not lead to rejection of out-groups. There are many examples where being a member of one group requires the rejection of other groups. There are also many examples where being a member of one group requires the valuing and respect for other groups. Outgroups need to be seen as collaborators and resources rather than competitors and threats. Express respect for diverse backgrounds and value them as a resource that increases the quality of your life and adds to the viability of your society. The degree to which your in-group identity leads to respect for and valuing of out-groups depends on developing a superordinate identity that includes both your own and all other groups.

Third, you develop a strong superordinate identity that transcends the differences between your own and all other groups. Being an American, for example, is creedal rather than racial or ancestral. The United States is a nation that unites as one people the descendants of many cultures, races, religions, and ethnic groups through an identification with America and democracy. And America has grown increasingly diverse in social and cultural composition. Each cultural group is part of the whole and members of each new immigrant group, while modifying and enriching our national identity, learn they are first and foremost Americans.

America is one of the few successful examples of a pluralistic society where different groups clashed but ultimately learned to live together through achieving a sense of common nationhood. In our diversity, there has always been a broad recognition that we are one people. Whatever our origins, we are all Americans.

Fourth, you adopt a pluralistic set of values concerning democracy, freedom, liberty, equality, justice, the rights of individuals, and the responsibilities of citizenship. It is these values that form the American creed. We respect basic human rights, listen to dissenters instead of jailing them, and have a multiparty political system, a free press, free speech, freedom of religion, and freedom of assembly. These values were shaped by millions of people from many different backgrounds. Americans are a multicultural people knitted together by a common set of political and moral values.

Diverse individuals from different cultural, ethnic, social class, and language backgrounds come together primarily in school, career, and community settings. Sometimes the results are positive and individuals get to know each other, appreciate and value the vitality of diversity, learn how to use diversity for creative problem solving and enhanced productivity, and internalize a common superordinate identity that binds them together. If diversity is to be a source of creativity and energy, individuals must value and seek out diversity rather than fear and reject it. Doing so will eventually result in cross-cultural friendships....

CLARIFYING MISCOMMUNICATIONS

Imagine that you and several friends went to hear a speaker. Although the content was good, and the delivery entertaining, two of your friends walked out in protest. When you asked them why, they called your attention to the facts that the speaker continually said "you guys" even though half the audience was women, used only sports and military examples, only quoted males, and joked about senility and old age. Your friends were insulted.

Communication is actually one of the most complex aspects of managing relationships with diverse peers. To communicate effectively with people from a different cultural, ethnic, social class, or historical background than yours you must increase your

1. *Language sensitivity:* knowledge of words and expressions that are appropriate and inappropriate in communicating with diverse groups. The use of language can play a powerful role in reinforcing stereotypes and garbling communication. To avoid this, individuals need to heighten their sensitivity and avoid using terms and expressions that ignore or devalue others.

2. *Awareness of stylistic elements of communication:* knowledge of the key elements of communication style and how diverse cultures use these elements to communicate. Without awareness of nuances in language and differences in style, the potential for garbled communication is enormous when interacting with diverse peers.

Your ability to communicate with credibility to diverse peers is closely linked to your use of language. You must be sophisticated enough to anticipate how your messages will be interpreted by the listener. If you are unaware of nuances and innuendoes contained in your message, then you will be more likely to miscommunicate. The words you choose often tell other people more about your values, attitudes, and socialization than you intend to reveal. Receivers will react to the subtleties conveyed and interpret the implied messages behind our words. The first step in establishing relationships with diverse peers, therefore, is to understand how language reinforces stereotypes and to adjust our usage accordingly.

You can never predict with certainty how every person will react to what you say. You can, however, minimize the possibility of miscommunicating by following some basic guidelines:

1. Use all the communication skills discussed in this book.
2. Negotiate for meaning whenever you think the other persons you are talking with misinterpreted what you said.
3. Use words that are inclusive rather than exclusive such as women, men, participants.
4. Avoid adjectives that spotlight specific groups and imply the individual is an exception, such as black doctor, woman pilot, older teacher, blind lawyer.
5. Use quotes, references, metaphors, and analogies that reflect diversity and are from diverse sources, for example, from Asian and African sources as well as from European and American.
6. Avoid terms that define, demean, or devalue others, such as cripple, girl, boy, agitator.
7. Be aware of the genealogy of words viewed as inappropriate by others. It is the connotations the receiver places on the words that are important, not your connotations. These connotations change over time so continual clarification is needed. There are loaded words that seem neutral to you but highly judgmental to people of diverse backgrounds. The word lady, for example, was a compliment even a few years ago, but today it fails to take into account women's independence and equal status in society and, therefore, is offensive to many women. Words such as girls or gals are just as offensive.

SUMMARY

In a global village highly diverse individuals interact daily, study and work together, and live in the same community. Diversity among your acquaintances, classmates, co-workers, neighbors, and friends is inevitable. You will be expected to interact effectively with people with a wide variety of characteristics and from a wide variety of backgrounds. In order to gain the sophistication and skills needed to do so you must accept yourself, lower the barriers to building relationships with diverse peers, recognize that diversity exists and is a valuable resource, ... and clarify misunderstandings.

All people need to believe that they are unique and separate individuals who are valued and respected in their own right. In order to do so, you must accept yourself as you are and build a coherent, stable, and integrated identity. Your identity helps you cope with stress, it provides stability and consistency to your life, and it directs what information is attended to, how it is organized, and how it is remembered. Your identity is built through your current relationships and identifications with real, historical, and fictional people. Actually, you have many interrelated identities. You have a family identity, a gender identity, and a country identity. An important aspect of your identity is your identification with your cultural, ethnic, historical, and religious background.

The more accepting you are of yourself, the more able you are to be accepting of others. But there are barriers to building positive relationships with diverse peers. The most notable barriers are prejudice, blaming the victim, and culture clash. Minimizing these barriers makes it easier to recognize that diversity exists and fundamental differences among people are to be both respected and valued. To do so you must respect your own heritage, respect the heritages of others, develop a superordinate identity that transcends the differences, and [adopt] a pluralistic set of values.

Accepting yourself, minimizing the barriers, and respecting and valuing diversity set the stage for actually gaining cross-cultural sophistication. Being able to relate effectively to people from a variety of cultures depends on seeking opportunities to interact cross-culturally, building trust, so that enough candor exists that you can learn what is and what is not disrespectful and hurtful to them. It is only through building friendships with diverse peers that the insights required to understand how to interact appropriately with people from a wide variety of backgrounds can be obtained. Two requirements for developing such friendships are highlighting cooperative efforts to achieve mutual goals and clarifying miscommunications that arise while working together.

REVIEW QUESTIONS

1. Explain what Johnson means—as specifically as you can—when he says that globalization has made diversity increasingly inevitable.
2. What is a self-schema? Give an example of one of your own self-schemas (see Chapter 3).
3. Explain the connection Johnson makes between prejudice and discrimination.
4. Explain how blaming the victim can contribute to stereotyping.
5. What does Johnson mean by "a strong superordinate identity that transcends the differences between your own and all other groups"?
6. What is a pluralistic set of values?

7. Give an example of how (a) language sensitivity and (b) awareness of stylistic elements of communication could enhance relationships with diverse others.

PROBES

1. People who belong to such organizations as a militia, skinhead, or Ku Klux Klan group often argue for the importance of ethnic purity and exclusivity. Members of men-only and women-only groups make similar arguments about gender exclusivity. Johnson's basic assumption in this reading is that these arguments for exclusivity are naïve, because diversity is a fact of the contemporary world. What specific examples can you cite to support Johnson's assumption? Where do you notice the concrete evidence of increasing diversity?
2. *Why* does Johnson say that the first step toward successfully interacting with diverse others is to learn to accept yourself?
3. Cognitive scientists pretty much agree that categorization is a basic human mental function. Our brains naturally and constantly categorize almost everything we perceive. If this is true, then we automatically categorize the people we perceive. How, then, can a person possibly avoid prejudice?
4. As Johnson defines *culture clash*, it is inevitable. Various cultures will naturally have conflicts over basic values. Tell how he suggests we respond to this inevitability.
5. Which of the previous readings in this book do you think could contribute most directly to your efforts to bridge differences with diverse others?

REFERENCE

Johnson, D. W. & Johnson, R. (1989). *Cooperation and competition: Theory and research.* Edina, MN: Interaction Book Company.

From Racism to Gracism
David A. Anderson

This was written by the pastor of one of the largest multicultural Christian churches in the United States. David Anderson also teaches cultural diversity for the University of Phoenix and several other educational institutions and hosts a nationally syndicated radio talk show called *Reconciliation Live*. His approach to the challenge of bridging cultural differences is straightforward—even simple—and it is also both profound and difficult to implement. As you would expect, he speaks from his perspective as a Christian, but whether you are religious or not, Christian or not, there are helpful ideas here. And as I've mentioned in the introductions to other writings that "take a position," I encourage you to read this one for understanding, remembering that understanding does not have to mean agreement.

David Anderson defines racism as speaking, acting, or thinking negatively about someone else solely based on that person's color, class, or culture. Anderson's basic idea is that racism can and should be countered with what he calls *gracism,* which is "the positive extension of favor on other humans based on color, class or culture." He argues that *gracism* is different from favoritism, because "favoritism is purposefully neglecting the needs of the many to accommodate the greeds of a few," and is "the exercise of exclusion," while *gracism* is "the art of inclusion," which means "showering extra grace on a few while having love for all."

The central part of this short excerpt from Anderson's book is an e-mail from a woman who provides an extended example of gracism. She reports the feelings of righteous indignation and "knowing full well that I was right" that she experienced when a Spanish-speaking family tried to barge into a boarding group line at an airport. Then she reports what happened when she invited the family to enter the line in front of her. This woman attributes the change she experienced to "a Holy Spirit smackdown," but whether that's how you would account for it or not, the e-mail does point out the precise difference between racist communication and "gracist" communication.

"A gracist," Anderson concludes, "reaches across ethnic lines and racial borders to lend assistance and 'extra grace' to those who are different, on the fringe or marginalized." As I mentioned, this is a simple idea and a potentially profound one. If you are inclined to dismiss this short reading as simplistic and naïve, I encourage you to explore how it might be specifically implemented in some of the interculturally challenging situations you experience.

MAIN IDEAS

- *Gracism* is the opposite of racism; rather than speaking, acting, or thinking negatively about someone based solely on that person's color, class, or culture (racism), *gracism* means the positive extension of favor on other humans based on color, class, or culture.
- *Gracism* is not favoritism because it is inclusive rather than exclusive: offering extra grace on a few while having love for all.
- *Gracism* is a Christian concept, *and* it can be understood and applied in both Christian and non-Christian contexts.
- *Gracism* can be practiced by both people in positions of power and those who are themselves marginalized.

I define racism as speaking, acting or thinking negatively about someone else solely based on that person's color, class or culture. A common definition for grace is the unmerited favor of God on humankind. Extending such favor and kindness upon other human beings is how we Christians demonstrate this grace practically from day to day. When one merges the definition of racism, which is negative, with the definition of grace, which is positive, a new term

From *Gracism: The Art of Inclusion* by David A. Anderson. Downers Grove, IL: InterVarsity Press, 2007. Reprinted by permission.

emerges—*gracism*. I define gracism as the positive extension of favor on other humans based on color, class or culture.

FAVOR OR FAVORITISM?

… The positive extension of favor toward certain people does not have to mean favoritism. When [New Testament author] James wrote about favoritism, he was writing in the context of loving all people and not discriminating against those who are under-resourced, low class or poor. "If you really keep the royal law found in Scripture, 'Love your neighbor as yourself,' you are doing right. But if you show favoritism, you sin and are convicted by the law as lawbreakers" (James 2:8–9).

To discriminate, exclude and not love everyone is sin. Notice that James's comments about favoritism in 2:9 follow the command to love your neighbor in 2:8. His point is that we are to love everyone and not discriminate against anyone. Does this mean that extending positive favor in an environment where everyone is loved and treated with equal respect is wrong? I say no.…

IS GRACISM FAIR?

Is it possible to extend favor and still be fair? Distinct from favoritism, whereby one is granted favor because of a special status, ethnic superiority or commonality, gracism reaches outside the box of elitism and special favors based on some fraternal code or secret handshake. Favor is showering extra grace on a few while having love for all. Favoritism is purposefully neglecting the needs of the many to accommodate the greeds of a few. While favor is the art of inclusion, favoritism is the exercise of exclusion. Christianity is an inclusive faith that bids all to come.

Yes, it is possible to extend favor without engaging in favoritism. There is a profound difference. One is from God and the other is from human beings.

A GRACIST LESSON LEARNED

I have been teaching on gracism for a few years now. I believe that the teaching takes a while to take root. It is a slow and dawning truth that becomes clearer the more one has the opportunity to act upon it. One woman who has been listening and learning about the concept of gracism wrote me an encouraging e-mail to explain how the teaching had a surprising effect on her during an encounter she had while awaiting a flight in an airport queue.

Dear David,

Last year I was in line at the airport waiting to board my flight on Southwest Airlines. I love Southwest for their cheap fares, but the one thing I don't like is that they have no assigned seats. You can print out your boarding group pass that will have an A, B or C on it and then you wait in line till your group is called. Everyone wants a good seat on the plane, so people will stand in that line for an hour if they have to, myself included.

I was holding tightly to my boarding group pass, which said "A," and I had been waiting in that line for at least a half hour, when a family—husband, wife and two young children—loudly made their way into the "waiting to board" area. You couldn't help but notice them. They seemed confused and were talking loudly in Spanish to one another, glancing at their tickets, waving their arms and pulling their bags and their kids into the huddle of travelers. I thought perhaps they were Mexican, and I began trying to understand what they were saying, but my very limited Spanish failed me.

It's funny how these boarding group lines may not look like lines at all in the literal sense. They snake around tables, chairs and luggage; they dip with younger travelers sitting down in the middle; they have big gaps where someone has stopped to talk on his cell phone or finish a page in her novel. But just to be clear—they are indeed lines. And it is understood who is in front of you and who is in back of you, and your place in the line is respected by the other travelers. Usually. The loud Spanish speaking family was trying to work their way into the A line and ended up just a few people ahead of me, looking very confused. They were hanging just to the right of the line and you could tell they were hoping to some-how get absorbed into a real spot. The others in line were not happy about this. I watched the people get closer to one another and even position the men with them to stand on the side like a defensive line on a football team.

The Mexicans kept trying to get in, all the while looking confused, glancing at their tickets and talking in Spanish. They tried to slip in a few different places, but this line was a united front—no one was moving. All eyes were on them, and though no one said a word, the sound was deafening. I could only imagine what was going through the minds of those in line. I could see them shaking their heads in disgust. "Stupid foreigners." "Who do they think they are coming over here and just butting in?" "They have no sense." It didn't matter that no one was speaking this stuff out loud. I had heard it so many times and I could see it on their faces and in their body language. And part of me was feeling it too. I have waited in this line all this time; no way are these people gonna just butt in front of me. That's not fair! Don't they know the rules? We just don't do that here. This is my place in line.

Just as I was perfecting my speech in my head, full of righteous indignation and knowing full well that I was—we all were—right, I had a Holy Spirit smackdown. That's when a completely different thought comes into your brain that you know is of God and it feels like a smack upside your head. I don't like Holy Spirit smackdowns. This time it was your voice, David, in my head, talking about gracism. Special favor for those who are disregarded. Special treatment, going above and beyond to extend grace to those who have been oppressed and dismissed in this world because of their race, class or culture.

It was such a powerful teaching and God used it to smack me upside the head in that moment. I prayed silently and asked God to help me be a gracist. He immediately showed me that my judgment of these people was wrong. Did it really matter who was in front of me in line? Who cares! What was most important here? What if you were in another country where you didn't speak the language and you were confused, tired and fearing you weren't going to make it in the plane? How would you feel? Wouldn't you be looking for someone to show you some kindness?

So I stuck my head out of line just enough to tap the Mexican woman on the shoulder. "Excuse me. Please come over here. You can get in line right here in front of me." I knew she didn't understand my words, but my message came through loud and clear. She smiled at me so big I thought she was going to cry. She grabbed her husband and kids and they all kept thanking me and bowing their heads. I saw relief come to them as they took their spot in line in front of me. They were so grateful and I was so ashamed. Why had it taken me so long to do the right thing?

David, thank you for teaching me about gracism. While I never thought I was a racist, I see how even being silent in those moments feeds the problem. Considering others who are different and giving them special favor is unnatural for most people, but it's clearly in the Word of God, and now that I have had the chance to apply it, I can say it feels like God too.

Humbled by grace,
T. Lynn

GOD IN FRONT

When one puts a G, which stands for God, in front of the negative concept of racism, then one has begun identifying solutions and resources to address the race problem in the world. It may sound simplistic, but I believe it is right. Who said that the solution had to be difficult? Admittedly, the implementation of the solution is the most difficult. Why is this? Race problems bring with them anger, bitterness, prejudice and pride. Conversion brings with it forgiveness, patience and access to available resources, such as the filling and the fruit of the Spirit.

When we repent of our sins personally, corporately and nationally, we then can begin to rebuild on a new foundation. Radical conversion and forgiveness change the heart of a person. Therefore, unless we go through repentance over the sin of racism, we Christians are battling the problem of race just like the world, namely without God. But if Christians put God in front of any problem, that problem will diminish because God is bigger than it. I am not saying that it will keep me as a black man from getting stopped by police officers when I'm traveling in neighborhoods that make them suspicious of me, but the God in me can give me the grace to handle such incidents with patience, kindness and forgiveness.

A gracist reaches across ethnic lines and racial borders to lend assistance and "extra grace" to those who are different, on the fringe or marginalized. This person or group can be of any color, culture or gender.

Are you a gracist? The heart of a gracist extends a helping hand to those who are outside the positive norms of a particular society. While the majority may enjoy the hidden rules of a particular sociological group, gracists build bridges of inclusion for those on the margins....

REVIEW QUESTIONS

1. Explain how what Anderson calls *gracism* is the opposite of racism.
2. Paraphrase Anderson's point that *gracism* is significantly different from favoritism.
3. What feelings did the author of the e-mail have to overcome in order to invite the Spanish-speaking family to enter the line in front of her?

PROBES

1. The author of this reading is African American. How do you believe his ethnic identity affects his main point?
2. This author argues that *gracism* is "the right thing to do" for religious, specifically Christian, reasons. What *communication-based,* nonreligious, and non-Christian rationale can you offer for practicing *gracism*?

"Which Is My Good Leg?": Cultural Communication of Persons with Disabilities

Dawn O. Braithwaite and Charles A. Braithwaite

This article reminds us that intercultural communication doesn't just happen with people who are different from us in ethnicity, gender, or age. The senior author is an authority on communication with disabled persons. She and her spouse use specific examples and important concepts to clarify the challenges of this kind of intercultural communicating and to suggest some important "Dos" and "Don'ts."

The essay begins with some reports from the experiences of persons with disabilities that underscore the kinds of communication difficulties they experience. This group gained significant national attention in 1990 with the passage of the Americans with Disabilities Act (ADA). Although as many as one in five people in the United States has some type of disability, this group was nearly invisible for many years. "In the past," the Braithwaites point out, "most people with disabilities were sheltered and many were institutionalized, but today they are very much a part of the American mainstream." This is another reason why it's important to learn about communicating with persons with disabilities.

The Braithwaites explain why "the distinctive verbal and nonverbal communication used by persons with disabilities creates a sense of cultural identity that constitutes a unique social reality." They also show how this cultural view helps clarify several challenges faced by communicators who are disabled.

Most disabled people see themselves as part of a minority group or a co-culture, the Braithwaites explain. Like other minorities, they have to engage in various "balancing acts" to cope with the pressures they confront. But there are also significant differences among members of this co-culture. All disabled people are not "the same," any more than all Asians or all women are the same.

The process of redefining oneself as part of a disabled culture occurs in steps or stages. As Christopher Reeve, an actor who played Superman and was disabled by an accident, explained, "You move from obsessing about 'Why me?' and 'It's not fair' and move into 'Well, what is the potential?'"

The article ends with a list of five "Don'ts" and five "Dos" to guide your communicating with people with disabilities. I hope you can recognize from this article that interpersonal relationships are just as possible with these people as they are with any others.

MAIN IDEAS

- A significant and growing percentage of the population is disabled and fewer are now institutionalized.
- Disabled persons constitute a culture, and communication between them and non-disabled people is a kind of intercultural communication.
- *Disability* is different from *handicap*.
- Most nondisabled people do not know how to communicate with those who are disabled.
- Most disabled people see themselves as members of a minority culture.
- Persons with disabilities grow into this culture through three steps: *stigma isolation, stigma recognition,* and stigma *incorporation.*
- Many disabled people view themselves as public educators on disability issues.
- Intercultural principles and skills can be helpfully applied to communication between nondisabled and disabled people.

Jonathan is an articulate, intelligent, 35-year-old professional man, who has used a wheelchair since he became paraplegic when he was 20 years old. He recalls taking a nondisabled woman out to dinner at a nice restaurant. When the waitress came to take their order, she looked only at his date and asked, in a condescending tone, "and what would *he* like to eat for dinner?" At the end of the meal, the waitress presented Jonathan's date with the check and thanked her for her patronage.[1]

Kim describes her recent experience at the airport: "A lot of people always come up and ask can they push my wheelchair. And, I can do it myself. They were invading my space, concentration, doing what I wanted to do, which I enjoy doing; doing what I was doing *on my own....* And each time I said, 'No, I'm doing fine!' People looked at me like I was strange, you know, crazy or something. One person started pushing my chair anyway. I said [in an angry tone], 'Don't touch the wheelchair.' And then she just looked at me like I'd slapped her in the face."

Jeff, a nondisabled student, was working on a group project for class that included Helen, who uses a wheelchair. He related an incident that really

"Which Is My Good Leg" by Dawn O. Braithwaite and Charles A. Braithwaite from *Intercultural Communication: A Reader*, 10th edition. Edited by Larry A. Samovar and Richard E. Porter. Copyright © 2003, Thomson Learning, Belmont, CA.

embarrassed him. "I wasn't thinking and I said to the group, 'Let's run over to the student union and get some coffee.' I was mortified when I looked over at Helen and remembered that she can't walk. I felt like a real jerk." Helen later described the incident with Jeff, recalling:

> At yesterday's meeting, Jeff said, "Let's run over to the union" and then he looked over at me and I thought he would die. It didn't bother me at all, in fact, I use that phrase myself. I felt bad that Jeff was so embarrassed, but I didn't know what to say. Later in the group meeting I made it a point to say, "I've got to be running along now." I hope that Jeff noticed and felt OK about what he said.

Erik Weihenmayer, the blind climber who recently scaled Mt. Everest, demonstrated another example of the regular use of nondisabled language by the disabled. During an interview with Matt Lauer on NBC's *Today Show* (June 12, 2001), he remarked that he was glad to get home so that he "could *see* his family."

Although it may seem hard for some of us to believe, these scenarios represent common experiences for people with physical disabilities and are indicative of what often happens when people with disabilities and nondisabled others communicate.

The passage of the Americans with Disabilities Act (ADA), a "bill of rights" for persons with disabilities, highlighted the fact that they are now a large, vocal, and dynamic group within the United States (Braithwaite & Labrecque, 1994; Braithwaite & Thompson, 2000). Disabled people represent one group within American culture that is growing in numbers. One in five people in the United States has some type of disability, which means that people with disabilities constitute a large segment of the American population (Cunningham & Coombs, 1997; Pardeck, 1998).

There are two reasons for increases in the numbers of persons with disabilities. First, as the American population ages and has a longer life expectancy, more people will live long enough to develop age-related disabilities. Second, advances in medical technologies now allow persons with disabilities to survive life-threatening illnesses and injuries, whereas survival was not possible in earlier times. For example, when actor Christopher Reeve became quadriplegic after a horse-riding accident in May 1995, newer advances in medical technology allowed him to survive his injuries and to live with a severe disability.

In the past, most people with disabilities were sheltered and many were institutionalized, but today they are very much a part of the American mainstream. Each of us will have contact with people who have disabilities within our families, among our friends, or within the workplace. Some of us will develop disabilities ourselves. Says Marie, a college student who became paralyzed after diving into a swimming pool:

> I knew there were disabled people around, but I never thought this would happen to me. I never even *knew* a disabled person before *I* became one. If before this happened, I saw a person in a wheelchair, I would have been uncomfortable and not known what to say.

Marie's comment highlights the fact that many nondisabled people feel extremely uncomfortable interacting with disabled people. As people with disabilities continue to live, work, and study in American culture, there is a need for both nondisabled and disabled persons to know how to communicate with one another.

DISABILITY AND CULTURAL COMMUNICATION

The goal of this chapter is to focus on communication between nondisabled persons and persons with disabilities as *intercultural communication* (Carbaugh, 1990). This claim is made because, as will be demonstrated later, persons with disabilities use a distinctive speech code that implicates specific models of personhood, society, and strategic action ... that are qualitatively different from those models used by nondisabled persons. Because persons with disabilities are treated so differently in American society, distinctive meanings, rules, and speech habits develop that act as a powerful resource for creating and reinforcing perceptions of cultural differences between persons with disabilities and nondisabled persons. The distinctive verbal and nonverbal communication used by persons with disabilities creates a sense of cultural identity that constitutes a unique social reality....

CHALLENGES FOR COMMUNICATORS WHO ARE DISABLED

When we adopt a cultural view and attempt to understand the communicative challenges faced by people with disabilities, it is useful to distinguish between "disability" and "handicap." Even though people often use these two terms interchangeably in everyday conversation, their meanings are quite different. The two terms implicate different relationships between persons with disabilities and the larger society. The term *disability* describes those limitations that a person can overcome or compensate by some means. Crewe and Athelstan (1985) identified five "key life functions" that may be affected by disability: (1) mobility, (2) employment, (3) self-care, (4) social relationships, and (5) communication. Some individuals are often able to compensate for physical challenges associated with the first three key life functions through assisting devices (e.g., using a wheelchair or cane), through training (e.g., physical therapy or training on how to take care of one's personal needs), through assistance (e.g., hiring a personal care assistant), or through occupational therapy to find suitable employment.

A disability becomes a *handicap* when the physical or social environment interacts with it to impede a person in some aspect of his or her life (Crewe & Athelstan, 1985). For example, a disabled individual with paraplegia can function well in the physical environment using a wheelchair, ramps, and curb cuts, but he or she is handicapped when buildings and/or public transportation are not accessible to wheelchair users. When a society is willing and/or able to create adaptations, disabled persons have the ability to achieve personal control and lead increasingly independent lives, which is important to their self-esteem and health (Braithwaite & Harter, 2000; Cogswell, 1977; DeLoach & Greer, 1981). For people with disabilities, personal control and independence are vitally important and "maintenance of identity and self-worth are tied to the perceived ability to control the illness, minimize its intrusiveness, and be independent" (Lyons et al., 1995, p. 134). This does not mean that people with disabilities deny their physical condition, but rather that they find ways to deal with it and lead their lives.

In fact, it is important to realize that the practical and technological accommodations that are made to adapt the physical environment for people with disabilities are useful for nondisabled people as well. Most of us are unaware of just how handicapped we would be without these physical adaptations. For example, our offices are located on the upper floors of our respective office buildings. We know that stairs take up a significant amount of space in a building. Space used for the stairwell on each level takes the place of at least one office per floor. So, the most space-efficient way to get people to the second floor would be a climbing rope, which would necessitate only a relatively small opening on each floor; however, very few of us could climb a rope to reach our offices on the second story, so we would be handicapped without stairs or elevators. When a student is walking with a heavy load of library books, automatic door openers, ramps, curb cuts, elevators, and larger doorways become important environmental adaptations that everyone can use and appreciate. Physical limitations become handicaps for all of us when the physical environment cannot be adapted to preempt our shortcomings.

Challenges to Relationships of People with Disabilities

Although it is possible to identify and to cope with physical challenges associated with mobility, self-care, and employment, the two key life functions of social relationships and communication are often much more formidable. It is less difficult to detect and correct physical barriers than it is to deal with the insidious social barriers facing people with disabilities. Coleman and DePaulo (1991) would label these social barriers as "psychological disabling," which is even more common in Western culture where "much value is placed on physical bodies and physical attractiveness" (p. 64).

When people with disabilities begin relationships with nondisabled people, the challenges associated with forming any new relationship are greater. For nondisabled people, this may be caused by a lack of experience interacting with people who are disabled. This leads to high uncertainty about how to talk with a person who is disabled. The nondisabled person feels uncertain about what to say or how to act because he or she is afraid of saying or doing the wrong thing or of hurting the feelings of the person with the disability, much like Jeff did with his group member, Helen, in the example at the beginning of this [essay].

As a result, people may feel overly self-conscious and their actions may be constrained, self-controlled, and rigid because they feel uncomfortable and uncertain (Belgrave & Mills, 1981; Braithwaite, 1990; Dahnke, 1983; Higgins, 1992). The nondisabled person may try to communicate appropriately, however, "Wishing to act in a way acceptable to those with disabilities, they may unknowingly act offensively, patronizing disabled people with unwanted sympathy" (Higgins, 1992, p. 105).

Interestingly, researchers have found that the type of disability a person possesses does not change the way nondisabled persons react to them (Fichten et al., 1991). So, high levels of uncertainty can negatively affect interaction and relationship development between people. It becomes easier to avoid that person rather than deal with not knowing what to do or say. Although Uncertainty Reduction Theory can be overly simplistic, especially when applied to ongoing relationships, it can help us understand some of the initial discomfort nondisabled people may have when interacting with a stranger or early acquaintance who is disabled.

Even when a nondisabled person tries to "say the right thing," wanting to communicate acceptance to the person with the disability, his or her nonverbal behavior may communicate rejection and avoidance (Thompson, 1982). For example, people with disabilities have observed that many nondisabled persons may keep a greater physical distance, avoid eye contact, avoid mentioning the disability, or cut the conversation short (Braithwaite, 1990, 1991, 1996). In this case, a person's disability becomes a handicap in the social environment because it can block the development of a relationship with a nondisabled person, who finds the interaction too uncomfortable. In all, nondisabled people hold many stereotypes of people from the disabled culture. Coleman and DePaulo (1991) discuss some of these stereotypes concerning disabled people:

> For example they often perceive them as dependent, socially introverted, emotionally unstable, depressed, hypersensitive, and easily offended, especially with regard to their disability. In addition, disabled people are often presumed to differ from nondisabled people in moral character, social skills, and political orientation. (p. 69)

Our long experience talking with nondisabled people about interacting with persons with disabilities has shown us that many nondisabled people find the prospect of these interactions uncomfortable. They tell us they are afraid of saying or doing the wrong thing and embarrassing or hurting the person who is disabled. In addition, nondisabled persons often find themselves with conflicting advice concerning what is expected of them or how to act. On the one hand, they have been taught to "help the handicapped" and, on the other hand, they were told to treat all people equally. Americans usually conceptualize persons as "individuals" who "have rights" and "make their own choices" (Carbaugh, 1988). When nondisabled persons encounter a person with a disability, however, this model of personhood creates a serious dilemma. For example, should one help a person with a disability open a door or try to help them up if they fall? Nondisabled persons greatly fear saying the wrong thing, such as "See you later!" to a blind person or "Why don't you run by the store on your way home?" to a person using a wheelchair. In the end, it simply seems to be easier to avoid situations where one might have to interact with a disabled person rather than face feelings of discomfort and uncertainty.

It should not be surprising to learn that most people with disabilities are well aware of these feelings and fears many nondisabled persons have. In fact, in research interviews, people with disabilities reveal that they believe they "can just tell" who is uncomfortable around them or not. They are able to describe in great detail both the verbal and nonverbal signals of discomfort and avoidance nondisabled persons portray that we described previously (Braithwaite, 1990, 1996). People with disabilities report that when they meet nondisabled persons, they would hope to get the discomfort "out of the way," and they want the nondisabled person to treat them as a "person like anyone else," rather than focus solely on their disability (Braithwaite, 1991, 1996). Most often they develop ways of communicating that allow them to have their needs met and, if possible, help reduce the uncertainty and discomfort of the nondisabled person (Braithwaite & Eckstein, 2000). For example, two men who are wheelchair users described how they avoid situations where they need to ask strangers for help getting out of their van in a parking lot:

> Well, I have a mobile phone. . . . I will call into the store and let the store manager or whoever know, "Hey, we're in a white minivan and if you look out your window, you can see us! We're two guys in wheelchairs, can you come out and help us get out of the van?"

These men described how they plan ahead to avoid putting nondisabled strangers in potentially uncomfortable communication situations. . . .

Redefining the Self as Part of the Disabled Culture

Most disabled people see themselves as part of a minority group or a co-culture. For some of the interviewees, this definition crosses disability lines; that is, their definition of "disabled" includes all those who have disabilities. For others, the definition is not as broad; when they think of disability they are thinking about others with the same type of disability they have. For example, some of the people with mobility-related disabilities also talked about blind and deaf people when they discussed disability, whereas others talked only about other wheelchair users. However narrowly or broadly they defined it, however, many do see themselves as part of a minority culture. For example, one of the interviewees described that being disabled "is like *West Side Story.* Tony and Maria; white and Puerto Rican. They were afraid of each other; ignorant of each others' cultures. People are people." Another man explained his view:

> First of all, I belong to a subculture (of disability) because of the way I have to deal with things, being in the medical system, welfare. There is the

subculture.... I keep one foot in the nondisabled culture and one foot in my own culture. One of the reasons I do that is so that I don't go nuts.

This man's description of the "balancing act" between cultures demonstrates that membership in the disabled culture has several similarities to the experiences of other American cultural groups. Many of the interviewees have likened their own experiences to those of other cultural groups, particularly to the experiences of American people of color. Interviewees described the loss of status and power that comes from being disabled, and they expressed that they believe many people were uncomfortable with them simply because they are different.

When taking a cultural view, it is important to recognize that not everyone comes to the culture the same way. Some people are born with disabilities and others acquire them later. For those people who are not born with a disability, membership in the culture is a process that emerges over time. For some, the process is an incremental one, as in the case of a person with a degenerative disease like multiple sclerosis that develops over many years. For a person who has a sudden-onset disability, such as breaking one's neck in an accident and "waking up as quadriplegic," moving from the majority (a "normal" person) to the minority (a person who is disabled) may happen in a matter of seconds. This sudden transition into the disabled culture presents many significant challenges of redefinition and readjustment in all facets of an individual's life (Braithwaite, 1990, 1996; Goffman, 1963).

If disability is a culture, when does one become part of that culture? Even though a person is physically disabled, how they redefine themselves, from "normal" or nondisabled to disabled, is a process that develops over time. It is important to understand that becoming physically disabled does not mean that one immediately has an awareness of being part of the disabled culture (Braithwaite, 1990, 1996). In fact, for most people, adjusting to disability happens in a series of stages or phases (Braithwaite, 1990; DeLoach & Greer, 1981; Padden & Humphries, 1988). DeLoach and Greer (1981) described three phases of an individual's adjustment to disability: stigma isolation, stigma recognition, and stigma incorporation. Their model helps us understand what is occurring in the process of adjustment to disability as acculturation. During this process, persons with disabilities progress from the onset of their disability to membership in the disabled culture.

The first phase, *stigma isolation*, occurs upon becoming disabled. At this time, individuals focus on rehabilitation and all of the physical changes and challenges they are experiencing. It is likely that they have not yet noticed the changes in their social relationships and communication with nondisabled others.

The second phase, *stigma recognition*, occurs when people who are disabled realize that their life and relationships have changed dramatically and they try to find ways to minimize the effects of their disability. They may try to return to normal routines and old relationships. This can be a frustrating phase because things have often changed more than the disabled people first realize. Especially when trying to reestablish old relationships, newly disabled people may find that their old friends are no longer comfortable with them or that, without shared activities, the friendships may lapse. At this point, people who are disabled start to become aware that they are now interacting as a member of a different culture than they were before, and they begin to assimilate the new culture into their identity and behavior (Braithwaite, 1990, 1996).

This begins the third phase, what DeLoach and Greer (1981) call *stigma incorporation*. At this point, people with a disability begin to integrate being disabled into their identity, their definition of self. They can see both the positive and negative aspects of being disabled and begin to develop ways to overcome and cope with the negative aspects of disability (DeLoach & Greer, 1981). In this stage of adjustment, people with disabilities develop ways of behaving and communicating so they are able to successfully function in the nondisabled culture (Braithwaite, 1990, 1996). This is what Morse and Johnson (1991) call "regaining wellness," when newly disabled individuals begin to take back control of their own lives and relationships, to live as independently as possible, and to adapt to new ways of doing things in their lives. At this point, they are able to develop ways of communicating with nondisabled others that help them live successfully as part of the disabled and nondisabled culture simultaneously (Braithwaite, 1990, 1991, 1996; Braithwaite & Labrecque, 1994; Emry & Wiseman, 1987) or what disability researcher Susan Fox has labeled as interability, intergroup communication (see Fox et al., 2000).

In this phase, then, persons with disabilities incorporate the role of disability into their identity and into their life. One man said: "You're the same person you were. You just don't do the same things you did before." Another put it this way: "If anyone refers to me as an amputee, that is guaranteed to get me madder than hell! I don't deny the leg amputation, but I am ME. I am a whole person. ONE." During this phase, people can come to terms with both the negative and positive changes in their lives. One woman expressed:

> I find myself telling people that this has been the worst thing that has happened to me. It has also been one of the best things. It forced me to examine what I felt about myself … my confidence is grounded in me, not in other people. As a woman, I am not as dependent on clothes, measurements, but what's inside me.

Christopher Reeve demonstrated the concept of stigma incorporation in an interview with Barbara Walters, four months after his devastating accident:

> You also gradually discover, as I'm discovering, that your body is not you. The mind and the spirit must take over. And that's the challenge as you move from obsessing about "Why me?" and "It's not fair" and move into "Well, what is the potential?" And, now, four months down the line I see opportunities and potential I wasn't capable of seeing back in Virginia in June … genuine joy and being alive means more. Every moment is more intense than it ever was.

We can see in this example that stigma incorporation, becoming part of the disabled culture, is a process that develops over time.

REDEFINING DISABILITY WITHIN NONDISABLED CULTURE

Finally, as people with disabilities redefine themselves as members of a culture, and as they redefine what it means to have a disabling condition, they are also concerned with trying to change the view of disability within the larger culture (Braithwaite, 1990, 1996).... Most people with disabilities view themselves as public educators on disability issues. People told stories about taking the time to educate children and adults on what it means to be disabled. They are actively working to change the view of themselves as helpless, as victims, or ill and the ensuing treatment such a view brings. One wheelchair user said:

> People do not consider you, they consider the chair first. I was in a store with my purchases on my lap and money on my lap. The clerk looked at my companion and not at me and said, "Cash or charge?"

This incident with the clerk is a story heard from *every* person interviewed in some form or another, just as it happened to Jonathan and his date at the beginning of this [reading]. One woman, who had multiple sclerosis and uses a wheelchair, told of shopping for lingerie with her husband accompanying her. When they were in front of the lingerie counter, the clerk repeatedly talked only to her husband saying, "And what size does she want?" The woman told her the size and the clerk looked at the husband and said, "And what color does she want?"

Persons with disabilities recognize that nondisabled persons often see them as disabled first and as a person second (if at all). The most common theme expressed by people with disabilities in all of the interviews is that they want to be *treated as a person first*. One man explained what he thought was important to remember: "A lot of people think that handicapped people are 'less than' and I find that it's not true at all.... Abling people, giving them their power back, empowering them." The interviewees rejected those things that would not lead to being seen as persons. A man with muscular dystrophy talked about the popular Labor Day telethon:

> I do not believe in those goddamned telethons ... they're horrible, absolutely horrible. They get into the self-pity, you know, and disabled folk do not need that. Hit people in terms of their attitudes, then try to deal with and process their feelings. And the telethons just go for the heart and leave it there.

One man suggested what he thought was a more useful approach:

> What I am concerned with is anything that can do away with the "us" versus "them" distinction. Well, you and I are anatomically different, but we're two human beings! And, at the point we can sit down and communicate eyeball to eyeball, the quicker you do that, the better!

Individually and collectively, people with disabilities do identify themselves as part of a culture. They are involved in a process of redefinition of themselves, and of disability. They desire to help nondisabled people internalize a redefinition of people of the disabled culture as "persons first."

CONCLUSION

The research we have discussed highlights the usefulness of viewing disability from a cultural perspective. People with disabilities do recognize themselves as part of a culture, and viewing communication and relationships from this perspective sheds new light on the communication challenges that exist. Some time ago, Emry and Wiseman (1987) first argued for the usefulness of intercultural training about disability issues. They call for unfreezing old attitudes about disability and refreezing new ones. Clearly, the interviews indicate that people who have disabilities would seem to agree....

We hope that you will be able to understand and apply intercultural communication concepts and skills and be able to adapt that knowledge to communicating with persons in the disabled culture. Finally, we believe that people with disabilities themselves will better understand their own experience if they study intercultural communication and come to understand the cultural aspects of disability.

For nondisabled persons who communicate with persons who are disabled, we suggest that taking an intercultural perspective leads to the following proscriptions and prescriptions:

Do Not:

- *Avoid* communication with people who are disabled simply because you are uncomfortable or unsure.
- *Assume* people with disabilities cannot speak for themselves or do things for themselves.
- *Force* your help on people with disabilities.
- *Use terms* like "handicapped," "physically challenged," "crippled," "victim," and so on unless requested to do so by people with disabilities.
- *Assume* that a disability defines who a person is.

Do:

- *Remember* that people with disabilities have experienced others' discomfort before and likely understand how you might be feeling.
- *Assume* people with a disability can do something unless they communicate otherwise.
- *Let people with disabilities tell you* if they want something, what they want, and when they want it. If a person with a disability refuses your help, don't go ahead and help anyway.
- *Use terms* like "people with disabilities" rather than "disabled people." The goal is to stress the *person first*, before the disability.

- *Treat* people with disabilities as *persons first*, recognizing that you are not dealing with a disabled person but with *a person* who *has* a disability. This means actively seeking the humanity of the person you are speaking with and focusing on individual characteristics instead of superficial physical appearance. Without diminishing the significance of a person's physical disability, make a real effort to focus on the many other aspects of that person as you communicate.

REVIEW QUESTIONS

1. Describe the two reasons the Braithwaites give for the increase in the number of persons with disabilities.
2. Explain what justifies the decision to treat persons with disabilities as a *cultural* group.
3. Explain the difference between a "disability" and a "handicap."
4. What is the primary relationship challenge that is faced by people with disabilities?
5. Explain the "balancing act" that many disabled people need to maintain.
6. Describe *stigma isolation, stigma recognition,* and *stigma incorporation.*

PROBES

1. How comfortable are you when communicating with a person with an obvious disability? If you are quite comfortable, how might you help others feel that way? If you are uncomfortable, what might you do to become less so?
2. If you are a nondisabled person, you might want to "say the right thing" but still end up communicating awkwardly with a person with a disability. What might you do to address this problem?
3. Disabled people strongly desire to be treated as a person first, not primarily as a disabled person. How can you support this desire in your own communicating with people with disabilities?

NOTE

1. The quotes and anecdotes in this chapter come from in-depth interviews with people who have visible physical disabilities. The names of the participants in these interviews have been changed to protect their privacy.

REFERENCES

Belgrave, F. Z., & Mills, J. (1981). Effect upon desire for social interaction with a physically disabled person of mentioning the disability in different contexts. *Journal of Applied Social Psychology, 11,* 44–57.

Braithwaite, D. O. (1990). From majority to minority: An analysis of cultural change from nondisabled to disabled. *International Journal of Intercultural Relations, 14,* 465–483.

Braithwaite, D. O. (1991). "Just how much did that wheelchair cost?": Management of privacy boundaries by persons with disabilities. *Western Journal of Speech Communication, 55,* 254–274.

Braithwaite, D. O. (1996). "Persons first": Expanding communicative choices by persons with disabilities. In E. B. Ray (Ed.), *Communication and disenfranchisement: Social health issues and implications* (pp. 449–464). Mahwah, NJ: Lawrence Erlbaum.

Braithwaite, D. O., & Eckstein, N. (2000, November). Reconceptualizing supportive interactions: How persons with disabilities communicatively manage assistance. Presented to the National Communication Association, Seattle, WA.

Braithwaite, D. O., & Labrecque, D. (1994). Responding to the Americans with Disabilities Act: Contributions of interpersonal communication research and training. *Journal of Applied Communication, 22,* 287–294.

Braithwaite, D. O., & Harter, L. (2000). Communication and the management of dialectical tensions in the personal relationships of people with disabilities. In D. O. Braithwaite & T. L. Thompson (Eds.), *Handbook of communication and people with disabilities. Research and application* (pp. 17–36). Mahwah, NJ: Lawrence Erlbaum.

Braithwaite, D. O., & Thompson, T. L. (Eds). (2000). *Handbook of communication and people with disabilities: Research and application.* Mahwah, NJ: Lawrence Erlbaum.

Carbaugh, D. (1988). *Talking American.* Norwood, NJ: Ablex.

Carbaugh, D. (Ed.). (1990). *Cultural communication and intercultural contact.* Hillsdale, NJ: Lawrence Erlbaum.

Cogswell, Betty E. (1977). Self-socialization: Readjustments of paraplegics in the community. In R. P. Marinelli & A. E. Dell Orto (Eds.), *The psychological impact of physical disability* (pp. 151–159). New York: Springer.

Coleman, L. M., & DePaulo, B. M. (1991). Uncovering the human spirit: Moving beyond disability and "missed" communications. In N. Coupland, H. Giles, & J. M. Wiemann (Eds.), *Miscommunication and problematic talk* (pp. 61–84). Newbury Park, CA: Sage.

Covert, A. L., & Smith, J. W. (2000). What is reasonable: workplace communication and people who are disabled. In D. O. Braithwaite & T. L. Thompson (Eds.), *Handbook of communication and people with disabilities: Research and application* (pp. 141–158). Mahwah, NJ: Lawrence Erlbaum.

Crewe, N., & Athelstan, G. (1985). *Social and psychological aspects of physical disability.* Minneapolis: University of Minnesota, Department of Independent Study and University Resources.

Cunningham, C., & Coombs, N. (1997). *Information access and adaptive technology.* Phoenix: Oryx Press.

Dahnke, G. L. (1983). Communication and handicapped and nonhandicapped persons: Toward a deductive theory. In M. Burgoon (Ed.), *Communication yearbook 6* (pp. 92–135). Beverly Hills, CA: Sage.

DeLoach, C., & Greer, B. G. (1981). *Adjustment to severe physical disability. A metamorphosis.* New York: McGraw-Hill.

Emry, R., & Wiseman, R. L. (1987). An intercultural understanding of nondisabled and disabled persons' communication. *International Journal of Intercultural Relations, 11,* 7–27.

Fichten, C. S., Robillard, K., Tagalakis, V., & Amsel, R. (1991). Casual interaction between college students with various disabilities and their nondisabled peers: The internal dialogue. *Rehabilitation Psychology, 36,* 3–20.

Fox, S. A., Giles, H., Orbe, M., & Bourhis, R. (2000). Interability communication: Theoretical perspectives. In D. O. Braithwaite & T. L. Thompson (Eds). *Handbook of communication and people with disabilities: Research and application* (pp. 193–222). Mahwah, NJ: Lawrence Erlbaum.

Goffman, E. (1963). *Stigma: Notes on the management of spoiled identity.* New York: Simon & Schuster.

Herold, K. P. (2000). Communication strategies in employment interviews for applicants with disabilities. In D. O. Braithwaite & T. L. Thompson (Eds). *Handbook of communication and people with disabilities: Research and application* (pp. 159–175). Mahwah, NJ: Lawrence Erlbaum.

Higgins, P. C. (1992). *Making disability: Exploring the social transformation of human variation.* Springfield, IL: Charles C Thomas.

Lyons, R. F., Sullivan, M. J. L., Ritvo, P. G, & Coyne, J. C. (1995). *Relationships in chronic illness and disability.* Thousand Oaks, CA: Sage.

Morse, J. M., & Johnson, J. L. (1991). *The illness experience: Dimensions of suffering.* Newbury Park, CA: Sage.

Padden, C., & Humphries, T. (1988). *Deaf in America: Voices from a culture.* Cambridge, MA: Harvard University Press.

Pardeck, J. T. (1998). *Social work after the Americans with Disabilities Act: New challenges and opportunities for social service professionals.* Westport, CT: Auburn House.

Thompson, T. L. (1982). Disclosure as a disability-management strategy: A review and conclusions. *Communication Quarterly, 30,* 196–202.

Worley, D. W. (2000). Communication and students with disabilities on college campuses. In D. O. Braithwaite & T. L. Thompson (Eds). *Handbook of communication and people with disabilities: Research and application* (pp. 125–139). Mahwah, NJ: Lawrence Erlbaum.

CHAPTER 12

Promoting Dialogue

Dialogue's Basic Tension
Karen E. Zediker and John Stewart

Especially over the past few decades, many elected officials, teachers, trainers, managers, and community activists have been calling for more "dialogue." Of course, the term means different things to different people. Elected officials at national and local levels want better two-way communication with voters. Teachers on campuses across the country want less lecturing and more active involvement and open communication in their classrooms. Managers at Ford, Boeing, Intel, and hundreds of smaller companies want to replace the command-and-control hierarchy with collaborative work teams, shared power, and "management by wandering around and talking." Community activists in Boston; Fargo; Albuquerque; Cupertino; London; Jerusalem; Aalborg, Denmark; Canberra, Australia; Cape Town, South Africa; and dozens of other cities encourage people with diverse backgrounds and radically different beliefs to talk respectfully and candidly with each other, rather than trying to shout each other down. They also try to replace distorted media campaigns, polarizing rhetoric, and violence with facilitated and mediated conversations among political enemies. But although specific definitions vary, in every case, proponents of dialogue have in mind the kind of communication that's being championed throughout this book.

For example, how might people bridge cultural differences (Chapter 11)? With dialogue. What often works in conflict (Chapter 10)? Dialogue. What's often the best communication with intimate partners (Chapter 8)? Dialogue. What's one useful and helpful way to define interpersonal communication (Chapter 2)? As dialogue. So this chapter draws from and contributes to a significant movement that's underway in many countries around the world, and it also summarizes a great deal of the rest of this book.

In this first essay my colleague and friend Karen Zediker and I talk about what we believe is the main feature or characteristic of dialogue—a tension between letting another person "happen to you" while you hold your own ground in the conversation.

The first point we make is that for us, the term *dialogue* labels a particular kind or quality of communication. Dialogue is what happens between people who are connecting with each other *as persons,* as unique, reflective, choosing, valuing, thinking-and-feeling beings.

Next, the essay explains what a "tension" is. Our main point here is that there is a "both/and" quality to the experience of communicating dialogically. When you're in a tension, you feel pulled in two directions at once, *and* each pull is affected by what it's pulling against. Dialogue, we argue, is this kind of tensional event.

Then we label what we believe is dialogue's basic tension, and we describe each "moment," "pole," or "end" of this tension. "Letting the other happen to me" means being open to and actually affected by the ways that the other person is *different from* you. It doesn't take a rocket scientist to understand this idea, but it's a little strange in the Western world, because westerners are usually interested mainly in the other pole of this tension. It can take some courage and patience to let yourself be subject to someone else's influence.

"Holding your own ground" is the other pole, and it means what it sounds like. You do this when you assert your position or express your ideas. The most important point we make after we sketch these two poles is that when they are lived tensionally, *each transforms the other*. You don't just let somebody happen to you; you do that as a person who's holding your own ground. And you don't just assert your position; you do that as a person who's letting the other happen to you. In the final part of this reading, we give some concrete examples of how this tension works in order to clarify what's at stake here.

We hope that this brief description will clarify what you'll need to do when you want to help dialogue happen. You've undoubtedly figured out by now that there is no set recipe for dialogue. But if you can live with this tension, and if your conversation partner can, too, the chances are good that this quality of communication will happen between you.

MAIN IDEAS

- "Dialogue" is defined here as virtually synonymous with "interpersonal communication" as it is defined in Chapter 2: As a kind or quality of communication that happens when the people involved are present to each other as persons.
- A primary feature of dialogue is tensionality, a both/and, push-pull quality.
- The main tension is a combination of *letting the other happen to me while holding my own ground.*
- Letting the other happen to me means experiencing another person as "Other," not me, fundamentally capable of surprising me.
- Holding my own ground means taking a stand and expressing it (see the second reading in Chapter 6).
- The important point is that the two poles of this tension need to be accomplished *simultaneously,* and when they are, each pole transforms the other.
- In the Martin Buber example, the text shows that each person allowed the other to happen to him, and that each also held his own ground—which turned out to be common ground.
- In the classroom example, Jim held his own ground in favor of sexual abstinence, the class understood and respected him, and he understood and respected their positions, all of which positively affected the general class understanding and opinion on this issue.

INTRODUCTION

It's exciting and confirming for us to learn about all the different people who are writing about dialogue today and trying to help dialogue happen in organizations, communities, and families. Our approach to dialogue is similar to some of theirs, and different from others'. Historically, we've been most influenced by Martin Buber's (e.g. 1970) writings, so we use the term "dialogue" to refer to a particular kind or quality of communication that happens when the people involved are present to each other as persons—as unique, reflective, choosing, valuing, thinking-and-feeling beings. So when one of us can perceive and listen to you as a person while being available as a person to you, and when you can do the same thing, then the communication between us can be called "dialogic" or "dialogue." When the opposite happens—when I am only focused on getting my own ideas out and you are not listening but "reloading"—only working out your response to my ideas—then the communication between us is "monologic" or "monologue."

One significant feature of dialogue as we understand it is tensionality. This means that dialogue is not a steady state, something that is stable and predictable. When people are in dialogue, they experience a dynamic, push-pull, both-and quality in their communication. There's more to dialogue than just this tensional quality, but we believe that it's important enough that we want to take the following pages to clarify what we mean when we say that dialogue is tensional and to explain and illustrate dialogue's most basic tension.

A dictionary or thesaurus provides two different images of tension—*anxiety* (associated with stress and strain) and *tautness* (associated with force, tightness and constriction). Most of us have experienced tension in both these senses. Some characterize tension as a struggle, being pulled from a variety of directions at once, somehow knowing that if one perspective has more pull, another will lose out. Others associate tension with a headache that grips both the base of your neck and the top of your eyebrows at the same time. Or the word "tension" makes some other people think of the rod that holds curtains in place in the shower by pushing in opposite directions against two walls. None of these images is exactly what we have in mind when we say that dialogue is tensional, but they do share some common features. When something is held in tension there are at least two points of contact, and there seems to be an inherent contradiction or push-pull set of forces.

Communication teachers Barbara Montgomery and Leslie Baxter (1996) highlight one important feature of tensionality when they talk about how communicators manage "the both/andness" of privacy and disclosure across the time line of a relationship. Montgomery and Baxter explain that usually privacy isn't the most important thing at one point and then open disclosure most important at another, but that at almost every moment in a relationship the people involved are experiencing some tension between *both* privacy *and* disclosure. Montgomery and Baxter say that this primary feature of dialogue "implicate[s] a kind of in-the-moment interactive multivocality, in which multiple points of view retain their integrity as they play off each other" (p. 160). Like the tension headache that hurts both at the base of your skull and your forehead at the same time, or the tension rod that pushes out against opposite walls and is held into place by the structure of the door or window frame, dialogic tensions are characterized by both/andness.

"Dialogue's Basic Tension" excerpted from "Dialogue as Tensional, Ethical Practice" by Karen E. Zediker and John Stewart.

THE PRIMARY TENSION

Our own communication experiences have taught us that moments of dialogue emerge most often when the people involved maintain one primary tension—the one between *letting the other happen to me while holding my own ground.* We are aware of other tensions as well, including one between univocality and multivocality and another tension between theory and practice. But in our opinion, other dialogic tensions are dependent on this primary tension.

If you were to diagram this tension, it might look something like this:

Letting the other happen to me ←————————→ Holding my own ground

In a few paragraphs, we'll highlight something misleading about this diagram. But first, let's clarify what this tension is by looking at its two ends.

Letting the Other Happen to Me

One moment in this dynamic—letting the other happen to me—consists of the concrete lived experience of what Buber and some other writers (e.g., Levinas, 1996) call experiencing the otherness of the Other. This means that you let someone happen to you when you allow who they are—especially their differences from you—to touch, connect with, and influence you. In his *Autobiographical Fragments,* Buber (1973)[1] reported that he recognized the basic quality of this moment when, as an 11-year-old, he cared for a "dapple-gray horse." When he was over 80 years old, he wrote,

> If I am to explain it now, beginning from the still very fresh memory of my hand, I must say that what I experienced in touch with the animal was the Other, the immense otherness of the Other, which, however, did not remain strange like the otherness of the ox and the ram, but rather let me draw near and touch it. When I stroked the mighty mane, sometimes marvelously smooth-combed, at other times just as astonishingly wild, and felt the life beneath my hand, it was as though the element of vitality itself bordered on my skin, something that was not I, was certainly not akin to me, palpably the other, not just another, really the Other itself; and yet it let me approach, confided itself to me, placed itself elementally in the relation of *Thou* and *Thou* with me. (p. 27)

In this fragment of his life, Buber provides a vivid example of letting the other happen to him. He realizes at a fundamental level that the horse is not an extension of himself, but something wholly other. Importantly, this lesson is one that Buber would have us learn about human beings as well. When we can experience other persons as unique individuals with opinions, beliefs, and values that are not simply extensions of our own, then we have the opportunity for genuine dialogue.

Another German writer named Hans-Georg Gadamer (1989) clarifies an important aspect of this first moment of this tension when he distinguishes between two German words for "experience," *Erlebnis* and *Erfahrung.* He explains that the first term labels experience that one "has" of something or someone. A person moves through life seeing, hearing, touching, tasting, and smelling things in order to grasp their meanings. So you might experience, in this *Erlebnis* sense, an encounter with a homeless person in which you could report where you saw her, what she said to you as you passed by, and how she smelled. *Erfahrung*, on the other hand, is the kind of experience that *happens to* one and that is the kind of experience that is consistent with Buber's notion of experiencing the otherness of the other. Gadamer describes *Erfahrung* as "experience as an event over which no one has control and which is not even determined by the particular weight of this or that observation, but in which everything is co-ordinated in a way that is ultimately incomprehensible" (p. 352). If you were to experience the homeless person in this second way, you'd experience her as a person rather than through a set of stereotypes or expectations. You might recall your eyes meeting and feeling for just that moment the sense of connection that you and she have as human beings despite the very real differences in your senses of security and community. "Experienced" people in this second sense are those who have become aware of what they have lived through, which means in part what has *happened to* them. And Gadamer notes that one form of experience as *Erfahrung* is experience of the other, "the Thou" (1989, p. 358).

Holding My Own Ground

The other moment in the primary tension of dialogue—holding my own ground—is easier for most people raised in Western traditions to understand, because of its connections with "rugged individuality." Understood as the label on one end of a continuum, holding my own ground is something that is done by an individual subject or intentional actor. You hold your own ground when you assert yourself or say exactly what's on your mind. One extreme version of this moment is present in communication teacher Barbara O'Keefe's (1997) description of the style of communication that is employed by the least developmentally sophisticated communicators she and her colleagues have studied. These people communicate in a way that O'Keefe calls "expressive." An infant communicates this way almost exclusively, but so do some adults. This way of communicating consists of

> simply thinking about the situation in relation to the self, evaluating thoughts in terms of whether they are disagreeable, repressing or misrepresenting disagreeable thoughts if uttering them might have negative consequences, but otherwise saying what comes to mind. (p. 104)

So, for example, if the baby feels bad, it cries, and if it feels good, it gurgles or smiles. What you see is what you get.

Holding my own ground presumes considerably more reflection, flexibility, and willingness to change than O'Keefe's expressive design logic, but, taken by itself, it strongly resembles what literature written in the 1970s and 1980s called "assertiveness." Assertiveness is behavior that "promotes equality in human relationships, enabling us to act in our own best interests, to stand up for ourselves without undue anxiety, to express honest feelings comfortably, to exercise personal rights without denying the rights of others" (Alberti and Emmons, 1990, p. 7). As the definition indicates, this literature encourages the assertive person to respect the "rights of others." But it emphasizes the two-step process of mental preparation and the development of behavioral skills that results in one being able to articulate and stand up for what one wants or believes.

By itself, standing my own ground can be viewed as being assertive or expressive, and letting the other happen to me can be understood as an experience that I receive or am subject to. This oppositional way of describing the tensional poles is useful, but it can also give the impression that both ends of the continuum are all about ME: what happens to me and what I make happen. Importantly, there is more to this primary tension of dialogue than the either/or of you happening to me or me happening to you.

So here's where we need to highlight what's misleading about the diagram we've provided: It makes the tension look like a connection between simple polarities, when it's not. The most important thing about poles in dialogue is that they are *in tension,* and this means that *both ends of the continuum are transformed by their interrelation.* So the other happens to me *while* and *as* I hold my own ground, and as a result, she happens to me in relation to my own position. In addition, I hold my own ground *in her presence* as she is happening to me. As a result, my own understanding of my position is fundamentally transformed by my experience of the other person. And vice versa; the other person's experiencing of me in relation to her is likely to transform her perception of her own identity and position. The constraints of language force us to talk about one end of this tension at a time, but our experience is that they are lived *together* or simultaneously.

This is an important point, so let us say it another way. When I live in this tension, my experience of the other person "happening to me" is strongly influenced by the position that I'm articulating (the ground that I'm holding), and the position that I'm expressing comes out as one that's strongly influenced by how the other is happening to me. In living communication, the two seemingly opposite moves (letting the other happen to me and holding my own ground) are *intimately interrelated.* And when lived in direct relation to one another, the two transform both the positions of the participants and their understanding of self and other.

Illustrations of the Tension

Here are two illustrations of how this works, one from Martin Buber's life and another from ours. Buber's autobiographical fragment called "Samuel and Agag" is a story of his lengthy conversation with "an observant Jew who followed the religious tradition in all the details of his life-pattern" (1973, p. 52). The two of them fell into a discussion of the section of the biblical book of Samuel in which Samuel delivered to King Saul the message that his dynastic rule would be taken from him by God because he had spared the life of Agag, the conquered prince of the Amalekites. Samuel's message to Saul was that obedience to God was more important than mercy. Buber told his conversation partner how, as a boy, he had been horrified to read how the heathen king Agag went up to Samuel with the words on his lips, "Surely the bitterness of death is past," and was butchered, "hewn to pieces" by Samuel. Buber writes that his "heart compelled me to read [this passage] over again or at least to think about the fact that this stood written in the Bible." He concluded, as he put it to his conversation partner, "I have never been able to believe that this is a message of God. I do not believe it." From one thoughtful Jew to another, it was very risky to assert that one did not believe something written in the Bible. Buber described what followed:

> With wrinkled forehead and contracted brows, the man sat opposite me and his glance flamed into my eyes. He remained silent, began to speak, became silent again. "So?" he broke forth at last. "So? You do not believe it?" "No," I answered, "I do not believe it." "So? so?" he repeated almost threateningly. "You do not believe it?" And I once again: "No." "What ... what ... ,"—he thrust the words before him one after the other—"what do you believe then?" "I believe," I replied without reflecting, "that Samuel has misunderstood God." And he, again slowly, but more softly than before: "So? You believe that?" And I: "Yes."
>
> Then we were both silent. But now something happened the like of which I have rarely seen before or since in this my long life. The angry countenance opposite me became transformed, as if a hand had passed over it soothing it. It lightened, cleared, was now turned toward me bright and clear. "Well," said the man with a positively gentle tender clarity. "I think so too." And again we became silent, for a good while. (pp. 52–53)

Buber and the man were both believers. The fact that Buber happened to the man is most apparent in the man's final reply: "I think so, too." But the fact that the man happened to Buber is also apparent in two things. The first is Buber's choice to include this fragment among the 20 key events of his 87-year life. The second is that in this conversation, Buber tested for the first time his previously unspoken decision, as he put it, to respond to the demand to choose between the Bible and God by choosing God (p. 53). Each also held his own ground, Buber in his disbelief and the man in his challenge. In addition, the dialogue transformed both moments for each man. Buber's experience of the man (and the man's experience of Buber) was transformed from that of a conversation partner to that of a co-conspirator in a potentially damning but personally compelling heresy. Buber's experience of his own position (and the man's experience of his) was transformed from one of lonely insistence to partnered confirmation.

There are also examples of this basic tension in our classrooms. As much as is possible, we work to foster dialogue in our classes by encouraging students to simultaneously let the other happen to them and to stand their own ground, and we attempt to do the same in relation to them. Some years ago, the primary challenge seemed to be the first moment in this tension. Students often found it difficult to listen to diverse others (let the others happen to them). Today the pole of standing one's own ground seems to be more challenging. Many students come to class with the conviction that political correctness means they have to be open to all views. Rather than engaging on issues with others who express positions they find incoherent or morally lacking, they smile, nod, and offer feedback focused on something safe like vocal delivery. When asked what they find compelling in an argument or to articulate substantive points of difference, they are often unable to do so. Superficial agreement often substitutes for engaged dialogue.

As a result, at the beginning of several of our communication courses, we attempt to enhance the potential for dialogue in two ways. Although we distribute a syllabus on the first day, almost all of the class time that day is spent exploring, not the course description, but the people in the room, beginning with us. Karen starts with a round of student responses to such questions as "What do you hope to get out of this class?" or perhaps "What do you most hope we do during this course, and what do you most hope we don't do?" Then she asks groups of two to three to form questions they would like answered about her. Often for a full class period she responds to questions about her academic background, experience teaching this course, spare-time activities, approach to teaching, test design, family history, expectations, and the degree to which she is excited about or disillusioned with contemporary students. There are also opportunities these first days to talk with, whenever possible, each person taking the course. At the end of the term, students often report that this time spent exploring *all* the people in class initiates and models a dialogic quality of contact, because both Karen and her students are put in positions where they let the others happen to them and they stand their own ground.

A second move we make is to help the class identify a limited number of topics they want to focus on throughout the term. These become topics for the speeches or discussions in public dialogue or group decision-making courses, for the research projects and case studies in a course on communication ethics, or for the series of "styles" assignments in the conflict course. This move permits sustained engagement on substantive issues, slows down some elements of the idea-pace of the course, and helps create the space for student self-reflection, enabling people taking the course to identify the beliefs and especially the values that filter their research and interpretations. This pedagogical move also helps students get beyond the stage of paraphrasing someone else's approach to an issue and into the experience of taking personal responsibility for the positions they advocate. In other words, we require assignments that offer students opportunities to stand their own ground by positioning themselves *ethically* in reference to some subject matter.

Here's one example of what sometimes happens. In a recent class of Karen's, a student we will call Jim took on the challenge of arguing in favor of sexual abstinence before marriage. He knew that his position was linked to his faith and his family's values, and he knew that his position was in the minority among his university peers. Others in the class were arguing against naïve "just say no" sex education programs, in favor of the morning-after pill and legalized prostitution. Jim knew that he had made an important choice for himself and that it would be an important choice for others to consider, but was unsure how to articulate his position in ways that enhanced dialogue. He knew that he did not want to portray himself as a preacher to his peers. He believed that quoting scripture would not be an effective way to engage his audience or persuade them to consider his position. Discussions with peers were part of the assigned preparation process, and in these discussions and e-mail conversations with Karen, Jim raised the concern that his position would be interpreted as a personal attack on or condemnation of his listeners. As he put it in an e-mail,

> The last thing that I want to do is make my audience feel as though I am preaching at them and telling them they are wrong and if they are having sex that they are all going to suffer huge consequences as a result of their actions.... All I am trying to do is make them ask questions and look inside themselves and see if what I present makes sense.

As Jim explored how to stand his ground, he realized that he did not want to give up his conviction or the opportunity to ask difficult questions simply to keep from offending anyone. One suggestion that he effectively incorporated into the first of his assigned speeches was to "steer away from being too apologetic for your position. You don't want to weaken it by worrying more about offending people than advocating for abstinence. I sense that you will get more respect than disdain."

And respect is what he gained. His listeners heard *him*—Jim—not just his position. They understood *him* and respected *him,* and this respect and understanding helped him achieve his communicative goal of getting them to ask questions and look inside themselves. Jim's ethical and moral presence helped generate the desired outcome, and the personal connection that occurred was more important than any one argument or persuasive appeal.

Importantly, Jim was also affected (transformed is only slightly too strong a word) by the communication events. As he let classmates and Karen happen to him, he was able to understand and articulate his position in ways he had not previously done. He moved from parroting the positions of his parents and the leaders of his faith community to choosing and explaining his own positions. Moments of anticipated and actual contact with others compelled Jim to reflect on his ground and to thoughtfully and assertively stand it.

The events of his preparation, presentation, and discussion of listener responses also transformed other aspects of the course. After Jim's talk, the topic of social perspectives on sex in this class was deepened beyond the superficial or selfish. Jim became a role model for standing your own ground while letting the other happen to you. Several students talked with Karen about how they too might advocate for positions they passionately and personally cared about in ways that were as direct, candid, and dialogically engaging as Jim had. They were particularly interested in prompting discussion that engaged not only arguments but also the value systems of the arguers themselves—as choice-making, ethically present persons.

CONCLUSION

In our experience, dialogue involves the negotiation of a variety of tensions, the most fundamental of which is holding my own ground and being open to the other-ness of the other. To say that dialogue is tensional reminds us that (1) it is a dynamic, emergent process rather than any kind of steady state (Cissna & Anderson, 1998) and (2) it can be understood as happening *between* distinguishable moments or poles, each of which transforms the other. We understand that not all communication is dialogic—in fact, much of it is a series of monologues in which one end of the continuum we identify is emphasized over the other. Either the persons involved are only standing their own ground—asserting or expressing to their heart's content, almost regardless of who is present—or they are going along with what's said, regardless of their true beliefs. Dialogue, however, is made manifest when the fundamental tension between letting the other happen to me and holding my own ground is in play for all the parties involved. This tension characterizes dialogue in every context where we have experienced it—intimate contact, student advising, psychotherapy, mentoring, group decision making, public deliberation, patient-provider contact, conflict management, mediation, and superior-subordinate negotiation.

REVIEW QUESTIONS

1. How do we define *dialogue*?
2. Explain what "letting the other happen to me" means. Give an example.
3. Explain what "holding my own ground" means. Give an example.
4. Give an example from your own communication experience of holding your own ground *while* you were letting the other happen to you, and of letting the other happen to you *as* you were holding your own ground.
5. Explain how having the class identify a limited set of topics for the term can help them experience dialogue's central tension.

PROBES

1. Before you work on the tension we discuss here, think about how you negotiate both "privacy" and "disclosure" in your dating relationship(s). Notice how you work both sides of this tension at the same time. Notice how your privacy moves are affected by your disclosures, and vice versa. All this is also true about the basic tension of dialogue.
2. Identify and briefly discuss two different kinds of *experience* you've had, one that is obviously what German speakers would call *Erlebnis* and one that is obviously *Erfahrung*.
3. Some time in the next 48 hours, make a real effort to live this tension in one of your communication encounters. Immediately afterward, write down what you experienced. Bring your reflections to class, and discuss them with one to two classmates who have tried the same thing. What do you notice?

NOTE

1. We find Buber's "Autobiographical Fragments," published in 1973 as the book *Meetings*, to be a particularly fruitful source for articulating the experiential bases of his key insights and concepts. Buber collected these fragments shortly before he died, in response to the request of the editors of the *Library of Living Philosophers* to write an intellectual biography for their volume on Buber. As Buber editor and translator Maurice Friedman notes, "These 'events and meetings' are in the fullest sense of the term 'teaching' and perhaps, in the end, the most real teaching that Martin Buber has left us.... Not only can one discover which tales 'speak to his condition,' but also the hidden teaching contained in the restraint with which Buber retells these 'legendary anecdotes' and in the order in which he has arranged them" (1973, pp. 4–5).

REFERENCES

Alberti, R. E., & Emmons, M. L. (1990). *Your perfect right: A guide to assertive living.* San Luis Obispo, CA: Impact.

Baxter, L. A., & Montgomery, B. W. (1996). *Relating: Dialogue and dialectics.* Mahwah, NJ: Lawrence Erlbaum.

Buber, M. (1970). *I and thou* (W. Kaufmann, Trans.). New York: Scribners.

Buber, M. (1973). *Meetings* (M. Friedman, Ed.). LaSalle, IL. Open Court Press.

Cissna, K. N., & Anderson, R. (1998). Theorizing about dialogic moments: The Buber-Rogers position and postmodern themes. *Communication Theory, 9*, 63–104.

Gadamer, H-G. (1989). *Truth and method* (2nd rev. ed.) (J. Weinsheimer & D. G. Marshall, Trans.) New York: Crossroads.

Levinas, E. (1996). *Emmanuel Levinas: Basic writings* (R. Bernasconi, S. Critchley, & A. Peperzak, Eds.). Bloomington: Indiana University Press.

Montgomery, B. W., & Baxter, L. A. (Eds.). (1998). *Dialectical approaches to studying personal relationships.* Mahwah, NJ: Lawrence Erlbaum.

O'Keefe, B. (1997). Variation, adaptation, and functional explanation in the study of message design. In G. Philipsen & T. L. Albrecht (Eds.), *Developing communication theories* (pp. 85–118). Albany: State University of New York Press.

Fostering Dialogue across Divides

Maggie Herzig and Laura Chasin

Martin Buber originally described "dialogue" as a kind of communication that can connect two individuals. These authors extend this vision to public issues. Maggie Herzig and Laura Chasin are two family therapists who, along with their colleagues, have developed an approach to public communication about difficult issues that has facilitated dialogue among people on opposite sides of such red-hot issues as abortion and gay-lesbian-bisexual-transgender rights.

The first part of this reading, taken from a publication titled *Fostering Dialogue across Divides,* clarifies how a two-person vision of dialogue can also work in public life. This is a kind of communicating that can actually be applied to some of the most toxic public events we experience, such as polarized political diatribes, abusive labor-management conflicts, and shouting matches at school board meetings. The authors mention in the fourth paragraph the importance of the "tension" that Karen Zediker and I describe in the article before this one.

Next, this essay explains what the Public Conversations Project means by "dialogue." For them, dialogue is a conversation in which "people who have different beliefs and perspectives seek to develop mutual understanding." When people are in relationships characterized by distrust, animosity, stereotyping, and polarization, dialogue requires careful planning, communication agreements, and skilled facilitation.

The reading continues by clarifying differences between dialogue and other kinds of communicating, especially debate. The cartoon "Anatomy of Two Conversations" visualizes some of these differences.

The final section of this reading applies dialogue to the current problem of political polarization in the United States—the "Red-Blue divide." These pages are written for people who are motivated to reach across this divide. It provides five suggestions or steps that can be taken, each of which applies ideas that are developed in earlier parts of this reading.

I strongly encourage you to extend your understanding of dialogue by consulting the materials created by the Public Conversations Project. Their website is comprehensive and valuable—www.publicconversations.org. They are one of the most effective organizations at demonstrating the practical applicability and power of the kind of interpersonal communication called "dialogue."

MAIN IDEAS

- Dialogue is a way to talk that reduces stereotyping and increases mutual understanding.
- The need for dialogue is less well-understood than the need for debate and activism.
- Today's polarized political climate makes dialogue more important than ever.
- At the Public Conversations Project, "dialogue" refers to a conversation in which people with different beliefs and perspectives seek to develop mutual understanding.
- Dialogue is very different from debate.
- There are five crucial elements of dialogue: listening with care, speaking respectfully, sharing airtime, learning about others' perspectives, and reflecting on one's own views.
- Two benefits include mutual understanding and the development of useful skills.
- Dialogue requires a genuine desire for mutual understanding, clarity about the conversation, some communication agreements, and a trained facilitator.
- Dialogue differs from debate in at least 11 ways.
- There are five important steps to take to promote dialogue.
- It's especially important to use questions dialogically.

THE ROLE OF DIALOGUE IN PUBLIC LIFE

The way we talk with each other makes a difference. And there is no single "best" way to talk.

Little League coaches shout simple instructions to young players.

Air traffic controllers speak in code with pilots.

Debaters cite evidence that supports their stand and counters an opposing position.

Activists proclaim short potent slogans to promote their causes.

In each case, there is a purpose to be served, and a distinctive way of talking serves that purpose. A baseball player instantly shifts his position on hearing the coach's abbreviated command. Collisions are averted through coded communication among people who speak different languages. Debaters argue for and against competing ideas. Activists' slogans energize allies and summon others to join the cause.

Dialogue is yet another way of talking that serves a distinct purpose. An effective dialogue reduces stereotyping and increases mutual understanding. Through dialogue, people who seem intractably opposed often change the way they view and relate to each other—even as they maintain the commitments that underlie their views. They often discover shared values and concerns which may lead to collaborative actions that were previously unthinkable.

Dialogue participants talk in ways that serve such purposes, communicating their views, experiences, and values without attacking their opponents personally or "trashing" opposing perspectives. Dialogue participants talk about the experiences and values underlying their own views. They ask real questions. They avoid interruptions. They listen.

The need for dialogue in our public life is less well understood than the need for debate and activism. In history and civics classes in the United States, debate and political activism are presented as time-honored tools in the toolbox of democracy, and rightly so. It was largely through these forms of public engagement that slavery and segregation were ended, women and African Americans got the vote, and the war in Vietnam was ended sooner rather than later.

Dialogue has a vital, if quieter, role to play in a resilient and civil democratic society. It can build bridges across divides in the body politic. It can promote healing in small communities that are struggling with a controversy. It can also reduce the likelihood of gridlock in the halls of Congress, hatred in the arena of public opinion, and potentially dangerous misrepresentations in our sound-bite saturated media.

Unbalanced by sufficient dialogue, the constructive impact of debate and activism has diminished in recent decades as public rhetoric has become riddled with polarizing assertions and demonizing stereotypes. Democratic life suffers as we increasingly gravitate to people who share our views and to media presentations that present us with the most offensive representatives of the other side. As we become selectively informed, we become selectively ignorant and increasingly unable to appreciate the extent of our ignorance.

In a polarized social and political climate, meaningful dialogue rarely happens without considerable thought and planning. In this guide we offer some of what we and our colleagues at the Public Conversations Project have come to regard as the nuts and bolts of effective dialogue design and facilitation. We hope this resource will be useful to people who are concerned about polarization and are working to bridge costly divides.

WHAT WE MEAN BY "DIALOGUE"

The word "dialogue" is used in many ways. It is sometimes used to refer to a heart-to-heart conversation between two people who care deeply about each other and who want their relationship to survive the tumult of a serious disagreement.

Some people call almost any exchange of different views a dialogue. For example, it may be used to attract an audience to an event that involves a debate between experts, followed by a Q&A session with the audience.

At PCP, we use the word "dialogue" to refer to a conversation in which people who have different beliefs and perspectives seek to develop mutual understanding. While doing so, they typically experience a softening of stereotypes and develop more trusting relationships. They often gain fresh perspectives on the costs of the conflict and begin to see new possibilities for interaction and action outside of the dialogue room.

Dialogue is very different from debate. In fact, participants in dialogue often agree explicitly to set aside argument so that they can focus on mutual understanding. Dialogue is also different from mediation, conflict resolution, and problem solving, although it may serve as a prelude to or an aspect of such processes. Finally, dialogue differs from group therapy and other conversations that have personal growth as their primary goal.

As we use the term, a dialogue can occur with little structure or planning among people whose bonds are stronger than their differences, among strangers who are genuinely interested in each others' views, and among people whose conflicts are neither intense nor long-standing. However, when people are in relationships characterized by distrust, animosity, stereotyping, and polarization, it may be very difficult to effectively pursue the goals of dialogue without

- careful, collaborative planning that ensures clarity about what the dialogue is and isn't, and also fosters alignment between the goals of the dialogue and participants' wishes.
- communication agreements that discourage counter-productive ways of talking about the issues and encourage genuine inquiry.

- meeting designs that include supportive structures for reflecting, listening, and speaking questions that invite new ways of thinking and talking about the issues.
- facilitation that is informed by careful preparation and responsive to the emerging needs and interests of the participants.

What Dialogue Is

The dialogues that PCP designs and facilitates are conversations in which the participants' primary goal is to pursue mutual understanding rather than agreement or immediate solutions. As participants pursue this goal, they sometimes decide to pursue other goals. For example, dialogue groups sometimes decide to become better informed together or to build consensus about ways that they can act on shared values.

What Dialogue Is Not

Dialogue is distinct from debate; in fact, participants in dialogue often explicitly agree to set aside persuasion and debate so that they can focus on mutual understanding. Dialogue is also different from mediation, conflict resolution, and problem solving although it may serve as a prelude to or aspect of such processes.

What Participants Do

- They listen and are listened to with care.
- They speak and are spoken to in a respectful manner.
- They share airtime so that all speakers can be heard.
- They learn about the perspectives of others.
- They reflect on their own views.

What Participants Gain

- Mutual understanding, which may stimulate new ideas for learning and action
- Communication skills that can be used in other difficult conversations

What It Takes

Dialogue is present any time people genuinely seek mutual understanding, setting aside for that time the urge to persuade or the pressure to decide. It can occur spontaneously, among friends, in classrooms, in organizations, or even among strangers. When people are experiencing polarized conflict, however, we have found that it is helpful if they

- have clarity and consensus about the purposes of the conversation.
- make communication agreements that will help them to achieve their purposes.
- have a facilitator whose sole responsibility is to help the participants honor their agreements and reach their shared purposes.

REACHING OUT ACROSS THE RED-BLUE DIVIDE, ONE PERSON AT A TIME

What This Guide Offers

This guide offers a step-by-step approach to inviting one other person—someone whose perspectives differ from your own—into a conversation in which

- you both agree to set aside the desire to persuade the other and instead focus on developing a better understanding of each other's perspectives, and the hopes, fears, and values that underlie those perspectives.
- you both agree to pursue understanding and to avoid the pattern of attack and defend.
- you both choose to address questions designed to open up new possibilities for moving beyond stale stereotypes and limiting assumptions.

Why Bother to Reach across the Divide?

Many people have at least one important relationship that has been frayed by painful conversations about political differences or constrained due to fear of divisiveness. What alternatives are there? You can let media pundits and campaign strategists tell you that polarization is inevitable and hopeless. Or you can consider taking a collaborative journey with someone who is important to you, neither paralyzed with fear of the rough waters, nor unprepared for predictable strong currents. You and your conversational partner will be best prepared if you bring (1) shared hopes for the experience, (2) the intention to work as a team, and (3) a good map that has guided others on similar journeys. We hope this guide will help prepare you to speak about your passions and concerns in ways that can be heard, and to hear others' concerns and passions with new empathy and understanding—even if you continue to disagree.

Are You Ready?

Are you emotionally ready to resist the strong pull toward polarization? What's at the heart of your desire to reach out to the person you have in mind? Is pursuing mutual understanding enough, or are you likely to feel satisfied only if you can persuade them to concede certain points? What do you know about yourself and the contexts in which you are able—or not so able—to listen without interrupting and to speak with care? Are you open to the possibility—and could you gracefully accept—that the other person might decline your invitation?

Are the Conditions Right?

Do you have a conversational partner in mind who you believe will make the same kind of effort you are prepared to make? Is there something about your relationship that will motivate both of you to approach the conversation with

Distinguishing Debate from Dialogue*

Debate	Dialogue
Premeeting communication between sponsors and participants is minimal and largely irrelevant to what follows.	Premeeting contacts and preparation of participants are essential elements of the full process.
Participants tend to be leaders known for propounding a carefully crafted position. The personas displayed in the debate are usually already familiar to the public. The behavior of the participants tends to conform to stereotypes.	Those chosen to participate are not necessarily outspoken leaders. Whoever they are, they speak as individuals whose own unique experiences differ in some respect from others on their side. Their behavior is likely to vary in some degree and along some dimensions from stereotypic images others may hold of them.
The atmosphere is threatening; attacks and interruptions are expected by participants and are usually permitted by moderators.	The atmosphere is one of safety; facilitators propose, get agreement on, and enforce clear ground rules to enhance safety and promote respectful exchange.
Participants speak as representatives of groups.	Participants speak as individuals, from their own unique experience.
Participants speak to their own constituents and, perhaps, to the undecided middle.	Participants speak to each other.
Differences within sides are denied or minimized.	Differences among participants on the same side are revealed as individual and personal foundations of beliefs and values are explored.
Participants express unswerving commitment to a point of view, approach, or idea.	Participants express uncertainties as well as deeply held beliefs.
Participants listen in order to refute the other side's data and to expose faulty logic in their arguments. Questions are asked from a position of certainty. These questions are often rhetorical challenges or disguised statements.	Participants listen to understand and gain insight into the beliefs and concerns of the others. Questions are asked from a position of curiosity.
Statements are predictable and offer little new information.	New information surfaces.
Success requires simple impassioned statements.	Success requires exploration of the complexities of the issue being discussed.
Debates operate within the constraints of the dominant public discourse. The discourse defines the problem and the options for resolution. It assumes that fundamental needs and values are already clearly understood.	Participants are encouraged to question the dominant public discourse, that is, to express fundamental needs that may or may not be reflected in the discourse and to explore various options for problem definition and resolution. Participants may discover inadequacies in the usual language and concepts used in the public debate.

*This table contrasts debate as commonly seen on television with the kind of dialogue we aim to promote in dialogue sessions conducted by the Public Conversations Project.

a positive spirit? Will you have a chance to propose a dialogue in ways that don't rush or pressure the other person? Will you be able to invite him or her to thoughtfully consider not only the invitation but the specific ideas offered here—ideas that you might together modify? Can you find a time to talk that is private and free from distraction?

If You Decide to Go Forward, Take It One Step at a Time

Extend the invitation with *clarity about its purpose* and a *spirit of collaboration.* If the invitation is declined, accept that response and talk to someone else.

Example—"I've been talking to people who share my general perspective about what's happening politically. I've hesitated to talk across the red-blue divide for fear of having a fruitless and divisive battle. Would you be willing to have a conversation with me, setting aside any impulse to persuade, instead focusing on better understanding each other and being understood for what we believe?"

[Pause for a response, continuing if appropriate.]

"I have a conversational roadmap, some questions, and also some suggested agreements. Would you be willing to look at them, and if you're interested, we can figure out together how to proceed?"

[If you decide to move forward ...]

Make some communication agreements.

Example—"I hope we can bring our best selves to what could be a hard conversation. Can we agree to

- *share speaking and listening time,* not interrupting each other and limiting ourselves to a preset amount of time (e.g., 4 minutes) for the opening questions?
- *speak for ourselves* from our personal experience, not trying to represent or defend an entire political party or ideological approach?
- *maintain the spirit of dialogue* by avoiding a critical or dismissive tone, aiming simply to understand (not to persuade)?"

Select some opening questions and take turns responding to them.

Example—"Here are some suggested questions for opening the dialogue (see page 576). The suggested format is to

- *read each question set*
- *take a couple minutes to reflect* on how we want to respond, then ...
- Each of us can *take a specified amount of time* (e.g., up to 3 or 4 minutes) for each set of questions. If one of us forgets about time, we can signal that person to wrap up. During this very structured part of the dialogue, we can jot notes to remember what we want to explore or ask about later in our conversation."

Anatomy of Two Conversations

Illustrated by J. Kline

Open the conversation to each other's questions and deeper exploration.

Example—"This is a less structured time, but it's still important to maintain agreements that we made. This is our chance to

- *ask each other questions*—not rhetorical questions—that reflect genuine curiosity about each other's experiences and perspectives;
- *pursue topics* that will help us further reflect on our own views, learn about each other's views, unpack the meanings we associate with certain terms, and, perhaps, identify common concerns and values.

First, let's see if we have questions for each other."

[If there are time constraints, agree to save a preset amount of time, perhaps 10 minutes, to close the conversation.]

Reflect on and close the conversation.

Example—"This is a time to say something about what this conversation was like and what we did or did not do that contributed in a positive way. We also can exchange parting words—perhaps words of appreciation, expressions of hope, or ideas about next steps."

Use Questions That Truly Open the Conversation and Avoid Narrow Debate

Some suggestions appear below. These questions are best used in the order presented here. Each question set involves one person speaking without interruption and the other listening, then the other answering the same questions, also without interruption. Take a couple minutes to reflect silently before answering questions. This is important! Thinking before speaking is a good idea, especially if you want to avoid the somewhat habitual and reactive exchanges common in polarized discussions.

Some Suggested Opening Questions:

First question set—your hopes for the dialogue and your underlying values:

- What hopes and concerns do you bring to this conversation?
- What values do you hold that lead you to want to reach across the red-blue divide?
- Where or how did you learn those values?

Second question set—sharing what's at the heart of your perspective:

- What is at the heart of your political leanings (e.g., what concerns or values underlie them) and what would you be willing to share about your life experiences that might convey what those things mean to you?

Third question set—reflecting upon complexities in your views:

- Within your general perspective on the issue(s), do you experience any dilemmas or mixed feelings, or are there gray areas in your thinking?
- In what ways have you felt out of step with the party or advocacy groups you generally support, or in what ways do those groups not fully reflect what's important to you?

Optional question set—stepping away from stereotypes:

- During divisive political debates, are there ways that your values and perspectives are stereotyped by the "other side"? If so, what is it about who you are and what you care about that makes those stereotypes especially frustrating or painful? Are there some stereotypes of your own party that you feel are somewhat deserved—even if they are not fully true—given the rhetoric used in political debates?

If you try these exercises, please let us know how it goes. Also let us know if you have invented other useful approaches or have questions that you'd like to share: e-mail **mherzig@publicconversations.org.**

REVIEW QUESTIONS

1. Describe these authors' version of the tension that Zediker and I explain in the previous reading.
2. Compare and contrast the contributions of debate and dialogue to democratic government.
3. Describe how dialogue is different from mediation and problem solving.
4. Explain how listening functions differently in debate and in dialogue.
5. Explain how questions function differently in debate and in dialogue.
6. Describe the differences in assumptions that ground debate and dialogue.

PROBES

1. Debate is widely recognized as an important feature of democracy. But as this article clarifies, it also can create problems. Describe the complementary role that dialogue can play in democratic decision making.
2. Paraphrase, and then respond to, these authors' argument for the value of reaching across the Red-Blue divide.
3. How does the form of questions affect communication?

Turning Enemies into Friends
Jonathan Sacks

This essay comes from a book titled *After Terror: Promoting Dialogue among Civilizations.* Its author, Jonathan Sacks, is chief rabbi of the United Hebrew Congregations of the Commonwealth. Sacks has been honored by many people including the Archbishop of Canterbury and has published seven books about the politics of hope.

The central idea of this essay is that a real hero is someone who uses communication to turn an enemy into a friend. In friendship, instead of fighting each other, the friends can fight the problems that confront them both, such as poverty, hunger, starvation, disease, and injustice. This might sound like a grandiose, impractical, and unrealistic idea, but Rabbi Sacks argues that it is both intensely practical and very possible.

I include this article because, as is obvious to anyone who observes the current world situation, the primary threat to peaceful prosperity in the world of the first half of the 21st century is conflict among religions. As I write this, almost 6,000 U.S. servicemen and -women have died in wars in Iraq and Afghanistan, conflicts that are anchored in and fueled by religious hatred. Civil war between Sunni and Shiite Muslims is killing thousands of additional people, as is civil war between Hamas and Fatah militants in Palestine. Jewish-Palestinian violence also continues, religiously based genocide rains terror in Darfur, and thousands of others are killed for their religious beliefs in Indonesia. Religion, which is supposed to be the main solution to hatred, is clearly a main problem today. Humans desperately need to reclaim the commitments to peace, justice, and love that are central to Islam, Christianity, Judaism, and other religions.

Rabbi Sacks suggests that the key is courage. Just as war demands physical courage, peace and reconciliation demand moral courage, "and that is far more rare." "In pursuit of peace, even great leaders are afraid to take the risk. The late [Egyptian president] Anwar Sadat and [Israeli prime minister] Yitzhak Rabin had the courage to take that risk, and both paid for it with their lives."

But national, regional, and local events demand this kind of courage, Sacks writes. You would think that religions would best promote forgiveness and reconciliation, but their efforts to enhance spiritual identity or an "Us" almost always also create a polarized "Them." Sacks uses an analysis of the biblical story of Cain and Abel to emphasize the necessity of dialogue to combat this division.

Sacks also argues that dialogic conversation can be considered to be "a form of prayer." "This is a radical idea," he notes, but he explains how it can be a helpful one. One insight offered by the three Abrahamic faiths of Judaism, Christianity, and Islam is that "language is holy." Language, or communication, or the ways people talk with one another can span "the metaphysical abyss between one center of consciousness [person] and another." This is an important idea that I hope you take from this book: How you talk and listen affects both you and others. There is a direct connection between the quality of your communication and the quality of your life (see Chapter 2).

In the final section of this article, Sacks argues that either religions will continue to be a source of long and bloody battles, which will lead people away from them to purely secular lives, or "religions will rise to the challenge." As a Jew, he understands that, for him, this means that, among other things, he must give up any vestige of hate for Germans because of their role in the Holocaust. This is an example of the kind of moral courage that is required.

The point of this article is that the huge, agonizing, and seemingly impossible problems that fill the news and define the "War on Terror" can be lessened, if not solved, with communication. It obviously is not as easy as that sentence implies, but it is actually possible for every person reading these words—for you—to do something about these problems. You can think globally and act locally. You can learn to communicate in the ways described by the writers in this book and to bring these ways into your everyday communicating.

MAIN IDEAS

- A real hero is one who turns an enemy into a friend.
- This kind of hero is desperately needed to reduce conflict in the world today.
- Moral courage, more than physical courage, is what is needed most.
- Religion can and does foster violence and division.
- Religion can and does also foster forgiveness and reconciliation.
- Dialogic conversation can be usefully viewed as a kind of prayer, because all three Abrahamic faiths—Judaism, Christianity, and Islam—believe that language is holy.
- Conflict among people of faith reveals a fundamental misunderstanding of religion.
- Forgiveness is required; even Jews must be able to forgive those responsible for the Holocaust.

Twenty centuries ago, Judaism's sages posed the question: Who is a hero? In most literatures until recent times, a hero was one who performed mighty deeds on the battlefield, who fought, killed, and perhaps died in a noble cause. A hero is one who defeats his enemies. The rabbis thought otherwise. *Who is a hero? One who turns an enemy into a friend.*

I find that answer profoundly wise. If I defeat you, I win and you lose. But in truth, I also lose, because by diminishing you, I diminish myself. But if, in a moment of truth, I forgive you and you forgive me, then forgiveness leads to reconciliation. Reconciliation leads to friendship. And in friendship, instead of fighting one another, we can fight together the problems we share: poverty, hunger, starvation, disease, violence, injustice, and all the other injuries that still scar the face of our world. You gain, I gain, and all those with whom we are associated gain as well. We gain economically, politically, but above all spiritually. My world has become bigger because it now includes you. Who is a hero? One who turns an enemy into a friend.

How different the world would look if that idea prevailed. In the summer of 1999 I stood in the streets of Pristina, in Kosovo, amidst the wreckage of war. The NATO operation had just come to an end. The Kosovan Albanians had returned home. But in the air there was an atmosphere of bitterness and anger. Months earlier, the Albanians were in terror of the Serbs. Now the Serbs feared reprisals from the Albanians. There was peace, but not real peace. War had ended, but reconciliation had not begun. Many of the soldiers with whom I spoke feared for the future. They thought that some day—perhaps not tomorrow, not next year, but sometime—the conflict would begin again, as it has so often in that part of the world.

It was there, surrounded by broken buildings and broken lives, that I understood how one word has the power to change the world: *forgiveness*. If we can forgive others, and act so that others can forgive us, then we can live with the past without being held prisoner by the past. But only if we forgive. Without that we condemn ourselves and our children to fight old battles again and again, with the same bloodshed, the same destruction, the same waste of the human spirit, the same devastation of God's world.

Breaking the cycle is anything but easy. War needs *physical* courage. Reconciliation demands *moral* courage, and that is far more rare. In war, ordinary people become heroes. In pursuit of peace, even great leaders are afraid to take the risk. The late Anwar Sadat and Yitzhak Rabin had the courage to take that risk, and both paid for it with their lives.

Yet if humanity is to survive the twenty-first century, there is no other way. Our capacity for destruction has grown too large. Our ability to use new communications technologies to transmit hate has grown too great. The time has passed when antagonisms were local, containable, limited in their reach. The primary beneficiary of globalization has been terror—anger felt in one place, translated into devastation in another. War is fought on a battlefield. Terror has no battlefield. It has become global. Though it can be contained by physical measures, ultimately it must be fought in the mind. In the short term, conflicts are won by weapons. In the long run, they are won by ideas.

Early in the Second World War the poet W. H. Auden said, "We must love one another or die." That may be too lofty a hope, but at the very least we must try to turn enemies into friends. We must turn the clash of civilizations into a conversation between civilizations. In this, the world's great faiths must take a lead.

IS RELIGION PRIMARILY A SOURCE OF CONFLICT?

Most religions value peace. Why, then, have they so often been a source of conflict? The word "religion" comes from the Latin root meaning "to bind." Religions bind people to one another and to God. They form a "We" greater than the "I." They create, in other words, group identity. That is precisely their power today. The twentieth century was dominated by the politics of ideology. The twenty-first century will be dominated by the politics of identity, and when it comes to identity, people turn to religion, for it contains humanity's deepest answers to the questions: Who am I? Why am I here? Of which narrative am I a part? How then shall I live?

However, the very process of creating an "Us" involves creating a "Them"—the people *not like us*, the other, the outsider, the infidel, the unredeemed, those who stand outside the circle of salvation. That is why, at the very time they are involved in creating community *within* their borders, religions can create conflict *across* those borders. That is why they both heal and harm, mend and destroy.

The Hebrew Bible contains a fateful warning at the beginning of its story of mankind. The first two human children, Cain and Abel, bring an offering to God—the first recorded act of religious worship. That led to rivalry, which led to animosity, which led to fratricide. The implication is unmistakable. Religion is like fire. It warms, but it also burns, and we are the guardians of the flame.

The original Hebrew text of the story of Cain and Abel contains an extraordinary verse which, because of its fractured syntax, is impossible to translate. Standard English versions have something like the following:

> Cain said to his brother Abel, "Let's go out to the field." And while they were in the field, Cain attacked his brother Abel and killed him. (Genesis 4:8)

However, the words, "Let's go out to the field" are not in the original text. Literally translated, the text reads:

> Cain said to his brother Abel ... And while they were in the field, Cain attacked his brother Abel and killed him.

"Cain said," but we do not discover what he said. The sentence breaks off midway. Words fail. Conversation ceases. The dialogue is interrupted. The two brothers can no longer speak to one another. In this subtle but unmistakable way the Bible is signaling one of its most fundamental truths. *When words fail, violence begins.*

It is a point the Bible makes more than once. It happens in the case of Joseph, Jacob's favorite son:

> When his brothers saw that their father loved him more than any of them, they hated him and could not speak a friendly word to him. (Genesis 37:4)

Their animosity festered. At one stage, the brothers thought of murdering Joseph. Eventually they sold him into slavery.

Centuries later, King David's son Absalom discovers that his half-brother Amnon has raped his sister Tamar. At the time, he said nothing:

> Absalom did not utter a word to Amnon, either good or bad; he hated Amnon because he had violated his sister Tamar. (2 Samuel 13:22)

This was the silence not of forgiveness but of cold calculation. Two years later, Absalom took revenge.

In the case of Joseph, the biblical text contains another nuance lost in translation. The Hebrew phrase translated as "they hated him and could not speak a friendly word to him" literally means "they could not *speak him to peace.*" As in the case of Cain and Abel, syntactic awkwardness signals a powerful message. Communication is our greatest tool of conflict resolution. If hostility is not discharged through dialogue, it will not disappear. Instead, it will grow. Speech leads to peace if we can keep the conversation going, not allowing it to falter or break down under the pressure of strong emotion. Pain expressed, listened to, heeded, can be resolved. Pain unheard and unheeded, eventually explodes. In the process, lives are lost.

CONVERSATION AS PRAYER

The Babylonian Talmud (*Berakhot* 26b) contains a phrase (*Ein sichah ela tefillah*) which literally means, "Conversation is a form of prayer." This is a radical idea. In conversation I open myself up to an other. Speaking, I give voice to my hopes and fears. Listening, I hear another self and momentarily experience the world from a different perspective. Through encountering the human other, I learn what it is to encounter the Divine Other, the ultimate reality beyond the self. Prayer is an act not only of speaking but also of listening. Conversation is a form of prayer. In the give-and-take of speech lies the heart of our humanity. Genesis 2:7 states: "And the Lord God formed man from the dust of the earth and breathed into his nostrils the breath of life, and man became a living being." An ancient translation reads the last phrase as "and man became *a speaking soul.*" Speaking is what makes us human. The human body is a mix of chemicals structured by DNA, what the Bible calls "dust of the earth." It is the use of language that infuses the body with the "breath of God." The highest definition of *Homo sapiens* is "the form of life that speaks."

It is often said that the Abrahamic faiths—Judaism, Christianity, and Islam—are the three great "religions of revelation." That is the wrong way to define their distinctiveness. *All* ancient faiths believed in revelation. They believed that the gods were to be found in phenomena of nature: the wind, the rain, the sun, the sea, the storm. What made the three Abrahamic monotheisms different is not that they believed that God reveals himself, but rather that he does so in *words*. They believe that *language is holy.*

Forces of nature signify power. Words signify meaning. Nature is indifferent to mankind. Language is the unique possession of mankind. What makes Judaism, Christianity, and Islam different from other faiths is that they conceive of God as personal, and the mark of the personal is that *God speaks.* Language is the only thing that spans the metaphysical abyss between one center of consciousness and another. It redeems our solitude, affirming that in the vast echoing universe we are not alone.

Therefore, to be true to our relationship with God, Jews, Christians, and Muslims must show that speech is greater than power, conversation more compelling than the use of force. God has taught us to listen to him for a reason: to teach us to listen to the other, the human other who, though not in our image, is nonetheless in his.

FROM CONFLICT AND VIOLENCE TO RECONCILIATION AND PEACE

Beginning in the sixteenth century, Europe embarked on a long process generally known as secularization. First science, then knowledge generally, then politics and power, and finally culture, sought and gained their independence from religion. Thus were born the secular university, the secular nation-state, and secular society.

The conventional wisdom is that these things happened because people stopped believing in God. In fact, it was not so. They happened because good, thoughtful, and reasonable people came to the conclusion that *people of God could not live peaceably with one another.* It was not God who failed but those who claimed to be his representatives on earth.

The closest analogy to the new international disorder of the twenty-first century is the age—the sixteenth and seventeenth centuries—of the great European wars of religion. Two stark choices lie ahead of us. Either religions will continue to be a source of conflict, in which case, after long and bloody battles, the world will be re-secularized, or religions will rise to the challenge. I have suggested that this challenge was implicit in the Abrahamic monotheisms from the very outset. The task God set and continues to set us was not to conquer and convert the world. That is the language of imperialism, not religious faith. It is to listen to the human other as if the Divine Other were speaking to us through him or her. I do not claim that this is easy. I do claim that it is necessary.

I am a Jew, and as a Jew, I carry with me the tears and sufferings of my grandparents, and theirs, through the generations. The story of my people is the story of a thousand years of exiles and expulsions, persecutions and pogroms, beginning with the First Crusade and culminating in the murder of two-thirds of Europe's Jews. For centuries, Jews knew that they, or their children, risked being murdered simply because they were Jews. How can I let go of that pain when it is written into my very soul?

Yet, for the sake of my children I must. Will I bring one victim of the Holocaust back to life by hating Germans? Does loving God more entitle me to love other people less? If I ask God to forgive me, does he not ask me to forgive others? The duty I owe my ancestors who died because of their faith is to build a world in which people no longer die because of their faith. I honor the past by learning from it, by refusing to add pain to pain, grief to grief. That is why we must answer hatred with love, violence with peace, and conflict with reconciliation.

Today God has given us no choice. There was a time when our ancestors lived surrounded by people who were like them. They could afford to say, "We are right. The rest of the world is wrong." We are no longer in that situation. We live consciously in the presence of difference. Our lives, our safety, our environment, our very future, are bound up with countries far away and cultures unlike our own. God has brought us eyeball to eyeball with the complex interdependence of his world, and now he is asking us: Can we recognize God's image in someone who is not in our image? Can you discern my unity in your diversity?

It took the death of 6 million people to bring Jews and Christians together in mutual dignity and respect. How many more people will have to die in the Middle East, Kashmir, Northern Ireland, the Balkans, before we understand that there are many faiths but God has given us only one world in which to live together. The time has come for us to replace the clash of civilizations with a respectful conversation between civilizations, and begin the hard but sacred task of turning enemies into friends.

REVIEW QUESTIONS

1. What is a rabbi?
2. "War needs _____ courage. Reconciliation demands _____ courage."
3. What conclusion does Sacks draw from his analysis of the biblical story of Cain and Abel?
4. Everybody knows that silence can be comforting. But the silence that Sacks discusses has the opposite effect. Explain.
5. List the three "Abrahamic faiths." What does "Abrahamic" mean?

PROBES

1. Sacks writes that one main beneficiary of globalization has been terror. What does he mean? How have enhanced worldwide transportation, the internationalization of business, the growth of global media, and the end of the Cold War all promoted terrorist activities?
2. Explain what Sacks means when he writes that "conversation is a form of prayer."
3. Explain the following quotation and paraphrase the point Sacks makes about it: "What makes Judaism, Christianity, and Islam different from other faiths is that they conceive of God as personal, and the mark of the personal is that *God speaks.*"
4. What kind of listening is Sacks urging when he says we should "listen to the human other as if the Divine Other were speaking to us through him or her"?
5. Sacks writes, "As a Jew ... the duty I owe my ancestors who died because of their faith is to build a world in which people no longer die because of their faith." Explain.

Elements of the Interhuman
Martin Buber

This book's approach to interpersonal communication is based primarily on the life work of Martin Buber, the author of this next essay. Even though his writings are challenging, I have included one here, because Buber is the primary source for almost everything in this book.

Buber was a Jewish philosopher and teacher who was born and raised in Austria and Germany and who died in 1965 in Israel. In many ways, he was very different from me, and he was probably also very different from you. He was a 19th-century European, a Jew who fled the Holocaust to Israel, and a world-renowned writer and speaker. His native language was German, and his writings in German, I am told, are difficult even for other German speakers to understand. But Buber recognized something about human life that has resonated with literally millions of people since he first expressed it in the early 1920s. His main book, *I and Thou*,[1] has been translated into over 20 languages, and for many years, it sold more copies worldwide than any books other than the Bible and the Quràn.

The idea that impressed so many people is that humans are born with the ability to connect with what's around us in two very different ways. Buber called them "I-It" and "I-Thou," and I call them "impersonally" and "interpersonally." Each is important. But, as Buber wrote late in his life, he was born into a world where "I-It" relating predominated, so he dedicated his creative and communicative energies to describing and encouraging the other alternative. This is where each of us can connect with Buber. If your experience is anything like mine, I-It relating predominates for you, too. And more I-Thou relating could enrich your life. This is why it can be worth it to read Buber carefully.

As I mentioned, because he was raised by his grandparents in Europe during the late-19th and early-20th centuries (Buber's parents were divorced), lived through both world wars, was active in several political movements, and was a well-known, even famous, citizen of Israel, his life experiences are different in many ways from yours and mine. But for me, Buber's peculiar genius is that he can sense the part of his experience that is universal and can project that universal knowledge about human meetings through his European heritage and his "foreign" native language in such a way that he talks to me directly. In other words, even though he is in many ways very different from me, he says, "This is my experience; reflect on it a little and you might find that it's your experience, too." Sometimes I stumble over Buber's language, the way he puts things. For example, like some other older authors in this book, Buber uses "man" when he means "human." But when I listen to him and do what he asks, I discover that he's right. It *is* my experience, only now I understand it better than I did before.

I don't know whether this one excerpt from Buber's writing will work this way for you. But the possibility is there if you open yourself to hear him. That's one thing about Buber's writings. Although he's a philosopher, some scholars criticize him because he doesn't state philosophical propositions and then try to verify and validate them with "proof." Instead, Buber insists that his reader try to meet him in a *conversation,* a dialogue. The main thing is for the reader to see whether his or her life experiences resonate with Buber's. This resonance is the main "proof" of the validity of Buber's ideas.

In almost all his writing, Buber begins by observing that each of us lives a twofold reality. One "fold" is made up of our interaction with objects—human and otherwise—in the world. In this model of living, we merely need to develop and maintain our ability to be "objective," to explain ourselves and the world with accurate theories and valid cause-and-effect formulations. But the other "fold" occurs when we become fully human *persons* in genuine relationships with others, when we meet another and "make the other present as a whole and as a unique being, as the person that he is."

The genuine relationship Buber talks about is the "highest form" of what I've been calling interpersonal communication. Buber's term for it is an *"I-Thou* relationship" or "dialogue."[2] According to Buber, the individual lives always in the world of *I-It;* the person can enter the world of *I-Thou.* Both worlds are necessary. You can't expect to communicate interpersonally with everyone in every situation. But you can only become a fully human person by sharing genuine interpersonal relationships with others. As Buber puts it, without *It,* the person cannot live. But he (or she) who lives with *It* alone is not a person.

This article is taken from a talk Buber gave when he visited the United States in 1957. It's especially useful because it is a kind of summary of much of what he had written in the first 79 years of his life (he died when he was 87).

In the "Main Ideas" section below I've outlined the article to simplify it and to show how clearly organized it actually is. As you can see from the outline, Buber's subject is interpersonal relationships, which he calls "man's personal dealings with one another," or "the interhuman." Like the rest of this book, Buber's article doesn't deal with some mystical spirit world in which we all become one. Rather, he's writing about communication between today's teachers and students, politicians and voters, dating partners, and between you and me. First, he explains some attitudes and actions that keep people from achieving "genuine dialogue." Then he describes the characteristics of this dialogue, or *I-Thou* relationship. In the outline, I've paraphrased each point that he makes.

A reminder about his language: I pointed out in the Introduction to this book that a few of the readings in *Bridges Not Walls* were written before we had learned about the destructive potential of the male bias in the English language. This is one of these readings. When I paraphrase Buber, I remove this bias, and I have tried to soft-pedal it when I quote him. But it's still part of his writing, at least as it is now translated. Given what he believed about human beings—and given the strong intellectual influence his wife, Paula, had on him—I am sure that Buber would have been quick to correct the gender bias in his language if he had lived long enough to have the opportunity. I hope you can overlook this part of his writing and can hear his insights about *persons.*

MAIN IDEAS

I. Interhuman relationships are not the same as "social relationships."
   A. Social relationships can be very close, but no *existential* or person-to-person relation is necessarily involved.
   B. This is because the collective or social suppresses individual persons.
   C. But in the interhuman, person meets person. In other words, "the only thing that matters is that for each of the two [persons] the other happens as the particular other, that each becomes aware of the other and is thus related to him in such a way that he does not regard and use him as his object, but as his partner in a living event, even if it is no more than a boxing match."

    D. In short, "the sphere of the interhuman is one in which a person is confronted by the other. We [i.e., Buber] call its unfolding the dialogical."

II. There are three problems that get in the way of dialogue.

    A. The first problem is the duality of *being* and *seeming*. Dialogue won't happen if the people involved are only "seeming." They need to try to practice "being."

        1. "Seeming" in a relationship involves being concerned with your image, or front—with how you wish to appear.

        2. "Being" involves the spontaneous and unreserved presentation of what you really are in your personal dealings with the other.

        3. These two are generally found mixed together. The most we can do is distinguish between persons in whose essential attitude one or the other (being or seeming) predominates.

        4. When seeming reigns, real interpersonal communication is impossible: "Whatever the meaning of the word 'truth' may be in other realms, in the interhuman realm it means that [people] communicate themselves to one another as what they are."

        5. The tendency toward seeming, however, is understandable.

            a. We *essentially* need personal confirmation—that is, we can't live without being confirmed by other people.

            b. Seeming often appears to help us get the confirmation we need.

            c. Consequently, "to yield to seeming is [the human's] essential cowardice, to resist it is his [or her] essential courage."

        6. This view indicates that there is no such thing as "bad being," but rather people who are habitually content to "seem" and afraid to "be." "I have never known a young person who seemed to me irretrievably bad."

    B. The second problem involves the way we perceive others.

        1. Many fatalist thinkers, such as Jean-Paul Sartre, believe that we can ultimately know *only* ourselves, that "man has directly to do only with himself and his own affairs."

        2. But the main prerequisite for dialogue is that you get in direct touch with the other, "that each person should regard his partner as the very one he is."

            a. This means becoming aware of the other person as an essentially unique being. "To be aware of a [person] ... means in particular to perceive his wholeness as a person determined by the spirit: it means to perceive the dynamic centre which stamps his every utterance, action, and attitude with the recognizable sign of uniqueness."

            b. But this kind of awareness is impossible so long as I objectify the other.

        3. Perceiving the other in this way is contrary to everything in our world that is scientifically analytic or reductive.

            a. This is not to say that the sciences are wrong, only that they are severely limited.

            b. What's dangerous is the extension of the scientific, analytic method to all of life, because it is very difficult for science to remain aware of the essential uniqueness of persons.

        4. This kind of perception is called "personal making present." What enables us to do it is our capacity for "imagining the real" of the other.

            a. Imagining the real "is not a looking at the other but a bold swinging—demanding the most intensive stirring of one's being—into the life of the other."

     b. When I *imagine* what the other person is *really* thinking and feeling, I can make direct contact with him or her.

  C. The third problem that impedes the growth of dialogue is the tendency toward imposition instead of unfolding.

     1. One way to affect a person is to impose yourself on him or her.

     2. Another way is to "find and further in the soul of the other the disposition toward" that which you have recognized in yourself as right.

       a. Unfolding is not simply "teaching," but rather *meeting*.

       b. It requires believing in the other person.

       c. It means working as a helper of the growth processes already going on in the other.

     3. The propagandist is the typical "imposer"; the teacher *can* be the correspondingly typical "unfolder."

     4. The ethic implied here is similar to Immanuel Kant's; that is, persons should never be treated as means to an end, but only as ends in themselves.

       a. The only difference is that Buber stresses that persons exist not in isolation but in the interhuman.

       b. For the interhuman to occur, there must be:

         (1) as little seeming as possible.

         (2) genuine perceiving ("personal making present") of the other.

         (3) as little imposing as possible.

III. Here is a summary of the characteristics of genuine dialogue:

  A. Each person must turn toward and be open to the other, a "turning of the being."

  B. Each must make present the other by imagining the real.

  C. Each confirms the other's being; however, confirmation does not necessarily mean approval.

  D. Each must be authentically him or herself.

     1. Each must say whatever she or he "has to say."

     2. Each cannot be ruled by thoughts of his or her own effect or effectiveness as a speaker.

  E. Where dialogue becomes genuine, "there is brought into being a memorable common fruitlessness which is to be found nowhere else."

  F. Speaking is not always essential; silence can be very important.

  G. Finally, all participants must be committed to dialogue; otherwise, it will fail.

Again, Buber's language sometimes can get in the way of understanding him. But if you listen carefully, I think at least some of what he says will resonate with you.

THE SOCIAL AND THE INTERHUMAN

It is usual to ascribe what takes place between men to the social realm, thereby blurring a basically important line of division between two essentially different areas of human life. I myself, when I began nearly fifty years ago to find my own bearings in the knowledge of society, making use of the then unknown concept of the interhuman, made the same error. From that time it became increasingly clear to me that we have to do here with a separate category of our existence, even a separate dimension, to use a mathematical term, and one with which we are so familiar that its peculiarity has hitherto almost escaped us. Yet insight into its peculiarity is extremely important not only for our thinking but also for our living.

We may speak of social phenomena wherever the life of a number of men, lived with one another, bound up together, brings in its train shared experiences and reactions. But to be thus bound up together means only that each individual existence is enclosed and contained in a group existence. It does not mean that between one member and another of the group there exists any kind of personal relation. They do feel that they belong together in a way that is, so to speak, fundamentally different from every possible belonging together with someone outside the group. And there do arise, especially in the life of smaller groups, contacts which frequently favour the birth of individual relations, but, on the other hand, frequently make it more difficult. In no case, however, does membership in a group necessarily involve an existential relation between one member and another. It is true that there have been groups in history which included highly sensitive and intimate relations between two of their members—as, for instance, in the homosexual relations among the Japanese samurai or among Doric warriors—and these were countenanced for the sake of the stricter cohesion of the group. But in general it must be said that the leading elements in groups, especially in the later course of human history, have rather been inclined to suppress the personal relation in favour of the purely collective element. Where this latter element reigns alone or is predominant, men feel themselves to be carried by the collectivity, which lifts them out of loneliness and fear of the world and lostness. When this happens—and for modern man it is an essential happening—the life between person and person seems to retreat more and more before the advance of the collective. The collective aims at holding in check the inclination to personal life. It is as though those who are bound together in groups should in the main be concerned only with the work of the group and should turn to the personal partners, who are tolerated by the group, only in secondary meetings.

The difference between the two realms became very palpable to me on one occasion when I had joined the procession through a large town of a movement to which I did not belong. I did it out of sympathy for the tragic development which I sensed was at hand in the destiny of a friend who was one of the leaders of the movement. While the procession was forming, I conversed with him and with another, a good-hearted "wild man," who also had the mark of death upon him. At that moment I still felt that the two men really were there, over against me, each of them a man near to me, near even in what was most remote from me; so different from me that my soul continually suffered from this difference, yet by virtue of this very difference confronting me with authentic being. Then the formations started off, and after a short time I was lifted out of all confrontation, drawn into the procession, falling in with its aimless step; and it was obviously the very same for the two with whom I had just exchanged human words. After a while we passed a café where I had been sitting the previous day with a musician whom I knew only slightly. The very moment we passed it the door opened, the musician stood on the threshold, saw me, apparently saw me alone, and waved to me. Straightway it seemed to me as though I were taken out of the procession and of the presence of my marching friends, and set there, confronting the musician. I forgot that I was walking along with the same step; I felt that I was standing over there by the man who had called out to me, and without a word, with a smile of understanding, was answering him. When consciousness of the facts returned to me, the procession, with my companions and myself at its head, had left the café behind.

The realm of the interhuman goes far beyond that of sympathy. Such simple happenings can be part of it as, for instance, when two strangers exchange glances in a crowded streetcar, at once to sink back again into the convenient state of wishing to know nothing about each other. But also every casual encounter between opponents belong to this realm, when it affects the opponent's attitude—that is, when something, however imperceptible, happens between the two, no matter whether it is marked at the time by any feeling or not. The only thing that matters is that for each of the two men the other happens as the particular other, that each becomes aware of the other and is thus related to him in such a way that he does not regard and use him as his object, but as his partner in a living event, even if it is no more than a boxing match. It is well known that some existentialists assert that the basic factor between men is that one is an object for the other. But so far as this is actually the case, the special reality of the interhuman, the fact of the contact, has been largely eliminated. It cannot indeed be entirely eliminated. As a crude example, take two men who are observing one another. The essential thing is not that the one makes the other his object, but the fact that he is not fully able to do so and the reason for his failure. We have in common with all existing things that we can be made objects of observation. But it is my privilege as man that by the hidden activity of my being I can establish an impassable barrier to objectification. Only in partnership can my being be perceived as an existing whole.

The sociologist may object to any separation of the social and the interhuman on the ground that society is actually built upon human relations, and the theory of these relations is therefore to be regarded as the very foundation of sociology. But here an ambiguity in the concept "relation" becomes evident. We speak, for instance, of a comradely relation between two men in their work, and do not merely mean what happens between them as comrades, but also a lasting disposition which is actualized in those happenings and which even includes purely psychological events such as the recollection of the absent comrade. But by the sphere of the interhuman I mean solely actual happenings between men, whether wholly mutual or tending to grow into mutual relations. For the participation of both partners is in principle indispensable. The sphere of the interhuman is one in which a person is confronted by the other. We call its unfolding the dialogical.

In accordance with this, it is basically erroneous to try to understand the interhuman phenomena as psychological. When two men converse together, the psychological is certainly an important part of the situation, as each listens and each prepares to speak. Yet this is only the hidden accompaniment to the conversation itself, the phonetic event fraught with meaning, whose meaning is to be found neither in one of the two partners nor in both together, but only in their dialogue itself, in this "between" which they live together.

BEING AND SEEMING

The essential problem of the sphere of the interhuman is the duality of being and seeming. Although it is a familiar fact that men are often troubled about the impression they make on others, this has been much more discussed in moral philosophy than in anthropology. Yet this is one of the most important subjects for anthropological study.

We may distinguish between two different types of human existence. The one proceeds from what one really is, the other from what one wishes to seem. In general, the two are found mixed together. There have probably been few men who were entirely independent of the impression they made on others, while there has scarcely existed one who was exclusively determined by the impression made by him. We must be content to distinguish between men in whose essential attitude the one or the other predominates.

This distinction is most powerfully at work, as its nature indicates, in the interhuman realm—that is, in men's personal dealings with one another.

Take as the simplest and yet quite clear example the situation in which two persons look at one another—the first belonging to the first type, the second to the second. The one who lives from his being looks at the other just as one looks at someone with whom he has personal dealings. His look is "spontaneous," "without reserve"; of course, he is not uninfluenced by the desire to make himself understood by the other, but he is uninfluenced by any thought of the idea of himself which he can or should awaken in the person whom he is looking at. His opposite is different. Since he is concerned with the image which his appearance, and especially his look or glance, produces in the other, he "makes" this look. With the help of the capacity, in greater or lesser degree peculiar to man, to make a definite element of his being appear in his look, he produces a look which is meant to have, and often enough does have, the effect of a spontaneous utterance—not only the utterance of a physical event supposed to be taking place at that very moment, but also, as it were, the reflection of a personal life of such-and-such a kind.

This must, however, be carefully distinguished from another area of seeming whose ontological legitimacy cannot be doubted. I mean the realm of "genuine seeming," where a lad, for instance, imitates his heroic model and while he is doing so is seized by the actuality of heroism, or a man plays the part of a destiny and conjures up authentic destiny. In this situation there is nothing false; the imitation is genuine imitation and the part played is genuine; the mask, too, is a mask and no deceit. But where the semblance originates from the lie and is permeated by it, the interhuman is threatened in its very existence. It is not that someone utters a lie, falsifies some account. The lie I mean does not take place in relation to particular facts, but in relation to existence itself, and it attacks interhuman existence as such. There are times when a man, to satisfy some stale conceit, forfeits the great chance of a true happening between I and Thou.

Let us now imagine two men, whose life is dominated by appearance, sitting and talking together. Call them Peter and Paul. Let us list the different configurations which are involved. First, there is Peter as he wishes to appear to Paul, and Paul as he wishes to appear to Peter. Then there is Peter as he really appears to Paul, that is, Paul's image of Peter, which in general does not in the least coincide with what Peter wishes Paul to see; and similarly there is the reverse situation. Further, there is Peter as he appears to himself, and Paul as he appears to himself. Lastly, there are the bodily Peter and the bodily Paul. Two living beings and six ghostly appearances, which mingle in many ways in the conversation between the two. Where is there room for any genuine interhuman life?

Whatever the meaning of the word "truth" may be in other realms, in the interhuman realm it means that men communicate themselves to one another as what they are. It does not depend on one saying to the other everything that occurs to him, but only on his letting no seeming creep in between himself and the other. It does not depend on one letting himself go before another, but on his granting to the man to whom he communicates himself a share in his being. This is a question of the authenticity of the interhuman, and where this is not to be found, neither is the human element itself authentic.

Therefore, as we begin to recognize the crisis of man as the crisis of what is between man and man, we must free the concept of uprightness from the thin moralistic tones which cling to it, and let it take its tone from the concept of bodily uprightness. If a presupposition of human life in primeval times is given in man's walking upright, the fulfillment of human life can only come through the soul's walking upright, through the great uprightness which is not tempted by any seeming because it has conquered all semblance.

But, one may ask, what if a man by his nature makes his life subservient to the images which he produces in others? Can he, in such a case, still become a man living from his being, can he escape from his nature?

The widespread tendency to live from the recurrent impression one makes instead of from the steadiness of one's being is not a "nature." It originates, in fact, on the other side of interhuman life itself, in men's dependence upon one another. It is no light thing to be confirmed in one's being by others, and seeming deceptively offers itself as a help in this. To yield to seeming is man's essential cowardice, to resist it is his essential courage. But this is not an inexorable state of affairs which is as it is and must so remain. One can struggle to come to oneself—that is, to come to confidence in being. One struggles, now more successfully, now less, but never in vain, even when one thinks he is defeated. One must at times pay dearly for life lived from the being; but it is never too dear. Yet is there not bad being, do weeds not grow everywhere? I have never known a young person who seemed to me irretrievably bad. Later indeed it becomes more and more difficult to penetrate the increasingly tough layer which has settled down on a man's being. Thus there arises the false perspective of the seemingly fixed "nature" which cannot be overcome. It is false; the foreground is deceitful; man as man can be redeemed.

Again we see Peter and Paul before us surrounded by the ghosts of the semblances. A ghost can be exorcized. Let us imagine that these two find it more and more repellent to be represented by ghosts. In each of them the will is stirred and strengthened to be confirmed in their being as what they really are and nothing else. We see the forces of real life at work as they drive out the ghosts, till the semblance vanishes and the depths of personal life call to one another.

PERSONAL MAKING PRESENT

By far the greater part of what is today called conversation among men would be more properly and precisely described as speechifying. In general, people do not really speak to one another, but each, although turned to the other, really speaks to a fictitious court of appeal whose life consists of nothing but listening to him. Chekhov has given poetic expression to this state of affairs in *The Cherry Orchard*, where the only use the members of a family make of their being together is to talk past one another. But it is Sartre who has raised to a principle of existence what in Chekhov still appears as the deficiency of a person who is shut up in himself. Sartre regards the walls between the partners in a conversation as simply impassable. For him it is inevitable human destiny that a man has directly to do only with himself and his own affairs. The inner existence of the other is his own concern, not mine; there is no direct relation with the other, nor can there be. This is perhaps the clearest expression of the wretched fatalism of modern man, which regards degeneration as the unchangeable nature of *Homo sapiens* and the misfortune of having run into a blind alley as his primal fate, and which brands every thought of a breakthrough as reactionary romanticism. He who really knows how far our generation has lost the way of true freedom, of free giving between I and Thou, must himself, by virtue of the demand implicit in every great knowledge of this kind, practice directness—even if he were the only man on earth who did it—and not depart from it until scoffers are struck with fear and hear in his voice the voice of their own suppressed longing.

The chief presupposition for the rise of genuine dialogue is that each should regard his partner as the very one he is. I become aware of him, aware that he is different, essentially different from myself, in the definite, unique way which is peculiar to him, and I accept whom I thus see, so that in full earnestness I can direct what I say to him as the person he is. Perhaps from time to time I must offer strict opposition to his view about the subject of our conversation. But I accept this person, the personal bearer of a conviction, in his definite being out of which his conviction has grown—even though I must try to show, bit by bit, the wrongness of this very conviction. I affirm the person I struggle with: I struggle with him as his partner, I confirm him as creature and as creation, I confirm him who is opposed to me as him who is over against me. It is true that it now depends on the other whether genuine dialogue, mutuality in speech arises between us. But if I thus give to the other who confronts me his legitimate standing as a man with whom I am ready to enter into dialogue, then I may trust him and suppose him to be also ready to deal with me as his partner.

But what does it mean to be "aware" of a man in the exact sense in which I use the word? To be aware of a thing or a being means, in quite general terms, to experience it as a whole and yet at the same time without reduction or abstraction, in all its concreteness. But a man, although he exists as a living being among living beings and even as a thing among things, is nevertheless something categorically different from all things and all beings. A man cannot really be grasped except on the basis of the gift of the spirit which belongs to man alone among all things, the spirit as sharing decisively in the personal life of the living man, that is, the spirit which determines the person. To be aware of a man, therefore, means in particular to perceive his wholeness as a person determined by the spirit; it means to perceive the dynamic centre which stamps his every utterance, action, and attitude with the recognizable sign of uniqueness. Such an awareness is impossible, however, if and so long as the other is the separated object of my contemplation or even observation, for this wholeness and its centre do not let themselves be known to contemplation or observation. It is only possible when I step into an elemental relation with the other, that is, when he becomes present to me. Hence I designate awareness in this special sense as "personal making present."

The perception of one's fellow man as a whole, as a unity, and as unique—even if his wholeness, unity, and uniqueness are only partly developed, as is usually the case—is opposed in our time by almost everything that is commonly understood as specifically modern. In our time there predominates an analytical, reductive, and deriving look between man and man. This look is analytical, or rather pseudo analytical, since it treats the whole being as put together and therefore able to be taken apart—not only the so-called unconscious which is accessible to relative objectification, but also the psychic stream itself, which can never, in fact, be grasped as an object. This look is a reductive one because it tries to contract the manifold person, who is nourished by the microcosmic richness of the possible, to some schematically surveyable and recurrent structures. And this look is a deriving one because it supposes it can grasp what a man has become, or even is becoming, in genetic formulae, and it thinks that even the dynamic central principle of the individual in this becoming can be represented by a general concept. An effort is being made today radically to destroy the mystery between man and man. The personal life, the ever-near mystery, once the source of the stillest enthusiasms, is levelled down.

What I have just said is not an attack on the analytical method of the human sciences, a method which is indispensable wherever it furthers knowledge of a phenomenon without impairing the essentially different knowledge of its uniqueness that transcends the valid circle of the method. The science of man that makes use of the analytical method must accordingly always keep in view the boundary of such a contemplation, which stretches like a horizon around it. This duty makes the transportation of the method into life dubious; for it is excessively difficult to see where the boundary is in life.

If we want to do today's work and prepare tomorrow's with clear sight, then we must develop in ourselves and in the next generation a gift which lives in man's inwardness as a Cinderella, one day to be a princess. Some call it intuition, but that is not a wholly unambiguous concept. I prefer the name "imagining the real," for in its essential being this gift is not a looking at the other, but a bold swinging—demanding the most intensive stirring of one's being—into the life of the other. This is the nature of all genuine imagining, only that here the realm of my action is not the all-possible, but the particular real person who confronts me, whom I can attempt to make present to myself just in this way, and not otherwise, in his wholeness, unity, and uniqueness, and with his dynamic centre which realizes all these things ever anew.

Let it be said again that all this can only take place in a living partnership, that is, when I stand in a common situation with the other and expose myself vitally to his share in the situation as really his share. It is true that my basic attitude can remain unanswered, and the dialogue can die in seed. But if mutuality stirs, then the interhuman blossoms into genuine dialogue.

IMPOSITION AND UNFOLDING

I have referred to two things which impede the growth of life between men: the invasion of seeming, and the inadequacy of perception. We are now faced with a third, plainer than the others, and in this critical hour more powerful and more dangerous than ever.

There are two basic ways of affecting men in their views and their attitude to life. In the first a man tries to impose himself, his opinion, and his attitude, on the other in such a way that the latter feels the psychical result of the action to be his own insight, which has only been freed by the influence. In the second basic way of affecting others, as man wishes to find and to further in the soul of the other the disposition toward what he has recognized in himself as the right. Because it is the right, it must also be alive in the microcosm of the other, as one possibility. The other need only be opened out in this potentiality of his; moreover, this opening out takes place not essentially by teaching, but by meeting, by existential communication between someone that is in actual being and someone that is in a process of becoming. The first way has been most power-fully developed in the realm of propaganda, the second in that of education.

The propagandist I have in mind, who imposes himself, is not in the least concerned with the person whom he desires to influence, as a person; various individual qualities are of importance only in so far as he can exploit them to win the other and must get to know them for this purpose. In his indifference to everything personal the propagandist goes a substantial distance beyond the party for which he works. For the party, persons in their difference are of signifi-cance because each can be used according to his special qualities in a particular function. It is true that the personal is considered only in respect of the specific use to which it can be put, but within these limits it is recognized in practice. To propaganda as such, on the other hand, individual qualities are rather looked on as a burden, for propaganda is concerned simply with *more*—more members, more adherents, an increasing extent of support. Political methods, where they rule in an extreme form, as here, simply mean winning power over the other by depersonalizing him. This kind of propaganda enters upon different rela-tions with force; it supplements it or replaces it, according to the need or the prospects, but it is in the last analysis nothing but sublimated violence, which has become imperceptible as such. It places men's souls under a pressure which allows the illusion of autonomy. Political methods at their height mean the effective abolition of the human factor.

The educator whom I have in mind lives in a world of individuals, a certain number of whom are always at any one time committed to his care. He sees each of these individuals as in a position to become a unique, single person, and thus the bearer of a special task of existence which can be fulfilled through him and through him alone. He sees every personal life as engaged in such a process of actualization, and he knows from his own experience that the forces mak-ing for actualization are all the time involved in a microcosmic struggle with counterforces. He has come to see himself as a helper of the actualizing forces. He knows these forces; they have shaped and they still shape him. Now he puts this person shaped by them at their disposal for a new struggle and a new work. He cannot wish to impose himself, for he believes in the effect of the actualiz-ing forces, that is, he believes that in every man what is right is established in a single and uniquely personal way. No other way may be imposed on a man, but another way, that of the educator, may and must unfold what is right, as in this case it struggles for achievement, and help it to develop.

The propagandist, who imposes himself, does not really believe in his own cause, for he does not trust it to attain its effect of its own power without his special methods, whose symbols are the loudspeaker and the television adver-tisement. The educator who unfolds what is there believes in the primal power which has scattered itself, and still scatters itself, in all human beings in order that it may grow up in each man in the special form of that man. He is confident that this growth needs at each moment only that help which is given in meeting and that he is called to supply that help.

I have illustrated the character of the two basic attitudes and their relation to one another by means of two extremely antithetical examples. But wherever men have dealings with one another, one or the other attitude is to be found to be in more or less degree.

These two principles of imposing oneself on someone and helping someone to unfold should not be confused with concepts such as arrogance and humility. A man can be arrogant without wishing to impose himself on others, and it is not enough to be humble in order to help another unfold. Arrogance and humility are dispositions of the soul, psychological facts with a moral accent, while imposition and helping to unfold are events between men, anthropological facts which point to an ontology, the ontology of the interhuman.

In the moral realm Kant expressed the essential principle that one's fellow man must never be thought of and treated merely as a means, but always at the same time as an independent end. The principle is expressed as an "ought" which is sustained by the idea of human dignity. My point of view, which is near to Kant's in its essential features, has another source and goal. It is concerned with the presuppositions of the interhuman. Man exists anthropologically not in his isolation, but in the completeness of the relation between man and man; what humanity is can be properly grasped only in vital reciprocity. For the proper existence of the interhuman it is necessary, as I have shown, that the semblance does not intervene to spoil the relation of personal being to personal being. It is further necessary, as I have also shown, that each one means and makes present the other in his personal being. That neither should wish to impose himself on the other is the third basic presupposition of the interhuman. These presuppositions do not include the demand that one should influence the other in his unfolding; that is, however, an element that is suited to lead to a higher stage of the interhuman.

That there resides in every man the possibility of attaining authentic human existence in the special way peculiar to him can be grasped in the Aristotelian image of entelechy, innate self-realization; but one must note that it is an entelechy of the work of creation. It would be mistaken to speak here of individuation alone. Individuation is only the indispensable personal stamp of all realization of human existence. The self as such is not ultimately the essential, but the meaning of human existence given in creation again and again fulfills itself as self. The help that men give each other in becoming a self leads the life between men to its height. The dynamic glory of the being of man is first bodily present in the relation between two men each of whom in meaning the other also means the highest to which this person is called, and serves the self-realization of this human life as one true to creation without wishing to impose on the other anything of his own realization.

GENUINE DIALOGUE

We must now summarize and clarify the marks of genuine dialogue.

In genuine dialogue the turning to the partner takes place in all truth, that is, it is a turning of the being. Every speaker "means" the partner of partners to whom he turns as this personal existence. To "mean" someone in this connection is at the same time to exercise that degree of making present which is possible to the speaker at that moment. The experiencing senses and the imagining of the real which completes the findings of the senses work together to make the other present as a whole and as a unique being, as the person that he is. But the speaker does not merely perceive the one who is present to him in this way; he receives him as his partner, and that means that he confirms this other being, so far as it is for him to confirm. The true turning of his person to the other includes this confirmation, this acceptance. Of course, such a confirmation does not mean approval; but no matter in what I am against the other, by accepting him as my partner in genuine dialogue I have affirmed him as a person.

Further, if genuine dialogue is to arise, everyone who takes part in it must bring himself into it. And that also means that he must be willing on each occasion to say what is really in his mind about the subject of the conversation. And that means further that on each occasion he makes the contribution of his spirit without reduction and without shifting his ground. Even men of great integrity are under the illusion that they are not bound to say everything "they have to say." But in the great faithfulness which is the climate of genuine dialogue, what I have to say at any one time already has in me the character of something that wishes to be uttered, and I must not keep it back, keep it in myself. It bears for me the unmistakable sign which indicates that it belongs to the common life of the word. Where the dialogical word genuinely exists, it must be given its right by keeping nothing back. To keep nothing back is the exact opposite of unreserved speech. Everything depends on the legitimacy of "what I have to say." And of course I must also be intent to raise into an inner word and then into a spoken word what I have to say at this moment but do not yet possess as speech. To speak is both nature and work, something that grows and something that is made, and where it appears dialogically, in the climate of great faithfulness, it has to fulfill ever anew the unity of the two.

Associated with this is that overcoming of semblance to which I have referred. In the atmosphere of genuine dialogue, he who is ruled by the thought of his own effect as the speaker of what he has to speak has a destructive effect. If, instead of what has to be said, I try to bring attention to my *I*, I have irrevocably miscarried what I had to say; it enters the dialogue as a failure and the dialogue is a failure. Because genuine dialogue is an ontological sphere which is constituted by the authenticity of being, every invasion of semblance must damage it.

But where the dialogue is fulfilled in its being, between partners who have turned to one another in truth, who express themselves without reserve and are free of the desire for semblance, there is brought into being a memorable common fruitfulness which is to be found nowhere else. At such times, at each such time, the word arises in a substantial way between men who have been seized in their depths and opened out by the dynamic of an elemental togetherness. The interhuman opens out what otherwise remains unopened.

This phenomenon is indeed well known in dialogue between two persons; but I have also sometimes experienced it in a dialogue in which several have taken part.

About Easter of 1914 there met a group consisting of representatives of several European nations for a three-day discussion that was intended to be preliminary to further talks. We wanted to discuss together how the catastrophe, which we all believed was imminent, could be avoided. Without our having agreed beforehand on any sort of modalities for our talk, all the presuppositions of genuine dialogue were fulfilled. From the first hour immediacy reigned between all of us, some of whom had just got to know one another; everyone spoke with an unheard-of unreserve, and clearly not a single one of the participants was in bondage to semblance. In respect of its purpose the meeting must be described as a failure (though even now in my heart it is still not a certainty that it had to be a failure); the irony of the situation was that we arranged the final discussion for the middle of August, and in the course of events the group was soon broken up. Nevertheless, in the time that followed, not one of the participants doubted that he shared in a triumph of the interhuman.

One more point must be noted. Of course it is not necessary for all who are joined in a genuine dialogue actually to speak; those who keep silent can on occasion be especially important. But each must be determined not to withdraw when the course of the conversation makes it proper for him to say what he has to say. No one, of course, can know in advance what it is that he has to say; genuine dialogue cannot be arranged beforehand. It has indeed its basic order in itself from the beginning, but nothing can be determined, the course is of the spirit, and some discover what they have to say only when they catch the call of the spirit.

But it is also a matter of course that all the participants, without exception, must be of such nature that they are capable of satisfying the presuppositions of genuine dialogue and are ready to do so. The genuineness of the dialogue is called in question as soon as even a small number of those present are felt by themselves and by the others as not being expected to take any active part. Such a state of affairs can lead to very serious problems.

I had a friend whom I account one of the most considerable men of our age. He was a master of conversation, and he loved it: his genuineness as a speaker was evident. But once it happened that he was sitting with two friends and with the three wives, and a conversation arose in which by its nature the women were clearly not joining, although their presence in fact had a great influence. The conversation among the men soon developed into a duel between two of them (I was the third). The other "duelist," also a friend of mine, was of a noble nature; he too was a man of true conversation, but given more to objective fairness than to the play of the intellect, and a stranger to any controversy. The friend whom I have called a master of conversation did not speak with his usual composure and strength, but he scintillated, he fought, he triumphed. The dialogue was destroyed.

REVIEW QUESTIONS

1. What distinction does Buber make between the social and the interhuman?
2. What feature of interpersonal contact does Buber say can characterize even "a boxing match"?

3. What does Buber mean when he says that "it is basically erroneous to try to understand the interhuman phenomena as psychological"?
4. Does Buber say that a person can practice "being" consistently, all the time? Explain.
5. Paraphrase the last sentence in the first paragraph under the heading "Personal Making Present." What is Buber challenging readers to do here?
6. Identify three possible things that a person who is imposing could impose on his or her conversational partner. In other words, what is (are) imposed when a person is imposing? What is unfolded when a person is unfolding?
7. What does Buber mean when he says that "to keep nothing back is the exact opposite of unreserved speech"?

PROBES

1. What does it mean to you when Buber says that social contacts don't involve an existential relation, but that interhuman contacts do?
2. For Buber, does "being" mean total honesty? Is "seeming" lying?
3. What circumstances make it difficult for you to "be"? How can you best help others to "be" instead of "seem"?
4. How do Buber's comments about the way we perceive others relate to the discussion of person perception in Chapter 5?
5. It sounds as if Buber is saying that science *cannot* be used to study human life. Is he saying that? Do you agree with him? Why or why not?
6. How is Buber's discussion of "imagining the real" related to what Stewart, Zediker, and Witteborn (Chapter 5) say about empathy?
7. Which teacher that you've had has functioned most as an "imposer"? Which teacher has been most consistently an "unfolder"?
8. What does "personal making present" mean to you? What do you need to do in order to perceive someone that way?
9. Have you ever experienced a silent "dialogue" of the kind Buber mentions here? What happened?

NOTES

1. You might also be interested in other things written by or about Buber. For starters I recommend Aubrey Hodes, *Martin Buber: An Intimate Portrait* (New York: Viking Press, 1971), or Hilary Evans Bender, *Monarch Notes: The Philosophy of Martin Buber* (New York: Monarch, 1974). Maurice Friedman has written the definitive Buber biography, and I'd especially recommend the third volume, *Martin Buber's Life and Work: The Later Years, 1945–1965* (New York: Dutton, 1983). Buber's most important and influential book is *I and Thou*, trans. Walter Kaufmann (New York: Scribner, 1970).

2. Buber's translators always point out that this "thou" is not the religious term of formal address. It is a translation of the German *Du*, the familiar form of the pronoun "you." As Walter Kaufmann, one of Buber's translators, explains, "German lovers say *Du* to one another and so do friends. Du is spontaneous and unpretentious, remote from formality, pomp, and dignity."

Ideas are clean. They soar in the serene supernal. I can take them out and look at them, they fit in books, they lead me down that narrow way. And in the morning they are there. Ideas are straight—
But the world is round, and a
messy mortal is my friend.
Come walk with me in the mud....

—*Hugh Prather*

Photo Credits

Index

abuse
    psychological, 337–338
acceptance
    of self, and identity, 97–99
accommodation, 135
accountability
    moral, 89
accountability shuffle, 52, 54
accountable self, 89
accounts, 137–138
accusations
    as defensive communication, 354
    as hurtful message, 335
acquired traits, 458
activity, language as, 106–108
addressability/addressivity, 32, 36
advice, as hurtful message, 335
affect, positive and intimacy, 275, 279, 281
affection
    emotions related to, 278, 279
    interpersonal, 279
Afifi, Walid A., 275–289
African Americans
    families, 235–236, 239
*After Terror: Promoting Dialogue among
    Civilizations* (Sacks), 506
aggression. *See also* violence
    verbal aggression, 336–337,
        374–381
Alexander, F., 43
alliance
    friendship and reliable, 258
all-or-nothing syndrome, 94–95
Allport, Gordon, 181
"always" in conversations, 227–228
Americans with Disabilities Act (ADA), 472
and, as marker and trigger, 141–143
Andersen, Peter A., 275–289

Anderson, Chris, 316
Anderson, David A., 465–470
anger
    facial expression and, 116
anxiety
    stereotyping and, 171
    tension and, 487
argumentativeness, 375–376
arguments. *See* conflict
Argyris, Chris, 225
Aristotle, 104–105
ascribed, identities as, 82
Ashvagosha, 190
assertiveness, 489–490
assumptions, 14, 23
attentive silence, 197
attributions
    attributional errors, 175–176
    in person perception, 171–172
Auden, W. H., 215
Autobiographical Fragments
    (Buber), 488
autoimmune diseases, 46
avowed, identities as, 82

back region of social performance, 87
Barrett, Martha, 241
Barrett, William, 22
Bavelas, Janet, 115
Baxter, Leslie, 487
behavior
    altering degenerative spiral and,
        405–406
    being and seeming, 519–521
belonging
    friendship and, 258
benevolence
    as motive for lying, 330, 331

531

betrayal
    consequences of, 334
    defined, 333
    gender and, 334
bias
    lie bias, 332
    truth bias, 332
blame
    accountability shuffle, 54
blaming the victim, 459–460
blended families, 237
blood pressure
    speech and changes in, 8
body movement
    couple types and, 122
    as nonverbal communication, 122–123
    posture, 122–123
both/and power, 363–364
Braithwaite, Charles, 470–483
Braithwaite, Dawn, 182, 470–483
break-up of relationships, 415–421
    degenerative spirals and, 404
    phases of, 416–419
    repair of relationship, 419–421
Brown v. *Board of Education*, 363
Buber, Martin, 8, 32, 487, 488, 490–491, 513–529
Burdette, Marsha Parsons, 333
Burke, Kenneth, 131, 181
Buss, David, 447

Campbell, Susan M., 423–427
cardiovascular disease
    interpersonal relationships and, 45–46
Carnegie, Dale, 262
categorizing, 457–458
causal attribution, 460
cause–effect thinking, 21–22
certainty
    as defensive communication, 357–358
Chasin, Laura, 495–505
Chekhov, Anton, 521
Cherry Orchard, The (Chekhov), 521
children
    degenerative spirals and, 404–405
    empathic listening and, 194
    of gay and lesbian parents, 240–241
    social skill deficits, 43–44
    suicidal behavior, 45
choice
    active and automatic, 23–24
    in communication, 17, 23–24
    ethical standards and commitment, 24
    family and, 238
    responses and, 80–81
clarifying question, 197
clarity, guidelines for, 226–228
cloning, uniqueness and, 32–33

closed question, 197
closed relationships, 210–211
closeness
    gender and, 293–294
    paradoxes and conundrums of, 408, 410
close relationship, 276
clothing
    as nonverbal cue for identification, 154
co-constructing selves, 73
Cody, Michael, 330
cognitive abilities
    social media and, 62–63, 66–67
cognitive processes, 170–174
cognitive schemata, 168–170
    person prototypes, 168–169
    scripts, 169–170
collaboration in communication, 22–23, 31
collectivism/collectivist societies, 441–452
    communication in, 445–446
    defined, 441
    face, 446
    family in, 441, 442–448
    future of, 451–452
    key differences from individualism, 448, 449
    marriage in, 447
    measuring, 441–442
    ranking of various countries, 443
    school and, 448–450
    shame and, 446
collusion, 330
comfort
    indirect ways of communicating, 282–283
    intimacy and communicating, 282–285
    nonverbal ways of communicating,
        283–284
command, as speech act, 106–107
communal identity, 78, 80
communication
    in collectivist and individualist societies,
        445–446
    complementary, 402
    continuum of, 31–33
    cultural communication of persons with
        disabilities, 470–481
    defensive, 352–358
    defined, 16–17
    diversity and clarifying miscommunication,
        462–463
    features of, 17–18
    high-context, 445–446
    intercultural, 473
    low-context, 445–446
    person centered, 171
    position centered, 171
    quality of, and quality of life, 6–9
    symmetrical, 402
communication agreement, 502

communication model
   social media and changes in, 64–66
communication skills
   power and, 366, 367–368
communication spirals, 399–412
   context for, 401
   degenerative spirals, 403–408
   elements of, 402
   generative, 402–403
   paradoxes and conundrums, 408–412
communication walls
   betrayal, 333–335
   deception, 329–333
   defensive communication, 352–358
   hurtful messages, 335–336, 340–349
   power and structure of conflict, 359–371
   verbal aggression, 336–338, 374–381
   violence, 338–339
communicator
   in communication model, 64
compadres/comadres, 446
competence
   identity and question of, 91, 93
complementary communication, 402
complexify your identity, 96–97
compliment, as speech act, 106–107
concentration, mindfulness and, 188
conclusions
   presented as truth, 226–227
conflict
   agreement and, 433–434
   arenas for, 393
   break-up of relationship, 415–423
   cycle of, 396
   definitions of, 391–392
   degenerative spirals, 403–408
   destructive conflict, 393–395
   different views, hearing, 423–427
   flexibility, 392
   fostering presence in, 427
   gay and lesbian couples, 309
   goals and, 391
   interaction and, 386–397
   as interactive behavior, 396–397
   interdependence of parties and, 393
   mixture of incentives, 392
   paradoxes and conundrums, 408–412
   to peace, 511–512
   perspective and, 423–427
   potential of, 387–391
   power as structure of, 359–372
   productive conflict, 393–395
   religion as primary source of, 508–510
   resolving issues, 428–437
   resurrecting old issues, 430–431
   rules for ruining discussion, 432–433
   steps in preparing to argue, 434–436

   terrain of relationships and, 431–432
   trust and, 426
   unfinished arguments, accumulation of,
      429–430
   verbal aggression, 374–381
   Women's Hotline case, 388–391
confrontation
   in collectivist and individualist societies,
      443–444
connection
   responses and, 80–81
connection and control, 249–250
Contact Quotient (CQ), 5–6
control
   of communication, 22–24
   connection and, 249–250
   deception and, 332
   defensive communication and, 355
   family and, 249–251
   resource control and power, 366–367
control touch, 121
conundrums of relationships, 408–412
convergence, 135
conversational hypertext, 132–133
conversations, 17. *See also* dialogue
   "always" and "never" in, 227–228
   clarity guidelines, 226–228
   conclusions presented as truth, 226–227
   difficult, and identities, 91–99
   don't rely on subtext, 223–225
   easing in, 225
   fierce, 52–60
   identities and, 74–77
   Me-Me And, 225–226
   as most influential communication event,
      28–29
   ordinary communication, 29
   prayer as, 510
   as relationship, 56–57
   say what you mean, 223–225
   self-sabotage, 221
   speak heart of matter, 222–226
   starting with Third Story, 218, 219–220
Coontz, Stephanie, 239
Coser, Lewis, 394
couples
   gay and lesbian, 308
   types of, and movement, 122
courage, 508
crackberry syndrome, 317
criticism, by family, 246–247
cues
   defined, 164
   primarily nonverbal cues, 116–123
   primarily verbal cues, 106–108
   selecting, organizing, and inferring, 164–168
cultural conditioning, 458

culture, 17. *See also* diversity
  collectivism, 441–452
  communication and, 24–26
  cultural communication of persons with
    disabilities, 470–481
  culture clash, 460
  defined, 25
  eye contact and, 117, 118, 195
  facial expressions and, 116
  God and Devil terms, 131
  grief and, 259
  individualism, 441–452
  perception and, 166–167
  power and, 364
  scripts and, 169–170
  touch, 120
  verbal aggression, 336–337
  verbal fighting, 364
culture clash, 460
Czikszentmihalyi, Mihaly, 191

dating
  culture and communication, 25
  social media and, 319–321
  violence in, 44
debate
  dialogue and, 501
deception, 329–333
  compared to betrayal, 333
  consequences of, 331–333
  motives for, 330–331
deep interactions
  intimacy and, 280
defensive communication, 352–358
  certainty and provisionalism, 357–358
  control and problem orientation, 355
  defined, 353
  evaluation and description, 354
  neutrality and empathy, 356–357
  significance of, 353
  strategy and spontaneity, 355–356
  superiority and equality, 357
degenerative spirals, 403–408
denial
  vulnerable identity and, 94–95
description speech, 354
destructive conflict, 393–395
Devil terms, 131
dialogic listening, 192–194, 200–206
  main obstacle to, 200–201
  metaphors, running with, 203–204
  mutual meanings, 201–206
  nexting and, 202–206
  "our" focus, 202
  paraphrase-plus, 202–203
dialogue. *See also* conversations
  being and seeming, 515, 519–521
  communication agreement, 502

conditions for, 500, 502
debate and, 501
defined, 487
disclosure and, 487
fostering across divides, 495–505
genuine, 525–527
holding my own ground, 489–490
imposition and unfolding, 523–525
invitation to, 502
letting the Other happen to me, 488–489
meanings of, 498–499
openness of, 504–505
participants in, 499
perceptions and, 515–516, 522–523
personal making present, 521–523
primary tension of, 488–494
privacy and, 487
questions for, 502–505
readiness for, 500
reasons for, 500
red-blue divide and, 500–505
requirements for, 499
role in public life, 497–498
tension in, 485–494
*Difficult Conversations: How to Discuss
    What Matters Most* (Stone, Patton,
    and Heen), 218
directives
  as hurtful message, 335
disabled persons
  challenges for disabled communicators,
    473–478
  cultural communication of, 470–481
  disability defined vs. handicap, 473–474
  labeled as disabled, 182
  redefining self in disabled culture, 476–480
  relationship challenges, 474–476
  stigma isolation, recognition, and
    incorporation, 477–478
disclosure
  tension in dialogue and, 487
discrimination
  blaming the victim, 459–460
  defined, 459
disgust
  facial expression, 116
disordered personal relationships, 43–48
divergence, 135
diversity. *See also* culture
  blaming the victim, 459–460
  clarifying miscommunications, 462–463
  collectivist and individualistic societies,
    439–452
  cultural communication of persons with
    disabilities, 470–481
  culture clash, 460
  difficulties with, 457–460
  fostering dialogue across divides, 495–505

gracism, 466–469
    prejudice and, 457–459
    recognizing and valuing, 461–462
    self-acceptance and, 455–457
divorce
    families of, 237
    homicide and, 45
    immune system and, 46
    risky health practices and, 47
    suicide and, 45
Divorce American Style, 248
dominance, posture and, 122
drug/alcohol abuse
    identities and, 81–82
Duck, Steve, 85–90, 127–139, 131, 150–156, 239, 254–266, 415–423
Durkheim, Émile, 45
dyadic phase of relationship break-up, 417, 418

easing in, 225
Easwaran, Eknath, 189
E-books, 68
education
    in individualistic and collectivist societies, 448–450
    unfolding and, 524–525
effects
    in communication model, 64–66
egoism
    as motive for lying, 330–331
either/or power, 361–363
embarrassment
    performance self and, 88–89
emotions
    eye behavior and, 117
    facial expression and, 116
    friends and emotional integration, 259–260
    gender differences in communicating, 167–168
    intimacy and, 278
    nonverbal communication to transmit, 154
    as unmeasurable, 34
empathy
    defensive communication and, 356–357
    facial expression and, 357
emphatic listening, 192–199
    attentive silence, 197
    clarifying question, 197
    encouraging skills, 196–198
    focusing skills, 195–196
    mirroring, 196–197
    paraphrasing, 198
    reflecting skills, 198–199
encouraging skills, 196–198
English language
    gender differences and, 110–111
    ongoing processes and, 110

entertainment factor
    perception, 174–175
equality
    defensive communication and, 357
essential function of talk, 133–134
ethical standards
    choice in communication, 24
ethnic identity, 456
ethnicity
    interracial marriages, 295–296
    relational development and, 296–298
ethnocentrism, 458
evaluation
    as defensive communication, 354
    as hurtful message, 335
everyday talk
    accounts, 137–138
    "and," 141–143
    conversational hypertext and hyperlinks, 132–133
    essential functions of, 133–134
    high code, 134–135
    indexical function of, 132
    instrumental function, 132
    low code, 134–135
    narration, 135–138
    "next," 143–145
    in relationships, 131–138
    ways of speaking, 134–135
exaggeration, vulnerable identity and, 95
expertise, power and, 366, 368
exploitation, as motive for lying, 330, 331
expression
    of desire, as hurtful message, 335
    entitled to, 220–222
    guidelines for clarity, 226–228
    speak heart of matter, 222–226
extended family, 441
eye contact
    as approach behavior, 117
    culture and, 117, 118, 195
    emphatic listening and, 195
    function of, 117
    as mixed cue, 113–114
    as nonverbal communication, 116–118

face
    in collectivist societies, 446
Facebook, 66
facework, 87
facial expression
    communicating comfort and support, 283
    culture and, 116
    empathy and, 357
    as nonverbal communication, 116
    relational messages and, 155
    with words as mixed cue, 113–114
false consensus bias, 458

Families We Choose (Weston), 238
family, 234–253
    changing views, 239–240
    choices and, 238, 239
    in collectivist societies, 441, 442–448
    connection and, 249–251
    control and, 249–251
    criticism by, 246–247
    description of, 235–242
    different views of, 235–238
    diversity of forms, 240–241
    divorced and blended families, 237
    extended, 441
    gay and lesbian, 236, 240–241
    hurtful messages and, 336, 348
    identities and, 81–82
    immune system malfunction, 46
    improving communication, 238–242
    in individualist societies, 441, 442–448
    interracial, 236–237
    learning from diversity, 241–242
    metamessages in talk, 243–253
    nuclear, 441
    paradox of, 252–253
    risky health practices, 47–48
    single-parent families, 239–240
    social skill development, 43–44
    stepfamilies, 237
    trends in families, 239–240
    without children, 237–238
fault-blame thinking
    continuous and collaborative
        communication, 22–23
    identification of, 20–21
    nexting and, 144–145
favoritism, 467
fear in facial expression, 116
feedback, vulnerable identity and, 95
fierce conversations, 52–60
    defined, 53, 57–58
Finzel, Ben, 146–150
Fisher, Walter, 136
Flow (Czikszentmihalyi), 191
focusing skills
    in emphatic listening, 195–196
    "our" focus, 202
Folger, Joseph P., 386–398
forgiveness, 508
fragmentation
    social media and, 316
Franklin, John Hope, 180
freedom
    paradoxes and conundrums of, 408
Freud, Sigmund, 78
friends/friendship, 254–266
    assistance and support from, 261–262
    belonging and, 258

features of, 257
losing a friend, 261, 264
nature of, 257–258
number of, 256–257
opportunities for communication about self,
    260–261
personality support, 263–264
process of friendship, 255–257
provisions of, 258–264
reassurance of worth, 262
reliable alliance, 258
rules of, 257
stability and, 259–260
front region of social performance, 87
fundamental attributional error, 175–176

Gadamer, Hans-Georg, 488–489
gays and lesbians
    conflict, 309
    factors predicting relationship quality,
        311–312
    family, 236, 240–241
    household labor, 308–309
    number of couples, 308
    perceived support of relationship, 310
    satisfaction in relationship, 310
    stability, 310–311
gaze, as nonverbal communication,
    116–118
gender/gender differences
    betrayal and, 334
    closeness and, 293–294
    communicating emotions, 167–168
    communication patterns, 111
    English language and, 110–111
    eye gaze and, 117
    intimacy and, 292–293
    perception and, 167–168
    power and, 364, 368
    relational development, 293–295,
        299–302
    supportiveness and, 292–293
    territory, 118
    use of term, 292
gender identity, 456
Generation Yers, 322–323
generative spirals, 402–403
genuine dialogue, 516, 525–527
gestures
    interactive, 115
    as nonverbal communication, 122–123
    with words as mixed cue, 114–115
Gibb, Jack R., 352–359
gift reciprocity, 261
globalization
    need for effective communication and, 455
    social media and, 67–68

goals
    conflict and, 391–392
    degenerative spirals and, 406
    self-disclosure and identifying, 213
God terms, 131
Goffman, Erving, 87, 215
goodness
    identity and question of, 91, 93
gracism, 466–469
grave dressing phase of relationship break-up, 417, 418
Gray, John, 111
greeting
    nonverbal rules to begin/end, 153
    as speech act, 106–107
Gross, Jane, 240
grounding your identity, 95–99
group
    in collectivist society, 444
Guerrero, Laura K., 275–289
guilt, in individualist societies, 446
Gutenberg Galaxy, The (McLuhan), 66

Hadjiwibowo, Raden Mas, 445
Haggerty, R. J., 46
Hall, Edward, 119, 445
handicap
    compared to disability, 473–474
happiness
    facial expression, 116
    relationships and, 410
health
    cardiovascular disease, 45–46
    immune system malfunctions, 46–47
    personal relationships and, 42–48
    risky health practices, 47–48
Heen, Sheila, 91–99, 218–230
Herzig, Maggie, 495–505
high code, 134–135
high-context communication, 445–446
Ho, David Yau-Fai, 446
Hocker, Joyce L., 359–374
Hofstede, Geert, 439–453
Hofstede, Gert Jan, 439–453
holding my own ground, 489–490
homicide, 45
horizontal media, 69
household labor
    gay and lesbian couples, 308–309
How to Win Friends and Influence People (Carnegie), 262
human contact, 9–10
hurtful messages, 340–351
    examination of, 343–344
    factors in level hurt from, 336, 345–347
    in family context, 336, 348
    impact of, 336, 347–348

    types of, 335–336
    typology of, 344
Hyde, Bruce, 200

I and Thou (Buber), 513
ideas
    conveyance of, 18–20
    perception of message and, 20
identities, 17
    accept yourself, 97–99
    accountable self and, 89
    all-or-nothing syndrome, 94–95
    audience and, 87–88
    avowed and ascribed, 82
    as bounded individual, 78
    changes in, 26–27, 80
    communal, 80
    communicating, 28
    complexify your identity, 96–97
    constructing, 73–83
    conversations and, 74–77
    core identity questions, 91, 93
    current views of, 77–79
    defined, 77
    denial and, 94–95
    difficult conversations and, 91–99
    embarrassment and predicaments, 88–89
    exaggeration and, 95
    family and, 81–82
    feedback and, 95
    grounding your identity, 95–99
    identify identity issues, 95–96
    identity quake, 93–94
    as multidimensional, 80
    negotiating, 27, 77
    older views of, 77–79
    past/present relationships and, 81–82
    performative self, 87–88
    personal, 80
    relational, 80
    responders, selves as, 81, 80
    self-acceptance and, 456
    self-schemas, 456–457
    as social or communal, 78–79
    transacted, 86, 89–90
identity message, 19, 27–28
I-It, 514
illusionary correlation, 458
Illusion of Technique, The (Barrett), 22
immediacy
    in everyday talk, 134
immediacy behaviors, 279
immune system
    interpersonal relationships and, 46–47
impersonal communication
    continuum of communication, 31–32

implicit personality theory, 170–171
  stereotypes and, 181–182
imposition, 523–525
impression formation, 170–171
impression management, 215
independent couples, 122
indexical function of talk, 128, 132
individualism/individualistic societies,
    441–452
  communication in, 445–446
  defined, 441
  family in, 441, 442–448
  future of, 451–452
  guilt and, 446
  key differences from collectivism, 448, 449
  marriage, 447
  measuring, 441–442
  ranking of various countries, 443
  school and, 448–450
inferring, in perception, 166–168
informational indigestion, 316
information disclosure
  as hurtful message, 335
ingratiation, 216
inhaling-exhaling, 11
  as metaphor for communicating, 158
  perception and, 162–178
inherited traits, 457–458
insider view
  paradoxes and conundrums of, 408–410
instrumental function of talk, 132
intentions
  complexity of, and identity, 98
interactions
  regulated by nonverbal communication, 153
  repeated interactions and intimacy, 281
interactive gestures, 115
intercultural communication, 473
interhumanity, 513–529
  being and seeming, duality of, 519–521
  genuine dialogue, 525–527
  imposition and, 523–525
  personal making present, 521–523
  social phenomena and, 517–519
  unfolding, 523–525
International Listening Association, 187
Internet. See also social media
  communication model changes, 65–66
interpersonal affection, 279
interpersonal communication, 31–37
  addressability, 36
  continuum of communication, 31–32
  defined, 32, 36–37
  features of the personal, 32–36
  reflection, 35–36
  response and, 34–35
  uniqueness and, 32–33
  unmeasurable elements, 33–34

interpersonal linkages
  power and, 366, 367
interpersonal warmth, 278
interracial families/marriages, 236–237, 295–302
interrogating questions
  as hurtful message, 335
intimacy
  comfort and social support, 282–285
  comfort with silence, 280
  defined, 277
  depth and, 280
  emotions and thoughts of, 278–279
  experiencing, 278–279
  expressing, 279–282
  eye gaze and, 117
  gender and, 292–293
  hurtful messages and, 347
  immediacy behaviors, 279
  in interethnic relations, 297–298
  interpersonal affection, 279
  listening and understanding, 281–282
  need for, 257
  paradoxes and conundrums of, 410
  person-centered messages, 284–285
  positive affect, 281
  positive involvement behaviors, 279
  relationships and risk, 410
  self-disclosure and, 280
  vs. sexual involvement, 277
  time and repeated interactions, 281
  uniqueness and, 279–280
intimate distance, 119
intrapsychic phase of relationship break-up,
    416–418
invitation, as speech act, 107
Itard, Jean-Marc Gaspard, 10
I-Thou relationship, 514

Janis, Irving, 394
Johnson, David W., 209–218, 453–465
jokes
  as hurtful message, 335–336
Jones, Stan, 121
Jones, Walter, 333
joy, 278

Kaiser, Robert, 55
Kant, Immanuel, 525
Kaplan, Abraham, 200
kinesics, 122
Knapp, Mark, 112, 121
Kurdek, Lawrence, 306–314

labels, relationships and, 411–412
language
  as activity, 106–108
  holiness of, 510
  interconnections with nonverbal
    communications, 152

perception and, 109–111
primarily verbal cues, 101, 116–123
Sapir-Whorf hypothesis, 109
as soup, 108–111
speech acts, 106–108
as system of symbols, 104–106
triangle of meaning, 105–106
Language as Symbolic Action (Burke), 181
Lasswell, Harold, 64, 65
Lee, Spike, 179–180
Leeds-Hurwitz, Wendy, 102
Leppo, Michael, 187
lesbians. *See* gays and lesbians
letting the Other happen to me, 488–489
LGBT communications
  words/phrases to avoid, 147–149
lie bias, 332
lies
  as hurtful message, 335–336
  reasons for, 330–331
life, quality of, 6–9
listening
  blood pressure and, 8
  dialogic, 192–194, 200–206
  emphatic, 192–199
  good listener, defined, 187
  intimacy and, 281–282
  mindful listening, 185–192
  in the moment, 188–192
Logan, Carole, 36, 101–127
loneliness
  degenerative spiral and, 404
  provisions of friendship and, 258,
    259, 262
Long Tail, The (Anderson), 316
love
  defined, 278
  identity and question of, 91, 93
low code, 134–135
low-context communication, 445–446
loyalty
  in collectivist society, 444
Lucas, Michelle, 187
Lynch, James J., 7–8

malevolence
  as motive for lying, 330, 331
Mao Zedong, 450
Marcour, Christoph, 319
marker
  and as, 141–143
  next as, 143–145
marriage
  in collectivist societies, 447
  in individualistic societies, 447
  interracial marriages, 236–237
  movement and gesture of couples, 122
  paradoxes and conundrums of, 410

Mars and Venus in Love (Gray), 111
Maslow, Abraham, 450
McDowell, Diane, 180
McGurl, Mark, 180
McLuhan, Marshall, 66
McMahan, David T., 85–90, 127–139,
    150–156
McNeill, David, 114–115
Mead, George Herbert, 79, 87
meaning, 17
  mutual, 201–206
  as outcome of selecting, organizing, and
    inferring, 166
  process of making, 18–23
  triangle of, 105–106
media. *See also* social media
  horizontal, 69
  vertical, 69
media literacy, 68
Medium Is the Massage, The (McLuhan), 66
Mehrabian, Albert, 117
Me-Me And, 225–226
Men Are from Mars, Women Are from Venus
    (Gray), 111
message
  in communication model, 64–66
  defined, 247–248
  hurtful, 335–336, 340–351
  as hurtful, 247–249
  match or fit of, 20
  metamessages, 245–253
  person-centered, 284–285
metacommunication, 248–249
  altering degenerative spiral, 406–407
  power and, 371
metamessages, 243–253
metaphor
  running with, 203–204
  soup metaphor for language, 108–111
Meyer, R. J., 46
mindful listening, 185–192
Miracle of Mindfulness, The (Thich Nhat Hanh), 189
mirroring
  as encouraging skill, 196–197
miscommunications
  diversity and clarifying, 462–463
mistakes, admitting, 97–98
mixed cues, 111–115
  in continuum, 103–104
  defined, 101
  facial expression and words, 113–114
  gestures and words, 114–115
  silence, 112–113
  voice, 112
monologue, 487
Montgomery, Barbara, 487
moral accountability, 89
moral courage, 508

movement
  as nonverbal communication, 122–123
multidimensionality of identities, 80
mutual meanings, 201–206

narration, 135–138
Nature of Prejudice, The (Allport), 181
negotiation, of identities, 77
network factors
  gender and relational development, 294–295
  in interethnic relations, 298
neutrality, as defensive communication, 356–357
"never" in conversations, 227–228
nexting, 18
  applying skill of, 30
  defined, 29–30
  dialogic listening and, 202–206
  fault-blame thinking, 144–145
  next as marker and trigger, 143–145
Nichols, Ralph G., 187
nonverbal communication
  body movement and gestures, 122–123
  of comfort and support, 283
  disabled persons and, 475
  emphatic listening and, 199
  eye contact and gaze, 116–118
  facial expression, 116
  functions of, 150–155
  to identify specific individuals, 154
  interconnections with verbal
    communication, 152
  intimacy expression, 279
  primarily nonverbal cues, 101, 116–123
  proximity or space, 118–120
  to regulate interactions, 152–153
  for relational meaning and understanding, 155
  silence, 112–113
  touch, 120–121
  to transmit emotional information, 154
nonverbal cues, primarily, 116–123
  body movement and gestures, 122–123
  in continuum, 103–104
  defined, 101
  eye contact and gaze, 116–118
  facial expression, 115
  proximity or space, 118–120
  touch, 120–121
nonverbal meaning-making, 21–22
nuclear family, 441

obesity
  attributional error and, 175–176
  implicit personality theory and, 181–182
offer, as speech act, 106–107
Ogden, C. K., 105
O'Hair, Dan, 330
O'Keefe, Barbara, 489

one-pointedness, 190
openness. *See also* self-disclosure
  defined, 210
  in dialogue, 504–505
  factors in, 211
  in relationships, 210
open questions, 197
open relationships, 210–211
opinions
  in collectivist and individualist societies, 444
ordinary communication, 29
organizing, in perception, 166
otherness of the Other, 488
Ottaway, David, 55
"our" focus, 202
outsider view
  paradoxes and conundrums of, 408–410
overload, perception and, 174

paradox
  of family, 252–253
  of relationships, 408–412
paralinguistics, 112
paraphrase-plus, 202–203
paraphrasing, 198
  benefit of, 228–229
  paraphrase-plus, 202–203
parents. *See* family
Parks, Malcolm, 42–52, 289–306
passion, 278
Patterson, Charlotte, 240–241
Patton, Bruce, 91–99, 218–230
peace, from conflict to, 511–512
Pearson, Judy, 118
perception, 162–178
  attribution, 171–172
  attributional errors, 175–176
  cognitive processes, 170–174
  cognitive schemata, 168–170
  cue in, 164
  defined, 163
  dialogue and, 515–516, 522–523
  entertainment factor, 174–175
  fast thinking and, 174
  gender and, 167–168
  ideas and, 20
  impression formation, 170–171
  inferring, 166–168
  as interpretive process, 163–168
  language and, 109–111
  organizing, 166
  overload, avoiding, 174
  person prototypes, 168–169
  problems of, 174–176
  scripts, 169–170
  selecting and, 164–165
  snap judgments, 175

stereotyping, 172–173
worldviews and, 167
performative self, 87–88
persistence
power of, 369–370
the personal, 32–36
personal distance, 119
personal identity, 80
personality
betrayal and, 334
friends and support for, 263–264
implicit personality theory, 170–171, 181–182
person centered communication, 171
person-centered messages, 284–285
person perception
attribution, 171–172
implicit personality theory, 170–171
person prototypes, 168–169
perspectives, conflict and, 424–427
philosophy, 14
philotimos, 446
physical courage, 508
physical violence, 338–339
Pinel, Philippe, 10
pitch, 112
Pond, K., 131
Poole, Marshall Scott, 386–398
position centered communication, 171
positive affect touch, 121
positive involvement behaviors, 279
posture
aiming, in emphatic listening, 195
dominance and submission, 122
forward leaning, 122–123
Powell, John, 8
power, 359–372
both/and power, 363–364
communication skills, 366, 367–368
culture and, 364
defined, 360–361
in distressed systems, 362–363
in effective systems, 363–364
either/or power, 361–363
expertise and, 366, 368
gender and, 364
individual power currencies, 365–368
interpersonal linkages, 366, 367
low-power positions, strategies of, 369–370
metacommunication and, 371
orientations to, 361–364
of persistence, 369–370
relational theory of, 364–365
relationships and, 266–273
resource control, 366–367
RICE acronym and, 365–368
Prather, Gayle, 428–437
Prather, Hugh, 428–437, 529

prayer, conversation as, 510
predicaments, performance self and, 88–89
prejudice
blaming the victim, 459–460
defined, 458
discrimination and, 459
diversity and, 457–459
ethnocentrism, 458
reducing, 459
stereotypes and, 458
primarily nonverbal cues, 116–123
body movement and gestures, 122–123
in continuum, 103–104
defined, 101
eye contact and gaze, 116–118
facial expression, 115
proximity or space, 118–120
touch, 120–121
primarily verbal cues, 104–111
in continuum, 103–104
defined, 101
language and perception, 109–111
language as activity, 106–108
language as soup, 108–111
language as system of symbols, 104–106
privacy
deception and, 332
tension in dialogue and, 487
problem orientation and defensive
communication, 355
productive conflict, 393–395
promise, as speech act, 106–107
provisionalism
defensive communication and, 357–358
proxemics, 118
proximity
close proximity communicating support, 283
intimate distance, 119
as nonverbal communication, 118–120
personal distance, 119
public distance, 120
social distance, 119–120
territory, 118
pseudoquestions, 197
psychological abuse, 337–338
psychosomatic disease, 43
Psychosomatic Medicine (Alexander), 43
public distance, 120
public life
role of dialogue in, 497–498

Qualman, Erik, 314–324
Quayle, Dan, 238, 239, 240
questions
clarifying question, 197
closed, 197
for dialogue, 502–505

questions—*Cont.*
open, 197
pseudoquestions, 197

race. *See* culture; ethnicity
racism, 459
defined, 466
gracism and, 466–469
Reaching Out: Interpersonal Effectiveness and Self-Actualization, 453
Reaching Out: Interpersonal Effectiveness and Self-Actualization (Johnson), 209
receiver, in communication model, 64–66
reciprocity, intimacy and, 279
reflection
emphatic listening and, 198–199
interpersonal communication, 35–36
regress, as motive for lying, 330, 331
regulators, 153
relational development
ethnicity and, 297–298
gender, 293–295, 299–302
network factors, 293–295, 298
sex differences, 293–295
relational identity, 80
relational theory of power, 364–365
relationship message, 19
relationshipping, 255–257
relationships. *See also* family; friends/friendship
break-up of, 415–423
change and, 412
close, 276
continuum of open to closed, 210–211
conunudrums, 408–412
conversation as, 56–57
disabled persons, challenges of, 474–476
everyday talk in, 131–138
failure to express self keeps you out of, 221–222
general norms and, 412
health and, 42–48
hurtful messages about, 345–346
identities and, 81–82
individual growth and, 411
insider view of, 408–410
interhuman vs. social relationships, 514–515, 517–519
labels in, 411–412
learning about, 412
natural forces on, 410
nonverbal communication as regulator, 155
openness in, 210
outsider view of, 408–410
paradoxes, 408–412
power and, 266–273
problems, dealing with, 416–420
redevelopment of, 419–421
self-disclosure and impact on, 212–213
self in, 410–411

unhappiness and, 410
words, and connotation of, 129–130
religion
conversation as prayer, 510
gracism, 466–469
language, holiness of, 510
peace, from conflict to, 511–512
as primary source of conflict, 508–510
request, as speech act, 106–107
resource control, power and, 366–367
responders, selves as, 80–81
response, interpersonal communication and, 34–35
responsibility, 23
rheumatoid arthritis, 46–47
RICE acronym, 365–368
Richards, I. A., 105
Richman, Phyllis, 247
risk
health practices and, 47–48
intimacy in relationships and, 410
self-disclosure and, 411
rituals, intimacy and, 281
Rogers, Carl, 194

Sacks, Jonathan, 506–512
sadness, facial expression and, 116
Sampson, Edward, 79
Sapir, Edward, 109
Sapir-Whorf hypothesis, 109
satisfaction
gay and lesbian couples, 310
Saussure, Ferdinand de, 102
schematas, 33
cognitive, 168–170
school
in individualistic and collectivist societies, 448–450
Scott, Susan, 29, 52–60
Scowcroft, Brent, 55
scripts, 169–170
seeming, and being, 519–521
selecting, in perception, 164–165
self
redefining self in disabled culture, 476–480
in relationships, 410–411
self-acceptance
benefits of, 457
diversity and, 455–457
self-actualization, 450–451
self-disclosure
appropriateness of, 214–215
benefits of, 213–214
characteristics of effective, 211–212
defined, 211
impact of, on relationships, 212–213
intimacy and, 280
self-presentation and, 215–217
self-presentation, 215–217

self-promotion, 216–217
self-sabotage
    in difficult conversations, 221
self-schema, 456–457
self-serving attributions, 460
self-verification, 217
selves. *See* identities
sender
    in communication model, 64–66
Senge, Peter, 29
separate couples, 122
sex
    versus intimate encounters, 277
    use of term, 292
sexism, 459
Shack, The (Young), 266–273
Shafir, Rebecca Z., 185–192
Shakespeare, William, 215
shame
    in collectivist societies, 446
Shotter, John, 26, 36
silence
    attentive silence, 197
    in collectivist societies, 445
    comfort with, and intimacy, 280
    as mixed cue, 112–113
    negative/positive uses of, 113
single-parent families, 239–240
Sinno, Abdul K., 61–71
Sinno, Rafic, 61–71
snap judgments, 175
social distance, 119–120
social media
    changes in access to mass media, 63–64
    cognitive abilities and, 62–63, 66–67
    communication model and, 65–66
    crackberry syndrome, 317
    dating and, 319–321
    difficulty with face-to-face interactions, 322–323
    fragmentation, 316
    future developments in, 67–68
    global connections through, 319
    horizontal and vertical media, 69
    increased productivity from, 317–318
    informational indigestion, 316
    popularity of, 316
social performance
    identities and, 87–88
social phase of relationship break-up, 417, 418
social phenomena, 517–519
social skills deficits, 43–44
soup, language as, 108–111
space, as nonverbal communication, 118–120
speech, rate of, 112
speech acts, 106–108
    features of, 106–107
    indirect, 107
    mutual construction of, 107

spirals, communication, 399–412
spontaneity and defensive communication, 356
spot touch, 121
stability
    friendship and, 259–260
    gay and lesbian couples, 310–311
stepfamilies, 237
stereotypes
    anxiety and, 171
    defined, 172–173
    implicit personality theory and, 181–182
    perception and, 172–173
    positive and negative, 173
    prejudice and, 458
    reasons for using, 181–182
    reducing, 459
    as totalizing others, 178–185
    vocal cues and, 112
Stewart, John, 14–42, 61–71, 73–82, 101–127,
        139–146, 162–178, 192–207, 328–340, 485–495
stigma isolation, recognition and incorporation,
        477–478
Stone, Douglas, 91–99, 218–230
storytelling, 135–138
strategic self-presentation, 216
strategy in defensive communication, 355–356
stress
    immune system and, 46
    self-disclosure, 214
Stutman, Randall K., 386–398
submission, posture and, 122
subtext, relying on, 223–225
suicide
    interpersonal relationships and, 44–45
superiority, as defensive communication, 357
support
    friendship and, 261–262, 263–264
    gay and lesbian couples, 310
    gender and, 292–293
    intimacy and communicating, 282–285
    verbal communication of, 284–285
surprise, facial expression and, 116
symbols
    arbitrariness of, 105
    language as system of, 104–106
symmetrical communication, 402
system
    language as system of symbols, 104–106

talk. *See* everyday talk; words
Tancer, Bill, 316
Tannen, Deborah, 111, 243–253
tautness, 487
teamwork, 88–89
tension
    conflict and, 392, 395
    defined, 487
    in dialogue, 485–494

territory, 118
Thich Nhat Hanh, 186, 189–190
Third Story, 218, 219–220
Thomas, Milt, 201
thoughts
    experienced with intimacy, 278–279
    word-thought relationship, 105–106
threat
    as hurtful message, 335
    as speech act, 106–107
totalizing, 178–185
touch
    communicating comfort and support, 283
    as nonverbal communication, 120–121
traditional couples, 122
transacted identities, 86, 89–90
Triandis, Harry, 446
triangle of meaning, 105–106
trigger
    and as, 141–143
    next as, 143–145
trust
    different views and, 426
truth
    conclusions presented as, 226–227
    genuine dialogue and, 525–526
    perception and, 163
truth bias, 332
Twitter, 62, 66, 69
Type A personality, 45

ultimate attribution error, 175–176
Uncertainty Reduction Theory, 475
understanding, intimacy and, 281–282
unfolding, 523–525
uniqueness
    as feature of personal, 32–33
    intimacy and, 279–280
unmeasurable elements
    of interpersonal communication, 33–34
utility, as motive for lying, 330, 331

value judgments
    with words, 131
Vangelisti, Anita L., 340–351
verbal aggression, 336–337, 374–381
    vs. argumentativeness, 375–376
    causes of, 377–378
    defined, 375
    solutions and benefits of, 378–381
verbal communication. See language
verbal cues, primarily, 104–111
    in continuum, 103–104
    defined, 101
    language and perception, 109–111
    language as activity, 106–108

language as soup, 108–111
    language as system of symbols, 104–106
vertical media, 69
victim, blaming, 459–460
violence
    interpersonal relationships and, 43–44
    physical, 338–339
    psychological abuse, 337–338
    verbal aggression, 336–337, 374–381
visual contact, as mixed cue, 114
vocal cues
    as mixed cue, 112
    stereotyped judgments and, 112
vocal quality, 112
von Andics, Margarethe, 45
Vygotsky, Lev, 79

Weihenmayer, Erik, 472
Weston, Kathy, 238
Whorf, Benjamin Lee, 109
Who's Afraid of Virginia Ham? (Richman), 247
Whyte, David, 56
Wigley, Charles J., III, 374–384
Wild Boy of Aveyron, 9–10
Wilmot, William W., 332, 359–374, 399–414
Wirth, Louis, 182
Witteborn, Saskia, 73–82, 162–178, 192–207,
    328–340
Wood, Julia T., 178–185, 234–243
words
    "and," 141–143
    to avoid in LGBT communications,
        147–149
    with facial expressions as mixed cue,
        113–114
    with gestures as mixed cue, 114–115
    God and Devil terms, 131
    high code, 134–135
    low code, 134–135
    "next," 143–145
    relationships and connotation of, 129–130
    triangle of meaning, 105–106
    value judgments and, 131
    word-thought relationship, 105–106
Words to Live By: Inspiration for Every Day
    (Easwaran), 189
worldviews, perception and, 167

Yarbrough, Elaine, 121
You Just Don't Understand: Woman and Men in
    Communication (Tannen), 111
Young, William Paul, 266–273

Zediker, Karen E., 73–82, 162–178, 192–207,
    328–340, 485–495
Zen Buddhism, 185, 189–190